Logic Pro® X Power!
The Comprehensive Guide

Kevin Anker

Cengage Learning PTR

Professional • Technical • Reference

Australia • Brazil • Japan • Korea • Mexico • Singapore • Spain • United Kingdom • United States

CENGAGE
Learning·

Professional • Technical • Reference

Logic Pro® X Power!: The Comprehensive Guide
Kevin Anker

Publisher and General Manager, Cengage Learning PTR: Stacy L. Hiquet

Associate Director of Marketing: Sarah Panella

Manager of Editorial Services: Heather Talbot

Senior Marketing Manager: Mark Hughes

Acquisitions Editor: Orren Merton

Project Editor: Kate Shoup

Technical Reviewer: Eli Krantzberg

Copy Editor: Kate Shoup

Interior Layout Tech: MPS Limited

Cover Designer: Mike Tanamachi

Indexer: Sharon Shock

Proofreader: Megan Belanger

For product information and technology assistance, contact us at
Cengage Learning Customer & Sales Support, 1-800-354-9706

For permission to use material from this text or product,
submit all requests online at **cengage.com/permissions**

Further permissions questions can be emailed to
permissionrequest@cengage.com

Library of Congress Control Number: 2013957886

ISBN-13: 978-1-305-07350-0

ISBN-10: 1-305-07350-9

Cengage Learning PTR
20 Channel Center Street
Boston, MA 02210
USA

Cengage Learning is a leading provider of customized learning solutions with office locations around the globe, including Singapore, the United Kingdom, Australia, Mexico, Brazil, and Japan. Locate your local office at:
international.cengage.com/region

Cengage Learning products are represented in Canada by Nelson Education, Ltd.

For your lifelong learning solutions, visit **cengageptr.com**

Visit our corporate website at **cengage.com**

Printed in the United States of America
2 3 4 5 6   21 20 19 18 17

This book is dedicated to the ever-growing Logic community—those who are just getting their feet wet and those who have been at it for the last 20-plus years. I also dedicate this book to Julli, Taylor, Xander, Mom, Dad, my late grandparents, Joann, and the rest of my family, who have supported me from day one.

Acknowledgments

As Sir Isaac Newton wrote so succinctly, "If I have seen further it is by standing on the shoulders of giants." The *Logic Power* books are, without question, an absolute reflection of their original author, Orren Merton. The foundations Orren laid—upon which I was lucky enough to help build through a couple of revisions of Logic—were so strong that without them, and without Orren's continued help and insight into the current version of Logic, this book would simply not be anywhere near as complete or thorough as it is. He is truly a giant whose knowledge and expertise are unparalleled. It is my honor to have worked with him, to have inherited his "baby," and to call him friend.

To spend your days writing books and your nights working gigs, not to mention disappearing for weeks at a time for work, you need a very special and incredibly patient support system. I can't thank my wife, Julli, and daughter, Taylor, enough for all the love and understanding they offer me. You guys rock. Also, my parents have always been in my corner, and I simply can't thank them enough. And who can't love a mother-in-law who's okay with her daughter marrying a musician? I am blessed to have such a wonderful, loving family.

I have also been fortunate to have the guidance, friendship, and support of a few experts in Logic and other related applications. My brother, Sean Anker, lent his experience and expertise to my understanding of video for this project, and to my understanding of computers in general since we first started programming in BASIC on an Apple II+ nearly 35 years ago. He is the geek I always aspired to be. Eddie Al-Shakarchi, a truly brilliant producer, musician, and rapper (Associated Minds), has not only helped me check various quirks in Logic on a regular basis through several Logic revisions, but has also helped me to blow off a lot of steam via iChat from day one. One of these days Edd….

I also have to acknowledge the music community that has been my extended family for more years than I can recall—particularly Marc Schonbrun, Harvey Cook, Lester Johnson, Tad Robinson, Steve Gomes, Robb Stupka, David Earl and the entire Severn Records crew, Jeff Chapin, Adam Jay Southerland, my late mentors Tony Jessup and Claude Sifferlen, and countless others who have worked with me, taught me, mentored me, and accepted me into the brotherhood.

Finally, I have to thank my editors. Kate Shoup's sense of ordering things and finding better ways to present the information that was there really elevated the quality of this project. I thank you for all your help making this book better! Eli Krantzberg, thank you so much for your insights. Your knowledge and thoroughness truly shone through in what was a hectic and unique revision. You pulled me back on the rails more than a few times, and this book is very much the better because of your insight.

About the Author

Kevin Anker, co-author of *Logic Pro 8 Power!* and *Logic Pro 9 Power!*, and author of *Using Logic Pro's Synthesizers*, is a longtime professional musician with more than a quarter century's experience in computer-based music production. He has performed, composed, sequenced, produced, engineered, and recorded for a variety of artists both nationally and internationally, including a long relationship with roots music label Severn Records and a variety of their acts, such as The Fabulous Thunderbirds; Tad Robinson; Darrell Nulisch; the late, great Lou Pride; Bryan Lee; and Ursula Ricks. He has been a Logic user since 2002. Kevin can be reached at logic@kevinanker.net.

Contents

Chapter 3 The Logic Project

Chapter 4 Global Elements of Logic

Contents

Contents

Chapter 7 Working with Audio and Apple Loops   227

Chapter 8 Working with MIDI

Contents

Chapter 12 Working with and Sharing Files

Contents

Introduction

If you've picked up this the book, you've probably already figured out that it deals with Apple's Logic Pro X digital audio workstation. This book takes a different angle than most others, however. In general, books written about Logic tend to be geared toward beginners and consist of a few hundred pages of incredibly basic information. If not, they are geared toward specific features of Logic and not the whole application. This book takes on a fairly ambitious task: to be a complete introduction and reference for Logic Pro X! It's a goal that no other Logic book really attempts, and although I make no claims of objectivity, I think this book achieves it nicely. I don't attempt to write everything about everything, but I make sure to cover those things that you are likely to run into while using Logic to make music and to explain them simply and thoroughly. Moreover, I attempt to go into the philosophy behind *why* Logic works the way it works. Hopefully you will not simply learn the mechanics of how to do something, but you'll really understand what you are doing so when you want to explore on your own, you'll be fully prepared—and successful!

Who This Book Is For

Who is this book for? Well, the glib answer is, "Anyone who owns Logic!" I'm sure some of you with older versions of Logic, Windows versions of Logic, different levels of Logic (Logic, Logic Silver, Logic Audio, Logic Gold, Logic Platinum, or Logic Express), and so on are wondering how much use you can get out of a book focused on the Macintosh OS X–only Logic Pro X. This is covered in more detail in Chapter 1, "Introducing Logic Pro X," but I'll quickly say this: Logic Pro X is one of the most incredible updates Logic has seen in a very long time. It offers many new and updated features, particularly with regard to audio and the fact that Logic is now a 64 bit–only application. Nonetheless, the basics of how Logic works have not fundamentally changed since the earliest days of Notator Logic for the Atari. Features get added and the look changes a bit, so the older your version, the fewer features your Logic version may have compared to this one. But the basic operating procedures and features in your Logic version should be covered here in a way that will help you. So if you're looking for help with Logic, this book can provide it.

As for what level of user this book is aimed at, really, I took pains to include everyone—from people trying to create music on a computer for the first time, to longtime GarageBand users, to experienced Logic users. The book opens with very basic information aimed at novices and beginners. The bulk of this book continues with more intermediate reference information, with expert tips and tricks sprinkled throughout. The final chapters discuss more esoteric, "expert" functions, but hopefully in a way that is accessible to intermediate users. If you are a beginner, don't feel that only the beginning will be appropriate for you; the chapters are written to bring you up to speed in no time! Intermediate and advanced users, don't feel the beginning of the book is wasted on you, although you're welcome to skip it. It's good stuff, with lots of historical and architectural information you may not be familiar with even if you're already fast and efficient with Logic and are just looking for a good reference book. My goal was to start simple, get more advanced, and hopefully leave nobody behind. This book really does try to offer something for everyone.

How This Book Is Organized

Every book on computer software starts with a number of assumptions and organizes the chapters accordingly. For this book, I start with the assumption that the reader has a very basic knowledge of sequencing and recording and little else. The beginning chapters are introductions—to digital audio, MIDI, sequencing, and Logic. From about Chapter 4, "Global Elements of Logic," onward, the book becomes far less basic. At that point, as I start getting into the meat of Logic Pro X, the thought is that you have a working knowledge of the basics and general layout discussed in the previous four chapters, that you have set up your template (don't worry, you'll know what that is soon!), and that you want to start composing, recording, and editing music.

Introduction

The general flow of the chapters follows a Logic project. After setting up Logic, you'll need to learn about the Transport and the main window. Then, you'll want to record and edit audio and MIDI, mix down your project, and finally save your project and organize your files. The final chapters are about more advanced, esoteric features of Logic that, as you create more complex compositions and build a more involved project studio, will become more important.

As for each chapter, there is no single model to which I adhere regarding the subdivisions of sections. It is the content that determines the organization of each individual chapter. One thing I do want to mention, however, is that every time a new Logic window or editor is introduced, we discuss each local menu in that window or editor. This gives you the advantage of getting an overview of many of the functions available in a window or editor before we go deeper into using those functions.

One More Note on Logic Pro X

Logic Pro X is an application in a state of flux, but in a great way. From Logic Pro X 10.0, to Logic Pro X 10.0.1, to the most recent release at this moment, Logic Pro X 10.0.4, features have been added and refined again and again, with each update improving Logic immensely. As a result, there may be things that are covered in this book that work differently because of an ensuing update. Therefore, it is important that as you update Logic, you pay attention to the release notes for each version of Logic Pro X to help you keep track of these changes.

Introducing Logic Pro X

F OR YEARS, LOGIC HAD A REPUTATION FOR BEING VERY COMPLEX. Over the last few versions of Logic, however, that situation has improved dramatically. With each new version, incredible new features have ensured that Logic maintained its place as an industry leader. Logic Pro X is no different in that regard. It is an incredibly deep, powerful, and feature-rich recording and production application that you can have up and running quickly. It has a unique and highly customizable set of tools that allows you to configure a workflow that suits your "logic." Its editing and processing tools are second to none, and its suite of effects and software instruments is truly complete. In this chapter, you'll learn what Logic is, where it's from, and its basic working premises.

What Is Logic Pro?

If you hear people discussing Logic, you're likely to hear terms such as "professional," "powerful," "flexible," and "steep learning curve" thrown around. So what is Logic Pro, really?

Put simply, Logic Pro is the most flexible, powerful, comprehensive, professional, and elegant application for producing music on a computer. Although some may consider that a rather contentious statement, after reading this book you will probably at least concede that this claim is not outrageous. A number of other powerful, professional, and worthy music-production programs are on the market today. I don't mean to downplay their functionality. Some applications have a feature or two that Logic lacks, or they implement one of the features that Logic also includes in a way that some prefer. Logic does, however, offer the best combination of features, flexibility, and power of all available music production applications.

Logic offers you:

▷ **Audio recording:** Record audio directly into Logic.
▷ **Audio editing:** Edit audio files using Logic's many editing tools, including sample-accurate editing, Flex Time, and Flex Pitch in the Tracks area.
▷ **MIDI recording:** Record and play back MIDI information.
▷ **MIDI editing:** Edit MIDI information in one of several MIDI editors.
▷ **MIDI notation editing:** Edit and print out professional scores and music charts.
▷ **Browsers:** Manage all your multimedia files right in the Logic Pro main window.
▷ **Global tracks:** Easily set up and edit project arrangement, marker, tempo, key signature, transposition, beat mapping, and video frame information.
▷ **Software instruments:** Use software instruments from within Logic.
▷ **Library:** Access complete channel strip settings and patches for your tracks in the Logic Pro main window.
▷ **Arranging:** View all your song elements as graphic regions and arrange them visually.
▷ **Mixing:** Mix your audio tracks and your MIDI tracks within the same song using Logic's completely customizable Mixer.
▷ **Processing:** Use Logic's professional offline and real-time processors and functions.
▷ **Control surface support:** Configure any hardware MIDI controller to be a hardware controller of any Logic function.
▷ **Environment:** Build an entire virtual studio and processing environment inside Logic.

For these features and more, Logic has earned its well-deserved reputation as the most complete professional music production application, and it continues to break new ground. What about that talk of Logic's steep learning curve? As with most applications that are as deep as this one, it helps to know the application's internal workings to more readily understand how to use it. To give you a solid grounding in the fundamental concepts of Logic, I'll start at the very beginning with Logic's origins and see how the functionality of those previous applications relates to the current version of Logic.

A Brief History of Logic

Once upon a time, in the mid-1980s, during what now would be considered the "prehistoric" era of computer music, a small German software company named C-LAB created a Commodore 64 program called Supertrack. Supertrack, like all early sequencers, was designed to allow users to store, edit, and play back the notes and performance information generated on MIDI synthesizers. (See the section "A Brief Overview of MIDI" later in this chapter for an explanation of MIDI.)

By 1987, this basic program evolved into Creator, and finally into Notator. Notator, which ran on the Atari ST, added a musical notation (or musical score) editor to Creator and became an instant power player in the burgeoning field of computer-based MIDI sequencers. Notator offered a clean, simple interface for four powerful MIDI editors: a real-time musical notation editor, an Event editor for displaying MIDI information in a scrolling list, a Matrix editor for displaying notes graphically, and a Hyper editor for editing non-note MIDI data (such as pitch bend). With these editors, you could play a song on your synthesizer or program it on your computer from scratch, then rearrange, edit, and manipulate your data as sheet music in the notation editor, in a text list, a graphic "piano roll," or a bar graph–style display.

As you can see in Figure 1.1, which shows an edit screen from the final version of Notator for the Atari, the program used the very same concepts and offered many of the same tools for manipulating MIDI information that are still used today. Notator's extensive editing options gave musicians powerful tools for creating and arranging music in an easy-to-use package. Notator won rave reviews from power users and hobbyists alike, and garnered a huge following among early MIDI musicians. Even 20 years after its final version, Notator still has a very lively following. In fact, there are websites and mailing lists on the Internet for people who still use Notator today.

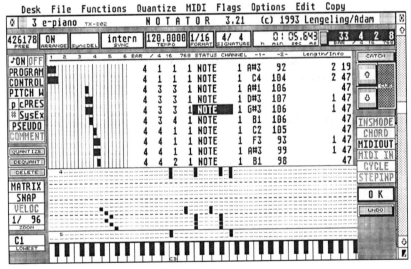

Figure 1.1 This screenshot from Notator Version 3.2.1 shows the Matrix and Event editors. Users of Notator would feel right at home with the evolved Matrix and Event editors of Logic, which are fundamentally the same two decades later.
© The Notator Users Group (www.notator.org).

By 1993, the principals who developed Notator left to form their own company, Emagic, and built upon their previous efforts by adding a graphical arrangement page and object-oriented editing, among other innovations. This product was named Notator Logic, and later simply Logic. Logic was soon ported to run on the Macintosh computer, which was quickly overtaking the Atari as the music computer of choice for professionals. This early version of Logic introduced the basic architecture and concepts that would form the basis for future iterations of Logic.

By the late 1990s, Logic's developers had ported Logic to run on Windows computers as well as the Macintosh, quietly discontinued the Atari version, and added to the program the ability to record and edit audio in addition to MIDI. To signify this, the developers modified the name of the application to Logic Audio. By the end of the 1990s, there were three versions of the application, each with an expanded feature set. Logic Audio Platinum had the most professional recording options, offering the most hardware options, including unsurpassed support for Digidesign's industry-standard hardware, Pro Tools TDM. Logic

Audio Platinum became nearly ubiquitous in the software lists of professional studios worldwide. Logic Audio Gold and Logic Audio Silver offered consumers more affordable versions of Logic with the same depth and power but fewer features. In addition, Emagic developed a separate application, MicroLogic, which was a basic and inexpensive derivative of Logic that offered beginners a way to get their feet wet in music production.

In July 2002, Apple Computer purchased Emagic. The Logic 6 release in February 2003 focused solely on the Macintosh, representing Emagic's return to single-platform development after a decade as a cross-platform application. The names of the three versions of Logic changed again, this time to Logic Platinum, Logic Gold, and Logic Audio. In 2004, Apple Computer streamlined Emagic's Logic line to only Logic Pro and Logic Express, and in late 2004, Apple Computer released Logic Pro 7 and Express 7. September 2007 saw the introduction of Logic Express 8 and the software suite Logic Studio, which included Logic Pro 8. In July 2009, Logic Pro 9 and Logic Express 9 were introduced. Logic Express was discontinued in December 2011 when Apple Computer moved all sales of Logic Pro 9 to its App Store. Logic Pro X continues to lead the way in professional music production on the Macintosh platform, garnering rave reviews.

As you can see, Emagic and Logic have a long and illustrious history in the computer-music field upon which Apple is building. To this day, the Event List and the Step, Score, and Piano Roll Editors of even the most recent Logic Pro X release would be instantly recognizable to an early Notator user, which speaks volumes about Apple's commitment to supporting its user community.

Will This Book Help You with Your Version of Logic?

The short answer is: Yes!

The long answer is that this book will offer you something no matter which version of Logic you are using. Exactly how much of the material is applicable depends on the specific platform and version number you are using. This book covers the features of the most current, feature-rich version of Logic, Logic Pro X. That means this book will cover features that are not found in any other version of Logic on any other platform. If you are using a previous version of Logic, the number of new features explained in this book will be considerable (although many will still be familiar), and the difference in appearance will be considerable as well.

Clearly, if you just purchased Logic Pro X, this book applies to your version. If you currently do not own Logic and you want to learn about it before purchasing it, this book will give you the ins and outs of the most current version of Logic. However, current users of different versions of Logic will find this book eminently useful as well.

The concepts and basic MIDI editing functionality in Logic haven't changed since the program's creation. In other words, users who have held onto Notator Logic 1.5 on their Atari ST could read this book and recognize many of the editors, the nomenclature, the architecture, and so on, even though the developers have seriously updated the look and added many features in the last couple decades. For users of more recent versions, the differences become even less pronounced. Through Logic 5.5, the features, look and feel, and operation of Logic were nearly identical whether it was running under Windows XP, Mac OS 9, or Mac OS X. Logic 7 was really the first version in nearly half a decade with significantly new design, and Logic 8 and Logic 9 carried that much further, but most operations themselves had not been fundamentally changed. Logic X continues the Logic tradition, adding more great features and improving and streamlining the look while keeping much of the feel of the application intact. As you can see by comparing Figure 1.2 and Figure 1.3, 2001's Logic Pro 5.5 running under Windows XP and 2013's Logic Pro X look different, yet clearly maintain a profound similarity.

In other words, users of previous versions of Logic looking for assistance with basic concepts and operational procedures will find it here. This book will, of course, address the newer features in Logic Pro X, but users of different versions can easily skip those discussions. In fact, users with earlier or less feature-rich versions of Logic can consider the coverage of the latest features a sneak peek at what the new version has to offer when making the decision about whether to upgrade!

A Brief Overview of MIDI

Musical Instrument Digital Interface (MIDI) was formally introduced in August 1983. The MIDI 1.0 protocol was absolutely revolutionary—it allowed MIDI instruments (such as synthesizers, drum machines, and sequencers) to communicate with, control, and be controlled by other MIDI instruments and MIDI controllers. The development of MIDI enabled the rise of electronic music and computer sequencers. MIDI makes possible much of what we use computers for in music production. If you

Logic Pro® X Power!: The Comprehensive Guide

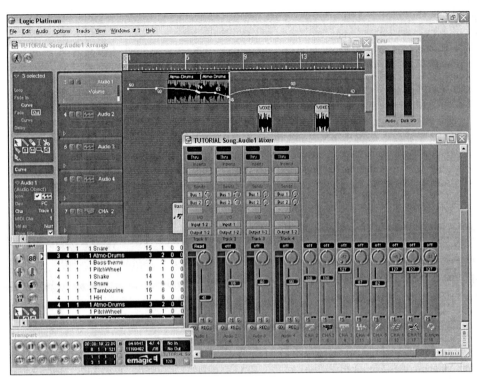

Figure 1.2 Logic Pro 5.5, the final version of Logic developed for Windows XP in 2001.
© Apple Inc.

Figure 1.3 Logic Pro X, the most recent version of Logic, running on Mac OS X. You can see that even with the integrated features of the main window, the two versions of Logic still resemble each other.
© Apple Inc.

are interested in a complete technical discussion of every aspect of the MIDI protocol, you should read *MIDI Power! Second Edition: The Comprehensive Guide* by Robert Guerin (Thomson Course Technology PTR, 2005), a very thorough and readable exploration of MIDI in depth. Using Logic doesn't require that sort of deep understanding of MIDI, but a basic knowledge of what MIDI is and how it works is invaluable.

The MIDI protocol specifies that every MIDI-compliant device that can both send and receive MIDI information must have a MIDI IN port to accept MIDI data, a MIDI OUT port to transmit MIDI data, and optionally a MIDI THRU port for transferring data between other MIDI devices. When you connect the MIDI OUT port of one device to the MIDI IN port of another device, the first device enables you to press a key, turn a dial, engage a control message, and so on, and the second device will receive the data.

In addition to providing hardware specifications that allow devices to send and receive MIDI, the MIDI protocol also defines how to pass data from one device to another. MIDI is a *serial protocol,* meaning that MIDI information is sent one *event* (or MIDI message) at a time. That may sound inefficient, but the speed of MIDI transfer is 31,250 bits per second (bps), where *bit* stands for *binary digit*. Because each MIDI message uses 10 bits (eight for the information, two for error correction), the MIDI protocol can send 3,906 bytes of data every second (31,250 divided by 8 bits to convert bits to bytes). Because one MIDI note can take up to 6 bytes, the protocol enables a device to play approximately 500 MIDI notes per second. This might seem like a lot of notes, but as soon as you add a couple five-note chords in a single 10-millisecond span of time, with multiple MIDI control messages, you might very well start seeing some compromised timing. That's why for the most demanding MIDI productions, there are MIDI time-stamping features on many MIDI interfaces to improve MIDI timing even further.

Even if you have no external MIDI hardware, MIDI is still the protocol that Logic uses for internal playback and automation of virtual instruments, so it's still useful to understand some basics about MIDI.

What MIDI Really Transmits

The most important thing to understand is that MIDI doesn't transmit any sound at all. It transmits only data. In other words, when you record digital audio, you're recording an actual file of digital information that will play back as sound. When you record MIDI data, you'll then need some sort of device—a synthesizer, drum machine, sampler, or software instrument—to actually hear that MIDI information. MIDI data can transmit the following:

▷ Performance events, such as when you play and release notes, and their velocities.

▷ The pressure with which you press the keys as you play (known as *aftertouch*).

▷ Information from MIDI controller wheels, knobs, pedal controls, ribbon controllers, pitchbend controllers, and so on that send parameters that affect performance.

▷ Channel settings. Each MIDI cable can support up to 16 channels, so each device can operate as 16 devices in one. Devices that can support multiple MIDI channels are called *multitimbral* devices.

▷ Synchronization information, so that all time-sensitive instruments or functions on various devices can operate from the same master clock and play in sync with each other.

▷ Program changes and sound-bank selections.

▷ MIDI Time Code (MTC), which allows MIDI devices to lock to devices that use Society of Motion Picture and Television Engineers (SMPTE)–format time code by translating SMPTE into something that the MIDI device can understand.

▷ System Exclusive messages, which are unique messages that can alter parameters and control of one specific MIDI device. Most MIDI synthesizers and some multitrack recorders offer unique System Exclusive commands.

MIDI Connections and Signal Flow

As described previously, connecting MIDI devices couldn't be simpler. The most basic type of MIDI connection, in which the MIDI OUT jack of one MIDI device is connected to the MIDI IN jack of another MIDI device, allows the first unit to send MIDI to the second unit, as shown in Figure 1.4.

Note that this type of connection does not allow for two-way communication, only one-way communication. This type of connection is most common when connecting a MIDI controller, which is a MIDI device that does not itself produce sounds (and doesn't *receive* MIDI), but can send MIDI to other devices, such as to a computer MIDI interface or another MIDI device.

An example of another simple but more dynamic MIDI connection is to connect both the MIDI IN and MIDI OUT of one device to the MIDI OUT and MIDI IN of another device, as shown in Figure 1.5.

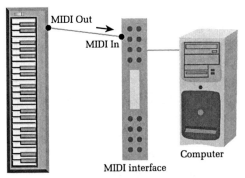

Figure 1.4 A basic MIDI connection between a MIDI OUT jack on a MIDI device and a MIDI IN jack on a MIDI interface, which is then connected to the computer. This type of MIDI connection allows the MIDI device to control MIDI software in the computer.
© Cengage Learning.

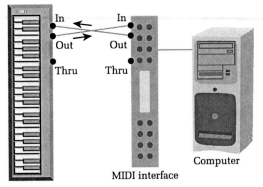

Figure 1.5 A new MIDI connection has been added to the system seen in Figure 1.4. The MIDI IN on the MIDI device has been connected to the MIDI OUT on the MIDI interface, allowing the MIDI software on the computer to control the MIDI device.
© Cengage Learning.

This enables two-way communication between MIDI devices, so each is capable of both sending and receiving data from the other. This is the most common form of routing between two devices capable of sending and receiving MIDI information, such as two synthesizers, or a computer and a synthesizer.

> **CAUTION:** When making connections like this, be sure both units have MIDI THRU and/or local control turned off, or else you might end up with a MIDI feedback loop. In a MIDI feedback loop, one unit sends a command to the other, which then sends the command back to the first unit, and on and on endlessly.

A final example of a basic MIDI connection illustrates how three MIDI devices might be connected via a MIDI THRU port. The MIDI OUT of the first device is connected to the MIDI IN of the second device, the MIDI OUT of the second device is connected to the MIDI IN of the first device, and the MIDI THRU of the second device is connected to the MIDI IN of the third device (see Figure 1.6).

In Figure 1.6, complete two-way communication between the first two devices is possible, and the first device (and often the second device) can also send MIDI information to the third device. Such connections are often used when a third MIDI device, such as a drum machine, is not being used to issue any MIDI messages, but only to receive them from the rest of the MIDI setup.

At this point, you should have a good understanding of what MIDI is and the importance of getting MIDI information into Logic. Because Logic can both send and receive MIDI, you will probably want a *MIDI interface*—a universal serial bus (USB)

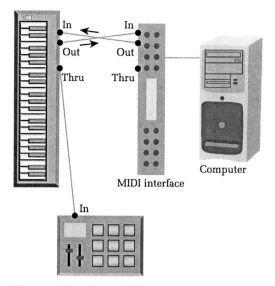

Figure 1.6 A new MIDI connection has been added to the system seen in Figure 1.5. The MIDI THRU on the original MIDI device has been connected to the MIDI IN on another MIDI device. This allows the MIDI software on the computer to control the second MIDI device.
© Cengage Learning.

device that accepts MIDI from MIDI devices and sends it into Logic—that has at least as many MIDI IN and MIDI OUT ports as you have MIDI devices. This will be discussed later in this chapter, in the section "A Brief Primer on Hardware."

A Brief Overview of Digital Audio

These days, recording digital audio is perhaps the most popular use of sequencers such as Logic Pro. In fact, the popular term to describe a computer used as the hub of a music production system is a *digital audio workstation (DAW)*. So what is digital audio? How does it differ from analog audio? Why is it important?

While a complete technical reference on the details of digital audio would result in a book almost as large as this one, it is important to know at least enough about the fundamentals of digital audio to be able to make a good recording. The following subsections should give you just enough of a background to get the most out of your audio recordings.

The Differences Between Analog and Digital Sound

We hear sound when our eardrums vibrate. If you read that carefully, you will realize that it did not say that we hear sound whenever *some object* vibrates. Many objects vibrate outside our ability to hear them (think of dog whistles or ultra-low subfrequencies). Our ears are theoretically capable of registering vibrations (also called *cycles*) that oscillate between 20 and 20,000 times a second. This is called the *frequency*—which is pretty logical when you think about it, because the term refers to the frequency of vibrations per second. Theoretically, then, humans can hear frequencies from 20 Hz to 20 kHz. (The measurement Hertz, or Hz, is named after Henry Hertz, who in 1888 developed the theory of the relationship between frequency and cycles.) In practice, hardly any adult's hearing reaches that theoretical maximum because people lose the ability to hear certain frequencies (high-pitched ones in particular) as they age, are subjected to loud noises, and so on.

If the frequency of vibration is slow (say, 60 vibrations per second, or 60 Hz), we perceive a low note. If the frequency of the vibration is fast (say, 6,000 vibrations per second, or 6 kHz), we would perceive a high note. If the vibrations are gentle, barely moving our eardrums, we perceive the sound as soft. The loudness and softness of the sound is called the *amplitude*, because the term refers to the volume, or amplification, of the sound. Thus we can graph sound as you see in Figure 1.7.

In the graph in Figure 1.7, the frequency is the distance between the oscillations of the waveform, and the amplitude is the height of the waveform. Most sounds we hear in the real world are complex ones that have more than a single frequency in them, as in the graph in Figure 1.8.

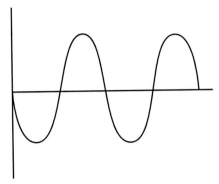

Figure 1.7 A graphical representation of a simple sound wave. This particular kind of even, smooth sound wave is known as a sine wave.
© Cengage Learning.

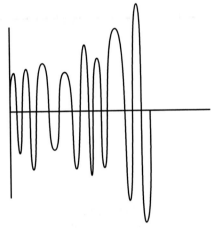

Figure 1.8 A more complex sound wave than the one seen in Figure 1.7. This example has more than a single tone in it, and not every frequency is being heard at the same volume (amplitude).
© Cengage Learning.

Now that you understand a little about sound waves, let's tie it into recording. One way to record sound is to make an exact replica of the original waveform on some other media. For example, you might carve an image of the waveform onto a vinyl surface or imprint the waveform on magnetic tape. In these cases, you have recorded an actual copy of the original sound wave. Now you just need a machine to amplify the sound so it's loud enough to listen to (or to rattle the windows, if that's your style). Because this type of recording results in a continuous waveform, it's called *analog recording. Analog* refers to any signal that is represented by a continuous, unbroken waveform.

Because a computer works using mathematical codes instead of actual pictures of objects, to use a computer for recording audio, we need to translate the actual analog signal into math. Luckily, sound can also be represented *digitally*—meaning by use of digits, or numbers. Basically, complex mathematical analysis has proven that if we sample a waveform twice in each cycle, or *period*, and record its variation in sound, we can reproduce the waveform. Now, each period is a full cycle, or vibration. That means if we wanted to reproduce a 60-Hz sound, which is 60 cycles, we'd need to take at least 120 samples. From this, you can see that if you want to capture the full range of human hearing—20 kHz, or 20,000 cycles—you have to take at least 40,000 samples.

What's Meant by Sampling Frequency and Bit Depth

From the preceding, we understand that we have to represent the sound wave as numbers to store it in the computer, and that by storing two samples per cycle we can represent that cycle. You've probably noticed that every recording interface and program that handles digital audio refers to sample rate and bit depth. I'll explain what these terms mean and how they affect your recording.

As explained, it takes two samples per cycle to represent each cycle accurately. It follows that the total number of samples taken of a waveform determines the maximum frequency that will be recorded. This is called the *sampling frequency* or *sampling rate.* For example, the sampling rate of the compact disc is fixed at 44.1 kHz, or 44,100 samples per second. It's a few thousand samples more than the minimum needed to represent the highest-frequency sound wave that humans can hear.

You've probably noticed that many audio interfaces today boast sampling rates of 96 kHz or even 192 kHz (kHz is short for kilohertz, or 1,000 Hz). That means these devices can represent sounds up to 48 kHz and 96 kHz. The obvious question is, why bother? We can only hear up to a theoretical 20 kHz anyway, right? Of course, it's not quite that simple. Although we may not be able to distinguish sounds accurately above a certain frequency, every sound also contains additional overtones, harmonics, spatial cues, and so on. These features enrich the sound, help us place it in space, and so on. When our sampling rate is too low to represent such features, they are simply discarded and lost forever. We may not consciously notice these "ultrasonic" frequencies when we listen to recordings, but many audiophiles and sound engineers believe that they contribute to a far more realistic listening experience.

That explains sampling rates, but what about bit depth? Remember, the sound wave has two components: the frequency and the amplitude. The mathematical representation of the amplitude at a particular instant in a particular cycle is stored in *bits.* A computer cannot interpolate information between the amplitudes you have stored—it only knows what the amplitude at a given instant in the cycle is if the amplitude is stored in a bit. The more bits used to store the amplitude per cycle, the more accurate the representation.

Finally, here is a loose—but good—analogy to give you a basic understanding of analog versus digital audio, sampling rate, and bit depth. If you make an analog recording, you are left with an actual copy of the audio waveform imprinted onto your media. If you make a digital recording, you are instead taking "snapshots" of the waveform and then attempting to re-create the waveform from those snapshots. Your sampling rate would be the number of snapshots you take every second, and your bit depth would represent the focus and color quality of each snapshot. As you can see, the higher the sampling rate and bit depth, the closer your snapshots will get to the actual sound wave, as follows in Figure 1.9.

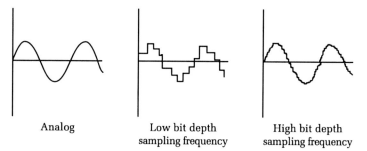

Analog   Low bit depth   High bit depth
                sampling frequency   sampling frequency

Figure 1.9 The higher the sampling rate and bit depth, the closer your snapshots will get to the actual sound wave. © Cengage Learning.

In analog recording, you record an accurate representation of the source, in this case a sine wave. In digital recording, the sample rate and bit depth directly influence the accuracy of the recording. With higher sample rates and bit depths, you can achieve a more accurate digital representation of the source than with lower sample rates and bit depths.

You should also keep in mind that as your bit depths and sampling rates increase, so do the processor, memory, and hard-drive requirements. The larger the bit depth and sample rate, the more CPU is required to process it, the more memory the audio requires during processing, and the more space on your hard disk the audio will require.

It is beyond the scope of this book to give comprehensive position papers on the merits of analog versus digital audio. The important things to remember are that any audio waveform that gets into your computer will be digital audio, and you need to be aware of sampling frequency and bit depth to get the most out of your hardware and out of Logic.

Audio and MIDI in Logic Pro

It's time to relate all of this to what it means for Logic. In its simplest description, Logic is a software MIDI and digital audio recorder. In other words, if you connect your MIDI devices to your computer, connect your audio devices to your computer, and then activate the Record function in Logic, you will record your audio and MIDI into Logic. If you then activate the Play function, you will hear the MIDI and audio you've just recorded. So far, this should be familiar to pretty much anyone who has ever used a DVR to record and watch their favorite shows.

For Logic to be able to record MIDI and digital audio information, you need a way to capture that information into the computer, and then a way to transfer that information out of the computer when you activate playback. In the case of audio, you capture and transfer this information through your *audio interface*. In the case of MIDI, you handle all of this with your *MIDI interface*.

Unlike a DVR, which requires little more setting up than telling it what channel to record at what time, Logic is famous (perhaps infamous) for the depth and breadth of setup and configuration options it offers. Logic Pro X's processes are streamlined so that you can configure your setup on a basic level very quickly, while still allowing the incredible amount of flexibility for which it is famous.

A Brief Primer on Hardware

It is beyond the scope of this book to give you a complete buyer's guide on computer hardware. It is also relatively pointless, because new products are introduced almost daily. But it is important to touch a little bit on the basic kinds of hardware you'll need to get the most out of Logic.

We'll assume that you already have any musical instruments or MIDI controller devices you will be using. If you already have your computer hardware as well and are ready to set it up, feel free to skip to Chapter 2, "A Quick Tour of Logic Pro."

How Fast Does Your Computer Need to Be?

The simple answer to this question is as fast as possible! The more detailed answer is that it depends on what sort of music production you expect to be doing and what your expectations are.

Apple's stated minimum requirements are for an Intel Macintosh computer. Apple goes on to recommend the following:

▷ A minimum of 4 GB of random access memory (RAM)
▷ A display with a resolution of 1,280×768
▷ The Mac OS X 10.8.4 or later operating system
▷ 5 GB minimum drive space

Logic also offers 35 GB of extra content—samples and loops—via an in-app download. The extra content is of a high enough level of quality that I would recommend making space on your drive for it.

If you intend to run a sizable number of effects and software synthesizers, your processor and RAM requirements will increase. Logic does have a Freeze function and Bounce in Place functions that can help conserve CPU power, but the more processor power and the more RAM you have, the better. (I'd recommend at least 8 GB of RAM if your system can handle it.)

If your computer is older and you are thinking of pushing the minimum, be warned: Slow computers not only have slower CPUs, but also usually have slower motherboards, hard drives, RAM, and so on. When you ask your computer basically to replace an entire building full of mixing desks, tape machines, effects units, and MIDI synthesizers, you're asking a lot. Although Logic Pro X is a very efficient program, it contains some very powerful, industry-leading tools that not only can inspire you and benefit your productions, but can bring even more recent computers to their knees fairly quickly. Keep that in mind.

My recommendation is that you get the fastest laptop or desktop Macintosh you can afford and load it with as much RAM as you can. You won't be sorry!

Different Types of Storage Drives

Traditionally, storage drives operate on the principle of a set of needles reading and writing data on magnetic platters that spin around incredibly fast. This type of platter hard drive (HDD) has been the industry standard for decades. The differences among the various types of HDDs are mainly in how fast these platters spin and what mechanism they use to connect to the rest of the computer. In recent years, solid-state drives (SSDs), basically large-capacity flash drives, have become more practical financially. SSDs have no moving parts and therefore offer the potential for much higher performance than HDD technology.

Storage drives use two mainstream transfer mechanisms to communicate with the host computer: Advanced Technology Attachment (ATA) and Small Computer Systems Interface (SCSI). Both formats have different performance subcategories, such as SATA, eSATA, ATA/66 or ATA/100, and SCSI-2 or SCSI-3. SCSI drives have higher top speeds, usually require an additional PCI Express expander or ExpressCard that supports the SCSI protocol (although some newer Macs support the USB Attached SCSI protocol), and generally cost more than similar-sized ATA drives. ATA is inexpensive, ubiquitous, and supported internally by every desktop and notebook system designed since 1998. eSATA is an external SATA standard that offers transfer rates that match that of internal SATA drives.

Recording audio files to an HDD can be a very disk-intensive task, and a faster hard drive can record and play back more simultaneous tracks. Most desktop and external hard drives these days spin at 7,200 RPM, which is fast enough to reliably handle songs with around 64 to 72 audio tracks—more than enough for most people. If you have a 7,200-RPM hard drive and you still need more tracks, you can either record audio to two different storage drives or get a faster drive. These days, hard drives running up to 15,000 RPM are available, although they are expensive and almost always require SCSI.

SSDs offer a few advantages over HDDs. First, because they have no moving parts, SSDs are silent in operation. If you work with your Mac Pro in the room with you, or with a laptop or iMac, eliminating any bit of extra computer noise is helpful. Second, SSDs have much faster read and write speeds. If a drive doesn't have to physically search for data or space to place data, it can work much more quickly and efficiently. Third, newer SSDs have longer projected life spans than HDDs. SSDs do have one major drawback: cost. For example, as of this writing, SSDs approaching 1 TB of storage cost $600 and more for just the drive, while 3-TB 7,200-RPM drives in external enclosures can be found for around $100.

If you are using a laptop with an internal HDD, it could spin at 5,400 RPM or 7,200 RPM. The MacBook Air series uses internal SSDs, and SSDs are an option you can configure when purchasing a new MacBook Pro, iMac, or Mac Pro. If you already have a MacBook Pro, many of the more recent ones allow easy access to the storage drive, enabling you to easily upgrade the capacity, speed, or type of drive installed. For high-performance mobile use, you should consider using an external HDD that runs at 7,200 RPM as your audio drive, particularly if you're running a slower internal drive. Several external HDDs are available in USB, FireWire, eSATA, or Thunderbolt enclosures that offer plug-and-play connectivity to all notebook computers with those ports. External SSDs are available, but their cost is, of course, very high at this time.

If your laptop doesn't have enough USB or FireWire ports but supports the use of an ExpressCard, you can buy an ExpressCard that will allow you to connect more USB or FireWire devices. You can also find eSATA ExpressCards that will allow you to use eSATA drives with your laptop. For Thunderbolt-equipped computers, you can buy hubs that offer USB, FireWire, Ethernet, and extra Thunderbolt ports, allowing you to connect several storage drives and peripherals to your computer.

Do You Need a Separate Storage Drive for Audio Files?

In general, the more a storage drive has to do, the less performance it has left over for audio. In other words, if your drive needs to read system files as well as audio files, it needs to divide its attention. If you have a drive devoted to nothing but recording audio files, that drive could dedicate 100 percent of its performance to audio-related tasks.

Clearly, having a separate drive for audio seems advantageous, but is it absolutely necessary? The answer to this depends on how audio-intensive your projects are. Even a slower hard disk should be able to run both system software and approximately 16–24 tracks of audio. If your needs are modest, you really shouldn't need a separate storage drive for your audio tracks. On the other hand, professional studios that need to record anything from solo singers all the way to full orchestras often have entire banks of storage drives. If you regularly work with songs in excess of 24 tracks or you can easily afford it, you should go ahead and buy a separate drive for audio files.

Even if you don't choose to buy extra drives for audio, I can't stress enough the importance of having at least one backup drive for your system. Regardless of the type of drive you use, drives do fail—typically in spectacular fashion at the worst possible moment. Back up, back up, back up.

MIDI Interfaces

Earlier, the section "A Brief Overview of MIDI" concluded by mentioning the MIDI interface. This device has the same MIDI IN and MIDI OUT ports that your MIDI hardware does and connects to your computer via USB to send that MIDI information from your external units into Logic, and vice versa. If you want Logic to be able to communicate with MIDI devices outside the computer, you need a MIDI interface.

So what size interface do you need? That depends completely on how many MIDI devices you have. Do you have only one controller keyboard? If so, then you just need a simple MIDI interface with one MIDI IN and one MIDI OUT port. It's also common for modern MIDI controllers to have their own USB MIDI connectors. If your needs are modest enough, your audio interface may already have all the MIDI ports you need. (See the following section, "Audio Interfaces.") Do you have a full MIDI studio and need 12 MIDI ports? In that case, you need to buy multiple MIDI interfaces of the largest size you can find (usually eight MIDI IN and eight MIDI OUT ports). Also think about whether you plan to expand your MIDI hardware over time. If you do, you might want to get a MIDI interface with more ports than you currently need.

Another thing to consider is whether your MIDI interface needs any professional synchronization features. Some of the more professional interfaces include a lot of video and hardware synchronization options that you might need if you do a lot of sound-to-picture work. Also, many of the larger interfaces include time-stamping functionality, which allows them to stamp the exact time that a MIDI event should occur as part of the MIDI message. Time stamping doesn't have a noticeable effect for small numbers of MIDI devices, but it can make a world of difference with MIDI studios containing large amounts of external hardware.

Finally, keep in mind that many different manufacturers make MIDI interfaces, and these interfaces are all equally compatible with Logic. As long as your interface has a USB connector and drivers for your Mac OS X, it should do the job.

Audio Interfaces

Because there are so many audio interfaces on the market, choosing one might seem daunting. Here are a few tips to help you with your selection.

First, consider how many audio channels you intend to record at one time. Do you see yourself recording a rock band or an entire symphony at once? If so, you will want to investigate those audio interfaces that enable users to daisy-chain more than one interface, so you can expand your system as your recording needs grow. Some systems today not only enable users to record 24 or more channels at once, but to connect two or three such boxes for a truly impressive audio recording system. On the other hand, do you see yourself recording only yourself or one stereo instrument at a time? If so, then a single interface with fewer inputs will do.

Next, consider how you would prefer or need your audio interface to connect to your computer. Are you using a laptop or an iMac? If so, you probably want an interface that connects to the computer via USB, FireWire, or Thunderbolt. All Intel Macintosh laptops and iMacs have USB connections. The availability of FireWire or Thunderbolt will depend on the age of your machine—for example, the newer MacBooks offer Thunderbolt and USB, but you can still use FireWire via a Thunderbolt-to-FireWire adapter. Older MacBooks are incompatible with Thunderbolt, but most offer FireWire. Some older MacBook Pros also allow you to select an ExpressCard format interface. If you have a Mac Pro, you might also prefer a USB, FireWire, or Thunderbolt interface, depending on what connections are available on your machine, because those interfaces don't require you to open up your machine and install anything. If you don't mind installing hardware in your older Mac Pro, you can choose an audio interface that is a Peripheral Component Interface Express (PCI Express) card. PCI Express options are usually more expandable and less expensive than USB, FireWire, and ExpressCard interfaces, but are more difficult to install. The newest Mac Pros no longer support internal expansion, but there are external Thunderbolt-based PCI Express expansion chassis on the market, which will also work with Thunderbolt-equipped MacBooks and iMacs.

You need to consider the sampling frequency and bit depth at which you want to record. Compact discs are standardized at 16 bits, with a sampling frequency of 44.1 kHz. Every audio interface available today can record at least at this level of fidelity. Do you want to be able to record at 24 bits, which is the industry standard for producing music? Do you want to be able to record at higher sampling frequencies, such as the 96 kHz that DVDs can use? All these decisions influence what kind of audio interface will fit your needs. Because the higher bit depths and sample rates capture a more accurate "picture" of the sound, as explained, you might want to record and process your audio at higher bit rates than your final format if you have the computer power to do so.

Finally, you should consider whether you want your audio interface to have additional features. For example, some audio interfaces have MIDI control surfaces and/or MIDI interfaces as part of a package. Does that appeal to you, or would you prefer to fill those areas with other devices?

Now that I've introduced Logic, some of its basic concepts, and the hardware you'll need, it's time to take "A Quick Tour of Logic Pro."

A Quick Tour of Logic Pro

2

NOW THAT YOU HAVE A BASIC UNDERSTANDING OF WHAT LOGIC CAN DO, it's time to start exploring. This chapter gives you a broad overview of the application, and the following chapters delve into the details of the individual areas. At this point, don't worry if you look at the various elements in Logic Pro X and are left with all sorts of questions. As you proceed, I promise that things will become clear!

Terminology in Logic

As you begin your examination of Logic, you should already be comfortable with some of the terms that are used in Logic to describe the most common functions and concepts. Of course, every sequencer uses its own terminology, and if you understand this, you'll find it far easier to comprehend the "logic" of the application, both figuratively and literally. Here are the key terms that you'll need to know to work with Logic effectively:

▷ **Project:** A Logic project contains information about all your editing, MIDI performances, mixing, and recording. A project can also contain audio files, sampler instruments, effects presets, and so on that are used by the song or songs that make up the project. These files are called the project's *assets*. Saving Logic projects with their assets (you'll learn more about that in Chapter 12, "Working with and Sharing Files") is a great way to keep every necessary piece of data used in one place.

▷ **Audio file:** Audio files are files on your computer that contain digital audio information. When you record into Logic, it saves your recording as a digital audio file on your storage drive. When you use Logic to manipulate audio data, that data will always originate from an audio file, regardless of whether it was initially recorded in Logic.

▷ **Track:** Audio and MIDI data are recorded into horizontal lanes in the Tracks area of the Logic Pro main window that are known as—wait for it—tracks. The term *tracks* is a holdover from the days of recording onto tape, where each separate strip of a tape recording was known as a *track* (so a stereo cassette would have two tracks, left and right, and an old eight-track tape had—you guessed it—eight tracks).

▷ **Audio region:** An audio region is a graphical representation of a section of audio from an audio file. These graphical representations appear in the Project Audio Browser and Project Audio window, Audio File editor, Audio Track editor, or Tracks area. An audio region can be as long as the entire audio file in which it is located, or it may be only a few milliseconds long. A single audio file can contain a virtually limitless number of audio regions. When you record or load audio into Logic, it will always contain at least one audio region that is, by default, the length of the entire audio file.

▷ **Audio channel:** Every audio channel strip in the Mixer is assigned to an audio channel internal to Logic, and every audio track in the Tracks area has an audio channel assigned to it. You can have more than one audio track assigned to the same audio channel, but only one at a time can be playing sound. There are 256 internal audio channels available in Logic.

▷ **Software instrument:** Software instruments are basically synthesizers that you can play, program, and record in Logic. Software instruments are controlled by MIDI, but produce audio. They use their own special software instrument channel strips in the Mixer, and software instrument tracks in the Tracks area. Logic includes a host of its own built-in instruments, such as Sculpture, ES2, and Vintage Electric Piano. It can also host software instruments from third-party vendors. We'll explore software instruments in detail in Chapter 9, "Working with Software Instruments."

▷ **Apple Loop:** An Apple Loop is a special type of region. I discuss Apple Loops in depth in Chapter 7, "Working with Audio and Apple Loops"; for now, just know that Apple Loops have digital audio information that has been specifically "tagged" so that they will automatically play back at the correct time and in the correct musical key as your Logic project, regardless of the tempo or key in which the original audio was recorded. Apple Loops may also contain MIDI and channel strip information in addition to audio information.

▷ **MIDI region:** Similar to audio regions, a MIDI region is a graphical representation of MIDI data. Unlike audio regions, however, MIDI regions are not necessarily related to any external information stored in a file on your hard disk. MIDI regions representing sections of MIDI data can be saved to files if you so choose, but they do not need to be stored anywhere other than the Logic project file. If you do save a MIDI file to your storage drive, the MIDI data will still remain in the Logic song as well. Software instrument and external MIDI instrument tracks utilize MIDI regions.

▷ **MIDI channel:** This refers to one of the 16 channels that each MIDI port can transmit, or all 16 channels if you have selected the All option. Every software instrument and external MIDI track is assigned to a MIDI channel except in the case of the All option, in which case the track itself is not assigned to a MIDI channel, but the individual messages are. You can have more than one software instrument or external MIDI track assigned to the same MIDI port and channel.

▷ **Event:** An event is a single occurrence of any MIDI message. This can be as simple as a single MIDI message, such as a program change, or it can be a note message, which is actually a compound MIDI message consisting of multiple MIDI messages that are represented as a single MIDI event in Logic.

▷ **Object:** The term *object* can broadly apply to nearly anything graphically represented on your display, but in Logic, *object* specifically refers to a virtual studio building block in Logic's MIDI Environment.

The Logic Pro Main Window

Those upgrading from pre–Logic 8 versions of Logic will notice that the former Arrange window, now called the Logic Pro main window, shown in Figure 2.1, has undergone a major transformation. Not only is it where you create tracks, record audio and MIDI, slice and splice MIDI and audio regions, and "arrange" them, but you can now access all the various editors, lists, and browsers directly in the Logic Pro main window! If you spent some time working with Logic 8 or 9, the main window in Logic X looks familiar, but there have been some significant changes. For those who are new to Logic, the Logic Pro main window is the first window you see when you launch Logic, and it is the window in which you will do the majority of your work. Figure 2.1 shows the Logic Pro main window in full-screen mode, which you access by clicking the arrows in the upper-right corner of the Logic Pro main window.

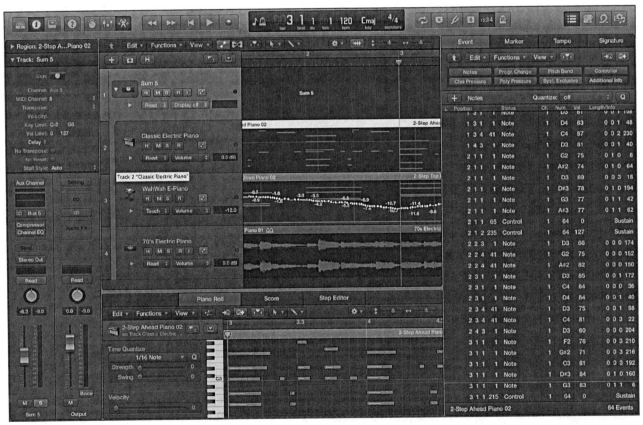

Figure 2.1 The Logic Pro main window, shown in full-screen mode, contains most of the commonly used setup, arrangement, recording, and editing functions.
© Apple Inc.

At the top of the main window is the control bar, a customizable selection of buttons for many common functions, such as accessing the Toolbar (now hidden by default in Logic Pro X) or accessing the main window Mixer and editors. The control bar also contains the transport controls, which have buttons to activate recording, turn on Cycle mode, and turn the metronome on and off, and it also includes the LCD, a display area that shows information about the position of the playhead, the project tempo and key, and so forth.

If you click the List Editors button or the Browser button at the right end of the control bar, a new pane will open on the right side of the main window, giving you access to items like the Event list and the Project Audio Browser. The Note Pads button gives you access to notes panes for your entire Logic project or for each individual track, and the Loop Browser button gives you access to your Apple Loops. Figure 2.1 shows the Lists area with the Event list displayed.

The left side of the screen includes the Inspector, which consists of a Region parameter box, a Track parameter box, and the main window channel strips. You can show or hide the Inspector by clicking the Inspector button in the control bar or by using the I key command. (Key commands are introduced later in this chapter in "The Key Commands Window.") If you click the Library button at the right end of the control bar, the Library will open on the left side of the main window. In the Library, you can view and select the available patches for the selected track. Clicking the Library button again will hide the Library. To the right of the Inspector is the track list, which shows the track headers for all tracks in your project and the global tracks. Global tracks are covered in Chapter 4, "Global Elements of Logic." The middle of the window is the Tracks area, which displays horizontal strips for each track and regions of audio or MIDI that are on your tracks. If you have automation mode on, as in Figure 2.1, you will also see track automation data in a track lane, meaning that track contains some automation data. The bar rule above the track list displays the measures of the song, and the playhead is the vertical line you see at measure 3, beat 1; it shows your exact location. The Tracks area is where you can perform Quick Swipe Comping, and you can also perform Flex Time and Flex Pitch directly in the Tracks area, along with much of your other region editing tasks.

You can also access the Mixer; the Audio Track and Audio File editors; the Piano Roll, Score, and Step editors; and the Smart Controls. As you can see, there are a lot of tools at your disposal, all in one window. In Chapter 6, "The Logic Pro Main Window," we'll explore in depth all the possibilities that the main window offers.

For those of you upgrading from GarageBand or who are new to computer-based recording entirely and who may feel overwhelmed by all the possibilities in Logic Pro X, you can work from a more manageable interface. It offers less access to the more powerful features in the main window, and less access to other windows available in Logic. As you become more comfortable with the features in Logic, you can add different capabilities selectively, growing your tools as you grow your knowledge. That said, this book will be diving into all the advanced features head first, so while you may want to manage the features while you do your own work, you will want full access to them while you work through this book. We'll cover all of that in more detail in Chapter 3, "The Logic Project." In the meantime, Figure 2.2 shows the Logic Pro main window with the advanced features disabled. Note that the MIDI editors at the bottom of the window offer one less option, and the browser on the right side of the window offers only the Media option.

The Mixer

The Mixer contains a separate channel strip for every audio and MIDI track in the Tracks area, along with Auxiliary and Output channel strips. Normally, it instantly adapts to your current tracks setup, adding, deleting, and rearranging channel strips based on the contents of the Tracks area. As you can see in Figure 2.3, the Mixer resembles a standard mixing desk, with a channel strip for each channel.

You can use the Mixer to mix the volume, panorama, routings, effects, and so on of the audio and MIDI tracks in your song. You can move effects from one slot to another either within or between channel strips in the Mixer. You can choose to view only certain types of channels, all your Tracks area channels, or every channel strip in your entire project. You can adjust single or multiple channel strips at the same time. Finally, you can print a final stereo or surround audio file of your entire song from the Mixer.

Using the Mixer to mix your song is explained further in Chapter 11, "Mixing in Logic."

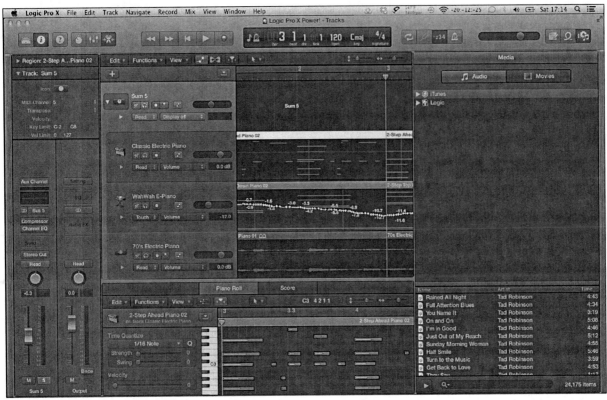

Figure 2.2 For those of you who are new to computer-based recording or who are making the move from GarageBand to Logic, you can choose to work in a more managed environment with fewer advanced options.
© Apple Inc.

Figure 2.3 The Mixer automatically adjusts itself to reflect the audio and MIDI channels currently in your Tracks area.
© Apple Inc.

The Project Audio Browser

The Project Audio Browser is a catalog of all the audio files and audio regions used in a given Logic song. The Project Audio Browser can be found in the Browsers area of the main window or opened as its own separate window, the Project Audio window. The Project Audio Browser may look unassuming compared to some of the others, but don't be fooled—as you can see in Figure 2.4, the Project Audio Browser is far more than a simple list of audio regions.

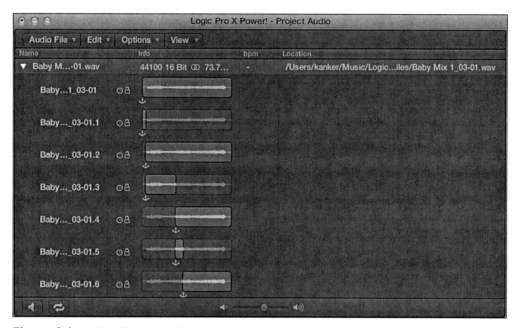

Figure 2.4 In the Project Audio Browser, shown here in its own separate window, you can add, subtract, loop, convert, and otherwise manipulate the audio files and regions in your Logic song.
© Apple Inc.

Using the various tools and menu options in the Project Audio Browser, you can audition, group, and adjust regions, as well as perform all sorts of file processes and conversions. You can also easily add audio regions to your Tracks area by simply dragging regions from the Project Audio Browser. The Project Audio Browser is easily one of the most important areas in Logic when you are using audio in your songs, as you'll see in Chapter 7.

The Audio Editors

For those of you who are upgrading from earlier versions of Logic, you read that right: *editors*. Previously, there were only two areas in Logic where you could do heavy audio editing: the Arrange area and the Sample editor. Logic Pro X not only changed the name of the Arrange area to the Tracks area, but the Sample editor is now known as the Audio File editor. Additionally, Logic Pro X has introduced the Audio Track editor.

When you manipulate audio regions in the Tracks area, you are really only editing Logic's pointers to a given audio file. The Audio Track editor gives you this same ability. However, in the Audio File editor, you can operate on the actual audio file itself. Both of these editors can be opened in the main window or in their own separate window. Figure 2.5 shows a stereo audio file in the Audio Track editor in the main window.

You can edit audio at the sample level in the Tracks area and both of the audio editors. One major benefit of using either audio editor is that you can work on your audio in a more focused setting, independent of all the other elements in your Tracks area. Additionally, the Audio File editor allows you to manipulate your audio destructively (in other words, permanently). Chapter 7 will give you more explanation on how to work with and edit audio in the Tracks area and both audio editors.

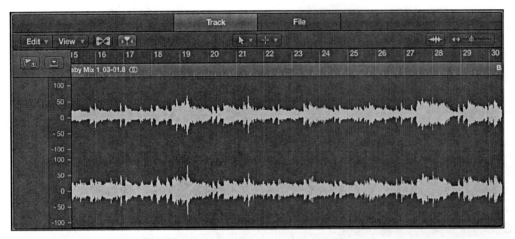

Figure 2.5 The Audio Track editor allows you to process and edit an audio file and offers amazingly precise resolution and editing tools.
© Apple Inc.

The Event List

As you would imagine, the Event list gives you a detailed list of all the events for the selected window or region. If you are looking at the entire main window, the Event list shows you what region is coming up next; if you're on a MIDI track, the Event list displays a detailed list of all the MIDI events in the track; and so on. Figure 2.6 shows an Event list of a MIDI track in the main window's Lists area. It can also be opened in its own separate window and as a one-line floating window.

The Event list is not simply a textual view of information. It is a very powerful editor, offering you precise access to more parameters than any other editor. The Event list is also an excellent tool to use in tandem with the other editors. For example, you can use an Event list window to give yourself a precise view of your data while using another editor to operate on your song. You'll learn more about methods of using the Event list in Chapter 8, "Working with MIDI."

The Piano Roll Editor

The Piano Roll editor is a MIDI note editor that displays MIDI note events as horizontal bars across the screen. The Piano Roll editor resembles a "piano roll" style of editor (so named because of its similarity to an old-time player piano song roll), with notes scrolling to the right of a graphic keyboard. It can be opened in the main window or in its own separate window, as shown in Figure 2.7.

If you want to program and edit your MIDI notes graphically, the Piano Roll editor is the place to do it. You not only can create and manipulate notes and control messages using the Piano Roll editor, but you can also use its more advanced features, including some new ones in Logic Pro X, which are detailed in Chapter 8.

The Step Editor

The Step editor (previously called the Hyper editor) is one of the least understood editors in Logic. It is a controller editor, a drum editor, and a grid editor all in one. It allows you to save event definitions as *lane sets*—or *MIDI view filter templates*, if you will—and complements the other Logic editors very well. Figure 2.8 shows a Step editor being used to create and edit MIDI controller data in the main window. It can also be opened in its own separate window.

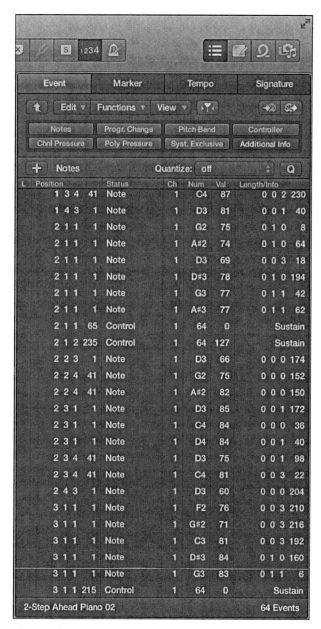

L	Position				Status	Ch	Num	Val	Length/Info
	1	3	4	41	Note	1	C4	87	0 0 2 230
	1	4	3	1	Note	1	D3	81	0 0 1 40
	2	1	1	1	Note	1	G2	75	0 1 0 8
	2	1	1	1	Note	1	A#2	74	0 1 0 64
	2	1	1	1	Note	1	D3	69	0 0 3 18
	2	1	1	1	Note	1	D#3	78	0 1 0 194
	2	1	1	1	Note	1	G3	77	0 1 1 42
	2	1	1	1	Note	1	A#3	77	0 1 1 62
	2	1	1	65	Control	1	64	0	Sustain
	2	1	2	235	Control	1	64	127	Sustain
	2	2	3	1	Note	1	D3	66	0 0 0 174
	2	2	4	41	Note	1	G2	75	0 0 0 152
	2	2	4	41	Note	1	A#2	82	0 0 0 150
	2	3	1	1	Note	1	D3	85	0 0 1 172
	2	3	1	1	Note	1	C4	84	0 0 0 36
	2	3	1	1	Note	1	D4	84	0 0 1 40
	2	3	4	41	Note	1	D3	75	0 0 1 98
	2	3	4	41	Note	1	C4	81	0 0 3 22
	2	4	3	1	Note	1	D3	60	0 0 0 204
	3	1	1	1	Note	1	F2	76	0 0 3 210
	3	1	1	1	Note	1	G#2	71	0 0 3 216
	3	1	1	1	Note	1	C3	81	0 0 3 192
	3	1	1	1	Note	1	D#3	84	0 1 0 160
	3	1	1	1	Note	1	G3	83	0 1 1 6
	3	1	1	215	Control	1	64	0	Sustain

2-Step Ahead Piano 02   64 Events

Figure 2.6 The Event list allows users to view and edit data in a text list.
© Apple Inc.

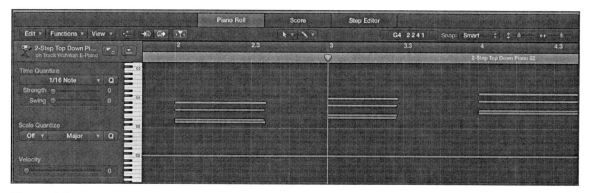

Figure 2.7 The Piano Roll editor is just one of the powerful MIDI editors in Logic. It allows you to edit MIDI notes and controller values graphically.
© Apple Inc.

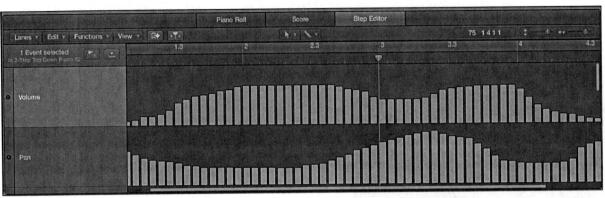

Figure 2.8 The Step editor can be a grid editor, a drum editor, or a controller editor. Here, it's being used to create and edit MIDI controller data.
© Apple Inc.

Don't worry if this definition seems a bit confusing right now. Chapter 8 will describe the many different uses for this powerful and often-overlooked MIDI editor. The Step editor might seem unusual at first, but its uniqueness and functionality are among the many features that set Logic apart from the pack.

The Score Editor

If you are comfortable working with musical notation, you will be comfortable with the Score editor. Logic's Score editor not only allows you to view, create, and edit MIDI as if you were writing on sheet music instead of a computer, but it allows you to print out professional-quality score charts as well. Figure 2.9 shows a piano part of a song displayed as musical notation in a Score editor window. You can also open a Score editor in the main window.

Figure 2.9 The Score editor allows you to create, view, edit, and print your MIDI tracks in musical notation.
© Apple Inc.

The Score editor offers traditional musicians and composers complete access to the world of sequencing in a familiar format, while being as customizable and powerful as the rest of Logic. For Score editor users upgrading from earlier versions of Logic, you'll be happy to know that the Score editor has seen improvements in Logic Pro X. You'll learn about it all in detail in Chapter 8!

The Loop Browser

As discussed earlier in this chapter, Apple Loops are a special kind of audio file. To help distinguish them from the normal audio files in your Project Audio Browser, Apple Loops get their own special browser, as shown in Figure 2.10.

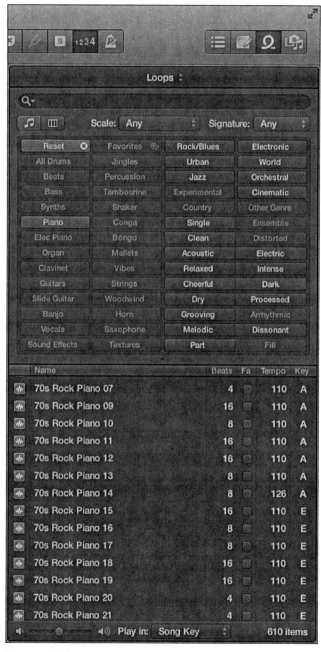

Figure 2.10 The Loop Browser lets you quickly locate and audition Apple Loops, as well as certain other types of loops such as ACID loops, and add them to the Tracks area.
© Apple Inc.

The Loop Browser allows you to quickly search, audition, and drag loops into your song. Apple Loops that you buy and drag onto the Loop window will automatically be indexed with the rest of your Apple Loops. You can index Apple Loops that you create however you choose. Other types of loops, such as ACID loops, may be accessible through the Loop Browser, but will not be indexed as thoroughly as Apple Loops. The Loop browser is available either as a tab in the main window or as its own window.

The Browsers

In addition to the Project Audio Browser, there are two other browsers that give you full access to all files on your computer or any connected drives that are usable in Logic. Figure 2.11 shows the contents of a folder in All Files view.

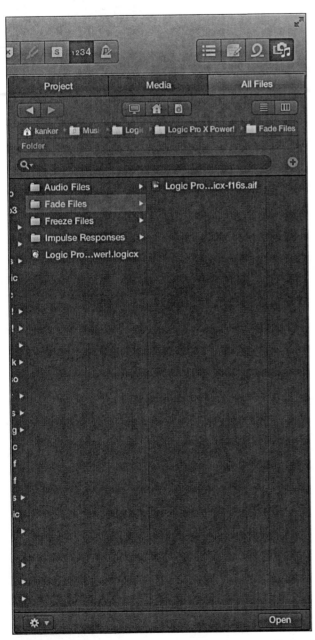

Figure 2.11 The browser gives you access to all the different files on your drives that Logic can use directly in the main window.

© Apple Inc.

The Media Browser allows you to see all the music and video files on your system, to audition audio files, and to add them directly to the Tracks area or to the Project Audio Browser for further processing. The All Files browser gives you access to your entire file system, allowing you to browse for and open other Logic or GarageBand projects, for example. We'll go into more depth about the browsers in Chapter 6.

The Library

Sifting through banks of presets across different instruments to find the perfect sound can be difficult at best. The Library tab in the main window, shown in Figure 2.12, makes this problem virtually disappear.

Figure 2.12 The Library makes finding the right plug-in preset fast and convenient, giving you instant access to all your Logic presets.
© Apple Inc.

The Library gives you immediate access to presets for all the Logic instruments and effects, channel strip presets, settings for your Audio Units plug-ins that you save via the plug-in control bar, and patches. Additionally, ReWire instruments and External MIDI instruments you have configured either in the Environment window or in Audio MIDI Setup (found in your /Applications/ Utilities folder) can be accessed in the Library.

A Note on Logic's Use of Mac OS X Directories: You may have already noticed that the Logic Pro file in your Applications directory does not have a folder around it, as some other programs you may own do. This is because Logic Pro follows Apple Inc.'s guidelines for where the support files for applications should go.

Logic Pro files are in one of two places:

▶ Factory presets and support files are in the "local" directory (meaning, at the level of your hard drive): /Library/Application Support/Logic.
▶ User presets and support files are in your user directory (with "~" being the UNIX symbol for the Home directory for a given user): ~/Library/Application Support/Logic. They can also be found in ~/Music/ Audio Music Apps.

As you see, there's really only a single folder to which you'll be adding information, and that's the user folder. It's also very convenient to back up just this one folder and know that all your presets, templates, sampler instruments, and so on have been backed up.

The Marker, Tempo, and Signature Lists

There are three other lists that can be found in the List Editors area of the Logic Pro main window—the Marker list, the Tempo list, and the Signature list. Each list allows you to create, edit, and delete events for its respective global track. Figure 2.13 shows a Marker list open in the List Editors area of the main window. Each of these lists can also be opened in a separate window. These lists will be covered in detail in Chapter 4.

Smart Controls

Smart Controls are one of the cool new features in Logic Pro X. Basically, Smart Controls give you access in the main window to the essential parameters for whatever plug-ins you have activated on the selected track. In other words, if you want to make quick edits to the effects on a given audio track or to a software instrument and the effects loaded in that track, opening that track's Smart Controls lets you work on all the plug-ins on a track simultaneously, without having to open each individual plug-in window. Figure 2.14 shows the Smart Controls for the channel strip patch Classic Electric Piano. This channel strip patch includes the Vintage Electric Piano software instrument and the Overdrive and Compressor effects. The Smart Controls for those three plug-ins are arranged left to right, respectively.

You can also edit existing Smart Controls and create your own Smart Controls for Logic's built-in instruments and effects and for third-party plug-ins and save them in a patch. You can map Smart Controls to your hardware controller, and even use Smart Controls to write track automation! Smart Controls also feature built-in access to the MIDI effect, Arpeggiator. Smart Controls are covered in detail in Chapter 6.

Track Stacks

Another powerful new feature in Logic Pro X is Track Stacks. A Track Stack is a handy way to group tracks for mixing and processing. You can combine several tracks into a stack, giving you a main track at the top of the stack that can be used to control all the other tracks in the stack.

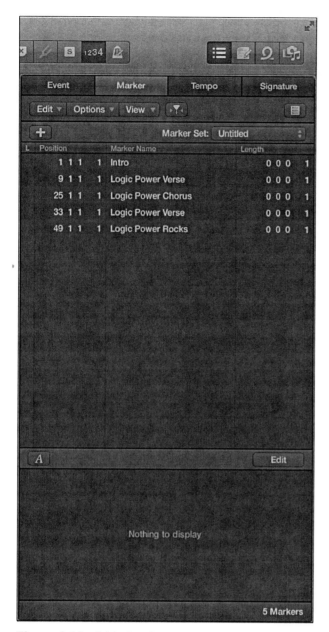

Figure 2.13 A Marker list open in the List Editors area of the main window. The Marker, Tempo, and Signature lists make creating, editing, and deleting events for their respective global tracks very easy.
© Apple Inc.

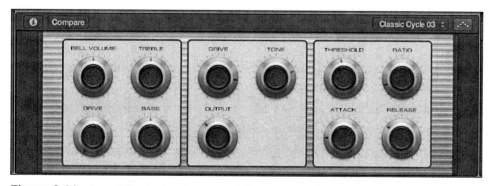

Figure 2.14 Smart Controls give you quick access to the most essential parameters of any software instrument and/or effects on a given track.
© Apple Inc.

There are two types of Track Stacks: Folder Stacks, which give basic control over volume, mute, solo, and automation for all tracks in the stack as a group, and Summing Stacks, which give you all the capabilities of the Folder Stack and let you process the output of all the tracks as a group. Figure 2.15 shows a Summing Track Stack in the Tracks area. Note the top track, Sum 5, contains three electric piano tracks, two with MIDI regions and one with an audio region. Also note that the left channel strip in the Inspector is the master channel strip for the Sum 5 Track Stack, and that it allows you to insert effects and route the output of the channel to sends.

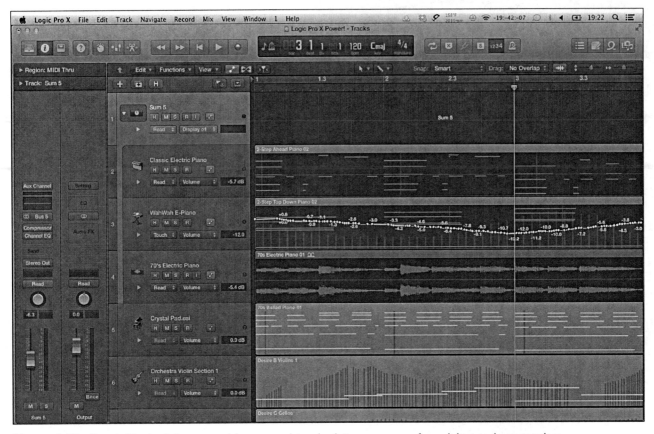

Figure 2.15 Track Stacks let you combine several tracks into one group for mixing and processing.
© Apple Inc.

Drummer

One other feature introduced in Logic Pro X is Drummer, a new type of track that is an editable virtual drummer. There are four different musical styles represented by Drummer, and multiple different "drummers" available per style. A Drummer track will contain at least one Drummer region, and a Drummer editor can be opened in the Editors area of the main window. Figure 2.16 shows a Drummer track with a Drummer region and the Drummer editor. You can also see some drum kit options in the Library, and the Drummer channel strip with pre-loaded effects.

Drummer also includes a Drum Kit Designer, allowing you to make custom kits. You can even have access to channel strips associated with each drum in the kit. Drummer will be covered in more detail in Chapter 6.

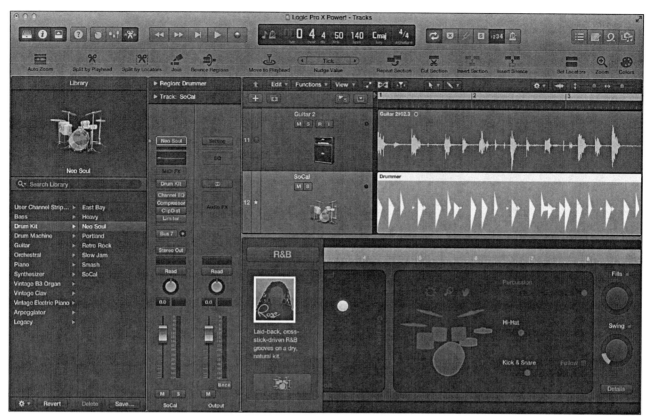

Figure 2.16 The new Drummer track puts a virtual drummer at your disposal, day or night.
© Apple Inc.

The Environment

The Environment is a window that offers you a library of graphical, onscreen objects that allow you to set up a virtual studio inside Logic, including all your studio objects and hardware routings (see Figure 2.17). The Environment also allows you to route external hardware with virtual processes and transformers. It's perhaps the most flexible, powerful, and (for some) daunting aspect of Logic.

For a long time, working in the Environment was essential to using Logic. Fortunately, the last few revisions of Logic have removed the need for most Logic users to ever have to tinker with the Environment. The introduction of Smart Controls with arpeggiators in the main window in Logic Pro X further distances the user from the need to work in the Environment. That said, if customizing your system for full control of a huge array of MIDI functions, including building a custom programming interface for your hardware synthesizers, then you will want to spend time learning about the power of the Environment. No other sequencer allows you to get under the hood to create unique devices and routings like Logic's Environment, and it will take time for you to feel comfortable using this power.

Notice that the Environment window itself is just an expansive open workspace, and that's exactly what the Environment offers you—an open surface on which to create your ideal studio. Let's look at another aspect of the Environment: layers.

Environment Layers

The Environment offers nearly infinite routing possibilities. Without some sort of organization, the Environment window would quickly become an unmanageably large space in which you would find yourself scrolling constantly to get to any structure you have created. To simplify and organize the Environment, Logic includes the concept of Environment layers. Notice that the left frame of the Environment window in Figure 2.17 includes a box called *Layer*. In this case, the layer is named SuperArp.

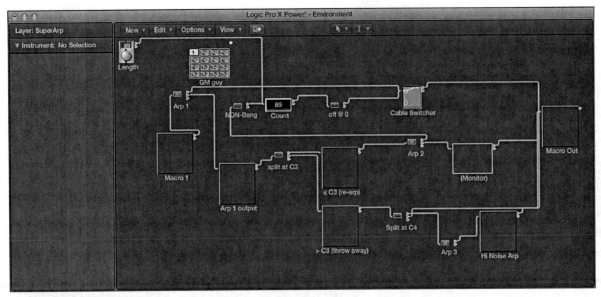

Figure 2.17 The Environment offers you nearly unlimited options for the construction of your own devices and routings inside Logic.
© Apple Inc.

If you click on the layer name, Logic displays a menu that contains all the available layers in that song's Environment, as shown in Figure 2.18.

Figure 2.18 This pop-up menu shows all the different layers available in the Environment of this song and enables you to create new layers on the fly.
© Apple Inc.

Layers allow you to organize your Environment into different levels, into which you can put as much or as little as you like to keep each Environment construction easily accessible. Putting different objects on different layers doesn't affect the way Logic processes the signals, but it does allow you to organize the Environment into more manageable sections.

You'll notice that Logic includes a few Environment layers out of the box. There is a special one worth looking at here: the Environment Mixer layer.

The Environment Mixer Layer

Every main window and Mixer channel strip has a corresponding Environment channel strip object. For your convenience, Logic automatically creates an Environment layer, called the *Mixer layer*, that consists of every audio, software instrument, input, output, aux, bus, and master channel strip in your project. By placing all these objects in the Mixer layer of the Environment, you keep the layer's contents separate from all the other layers in the Environment. You can access this layer from the Layer pop-up menu. Figure 2.19 shows a Mixer layer for a Logic project.

Figure 2.19 The Mixer layer of the Environment contains a complete mixer representing every audio and MIDI channel and routing for your current project.
© Apple Inc.

At first blush, this screen looks a lot like the Mixer shown in Figure 2.3, but the Environment Mixer layer doesn't contain any MIDI channel strips. You'll learn more about both mixers later; for now, you should just know you have a choice.

Unfortunately, exploring the full potential of the Environment is outside the scope of this book. For those of you who are keen to master the potential of the Environment, there are resources on the Internet, such as www.logic-users-group.com. Here, you can find expert Environment users willing to answer questions from beginners to very advanced users.

The MIDI Transform Window

The MIDI Transform window allows you to alter events according to definable parameters. If that sounds confusing, you're not alone—the MIDI Transform window is definitely complicated. To give you a quick example of a use for the MIDI Transform window, if you wanted to change all the D#2 notes in a given track to F#2 without manually editing the notes, you could quickly perform that action in the MIDI Transform window, as shown in Figure 2.20.

You can design your own transformations using amazingly complex data manipulations involving multiple criteria and data mapping, or use the transformations that Apple includes for you with Logic. If all that sounds difficult, don't worry; Chapter 8 explains this feature in detail.

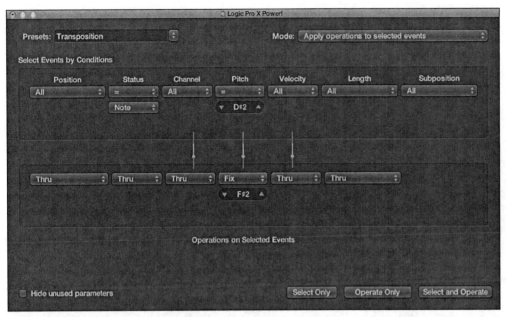

Figure 2.20 The MIDI Transform window is powerful enough to make complex global data transformations based on a custom set of criteria. You can also use it to make relatively uncomplicated changes, such as the simple note transposition here.
© Apple Inc.

The Key Commands Window

Every program allows you to access its features through keyboard shortcuts in addition to selecting commands with the mouse. This is nothing new. However, Logic makes more extensive use of key commands than most applications. In fact, the Key Commands window by itself offers many more options than most applications, as you can see in Figure 2.21.

For most users, accessing functions via key commands is much quicker than using the mouse, so most professional applications offer a vast selection of their functions via key commands. The more flexible applications often allow users to define their own keys to personalize the application to reflect their preferences. Logic takes this a step further—not only can nearly every feature be accessed via a key command, but, in fact, many commands in Logic can *only* be accessed via key command. Also, many key command–only functions do not come with those commands preassigned to keys, so to access such commands, the user first must define them. Setting up your own key commands in Logic is discussed in the following chapter.

It might seem counterintuitive for some commands to be available only via key commands, fueling Logic's reputation for being difficult to learn. In truth, it is for ease of use that some of the advanced, expert features are available only via key commands. Rather than crowd each menu with large numbers of commands that most people would never use, Logic makes the least accessed and most obscure functions available for those who need them, but keeps them out of the way of everyone else.

Right-Mouse Button Preferences

If you are using a two-button mouse, you can configure Logic to perform one of four functions when you right-click (or Control-click):

- ▷ You can assign it to a specific tool.
- ▷ You can assign it to open the Tool menu.
- ▷ You can assign it to open contextual shortcut menus.
- ▷ You can assign it to open combined Tool and contextual menus.

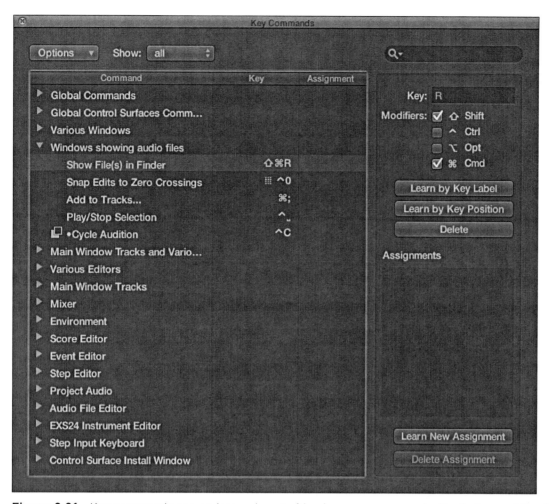

Figure 2.21 Key commands are an integral part of Logic, as you can see by the features of the Key Commands window and the number of commands that are available only as key commands.
© Apple Inc.

If you are using a trackpad, you can assign a secondary click gesture in the System Preferences Trackpad pane to access the right-mouse button preference you assign. Each option has its uses, but it's up to you to decide which one works best for you.

It's easy to configure your right-click preference in Logic. Simply open the Editing tab in the General Preferences window by selecting Logic Pro > Preferences > General or by choosing General in the Preferences menu in the Toolbar and selecting the Editing tab. Figure 2.22 shows the Editing tab of the General Preferences window. Then open the Right Mouse Button pop-up menu and choose one of the following:

▷ If you choose Is Assignable to a Tool, you will have three tool options at your immediate disposal at all times—one for when you click, one for when you Command-click, and one for when you right-click.
▷ If you select Opens Tool Menu, then every time you click the right mouse button, a menu will open in which you can select the tool you would like to use.
▷ If you want to have access to contextual menus with your right mouse button, then select the Opens Shortcut Menu option.
▷ If you think that having access to both tools and contextual menus would work best, you can assign your right-click preference to Opens Tool and Shortcut Menu, like the one shown in Figure 2.23.

It's important to note that the Tool menu and Shortcut menu contents will vary depending on the window, and sometimes even the area of the window, in which you are working, and that not all shortcut menus will have tools. (If it's not the Tracks area or an editor, it's likely not to have tools.) Also remember that although you may choose to assign the right-click preference to a

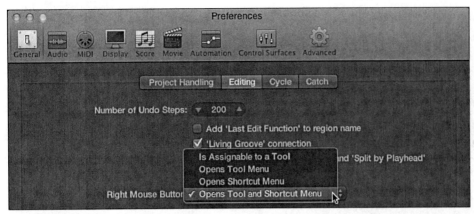

Figure 2.22 The Editing tab of the General Preferences window. You can configure your right-click preference in the Right Mouse Button pop-up menu.
© Apple Inc.

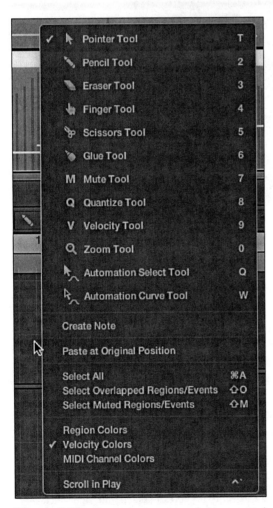

Figure 2.23 If you assign your right–mouse button preference to Opens Tool and Shortcut Menu, then whenever you right-click, a menu featuring both tools and contextual shortcuts will open.
© Apple Inc.

third tool or to access the Tool menu, whenever you see the phrase "right-click" in this book, it means any of the different methods you can use to open a contextual menu: right-click, Control-click, or your assigned trackpad gesture. For the purposes of this book, I will be using the Opens Shortcut Menu setting to cover the different contextual menu items available the majority of the time. In my own general workflow, I find having both the tools and the menus available to be the more elegant approach.

Screensets

Most sequencers allow you to arrange the various windows and editors onscreen and save these screen formats. As with key commands, however, Logic takes the concept and runs with it in its own uniquely powerful ways. Screensets are not simply an available option in Logic; they are an integral part of how you use the application. Notice that a number appears in the Logic menu bar, as shown in Figure 2.24. This number (4 in Figure 2.24) indicates the designated number of the screenset that you are currently accessing. You can access up to 90 screensets directly from the numeric keypad, and you can access additional screensets from the Next Screenset and Previous Screenset key commands. As you open, close, and move windows around, Logic automatically remembers them; the next time you launch your Logic song, it will automatically have the same windows, open in the same location, in each screenset.

Figure 2.24 Screensets are not an afterthought or a hidden option in Logic. The active screenset is prominently displayed in Logic's menu bar. Here the menu bar shows that screenset 4 is active.
© Apple Inc.

Setting up your screensets helps you create your own ideal workspace and is one of the ways in which Logic is unique—allowing every user to customize Logic to suit himself or herself. In fact, setting up screensets is one of the first things you'll want to do as you customize Logic for yourself, as you will see in the next chapter.

Speaking of customizing Logic to suit your needs, now that you have an idea of the possibilities of Logic, it's time to set up your default template. The next chapter, "The Logic Project," will explain how.

The Logic Project

3

A N IMPORTANT DISTINCTION BETWEEN LOGIC AND OTHER MUSIC WORKSTATION APPLICATIONS is just how much information is stored in each document file, which is called a *project* in Logic. In most applications, you set up the application the way you want to by arranging windows, toolbars, and so on. When you load a document, that document uses the application configuration. In Logic, the *project* contains everything about your studio—the setup of all your instruments, editors, windows, screensets, and everything else that is configurable in Logic. In fact, each project in Logic is a self-contained virtual studio. That means if you create a project in your copy of Logic and then open it in someone else's copy of Logic, you will still find your own familiar virtual studio waiting for you.

When you launch Logic for the first time, it automatically presents you with a selection of different templates in the Project Chooser. These templates represent Apple's effort to provide an array of ready-made project setups that people will find generally useful. Figure 3.1 shows the Project Chooser.

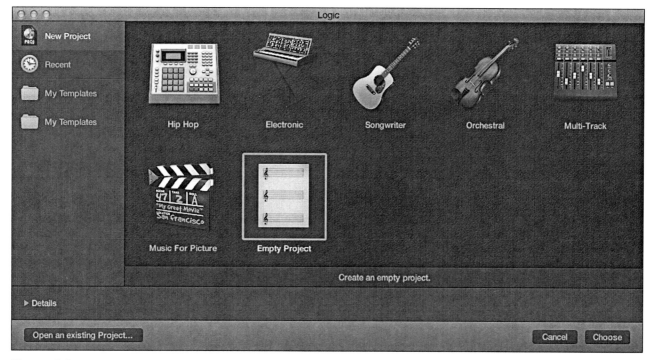

Figure 3.1 The Project Chooser. When you first launch Logic, or when you use the File > New command, the Project Chooser opens.
© Apple Inc.

Templates are blank songs with a specific configuration from which you might want to start. Apple's templates are stored in the Application Support folder for Logic, which you can find at /Library/Application Support/Logic/Project Templates. This chapter deals with creating and saving your own custom template, which will help you get right down to the business of creating music every time you open Logic.

You should explore the templates that Apple includes with Logic to get a feel for the myriad ways you can configure Logic. Apple has included templates for uses as varied as electronic music composition, music for picture, and multi-track recording. To open a template in the Project Chooser, simply click on its icon and then click the Choose button. Each time you close a template, you can access the Project Chooser by selecting File > New from Template or pressing Command+N.

After you have explored some of these templates, open an empty project by doing the following:

1. Select File > New from Template or press Command+N.
2. Click on the Empty Project option.
3. Click the Choose button.

> **TIP:** You can also access an empty project by selecting File > New or by pressing Shift+Command+N.

You'll use this empty project to create your template. When complete, you will be able to select this template to have Logic immediately open into your personal virtual studio instead of a general default song.

Don't worry about the Details area that you access by clicking the disclosure triangle at the bottom-left corner of the Project Chooser. Some of its options are unnecessary for a template, and the other options you'll set up manually to help you understand how to change things like your audio inputs and outputs when needed. The Details area is covered in Chapter 12, "Working with and Sharing Files."

Trust me on this: Creating your template project is one of the most important things you will do in Logic! The actual mechanics involved in creating a template couldn't be simpler:

1. You set up a Logic project.
2. You name the Logic project.
3. You select File > Save As Template.

Exactly *how* you set up the template, however, involves some serious thought and preparation. Creating your template project is a continuous process. As you learn more about Logic and your working preferences, you can always go back and change your template project accordingly. You can even create a number of different templates designed for different purposes, much like the templates that Apple has included with Logic. To get you started, here are a few points that you need to consider.

Visualizing Your Workspace

The first and most important aspect of creating a template project is to have a general idea of what aspects of the program you'll want to access. Chapter 2, "A Quick Tour of Logic Pro," gave you an overview of some of the windows and editors in Logic. Did you already get a sense of which ones you expect to use the most? Do you imagine yourself needing the main window and the Audio File editor all the time, the Piano Roll editor a little, and the Score editor not at all? Do you imagine that your most important windows will be the Score editor and Event List editor, and then the main window and the Mixer? Do you need to access Environment objects creatively for each composition? You don't need to know how to use all the windows and editors yet—that's what the rest of the book is for. For now, consider how you might want to work and which windows you'll want to have readily available.

Next, consider how much screen real estate you have. Do you have dual 27-inch screens so you can spread out everything you'll need at once? Are you making do with a 13-inch laptop screen? Do you like to work with one single window on the screen at one time, or do you like to have each editor in its own separate window? Luckily, Logic's screensets allow you to build your template project to fit any of these configurations; all you need to have is a general idea of where you'd like to start.

Remember, the core idea behind Logic is to be as configurable as possible to allow you the flexibility to create your own ideal workspace. If you have an inkling of what the makeup of that ideal space will be, then it will be that much easier to create it. The name of the game here is experimentation. If you're not sure you'll have enough room for an editor, open the editor in the Editors area of the main window. You could even open it in its own window, resize it, move it around, and see how it feels to use it in that size and position. When you're comfortable with Logic, rearranging your template will be as simple as opening the application, placing the window you need in the screenset you desire, perhaps locking the screenset (explained later in this chapter in the section "Setting Up Screensets"), and resaving the project. For now, with just what has already been discussed and a bit of careful planning, you can already set up an almost optimal template project.

Creating Your Template

Not too long ago, creating a new workspace from scratch in Logic meant getting your hands dirty and digging around in menus and the Environment. Having to figure out how to create and configure instrument objects, audio objects, Environment Mixers, and so forth helped add to the impression that Logic was an application with a very steep learning curve. The process is so much simpler these days that getting a template started with a full complement of audio, software instrument, and external MIDI tracks takes little more than a few mouse clicks and keystrokes.

To begin creating your template project, select Empty Project in the Project Chooser (if you do not already have an empty project open). When you create an empty project, you are greeted with an empty main window showing a New Tracks dialog box, as shown in Figure 3.2. In the New Tracks dialog box, you can add and configure audio, software instruments, Drummer tracks, guitar or bass tracks, and external MIDI tracks. Let's begin by adding some audio tracks to the empty project.

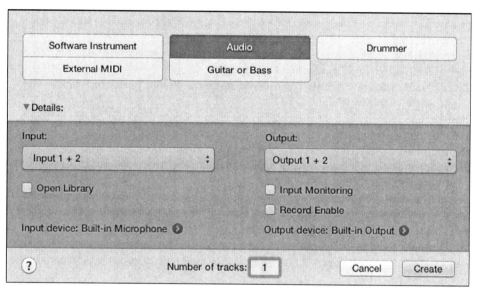

Figure 3.2 The New Tracks dialog box.
© Apple Inc.

Adding Audio Tracks

To add audio tracks to your project, click the Audio button in the New Tracks dialog box. Figure 3.2 shows the new audio track options. In the Number of Tracks field, enter the number of audio tracks you would like to add to your project. (Don't worry about getting it right the first time. You can always add more tracks later.) You then need to configure your audio tracks. Click the Details disclosure triangle to access the configuration parameters. The New Tracks dialog box gives you the following options for configuring your audio tracks so they'll be ready to go immediately after creation:

▷ **Input:** The Input menu allows you to assign hardware inputs, buses, or no input to your new audio tracks. With no-input tracks, you can configure the input later if desired. If you select a single input, Input 1 for example, all your new audio tracks will be mono. If you choose a paired input—for example, Input 1 + 2—your new audio tracks will be stereo. If you choose Surround as the format for your new audio tracks, Logic will configure your hardware inputs per the assignment in the Input screen of the I/O Assignments tab of the Audio Preferences window, covered in the section "Configuring Surround Inputs" later in this chapter. You also have the option of selecting No Input or a bus for the input of surround audio tracks. If you are creating more than one new audio track assigned to hardware inputs or to buses and you select the Ascending option at the top of the Input menu, Logic will automatically assign hardware inputs or buses to your new audio tracks in ascending order. Alternatively, suppose you are assigning your new audio tracks to hardware inputs and are creating more new audio tracks than you have hardware inputs. In that case, after Logic has assigned all your hardware inputs to audio tracks, Logic will start back at hardware input 1 and continue assigning subsequent inputs in ascending order. Therefore, if you create 10 new mono audio tracks and select the Ascending option, but you have only eight hardware inputs, Logic will assign audio tracks 1–8 to hardware inputs 1–8, respectively, and then assign audio track 9 to hardware input 1 and audio track 10 to hardware input 2.

▷ **Output:** The Output menu allows you to assign your new audio tracks to hardware outputs, buses, no output, or surround. If you select No Output, you can configure the output later if desired. As with the Input menu, if you select a single output or a paired output, all subsequent outputs will be mono or stereo, respectively. If you select Surround as your output format, Logic will configure your hardware outputs per the assignment in the Output screen of the I/O Assignments tab of the Audio Preferences window. Surround outputs and the Output screen of the I/O Assignments tab of the Audio Preferences window are covered in detail in Chapter 11, "Mixing in Logic." If you are creating more than one new audio track assigned to hardware outputs or to buses and you select the Ascending option at the top of the Output menu, Logic will automatically assign hardware outputs or buses to your new audio tracks in ascending order. Alternatively, suppose you are assigning your new audio tracks to hardware outputs and are creating more new audio tracks than you have hardware outputs. In that case, once Logic has assigned all your hardware outputs to audio tracks, Logic will start back at hardware output 1 and continue assigning subsequent outputs in ascending order.

▷ **Input Monitoring:** Selecting the Input Monitoring checkbox activates your new audio tracks' input monitoring buttons, allowing you to monitor signals passing through your new audio tracks' channel strips when the audio tracks are not record enabled. Beware that if you have any live mic sources hooked up and your monitoring is turned on—for example, you are working on your laptop and the built-in mic is your input device and the built-in speakers are your output device—expect to get a good dose of feedback. Always be mindful of your levels!

▷ **Record Enable:** Selecting the Record Enable checkbox activates your new audio tracks' Record Enable button, allowing you to begin recording to your new audio tracks almost immediately.

▷ **Open Library:** Selecting the Open Library checkbox opens the Library in the main window when you create your new audio tracks, allowing you to instantly access channel-strip settings for your new audio channel strips.

▷ **Input Device:** The Input Device field shows the currently selected input device for Logic. Clicking the right-arrow button to the right of the currently selected input device opens the Devices tab of the Audio Preferences window. This tab is covered in the section "Setting Up Your Hardware" later in this chapter.

▷ **Output Device:** The Output Device field shows the currently selected output device for Logic. Clicking the right-arrow button to the right of the currently selected output device opens the Devices tab of the Audio Preferences window. After you have configured all the options in the New Tracks dialog box, click the Create button, and the specified number of new audio tracks will be created. Your new audio tracks will be visible in the main window and channel strips for each new audio track will be added to the Mixer. Channel strips will also be created in the Mixer layer of the Environment for each new audio track.

What if you created eight mono audio tracks, but you would like to add eight stereo audio tracks? You can open the New Tracks dialog box by doing one of the following:

▷ Clicking the left-most plus symbol(+) at the top of the track list
▷ Selecting Track > New Tracks
▷ Pressing Option+Command+N

If you want to add a track that is identical to a track you have selected in the track list, you can do one of the following:

▷ Select Track > Other > New Track With Duplicate Settings.
▷ Press Command+D.
▷ Click the right-most plus symbol at the top of the track list.

The new tracks will appear directly below the selected track in the track list, and the new track will be selected.

Configuring the Audio Track Inspector

Although all the parameters you need to get started are configured using the New Tracks dialog box, there are a couple of other options you may want to change in the Track Inspector. Each track has its own Track Inspector, although if a track shares a channel strip with other tracks, then they all share the same Track Inspector. Figure 3.3 shows an audio track and its Track Inspector.

The audio Track Inspector options are as follows:

▷ **Track name:** If you know what sources you are going to assign to a particular audio track, you can double-click on the default name to the right of the disclosure triangle—Audio 7 in Figure 3.3. Logic will display a text box in which you can type the new track name. For example, if you know Audio 7 will always be a kick drum, you could name the track "Kick Drum."

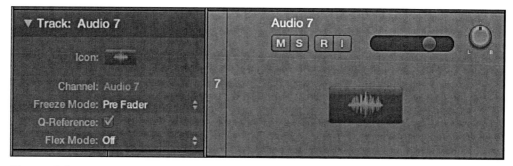

Figure 3.3 An audio track and its Track Inspector.
© Apple Inc.

▷ **Icon:** Use this setting to select the icon you want to represent the audio track. If you click and hold the mouse pointer on the image, Logic will display a menu of available icons, categorized by type. If you know that certain audio tracks will always be for a particular purpose—for example, audio track 1 will always be a vocal track and audio track 2 will always be the bass track—then feel free to assign an appropriate icon to each track.

▷ **Freeze Mode:** The Freeze Mode parameter lets you specify whether the track will include effects in the resulting Freeze file if you freeze the track. The Freeze Mode parameter and Freeze tracks are covered in Chapter 6, "The Logic Pro Main Window."

▷ **Q-Reference:** Logic Pro X lets you easily quantize audio. With the Q-Reference button selected, the audio track will give its region's transients as quantization reference points. Q-Reference and quantizing audio are covered in Chapter 6.

▷ **Flex Mode:** In addition to quantizing audio, Logic Pro X lets you treat audio in an elastic manner, changing the timing of an audio file in a nondestructive manner. The Flex Mode parameter helps you define what kind of Flex Time editing process will work on the audio. You can also select Flex Pitch Editing mode using the Flex Mode parameter. Flex Time and Flex Pitch editing and the Flex Mode menu are covered in Chapter 6.

Adding Guitar and Bass Tracks

In the New Tracks dialog box, you can add guitar and bass tracks by clicking the Guitar or Bass button. The new guitar and bass tracks options are identical to those offered when you add new audio tracks. The only difference is that when you select the Open Library checkbox and click Create, the channel strip associated with the new guitar or bass track will be loaded with guitar-oriented effects like Pedalboard and Amp Designer.

Adding Software Instrument Tracks

The software instrument track represents a simple MIDI device that plays on only one MIDI channel, but that produces audio via software instruments. To add software instrument tracks to your project, click the plus symbol at the top of the track list, select Track > New Software, or press Option+Command+N. Then click the Software Instrument button in the New Tracks dialog box that appears, as shown in Figure 3.4.

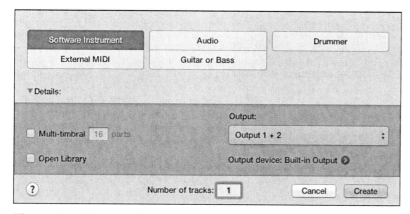

Figure 3.4 The New Tracks dialog box configured for creating new software instrument tracks.
© Apple Inc.

When you click the Software Instrument button, the New Tracks dialog box presents you with the following options:

▷ **Multi-Timbral:** Selecting the Multi-Timbral checkbox and entering a number in the Parts field creates your new software instrument as a multitimbral instrument with the number of parts you entered. Creating and using multitimbral software instruments is covered in Chapter 9, "Working with Software Instruments."

▷ **Output:** The Output menu allows you to assign your new software instrument tracks to specific hardware outputs or buses. If you select the Ascending option at the top of the Output menu, Logic will automatically assign hardware outputs or buses to your new software instrument tracks in ascending order.

▷ **Open Library:** Selecting the Open Library checkbox opens the Library in the main window when you create your new software instrument tracks, allowing you to instantly access channel-strip settings for your new software instrument channel strips. It also pre-loads the software instrument channel strips with an instrument and effects. Unless you know you want a lot of instances of Vintage Electric Piano in your template, it's probably best to keep this option unchecked. Chapter 9 will teach you how to add software instruments to your software instrument channel strips.

▷ **Output Device:** The Output Device field shows the currently selected output device for Logic. Clicking the right-arrow button to the right of the currently selected output device opens the Devices tab of the Audio Preferences window.

After you configure the New Tracks dialog box to create your software instruments, click the Create button. The specified number of software instrument tracks will be created. Your new software instrument tracks will be visible in the main window, and channel strips for each new software instrument track will be added to the Mixer. Channel strips will also be created in the Mixer layer of the Environment for each new software instrument track.

If you need to create any more software instrument tracks, you can use any of the methods described earlier for creating more audio tracks, although the key command for creating a duplicate software instrument track is Option+Command+S.

Configuring the Software Instrument Track Inspector

Because a software instrument track is a hybrid track that incorporates both MIDI sequencing capabilities and audio output, it has a wider range of track parameters than an audio track does. Figure 3.5 shows a newly created software instrument track and its Inspector.

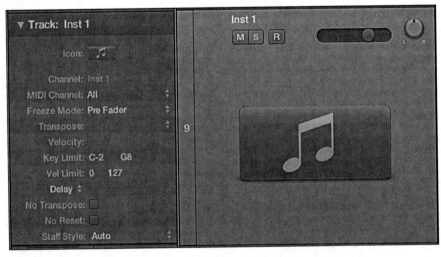

Figure 3.5 A software instrument track with its Inspector.
© Apple Inc.

The software instrument track parameters are as follows:

▷ **Track name:** If you know what software instrument you are going to assign to a particular software instrument track, double-click on the default name to the right of the disclosure triangle—Inst 1 in Figure 3.5. Logic will display a text box in which you can type the new track name. For example, if you know you will be adding Sculpture to software instrument track 1 of your template, you could name software instrument track 1 "Sculpture."

▷ **Icon:** Use this setting to select the icon you want to represent the software instrument track. If you know you'll be dedicating a software instrument track to a specific software instrument, feel free to assign an icon to that software instrument track. If you click and hold the mouse pointer on the image, Logic will display a menu with categorized picture options. Find one that represents your software instrument in some way. For example, if the software instrument is Vintage Electric Piano, you can use an electric piano image; if it's Ultrabeat, you could use one of the available drums options; and so on.)

▷ **MIDI Channel:** This parameter assigns the MIDI channel for your software instrument track. If you set the MIDI Channel parameter to All, then your software instrument will respond to any MIDI input when its track is selected. If you set the MIDI Channel parameter to a specific MIDI channel—channel 3, for example—then your software instrument will respond only to MIDI input on MIDI channel 3 when its channel is selected.

▷ **Freeze Mode:** The Freeze Mode parameter lets you specify whether the track will include effects in the resulting Freeze file if you freeze the track. The Freeze Mode parameter and Freeze tracks are covered in Chapter 6.

▷ **Transpose:** If you enter a value here, every time you play this software instrument, Logic will automatically transpose the note it sends the software instrument up or down by the amount you specified. You can either double-click in the space to the right of Transpose to display a text box or drag the mouse pointer up or down to add or subtract up to 96 steps (a full eight octaves!) from the original value or half-step increments. If you click on the double-arrows to the right, you can quickly shift up to three octaves up or down.

▷ **Velocity:** If you enter a value here, every time you play this software instrument, Logic will automatically increase or reduce the velocity of the MIDI note it sends to the software instrument by this value. You can double-click to the right of Velocity to display a text box or drag the mouse pointer up or down to increase or reduce the velocity of the MIDI note by up to 99 steps. (MIDI values are represented from 0 to 127, so this parameter can be used to adjust velocities through nearly the entire velocity range.)

▷ **Key Limit:** This parameter sets the upper- and lower-note boundaries of the software instrument. You can use this parameter to make certain that you do not send a software instrument a note outside of its range or to artificially reduce the range of the notes you choose to send a software instrument. For example, even though Vintage B3 Organ is capable of reproducing notes outside the actual range of a Hammond B-3, you might want to limit the notes to a Hammond's real range to ensure a realistic organ sound. As with the previous two parameters, you can either double-click on the values to display a text box or click and hold on either value to use the mouse to raise or lower the value.

▷ **Vel Limit:** This parameter sets up the upper and lower velocity boundaries of the instrument. As with the previously discussed parameters, you can double-click on each value to display a text box or click and hold on the value to use the mouse to raise or lower the values.

▷ **Delay:** The term *delay* has many meanings in a musical (and even in a MIDI-related) context. In this context, it warrants further explanation. Basically, this Delay parameter allows you to send MIDI information to this software instrument either early or late, depending on the setting. This parameter is not a MIDI echo that enables you to create doubling or echo effects that are also often called delays. This parameter only adjusts the point at which Logic will commence sending data to your software instrument. Clicking on the arrows lets you select between delaying in ticks and delaying in milliseconds. You can double-click in the space to the right of Delay or click and hold the mouse pointer to raise or lower the value between −99 and +99 ticks or −500.0 and +500.0 ms, depending on your Delay value setting. (A *tick* is the smallest amount of distance possible on the main window's Time ruler.)

▷ **No Transpose:** If you select this checkbox, the software instrument is set to No Transpose. That means even if you are transposing all MIDI tracks globally or with the Transpose setting in the Region Inspector, the process will not affect this instrument. This checkbox is especially valuable for software instrument percussion tracks, where transposing notes often results in selecting completely different sounds.

▷ **No Reset:** If you select this checkbox, this software instrument will not respond to MIDI reset messages such as mod wheel and pitchbend resets, even if they are sent to all devices.

▷ **Staff Style:** This parameter is set to Auto by default. If you click and hold the arrows to the right of the parameter name, Logic displays a list of all the available default Score editor styles. In the Auto style, Logic picks an appropriate style based on the pitch range of the notes on the track. If you do not use the Score editor, you can ignore this parameter.

Adding External MIDI Tracks

If you are planning to use external MIDI devices such as a MIDI keyboard as a sound source, or if you are planning to use ReWire to pipe audio into Logic, you need to use external MIDI tracks. To add external MIDI tracks to your project, click the plus symbol at the top of the track list, select Track > New, or press Option+Command+N. Then Click the External MIDI button. Figure 3.6 shows the New Tracks dialog box with the External MIDI button selected.

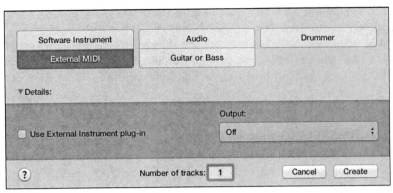

Figure 3.6 The New Tracks dialog box configured for creating new external MIDI tracks.
© Apple Inc.

As you can see in Figure 3.6, the only options available when you click the External MIDI button in the New Tracks dialog box are the Number of Tracks field, the Use External Instrument Plug-in checkbox, and an Output menu.

An external instrument is a software instrument that lets you merge the audio coming in from an external MIDI device with the MIDI that Logic sends to the external MIDI device on a single track. If you didn't use the external instrument, you would need one external MIDI track for Logic to send MIDI information to the device and a separate audio track to get the external MIDI device's audio back into Logic. External instruments are covered in Chapter 9.

The Output menu lets you select the MIDI OUT port and channel for the new external MIDI track. If you are creating multiple external MIDI tracks, select the Ascending option at the top of the Output menu, and Logic will automatically assign a new MIDI channel to each new external MIDI track ascending from the MIDI channel assigned in the Output menu. If you have multiple MIDI OUTs available, each OUT will have its own submenu giving you access to all the OUTs your MIDI interface offers. Working with MIDI ports is covered in more detail in the section "Setting Up Your MIDI Hardware" later in this chapter.

How many external MIDI tracks you should add depends on how many MIDI OUT ports your MIDI interface has or how many ReWire instruments you want to use. For each MIDI OUT you have, you can access 16 MIDI channels. It is very beneficial to have a dedicated MIDI connection for each of your external MIDI instruments, as this gives you access to all the power Logic offers for utilizing all your external MIDI hardware to the fullest. This is particularly true of multitimbral external MIDI equipment, which can allow you to access up to 16 MIDI channels simultaneously from one MIDI instrument.

When you create a new external MIDI track, Logic creates a General MIDI multi-instrument object (GM device) in the Environment, as shown in Figure 3.7. Don't worry that it's a GM device; you can always reconfigure it for your specific piece of MIDI hardware, as you'll see a little later in this chapter.

Figure 3.7 A General MIDI multi-instrument object in the Environment. When you create an external MIDI track, a multi-instrument object is automatically created in the Environment.
© Apple Inc.

Logic automatically creates a new GM device for each new set of 16 tracks. Note that the number of GM devices created depends on the number of MIDI OUT ports you have available on your MIDI interface. Therefore, if you have four MIDI OUT ports on your MIDI interface, you can create up to 64 external MIDI tracks in the New Tracks dialog box and have four GM devices automatically added to the Environment. You can always add more instrument objects and GM devices in the Environment later if need be. To add duplicate external MIDI tracks, use the Track > New External MIDI command or press Option+Command+X.

Setting Up the GM Device

A multitimbral instrument is an instrument that can play sounds on up to 16 MIDI channels simultaneously. When you first create new external MIDI tracks, you should open an Environment window (Command+0) and configure the GM device that communicates with your multitimbral instrument. Click the downward-pointing triangle button in the upper-left corner of the Environment window to open the Layer menu; then choose the MIDI Instr. layer to view your GM device(s) and the Inspector shown in Figure 3.8.

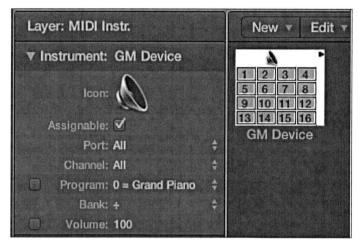

Figure 3.8 A GM device and its Inspector.
© Apple Inc.

The functions of the parameters in the GM Device Inspector are as follows:

▷ **Instrument name:** To give your new multi instrument a name, click on the word (GM Device) to the right of the disclosure triangle. Logic will display a text box in which you can type the new name.

▷ **Icon:** The added visual cue of an icon can help you visualize your device. You might as well take care of assigning one while configuring your GM device. Selecting an icon was discussed earlier, in the section "Configuring the Software Instrument Track Inspector."

▷ **Port:** You'll want to make sure your instrument is set to the correct port. Click the number (or it might be the word "All," as in Figure 3.8) next to the Port parameter, and you'll see a list of all available MIDI ports. Choose the one to which your device is connected. MIDI ports are covered in more detail later in this chapter, in the section "Selecting MIDI Ports."

▷ **Channel:** If your device is capable of operating on only a single MIDI channel, or if your instrument represents only a single patch on a synth, be sure to select that channel in the Channel parameter. Click the number next to Channel and select the proper MIDI channel, from 1 to 16. If you want the notes in your MIDI regions to determine the MIDI channel, set the Channel parameter to All.

▷ **Program:** Select this checkbox and select a program number between 0 and 127 if you want this instrument to always select a specific patch in your MIDI device.

▷ **Bank:** Most modern MIDI devices include several banks of sounds, generally at 128 presets per bank. If your MIDI device recognizes bank select messages, you can use the Bank parameter to send the desired message to access the desired preset on your MIDI device.

▷ **Volume:** Select this checkbox and select a MIDI volume level between 0 and 127 if you want this instrument to always set your MIDI device to a specific volume.

After you have set parameters for the GM device as a whole, it's time to activate its individual subchannels. If any boxes in the GM device have lines through them, it's because those subchannels are turned off by default. You'll want to activate as many subchannels as your instrument supports. For example, if your synth is eight-part multitimbral, you'll activate eight subchannels in the multi instrument by clicking on them. Figure 3.9 shows the GM device with all channels activated.

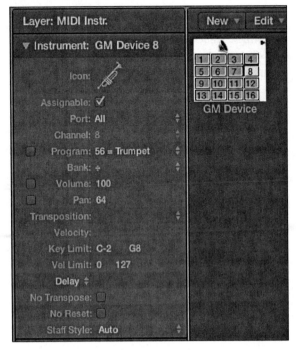

Figure 3.9 A GM device with all subchannels activated. The Inspector shown is the unique Inspector for subchannel 8.
© Apple Inc.

Notice that each subchannel has its own on/off toggle and associated Inspector. Most of the parameters you see in the Inspector are identical to those in the software instrument Track Inspector previously discussed, and they function identically. Additionally, each GM device channel has Program and Bank parameters for loading specific presets per MIDI channel. There's also a Pan parameter for setting a panorama placement for each channel via MIDI. Because each subchannel of a GM device is basically a unique single-channel MIDI instrument, you get a set of six general parameters for the entire MIDI instrument, but you might want each subchannel to be completely unique. If you already know how you want to set up your subchannels, go ahead and set the Inspectors as you activate the channels. Be careful about setting a global port value, however, because it applies to the entire multi instrument.

The Multi Instrument Window

The other window that you can access from a GM device is the Multi Instrument window. If you double-click any GM device, Logic displays this window, shown in Figure 3.10. Here you can set up the banks and patch names of your GM device.

You can set several parameters in this window:

▷ **Device Name and Short Device Name:** The device name is simply the name of your multi-instrument object. You should have already named your multi instrument, and that name should already appear in the Device Name box. In the Short Device Name box, you can type a short abbreviation of the instrument name that will appear in the main window track list when a multi instrument's program name is also being displayed.

▷ **Bank:** This menu enables you to select among banks of patches on your MIDI device. Each multi-instrument object allows up to 15 banks, numbered 0–14. If you choose Bank 1–14, Logic asks whether you want to initialize the bank. If you want to enter your own bank names, press Return. If you want to use the generic General MIDI names, starting with Bank 0, click Cancel. In general, unless your instrument is specifically a General MIDI device, you'll want to enter your own names (See the upcoming "Program Names" entry in this list).

▷ **Bank Message:** This menu allows you to select among different MIDI messages that will be sent to your MIDI device when you switch banks. Different manufacturers and devices use different messages to switch banks, so you need to consult your MIDI device's documentation to see which selection is appropriate for each device.

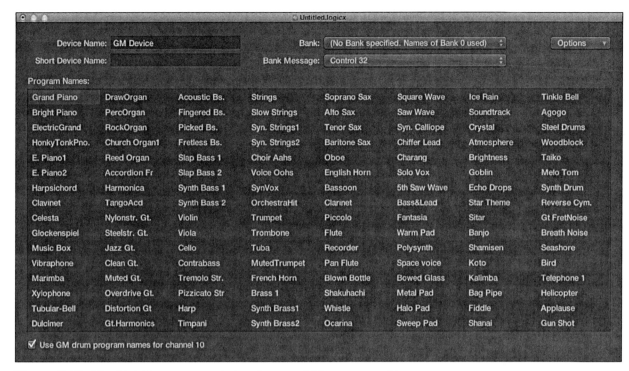

Figure 3.10 The Multi Instrument window for a multi-instrument object.
© Apple Inc.

▷ **Program Names:** You'll notice that 128 program names are visible in the Multi Instrument window for each bank. You can enter the specific names for the various programs of your device here. You can do this in a number of ways:

   ▷ Double-click on each program name one by one and manually type the new program name in the text boxes that appear.

   ▷ Copy data from the Clipboard by using the Options menu to the right of the Bank Message menu (see Figure 3.11). You can easily type the program numbers and names into a word-processing program and simply use the menu to copy them all to the correct program. You can also copy and paste program names from another multi-instrument object by using either this menu or the Copy and Paste global commands. If the device's manufacturer has a preset list in PDF format, you may also be able to copy and paste it in from the PDF, perhaps after a little editing in a word processor.

Figure 3.11 The Options menu in the Multi Instrument window.
© Apple Inc.

   ▷ If you want program numbers instead of names, select Options > Init Names as Numbers.

   ▷ If you wish to use General MIDI program names, select Options > Init General MIDI Names.

▷ **Use GM Drum Program Names for Channel 10:** In General MIDI devices, channel 10 is reserved for drums. The General MIDI drum kit also contains a standard set of drum kits. If you select this checkbox, Logic automatically uses the standard drum set names for subchannel 10.

Once you have configured all your GM devices, you can easily reassign external MIDI tracks to different MIDI devices and different MIDI channels in those devices using the Library in the main window. Simply open the Library by clicking the Library button in the control bar and browse the different folders that represent your GM devices.

> **TIP:** The best part about customizing the program names for your GM devices is that if you select the GM device in a track in the main window and your track header has enough room, it will display the actual track name. Also, if you have the Program button (one of the performance parameters in the instrument Track Inspector mentioned but not detailed earlier) checked for that subchannel, you can send your device program changes from the main window by clicking on program names (and scroll through your synth's programs by scrolling through the program names in the main window). Because you have all the names typed in, you can send changes by name rather than by number. For this reason, even for mono synths that are not multitimbral, you should seriously consider using a GM device for the MIDI device and only activating one subchannel. This might seem like overkill, but it conveniently enables you to customize patch names, which is worth the minimal additional effort.

Adding Drummer Tracks

Drummer is one of the major new features in Logic Pro X, and a really cool one to boot. Drummer gives you access to a highly configurable, specialized instrument and track that include detailed drum samples of a number of different kits in several styles with automatically generated drum parts. To add a Drummer track, click the plus symbol at the top of the track list, select Track > New, or press Option+Command+N. Then click the Drummer button. Figure 3.12 shows the New Tracks dialog box with the Drummer button selected.

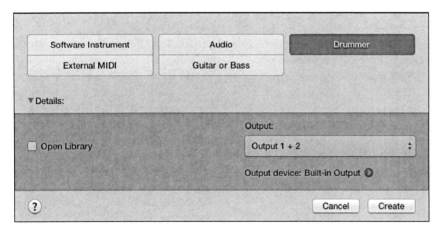

Figure 3.12 The Drummer options in the New Tracks dialog box.
© Apple Inc.

The options in the New Drummer dialog box are familiar. Selecting the Open Library checkbox opens the Library in the main window after you create the new Drummer track, letting you browse the different drum kits. The Output menu lets you select the hardware outputs for your Drummer track. The Output Device field displays the currently selected output device, and the right-arrow button gives you access to the Devices tab of the Audio Preferences window.

Drummer is similar to a software instrument, but it automatically adds regions to the Drummer track when you click Create. Drummer's specialized editor also opens when you create a new Drummer track. Figure 3.13 shows a Drummer track with its specialized regions and editor.

Configuring the Drummer Track Inspector

The Drummer Track Inspector is basically a stripped-down version of the software instrument Track Inspector, with the options in the Drummer Track Inspector functioning identically to the same options in the software instrument Track Inspector. Figure 3.14 shows the Drummer Track Inspector.

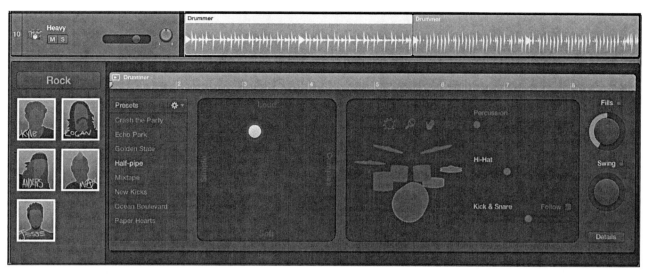

Figure 3.13 A Drummer track and the Drummer editor.
© Apple Inc.

Figure 3.14 The Drummer Track Inspector offers many of the same options as the software instrument Track Inspector.
© Apple Inc.

If you're planning to do a lot of writing in Logic or are otherwise hoping to use real drum sounds in your projects, but won't always have access to a real drummer or simply won't have the capabilities to record a real drummer, having Drummer ready to go in your template is an excellent idea. Because Drummer is such a major new feature in Logic, and because it involves many different aspects of the main window, I'll dive deeper into Drummer and its capabilities in Chapter 6.

Adding ReWire Tracks

Although adding and configuring ReWire tracks is covered in detail in Chapter 9, if you know you will be using a ReWire slave with Logic, you may want to add some ReWire tracks to your template project.

To add ReWire tracks to your project, you need to create some new—or configure some existing—external MIDI tracks. To configure your external MIDI tracks for ReWire use, select the external MIDI track you wish to configure. Then launch the desired ReWire application. Once the ReWire application has launched, you can access any available ReWire instruments in the Library, as shown in Figure 3.15, and assign a ReWire instrument to your selected external MIDI track.

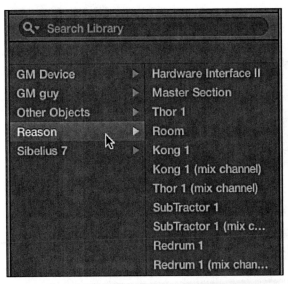

Figure 3.15 You can use the Library to assign the instruments available in your ReWire applications to external MIDI tracks.
© Apple Inc.

After you have configured your external MIDI tracks for ReWire transmission, you can play and sequence the instruments in your ReWire applications from Logic. To route the audio from your ReWire applications into Logic, you will need to create and configure auxiliary channel strips. Creating auxiliary channel strips is covered in the next section of this chapter. Configuring auxiliary channel strips for ReWire audio transmission is covered in detail in Chapter 9. Note that your ReWire slave has to run in 64-bit mode for Logic to access it.

Adding Auxiliary Tracks

Auxiliary channel strips, or aux channel strips, are destinations for buses in Logic. For those unfamiliar with auxes and buses, they are covered in Chapter 11. Briefly, a *bus* is used to transmit audio from one or more channel strips to another channel strip in Logic. An *aux* is the most common destination for a bus. One common use of an aux channel strip is to instantiate a reverb effect in the aux channel strip and to send audio from a variety of audio or software instrument tracks through a bus to the aux, allowing them all to utilize the same reverb effect. If you are familiar with auxes and buses, or you think you can see the value of having a few auxes in your template, then you may want to add a few to your template.

Creating Auxiliary Channel Strips

To create a new aux, open the Mixer either in the main window by clicking the X button or in a Mixer window by selecting Window > Mixer or by pressing Command+2. From the Mixer's local Options menu, select Create New Auxiliary Channel Strips; alternatively, press Control+N. This will create a new auxiliary channel strip. You can create more auxes via the Create New Auxiliary Channel Strips command.

> **NOTE:** When I say *Mixer,* that's exactly what I mean: the separate window called Mixer or the Mixer that's integrated in the main window. I do not mean the Mixer layer of the Environment. If you think you opened the Mixer window but you see the Layer menu, make sure you didn't open the Environment Mixer! For more on this distinction, check out Chapter 11.

Adding Auxiliary Tracks to the Main Window

Now that you have created some aux channel strips, you can add auxiliary tracks to the Tracks area in the main window. Having auxiliary tracks in the main window can be valuable because it enables you to easily automate and edit the automations for a wide variety of aux channel strip parameters and insert effect parameters, as you'll explore in Chapter 10, "Using Automation in Logic."

In the Tracks area, create a new track for each aux you would like to have in the main window. It doesn't matter what type of tracks you create because you will be reassigning them. To reassign a track to an aux, follow these steps:

1. Right-click on the selected track header. This will open the menu shown in Figure 3.16.

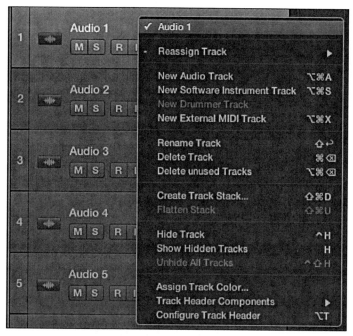

Figure 3.16 Right-clicking on a track header opens this menu.
© Apple Inc.

2. Choose Reassign Track > Mixer > Aux and select the aux channel strip you want to assign to the current track, as shown in Figure 3.17.

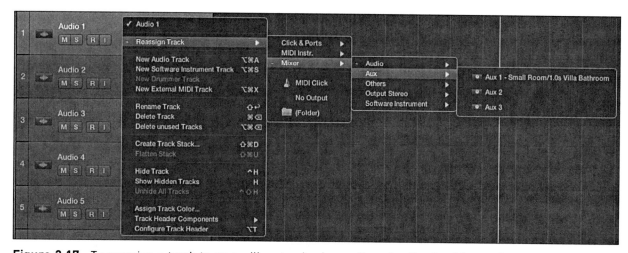

Figure 3.17 To reassign a track to an auxiliary track, choose Reassign Track > Mixer > Aux and select the aux you wish to assign to the track.
© Apple Inc.

Setting Up Your Main Window

We've spent quite a few pages discussing the basic setup of your template project, but no less important is setting up the main window. For example, Figure 3.18 contains the main window generated by the Electronic template from the Project Chooser.

Figure 3.18 An example of a main window generated by the Electronic template. Most likely, you will prefer a different configuration for your own personalized template.
© Apple Inc.

Does this look like your ideal workspace? Or do you imagine yourself using a different combination of tracks—perhaps with different instrument names? Do you want your track lanes to have more room? The main windows in the provided templates are designed to offer users a sampling of available track types and configurations, in the hopes that some of what they need might be included in a particular template. For your template, you want your main window to represent *your* personal working needs.

> **TIP:** As you can see, using key commands in Logic is a major timesaver. Creating tracks isn't fun, creative work—it's an administrative task that most people just want to finish as soon as they can. If you are creating 50 or more tracks of different types using menus, that means you have to navigate to the menu option, then re-navigate to the menu option, then re-navigate to the menu option. If you use the key command, however, creating each new track is as rapid as tap, tap, tap! I'll continue to show you the menu options as well as the default key commands throughout this book, but you should commit some time to learning to use Logic via the key commands. Now is an excellent time to start!

Setting Up Tracks

Although many of the steps involved in creating your tracks are simplified and streamlined in Logic, there are still a few more things you may want to set up to finish configuring your template.

Naming Tracks

Now that you've created as many tracks as you think you'll need, you might want to think about giving them slightly more descriptive names than simply audio 1, audio 2, and so on. Of course, you probably don't know what your final track names will be, but perhaps you expect you will need 12 separate audio tracks for your drums, for example. If so, you might rename audio 24–36 (or whichever tracks you choose) drums 1–12. Did you only need eight MIDI tracks divided between two separate MIDI synths, such as a Roland and a Korg synth? Why not name the MIDI tracks Korg 1–Korg 4 and Roland 1–Roland 4 to be more descriptive? Remember, customizing your main window to be your personal workspace is the name of the game!

The easiest way to name tracks is to click the track name in the Track Inspector or to double-click the name in the track header. As soon as you do, a text box will appear with the current name of the track highlighted, as shown in Figure 3.19. Type any name you want, then press Return, press Esc, or click anywhere outside the text box.

Figure 3.19 To rename a track in your track list, click the track name next to the triangle in that track's Inspector or double-click the track name in the track header as shown. When the text box appears, type the new name.
© Apple Inc.

You can also use a menu command to name tracks—Track > Rename Track—or press Shift+Return. If you change track names using the menu command, you are actually naming the *track itself*. By default, this distinction makes no difference; however, if you decide to display the additional names of your tracks by selecting the checkbox in the Additional Name Column section of the Track Header Configuration dialog box, you can configure Logic to display not only the track name or the name created with the Rename Track command, but a variety of different name types for either the first or second track name. To open the Track Header Configuration dialog box, do one of the following:

▷ Select Track > Configure Track Header.
▷ Right-click on the track header and select Configure Track Header from the menu that appears.
▷ Press Option+T.

Figure 3.20 shows the Additional Name Column section of the Track Configuration dialog box.

Figure 3.20 The Additional Name Column section of the Track Header Configuration dialog box. Selecting the checkbox displays the second names of your tracks.
© Apple Inc.

The menu in the Additional Name Column section of the Track Header Configuration dialog box offers these options:

▷ **Automatic:** This option names your tracks based on the following criteria, in order: user-entered names, channel-strip settings or software instrument names, and in the absence of one of the previous options, the parent channel strip's name.
▷ **Patch or Channel Strip Setting Name:** This option displays the patch or channel strip setting name for the parent channel strip of each track. A channel strip's setting involves only a single channel strip. A patch can include aux channel strips and Smart Controls, and even Track Stacks. You'll look at channel strip settings and patches in more detail in Chapter 11.
▷ **Software Instrument Setting Name:** This option displays the software instrument setting name for each software instrument track.
▷ **Channel Strip Name:** This option displays the channel strip name of each track's parent channel strip in the Mixer.

▷ **Channel Strip Type and Number:** This option displays the type and number of each track's parent channel strip. For example, if a track's parent channel strip is the third auxiliary channel strip, the track's name will be aux 3.

When you enable the additional name, the additional name is displayed over the Volume slider in the track header. Thus, you could have a track named Nord Electro on a track named Wurly, for example, or a track named Ambient Guitar on a track named audio 6. Figure 3.21 shows a track with this view enabled.

Figure 3.21 If you have chosen to display additional names in the track header, you'll see the additional name you designated in the menu found in the Additional Name Column section of the Track Header Configuration dialog box. © Apple Inc.

You can also access the Additional Name Column options by right-clicking on the track header, selecting Track Header Components > Additional Name Column, and choosing one of the Additional Name Column options.

> **NOTE:** For ages, Logic had fairly unintuitive track and channel-strip naming practices. Naming a track didn't name its channel strip, and naming a channel strip didn't name its track. It was often a confusing mess getting your Arrange window (the old name of the main window) and your Mixer names unified. Since the introduction of Logic Pro 9, you can easily name your tracks in the main window using the track header, the Track Inspector, or the selected track's main window channel strip; in the Mixer; or in the Environment Mixer layer. The name of a track is unified across the entire application!

Coloring Tracks

As a final method of customizing your template tracks, you might want to think about coloring them. Certainly it won't affect your music or creativity in any way if you do or do not use a unique color for each track, but it does help to keep tracks separate and to visually group tracks that you want to keep together, such as tracks for the same MIDI instrument or for similar types of audio recordings. For example, you might color all your drum tracks the same color.

First, to see the colors you are choosing before each track lane has any regions on it, make sure Track Color Bars is selected in the Track Header Configuration menu. To access the Track Header Configuration menu (covered in full detail in Chapter 6), right-click in any track's track header or press Option+T. Alternatively, select Track Header Components > Show Track Color Bars in the right-click track header menu. With Track Color Bars selected, you will see a small line at the left of each track header that shows you the color for that track. To change the color, display the Color palette by doing one of the following:

▷ Selecting View > Show Colors
▷ Selecting Track > Assign Track Color
▷ Choosing Assign Track Color in the track header right-click menu
▷ Pressing Option+C.

Logic presents its Color palette, as shown in Figure 3.22. When you click on any of the palette's colors, you will see the line of color change to the selected color.

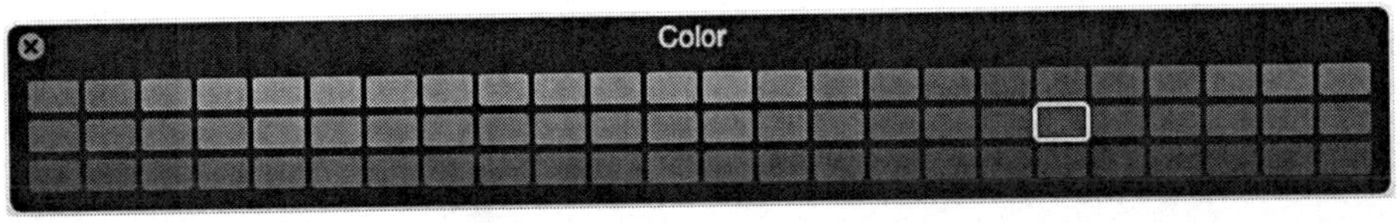

Figure 3.22 Logic's Color palette. Click on a color to choose it for the selected track in the main window. © Apple Inc.

Configuring the Initial Zoom and Automation Settings

You may want all of your track lanes to be wider or thinner than the default tracks that Logic creates in the main window. Basically, the skinnier the track lane, the more tracks will fit in the track list—but the less detail you will see for each track. You may also want the horizontal zoom in the Tracks area to be more zoomed in (for more precise detail) or more zoomed out (for an overview of an entire song).

Many Logic users choose to set up an initial screenset with a main window with wider track lanes and a tight horizontal zoom to focus on a specific group of tracks, and then another screenset with a main window with very skinny track lanes horizontally zoomed out for viewing the whole song at once.

To accomplish this, you can use the zoom sliders at the upper-right corner of the Tracks area (see Figure 3.23). The slider on the left controls vertical zoom. Dragging the slider to the right increases the track lane height, and dragging the slider to the left decreases the track lane height. The slider on the right controls horizontal zoom. Dragging the slider left decreases how much horizontal space is shown between each bar/SMPTE location, and dragging the slider right increases how much horizontal space is shown between each bar/SMPTE location. You can also use the zoom key command, Control+arrow. Press the appropriate arrow key, depending on whether you are increasing (up) or decreasing (down) the vertical zoom or increasing (right) or decreasing (left) the horizontal zoom.

Figure 3.23 The vertical and horizontal zoom sliders allow you to adjust vertical and horizontal zoom for the entire Tracks area.
© Apple Inc.

Logic also offers a number of ways to vertically resize individual tracks without resizing the other tracks in the Tracks area. If you move the mouse pointer to the bottom edge of a track header, the cursor will turn into a resize cursor, as shown in Figure 3.24. The resize cursor lets you click and drag the mouse vertically to increase or decrease the height of that individual track. A help tag opens to show you a numeric value for your individual track zoom setting, also shown in Figure 3.24. You can also select a track and use the key commands for Individual Track Zoom In (Control+Option+Command+up arrow) and Individual Track Zoom Out (Control+Option+Command+down arrow). Finally, you can activate the Auto Track Zoom feature in the local Tracks area View menu or by pressing Control+Z. Auto Track Zoom will increase the size of whichever track in the Tracks area you have currently selected, leaving all unselected tracks at their normal height.

Figure 3.24 If you move the cursor to the bottom of a track header, the cursor will turn into a resize cursor, indicating that you can adjust the height of the track by dragging up or down with your mouse. A help tag opens, giving a numeric value for the size of the track.
© Apple Inc.

Setting Up Screensets

We've already discussed screensets, which are one of Logic's indispensable customization tools. Using screensets, you can set up each view in Logic to have its own unique set of editors and windows, and you can easily switch between the views by using the number keys. Press a number key or two to get a quick glimpse at what screensets can do for you. It's kind of like having multiple workflows or templates within your projects.

Setting up screensets couldn't be simpler: You simply press a number key to go to a screenset and organize the various windows and editors as you like. Then, when you save your template project, all your screensets will be automatically saved as well. No muss, no fuss! There are only a couple of special options for creating screensets that you might want to consider using, and they are discussed in this section.

First, if you open the Screenset menu (the number displayed between the Window and the Help menus), you'll notice a list of current screensets and, below that, a menu of screenset options. You can see this in Figure 3.25, which shows the screensets of the Electronic template.

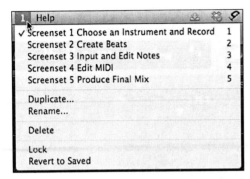

Figure 3.25 The Screenset menu displays a list of your screensets plus screenset options.
© Apple Inc.

The screenset options are as follows:

▷ **Duplicate:** If you want to create a new screenset using the current screenset as a base, select Duplicate. This opens the Duplicate Screenset dialog box, where you can assign the duplicate screenset to the number of your choice and name the screenset.

▷ **Rename:** Selecting the Rename option opens the Rename Screenset dialog box, where you can rename your screenset.

▷ **Delete:** You can use the Delete command to delete the current screenset. Be advised that there is no warning dialog box when you use this command.

▷ **Lock:** If you know that, even if you open and close windows while using Logic, you'll want the windows of a particular screenset to never change from Logic session to Logic session, you can choose to lock the screenset using the Lock menu command.

▷ **Revert to Saved:** The Revert to Saved command simply returns the current screenset to its original state, just like you used the key command for selecting that particular screenset.

Setting up your screensets in your template is really this easy! Trust me—using screensets is one of the best ways to configure Logic to reflect how you want to work.

Defining Key Commands

Don't worry. You're not going to give every command in Logic a key command at this point. But as you work on your template, you should begin to get a feel for which commands you might like to access from the keyboard instead of the menus so you can begin defining your own key commands. Logic makes this process simple with its extremely powerful and intuitive Key Commands window. To access the Key Commands window (see Figure 3.26), select Logic Pro > Preferences > Key Commands or press Option+K.

You will notice that the key commands are grouped into commands relating to specific windows and editors in the Command list. You can click any of the disclosure triangles from any or all of the groups to see what key commands are available for that window or editor.

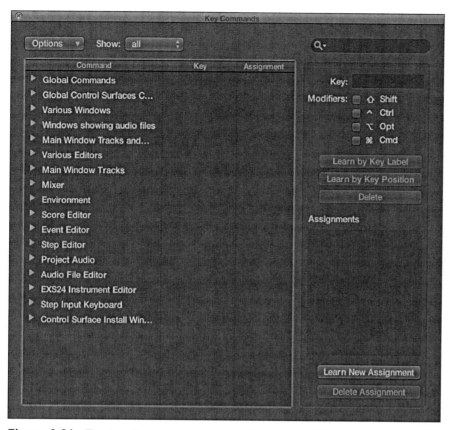

Figure 3.26 The Key Commands window offers many different methods to search for and assign key commands.
© Apple Inc.

The easiest way to define a key command is simply to search for the command and then inform Logic as to which key you wish to use as the key command. For example, suppose you want to assign a key command to the Duplicate Screenset command. In that case, do the following:

1. Type the word screenset in the Search field in the Key Commands window, as shown in Figure 3.27. Logic will display a list of all key commands with the word "screenset" in their name.
2. When you have found the correct command, select it. In this example, select the Duplicate Screenset command.
3. Assign a key to a command by doing one of the following.
   ▷ **Click the Learn by Key Label button:** This "learns" key sequences based on the label of the key you press. In other words, if you press a key labeled 3, then 3 will be assigned to that command. In this example, click the Learn by Key Label button, then press Command+Shift+2. You will see the Key field and Modifiers boxes reflect your choice, as shown in Figure 3.28. You can now press Command+Shift+2 (the 2 on either the keyboard or the numeric keypad) to lock or unlock a screenset. Your new key command is listed in the Key column of the Command list. Make sure you disengage the Learn by Key Label button before you press any other keys!

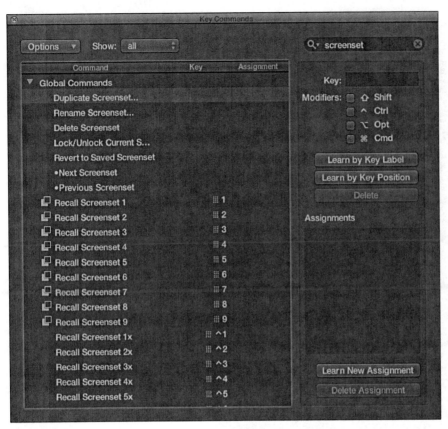

Figure 3.27 To search for key commands, type a search word into the Search field of the Key Commands window.

© Apple Inc.

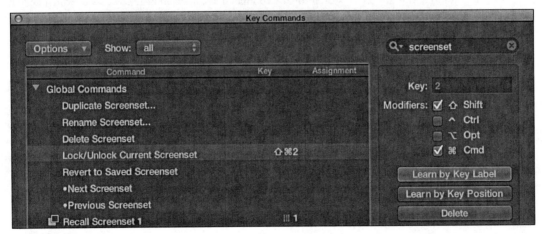

Figure 3.28 If you click the Learn by Key Label button and then press Command+Shift+2, the Key field and Modifiers boxes will reflect your choice.

© Apple Inc.

▷ **Click the Learn by Key Position button:** This key command option allows you to assign a key command not based on the label on the key, but based on the position of the key on the keyboard. The advantage of this is that you can assign different key commands to the number 2 above the keyboard and the number 2 in the numeric keypad. It also means that if you switch between different languages, your key assignments will remain the same. Using the same example, if you click the Learn by Key Position button and press Command+Shift+2, the Key Assignment field will reflect the location code (or scan code) of the key pressed (in this case, the number 2 above the keyboard, not the numeric keypad), and only those exact keys will be assigned to the command, as shown in Figure 3.29. Your new key command is listed in the Key column of the Command list.

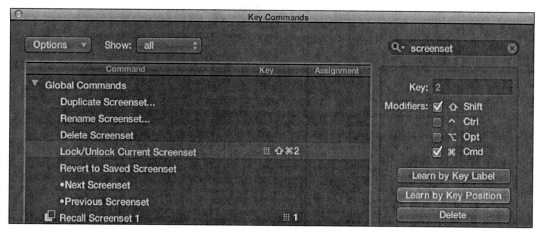

Figure 3.29 Learn by Key Position memorizes the specific keys you have pressed and assigns that sequence to your key command—in this case, Command+Shift+2 (above the keyboard, not on the numeric keypad).

© Apple Inc.

▷ **Click the Learn New Assignment button:** If you want to assign a command to a control surface, click this button, then move or press the control on the control surface to which you wish to assign this command. The Assignments pane will reflect what you moved or pressed, as shown in Figure 3.30.

That's it! You've just activated a new key command! As you become more familiar with Logic, you will use these methods not only to activate key commands that do not have defaults, but also to assign different key commands than the Logic default key sequences to better suit your own working methods.

NOTE: If you are unfamiliar with Logic's key commands and want to get in the habit of using them, a great way to learn key commands is to make yourself a cheat sheet of your most-used key commands and leave it right next to your keyboard. This can be an index card, a sheet of paper, or any other material that works for you. You can also select Show > Used in the Key Commands window, then select Options > Copy Key Commands to Clipboard, and finally paste the list into a word processor for printout. Use cheat sheets to help familiarize yourself with key commands until they become second nature to you!

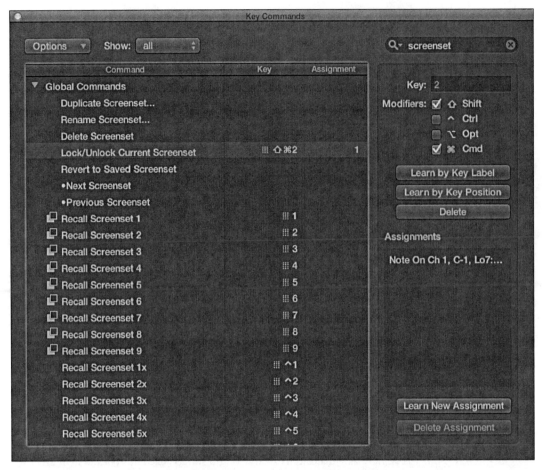

Figure 3.30 You can assign key commands to control surfaces as well as keyboards and MIDI devices by using the Learn New Assignment button.

© Apple Inc.

Setting Up Your Hardware

These days, there are many options for hardware that can interface with a DAW, and having Logic configured to work with your hardware is essential to ensuring the kind of ease of use that keeps inspiration flowing when it hits. Before you finalize your initial setup of Logic, you need to look at configuring your audio interface, your MIDI gear, and any control surfaces you may be using.

Interfaces and Drivers

Sometimes, simply plugging your audio interface into your computer is enough to enable your computer to recognize the interface so that you can start using it. Other times, the audio interface comes with *drivers*—files that explain to your computer how to communicate with your interface. For example, with Mac OS X, audio and MIDI interfaces that support the standard USB, FireWire, or Thunderbolt class–compliant drivers that are built into Core Audio (explained in the next section) and Core MIDI do not require additional drivers, whereas all other audio and MIDI devices require installation of manufacturer-supplied drivers. If your hardware requires manufacturer-supplied drivers, you may need to make sure they offer 64-bit bit drivers.

In general, most of the configuration of audio and MIDI devices is done inside Logic, so driver installation is usually a very straightforward process of inserting the CD that came with your hardware or (more likely) downloading drivers from the Internet, and then launching an installation application. Most device-driver installations require you to restart your computer at the end of the process because most operating systems scan for new drivers only when the system starts up.

Configuring Your Audio Device

To get the most out of your system, you will need to tell Logic exactly how you want to use your hardware. You can configure how Logic will interact with your audio interface in the Devices tab of the Audio Preferences window, which you can access by choosing Logic Pro X > Preferences > Audio and then clicking on the Devices tab. The Devices tab of the Audio Preferences window is shown in Figure 3.31.

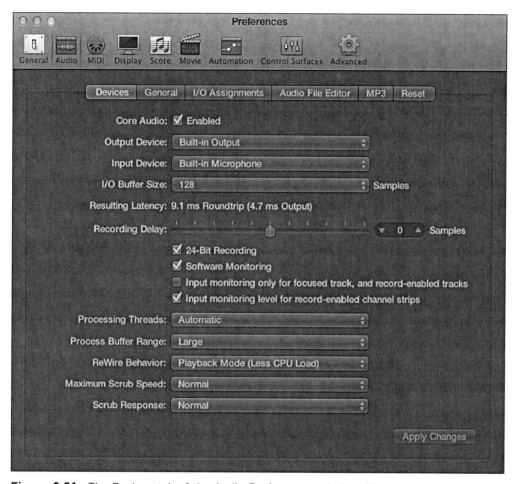

Figure 3.31 The Devices tab of the Audio Preferences window. Here you can configure how you want Logic to use your audio device.
© Apple Inc.

Some of the options in the Devices tab are self-explanatory; others are less so. I'll briefly go over all of the options here. Because the I/O Buffer Size and Process Buffer Range options are more complex and require detailed explanation, each will get its own section later in this chapter. The Software Monitoring setting is discussed in Chapter 5, "Transport Controls and Recording."

▷ **Core Audio:** Select the Core Audio checkbox if your audio interface uses the Core Audio driver.
▷ **Output Device:** Use this menu to select the audio device to which Logic will output audio.
▷ **Input Device:** Use this menu to select the audio device from which Logic will receive audio.
▷ **I/O Buffer Size:** This is explained in detail in the "I/O Buffer Size" section later in this chapter.
▷ **Resulting Latency:** This tells what your I/O latency will be at the current I/O Buffer Size setting, along with the specific value of the output latency.
▷ **Recording Delay:** If your audio interface properly discloses how long it takes for audio to travel from its inputs into the computer, Logic can automatically compensate for this delay to make sure that everything you record appears in Logic's Tracks area exactly at the instant you recorded it. However, some devices do not report their delay, so Logic would have no way of knowing exactly how to compensate for the record offset caused by your hardware. The Recording Delay

parameter enables you to manually adjust Logic's recording offset compensation so that you can even compensate for devices that do not report their delay. If this sounds complicated, and/or if your tracks don't sound like they are out of time, you don't need to worry about this parameter. For most modern interfaces, you won't need to adjust this.

▷ **24-Bit Recording:** If you want to record into 24-bit audio files, keep this checkbox checked. Using 24-bit files takes up more processing power and hard disk space, so some users prefer to record at 16-bit to conserve their CPU and hard disk. In addition, some older or inexpensive audio interfaces do not have 24-bit recording capability. These days, almost every device is capable of 24-bit recording. As explained in Chapter 1, "Introducing Logic Pro X," it is advantageous to use the highest bit rate you can, so you should keep this option selected if your system is capable.

▷ **Software Monitoring:** This option selects or deselects software monitoring. Software monitoring is explained in detail in Chapter 5.

▷ **Input Monitoring Only for Focused Track, and Record-Enabled Tracks:** This option enables software monitoring for the currently selected track and/or any record-enabled tracks.

▷ **Input Monitoring Level for Record-Enabled Channel Strips:** Selecting this option enables you to set a separate record-monitoring level for a record-enabled track. You can record-enable a track, then set the level fader for that track to the level at which you wish to monitor while recording. When you disengage the Record button for that track, the level fader will return to its previous setting. This does not affect the input level of your source! Therefore, you must still take care to properly set your input levels on your audio interface to avoid overloading your converters.

▷ **Processing Threads:** The Processing Threads setting determines how many of your available processing cores will be used for rendering audio. The Automatic setting gives Logic the ability to automatically decide how many processing threads will open. If you want, you can designate the number of cores Logic will use by selecting a number from the menu. How many cores you can access depends on your computer's processor.

▷ **Process Buffer Range:** The Process Buffer Range setting is explained in detail in the "Process Buffer Range" section later in this chapter.

▷ **ReWire Behavior:** ReWire is a technology developed by Propellerhead Software (the Swedish audio software company famous for ReCycle, ReBirth, and Reason) to allow separate standalone audio applications to interoperate. Setting up Logic as a ReWire host is addressed in detail in the section "Using ReWire 2 Instruments" in Chapter 9. This setting determines whether Logic utilizes ReWire in Playback mode, which takes up less CPU processing, or in Live mode, which allows you to send MIDI from Logic to your ReWire applications with lower latency, at the expense of a high CPU load.

▷ **Maximum Scrub Speed:** *Scrubbing* refers to using the mouse to move the playhead over an audio file while Logic is paused to play it back as opposed to simply clicking Play. You can also scrub if you click and drag on a region with the Scissors tool. This option is particularly useful if you are doing some very fine editing and are listening for a specific point in the song. The Maximum Scrub Speed option determines the maximum possible playback speed when you scrub: Normal or Double Speed. When you select Normal, even if you scrub your mouse as quickly as you can across a section of audio, you'll never hear it faster than real time. If you select Double, you will hear the section play back at double the normal speed. You might want to change the scrub speed if you want to be able to quickly scrub through your song.

▷ **Scrub Response:** This setting determines how quickly the scrub function will react to changes in your mouse speed. Your options are Slow, Normal, Fast, and Faster. The faster the response, the more the playback reflects your actual speeding up and slowing down, but the more jerky the sound will be if you don't keep your speed extremely steady.

Adjusting the Audio Hardware Buffers

One of the most important reasons to open the Devices tab of the Audio Preferences window is to adjust the various input and output buffers. Adjusting buffers is how you fine-tune Logic's performance to get the most out of your system. To do this properly, it is important to know what each of the buffers does so you can tailor the settings to meet your requirements exactly.

The fundamental concept is that it takes a set amount of time for the CPU to perform a given amount of work. Because timing is so integral to making music, having control over the exact amount of time it takes the CPU to complete a given task is crucial. Logic allows users to have independent control over two separate but related audio buffers: the input/output (I/O) buffer and the process buffer.

I/O BUFFER SIZE

When you record audio into Logic, it naturally takes a certain amount of time before you hear it played back through the audio interface's outputs. First, the audio has to travel from your audio interface into the audio driver of your audio interface. The driver then passes the signal information to Logic. After Logic records the audio onto your hard drive, Logic returns the audio to your audio driver for output, and finally the driver sends the audio to your interface. This is shown in Figure 3.32.

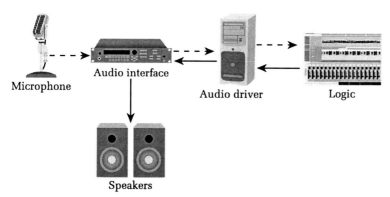

Figure 3.32 The signal flow of audio into and out of your computer.
© Cengage Learning.

As this figure shows, the audio driver is in charge of regulating the input and output of audio to and from the application. To do this effectively and in perfect synchronization, the audio driver passes to Logic a chunk of audio that consists of a variable number of samples, and Logic then sends to the driver chunks of audio with that same number of samples. The amount of time that elapses in this process is called *latency*.

If the number of samples in each chunk of audio is very small, the latency will be very low. The drawback is that the audio driver has to work very quickly to keep those small chunks of audio moving. This requires more CPU power and, if the audio drivers are not well written, can cause audible crackles and pops as the audio driver struggles to keep up with the demands placed on it. If the number of samples in each chunk is very large, the driver does not need to work nearly as hard, resulting in a far lower CPU drain and better performance from audio drivers. However, large buffers result in a higher latency.

You can set the size of the buffer using the I/O Buffer Size menu in the Devices tab of the Audio Preferences menu. Figure 3.33 shows the I/O Buffer Size menu.

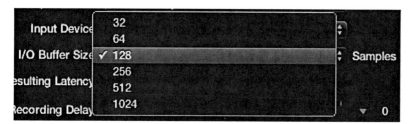

Figure 3.33 You can select any of these different buffer sizes in the I/O Buffer Size menu.
© Apple Inc.

There are a number of situations in which you need your latency to be as low as possible:

▷ To get the most out of software monitoring (see the "Recording, Software Monitoring, and Latency" section in Chapter 5)
▷ To play virtual instruments in real time
▷ To use external hardware alongside playback from Logic

In these cases, you should set your buffer as low as your system can handle without glitches (audible pops and crackles during playback), which usually ranges between 64 and 256 samples. Otherwise, you can set your buffer to a high setting because higher settings usually offer the best CPU performance—try 512 and 1,024 samples. As a rule, you should start with as low a setting as you can, and if you notice audio glitches or sluggish computer performance due to the CPU strain, slowly raise the I/O Buffer Size value until you reach the lowest comfortable setting. After you change the buffer size, you must then click on Apply Changes. Logic Pro will reset the driver and reload any software instrument's data that exists in the project, which can take a little while in a full project.

PROCESS BUFFER RANGE

When you use a native audio engine, your computer's CPU handles all the audio processing. Just as the audio drivers handle audio in chunks to increase efficiency, the CPU also handles audio processing in chunks. The size of these chunks is set with the

Process Buffer Range menu. The Process Buffer Range setting may be Small, Medium, or Large. The smaller the buffer, the faster audio is processed, but the more CPU is required, leaving less total CPU power available for other processing. The larger the buffer, the slower the CPU processes audio, which leaves more power available for everything else, such as playing tracks, doing screen redraws, etc.

If your process buffer is too small for your system, your system will quickly run out of power, presenting you with cryptic messages such as "Error: Core Audio too slow" and the like. Regardless of the exact text, the reason is the same: Logic can't keep up with everything you're asking it to do. If your buffer is too large, you may find that some operations that rely on a fast response—such as external storage devices, recording, or real-time processing—will become out of sync because each chunk is too large to keep up with the rest of the song. You have to adjust this setting to find the ideal buffer size for your particular system, but in general you should keep the Process Buffer Range setting as small as possible. Most modern computers should be able to handle a Process Buffer Range setting of Small or Medium without a problem. Start with a setting of Small, and then increase it as necessary to find the ideal setting.

Setting Up Your MIDI Hardware

Because most MIDI devices don't have many configurable options, setting them up is far more straightforward than with audio devices. When connecting your MIDI hardware to your MIDI interface, however, you need to be conscious of MIDI ports.

Selecting MIDI Ports

The most basic MIDI interfaces have a single MIDI IN and a single MIDI OUT jack. However, many MIDI interfaces have multiple jacks (usually two to eight of each). Each pair of IN and OUT jacks is referred to as a *MIDI port*. You'll need to keep track of which device you have plugged into which port. Although Logic can detect that something is connected to a MIDI port, it's up to you to tell Logic what that device is and what it can do. This becomes especially important when you add devices or change the port to which they are connected. You can run into problems such as devices not being detected or, if you select the wrong MIDI port, MIDI data being sent to the wrong devices.

Every external MIDI track in Logic has an Inspector; the second parameter (right under the Icon checkbox) is the Port setting. Figure 3.34 shows an external MIDI track in the main window with its port set to port 2.

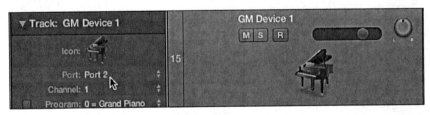

Figure 3.34 By looking at the Port setting in the Inspector of this MIDI object, you can quickly determine that the device is connected to port 2 of the MIDI interface.
© Apple Inc.

If you change the MIDI ports to which your MIDI devices are connected, make sure that the Port settings of your external MIDI tracks are still accurate. While audio settings are global for all Logic songs, MIDI settings are project-specific and may need to be updated. Ideally, you want to keep your MIDI equipment configured the same way all the time to increase the effectiveness and efficiency of your template. If you remove devices that are being sent MIDI data from Logic, or perhaps you get a new piece of MIDI equipment, be sure to set the MIDI port on those external MIDI tracks to the new device to which you'd like the signals sent. Keeping Logic and your template properly up to date with what MIDI device is connected to which MIDI port is an essential part of setting up and maintaining your system.

Logic Pro and Surround

Surround material is pervasive in modern music and video, from 5.1 DVD-Audio releases to 7.1 SDDS movie releases. Logic Pro offers full surround support, including recording, bouncing, mixing, and processing in a wide variety of surround and legacy formats. Although topics such as surround mixing and bouncing are covered in Chapter 11, knowing what the supported surround formats are and how you can configure your audio interface for surround input is necessary if you are considering using surround in Logic.

Supported Surround Formats

Logic offers the following surround format options:

▷ **Quadraphonic:** Quadraphonic, or Quad, is a fairly old format whose height of popularity was in the 1970s. The format uses four channels: one right, one left, one right rear, and one left rear.

▷ **LCRS (Pro Logic):** LCRS is the original Dolby Pro Logic Surround format, which is another four-channel format consisting of left, center, right, and surround (rear) channels.

▷ **5.1 (ITU 775):** This is the surround format most commonly in use today. This is the format that 5.1 DVD-Audio uses, and it is typical in home theater systems. This format uses a total of six channels: left, center, right, left rear, right rear, and LFE (low frequency effect).

▷ **6.1 (ES/EX):** This setting is used for the DTS ES or Dolby Digital EX format. This is a seven-channel format utilizing left, center, right, left rear, surround, right rear, and LFE channels.

▷ **7.1 (3/4.1):** This is a common cinema format similar to 5.1, but with two more surround channels: a left side channel and a right side channel.

▷ **7.1 (SDDS):** SDDS is a Sony format used in movie theaters. It consists of eight channels: left, left center, center, right center, right, left rear, right rear, and LFE.

Setting the Project Surround Format

To set the surround format for your project, you need to open the Audio tab of the Project Settings window by doing one of the following:

▷ Choosing File > Project Settings > Audio

▷ Pressing Option+P to open the Project Settings window and selecting the Audio tab.

Figure 3.35 shows the Audio tab of the Project Settings window. To assign a surround format to your project, simply select your desired format from the Surround Format menu.

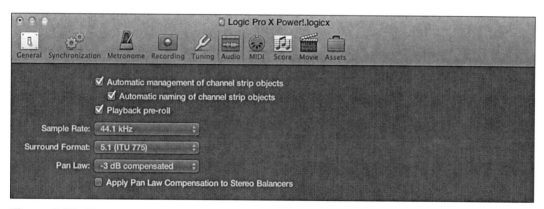

Figure 3.35 The Audio tab of the Project Settings window. You can assign a surround format to your project from the Surround Format menu.

© Apple Inc.

Configuring Surround Inputs

To set the surround input format, open the Input screen of the I/O Assignments tab of the Audio Preferences window (see Figure 3.36). Use the Show As menu to set the desired surround format. Selecting a surround format automatically configures the various input assignment menus to the default input settings for the chosen format. In Figure 3.36, the surround format is 5.1 (ITU 775), and the input assignment menus reflect the default settings. You can reassign any channel to any available input. You can configure surround outputs in the Output screen of the I/O Assignments tab in the same fashion.

Setting Up Your Control Surface

If you have a software controller, you are in for a special treat. A control surface can actually be any MIDI device capable of sending and receiving MIDI in order to control functions within Logic. The most common control surfaces, however, resemble

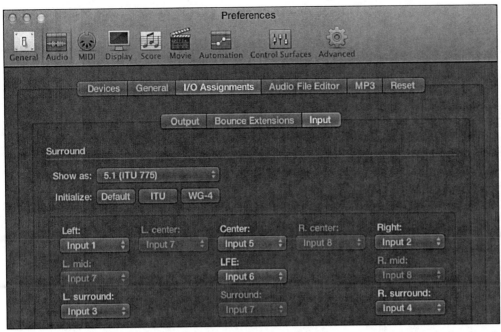

Figure 3.36 The Input screen of the I/O Assignments tab of the Audio Preferences window. You can configure your audio interface for surround input in this screen.
© Apple Inc.

hardware mixers, except instead of controlling audio, they control your Logic software. A full explanation of how to use your control surface is beyond the scope of this book; this section will just focus on how to set up your control surface to work with Logic.

Setting Up a Supported Control Surface

Logic already has complete built-in support for a number of popular control surfaces. As of this writing, Logic Pro X ships with built-in support for the following devices:

▷ **CM Labs:** Motor Mix
▷ **Euphonix:** MC Professional and Artist series controllers
▷ **Frontier Design:** TranzPort
▷ **JL Cooper:** CS-32 MiniDesk, FaderMaster 4/100, MCS3
▷ **Korg:** microKONTROL, KONTROL49
▷ **M-Audio:** iControl
▷ **Mackie Designs:** Baby HUI, HUI, Logic Control (Mackie Control), Logic Control XT (Mackie Control XT), Mackie Control C4
▷ **Radikal Technologies:** SAC-2k
▷ **Recording Light:** Offers MIDI control of a "Recording" light to let people know your session is in live recording mode
▷ **Roland:** SI-24
▷ **Tascam:** FW-1884, US-224, US-428, US-2400
▷ **Yamaha:** 01V96, 02R96, DM1000, DM2000

> **NOTE:** Apple is always adding support for new control surfaces, so if you have a control surface that is not listed here, keep checking with Apple to see whether support for it has been added.

Depending on your control surface, you may need a MIDI interface to connect it. (See your control surface's owner's manual for instructions on proper hookup.) Logic will automatically detect most control surfaces when you connect them to your system.

You will be presented with the Control Surface Setup window when Logic launches, shown in Figure 3.37. This indicates that Logic was able to sense that you had a control surface plugged in and that all is well.

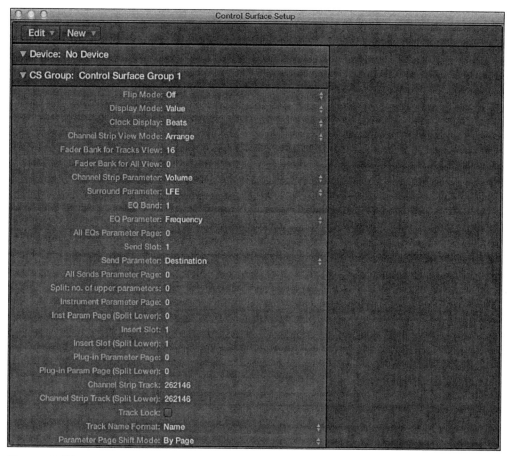

Figure 3.37 The Control Surface Setup window. If Logic automatically opened to this window, you're home free. Otherwise, you may need to connect to your control surface manually.
© Apple Inc.

If this window does not detect your control surface immediately, don't worry, as all is not lost. Simply select New > Scan All Models from the Control Surface Setup window, and Logic will rescan your MIDI interface to find any connected control surfaces. If your control surface does not support automatic scanning, then you need to add it manually by doing the following:

1. Choose New > Install from the Control Surface Setup window.
2. Choose your control surface from the list.
3. Click Add.

If your control surface is found but does not seem to be responding, open the global Logic Pro menu and choose Logic Pro X > Control Surfaces > Rebuild Defaults. That should do the trick. If this works, it means that Logic always knew where your control surface was among your devices, but it was simply not connecting. If this doesn't work, you'll need to start looking for loose cables and hardware connections, then try again. If nothing works, don't be afraid to contact the controller manufacturer's tech support and ask them to walk you through the connection process.

Once Logic senses your control surface, you're ready to go. Close the window and bask in the joy of your control surface!

Setting Up Any MIDI Device as a Control Surface

As mentioned, if your control surface is not supported, you can still configure Logic to use it to control the application. If you want to use an unsupported control surface, you will need to set up what each knob, fader, and button on your controller does. The basic procedure is to first click on an onscreen control or menu option. After you have done this, immediately select Logic

Pro X > Control Surfaces > Learn Assignment For. (You will notice that the word following "For" will be the control or command you just selected.) Figure 3.38 illustrates how this should work.

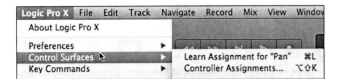

Figure 3.38 In this example, the volume slider of the first track in the track Mixer was clicked. As you can see, the Learn Assignment parameter now says "Learn Assignment for 'Pan,'" reflecting that any controller assignment you make will be mapped to the panorama of that track.
© Apple Inc.

After you select the Learn Assignment command (or press Command+L), you will be presented with the Controller Assignments dialog box shown Figure 3.39. At this point, click the Learn button and twist, press, slide, or otherwise manipulate a control on your MIDI controller, and it will be automatically assigned to the chosen control or command in Logic. You can use this to assign each button, knob, and fader on your MIDI controller to control a function in Logic.

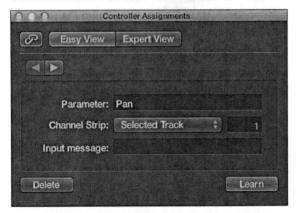

Figure 3.39 When you execute the Learn Assignment command, you will be presented with the Controller Assignments window. Click Learn and move a control on your MIDI device, and it will be assigned to that control or command.
© Apple Inc.

As you can see, this is an amazingly powerful feature in Logic, allowing virtually every aspect of the application to be remotely controlled! As you can also see, going into every detail of this extremely powerful feature would take a whole chapter by itself, and it's beyond the scope of this book. This description should be enough to get you started with a basic setup. When you want to get into more complex and esoteric assignments, the *Logic Pro X Control Surfaces Support* online help manual offers a complete description of the Controller Assignments feature.

Saving Your Template

When you are ready to save your template project, select File > Save As Template. You will be presented with the Save As dialog box, already opened to the Project Templates folder in the user directory. Click Save, and your template will be ready for you to use as a starting point any time you need it!

TIP: Being that your template is so important and painstakingly constructed, you most likely will want to save it from being accidentally modified. Luckily, the Mac OS offers two easy methods to protect a file. For either, you'll need to select your template in the Mac OS Finder and choose File > Get Info, press Command+I, or right-click your template and select Get Info. When the Get Info box appears, you'll notice two checkboxes. If you select the Stationary Pad checkbox, Logic will open a copy of your template and name it "Untitled" instead of your actual template file; that way, if you accidentally press Return, it creates a new file and doesn't overwrite your previous template. You may also want to select the second checkbox in the Get Info window, labeled Locked. With this selected, you simply cannot make any changes to the template file without unlocking the file in the Finder first. Either method will protect your template from accidental changes.

Logic's Use of Mac OS X Directories: You may have already noticed that the Logic Pro X file in your Applications directory does not have a folder around it, as some other programs you may own do. This is because Logic Pro follows Apple's guidelines for where the support files for applications should go. Logic Pro files are in one of two places.

Factory presets and support files are in the local directory (meaning, at the level of your hard drive):

▶ /Library/Application Support/Logic

User presets and support files are in your user directory, with ~ being the UNIX symbol for the Home directory for a given user:

▶ ~/Library/Application Support/Logic
▶ ~/Music > Audio Music Apps

As you can see, there's really only a single folder to which you'll be adding information, and that's the user folder. It's also very convenient to back up just this one folder and know that all your presets, templates, sampler instruments, and so on have been backed up.

You should now understand the basics of what Logic is and what Logic can do. You should also have completed the basic configuration of your template project. From this point forward, the focus shifts from explaining to exploring. As such, you will encounter many details very quickly. Don't feel intimidated if you need to slow down or reread a section a few times before you are comfortable with the information. Logic is a very deep program, and it takes time to absorb. In the next chapter, you will start exploring some of the global functions, options, menus, and tracks Logic has to offer. As you learn about new functions in Logic, remember to incorporate those things you find useful into your template and its screensets!

Global Elements of Logic

F OR LONG-TIME LOGIC USERS, the system of global and local menus used in Logic has become second nature. Logic Pro X has changed this paradigm significantly, so if you're upgrading from a previous version of Logic, you may be searching a bunch of new and different menus in locations you would not expect to find commands you've used for years. Some commands have been moved from local menus to global menus; indeed, there are numerous new and different global menus. Some menus seem to have disappeared entirely. Don't worry; those commands can still be accessed, just in new or renamed menus. Reading this chapter will be essential to working with Logic Pro X not just for users who are new to Logic, but also for long-time users, who might normally skip this chapter.

Many of Logic's commands and options make sense only within the specific window where the command or feature is used. For example, having a function to select notes wouldn't make sense in the Mixer, and having a way to adjust the stereo field of an audio track isn't useful in the Score editor. That's why many commands and tools in Logic reside in *local* menus—menus specific to the window or area of the main window you are using. This allows Logic to put many more commands at your fingertips than if it were limited only to the menus in the OS X menu bar. Many of these commands are also available in right-click menus within each specific area.

There are some functions that apply to more than one window, affect the entire song, or affect the whole application. These elements of Logic can be considered *global*. However, there has been a shift of focus in Logic Pro X to the main window. Many functions that previously resided only in local menus in the former Arrange window (current main window) now exist in both local and global menus. Before covering the more specific elements of Logic Pro X, I'll use this chapter to give you one more broad view of the kinds of options and features available to you in Logic.

What Do You Know?: Logic Pro X's organizational change from previous iterations has made organizing this book more challenging. Believe it or not, determining where to put this chapter in the book and what to include in it were actually two of my tougher decisions. The change in content and structure among many global and local menus is significant. For intermediate and advanced music software users, it's not that intimidating—you're familiar with the concepts of global menus, local menus, using tools from a Tool menu, and so on. Intermediate and advanced Logic users may already understand what most of the features, functions, and concepts are all about. Experienced Logic Pro X users simply have to become familiar with the new paradigm. For a beginner or someone migrating from GarageBand, on the other hand, reading about these menus— some having specific functions in the main window while having no purpose in other windows—and later learning how to create and manipulate data in global tracks might seem overwhelming.

In the end, I decided that because the global tracks and some of the global menus play a part in almost every section after this one, those items needed to be covered here. Because some local commands have been moved to global menus, those will be covered in detail when we get to those specific areas of focus later in the book. For example, it would be hard to discuss the Record Button Options command in the global Record menu without dealing with the Transport controls as a whole; the Transport controls have a dedicated chapter. Conversely, because the marker track functions across your whole project, it is truly global and it is covered in this chapter. As these features are mentioned, I'll list the sections that cover the issues more in depth so you can find answers to any questions you might be left with. Hopefully, for those of you who are a bit perplexed, after you've read a little further, you can come back to this chapter and everything will be clearer.

The Global Menus

You've already looked at and used commands from both global and local menus. The following chapters explore all of the local menus throughout the various editors, windows, and tabs in Logic in depth. Detailed information on many functions of the global menus will be offered later on in the appropriate chapters. This chapter offers a brief description of each global menu and its contents. When menu commands have default key commands, these will also be listed with the menu command.

The Logic Pro X Menu

The Logic Pro X menu, shown in Figure 4.1, contains commands and options that affect the entire application.

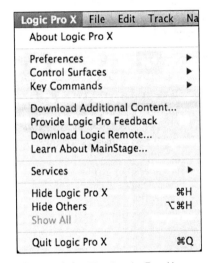

Figure 4.1 The Logic Pro X menu.
© Apple Inc.

It contains the following commands and submenus:

▷ **About Logic Pro X:** Obsessed with trying to figure out whose name is on the platinum album on the Logic Pro X splash screen? You can get another look at the splash screen by selecting this command. To close the splash screen, simply click anywhere inside it.

▷ **Preferences:** The Preferences submenu, detailed in the next section, "The Preferences Submenu," offers shortcuts to the main tabs in the Preferences window. The preferences themselves are described throughout this book, where appropriate.

▷ **Control Surfaces:** This submenu, explained in the section "The Control Surfaces Submenu," contains options for configuring and using MIDI control surfaces with Logic.

▷ **Key Commands:** The Key Commands submenu lets you change your default keyboard language and gives you access to the Logic 9 key commands (for those of you who are used to them) via the Key Commands > Presets command. It also offers the command to open the Key Commands window. Chapter 3, "The Logic Project," discussed the Key Commands window. The key command for this is Option+K.

▷ **Download Additional Content:** Logic Pro X has tens of gigabytes of additional content—Apple Loops, samples, Drummer kits, impulse responses, and so forth—which you can download from Apple using this command. If you have the storage space for all of this content, it is well worth the effort to download it.

▷ **Provide Logic Pro Feedback:** Selecting this command will open your Web browser and take you to a page on the Apple website where you can submit feedback to Apple about Logic Pro. I can't stress how important it is for you to use this feature to submit new ideas and report any bugs you may encounter.

> NOTE: There are bugs in nearly every program that won't crash the program but may affect your workflow. Because they don't show up in crash logs, the only way a developer can fix these bugs is from user feedback, detailing what the bug is and how to reproduce it. Believe me when I say that developers appreciate this kind of user feedback. No one tries to write bugs into their software, and Apple does listen to your feedback, be it about wish-list features or any bugs. Many of the features you will learn about in this book are a direct result of user feedback.

▷ **Download Logic Remote:** Those of you with an iPad 2 or greater running iOS 6.0 or greater can download the Logic Remote app, which offers a fairly full complement of touch-based controls for things like the Mixer and Logic's software instruments. Highly recommended.

▷ **Learn About MainStage:** Selecting this command opens your Web browser to a page detailing Apple's live performance spin-off of Logic, MainStage. MainStage offers all the included Logic effects and software instruments in a purpose-built application for use on stage. Its flexibility is amazing, and its $30 price makes it truly a bargain.

▷ **Services:** This is a standard Mac OS X submenu included by the system in every Mac OS X application. This submenu is of no use in Logic.

▷ **Hide Logic Pro X:** This command will remove all the Logic Pro windows from your screen until you select the application in the Finder or the Dock. The key command for this is Command+H.

▷ **Hide Others:** You can hide every application except Logic Pro with this command. The key command for this is Option+Command+H.

▷ **Show All:** You can reveal all applications, including those that are hidden, with this command.

▷ **Quit Logic Pro X:** Use this command to quit Logic Pro. The key command for this is Command+Q.

The Preferences Submenu

The Preferences submenu, shown in Figure 4.2, gives you access to the individual tabs of the Preferences window and other global preference-related elements of Logic Pro. Preferences govern the application as a whole, and therefore apply to any project open within the application.

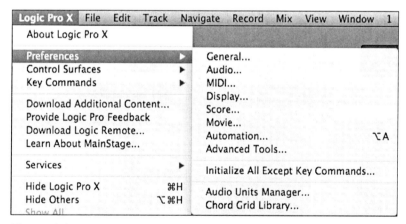

Figure 4.2 The Preferences submenu. Selecting any of these options will open the Preferences window to that particular tab.
© Apple Inc.

The commands in the Preferences submenu are as follows:

▷ **General, Audio, MIDI, Display, Score, Movie, Automation, and Advanced Tools:** Each of these opens the Preferences window to the specific tab you have selected. Each tab has a number of sub-tabs to which you can navigate from there. The different tabs are explained in the chapter appropriate for each particular set of preferences. The Advanced Tools option is covered further in the next section.

▷ **Initialize All Except Key Commands:** You can reset every preference except your key commands by selecting this command.

▷ **Audio Units Manager:** You can launch the Audio Units Manager with this command. The Audio Units Manager allows you to turn on and off individual Audio Unit plug-ins within Logic, as well as scan them for compatibility. Chapter 11, "Mixing in Logic," details the functions of the Audio Units Manager.

▷ **Chord Grid Library:** Selecting this command opens the Chord Grid Library, which contains more than 4,000 different guitar chords displayed in tablature for use in the Score editor. You can also use the Chord Grid Library to create your own guitar chord tablature for use in the Score editor. The Chord Grid Library is covered in detail in Chapter 8, "Working with MIDI."

THE ADVANCED TOOLS PREFERENCES

Logic Pro X is, as you are discovering, an incredibly deep and powerful application. Although this book deals with Logic Pro wide open—with all Advanced Tools available—you may want a more managed experience when you use Logic. The Advanced Preferences window, shown in Figure 4.3, which you access by choosing Advanced Tools from the Preferences submenu, gives you ample control over what tools are available to you in Logic.

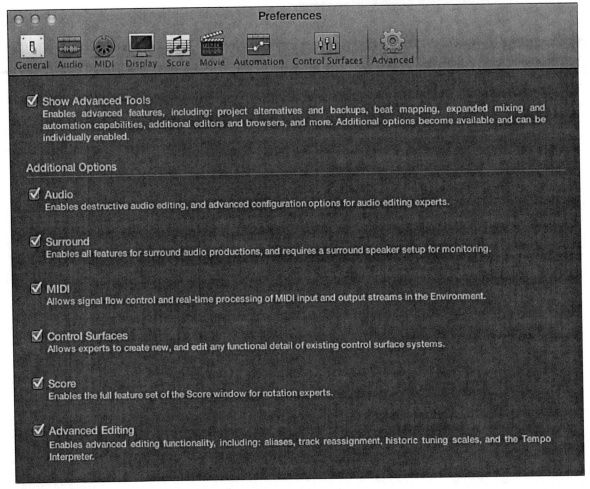

Figure 4.3 The Advanced Preferences window.
© Apple Inc.

The Advanced Tools Preferences are as follows:

▷ **Show Advanced Tools:** This checkbox turns on or off access to all advanced tools. When it is selected, you have access to the additional options shown in Figure 4.3. If you deselect this checkbox, the additional options are no longer available, and Logic runs in a very basic mode with limited editing parameters and global tracks, among other things. If you recall, Figure 2.2 in Chapter 2, "A Quick Tour of Logic Pro," showed how Logic looks when Show Advanced Tools is disabled—simplified, but with all the basics covered. For those of you transitioning from GarageBand who want something more like "GarageBand Pro" than the full Logic Pro experience, working with Show Advanced Tools disabled is a great option. It is also an excellent option if you are turning over control of Logic to someone with much less knowledge for a bit while working on a project. You can turn all the advanced tools on and off at any time, even while a project is open!

▷ **Audio:** Selecting the Audio checkbox lets you access the Audio File editor. The Audio File editor works on audio files destructively; the original audio file is permanently altered when using the Audio File editor. You also have full access to all audio configuration options, like full control of surround inputs and outputs.

▷ **Surround:** The Surround option lets you enable or disable surround entirely.

▷ **MIDI:** This MIDI option gives you access to the Environment and MIDI Transform windows.

▷ **Control Surfaces:** This option gives you full access to all commands in the Logic Pro X > Control Surfaces submenu and all parameters in the Control Surfaces Setup window.

▷ **Score:** This option gives you access to all the features in the Score editor.

▷ **Advanced Editing:** This option gives you access to advanced editing features like track reassignment (covered in Chapter 3) and the Tempo Interpreter, which is covered in Chapter 13, "Advanced Tempo Operations."

The Control Surfaces Submenu

The Control Surfaces submenu, shown in Figure 4.4, offers commands relating to the use and configuration of MIDI devices to be used as control surfaces for Logic.

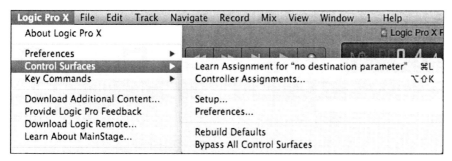

Figure 4.4 The Control Surfaces submenu of the Logic Pro X menu.
© Apple Inc.

The commands in this submenu include the following:

▷ **Learn Assignment For:** This command launches the Controller Assignments window for the selected option or command. This was discussed in Chapter 3. The key command for this is Command+L.

▷ **Controller Assignments:** You can launch the Controller Assignments window without previously selecting an option or command here. The Controller Assignments window was discussed in Chapter 3. The key command for this is Option+Shift+K.

▷ **Setup:** This launches the Control Surface Setup window. This window was discussed in Chapter 3.

▷ **Preferences:** You can set a number of preferences for how your control surface interacts with Logic here.

▷ **Rebuild Defaults:** This will reset the preferences for your control surface.

▷ **Bypass All Control Surfaces:** When selected, this option disables your control surface.

The File Menu

Not surprisingly, the File menu, shown in Figure 4.5, contains options and commands that involve files. Most commands here will get files either into or out of Logic. If not otherwise noted, most of these commands will be explored in more detail in Chapter 12, "Working with and Sharing Files."

The following list describes the entries in the File menu:

▷ **New:** This command opens a completely empty Logic project. In a break with Apple's own system-wide key-command conventions, the key command for New is Shift+Command+N.

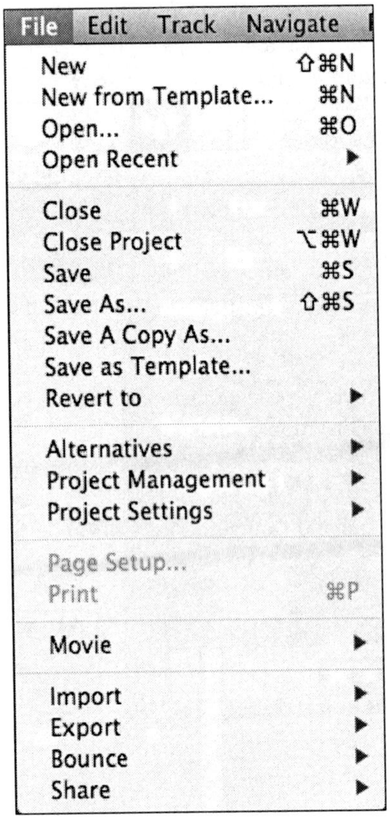

File	Edit	Track	Navigate	
New			⇧⌘N	
New from Template...			⌘N	
Open...			⌘O	
Open Recent			▶	
Close			⌘W	
Close Project			⌥⌘W	
Save			⌘S	
Save As...			⇧⌘S	
Save A Copy As...				
Save as Template...				
Revert to			▶	
Alternatives			▶	
Project Management			▶	
Project Settings			▶	
Page Setup...				
Print			⌘P	
Movie			▶	
Import			▶	
Export			▶	
Bounce			▶	
Share			▶	

Figure 4.5 The File menu.
© Apple Inc.

▷ **New from Template:** This command opens the New window, which was covered in Chapter 3. The key command for this is Command+N.

▷ **Open:** The Open command opens a song or project created by Logic (any version or platform of Logic from Logic 5 to Logic X). It can also open all the other file types Logic supports—GarageBand, MIDI, AAF, and XML (Final Cut Pro). The key command for this is Command+O.

▷ **Open Recent:** The Open Recent submenu contains a list of your recently opened projects. If the list gets too long, you can use the Clear Menu option in the Open Recent submenu to clear the Open Recent list.

▷ **Close:** This command closes the upper-most open window. If only one window is open, it prompts a Save dialog box, allowing you to close the current project. It will not close a floating window, but you can use it to close a plug-in window if the plug-in window has been selected. The key command for this is Command+W.

▷ **Close Project:** This command closes the current project. The key command for this is Option+Command+W.

▷ **Save:** This will save the current project. The key command for this is Command+S. The first time you save your project, the Save command functions like the Save As command.

▷ **Save As:** This command brings up a Save dialog box for you to name and save your project. The key command for this is Shift+Command+S.

▷ **Save a Copy As:** This command brings up a Save dialog box for you to save a copy of your project.

▷ **Save as Template:** This command saves the current project as a template.

▷ **Revert To:** If you aren't happy with the current state of your project, Revert To will reload the last saved version of your project. Obviously, this only works if you've previously saved your project!

▷ **Alternatives:** The Alternatives submenu offers ways of saving and accessing different versions of a project—for example, different mixes, different arrangements, or different instrumentations—contained within the project.

▷ **Project Management:** The Project Management submenu offers you a few options for managing Logic projects:

  ▷ **Clean Up:** You can use this command to find and display unused project files, enabling you to selectively delete them.

  ▷ **Consolidate:** You can take a Logic song that does not have its dependent files in the proper project folder structure and consolidate it into the correct structure with this command.

▷ **Rename:** This allows you to rename a project.

▷ **Show in Finder:** This command opens a Finder window to the location of your Logic project within your file structure.

▷ **Project Settings:** The Project Settings submenu, described in further detail in the next section, allows you to open the Project Settings window to a specific tab. Project settings are specific to the particular project in which you are working.

TIP: If you have a preferred, standard set of project settings, save them as a part of your template. You can then alter them on a per-project basis as needed.

▷ **Page Setup:** This command opens the Page Setup window for your printer driver.

▷ **Print:** This prints the contents of the selected window. This is useful if you want to print musical notation from the Score editor, for example. The key command for this is Command+P.

▷ **Movie:** The Movie submenu offers a few options for working with movie files, including the Open Movie command. While the movie track is discussed briefly at the end of this chapter, you'll find much more information on using movies in Logic in Chapter 14, "Working with Video."

▷ **Import:** The Import submenu gives you options for importing any supported file type into Logic.

▷ **Export:** In the Export submenu, you can export your Logic project into any of the aforementioned formats that Logic supports except GarageBand. You can also export a single region, track, or all of your tracks into individual files. The various Export options are discussed in Chapter 7, "Working with Audio and Apple Loops," and Chapter 12, "Working with and Sharing Files."

▷ **Bounce:** The Bounce submenu gives you options for bouncing all or part of your project to audio files. The File > Bounce > Project or Section command is discussed in Chapter 11, "Mixing in Logic." The other Bounce submenu commands are covered in Chapter 6, "The Logic Pro Main Window."

The Project Settings Submenu

When you set Logic's preferences, those settings apply to the entire application, regardless of the project. Project settings, on the other hand, apply only to the current project. The Project Settings submenu is shown in Figure 4.6.

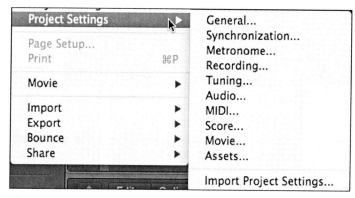

Figure 4.6 The Project Settings submenu.
© Apple Inc.

▷ **General:** The General command opens the General tab in the Project Settings window. This tab offers one option: the Project Type checkbox. This lets you choose between using a musical grid in the Tracks area and editors—bars and beats in the ruler—and a time-based ruler. When Use Musical Grid is enabled, tempo information will be embedded in your audio files. If you are recording music with Logic, you will generally want to enable the Use Musical Grid checkbox.

▷ **Synchronization:** You can open the Project Settings Synchronization tab here. Some synchronization settings are discussed in Chapter 13.

▷ **Metronome:** You can open the Project Settings Metronome tab here. These settings are described in Chapter 5, "Transport Controls and Recording."

▷ **Recording:** You can open the Project Settings Recording tab here. These settings are described in Chapter 5.

> **Tuning:** You can open the Project Settings Tuning tab here. In addition to a global master tuning option for software instruments used in your project, you can also use and create alternate tuning systems via the tuning settings.
> **Audio:** You can open the Project Settings Audio tab here. These settings are described in Chapter 6.
> **MIDI:** You can open the Project Settings MIDI tab here. These settings are described in Chapter 6.
> **Score:** You can open the Project Settings Score tab here. These settings are described in Chapter 8.
> **Movie:** You can open the Project Settings Movie tab here. These settings are described in Chapter 14.
> **Assets:** You can open the Project Settings Assets tab here. These settings are described in Chapter 12.
> **Import Project Settings:** This command allows you to import the project settings of another Logic project. Selecting this command brings up a File dialog box, where you can choose the project from which you want to import settings. You may choose to import any or all of the following: screensets, transform sets, lane sets, score instrument sets, score styles, and/or score settings.

The Edit Menu

The Edit menu, shown in Figure 4.7, includes a standard set of global editing, moving, selection, and undo commands.

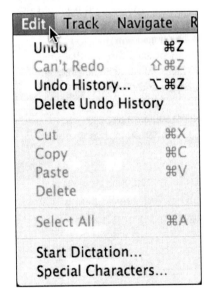

Figure 4.7 The Edit menu.
© Apple Inc.

The commands in the Edit menu are as follows:

> **Undo:** If you are not happy with your most recent action, Undo will revert Logic to the condition before that action. Not all actions can be undone. If you try to undo an action that cannot be undone, the command will be grayed out and will read "Can't Undo." The key command for Undo is Command+Z.
> **Redo:** If you have undone an action and you want to bring it back, you can use the Redo command. Not all actions can be redone. If you try to redo an action that cannot be redone, the command will be grayed out and will read "Can't Redo." The key command for this is Shift+Command+Z.
> **Undo History:** Logic has multiple levels of undo. Each action gets stored in the Undo History window. At any time, you can go back and undo as many actions as you'd like. The Undo History window is explored in more detail in Chapter 6. The key command for this is Option+Command+Z.
> **Delete Undo History:** Use this command to empty the Undo History window and start over with a brand-new list of actions.

▷ **Cut:** This command removes the selected data from its current location and adds it to the Clipboard. The key command for this is Command+X.

▷ **Copy:** This command adds the currently selected data to the Clipboard without removing it from its current location. The key command for this is Command+C.

▷ **Paste:** This command pastes the data in the Clipboard at the current playhead location. Note that this works only for compatible data. For example, if an audio file is in the Clipboard, you can't paste it into the Score editor. You can, however, paste it into the Audio window, Sample editor, or main window, as these windows can contain audio data. The key command for this is Command+V.

▷ **Delete:** This command will delete the selected data without adding it to the Clipboard.

▷ **Select All:** This command will select all of the data in the current window. The key command for this is Command+A.

▷ **Start Dictation:** The Start Dictation command lets you speak into your computer's microphone. Your computer will send that audio to Apple's servers for analysis, then return it to your computer as text.

▷ **Special Characters:** The Special Characters command gives you access to a host of non-standard characters.

> **NOTE:** There may be more commands available in the main Edit menu. This depends on the currently selected window or on what area is in focus in the main window.

The Track Menu

The Track menu, shown in Figure 4.8, contains a number of commands for creating and working with tracks. You're already familiar with some of these commands from setting up your template. Many of the others will be covered in Chapter 6. The Global Tracks submenu options are covered in detail in the "Global Tracks" section later in this chapter.

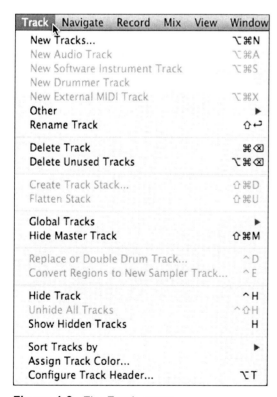

Figure 4.8 The Track menu.
© Apple Inc.

The Navigate Menu

The Navigate menu offers a number of commands for navigating your project. Many of the Navigate menu commands are covered elsewhere in this book. The commands that deal with markers in the Navigate menu and its Go To submenu are covered in the section "The Marker Track" later in this chapter.

The Record Menu

The Record menu offers a number of recording options, which are covered in Chapter 5.

The Mix Menu

The Mix menu offers a number of automation- and mix-related commands, which are covered as needed throughout this book.

The View Menu

The View menu offers a number of main window view options. It is covered in Chapter 6.

The Window Menu

The Window menu, shown in Figure 4.9, contains commands related to opening and manipulating windows.

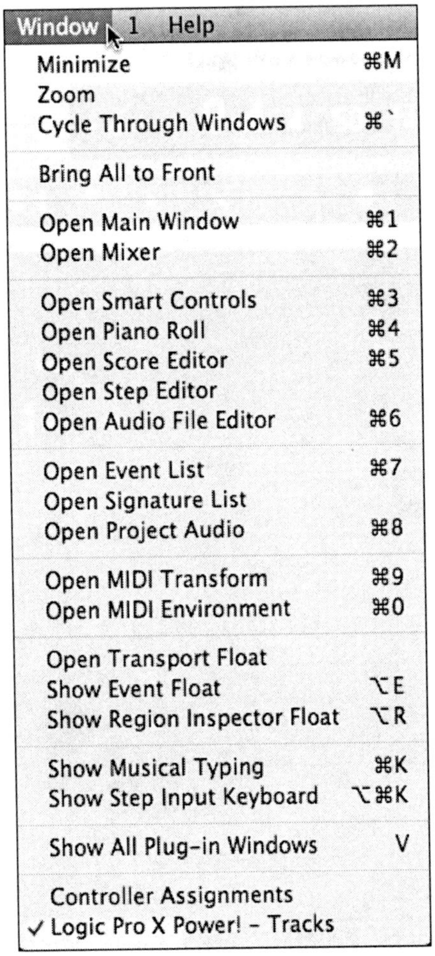

Window	1	Help	
Minimize			⌘M
Zoom			
Cycle Through Windows			⌘`
Bring All to Front			
Open Main Window			⌘1
Open Mixer			⌘2
Open Smart Controls			⌘3
Open Piano Roll			⌘4
Open Score Editor			⌘5
Open Step Editor			
Open Audio File Editor			⌘6
Open Event List			⌘7
Open Signature List			
Open Project Audio			⌘8
Open MIDI Transform			⌘9
Open MIDI Environment			⌘0
Open Transport Float			
Show Event Float			⌥E
Show Region Inspector Float			⌥R
Show Musical Typing			⌘K
Show Step Input Keyboard			⌥⌘K
Show All Plug-in Windows			V
Controller Assignments			
✓ Logic Pro X Power! – Tracks			

Figure 4.9 The Window menu.
© Apple Inc.

The Window menu contains the following commands:

▷ **Minimize:** This command minimizes the currently selected window to the Dock. The key command for this is Command+M.

▷ **Zoom:** You can instantly resize a window to fill the entire screen using this command.

▷ **Cycle Through Windows:** You can switch from the current window to the next unselected window using this command. The key command for this is Command+`.

▷ **Bring All to Front:** Selecting this command brings all Logic windows to the front of any other open windows.

▷ **Open Main Window:** This command launches the main window. The main window is the focus of Chapter 6. The key command for this is Command+1.

▷ **Open Mixer:** This command launches a Mixer window. The Mixer is discussed in Chapter 11. The key command for this is Command+2.

▷ **Open Smart Controls:** This command opens Smart Controls for the selected track at the bottom of the main window. Smart Controls are covered in Chapter 6. The key command for this is Command+3.

▷ **Open Piano Roll:** This command launches the Piano Roll editor. The Piano Roll editor is discussed in Chapter 8. The key command for this is Command+4.

▷ **Open Score Editor:** This command launches the Score editor. The Score editor is discussed in Chapter 8. The key command for this is Command+5.

▷ **Open Step Editor:** This command launches the Step editor, formerly called the Hyper editor. The Step editor is discussed in Chapter 8.

▷ **Open Audio File Editor:** This command opens the Audio File editor, formerly known as the Sample editor. The Audio File editor is explored in Chapter 7. The key command for this is Command+6.

▷ **Open Event List:** This command launches the Event list. The Event list is discussed in Chapter 8. The key command for this is Command+7.

▷ **Open Signature List:** This command launches the Signature list. This window is used for entering time-signature and key-change information. This window is explored in "The Signature Track" section later in this chapter.

▷ **Open Project Audio:** This command opens the Project Audio window, formerly called the Audio bin. The Project Audio window is explored in Chapter 7. The key command for this is Command+8.

▷ **Open MIDI Transform:** This command launches a Transform window. The Transform window is discussed in Chapter 8. The key command for this is Command+9.

▷ **Open MIDI Environment:** This command launches an Environment window. The key command for this is Command+8.

▷ **Open Transport Float:** This command launches a Transport window. The Transport window is discussed in Chapter 5.

▷ **Show Event Float:** If you want a one-entry Event list in a floating window to always show you the currently selected data, you can launch one with this command. The key command for this is Option+E.

▷ **Show Region Inspector Float:** Selecting this command opens a floating Region Inspector, which will display the playback parameters for the selected region. The floating Region Inspector is an exact duplicate of the Region Inspector in the Inspector pane, which is covered in Chapter 6. The key command for this is Option+R.

▷ **Show Musical Typing:** This command opens the unfortunately named Musical Typing window, formerly the much hipper Caps Lock Keyboard window. Musical Typing lets you use your computer keyboard for real-time performance, albeit in a much more limited fashion than you can achieve with a MIDI controller. Still, it's very handy in a pinch! The key command for this is Command+K.

▷ **Show Step Input Keyboard:** This command opens the Step Input Keyboard window, which can be used to input MIDI note information into the Event list and Score and Piano Roll editors. The key command for this is Option+Command+K.

▷ **Show All Plug-in Windows:** This command lets you show any plug-in windows you have open. It also lets you close all open plug-in windows. The key command for this is V.

▷ **Controller Assignments:** This command opens the Controller Assignments window, covered in Chapter 3.

▷ **List of open windows:** At the bottom of the Window menu is a list of all the windows currently open in Logic. In Figure 4.9, for example, the open window is the Tracks window, or the main window from the Logic X Power! Project. If you have several windows open in Logic, they all will be listed here, and you can select one of those windows to bring that window to the front.

The Screenset Menu

This menu includes commands relating to screensets. This menu was explored in Chapter 3.

The Help Menu

The Help menu is the standard Mac OS X Help menu with some great added features. In addition to the Help menu's Search field, the Help menu gives you direct access to all your Logic Pro manuals on the Internet. The Help menu also contains a number of other useful Logic Web links.

Global Tracks

Global tracks are unique tracks that contain information that pertains to the entire Logic project, such as the project's tempo, key signature, time signature, arrangement, song markers, thumbnails of video for which you are composing audio, and so on. Global tracks can be displayed in the main window and in the Piano Roll, Score, and Step editors. There are seven types of global tracks:

▷ **Arrangement track:** The arrangement track contains arrangement markers that can be used not only to name sections of your project, but to actually arrange them and the regions within them quickly and easily.

▷ **Marker track:** This track contains song markers, or position holders you can use to label and separate sections of your project.

▷ **Movie track:** This track contains thumbnail frames of QuickTime movie in sync with Logic.

▷ **Signature track:** This track contains all your time signatures and key signatures for your project.

▷ **Transposition track:** This track shows any global transposition events—in other words, any chord changes or note transpositions that would result in all MIDI regions and Apple Loops being transposed from their original pitch.

▷ **Tempo track:** This track contains the tempo and tempo changes for your project.

▷ **Beat mapping track:** This powerful addition to Logic allows you to use any audio or MIDI region with strong rhythmic accents to create a beat map that Logic will use to adjust the musical timeline.

Figure 4.10 shows all the global tracks open in the Tracks area.

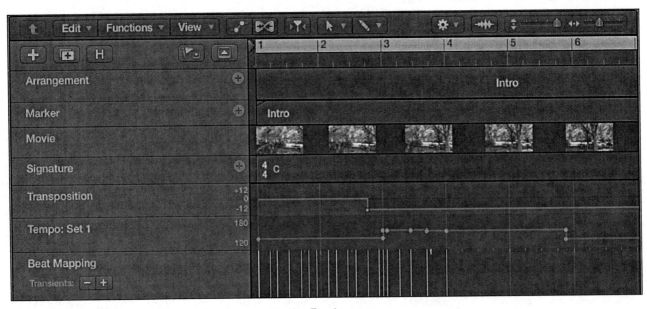

Figure 4.10 The seven global tracks displayed in the Tracks area.
© Apple Inc.

As you can see in Figure 4.10, even in a more minimized state, global tracks can eat up your screen real estate quickly! Don't worry—you don't need to view them all at the same time. They can be easily shown or hidden using the G key command or the

Hide/Show Global Tracks button (the right-most button at the top of the Track list in Figure 4.10), and they can be resized. The Track > Global Tracks submenu includes the Configure Global Tracks command. You can also right-click any global track header and select this command from the shortcut menu or press Option+G key. This will bring up a sliding window allowing you to choose to show only those global tracks that you want to see (see Figure 4.11). There are also key commands to toggle each global track on or off, commands for this in the Track > Global Tracks submenu, and hide/show individual global tracks options in the global tracks right-click shortcut menu. Using the Global Tracks Configuration window, you can, for example, choose to view only the marker and movie tracks, or you might choose to show the tempo track in the main window but not in the Score editor.

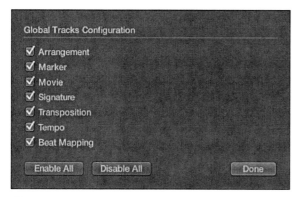

Figure 4.11 The Global Tracks Configuration sliding window lets you select which global tracks you would like to show.
© Apple Inc.

If you want to rearrange your displayed global tracks, you can do this by grabbing a global track in the Track list and dragging it to its new location. Also, when you move the cursor to the bottom border of a global track, it turns into a resize cursor, and you can drag that track to resize it. Figure 4.12 gives an example of these global track features.

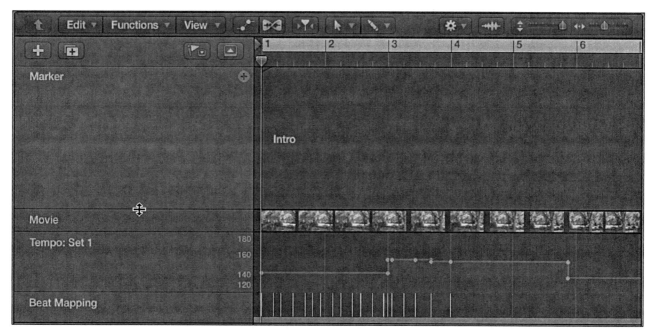

Figure 4.12 Here, only four of the seven global tracks are showing. The marker track has been resized to its maximum size via the resize cursor (shown). The movie and beat mapping tracks have been resized to their smallest setting. Finally, the tempo track is expanded to a medium setting.
© Apple Inc.

Common Features of Global Tracks

The movie and beat mapping tracks are unique in their functions and features, but the other five global tracks share a number of common features. The data on these global tracks consists of *global events*. These global events are different types of data depending on the specific global track, but they can be created, moved, copied, and deleted similarly. The next sections explain how.

Creating a Global Event

To create a global event on a global track, simply click with the Pencil tool at the desired position in the track. As the mouse button is down, a help tag with the exact position (and value, if applicable to that global track) will be displayed below the cursor. Figure 4.13 illustrates creating a global event in the tempo track.

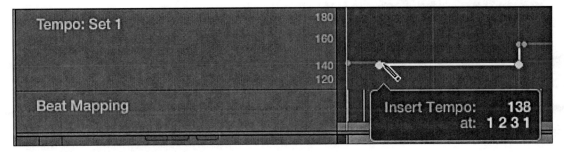

Figure 4.13 Inserting global events in the tempo track. Just click in the track with the Pencil tool to create the event. The help tag below the Pencil tool displays information about your action, including position information.
© Apple Inc.

If you have not changed the default tool to the Pencil tool, you can access the Pencil tool with the Command key by assigning the secondary Tool menu to the Pencil tool.

You can also access the Tool menu by pressing T. If you have set the Right Mouse Button preference in the Logic Pro > Preferences > Global > Editing tab to Opens Tool Menu or Opens Tool and Shortcut Menu, you can use your right mouse button to access the Tool menu and select the Pencil tool.

> **NOTE:** If the concepts of tools and Tool menus aren't familiar to you, you might want to skip to Chapter 6, which, in the context of the main window tools, discusses the Tool menu and the Pencil tool in detail.

The arrangement, marker, and signature tracks offer one other method of creating new global events. Clicking the plus (+) button at the right side of those global track headers creates a new global event for that track at the current playhead position. Signature track events created this way are automatically rounded to the nearest bar.

Selecting and Moving Global Events

You can select global events using the common selection methods you are familiar with from other applications. Click on an event with the mouse pointer to select it. To select multiple global events, Shift-click on the events you want to select. If you want to make a "rubber band" (sometimes called a *lasso*) selection, you can click and drag the cursor over a group of events, although this method does not work on the beat-mapping, signature, and marker tracks. If you click the track header of the global track in the Track list, you will select all the events on that track.

Once selected, you can move and/or change global events simply by dragging them. When the mouse button is down, a help tag with the exact position (and value, if applicable to that global track) of your global event will be displayed below the cursor. Figure 4.14 shows a global event on the tempo track being moved.

Copying and Deleting Global Events

You can copy and delete global events using the standard Macintosh methods for copying and deleting information.

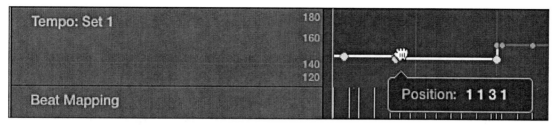

Figure 4.14 A global event on the tempo track has been selected and is being moved to the right.
© Apple Inc.

To copy data using the mouse, Option-drag any selected data. You can also use the Edit menu and keyboard commands for Cut and Paste or Copy and Paste.

To delete data using the mouse, click on the data with the Eraser tool from that window's Tool menu. You can also use the Delete or Backspace key on your keyboard. Finally, you can use the Delete command in the Edit menu.

The Arrangement Track

The arrangement track is a very welcome addition to Logic Pro X. The arrangement track lets you experiment with and create new arrangements of your project on the fly. Want to hear what a double-chorus would sound like before the bridge? Think that perhaps you want to delete that last verse? Previously, this kind of stuff would involve copying and pasting entire sections, moving entire sections, and/or deleting entire sections by selecting all the regions in those sections and manipulating them and the playhead to move all your regions where you wanted them. With the arrangement track, all of this is done quickly and easily—once you create your arrangement markers. The arrangement track also influences the Drummer track, covered in Chapter 6. Figure 4.15 shows the arrangement track over a project in the main window.

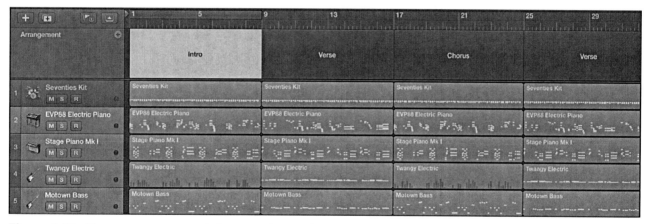

Figure 4.15 The arrangement track lets you change the arrangement of your project quickly and easily.
© Apple Inc.

Creating Arrangement Global Events

You can create arrangement markers by using the methods described earlier in the section "Creating a Global Event." Use the plus sign in the arrangement track header to create a new arrangement marker. By default, arrangement markers made using this method are eight bars long when using the musical grid. They are also named by default, starting with "Intro," "Verse," "Chorus," "Bridge," and "Outro" as you create more arrangement markers. Don't worry, you can rename them, as you'll discover in the next section. If you create an arrangement marker using the Pencil tool, it will begin wherever you click with the Pencil tool. If you click the Pencil tool on an area in the arrangement track that already has an arrangement marker, the new marker will be placed where you click the Pencil tool and the previous marker will be automatically resized to end at that point. By default, arrangement markers created using the Pencil tool are four bars long and are named "marker" with a number describing its order among the other markers. Figure 4.16 shows a marker created with the Pencil tool. It is named marker 3 because it is the third marker in the arrangement track. Note that the Verse marker from Figure 4.15 has been automatically resized to accommodate the new marker.

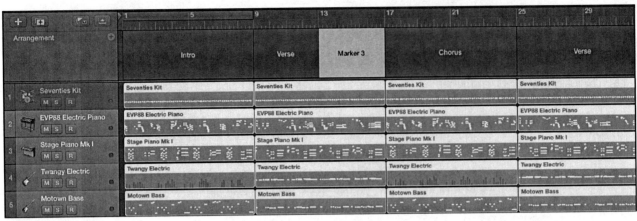

Figure 4.16 Marker 3, created with the Pencil tool, is numbered per its position among the markers in the arrangement track.
© Apple Inc.

Renaming Arrangement Markers

Given the automatic marker naming in the arrangement track, it's likely you will want to rename some or all of your arrangement markers almost immediately. Renaming arrangement markers is incredibly easy. If you're fine with the basic Intro, Verse, Chorus, Bridge, and Outro names for your arrangement, but you simply want to rename a marker to one of those options, click on the name of the marker you wish to change. A menu opens giving you access to each of these options, as shown in Figure 4.17.

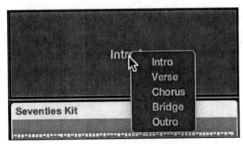

Figure 4.17 To change the name of a marker to one of the basic names provided in Logic, click on the name of the marker you wish to change and select another option from this menu.
© Apple Inc.

This method works for arrangement markers created using either the plus button or the Pencil tool. To change the name of any arrangement marker to some other, more specific name, double-click somewhere in the marker outside the marker name area. A text input window opens where you can name the marker anything you choose. Enter the name, press Return, and your marker is renamed.

Copying, Resizing, Moving, and Deleting Arrangement Markers

The processes for copying, resizing, moving, and deleting couldn't be easier:

▷ To copy an arrangement marker to a new location, Option-drag the selected marker to its new location. Your original marker stays in its original location, and a copy of that marker and all the regions within that marker are placed in the new location.

▷ To resize a marker, simply move the cursor to the right or left edge of the marker you wish to resize. A resize cursor will appear. Click and drag the edge of the marker to resize the marker to the desired length.

▷ To move an arrangement marker, drag the marker to its new location; the marker and all the regions within it are moved accordingly.

▷ Deleting an arrangement marker is a little more involved. When you press the Delete key the first time, all the regions within the marker are deleted but the marker remains. Pressing Delete again removes the marker. If you delete an arrangement marker between two other markers, the markers to the right are moved to the left with their dependent regions, closing the gap in your project. If you delete the first arrangement marker in your project, all other markers and their dependent regions are shifted to the left, with the new first marker placed at the beginning of your project. You can delete multiple arrangement markers by Shift-clicking the markers you want to delete. Again, pressing Delete once removes the regions within the selected markers, and pressing Delete again removes the actual markers, with all gaps among remaining markers automatically eliminated.

Remember, if you accidentally perform any of these operations on an arrangement marker, the Undo command, Command+Z, will undo the action.

The Marker Track

The marker track displays project markers. While this may sound like it's identical to the arrangement track, their functions are quite different. Arrangement track markers can help you easily change a song's arrangement. Marker track markers, on the other hand, are very useful placeholders for locations or sections of your project. They can appear as short placeholders with a line of text in the marker track or as much longer messages in their own Marker Text window. The background and text of the markers can be colored if you wish. Figure 4.18 shows the Piano Roll editor with the marker track displayed.

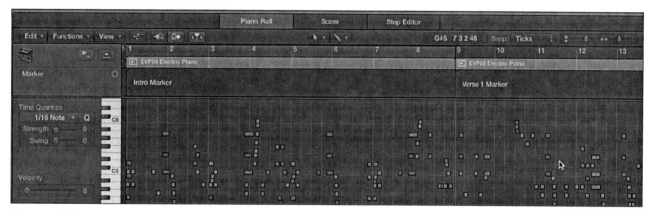

Figure 4.18 This Piano Roll editor has a marker track displaying song markers at the top of the editor.
© Apple Inc.

The marker track has its own hide/show button—it's the button with the flag in it next to the Hide/Show Global Tracks button. If you click the Hide/Show Marker Track button, the marker track will be shown, and any other currently displayed global tracks will be hidden. Clicking the button again hides the marker track, and all other global tracks remain hidden.

Markers are an invaluable aid in organizing and navigating your project. They are very easy to create and use, as you will soon see. They are even embedded in any audio files you bounce or export from Logic, allowing you to use them across multiple projects.

The Marker List

In addition to being visible in the marker track, Logic stores the locations of all of a song's markers in a specialized Event list called the Marker list, available in the List Editors area of the main window or as its own window. The Marker list displays all the markers currently in your project. It allows you to edit the positions of markers, create markers, and perform some additional functions as well. You can bring up the Marker list window by choosing Navigate > Open Marker List or by click-dragging the Marker tab in the List Editors area. To display the Marker list in the main window, open the List Editors area in the main window by clicking the List Editors button or pressing D and then clicking the Marker tab. Figure 4.19 shows a Marker list window.

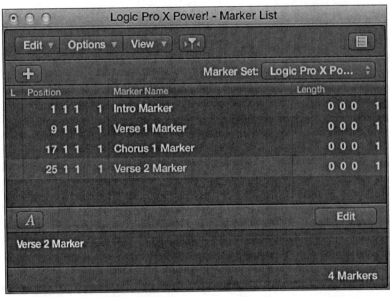

Figure 4.19 In the Marker list, you can add markers, edit their position and length, and more.
© Apple Inc.

The Marker list serves as a single location to quickly view all your markers. If you like to navigate or edit markers from a list, the Marker list serves that purpose, too. If you make regular use of markers, a Marker list window can be an invaluable addition to your screensets.

The Marker list incorporates some unique buttons and menus, which you will now explore.

THE EDIT MENU

The Marker list Edit menu, shown in Figure 4.20, features many of the same functions as the global Edit menu. Refer to the section on the global Edit menu for information on these functions.

Figure 4.20 The Marker list Edit menu.
© Apple Inc.

THE OPTIONS MENU

The Options menu contains commands for creating and altering markers. Figure 4.21 shows the Marker list Options menu.

Figure 4.21 The Marker list Options menu.
© Apple Inc.

The Marker list Options menu commands are as follows:

▷ **Create:** The Create command creates a new marker at the bar nearest to the current playhead position. The key command for this is Option+' (apostrophe).

▷ **Create Without Rounding:** The Create Without Rounding command creates a new marker at the current playhead position. The key command for this is Control+Option+' (apostrophe).

▷ **Lock SMPTE Position:** This command locks your marker to its current SMPTE position. The key command for this is Command+Page Down.

▷ **Unlock SMPTE Position:** If you have a marker locked to a SMPTE position, you can unlock it using this command. This is particularly applicable to video markers, which are covered in more detail in the section "The Movie Track" later in this chapter and in Chapter 14. The key command for this is Command+Page Up.

▷ **Convert to Scene Marker:** This command converts a standard marker into a movie scene marker.

▷ **Convert to Standard Marker:** This command converts a movie scene marker into a standard marker.

THE VIEW MENU

The View menu contains a couple of options to change the display of information in the Marker list. Figure 4.22 shows the Marker list View menu.

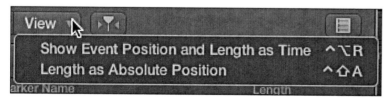

Figure 4.22 The Marker list View menu.
© Apple Inc.

The Marker list View menu options are as follows:

▷ **Show Event Position and Length as Time:** This command changes the Position and Length columns in the Marker list from displaying information in bars to SMPTE. This is very useful when working with movie scene markers. The key command for this is Control+Option+R. If you are not using the musical grid in a project, the Marker list will use time by default.

▷ **Length as Absolute Position:** This command changes the Length column from displaying the relative length of the marker to the actual bar position of the end of the marker. The key command for this is Control+Shift+A.

THE MARKER SET MENU

The Marker Set menu, shown in Figure 4.23, lets you manage multiple sets of markers. As you learn to work with markers and begin using them to navigate your projects, you'll see the advantage of, for example, having one set of markers ready for navigating vocal overdubs while another set is ready for the lead guitar track. The Marker Set menu makes managing sets of markers simple.

Figure 4.23 The Marker Set menu lets you manage and access multiple sets of markers.
© Apple Inc.

The menu commands are self-explanatory:

▷ Create a new marker set (an empty Marker list) with the New Set command.
▷ To switch marker sets, choose the desired set at the top of the Marker Set menu.
▷ Delete the selected set with the Delete Set command.
▷ Rename the selected set with the Rename Set command.

It's that simple! You can also access this menu by clicking on the Marker fields in the marker track header.

THE MARKER LIST BUTTONS

The Marker list has three buttons. Brief explanations of their functions follow:

▷ **Catch Playhead:** When lit, this button (next to the View menu) ensures the Marker list follows along the playhead.
▷ **Edit Marker:** This button, in the upper-right corner of the Marker list, opens the Marker Text area at the bottom of the Marker list. The Marker Text area is covered later in the section "The Marker Text Area" later in this chapter.
▷ **Create:** Clicking the plus button creates a new marker at the beginning of the division nearest the current playhead position. Divisions and the Division setting in the Transport are covered in Chapter 5.

Marker Commands in the Navigate Menu

In addition to the commands available in the Marker list, there are also commands pertaining to the creation and use of markers in the global Navigate menu, as shown in Figure 4.24.

The Navigate menu marker commands are as follows:

▷ **Go To:** The Go To submenu, shown in Figure 4.25, contains the following marker commands:
  ▷ **Next Marker:** The Next Marker command lets you navigate your project via markers. Selecting Next Marker moves the playhead to the next marker. The Go To marker key commands are particularly good ones to learn. The key command for Next Marker is Option+. (period).
  ▷ **Previous Marker:** The Previous Marker command moves the playhead to the previous marker. The key command for this is Option+, (comma).
  ▷ **Marker Number:** The Marker Number command opens the Go to Marker dialog box. Simply type a marker number in the Go to Marker Number field, click OK, and the playhead will move to that marker. The key command for this is Option+/ (forward slash).

Figure 4.24 The Navigate menu.
© Apple Inc.

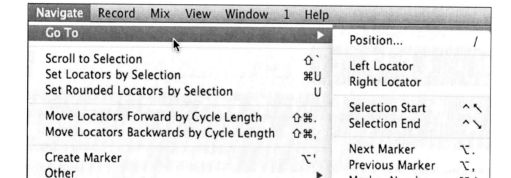

Figure 4.25 The Go To submenu.
© Apple Inc.

▷ **Create Marker:** The Create Marker command creates a new marker at the bar nearest to the current playhead position. The key command for this is Option+' (apostrophe).

▷ **Other:** The Other submenu, shown in Figure 4.26, contains a number of useful marker commands:

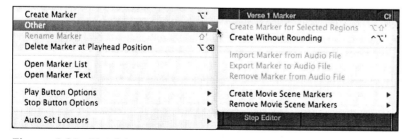

Figure 4.26 The Other submenu.
© Apple Inc.

▷ **Create Marker for Selected Regions:** This command creates new markers at the position of each selected region. The markers also span the length of each selected region and take on the name of their respective parent region. The key command for this is Option+Shift+' (apostrophe).

▷ **Create Without Rounding:** The Create Without Rounding command creates a new marker at the current playhead position. The key command for this is Control+Option+' (apostrophe).

▷ **Import Marker from Audio File:** When you record or bounce an audio file in Logic, the marker information that falls within the borders of that audio file is included in the bounced file. The Import Marker from Audio File command lets you import this information into your Logic project—a handy feature if you want to share markers across multiple projects. You'll learn more about bouncing audio in Chapter 11.

▷ **Export Marker to Audio File:** The Export Marker to Audio File command allows you to export marker information directly into an audio region.

▷ **Remove Marker from Audio File:** The Remove Marker from Audio File command removes the marker information from an audio file, which is helpful if you are sharing audio across projects and want to remove marker information from the audio on a per-project basis.

▷ **Create Movie Scene Markers:** The Create Movie Scene Markers submenu offers a variety of options for creating movie scene markers. It's covered in Chapter 14.

▷ **Remove Movie Scene Markers:** The Remove Movie Scene Markers submenu offers a variety of options for removing movie scene markers. It's also covered in Chapter 14.

▷ **Rename Marker:** The Rename Marker command lets you rename the selected marker. When you use this command, a text window opens above the marker in the marker track lane, where you can input a new name and then press Return. The key command for this is Shift+' (apostrophe).

▷ **Delete Marker at Playhead Position:** This command deletes the marker at the current playhead position. The key command for this is Option+Delete.

▷ **Open Marker List:** The Open Marker List command opens a Marker list window.

▷ **Open Marker Text:** The Open Marker Text command opens a Marker Text window. The Marker Text window is discussed in the section "The Marker Text Area" later in this chapter.

Creating, Copying, Resizing, Moving, and Deleting Markers

As discussed, markers are global events and can be created, copied, moved, resized, and deleted in the same way as any global event on a global track. The Marker list gives you the ability to accomplish the same things in a text-based editor using standard Edit menu commands, mouse input, and keyboard input. The marker commands in the Navigate menu offer a number of other ways to work with markers. In addition to the methods discussed earlier, Logic offers a few additional ways to work with markers in your project:

▷ You can use the Create Marker, Rename Marker, and Delete Marker commands by Control-clicking when mousing over the marker lane to open a shortcut menu.

▷ You can drag one or more regions from the main window into the marker track. A marker will be created with the same length and position as the dragged region(s).

▷ You can click the Marker field in the marker track header to open a menu that offers the Create Markers from Regions command.

▷ Markers that you create using regions may be rounded to the closest bar line. If you want your marker to be at the exact position of the regions, even if they are not on a bar line, you can choose Navigate > Other > Create Without Rounding. The key command for this is Control+Option+' (apostrophe).

▷ You can create a marker that corresponds to a cycle area if Cycle mode is on (see Chapter 5) and the marker track is shown by dragging the cycle area down into the marker track or down into the bottom third of the Bar ruler.

If you attempt to create a marker where one already exists within a quarter note in either direction, Logic will not create the new marker. If you want to assign a marker to an absolute time position regardless of the song's tempo (this is very useful for film scoring and audio post-production for video), create a marker or select a previously created marker and use the Lock SMPTE Position command from the Tracks areas's local Functions menu. The key command for this is Command+Page Down.

If you decide that you no longer need a marker, deleting it is very simple. You can simply select the marker in the marker track and press Delete. Alternatively, you can delete it from the Marker list. Lastly, you can move the playhead to the marker you would like to delete and choose Navigate > Delete Marker at Playhead Position.

Adding or Changing Marker Color

You can easily add or change the color of a marker on the marker track:

1. Choose View > Show Colors or press Option+C to open the Color palette.
2. Select one or more markers.
3. Click the color in the palette you wish to add to the marker(s). The color will be applied to the selected marker(s).

The Marker Text Area

The Marker Text area, shown in Figure 4.27, is found at the bottom of the Marker list. It is where you customize the look and feel of the marker you have created.

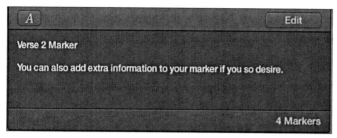

Figure 4.27 The Marker Text area contains all your options for customizing markers.
© Apple Inc.

As you can see in Figure 4.27, there are two buttons above the text-entry area. These buttons have the following functions:

▷ **A:** This button opens a Font window containing options for selecting a font, resizing the font, and choosing the font style and color.
▷ **Edit/Done:** Click the Edit button to edit the text for the selected marker. After you click the Edit button, it toggles to a Done button. When you are finished entering the marker text, click the Done button.

You can also double-click in the Marker Text area to enter text. If you have text in the Clipboard, you can paste it into a marker, or you can copy the text here in the Marker Text area into the Clipboard to paste it elsewhere.

Keep in mind that in the main window, the marker space in the marker track may be too small to display anything more than the name and color of your marker. You can resize an expanded marker track to display all the text if desired. You'll need to keep the Marker Text window open in your screenset to view customized marker text; the marker track itself uses only its default font.

> **TIP:** Clearly, the markers in the global track are not designed for large amounts of text. They are perfect for a quick title and maybe a note or a lyric or two, but not much more than that. If you want your markers to contain extensive notes and information for collaborators, future reference, and so on, you would be better off to keep the Marker Text window open permanently. A great way to do this is to select Navigate > Open Marker Text. This creates the Marker Text window as a floating window, meaning it will not get lost behind other windows and will always be visible. One thing to keep in mind, however, is that with the Notes feature, there is far less need to use markers for extensive notes. You can read about the Notes feature in Chapter 6.

Using Markers

This chapter has already discussed using markers as a visual cue to organize your project or to create extensive text boxes filled with notes, lyrics, and such that will automatically follow your song. You can also use markers to move the playhead and set a cycle area.

If you Option-click on a marker in the marker track, the playhead moves to the start of the marker. If you drag a marker to the Bar ruler, it will set the locators and turn on Cycle mode for the length of that marker.

Importing Markers from Other Projects

One very cool feature in Logic is the ability to import settings from one project directly into another. While templates do a great job of giving you a customized blank slate from which to start, sometimes you'll find that you'd really like to import things like aux routings, entire mixer configurations, and global tracks. In addition to being able to import markers from an audio file, you can import the marker track from one project into another in the All Files Browser. This is covered in detail in Chapter 12.

The Signature Track

The signature track shows any time and key signatures associated with the song. If you haven't set any, Logic will default to a time signature of 4/4 and a key of C. If you import a GarageBand song, your initial key and time signature settings from GarageBand will be carried over. If you are not familiar with music notation or otherwise do not generally use time and key signatures in your music, you most likely will not use the signature track very often. Figure 4.28 shows a signature track open in the Score editor.

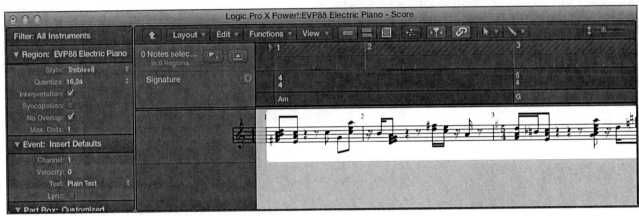

Figure 4.28 A signature track with a time and key signature change displayed in the Score editor.
© Apple Inc.

In general, information in the signature track is more for display purposes than anything else. Any key-signature changes after the initial key signature affect the display of MIDI notes in the Score editor but don't have any effect on playback. Similarly, even time-signature changes don't affect playback, only the display of measures in the Score editor and the Bar ruler and the emphasis of the metronome.

The signature track does interact with the transposition track. When you create signature events and transposition events, the transposition events will automatically reflect your signature events. The reverse is not true: Transposition events you create are not reflected on the signature track. Apple Loops and transposable MIDI regions will be transposed based on the setting in the transposition track. These settings determine whether there will be any transposition relative to the current key signature shown in the signature track. If no events are available in the transposition track, the global playback key for Apple Loops and MIDI regions is determined by the very first key signature.

Creating Time- and Key-Signature Global Events

You can create time and key signatures by creating global events in the signature track as described in the "Creating a Global Event" section earlier in this chapter. If you click with the Pencil tool in the top half of the signature track, you will see the dialog box shown in Figure 4.29, for adding a time-signature event. You can also access the Time Signature dialog box by clicking the plus button in the signature track header. If you click the Pencil tool in the bottom half of the signature track, you will be shown the dialog box in Figure 4.30 to add a key-signature event.

If you collapse the signature track height to the point that the time and key signatures are merged onto the same line, you won't be able to create signature events with the Pencil tool. Only when the signature track is expanded will both lines for time and key signatures be visible.

Time and key signatures can also be added in the Score editor. This is discussed in Chapter 8.

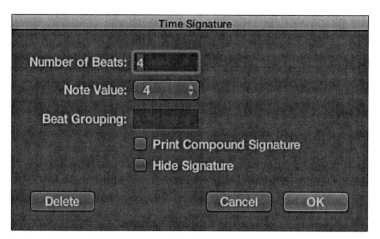

Figure 4.29 When you use the Pencil tool or the plus button to create a time-signature event, this dialog box lets you enter the time-signature information. When you click OK, the time signature will be added to the signature track.
© Apple Inc.

Figure 4.30 When you use the Pencil tool to create a key-signature event, this dialog box lets you enter the key-signature information. When you click OK, the key signature will be added to the signature track.
© Apple Inc.

Copying, Resizing, Moving, and Deleting Signatures

Events on the signature track can be selected, moved, deleted, and copied in the same way as other global events. If you want to edit an existing signature, double-click it, and the corresponding dialog box shown in Figures 4.29 and 4.30 will open. If you Shift-double-click anywhere in the signature track, you will open the Signature list window, shown in Figure 4.31. The Signature list is also available in the List Editors area of the main window. Time and key signatures are shown in a list-style editor, much like the Marker list. Any other score symbols, such as repeat signs, double bar lines, and so on, are also shown in this list. You can also open the Signature list in its own floating window by dragging the Signatures tab in the List Editors area.

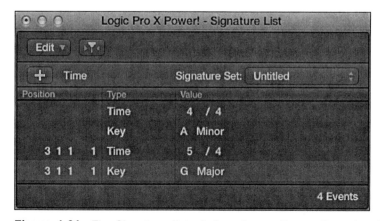

Figure 4.31 The Signature list window shows all your time signatures and key changes in a list format.
© Apple Inc.

The Edit menu in the Signature list is a typical Edit menu, full of familiar commands. You can create new signature events by clicking the plus button in the Signature list. You can select what kind of event is created when you click the plus button by clicking the text field next to the plus button (it reads "Time" in Figure 4.31). The Signature Set menu in the Signature list gives you access to signature sets, which are similar to marker sets in that you can create, rename, delete, and switch between signature sets. You can also access commands related to signature sets by clicking on the Signature field in the signature track header.

Cutting Measures in the Signature Track

If you want to cut measures in the signature track—for example, if you want to divide one 5/4 measure into a 3/4 measure and a 2/4 measure—you can select the Scissors tool from the Tool menu of the selected window and click at the desired location. If you make a cut in the middle of a bar in which there are no time-signature changes, you will create two shorter measures with the original time. You can also merge two measures into one longer measure by using the Glue tool in the signature track.

Importing Signature Tracks from Other Projects

Like marker tracks, signature tracks can be imported from one project into another in the All Files Browser. This is covered in Chapter 12.

The Transposition Track

The transposition track shows global transposition events that affect the transposition of Apple Loops and MIDI regions. In MIDI regions, the MIDI events themselves are changed, but nondestructively, meaning that the original data is not deleted. If you remove the transposition, the original data will return. Apple Loops will be pitch-shifted based on the transposition events on the transposition track. Regular audio regions and Apple Loops with no key information will not be transposed. Figure 4.32 shows the transposition track in the main window.

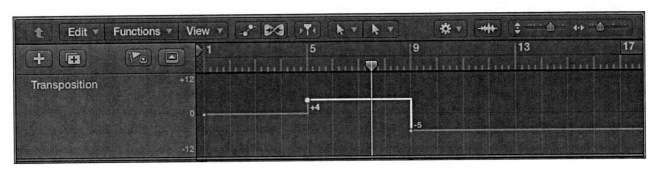

Figure 4.32 The transposition track in the main window.
© Apple Inc.

If you do not want a MIDI region to transpose, click the No Transpose checkbox in its Region Inspector. The current key signature in the signature track determines the zero position of the transposition track. If the key signature changes during a song, the zero position of the transposition track also changes.

Editing Events in the Transposition Track

Transposition events on the transposition track take the form of nodes (round dots). These transposition events are connected with vertical and horizontal lines. The transposition event determines the global transposition value until the song position reaches the next transposition event (node) during playback.

You can create, copy, move, and delete transposition events as described in the "Common Features of Global Tracks" section earlier in this chapter. Transposition events are limited to being moved horizontally (along the timeline) or vertically (by the transposition value), not diagonally. The help tag will appear below the cursor when you drag a transposition node or the transposition line, with the exact transposition value or bar position of the current transposition event displayed, depending on the direction of the drag.

Pressing Control+Option+Command while clicking in the transposition track opens a text window, as shown in Figure 4.33. You can directly enter a transposition value in the box and press Return. This creates a transposition event of the typed value at the clicked position. The scale range for the display of transposition events is +/−12 semitones.

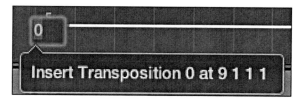

Figure 4.33 If you Control+Option+Command-click on the transposition track, a text window will appear. When you type a value and press Return, a transposition event will be created at that location.
© Apple Inc.

The Tempo Track

Tempo, meaning speed or pace, is one of the most important elements in music. Tempo management can be as simple as agreeing on the tempo of a song and asking all the musicians to play in time, or as complicated as keeping track of multiple tempo changes throughout a musical movement or even continuous tempo changes. With digital audio sequencers being the nerve center for both electronic and acoustic programmed and performed tracks, it becomes vital that the sequencer keeps everything synchronized and that it gives the user the tools to fully implement whatever tempo requirements they have. The tempo track gives you a visual track for displaying, setting, and editing tempo events for your song. Figure 4.34 shows the tempo track in the main window.

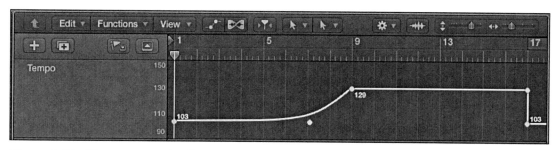

Figure 4.34 The tempo track offers both a visual display and a convenient editing track for tempo changes in your song.
© Apple Inc.

Like the transposition track, the tempo track is made up of nodes along a line. These nodes are tempo events, and the line is the current tempo.

Inserting, Deleting, Moving, and Copying Tempo Changes

You can insert tempo changes like any other global event: by clicking in the tempo track with the Pencil tool to create a tempo change at the current position. Pressing Control+Option+Command while clicking in the tempo track opens a text window, as shown in Figure 4.35. You can directly enter a tempo value in the box and press Return. This creates a tempo change of the typed value at the clicked position.

Figure 4.35 If you Control+Option+Command-click on the tempo track, a text window will appear. When you type a value and press Return, a tempo change will be created at that location.
© Apple Inc.

You can also record tempo changes in real time, as explained in Chapter 13; they will be reflected in the tempo track.

Moving, copying, and deleting tempo changes is handled exactly the way other global events are handled. If you want to create a continuous transition between two tempi, select the node at the tip of the right angle formed by the first and second nodes and drag it inside the angle. A curve or diagonal line will form. The Tempo > Resolution menu, available by clicking on the Tempo field in the tempo track header, defines the minimum division size for tempo changes along the project timeline. Shorter divisions mean more tempo changes; longer divisions mean fewer tempo changes. You can define this differently for each node. You can also define a quantization setting for tempo nodes in the Tempo > Quantization menu in the tempo track header.

The range for the display of tempo events adjusts automatically: Dragging a tempo event beyond the current upper and lower boundaries of the tempo track results in an automatic adjustment of the range. You can manually define the maximum and minimum of the tempo scale by grabbing the maximum and minimum values in the tempo track header and dragging them vertically or by double-clicking on them and typing the desired value into the text window that appears.

Tempo Sets

Tempo sets work similarly to the marker sets discussed earlier in this chapter. You can also access, create, delete, and rename tempo sets in the Tempo > Tempo Sets menu in the tempo track header and in the Tempo list, which is covered in Chapter 13.

Importing Tempo Tracks from Other Projects

Like marker and signature tracks, tempo tracks can be imported in the All Files Browser.

Accessing Logic Pro's Advanced Tempo Functions from the Tempo Track

Logic Pro X offers a number of more advanced tempo features, a few of which can be accessed directly from the tempo track. These are discussed in Chapter 13.

You can Shift-double-click in the tempo track to open the Tempo list, which is a list view of your project's tempo changes. The Tempo list opens in the List Editors area of the main window.

The tempo track has a close relationship with the beat mapping track, described in a the next section. After you use the Beat Mapping function in the beat mapping track, do not make any more changes in the tempo track!

The Beat Mapping Track

The beat mapping track is perhaps one of the most unusual and powerful global tracks in Logic. It does exactly what the name implies: It maps Logic's tempo to a beat. Suppose you recorded a fantastic audio or MIDI performance of an instrument, but the timing was a bit off the metronome click. Or maybe you recorded a live band without any metronome at all. The beat mapping track analyzes the performance and creates a musically meaningful tempo map so that the bars and measures will fall in useful places. The performance is in no way moved or altered; it is only Logic's tempo map and Bar ruler that are adjusted to fit the performance. Beat mapping allows you to then use a metronome that will follow the tempo of your recorded performance. You can quantize other regions to the performance thanks to the beat mapping track; loops will lock to the rest of the project, and so on. Figure 4.36 shows the beat mapping track.

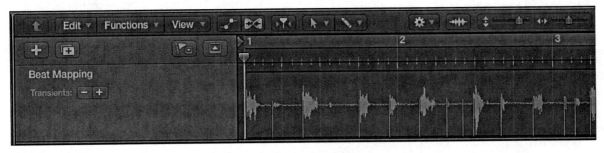

Figure 4.36 The beat mapping track shown in the main window.
© Apple Inc.

> **NOTE:** For new Logic users, a common mistake is to think that beat mapping is the same thing as Logic's audio tempo manipulation features, collectively called *Flex Time*. In fact, beat mapping and Flex Time are the exact opposite. Beat mapping conforms Logic's tempo map to the existing tempo of your performance. Flex Time conforms your performance to Logic's tempo map. You'll learn more about Flex Time in Chapter 6.

Beat-Mapping Process

The beat-mapping process basically consists of two steps:

1. You graphically link musical events (MIDI notes or audio transients, which correspond to the initial accent of rhythmically important notes) to the desired bar positions in the beat mapping track.
2. You tell the beat mapping track which measures to line up with which beat position lines. Logic will automatically insert tempo changes, causing the musical bars to correspond to the positions of the beat position lines.

As you can imagine, manually adding each and every beat position line for a song that is hundreds of bars long would require massive amounts of work! Luckily, Logic offers a number of automatic beat-mapping functions to make this process as fast and intuitive as possible.

BEAT MAPPING FROM MIDI REGIONS

Beat mapping from MIDI regions is simple:

1. Select a MIDI region for Logic to beat map. As soon as you select a MIDI region, beat position lines for each MIDI note, similar to those found in the Piano Roll editor, will appear in the beat mapping track, as shown in Figure 4.37.

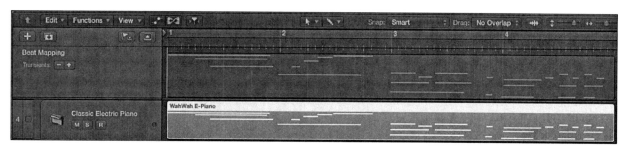

Figure 4.37 The beat mapping track uses beat position bars identical to those in the selected region.
© Apple Inc.

2. Tell Logic exactly which position on the Bar ruler you want to correspond to each note. At the first position where you want to assign to a MIDI note, click and hold the mouse button. A white vertical line will appear in that location, as shown in Figure 4.38.

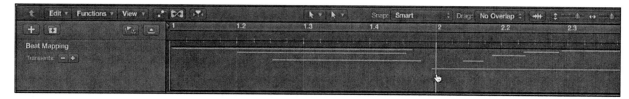

Figure 4.38 Click and hold the mouse at the first position on the Bar ruler where you want to assign a MIDI note.
© Apple Inc.

3. Drag the vertical line toward the beat position line to which you want to assign the selected bar position. Another line will extend from the selected bar position location to the beat position line you have selected, as shown in Figure 4.39. The help tag will reflect your action and the pointer's exact location.

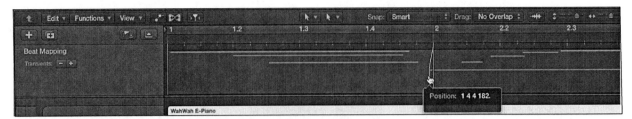

Figure 4.39 Drag the vertical line to the beat position line you want to assign to your selected bar position. A line will extend from the original vertical line to the beat position line.
© Apple Inc.

4. Release the mouse button. Logic inserts a tempo change to shift the Bar ruler so that the position you chose is linked to the note you chose, as shown in Figure 4.40.

Figure 4.40 When you release the mouse button, a tempo change is created to shift the Bar ruler to match the beat position. Notice that the entire Bar ruler has moved over. No musical events have been affected, however—only the tempo map.
© Apple Inc.

That's the whole procedure! Simply repeat these steps for any additional Bar ruler positions you want to map to MIDI notes. If you want connect a bar position line to a position in which there is no beat position line, drag the yellow vertical line while pressing the Control key.

If you are not happy with a mapped beat, you can erase any beat allocation by double-clicking on it, clicking on it with the Eraser tool from the selected window's Tool menu, or selecting it and pressing Delete. You can erase all your beat mapping by clicking in the Track list of the beat mapping track (except, obviously, the buttons or menus) and pressing Delete.

> **TIP:** This example illustrated beat mapping a MIDI region on the main window. Keep in mind that the global tracks all appear in the Piano Roll, Score, and Lane editors. You might find it more convenient to beat map MIDI regions in one of these MIDI editors, where you have a much better view of the actual MIDI notes.

BEAT MAPPING FROM AUDIO REGIONS

Beat mapping from audio regions follows the same procedure as beat mapping from MIDI regions: You click on a Bar ruler position to create the vertical line, drag it to the vertical beat position line to which you wish to allocate that bar position, then release the mouse, repeating this procedure until you have completed the beat map. There is one very significant difference between beat mapping a MIDI region and an audio region, however. Whereas the notes of the selected MIDI region(s) will automatically generate beat position lines in the beat mapping track, audio regions must be *analyzed* first. That means Logic must search the audio region for transients, or the initial attack of strong notes. (In the waveform, these transients look like spikes in the signal.) Generally, the more rhythmic the instrument (drums, percussion, and so on), the more distinct and accurate Logic's analysis of the transients will be.

To do this, follow these steps:

1. Select an audio region (or regions).
2. Click in the Beat Mapping field in the beat mapping track header.
3. Select Analyze Transients in the Beat Mapping menu.

Logic will analyze the region(s) for transients and generate corresponding beat position markers in the beat mapping track. You can also drag an audio region (or regions) directly onto the beat mapping track to begin the analyzing process.

The Transients buttons in the track header of the beat mapping track (see Figure 4.36) allow you to change the sensitivity to transients of the beat-mapping algorithm. You can click on these buttons to increase or decrease the sensitivity of the detection algorithm to transients. Generally, the most useful results will happen within a couple of clicks up or down from the default analysis. High Transients settings work well for regions with less distinct accents, but will detect too many peaks as transients in other files. If even a Transients setting somewhere in the middle of the range detects extraneous transients that are not musically useful, you can try a lower Transients setting. After you analyze transients, you can click through the entire Transients range to find a setting that works for your selected region.

BEATS FROM REGIONS

Selecting this option in the Beat Mapping menu creates a metronome region that you use to guide the beat mapping track as to where to generate beat position lines. For veteran Logic users, this is almost identical to using a guide region in the Reclock function. The advantage to using Beats from Regions is that the metronome region you create will often be easier for the beat mapping track to detect beats from, resulting in more accurate beat mapping. For example, you might want to beat map your song to an acoustic guitar part, but the accents may be too soft to accurately analyze. In that case, creating a metronome region with the same timing as the acoustic guitar track and using Beats from Regions will result in the beat map you want.

To use this option, follow these steps:

1. Create a MIDI track with an appropriately distinct rhythm, tapping out the exact beat to which you want Logic to beat map. If your metronome region isn't exactly right, you can use the MIDI editors to shift notes or keep trying until you get it right.
2. When you are satisfied with the metronome region, click the Beats from Region button. You will be presented with the Set Beats by Guide Region(s) dialog box shown in Figure 4.41.

Figure 4.41 Choose the note division of your metronome region in the Set Beats by Guide Region(s) dialog box.
© Apple Inc.

3. Select the note division you want for your metronome region and click OK. The Bar ruler of your song will be beat mapped to the metronome region, as shown in Figure 4.42.

BEAT MAPPING TO MARKERS

You can beat map to the markers in the marker track, if that track is visible. Simply select one or more markers, and the beginning of the marker(s) will appear as beat position lines in the beat mapping track. This works with standard markers and with scene markers.

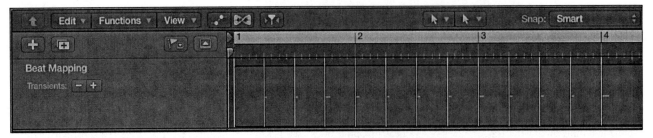

Figure 4.42 After the Beats from Regions process, your Bar ruler will be mapped to the beats of your metronome region.
© Apple Inc.

Beat Mapping to Scene Markers

This feature of the beat mapping track is especially useful for scoring to picture. If you are using a movie track with a loaded QuickTime movie and you have used the Create Marker Set from Scene Cuts or the Add Scene Cuts to Marker Set function on the movie track (see the section "The Movie Track" later in this chapter), the detected scene cuts will create markers, which can be used to generate beat position lines in the beat mapping track. If you want to define cut positions as the first downbeat of a bar, simply allocate the bar position to the beat position line as described in the "Beat Mapping from MIDI Regions" section earlier in this chapter.

Protecting MIDI Event Positions

When you beat map an audio region, all MIDI events also move to reflect the new tempo map. However, this is not always a desirable result. For example, suppose you have a MIDI drum pattern that needs to line up correctly with a piano audio region you are beat mapping. To maintain the absolute position of all your MIDI events relative to the Bar ruler, you can select the Protect MIDI option in the beat mapping track header menu.

The Movie Track

The movie track, unlike the other global tracks, does not contain any global events. Instead, it contains thumbnail images of single frames of a QuickTime movie loaded with your song. This track is especially for users who are doing sound for picture. Figure 4.43 shows the movie track displayed in the main window.

Figure 4.43 The movie track shows thumbnails of a QuickTime movie.
© Apple Inc.

You can open a QuickTime movie by choosing the Open Movie option in the Movie menu of the movie track header, by selecting File > Movie > Open Movie, or by clicking in the movie track with the Pencil tool of the window you are in to insert a movie into the movie track at the current mouse pointer position.

You can also use the Movies tab in the Media area of the browsers in the main window to search for and preview movie files on any connected volume. You can open a movie from the Movie tab of the Media Browser by dragging the movie file directly into the Tracks area at the desired position. All of these methods open the Open Movie dialog box, shown in Figure 4.44. In this dialog box, you can choose to open the movie, extract its audio, or both.

The number of thumbnails you see depends on the current zoom level. The frames are always left aligned, with the exception of the final movie frame, which is right aligned. In other words, the left border of every frame except the final frame represents the correct song position for that frame. The final frame is right aligned to ensure that regardless of your zoom level, at least the first and last frames of a movie will be visible. No video editing operations are possible on movie thumbnail tracks.

Figure 4.44 The Open Movie dialog box.
© Apple Inc.

Because the movie track doesn't contain any global events, you can't do any editing. You can, however, use the Create Marker Set from Scene Cuts or the Add Scene Cuts to Marker Set functions in the movie track header menu, both of which search for scene cuts in the movie. Both of these commands create movie scene markers, which are special markers locked to a specific SMPTE time and which can be deleted if the movie is removed from the song. Create Marker Set from Scene Cuts creates an entire new marker set from the detected scene cuts. Add Scene Cuts to Marker Set adds detected scene cuts to the current marker set. Finally, as described in the section "The Beat Mapping Track," you can use the detected cut scenes from a movie track to generate beat position lines in the beat mapping track.

Now that you are familiar with some of the global options that you can access from several areas of Logic Pro X, it's time to start exploring the individual program areas, starting with the Transport in the next chapter.

Transport Controls and Recording

T HE TRANSPORT CONTAINS PERHAPS THE MOST FUNDAMENTAL FUNCTIONS IN LOGIC—the controls for recording, playback, and project position. The Transport is modeled after the transport section of a tape machine, so named because pressing the buttons physically moves (transports) the magnetic tape. Of course, there's no tape in your computer, but because the metaphor of the tape machine transport for these controls is quite intuitive, it has found its way into Logic (and, in fact, almost all modern software-based audio applications). Figure 5.1 shows the default Logic Pro X Transport.

Figure 5.1 In the Transport, you can control recording, playback, and related functions. The Transport also offers project position display and other data viewing options.
© Apple Inc.

Notice that the Transport in Logic offers many more options than a standard tape machine. This is because Logic offers far more functionality than simply recording and playing back. Logic Pro X brings some changes to the Transport, including the moving of the Transport to the control bar at the top of the main window, and multiple preset display modes for the LCD. All of the functions accessible on the Transport are directly related to playback or recording, as you'll discover in the next sections.

The Transport Buttons

The most immediately noticeable features of the Transport are the Transport buttons themselves. These are the buttons that directly correspond to those buttons on a tape machine that "transport" the tape. When you record on a computer, no actual tape is physically moved, so Logic uses a playhead—a vertical line in the main window from the Bar ruler to the bottom of the Tracks area—to indicate the current playback location in the song. Figure 5.2 shows the default Transport buttons.

Figure 5.2 The default Transport buttons.
© Apple Inc.

If you have help tags enabled, holding the mouse pointer over these buttons will reveal the names of the buttons. Although the functions of these buttons are self-evident if you've previously used a tape recorder, here is specific information about how these buttons function in Logic, starting from left to right in the Transport shown in Figure 5.2.

▷ **Rewind:** Clicking this button moves the playhead backward. If you click and hold this button, the playhead moves backward more quickly. The key command for this is Shift+, (comma). If you *short-click* the button (that is, click the button very quickly), the playhead jumps back one bar. The key command for this is , (comma). If you click and hold the button and drag your mouse to the left or right, you can shuttle the playhead backward *or* forward. If you Command-click on the Rewind button, you will move the playhead to the previous marker. The key command for this is Option+, (comma).

TIP: It might be easier to remember these Rewind commands by thinking of them as using the less than (<) key rather than the comma, as this key resembles the left-facing arrows of a Rewind button on a tape, CD, or DVD player's transport controls.

▷ **Fast Forward:** This button moves the playhead forward. If you click and hold this button, the playhead moves forward more quickly. The key command for this is Shift+. (period). If you short-click the button, the playhead jumps forward one bar. The key command for this is . (period). If you click and hold the button and drag your mouse to the left or right, you can shuttle the playhead forward *or* backward. If you Command-click on the Fast Forward button, you will move the playhead to the next marker. The key command for this is Option+. (period).

TIP: It might be easier to remember these Fast Forward commands by thinking of them as using the greater than (>) key rather than the period, as this key resembles the right-facing arrows of a Fast Forward button on a tape, CD, or DVD player's transport controls.

▷ **Stop:** By default, clicking Stop halts playback or recording. If Logic is not playing or recording when you click Stop, the playhead will return to the first bar of the project or cycle. The key command for this is 0. The Stop button has a shortcut menu, which you can reveal by clicking and holding or right-clicking on the Stop button. The Stop shortcut menu is covered in the section "The Stop Button Shortcut Menu" later in this chapter. You can also toggle playback with the spacebar.

▷ **Play:** By default, clicking this button begins playback at the current playhead or from the left locator. If you are in Cycle mode, playback begins at the start of the cycle. The key command for this is the Enter key on the numeric keypad. You can also toggle playback with the spacebar. The Play button has a shortcut menu, which you can reveal by clicking and holding or right-clicking on the Play button. The Play shortcut menu is covered in the section "The Play Button Shortcut Menu" later in this chapter. You can also toggle playback with the spacebar.

▷ **Record:** When you click this button, it turns red, along with the LCD, and Logic begins recording. The key command for this is R. If you have designated a count-in or a pre-roll, covered later in this chapter, Logic will play the count-in or pre-roll before engaging record. Any data sent by connected MIDI controllers is recorded on the selected MIDI track in the main window. Any audio sent into one or more channels of your audio interface is recorded as audio on record-enabled audio tracks with one of those channels selected as an input. Logic creates a region in the Tracks area for each track you record. The region will span the actual length of the time you recorded, from the end of the pre-roll (if applicable) to the moment Stop was clicked. If you click and hold down the Record button or right-click on it, you can access the Recording Settings window, which is explained in the section "The Recording Settings Window" later in this chapter.

TIP: Remember, Logic is designed to allow users to really fly by using key commands everywhere possible. That means not only are there key commands for all the Transport buttons, but there are key commands relating to Transport functions that offer even more functionality. For example, simply clicking Play will start playback at the current playhead position or at the beginning of a cycle, but there are also key commands for Play from Beginning (to begin playback from the start of the song), Play from Previous Bar (to begin playback one bar behind the current playhead position), Play from Selection (to begin playback from the start of a selected region), and so on. You can use a key command for the Stop and Go to Left Locator command or for the Stop and Go to Last Play Position command, and there are key commands to increase or decrease the fast-forward and rewind speed. Assigning and using these and other Transport-related key commands will vastly speed up your workflow. Give them a try!

Mode Buttons

The mode buttons, located under the Transport buttons, toggle Logic's playback and/or record mode. Figure 5.3 shows the default mode buttons.

Figure 5.3 From left to right: the Cycle, Replace, Tuner, Solo, Count In, and Metronome mode buttons.
© Apple Inc.

If you have help tags enabled, holding the mouse pointer over these buttons will reveal their functions. From left to right, here is a description of the first three of these buttons:

▷ **Cycle:** This button toggles Cycle mode on or off. Basically, in Cycle mode, playback and recording repeat within a given range defined by the left and right locator positions. You can numerically input the boundaries of the cycle in the Locator display (see the "Locators" section later in this chapter), or you can graphically set the cycle boundaries in the main window, among other methods. The Cycle button has a shortcut menu, which you can reveal by clicking and holding or right-clicking on the Cycle button. Cycle mode and the Cycle button shortcut menu are explained in more detail in Chapter 6, "The Logic Pro Main Window."

▷ **Replace:** This button toggles Replace mode on and off. In Replace mode, any data you record onto a track will supersede previously recorded data on that track. In other words, if you record a region on a track, turn on Replace mode, and then record over that original region, the old data will be gone and the new data will be all that is left on that track. If Replace mode is off, recording over a region on a track leaves the original region intact. The old region is still present but will not play back until you move it to an empty track. If you are using Replace mode and Cycle mode simultaneously, an existing region is deleted only on the first pass. As you continue to cycle, each subsequent pass is retained.

▷ **Tuner:** If you have an audio track selected, you can click the Tuner button, and Logic Pro's Tuner will open, letting you tune your source instrument.

There are three more mode buttons: Solo, Count In, and Metronome. These buttons require the additional explanation provided in the following subsections.

The Solo Button

Next to the default mode buttons is the Solo button, which appears like an S in a box, as shown in Figure 5.4. When Solo mode is active, you may play back your song while only listening to the selected regions you wish to hear.

Figure 5.4 The Solo button. Click it once to turn Solo on. Click again to turn Solo off.
© Apple Inc.

In Logic Pro, you have two ways to solo tracks or regions in the Tracks area:

▷ You can select one or more regions and click the Transport Solo button, or use the key command Control+S.

▷ You can click the Solo button on a track to solo the entire track.

You can also press the key command S to toggle track solo on and off. If you press Shift while the Transport Solo button is engaged, you can solo the regions on multiple tracks by clicking in their track headers, which selects all regions on all selected tracks.

If Solo mode is active and all selected regions are being soloed, what if you want to select a region for editing or moving but you don't want it to be soloed? Logic facilitates this by offering a Solo Lock feature. If you Option-click the Solo button, you will activate Solo Lock, which locks the Solo function to those regions already selected. You can also access the Solo Lock function by clicking and holding or right-clicking the Solo button and selecting Solo Lock from the shortcut menu that opens. Figure 5.5 shows the Solo button shortcut menu.

Figure 5.5 The Solo button shortcut menu, which contains the Solo Lock function. You can access this menu by clicking and holding or Control-clicking on the Solo button.
© Apple Inc.

With Solo Lock active, you can manipulate any other region without changing the solo selection. If you want to return to selecting only the soloed regions, you can use the key command for Reselect Solo-Locked Objects, Option+Shift+S.

When Solo is activated, the Solo button, the LCD, and the soloed regions glow yellow. When Solo Lock is activated, the button icon changes to a small padlock image with an S in it, as you can see in Figure 5.5.

The Solo function is one that spans multiple windows and has some deeper functionality, which you will explore in Chapter 6, "The Logic Pro Main Window," and Chapter 11, "Mixing in Logic."

The Count In and Metronome Buttons

The Count In and Metronome buttons, shown in Figure 5.6, turn the count in and the metronome on and off, respectively. You can also press the key command K to toggle the metronome on and off, and Shift+K to toggle the Count In feature. The metronome emits a constant click at the current song tempo.

Figure 5.6 The Count In and Metronome buttons. These turn the pre-roll count in and the metronome on and off. Additionally, the Metronome button also gives you access to the Metronome Settings dialog box.
© Apple Inc.

If you hold the mouse button down over the Metronome button or right-click on it, Logic displays a menu (see Figure 5.7) that lets you open the Metronome Settings window.

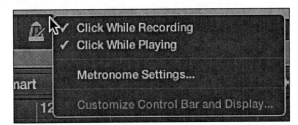

Figure 5.7 Clicking and holding the Metronome button opens this menu.
© Apple Inc.

Metronome Settings

The Metronome Settings window, shown in Figure 5.8, consolidates all the various settings that affect the metronome. The MIDI settings can also be accessed from the metronome object's Inspector in the Environment. The Recording Settings window, covered later in this chapter, offers added control of the metronome on count-in or record pre-roll.

You can access the Metronome Settings window by doing one of the following:

▷ Clicking and holding the Metronome button
▷ Right-clicking the Metronome button and selecting Metronome Settings from the menu that appears (refer to Figure 5.7)
▷ Selecting Record > Metronome Settings
▷ Selecting File > Project Settings > Metronome

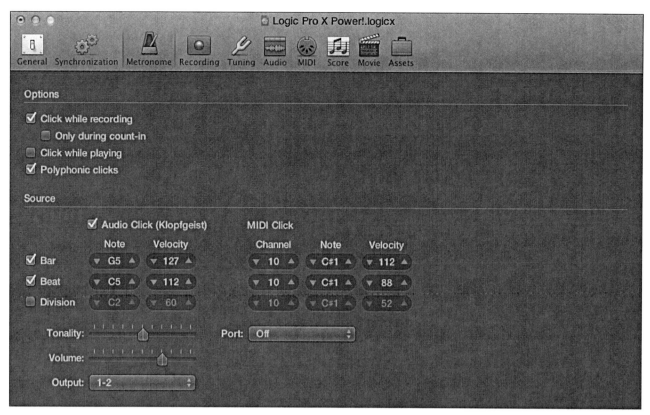

Figure 5.8 The Metronome Settings window.
© Apple Inc.

All the parameters in the lower right of the Metronome Settings window under the MIDI Click heading allow you to configure an external MIDI synthesizer to be your metronome. You can set the MIDI port of a hardware synth; determine whether you want different MIDI notes to be played on the bar, beat, or division; and set the channel, note, and velocity of each metronome note.

Most often, however, you will probably want to use Logic's internal click as a metronome. It's not only more convenient, but because an internal Logic software instrument generates the click, the timing is always sample-accurate, which means that the beat will always occur precisely when the master digital clock tells it to occur, not early or late. (MIDI timing has a *significantly* lower resolution than sample-accurate timing.) To use the internal software instrument for your metronome, select the Audio Click (Klopfgeist) checkbox at the top left of the Source area. Klopfgeist is the name of the metronome software instrument in Logic. *Klopfgeist* translates literally to "knocking ghost," so when you use it, you can honestly say there is a ghost in the machine!

As with the MIDI metronome object, you can have different notes for different time divisions, and you can set the note and velocity. You also have a Tonality control, which allows you to tone-shape the sound from Klopfgeist to a limited degree, and a Volume control, which sets the volume of the software instrument. Finally, you can select the output from which Klopfgeist will sound.

The Options area of the Metronome Settings window contains checkboxes that determine when you will hear the metronome. If you select the Click While Recording checkbox, you'll hear the click when you are recording. Selecting the Click While Playing checkbox ensures that you'll hear the click when you're playing. These two options can also be selected in the Metronome button menu, as shown in Figure 5.7. If you select the Only During Count-In checkbox, the click will play only during the count-in, or the measures before the recording begins.

You can set your click to be monophonic (one voice) or polyphonic (more than one voice) by selecting or deselecting the Polyphonic Clicks checkbox. If you are using Klopfgeist, this setting will have no effect.

The LCD

Between the Transport buttons and the mode buttons is the LCD, the most important source of meaningful information in the Transport. You can enter the tempo directly in the LCD, set Cycle regions, move the playhead, and perform myriad other functions within the LCD. Figure 5.9 shows the LCD.

Figure 5.9 The LCD in the Transport gives you vast amounts of feedback and control over your project.
© Apple Inc.

The LCD has five different display modes, accessible in the menu that opens when you click the left end of the LCD (where the musical note and metronome symbol are in Figure 5.9). Figure 5.10 shows the LCD menu.

Figure 5.10 The LCD menu.
© Apple Inc.

As you can see, in addition to the five different display modes, there are three other options in the LCD menu. The eight LCD menu options are as follows:

▷ **Beats & Project:** Selecting this option configures the LCD to display the current bar/beat/division/tick position, along with the project tempo, key signature, and time signature. Figure 5.11 shows this option.

Figure 5.11 The Beats & Project option of the LCD menu.
© Apple Inc.

▷ **Beats & Time:** Selecting this option configures the LCD to display the current bar/beat/division/tick position, along with the current SMPTE time position. SMPTE (short for Society of Motion Picture and Television Engineers) is the standard format used for synchronizing sound to pictures. Figure 5.12 shows this option.

Figure 5.12 The Beats & Time option of the LCD menu.
© Apple Inc.

▷ **Beats:** Selecting this options configures the LCD into a large display of the current bar/beat/division/tick position. Figure 5.13 shows this option.

Figure 5.13 The Beats option of the LCD menu.
© Apple Inc.

▷ **Time:** Selecting this option configures the LCD into a large display of the current SMPTE time position. Figure 5.14 shows this option.

Figure 5.14 The Time option of the LCD menu.
© Apple Inc.

▷ **Custom:** Selecting this option configures the LCD into a customizable display. For Logic users transitioning from older versions of Logic, this is the LCD view that offers the same functionality the Transport offered. Although all the other LCD views have their uses, the Custom view offers the most flexibility and power. The following sections deal with the options available in the Custom view. As you can see in Figure 5.15, the default Custom view offers many more features than any other LCD view.

Figure 5.15 The Custom option of the LCD menu.
© Apple Inc.

> **NOTE:** The only "problem" with the Custom view is that it can take up a lot of space in your control bar. Logic compensates for this by reducing the Transport buttons to just the essentials (Stop, Play, and Record), reducing the number of available mode buttons, and putting any displaced controls—including the list editors, Note Pad, Apple Loops, and Browser buttons—in a menu that can be accessed at the far-right end of the control bar. You'll explore this in Chapter 6.

▷ **Open Giant Beats Display:** Selecting this option opens a separate, resizable window with a very large display of the current bar/beat/division/tick position. Figure 5.16 shows this display.
▷ **Open Giant Time Display:** Selecting this option opens a separate, resizable window with a very large display of the current SMPTE time position. Figure 5.17 shows this display.

Figure 5.16 The Giant Beats Display option in the LCD menu opens a separate giant bar display window.
© Apple Inc.

Figure 5.17 The Giant Time Display option in the LCD menu opens a separate giant SMPTE time display window.
© Apple Inc.

▷ **Use SMPTE View Offset:** This option allows you to display a different SMPTE time for the start of your song rather than the true SMPTE start time that an external device is sending to Logic. For this to work, you need to check the Enable SMPTE View Offset option in the General tab of the Synchronization Settings window. To access this window, choose File > Project Settings > Synchronization. You can then choose Use SMPTE View Offset.

The Positions Display

To the right of the LCD menu is the Positions display, shown in Figure 5.18. This display shows you a numeric representation of where the playhead currently is in your song. The top number is shown in SMPTE time format (hours:minutes:seconds:frames/subframes), and the bottom number is in bar position format (bar/beat/division/tick). The bar position format is so named because it follows the musical notation structure of bars and beats. This is the same format shown in the main window on the Bar ruler, unless you choose to show SMPTE time format in the Bar ruler.

Figure 5.18 The Positions display, located to the right of the LCD menu.
© Apple Inc.

Positions Display Format Preferences

You have some options in how you display the two formats. If you select Logic Pro > Preferences > Display and click the General tab, you'll see two menus that enable you to customize the display of the two formats. You can adjust the display of SMPTE time via the Display Time As menu, shown in Figure 5.19.

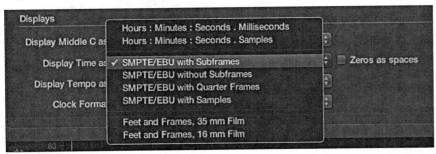

Figure 5.19 The Display Time As menu in the Display Preferences window's General tab alters the way the SMPTE format appears in the Positions display.
© Apple Inc.

These options change the way SMPTE appears in the Positions display. You also can opt for zeros to be displayed as spaces by selecting the Zeros as Spaces checkbox. Change the default SMPTE display only if you need a different format to synchronize your Logic song to a picture in that format.

If you open the Clock Format menu, Logic displays the various clock formats shown in Figure 5.20. These options allow the clock to take on a slightly different look. It's worth browsing through the different options here so you can find out which one you prefer working with.

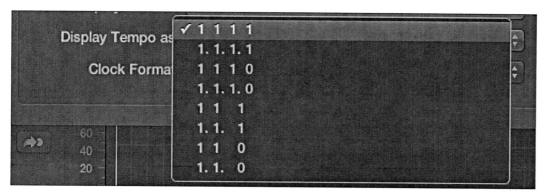

Figure 5.20 The Clock Format menu in the Display Preferences window's General tab. These parameters allow you to change the look of the clock in the Positions display.
© Apple Inc.

Using the Positions Display to Move the Playhead

In addition to offering a numeric visual reference to the location of the playhead, the Positions display has another function. If you double-click one of the numbers, the display becomes a text box, as shown in Figure 5.21. Enter the desired numeric location here; when you press Return, the value of both numeric displays will change, and the playhead will jump to the specified location.

Figure 5.21 If you double-click on one of the numeric displays, the Positions display allows you to enter a new playhead location.
© Apple Inc.

You can also click and drag vertically on any component of either the SMPTE display or the clock display to move the playhead in those units. In other words, if you click and drag on the division area in the clock display, you can move the playhead backward and forward in divisions.

Locators

Directly to the right of the Positions display is a display window for the locators. Figure 5.22 shows the Locators display. The locators define the start and end for Cycle mode. As with the Positions display, if you double-click the numeric values, you can enter the position of each locator. Also, as in the Positions display, clicking and dragging vertically on any component of either the start or end locator allows you to alter the position of that locator.

Figure 5.22 The locators are displayed numerically to the right of the Positions display.
© Apple Inc.

The Tempo/Project End Display

To the right of the Positions display is the Tempo/Project End display, shown in Figure 5.23. The Tempo portion, on top, displays the tempo of the current song in either beats per minute (BPM), frames per second, or quarter notes per minute.

Figure 5.23 The Tempo/Project End display.
© Apple Inc.

You can choose how tempo will be displayed in the Display Tempo As menu in the General tab of the Display Preferences window (see Figure 5.24), which you access by choosing Logic Pro > Preferences > Display.

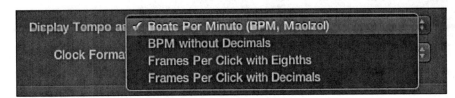

Figure 5.24 The Display Tempo As menu in the General tab of the Display Preferences window.
© Apple Inc.

The first two options are BPM (beats per minute) options, while the second two are SMPTE options. Logic offers a BPM range of 5–990 BPM, with four-decimal-place precision, which should be enough tempo range for most users! You can change the tempo of the project inside the LCD in two ways:

▷ By double-clicking the tempo value to bring up a text box and then entering the new value

▷ By clicking on the tempo number and dragging the mouse up or down. Logic allows for more complicated tempo programming and changes using either the Tempo track in the global tracks discussed in Chapter 4, "Global Elements of Logic," or the other tempo functions explored in Chapter 13, "Advanced Tempo Operations."

The Project End display below the Tempo display shows you the final bar in the song. When the playhead reaches this measure, Logic stops playback. You can double-click in this box to open a text box in which you can change the value, or click and drag on the Project End display. The maximum project length in Logic is around 12 hours; exactly how many bars this adds up to depends on the time signature and tempo of your project.

The Signature/Division Display

To the right of the Tempo/Project End display is the Signature/Division display, shown in Figure 5.25. The Signature value represents the time signature at the currently selected measure in the project. You can add as many time-signature changes as you like to your project using the signature track as described in Chapter 4, or the Score editor, which is discussed in Chapter 8, "Working with MIDI." You can also change the Signature display value to create a signature track event at the current playhead position. If you want to remove a time-signature change, simply change the time signature back to its original value.

Figure 5.25 The Signature/Division display.
© Apple Inc.

The Division value lets you determine what note value will get the third position in the bar/beat/division/tick display. This also will affect the resolution of the Bar ruler in the main window. You can assign key commands to raise and lower this division value quickly.

The MIDI Activity Display

To the right of the Time Signature/Division display is the MIDI Activity display, shown in Figure 5.26. This display gives you visual feedback as to whether Logic is sending or receiving MIDI events. If the MIDI events being sent are a chord, Logic's Auto Chord Recognition feature will show you the proper name for the chord rather than showing you all of the individual notes. If your MIDI devices get stuck notes (in other words, they can't stop playing) or are otherwise unresponsive, you can click in the MIDI monitor to send a MIDI Reset command to them. If that doesn't work, you can double-click to send a MIDI Panic Off message; basically, this sends individual note-off commands for every note on every channel.

Figure 5.26 The MIDI Activity display.
© Apple Inc.

The Load Meters

The load meters, shown in Figure 5.27, display the CPU and storage drive loads of your project in real time. Double-clicking on the load meters opens the System Performance window, which displays your project's loads in greater graphic detail in a floating window. Figure 5.28 shows the System Performance window.

Figure 5.27 The load meters display the CPU and storage drive loads of your project.
© Apple Inc.

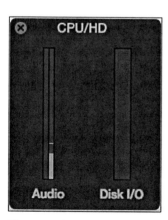

Figure 5.28 Double-clicking the load meters opens the System Performance window.
© Apple Inc.

Although Logic saves the position of every window and song setting with each project, it doesn't save the position of the System Performance window because it seems to view that window as global to Logic, not specific to a project. In other words, if you close a project with the System Performance window open, all your project's windows will close, but the System Performance window will remain open, ready for the next project you open. The upshot of this is if you like to display it, you'll need to relaunch it every time you open Logic.

The Master Level Slider

To the far right of the Transport area is the Master Level slider. This slider, shown in Figure 5.29, is directly linked to the master channel strip in the Mixer, controlling the level of your entire Logic project.

Figure 5.29 The Master Level slider in the Transport.
© Apple Inc.

Customizing the Transport

If you right-click in an empty area of the Transport, the Customize Control Bar and Display menu, shown in Figure 5.30, will open. The Customize Control Bar and Display option is also accessible from any of the other shortcut menus available in the Transport.

Figure 5.30 Right-clicking in the Transport opens the Customize Control Bar and Display menu.
© Apple Inc.

Selecting Customize Control Bar and Display causes Logic to open the Customize Control Bar and Display dialog box, shown in Figure 5.31. This dialog box allows you to customize the display of the Transport.

Three columns in the Customize Control Bar and Display dialog box are directly related to the three different areas of the Transport:

▷ **Transport:** The Transport column allows you to customize what Transport buttons will be displayed.
▷ **LCD:** The LCD column options affect the LCD display area. The menu at the top of the LCD column gives you another means to select your display mode. Only the Custom option gives you access to a customized LCD display.
▷ **Modes and Functions:** The Modes and Functions column gives you access to a variety of mode area buttons.

> **NOTE:** The column to the left, Views, is covered in Chapter 6.

Although there are many unique and valuable functions that you can add to the Transport via this dialog box, covering all of them here would be impossible. Rest assured, most of these functions are covered throughout this book, and anything not covered can be found in the manual. That said, there is one very important mode button, one very important display mode, and one function that adds both a button and a display option accessible in the Customize Transport dialog box, which are covered now.

The Sync Button

Selecting the Sync checkbox in the Modes and Functions column of the Customize Control Bar and Display dialog box adds a Sync button to the Transport, as shown in Figure 5.32. Clicking this button toggles on Sync mode, which allows you to slave the

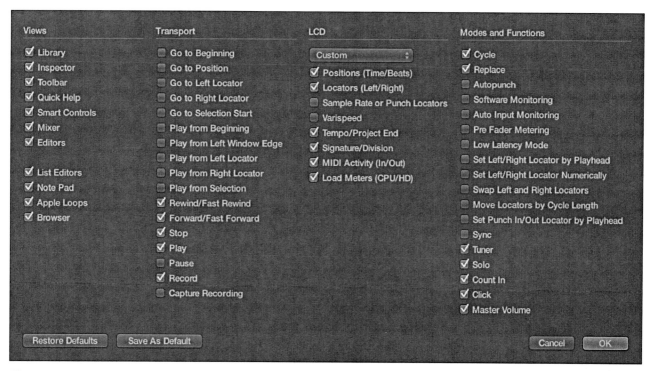

Figure 5.31 The Customize Control Bar and Display dialog box allows you to create highly customized Transports, giving you access to a wide range of Transport buttons, LCD fields, and mode buttons.
© Apple Inc.

sequencer in Logic Pro to external hardware, such as tape machines, external hard disk recorders, hardware sequencers, and any other device that is capable of sending compatible timecode, as well as internal software applications that receive MIDI Clock via Core MIDI. If Logic is the slave, that means Logic is taking its tempo cues from the external hardware. If you don't have any external hardware that generates its own tempo, or if all your external devices are slaves and Logic is the master, you will not need to use Sync mode in Logic.

Figure 5.32 The Sync button. Turn on Sync mode to slave Logic Pro to an external tempo.
© Apple Inc.

Holding down the Sync button opens a menu of synchronization options. These options allow you to select the type of sync that Logic will send, give you access to tempo editors, and so on.

The Sample Rate or Punch Locators

Selecting the Sample Rate or Punch Locators checkbox in the LCD column of the Customize Control Bar and Display dialog box adds the Sample Rate or Punch Locators display to the LCD display area, as shown in Figure 5.33.

Figure 5.33 The Sample Rate or Punch Locators display.
© Apple Inc.

If you do not have Autopunch mode engaged, then the Sample Rate or Punch Locators display shows the project sample rate. You can change this by clicking on the sample rate and selecting a new sample rate from the menu that opens. When you engage Autopunch mode, the display changes to show the punch locator positions, as in Figure 5.33.

The Varispeed Display and Button

Selecting the Varispeed option in the LCD column of the Customize Control Bar and Display dialog box adds the Varispeed display and Varispeed button to the Transport. Figure 5.34 shows a Transport customized to show the Varispeed display and the Varispeed button next to each other.

Figure 5.34 The Varispeed display and button.
© Apple Inc.

Varispeed is a very powerful feature, enabling you to speed up or slow down your entire project nondestructively and instantaneously. For example, you can use Varispeed to slow down the project a little bit to practice a part or speed it up to see how it feels at a faster tempo. Varispeed and the Varispeed display and button are covered in the "Using Varispeed" section later in this chapter.

Hiding the Transport

Although the Transport is a very handy tool with many important functions, there are times when you may want to hide it. Perhaps you have all your necessary Transport key commands assigned and memorized, or maybe you have a control surface that has all the necessary Transport controls configured. Possibly you're in the middle of a large project and you find you need the extra bit of screen real estate in the main window that hiding the Transport would offer.

Hiding the Transport is not difficult; simply select View > Hide Control Bar. Alternatively, place your cursor at the bottom of the Transport or control bar and your cursor will become a Resize cursor. If you find you want the Transport at some times in a project but not at other times, or if you want certain configurations of the Transport for different purposes—tracking as opposed to mixing, for example—save your different Transport configurations in screensets!

Opening the Transport Window

Having the Transport display directly in the main window is convenient as long as you are working in the main window. However, there may be times when you are working in a screenset that doesn't include the main window, or you may want to have multiple Transports open displaying different things, such as a conventional Transport, a Giant Beats display, and a Giant Time display. You can open separately movable, resizable, and configurable Transport windows by selecting Window > Open Transport Float from the global Window menu.

> **TIP:** If you select the Giant Time Display or the Giant Beats Display option, you will lose all the other functions of the Transport. But never fear: Logic allows you to open as many of each kind of window as you like, so you can also open multiple Transports if you want. For example, you could open one Transport and configure it as a Giant Beats display, and then open a second, fully featured Transport.

Resizing the Transport Window

To resize a Transport window, click and hold the mouse on the lower-right corner and drag the Transport to the desired size, as shown in Figure 5.35. Note that the Transport window can only be resized horizontally.

Figure 5.35 To resize the Transport window, simply drag the lower-right corner with your mouse.
© Apple Inc.

Recording

For the purposes of this book, the most basic definition of recording is capturing performances with Logic. Logic Pro offers a large number of recording modes and options. To record in Logic, you need to select a MIDI track or record-enable one or more audio and/or software instrument tracks. (This is explained further in the next chapter.) If you are recording a single audio track, the selected audio track will automatically record-enable when you click Record. To activate the normal Record mode, simply click the Record button. After the count-in, set in the Metronome Settings window, Logic begins capturing data. MIDI information and arrangement data (such as automation that you record live, tempo changes, and so on) are stored in the Logic project itself, while audio is saved onto your storage drive. All of this immediately shows up in the main window of Logic. Figure 5.36 shows a recording in progress.

Figure 5.36 Logic Pro X, recording away!
© Apple Inc.

The Record Button Shortcut Menu

In the good (but featureless) old days, there was only one record option: You clicked the Record button, and the tape started rolling, ready to print your performance. Now, however, we are in the software age, and Logic Pro offers myriad recording and monitoring options. If you hold down the Record button or right-click it, Logic displays the menu shown in Figure 5.37.

Figure 5.37 You access this menu by clicking and holding down the Record button in the Transport.
© Apple Inc.

Here is an explanation of the menu options:

▷ **Record:** This starts the normal Record mode. Selecting this is the same as simply clicking the Record button. The key command is R.

▷ **Record/Record Toggle:** Record Toggle switches between Record and Playback modes. The key command for this is the * (asterisk) on the numeric keypad. If your keyboard doesn't have a numeric keypad, you can reassign this command.

▷ **Record/Record Repeat:** This option starts recording at the previous drop or record-start point, and replaces the previous recording.

▷ **Allow Quick Punch-In:** If you are recording audio, normally you set up a track and start recording from the beginning of the song or you set recording to begin at predetermined drop locators or with the playhead. If you turn on Allow Quick Punch-In, you can be in Play mode and simply switch into Record mode immediately. It's a quick punch-in because you did not previously configure Logic to record at the specific location you chose. You should perform quick punch-ins sparingly because it's pretty taxing on your computer's resources to punch in completely cleanly without clicks or gaps. Instead, you should use the drop locators to set locator points in advance so that Logic can allocate and conserve the resources ahead of time. Also, keep in mind that even though you are quick punching in, you still need to have an audio track record-enabled to record your punch-in.

> **NOTE:** The term *punch-in* comes from the fact that when recording to tape, to start recording on the fly, engineers would "punch in" (not literally) the recording head while the playback head was operating. With digital recording, there are no tape heads to punch, but Logic still has to switch instantly from Playback to Record mode, which in itself is quite a task.

> **TIP:** To do true "tape-recorder style" punch-in/punch-out without stopping and starting the sequencer, use the tandem of Quick Punch-In and Record/Record Toggle.

▷ **Auto Input Monitoring:** This allows you to monitor in Logic what is coming in through the hardware inputs when Logic is stopped and in Record mode. When in Playback mode, Logic plays any prerecorded audio regions on the audio track that are record-enabled. You'll almost always leave this option on unless your audio hardware has a special monitoring mode or you want to free additional resources in the host computer. As discussed in Chapter 2, "A Quick Tour of Logic Pro," whenever you are monitoring audio through software, there is some latency.

▷ **Recording Settings:** This brings up the Recording Settings window. You can also access this window by selecting File > Project Settings > Recording. The Recording Settings window is explored further in the next section.

You can also access many of these options in the global Record menu, which is covered right after the Recording Settings window.

The Recording Settings Window

The Recording Settings window, shown in Figure 5.38, presents a number of options to customize how you record with Logic. Some of these parameters are explained elsewhere in the book, and some parameters appear in other windows as well.

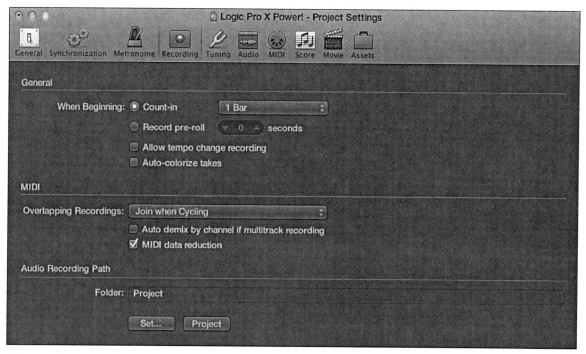

Figure 5.38 The Recording Settings window.
© Apple Inc.

Following are brief descriptions of some of these parameters:

▷ **Count-In/Record Pre-Roll:** Use these option buttons to determine how many bars or seconds Logic will rewind the playhead when you start recording.

▷ **Allow Tempo Change Recording:** Selecting this checkbox enables you to record tempo changes.

▷ **Auto-Colorize Takes:** When you select this checkbox, Logic auto-colorizes each take in a folder when take recording. Take recording is covered later in this chapter.

▷ **Overlapping Recordings:** The settings in this menu—Create Take Folders, Join with Selected Regions, Join when Cycling, Create Tracks when Cycling, and Create Tracks and Mute when Cycling—relate to MIDI recording only. The Create Take Folders setting is covered later in this chapter. The rest of these settings control how Logic records when in Cycle mode. These parameters are defined in the "Cycle Mode" section of Chapter 6.

▷ **Auto Demix by Channel If Multitrack Recording:** If this checkbox is selected and you are recording on more than one MIDI channel at a time to more than one record-enabled MIDI track at a time, Logic will automatically demix the MIDI channels to the record-enabled tracks. Each MIDI track will contain a single MIDI region with all of the information recorded from that channel.

▷ **MIDI Data Reduction:** If this checkbox is selected, Logic thins incoming MIDI information to allow for smoother playback of complex performances of MIDI-rich projects.

▷ **Folder:** By default, Logic will use your project folder as the audio record path. In other words, any audio you record in a project will be automatically stored in the project folder. If you want to set a different audio record path, click the Set button to open a dialog box; there, you choose the directory in which your audio files will be saved. To revert to the project folder, click Project. The Set command may be useful for some specific projects, but in general—and more specifically for your template—the Project option is likely the best option.

The Record Menu

The global Record menu, shown in Figure 5.39, offers quick access to a number of different commands related to recording.

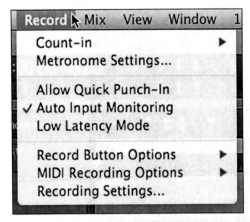

Figure 5.39 The global Record menu.
© Apple Inc.

Most of these functions are covered in depth throughout this chapter, but briefly, these commands are as follows:

▷ **Count-in:** This submenu let you define the length of the count-in when the Count-In button is enabled as well as the time signature of the count-in.

▷ **Metronome Settings:** This lets you access the Metronome Settings window, covered earlier in this chapter.

▷ **Allow Quick Punch-In:** This allows you to perform quick punch-ins, covered in the section "The Record Button Shortcut Menu" earlier in this chapter.

▷ **Auto Input Monitoring:** This enables Auto Input Monitoring, covered in the section "The Record Button Shortcut Menu" earlier in this chapter.

▷ **Low Latency Mode:** This enables Low Latency mode, covered in the section "Low Latency Mode" later in this chapter.

▷ **Record Button Options:** The Record Button Options submenu contains the three Record button mode options available in the Record button shortcut menu.

▷ **MIDI Recording Options:** This submenu offers the same five commands found in the Overlapping Regions menu in the Recording Settings window.

Recording Using Key Commands

Although Logic's menus offer a large selection of recording modes and parameters, if you want to record quickly, you should assign key commands to all of the modes, functions, and options that you access regularly. In addition, some powerful recording functions are available only via key commands. For example, Record Off for All, a key command that turns off the record status of all record-enabled tracks, is available only via key command. As you are starting to see, the more key commands you assign and use while recording, the faster and more efficiently you will be using Logic.

Method Tip: How to Record in Logic: Don't let all these recording options confuse you into thinking that basic recording of audio or MIDI in Logic is difficult. It's not. The basic procedure couldn't be easier:

▶ **To record audio:** Select one or more audio tracks in the main window. Record-enable the audio tracks and start recording (via Transport button, key command, control surface, and so on). To arm more than one audio track at a time, each track must be assigned to a different input.

▶ **To record MIDI:** Select a MIDI track and start recording.

▶ **To record MIDI and audio at the same time:** Record-enable one or more audio tracks and then record-enable an external MIDI or software instrument track. With all your audio tracks record-enabled and your MIDI track selected, start recording. The next chapter gets into more detail about record-enabling audio tracks.

Recording, Software Monitoring, and Latency

Whenever you record audio into a computer, you will have to deal with latency. Why? Physics, I'm afraid—and as Scotty told Captain Kirk so many times, "I cannot change the laws of physics!"

Here is the simplest explanation that I can give. When recording audio onto a tape machine, the instant the Record button is clicked, the record head engages the tape, and any material streaming through the record head is printed onto the tape. There is no delay inside that tape head; the audio material instantly streams through the record head.

When you record audio into a computer, first that audio is converted into a digital signal inside your audio interface. This process requires the interface to process a number of samples before it can stream the digital audio. (See the section "The Differences Between Analog and Digital Sound" in Chapter 1 for a full explanation of digital audio, samples, and so on.) Next, the digital audio streams into your computer. In this case, the digital audio then needs to go through the Mac OS X operating system to get into Logic Pro. Core Audio, the Mac OS X audio system, also needs to hang onto a few samples' worth of information before it can pass it onto Logic. After that, to most efficiently process the streaming audio, Logic buffers the audio and processes it in chunks. How much time this takes depends on the size of the buffer. All these samples of delay are called the *recording latency*, or the time lag between when a sound enters your audio interface and when it ends up in the Logic Tracks area. The exact amount of time will depend on the total number of samples divided by the sample rate at which you are recording.

Recording latency, however, is only half the story. If you want to hear what you are recording—in other words, to monitor your recording—you will have to deal with monitoring latency as well. There are basically two types of monitoring. The first, hardware monitoring, means that you monitor what you are recording before the signal passes through Logic. The second, software monitoring, means that you are monitoring your signal after it is recorded into Logic.

How Recording Latency Can Cause Recording Offset

Suppose you are using a 4/4 drum loop in which every beat is exactly on the bar. You start recording. The first beat hits at 1.1.1.0. You play the part you wish to record exactly on time. However, your recording latency is 441 samples. If Logic were to place the digital audio at the exact point in the track that it appeared in Logic, there would be a *recording offset*—a difference between when the source audio was recorded and when the digital audio was placed on the track—of 441 samples.

Thankfully, Logic is extremely smart regarding recording offset. All audio interfaces report how many samples they take to do their processing to Core Audio. Core Audio then adds to that number how many samples it uses to process the audio and passes that information to Logic. Logic takes that number from Core Audio, adds the setting of its own audio buffer to it, and then places that digital audio on the track at the correct spot. So using this earlier example, Logic would figure out that there was a recording latency of 441 samples and move the audio backward to 1.1.1.0 on the track, thus eliminating the recording offset. Your performance is exactly in time with the drum loop!

However, not all audio drivers report the correct recording offset to Core Audio. In this situation, Logic does the only thing it can: It places the audio where it *thinks* it should go based on the inaccurate numbers it has to work with. If you play back what you just recorded and it sounds off, as if your recording is consistently early or late, this may very well be the reason.

If you discover there is a recording offset, the first thing to do is to fire off an email to the manufacturer of your audio interface informing them of the problem. If you are an advanced user and have used the Logic Pro Audio File editor to count exactly how many samples of recording offset there are, be sure to send that information as well. Hopefully, this will help the manufacturer write a new Core Audio driver that reports the correct sample delay.

Fortunately, you're not simply left at the mercy of the manufacturer. In the Audio Preferences window's Devices tab (choose Logic Pro X > Preferences > Audio > Devices), Logic offers a Recording Delay slider (see Figure 5.40). You can use this to manually adjust Logic's recording offset correction amount. So if, for example, you have determined that all your audio is being placed 140 samples early, you can use this slider to delay the placement of the audio by 140 samples. If you determine that the

Figure 5.40 The Recording Delay parameter in the Audio Preferences window's Devices tab lets you manually adjust for recording offset.
© Apple Inc.

audio is being placed 140 samples late, you can use this slider to subtract 140 samples. If you're not sure, just experiment with different amounts until you get as close to zero as you can.

Hardware Monitoring Versus Software Monitoring

As mentioned, in addition to dealing with recording latency, you also have to deal with latency when listening to what you are recording. One of the ways you can deal with it is to virtually eliminate it by using hardware monitoring. That means directly listening to the source you are recording in hardware, before it hits the Logic Pro software.

This can be done in a couple of ways. Many audio interfaces offer direct monitoring or direct hardware monitoring. That means the interface sends the source audio signal both into your computer and out of one of its hardware outputs. The audio fed directly from the audio input to the audio output incurs virtually no delay at all. I say "virtually" because there may still be a small delay from digital-to-audio and audio-to-digital conversion, but this will be negligible. If your audio interface allows direct monitoring, there will be a physical switch or button on your interface or a software mixer included with your interface to set this up. Read the manual for your audio interface for more information. Suppose you do not have an interface capable of hardware monitoring. In this situation, you have two choices: Buy an external mixer and send one signal from the mixer to your audio interface and another to your speakers/headphones, or use software monitoring. There are other reasons to use software monitoring, too. If you want to monitor through Logic's effects—for example, if you want to record your guitar using Amp Designer and Pedalboard as your guitar amp and effects—you have no choice but to use software monitoring. Also, when you monitor through hardware, you can't be sure exactly what the signal sounded like as Logic recorded it—perhaps your mic preamp levels were too high, and so on. But when you monitor through software, you are monitoring exactly what is going through Logic, so you can stop the recording immediately to fix any problems. You can engage software monitoring via the Software Monitoring checkbox in the Devices tab of the Audio Preferences window (choose Logic Pro X > Preferences > Audio > Devices); via key command; or via the Software Monitoring button on the Transport (if you have customized your Transport to include it).

The major drawback to software monitoring is that all of the delay you incurred earlier with recording latency, you incur again. The signal goes back through Logic's buffer, through Mac OS X, into your audio interface's converters, and so on. That means if you use software monitoring, your monitoring latency is double your recording latency. Also, if you are using plug-ins that cause latency, software monitoring really messes with Logic's ability to compensate for recording offset. This shortcoming of software monitoring can be addressed using Low Latency mode (see the next section), but in general, the drawbacks of software monitoring are severe enough that I *highly* recommend that when you record, you use hardware monitoring whenever possible.

Low Latency Mode

As explained, Logic can correct for recording offset created by your audio interface, Core Audio, and Logic's own buffer. However, when you record through plug-ins that cause delay (plug-in delay is discussed in Chapter 11), that delay happens after Logic has internally compensated for recording offset. In other words, your recording will be placed on the track late and won't sync up with the rest of your audio.

When Low Latency mode is engaged, Logic creates an alternate signal path that completely ignores plug-ins that cause more than a user-defined amount of delay. In other words, if you manually set the delay limit for 5 milliseconds (ms), and if there are plug-ins that cause more than 5 ms of delay in the signal path, turning on Low Latency mode will create an alternate signal path without those plug-ins.

This guarantees that the total plug-in delay of the entire signal flow of the selected channel, including any aux channel strips and output channel strips, stays under this user-defined maximum value.

To set the maximum plug-in delay for Low Latency mode, open the General tab of the Audio Preferences window and adjust the Limit value in the Plug-In Latency area (see Figure 5.41). To engage Low Latency mode, click the Low Latency Mode button in a custom Transport or click the Low Latency Mode checkbox in the General tab of the Audio Preferences window, also shown in Figure 5.41.

With Low Latency mode engaged, your recording will be placed far closer to its "correct" position when recording through delay-causing effects. I say "closer" because depending on your latency threshold, there may still be some amount of offset, but not enough for you to notice.

You should be aware that engaging Low Latency mode will most likely change the sound of your track, perhaps drastically, because you are bypassing plug-ins that would otherwise affect your track's sound. For this reason, you should engage Low Latency mode only very briefly, to specifically record tracks through delay-causing plug-ins when you have software monitoring

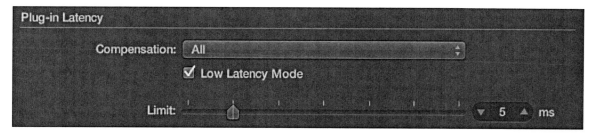

Figure 5.41 Set the maximum plug-in delay limit for Low Latency mode in the General tab of the Audio Preferences window.
© Apple Inc.

turned on. If you are not using software monitoring, you will not need Low Latency mode. Ditto if you are not recording through effects that cause delay.

Software Monitoring and I/O Buffer Size

As explained, when you record through software monitoring, your monitoring latency is double your recording latency. If this latency is too high, it will actively hinder your performers because there will be a noticeable and jarring delay between when an instrument is played or a lyric is sung and when that performance is heard. Clearly you want your total monitoring latency to be as low as possible to avoid inhibiting your performers.

The main parameter for reducing latency is the I/O Buffer Size menu, found in the Devices tab of the Audio Preferences window (choose Logic Pro X > Preferences > Audio > Devices) and shown in Figure 5.42. The lower the buffer size, the fewer samples are processed at a time, and the less latency you will experience.

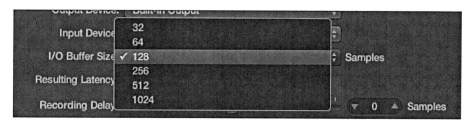

Figure 5.42 The I/O Buffer Size menu lets you choose the size of the audio buffer Logic uses when streaming digital audio into and out of Logic.
© Apple Inc.

The temptation is to use the smallest audio buffer available, which is 32 samples. Unfortunately, not all audio interfaces can operate efficiently when the number of samples is too small, which can result in crackles and pops in your recorded audio. Also, the smaller the buffer, the more CPU power is required to stream audio into and out of your Mac. Depending on how much processing power your computer has and how much processing power your Logic project is using, setting your I/O buffer size too low can result in crackles and pops in your recorded audio, or overload errors, which will stop recording.

To help you determine what monitoring mode and buffer size to use, Logic reports the total I/O latency in milliseconds beneath the I/O Buffer Size menu. The Resulting Latency area tells you the roundtrip latency as well as what your output latency is for the current buffer setting. While these things won't tell you exactly how to use your system, they can be beneficial aids in balancing what latency you incur at different buffer settings with your monitoring needs.

Recording Takes

In the world of multitrack recording, it's fairly common to record a particular section of a song repeatedly. Perhaps you are looking for a few different vocal recordings to work with on a chorus, or you would like to have a number of different piano solo options from which you can choose. You may even want to use multiple performances of the same section of the song to compile a single performance from the best bits of the different recordings. Recording multiple performances of the same material is known as recording *takes*. With Logic's take recording, recording and managing audio and MIDI takes has been simplified and streamlined to an amazing degree.

Recording Audio Takes

Recording audio takes in Logic Pro X requires no special configuration. The ability to easily record, edit, and manage takes is the default behavior in Logic. So why bother covering recording audio takes, then? Because how Logic handles audio takes, and the things you can do with your audio takes—such as Quick Swipe Comping (covered in Chapter 6)—are likely to become integral parts of your workflow.

To record audio takes, you need to engage Cycle mode and record more than one pass in the cycle or record over at least 50 percent of an existing audio region. Logic automatically creates a take folder for that region. An audio take folder is actually a single audio file containing all your passes over a particular region. In the Tracks area, a take folder resembles a typical audio region with three very important differences: There is a disclosure triangle in the upper-left corner of the take region, to the right of that is a field featuring either a letter or a number that gives you access to the Take Folder menu, and next to the Take Folder menu is the Quick Swipe Comping button. Figure 5.43 shows a take folder in the main window.

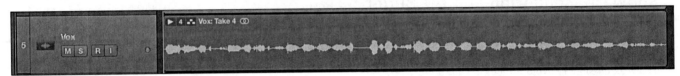

Figure 5.43 An audio take folder in the main window.
© Apple Inc.

Opening an Audio Take Folder

Clicking the disclosure triangle in the upper-left corner of a take folder opens the take folder. You can also open a take folder by double-clicking it or by pressing Option+F. Figure 5.44 shows an open take folder.

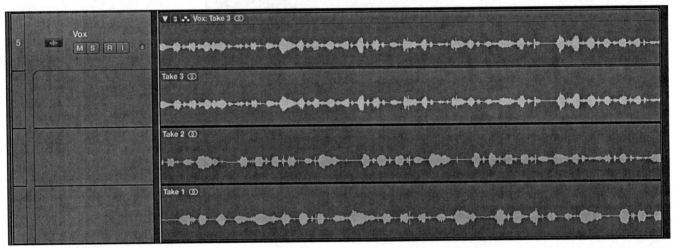

Figure 5.44 Clicking the disclosure triangle in the upper-left corner of a take folder opens the take folder.
© Apple Inc.

You can select different takes for playback in an open take folder by clicking on the desired take. Be aware that the top level still represents the current selections in the take folder (this will become more apparent when you start Quick Swipe Comping), and the individual takes are displayed below the take folder. The last take is displayed just below the take folder, the first at the bottom. You can also select the desired take from either an open or a closed take folder by choosing it from the Take Folder menu or from the menu that appears when you right-click on a take folder. You can reorder takes by dragging a take onto the take folder. That take will then be the first take in the take folder.

The Take Folder Menu

Clicking on the take number/letter field in the upper-left corner of a take folder opens the Take Folder menu, shown in Figure 5.45.

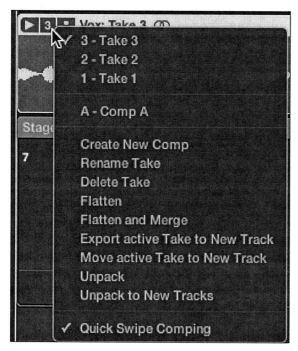

Figure 5.45 The Take Folder menu.
© Apple Inc.

The functions of the commands in the Take Folder menu are as follows:

▷ **Takes and Comps list:** At the top of the Take Folder menu is a list of the takes and composite takes, called *comps*, in the selected take folder. To switch takes or comps, simply select a different take or comp from the list.

▷ **Create New Comp:** This command saves a comp you have created in a take folder and adds it to the Takes and Comps list. If you have created a comp, and the comp is selected in the Takes and Comps list, this command becomes the Duplicate Comp command, which saves the current comp and creates a duplicate of the comp. Logic's comping features are covered in Chapter 6.

▷ **Rename Take/Comp:** This command opens the Rename Take or Rename Comp dialog box, depending on whether you have a take or a comp selected. You can rename the selected take or comp in this dialog box. The key command for this is Shift+T.

▷ **Delete Take/Comp:** This command deletes the selected take or comp. The key command for this is Option+Shift+Delete.

▷ **Delete All Other Comps:** This command is displayed only if you have more than one comp, and you have one comp selected. The Delete All Other Comps command deletes all but the selected comp.

▷ **Flatten:** The Flatten command replaces the take folder with regions created from the comp selections you have made from your takes. The new regions are independent of each other and therefore can be moved, copied, pasted, and edited individually. The key command for this is Option+Shift+U.

▷ **Flatten and Merge:** The Flatten and Merge command creates a single new audio region from the comps you have made in your take folder. The new region is the same length as its parent take folder. The key command for this is Option+U.

▷ **Export Active Take/Comp to New Track:** The Export Active Take/Comp to New Track command exports either the selected take or the current comp to a new audio track using the same channel strip as the parent track. Because the take/comp has been exported, the take/comp also remains in the take folder.

▷ **Move Active Take/Comp to New Track:** The Move Active Take/Comp to New Track command moves either the selected take or the current comp to a new audio track using the same channel strip as the parent track. Because the take/comp has been moved, the take/comp no longer exists in the take folder.

▷ **Unpack:** The Unpack command creates new tracks for each take and each comp in the selected take folder using the same channel strip as the parent track. Because all the takes and comps share the same channel strip, this command also mutes all but the currently active take or comp. The key command for this is Control+Command+U.

▷ **Unpack to New Tracks:** The Unpack to New Tracks command creates new tracks for each take and comp in the selected take folder using new, unmuted channel strips for each new track, but with the settings of the parent track's channel strip. The key command for this is Control+Shift+Command+U.

▷ **Quick Swipe Comping:** The Quick Swipe Comping option lets you toggle Quick Swipe Comping mode. When Quick Swipe Comping is engaged, you can create and edit comps. When Quick Swipe Comping is disengaged, you can't create or edit comps, but you can access Logic's full complement of editing features, including the new Flex Audio features. You can also toggle Quick Swipe Comping mode by clicking the Quick Swipe Comping button or by pressing Option+Q.

Audio Take Folder Behaviors

Because recording takes and creating take folders involves recording over existing regions, there are some behaviors that are unique to recording takes and take folders. The behaviors are designed to be helpful, but because there is a wide variety of ways you can employ take recording, there are some specific guidelines you need to be aware of to understand recording takes and using take folders.

If you are working on a project alone or you are having a musician perform the same section over a few times, then using cycle recording to record a section repeatedly has obvious benefits. As mentioned earlier, cycle recording an audio track automatically creates a take folder after the second pass. What happens when you stop cycle recording? That depends on where you stop in the cycle. If you stop recording in the first bar of a cycle, Logic will automatically discard the "extra" bit that went into the next cycle and truncate the recording to the end of the previous cycle. If you stop recording after the first bar of a new cycle, Logic will automatically add the small section of the new cycle with the previous cycle. This can be handy if you don't like what you played at the start of a cycle, and you decide you can fix it by playing into the next cycle.

If you have already created a take folder on a track and you record over the take folder, then the new region is automatically added to the existing take folder. If your new region starts before or ends after the take folder—in other words, with Cycle mode disengaged—then the take folder is lengthened to match the length of the new audio region. If the new region begins and ends inside the boundaries of the take folder, a new comp is made of the new recording and the previous take or comp.

If you record over multiple take folders in a single track lane, then the new audio file is split into separate takes at the beginning of each take folder, and the resulting takes are added to those take folders. If there were any gaps between the take folders previously, the take folders are lengthened to match their new takes.

You can also add existing audio regions to a take folder by simply dragging them to the take folder and dropping them at the desired position. If the new region is the same length as the take folder, then it is added as a take. If the new region is longer than the take folder, the take folder is lengthened to match the length of the new region. If the new region is shorter than the take folder, a new comp is created from the new region and the existing take or comp.

It is also possible to multitrack takes. For example, suppose you need the bass player and the guitarist to record a few new takes on the second verse of a song. You can record their takes at the same time, and the new regions will be added to take folders on their respective tracks, allowing you to create edits later.

Finally, you cannot record takes with Replace mode engaged, because Replace mode discards any previously recorded audio.

Can I Disengage Audio Take Recording?: Takes offer extremely powerful and intuitive organization and editing tools. I highly recommend that you learn to integrate Logic's takes features into your workflow.

Those who started using Logic before the takes feature may be set on older ways of working. There is no preference to turn off audio take recording. However, once you have recorded audio, you can use the Unpack to New Tracks command in the Take Folder menu or press Control+Shift+Command+U to unpack your take folder to new audio tracks. If you are determined to never get used to take folders, you can unpack every take folder via key command as soon as it's created, even on the fly.

There have been complaints that the takes feature can't be turned off, but frankly, these complaints are unfounded. This requires a grand total of one extra key press after recording. And again, I highly recommend everyone give take recording a chance—I believe it's worth the effort.

Recording MIDI Takes

Although there are similarities between audio take recording and MIDI take recording, there are some aspects of MIDI take recording that are different. First of all, because the default behavior in Logic is to add any new events to an existing MIDI region when recording, you actually have to tell Logic that you want to record MIDI takes. To do this, simply open the Recording Settings window by selecting File > Project Settings > Recording. In the Overlapping Recordings menu, select Create Take Folders (see Figure 5.46).

Figure 5.46 The Overlapping Recordings menu of the Recording Settings window. Selecting Create Take Folders allows you to record MIDI takes.
© Apple Inc.

With Create Take Folders selected, recording in Cycle mode or recording over a MIDI region creates a MIDI take folder. Figure 5.47 shows a MIDI take folder.

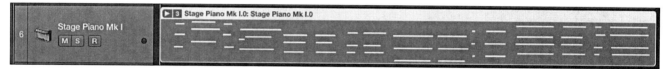

Figure 5.47 A MIDI take folder.
© Apple Inc.

Like audio take folders, MIDI take folders also have a disclosure triangle for opening the take folder and a number field for opening the Take Folder menu. Figure 5.48 shows the Take Folder menu.

Figure 5.48 The Take Folder menu for a MIDI take folder.
© Apple Inc.

As you can see, the functions in the Take Folder menu of a MIDI take folder are identical to some of the functions in the Take Folder menu of an audio take folder. You can reference the section "The Take Folder Menu" earlier in this chapter for an explanation of these commands. However, there is one big difference worth noting: The Flatten command replaces the take folder with the currently selected take.

MIDI Take Folder Behaviors

Recording over an existing MIDI take folder adds the new MIDI region to the MIDI take folder. If you record over multiple MIDI regions, the existing regions will be merged and will show as the first take, and the new region will show as the newest take. If you are recording to multiple MIDI tracks, the regions will be merged into take folders per track. Recording over existing MIDI take folders will merge the existing folders into first takes per track, and the new region will show as the newest take.

MIDI take folders do not offer the comping functionality of audio take folders. However, you can unpack MIDI takes, open individual takes in Logic's powerful MIDI editors and use the editors to create your own MIDI comps by selecting and deleting sections from different MIDI takes to create the perfect performance! Logic's MIDI editors are covered in detail in Chapter 8.

Auto-Colorizing Takes

By default, all takes assume the color of the parent region. You can also colorize individual takes using the Colors menu by selecting View > Show Colors (or pressing Option+C), selecting a color, and clicking on a take. Logic also will automatically make each take a different color when you select the Auto-Colorize Takes option in the General area of the Recording Settings window (refer to Figure 5.38). This option is particularly helpful for keeping track of which parts of a comp come from which take.

The Play Button Shortcut Menu

If you click and hold or right-click on the Play button, the Play button shortcut menu opens, giving you a variety of options for what happens when you click Play. Figure 5.49 shows the Play button shortcut menu.

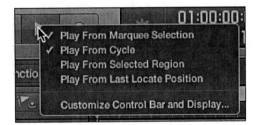

Figure 5.49 The Play button shortcut menu lets you control the behavior of the Play command.
© Apple Inc.

The Play button shortcut menu options are as follows:

▷ **Play from Marquee Selection:** Playback will start from the beginning of your Marquee selection and end at the end of your Marquee selection. Marquee selections and the Marquee tool are covered in Chapter 6.

▷ **Play from Cycle:** Playback will start from the beginning of the cycle area when Cycle mode is engaged and will continue to cycle until it is manually stopped.

▷ **Play from Selected Region:** Playback will begin at the beginning of the selected region.

▷ **Play from Last Locate Position:** Playback will begin at the last point Play was engaged. You can also accomplish this by double-clicking the Play button.

These are only some of the Play options available to you in Logic. There are more Play options available in the Key Commands window. You should check them out and maybe even assign a few you find useful to key commands.

The Stop Button Shortcut Menu

The Stop button has its own shortcut menu, which you can access by clicking and holding or right-clicking the Stop button. Figure 5.50 shows the Stop button shortcut menu.

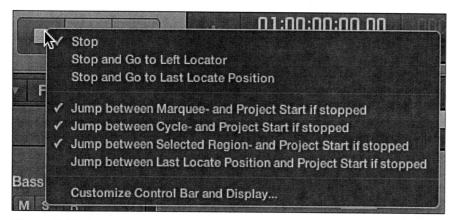

Figure 5.50 The Stop button shortcut menu gives you options to control the Stop command's actions.
© Apple Inc.

The Stop button shortcut menu has the following options:

▷ **Stop:** Playback stops at the current playhead position when you click Stop.

▷ **Stop and Go to Left Locator:** The playhead moves to the left locator when you click Stop.

▷ **Stop and Go to Last Locate Position:** The playhead returns to the last locate position when you click Stop. For example, if you were playing a Marquee selection and clicked Stop with this mode engaged, the playhead would return to the beginning of the Marquee selection.

▷ **Jump Between Marquee and Project Start If Stopped:** With this option selected, you can toggle the playhead position between the project start and the start of your Marquee selection by clicking Stop.

▷ **Jump Between Cycle and Project Start If Stopped:** With this option selected, you can toggle the playhead position between the project start and the start of your cycle area by clicking Stop.

▷ **Jump Between Selected Region and Project Start If Stopped:** With this option selected, you can toggle the playhead position between the project start and the start of your selected region by clicking Stop.

▷ **Jump Between Last Locate Position and Project Start If Stopped:** With this option selected, you can toggle the playhead position between the project start and the last locate position by clicking Stop.

Using Varispeed

As mentioned, Varispeed lets you alter the speed of your entire project instantly and nondestructively. You can slow down a project by up to half or speed it up to a maximum of double speed.

To use Varispeed, first customize your Transport to include the Varispeed controls. Then, to turn Varispeed on, simply click the Varispeed button. You can then adjust your project speed by clicking and dragging the Varispeed value in the Varispeed display or by double-clicking the Varispeed value and entering a value manually. If you click on the top half of the Varispeed display, where the Varispeed mode appears, a menu opens, giving you a few Varispeed options. Figure 5.51 shows the Varispeed Mode menu.

Figure 5.51 The Varispeed Mode menu.
© Apple Inc.

The Varispeed Mode menu options are as follows:

▷ **Speed Only:** If you select this option, changing the Varispeed value only affects the speed of playback, not the pitch. This mode is best for checking how the project sounds and feels at different tempos and for practicing or recording difficult sections of a project.

▷ **Varispeed (Speed and Pitch):** With this option enabled, Varispeed functions like an analog tape machine or a record player would, where speeding up or slowing down the playback also affects pitch. This mode is particularly good for working with vocal performances, enabling you to slow the speed and lower the pitch to help a singer in more difficult sections. The speed can be decreased up to half and increased up to double the original speed. Slowing the speed down by half lowers the pitch an octave, and speeding it up to double raises the pitch an octave. Obviously, the further you get from the actual pitch, the less desirable the results may be.

▷ **Varispeed and MIDI:** The Varispeed and MIDI mode transposes any MIDI tracks (other than drum tracks) to match the pitch change your audio incurs using Varispeed. If you are using MIDI tracks and trying to alter the speed and the pitch of the project, this is the mode to use.

You can alter the display of the Varispeed value in the Varispeed Value menu, which you open by clicking the percent symbol in the Varispeed value field. Figure 5.52 shows the Varispeed Value menu.

Figure 5.52 The Varispeed Value menu.
© Apple Inc.

The Varispeed Value menu options are as follows:

▷ **Percentage:** This displays the Varispeed value as a percentage of the original tempo.

▷ **Resulting Tempo:** This displays the Varispeed value as the tempo that will result from the current Varispeed setting. This view mode is good for trying out new tempos.

▷ **Detune (Semitones.Cents):** This displays the Varispeed value as the amount of detuning incurred in semitones and cents.

▷ **Tuning Reference (Hz):** This displays the Varispeed value as the actual tuning of the project compared to 440.0 Hz. This mode is great for working with instruments tuned to a different standard than A440 and having them fit in projects recorded with A440 as the standard tuning note.

Now that you have a good sense of how to use the Transport, how to use some of Logic's playback features, and how to record takes, it's time to dig into the next chapter on the main window, including more detail on comping.

The Logic Pro Main Window

T HE MAIN WINDOW IS THE CENTRAL WINDOW IN LOGIC. As mentioned in Chapter 2, "A Quick Tour of Logic Pro," the main window has seen some significant changes since Logic Pro 9. The main window, formerly called the Arrange window, gives you integrated access to all the editors, browsers, and lists, as well as to Smart Controls and the Drummer editor. Here you create and manipulate all the various tracks of your project, along with those tracks' adjustable parameters. You can record data onto tracks in the Tracks area, and that data is graphically represented in track lanes as one or more regions. These regions can then be arranged (that is, manipulated into new organizations that do not necessarily reflect the original data organization), processed, and automated. You can use the Tracks area in the main window to give you an overview of an entire project or a sample-accurate close-up of a few tracks. You can play your Logic project from beginning to end or set up project locators at any two points and just focus on your project from there. Figure 6.1 gives you a look at a Logic main window showing a selection of audio and MIDI tracks along with their regions, some automation, a global track (an expanded marker track), and the Project Audio Browser and Smart Controls for a track.

Figure 6.1 The main window in Logic Pro X. You will spend much of your time using this window, so getting comfortable with it will make your Logic experience a productive one.
© Apple Inc.

You will find that you spend much of your time using Logic in the main window, so you'll need a solid understanding of what functions and features are available to you here.

An Overview of the Main Window

While every different area in the main window is covered in depth throughout this book, this chapter will touch on each area briefly before going into detail on the more "traditional" functions in the main window. With the exception of the Track list and the Tracks area, all other areas in the main window can be hidden if desired. The main window interface consists of the following different areas:

▷ **Tracks area:** The Tracks area is the central area of the main window. Here you find the Track list, global tracks, local menus, and track lanes. This is the area where you perform the bulk of your editing and arranging tasks. Figure 6.2 shows the Tracks area.

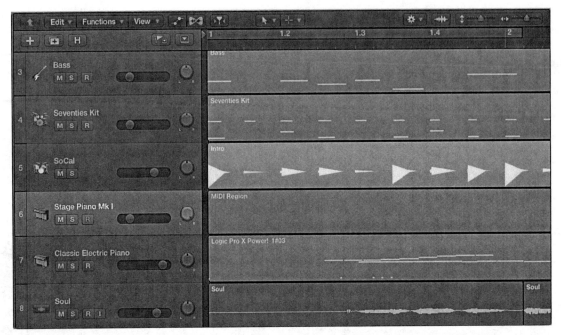

Figure 6.2 The Tracks area is where you will perform most editing and arranging tasks.
© Apple Inc.

▷ **Control bar:** The control bar is a customizable area that sits across the top of the main window. In it, you can place mouse shortcuts for different commands and windows, and for the Lists and Browsers areas. It also contains the Transport controls and the LCD display, and you can access a Toolbar area underneath the control bar. The control bar is covered in the section "The Control Bar" later in this chapter.

▷ **Inspector pane:** The Inspector pane is found on the left side of the main window. It consists, from top to bottom, of the Region Inspector, the Track Inspector, and the Inspector channel strips. You can toggle the Inspector pane by selecting View > Inspector, by clicking the Inspector icon in the control bar, or by pressing the key command I. Each component of the Inspector gives you some added control over individual tracks or regions in the Tracks area. The different components of the Inspector are covered in detail in the "Track Parameters" and "The Inspector Channel Strips" sections later in this chapter. Figure 6.3 shows the main window Inspector pane.

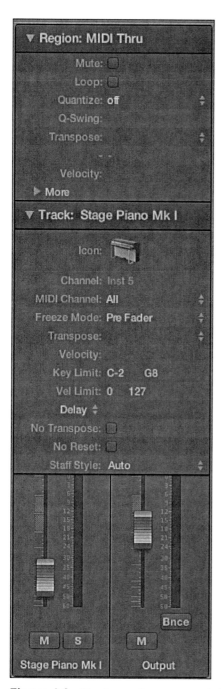

Figure 6.3 The Inspector pane contains the Region Inspector, the Track Inspector, and the Inspector channel strips.
© Apple Inc.

▷ **Library:** The Library is found on the left side of the main window when the Library button in the control bar is selected or when you select View > Library. The Library gives you access to patches and settings for the currently selected track, along with a Save command for patches, among other things. Patches are new to Logic Pro X, and are covered later in this chapter. Figure 6.4 shows the Library.

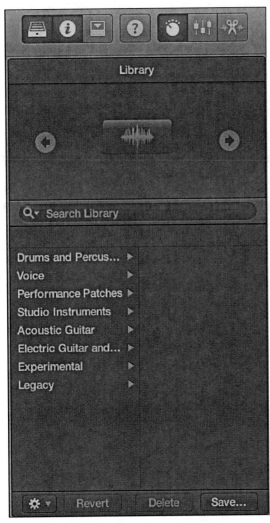

Figure 6.4 The Library in the main window gives you access to patches and settings for the current track.
© Apple Inc.

▷ **Note Pad area:** The Note Pad area is found on the right side of the main window. This area lets you create notes for individual tracks or for your project as a whole, making it very easy to create specific reminders for yourself or for your collaborators. Figure 6.5 shows the Note Pad area.

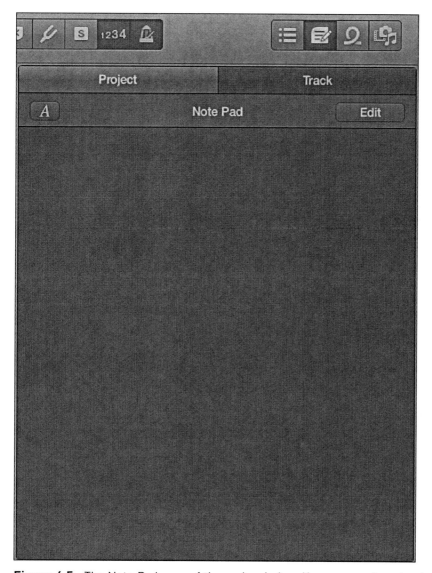

Figure 6.5 The Note Pad area of the main window. You can create notes for individual tracks or for the project as a whole in this area.
© Apple Inc.

▷ **Lists area:** The Lists area occupies the same space as the Note Pad area. This area is used for editing different types of data in a text-based interface. It contains tabs for the Event, Marker, Tempo, and Signature lists, as shown in Figure 6.6.

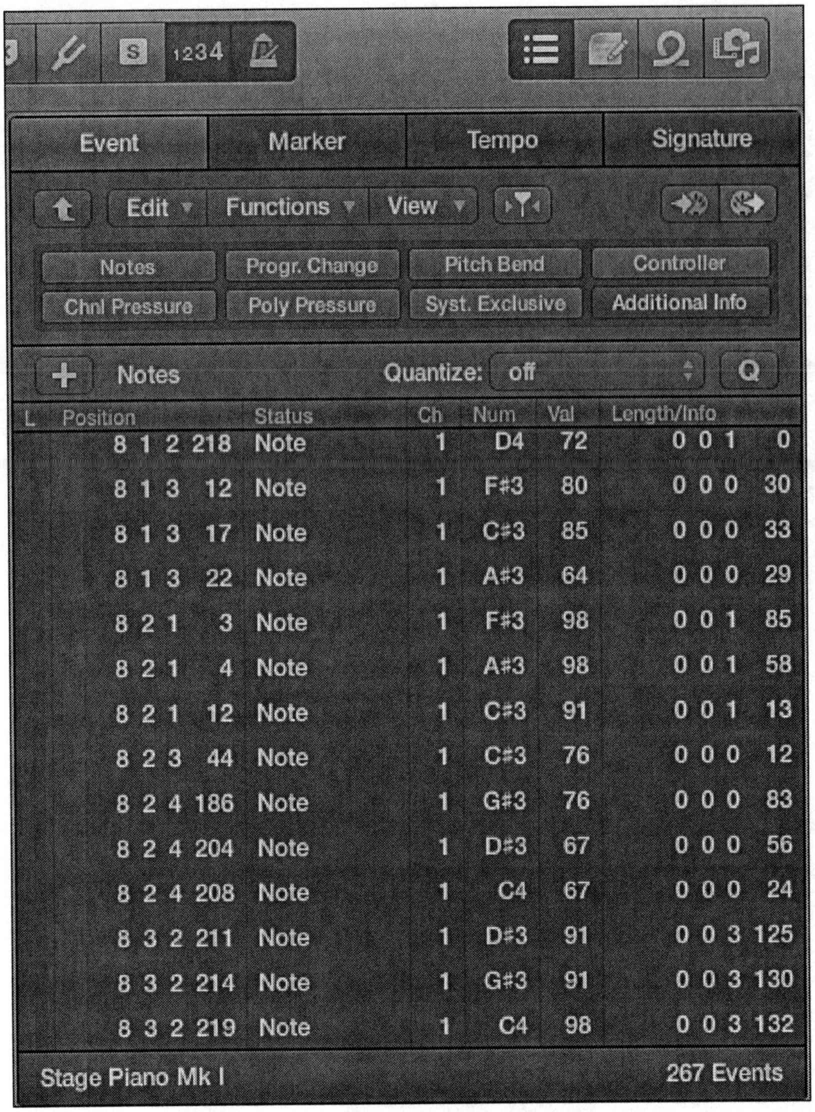

Figure 6.6 The Lists area of the main window. Here you can access the Event, Marker, Tempo, and Signature lists directly in the main window.

© Apple Inc.

▷ **Browsers area:** The Browsers area occupies the same space as the Note Pad and Lists areas. Selecting a component of any of these areas while a component of the other area is showing automatically hides the first. For example, if you are working in the Event list in the Lists area and you open the Media tab of the Browsers area, the Event list will be hidden and the Media Browser will be shown. The Browsers area is a repository of browsers for different media files, such as audio files, video files, and effect presets. The Browsers area contains tabs for the Project Audio Browser, the Media Browser, and the All Files Browser, as shown in Figure 6.7.

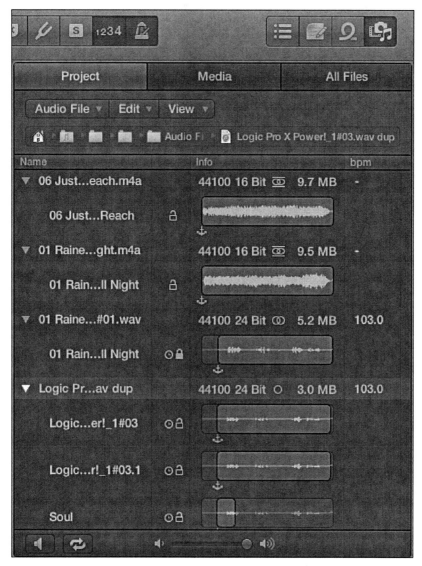

Figure 6.7 The Browsers area of the main window. Here you can access the Project Audio Browser, the Media Browser, and the All Files Browser.
© Apple Inc.

▷ **Loops Browser:** The Loops Browser gives you access to all your Apple Loops. Figure 6.8 shows the Loops Browser.

Figure 6.8 The Loops Browser gives you access to all your Apple Loops.
© Apple Inc.

▷ **Editor area:** At the bottom of the Tracks area is the Editor area. You can access the different editors via varying control bar buttons, key commands, and Tracks area selections, as you'll learn throughout this chapter. The Editor area can display the Mixer, Audio Track, and Audio File editors; the Piano Roll, Score, and Step editors; as well as Smart Controls and the Drummer editor. Figure 6.9 shows the Editor area.

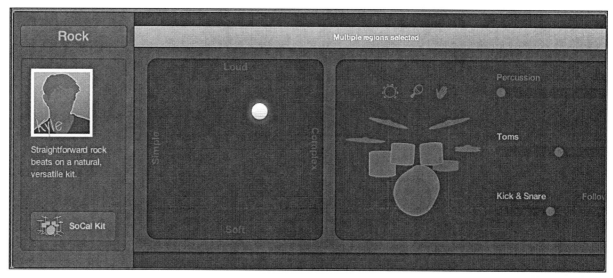

Figure 6.9 The Editor area of the main window gives you access to the Mixer, Audio Track, and Audio File editors; the Piano Roll, Score, and Step editors; plus Smart Controls and the Drummer editor. In this figure, the Drummer editor is open in the Editor area.
© Apple Inc.

Local Menus

Every editor and window in Logic has its own local menus. These menus conveniently contain commands users need within that window and editor. (Keep in mind that some commands that can be used in a particular window will not be in local menus because they are already located in the global application menus or because the given function is only available using key commands.)

The following sections describe the local menus in the Tracks area of Logic and the commands that they contain.

The Edit Menu

The Edit menu, shown in Figure 6.10, is the first local menu in the Logic Tracks area.

Figure 6.10 The Edit menu in the Tracks area.
© Apple Inc.

Following are descriptions of each command in the Edit menu. Whenever a key command is defined by default, it is listed at the end of the definition. Remember that even for menu commands that do not have default key commands assigned, you can assign one yourself in the Key Commands window.

▷ **Undo:** This command will undo the last action in Logic. Be careful about relying on Undo, however; not every action can be undone. If an action cannot be undone, this command will be grayed out and will change to Can't Undo. The key command is Command+Z.

▷ **Redo:** This command will redo the action previously undone. Be careful about relying on Redo, however; you cannot redo every option that you can undo. If an action cannot be redone, this command will be grayed out and will change to Can't Redo. The key command is Shift+Command+Z.

▷ **Undo History:** Logic offers multiple levels of undo. It maintains a list of actions that have been performed, and you can choose to undo any or all of them at any point. And this does mean at *any* point—your undo list is saved with your project, so the list of all your undoable actions is always available (unless you choose to delete it; see the description of the Delete Undo History command). You determine how many levels deep your Undo History will be via a preference in the Editing tab of the General Preferences window, which you can access by selecting Logic Pro X > Preferences >

General. You can choose any number up to 200 steps. When you select this command, you are presented with the Undo History window shown in Figure 6.11.

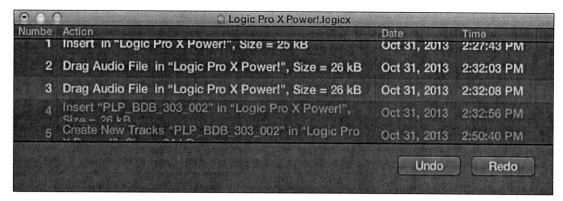

Numbe	Action	Date	Time
1	Insert in "Logic Pro X Power!", Size = 25 kB	Oct 31, 2013	2:27:43 PM
2	Drag Audio File in "Logic Pro X Power!", Size = 26 kB	Oct 31, 2013	2:32:03 PM
3	Drag Audio File in "Logic Pro X Power!", Size = 26 kB	Oct 31, 2013	2:32:08 PM
4	Insert "PLP_BDB_303_002" in "Logic Pro X Power!", Size = 26 kB	Oct 31, 2013	2:32:56 PM
5	Create New Tracks "PLP_BDB_303_002" in "Logic Pro	Oct 31, 2013	2:50:40 PM

Figure 6.11 The Undo History window. In this example, you can undo action 3 and below by clicking the Undo button. If you undo these actions, you can redo them by clicking the Redo button.
© Apple Inc.

The obvious features of the Undo History window are a list of your previous actions in Logic and two buttons in the bottom-left corner, labeled "Undo" and "Redo." When you click on an option inside the window, that option is highlighted. You can change what step you have highlighted by either clicking on another step or pressing the up or down arrow key. The actions above the selection appear as normal, and those below the selection are grayed out. This indicates that if you were to click the Undo button, all the options below the line would be undone. If you want to redo those actions, clicking the Redo button will redo them. Clicking Undo or Redo moves the highlighted area up or down a step accordingly. Keep in mind that you can redo what you have just undone only if you have not already gone ahead and performed other actions. If you have, these new actions start where your Undo action left off, and you'll no longer have Redo as an option. As with the single Undo and Redo commands, not every action will appear in your Undo History, as not every action can be undone or redone. The key command to open this window is Option+Command+Z.

▷ **Delete Undo History:** This option completely empties the Undo History window for the project. After this, no previous actions will be undoable. The Undo History window immediately starts recording all undoable actions after the Delete Undo History command, and those subsequent actions remain undoable until the next time you select Delete Undo History.

▷ **Cut:** The Cut command removes the contents of any selection you make in a text box or track lane of the Tracks area and places it onto the Clipboard. You can then use the Paste command to replace the cut selection. The key command for the Cut function is Command+X.

▷ **Copy:** The Copy command copies the contents of any selection you make in a text box or track lane of the Tracks area and places it onto the Clipboard. The original data is not removed. You can then use the Paste command to insert a copy of the data on the Clipboard. The key command for the Copy function is Command+C.

▷ **Paste:** Paste inserts the data from the Clipboard at the current playhead location. Keep in mind that if you have text on the Clipboard, you have to paste it into a text window, and if you have a region from a track lane on the Clipboard, you cannot paste that into a text box. The key command is Command+V.

▷ **Paste Replace:** Instead of inserting the regions from the Clipboard at a given location, Paste Replace overwrites any regions that occur at the same point in the timeline with regions from the Clipboard. The key command is Shift+Command+V.

▷ **Paste at Original Position:** If you select Paste at Original Position, the regions on the Clipboard will be pasted to the exact position they were cut or copied from instead of at the current project location.

▷ **Delete:** Delete erases any currently selected regions. The key command is, obviously, Delete.

▷ **Select:** The Select submenu is covered later in this chapter in "The Select Submenu" section.

▷ **Hide/Show Flex Pitch/Time:** This command toggles the Enable Flex buttons on audio track headers. The key command for this is Command+F.

▷ **Repeat:** This command repeats the selected region. Selecting it opens a small dialog box for you to specify the number of repetitions, whether you want real or alias copies, and whether you want to quantize the copies (in other words, force the repeats to end on an exact bar line, even if the original does not). The key command is Command+R.

▷ **Split:** This submenu includes two commands that divide regions in different ways:

    ▷ **Split Regions at Playhead:** This command splits any selected regions at the current playhead position. The key command is Command+T.

    ▷ **Split Regions at Locators:** This command creates a split in any selected regions at the current locator positions. The key command is Control+Command+T.

▷ **Join:** This submenu offers a couple of options for joining regions:

    ▷ **Regions:** This command joins the data from any selected regions into a single region. The new object will be given the same name and will be on the same track as the track of the first selected object. If you have MIDI regions on different tracks, the merged data will retain its position in time but not its MIDI channel. The MIDI channel on which the newly created MIDI region will transmit its data will be the MIDI channel that the instrument on the selected track is using. If you use this command on noncontiguous audio regions, Logic will create a new audio file containing the joined regions, just as if you had used the Glue tool (described in the section "The Tracks Area Tool Menu" later in this chapter). The key command is Command+J.

    ▷ **Regions Per Tracks:** This is the same as the preceding option, except that if the selected objects are on different tracks, rather than a single region being created on the track of the first region, Logic will create regions on each track on which there are selected regions. That means merged MIDI regions will transmit their data on their original MIDI channel because they are not changing MIDI instruments. New audio files will be created for merged audio regions on their respective tracks. The key command is J.

▷ **Move:** See the section "The Move Submenu" later in this chapter.

▷ **Trim:** See the section "The Trim Submenu" later in this chapter.

▷ **Convert:** The Convert submenu offers the following options for converting regions:

    ▷ **Loops to Regions:** This command turns any loops of the selected region into an actual copy of the selected region. The key command is Control+L.

    ▷ **MIDI Loops to Aliases:** This command turns any loops of the selected MIDI region into aliases of the selected MIDI region.

    ▷ **Audio Regions to New Regions:** This command makes independent audio regions in the Project Audio Browser for regions previously considered subregions of a "parent" audio region (meaning audio regions carved from what was one initial audio region). The key command is Option+Command+R.

    ▷ **Audio Regions to New Audio Files:** This command saves all the audio regions you select as separate audio files on your hard disk. This command is incredibly useful if you want to export specific regions to other audio applications. You may also need to use this command if you want to make an Apple Loop of a specific region that is a part of a longer audio file. The key command is Option+Command+F.

▷ **Time Stretch:** The Time Stretch submenu includes the following options:

    ▷ **Time Stretch Region to Locators:** When you select an audio region and choose this command, Logic will time stretch or compress your audio to the length of the locators. Note that no audio region can be stretched more than 400% or compressed to less than 25% of its original length. The key command is Option+Command+L.

    ▷ **Time Stretch Region to Nearest Bar:** This command results in Logic using time stretching or compressing to adjust the length of a selected audio region to the nearest bar. Note that no audio region can be stretched more than 400% or compressed to less than 25% of its original length. The key command is Option+Command+B.

    ▷ **Time Stretching Algorithm:** When Logic time stretches or compresses an audio region, it uses unique and high-quality algorithms created for its Time Machine in the Audio File editor, which is explored in the next chapter. The Time Stretching Algorithm submenu is explained in the section "The Time Stretching Algorithm Submenu" later in this chapter.

▷ **Copy MIDI Events:** This command opens the dialog box shown in Figure 6.12. From this dialog box, you can select exactly where your data to copy is, if you want to copy it to the Clipboard or to another location in the Tracks area, what type of copy mode (merge, replace, and so on) you wish for your MIDI data, and how many copies you want to make. This command is a very powerful way to move large amounts of MIDI data around your project. If you work with MIDI a lot, assigning this command to a key command is a must.

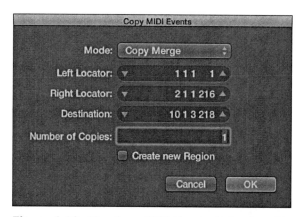

Figure 6.12 The Copy MIDI Events dialog box. Use this to copy or move large amounts of MIDI data around your project.
© Apple Inc.

▷ **Delete MIDI Events:** This submenu contains the following options for deleting MIDI events in a track:
  ▷ **Duplicates:** This command erases all duplicate MIDI events (meaning, similar events at the same time position in your project) in selected regions. The key command for this is D.
  ▷ **Inside Locators:** This command erases all MIDI events in selected regions inside the left and right locators.
  ▷ **Outside Locators:** This command erases all MIDI events outside of the left and right locators in selected regions.
  ▷ **Outside Region Borders:** Use this command to erase all of the MIDI events outside the borders of a selected region.
  ▷ **Unselected Within Selection:** This command erases all the unselected MIDI information inside an area you have selected.

▷ **Separate MIDI Events:** The Separate MIDI Events submenu contains the following commands:
  ▷ **By Event Channel:** If you have a MIDI region selected, this command creates a new track for each MIDI channel used by events in the parent region. Each new track will contain the events from the original region that were on that MIDI channel. This command is useful for recording many different MIDI parts on different MIDI channels at once and then moving each part to its own track afterward. Remember that if you select a track header, all the regions on that track are selected, allowing you to separate an entire track with one command.
  ▷ **By Note Pitch:** If you have a MIDI region selected, this command creates a new track for every MIDI note in the parent region. This command is especially useful for recording a MIDI drum performance, in which each note is a separate drum, and then placing each drum note on its own separate track afterward.
  ▷ **By Articulation ID:** Articulations are a means of getting different timbres out of an instrument. For example, a violin can be played using many different bowing techniques. In this example, articulations allow you to access different bowing techniques from one software instrument. This is much more elegant than having to have one software instrument for long bowing and another one for tremolo. Different articulations have different IDs—MIDI commands that tell the software instrument to use a particular articulation. The By Articulation ID command lets you separate all MIDI data to tracks based on articulation ID.

▷ **Cut/Insert Time:** This submenu includes these commands that add or remove time from the project:
  ▷ **Cut Section Between Locators:** This command removes an amount of time determined by the project locators. Regions after the right locator move to the left locator, and all information between the locators is removed from the project to the Clipboard. The key command for this is Control+Command+X.
  ▷ **Insert Section at Playhead:** This command inserts all the information cut by the Cut Section Between Locators command back into the project at the current playhead position. All regions to the right of the inserted objects are moved to the right in the Tracks area so they begin at the end of the inserted regions. The key command for this is Control+Command+V.
  ▷ **Insert Silence Between Locators:** This command creates a gap of empty space between the two locators. Any regions between the locators move to the right of the right locator. The key command for this is Control+Command+Z.
  ▷ **Repeat Section Between Locators:** This command takes all selected regions inside the locators and any sections of any selected regions inside the locators and copies them to the right of the right locator. The key command for this is Control+Command+R.

▷ **Tempo:** The Tempo submenu contains a number of commands for performing tempo-related operations. It is covered in detail in Chapter 13, "Advanced Tempo Operations."

▷ **Open In:** If you have configured Logic to use an external sample editor, this command lets you open audio regions in that editor from Logic. Configuring Logic to use an external sample editor is covered in the next chapter.

▷ **Snap Edits to Zero Crossings:** This command sets a preference to search selected audio regions for points at which the amplitude of the audio wave crosses the zero line. Any subsequent attempts to edit the length of an audio region will be restricted to zero crossings. This is useful in matching up audio edits.

The Select Submenu

The Select submenu, shown in Figure 6.13, contains numerous commands for selecting regions and events in the Tracks area.

Figure 6.13 The Select submenu.
© Apple Inc.

The Select submenu commands are as follows:

▷ **All:** This command selects all regions on every track lane. The key command is Command+A.

▷ **All Following:** If you select a region in the Tracks area, this command selects all other regions on every track lane beyond the selected region. This command does not select any region whose starting point comes before your originally selected region, even if the end of the region extends to (or past) the selected region. The key command is Shift+F.

▷ **All Following of Same Track:** If you select a region in the Tracks area, this command selects all other regions beyond the selected region on the same track lane. This command does not select any region whose starting point comes before your originally selected region, even if the end of those regions extends to (or past) the selected region. The key command is Option+Shift+F.

▷ **All Inside Locators:** This command selects all regions that are between the left and right locators. The key command is Shift+L.

▷ **Muted Regions:** You can use this command to select all the regions that you have previously muted in the Tracks area. The key command is Shift+M.

▷ **Overlapped Regions:** This command selects every region that is overlapping (or overlapped by) another region.

▷ **Equal Colored Regions:** If you are using color to organize your tracks in the Tracks area, this command will select all the regions that have the same color. The key command is Shift+C.

▷ **Empty Regions:** If you have regions that do not contain any data, this command selects them. Because empty regions typically don't serve much purpose, this command is often used in tandem with Delete (or the Delete key) to remove unnecessary regions from the main window.

▷ **Similar Regions:** If you select a region, this command selects regions that process the same type of MIDI data as the one you have selected.

▷ **Equal Regions:** If you select a region, this command selects regions identical to the region you have selected. For example, if you have copied and pasted a region a number of times, this will select each of the copied regions.

▷ **Next Region:** This command selects the region to the right of the selected region on the selected track. The key command for this is right arrow.

▷ **Previous Region:** This command selects the region to the left of the selected region on the selected track. The key command for this is left arrow.

▷ **Deselect All:** Any selected regions will be deselected with this command. The key command is Option+Shift+D.

▷ **Deselect Global Tracks:** This command will deselect any global tracks and/or global events on global tracks that have been selected.

▷ **Deselect Outside Locators:** When you select this command, any regions you've previously selected outside the left and right locators will be deselected. Regions between the two locators will be unaffected.

▷ **Invert Selection:** This powerful command toggles the selection status of regions in the Tracks area. In other words, if you currently have four regions selected, this command deselects those four regions and selects every other region in the Tracks area. The key command is Shift+I.

The Move Submenu

The Move submenu offers a number of commands for moving regions in the Tracks area. Figure 6.14 shows the Move submenu.

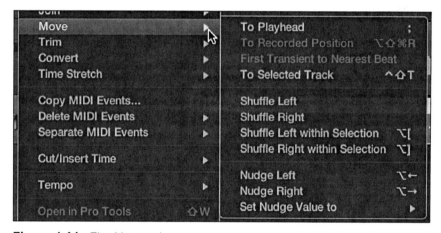

Figure 6.14 The Move submenu.
© Apple Inc.

The Move submenu commands are as follows:

▷ **To Playhead:** This command moves the selected regions to the current playhead position. The region(s) farthest to the left will be placed at the location of the playhead, and any regions beginning after the left-most regions will be placed at their same relative positions. The key command for this is ; (semicolon).

▷ **To Recorded Position:** This command returns a region that has been moved to the position in the Bar ruler where it was originally recorded. The key command for this is Option+Shift+Command+R.

▷ **First Transient to Nearest Beat:** This command moves the first transient of the selected region to the nearest beat.

▷ **To Selected Track:** This command moves any selected regions to the selected track. The key command for this is Control+Shift+T.

▷ **Shuffle Left:** This command moves the selected regions left to close any gaps between them and the regions to their right.

▷ **Shuffle Right:** This command moves the selected regions right to close any gaps between them and the regions to their left.

▷ **Shuffle Left Within Selection:** This command moves the selected regions left to close any gaps between them and the regions to their right. The key command for this is Option+[(left bracket).

▷ **Shuffle Right Within Selection:** This command moves the selected regions right to close any gaps between them and the regions to their left. The key command for this is Option+] (right bracket).

▷ **Nudge Left:** The Nudge Left command moves selected regions left by the amount defined in the Set Nudge Value To submenu, covered after the Nudge Right command. The key command for Nudge Left is Option+left arrow. Note that this is also a system-wide key command; as of this writing (which covers Logic 10.0.4), you will need to either deactivate the key command in the Keyboard Shortcuts tab in the Keyboard pane of the System Preferences window or reassign the key command in the Key Commands window. Hopefully this gets fixed in a future Logic update.

▷ **Nudge Right:** The Nudge Right command moves selected regions right by the amount defined in the Set Nudge Value To submenu. The key command for this is Option+right arrow. Note that, like Nudge Left, this is also a system-wide key command, so as of this writing (which covers Logic 10.0.4), you will need to either deactivate the key command in the System Preferences window or reassign the key command in the Key Commands window. Hopefully this gets fixed in a future Logic update.

▷ **Set Nudge Value To:** This submenu lets you define the nudge value used by the Nudge Left and Nudge Right commands. You can use this submenu to set the nudge value by bar (Control+Option+M), beat (Control+Option+B), division (as defined in the Division field of the Custom LCD display) (Control+Option+D), tick (Control+Option+T), five frames (a SMPTE nudge value), one frame (Control+Option+F), a half frame (Control+Option+H), SMPTE bit, 10 ms (Control+Option+0), 1 ms (Control+T), or sample (Control+Option+S). Figure 6.15 shows the Set Nudge Value To submenu.

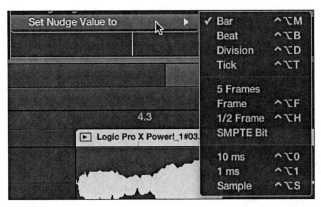

Figure 6.15 The Set Nudge Value To submenu of the Move submenu.
© Apple Inc.

The Trim Submenu

The Trim submenu, shown in Figure 6.16, includes a number of commands for trimming the size of regions.

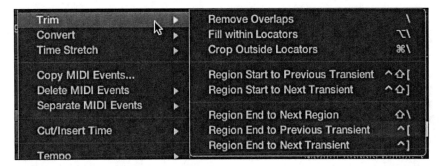

Figure 6.16 The Trim submenu.
© Apple Inc.

The Trim submenu commands are as follows:

▷ **Remove Overlaps:** If you have overlapping regions selected, this command shortens the length of the earlier region to stop at the beginning of the later region. The key command is \ (backslash).

▷ **Fill Within Locators:** This command elongates all regions between the locators on the same track so there are no gaps between them. The key command is Option+\ (backslash). When applied to regions on separate tracks, the regions will simply be extended to the locators.

▷ **Crop Outside Locators:** This command crops any part of a selected region that is outside the locators. The key command for this is Command+\ (backslash).

▷ **Region Start to Previous Transient:** This command extends the beginning of an audio region with analyzed or created transients to the previous transient within that region. This command will not extend an audio region beyond its beginning. The key command for this is Control+Shift+[(left bracket).

▷ **Region Start to Next Transient:** This command shortens the beginning of an audio region with analyzed or created transients to the next transient within that region. The key command for this is Control+Shift+] (right bracket).

▷ **Region End to Next Region:** This command extends all selected regions so that they end at exactly the beginning of the subsequent region on the track. For audio regions, this works only if the audio file is long enough for the region to extend to the beginning of the subsequent region. The key command is Shift+\ (backslash).

▷ **Region End to Previous Transient:** This command shortens the end of an audio region with analyzed or created transients to the previous transient within that region. The key command for this is Control+[(left bracket).

▷ **Region End to Next Transient:** This command lengthens the end of an audio region with analyzed or created transients to the next transient within that region. This command will not extend an audio region beyond its end. The key command for this is Control+] (right bracket).

The Time Stretching Algorithm Submenu

You can choose from several time stretching algorithms, each of which is optimized differently. Figure 6.17 shows the options available from the Time Stretching Algorithm submenu.

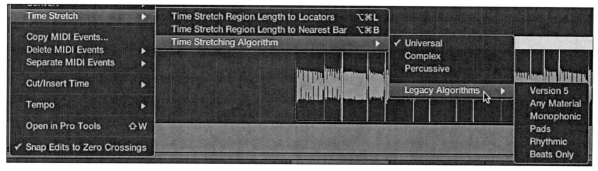

Figure 6.17 The Edit > Time Stretch > Time Stretching Algorithm submenu.
© Apple Inc.

You can select from the following algorithms:

▷ **Universal:** This algorithm is designed to supplant the Any Material algorithm. Most of your time stretching and compressing needs can be addressed with this setting.

▷ **Complex:** This algorithm is designed to time stretch or compress particularly dense and complex material.

▷ **Percussive:** This algorithm is designed to maintain the rhythmic integrity of your more percussive audio material when time stretching or compressing. Don't let the name fool you; this algorithm works beautifully on percussive material played on harmony instruments as well as drums and other percussion instruments.

▷ **Legacy Algorithms:** The algorithms in this submenu come from earlier versions of Logic. The Legacy algorithms are as follows:

   ▷ **Version 5:** This is the time stretching algorithm from Logic 5.

   ▷ **Any Material:** This algorithm gives high-quality results when stretching and compressing audio regions containing any variety of material.

   ▷ **Monophonic:** This algorithm is optimized for material that uses only a single voice (such as a single singer, wind instrument, mono synthesizer, and so on).

   ▷ **Pads:** This algorithm is optimized for polyphonic material, such as pads, choirs, and so on.

   ▷ **Rhythmic:** This algorithm is optimized for instruments with dramatic rhythmic peaks, such as percussion, steel drums, pulsing rhythmic synths, and so on.

   ▷ **Beats Only:** This algorithm is for non-pitched material with strong rhythmic peaks, such as drums. You can use this algorithm to adjust the spaces between peaks, which produces excellent results on drums and such. However, the algorithm is often ineffective or unusable on melodic audio parts.

One of the advantages of the way Logic implements its Time Machine is that third parties can release their own extremely high-quality time stretching algorithms that you can use within Logic. If you have any third-party algorithms installed, such as the iZotope Radius AU or Serato Pitch 'n Time LE AU, you will see their available algorithms in this menu, and you can use these algorithms seamlessly in the Time Machine. They will also be available to you in the Time and Pitch Machine in the Audio File editor.

At this time, there are other high-quality algorithms being developed by other companies as well, so be sure to do some research as to the current state of the art if you are looking for some professional time stretching algorithms. Finally, make sure that whatever third-party AU you purchase offers 64-bit compatibility.

The Functions Menu

The Functions menu options primarily deal with different ways of handling properties of regions, such as region names, colors, and the contents of the regions. Figure 6.18 shows the Functions menu.

Figure 6.18 The Tracks area Functions menu.
© Apple Inc.

The Functions menu options are as follows:

▷ **Rename Regions:** This command opens a text box in the selected region's header, allowing you to rename the selected region. The key command for this is Shift+N.

▷ **Name Regions by Track Name:** When you select a track and then use this command, all of the regions on that track will be given the name of the track. The key command is Option+Shift+N.

▷ **Name Track by Region Name:** When you select a region and then use this command, the track will be given the name of the selected region. The key command is Option+Shift+Command+N.

▷ **Color Regions by Track Color:** When you select a track and then use this command, all of the regions on that track will be given the same color as the track. The key command is Option+Shift+C.

▷ **Color Track by Region Color:** When you select a region and then use this command, the track will be given the same color as the selected region. The key command is Option+Shift+Command+C.

▷ **Remove Silence from Audio Region:** When you select an audio region, you can choose this command, also known as Strip Silence, to scan the audio region for points in which the audio material is below a threshold you define, and then create a number of new audio regions out of those regions above the threshold. This command is extremely useful for removing any pauses in a recording. This command is covered in more detail in Chapter 7, "Working with Audio and Apple Loops." The key command is Control+X.

▷ **Show Audio File in Finder:** This command opens a Finder window showing you the actual file on your hard drive referenced by the selected audio region. The key command is Shift+Command+R.

▷ **Open in Apple Loops Utility:** This command opens the Open Audio File in Apple Loops Utility dialog box, which lets you define the length in bars of the selected audio region before opening the Apple Loops Utility. This command is covered in detail in Chapter 7.

▷ **MIDI Region Parameters:** This submenu contains a number of commands that relate to the parameters specific to MIDI regions. The following are descriptions of the MIDI Region Parameters submenu's options:

   ▷ **Apply Quantization Permanently:** This command permanently applies the playback quantize value assigned to the MIDI region in its Inspector. The key command is Control+Q.

   ▷ **Apply All Parameters Permanently:** This command permanently adjusts the values in the Inspector of a MIDI region. The key command is Control+N.

   ▷ **Apply All Except Channel:** This command permanently adjusts the values in the Inspector of a MIDI region except the MIDI channel value setting.

   ▷ **Apply All Except Channel and Delay:** This command permanently adjusts the values in the Inspector of a MIDI region except the MIDI channel or the MIDI delay settings.

▷ **MIDI Transform:** The MIDI Transform submenu offers shortcuts to the functions in the MIDI Transform window. Selecting one of the options in the MIDI Transform submenu opens the MIDI Transform window, with the selected MIDI Transform process ready to be used. The MIDI Transform window is covered in Chapter 8, "Working with MIDI."

▷ **Region Alias:** The Region Alias submenu is covered in the next section.

▷ **Insert Instrument MIDI Settings as Events:** When you select a MIDI track, choosing the Insert Instrument MIDI Settings as Events command creates MIDI events for program, volume, and pan if they are selected in the Track Inspector and places those events in the track.

▷ **Copy as ReCycle Loop:** If you want to copy audio in your Tracks area for use in Propellerhead's ReCycle, you can select the audio files and copy them to the Clipboard using this command.

▷ **Paste ReCycle Loop:** If you have copied a REX or REX2 loop to the Clipboard, you can paste it at the current playhead position using this command.

▷ **Lock SMPTE Position:** This command locks any selected region to its SMPTE position. That way, any changes in bar length, tempo, meter, and so on will not affect those regions' time positions, even as their bar location changes. The key command is Command+Page Down.

▷ **Unlock SMPTE Position:** This command unlocks the selected regions from their SMPTE position. At this point, these regions are tied to their bar position, like every other region. The key command is Command+Page Up.

▷ **Folder:** The Folder submenu is covered in the upcoming section "The Folder Submenu."

The Region Alias Submenu

Aliases are regions that do not themselves contain data, but are pointers to other regions that contain data. This submenu offers a selection of commands relating to the creation and selection of aliases. Figure 6.19 shows this submenu.

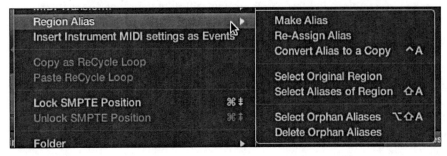

Figure 6.19   The Region Alias submenu of the Functions menu.
© Apple Inc.

An explanation of the commands in the Alias submenu follows:

▷ **Make Alias:** This command makes an alias of the selected region.

▷ **Re-Assign Alias:** If you select an alias and the desired region to which you wish to reassign that alias, choosing this command will reassign the selected alias to point to the selected region instead of the initial region to which the alias pointed.

▷ **Convert Alias to a Copy:** This command turns an alias into a real copy of the original region. In other words, it will now contain data identical to that of the original region and not simply a pointer to the original region. The benefit of this command is that you can then edit events in the new region copy or the region as a whole. The key command is Control+A.

▷ **Select Original Region:** If you select an alias and then choose this command, the original region to which the alias is pointing will be selected as well.

▷ **Select Aliases of Region:** If you select a region and choose this command, all the aliases of the original region will be selected as well. The key command is Shift+A.

▷ **Select Orphan Aliases:** If you have unassigned aliases in your Tracks area because you deleted the original region to which they pointed, this command selects those aliases. The key command is Option+Shift+A.

▷ **Delete Orphan Aliases:** This command deletes all aliases that point to deleted regions.

The Folder Submenu

Logic Pro uses two different kinds of folders. Folder tracks are tracks that use folders as containers for the data of one or more other tracks. They allow you to organize tracks into their own little Tracks area groups and move and edit the entire group on a single track. For example, you could keep your "main" Tracks area organized by creating folder tracks for all your drum loops, synth lines, backup vocals, and so on. I will explain folder tracks in more depth later in this chapter.

Folders are also used for recording takes. Takes are multiple recordings of the same section of a project on the same track. Take recording and take folders were covered in Chapter 5, "Transport Controls and Recording." The Folder submenu, shown in Figure 6.20, contains commands that operate on folder tracks and take folders.

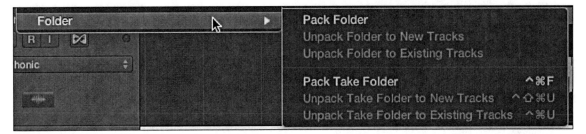

Figure 6.20   The Folder submenu of the Functions local menu.
© Apple Inc.

The commands in the Folder submenu are as follows:

▷ **Pack Folder:** This command combines all the selected tracks into a single folder track.

▷ **Unpack Folder to New Tracks:** When you select a folder track, this command removes each track from the folder and creates a new track in your Track list for each track in the folder.

▷ **Unpack Folder to Existing Tracks:** This command also removes each track from the selected folder. If you do not have any existing tracks in your Tracks area that match the folder track, it creates new tracks. If empty tracks already exist that match the name of the folder track, it places the contents of each track on the matching empty track.

▷ **Pack Take Folder:** This command places all selected regions in a new take folder. Take folders were covered in more detail in Chapter 5. The key command for this is Control+Command+F.

▷ **Unpack Take Folder to New Tracks:** This command unpacks a take folder to new tracks, all with their own channel strips but with the original track's channel strip setting. The key command for this is Control+Shift+Command+U.

▷ **Unpack Take Folder to Existing Tracks:** This command also removes each take from the selected take folder. The takes will be placed on new tracks assigned to the parent track's channel strip. The key command for this is Control+Command+U.

The View Menu

The View menu is loaded with options you can use to specify what you will see in your Tracks area. Most of these options simply allow you to select or deselect various items to determine whether they will appear in your Tracks area. Figure 6.21 shows all the various items that you can choose to view or not to view in the Tracks area.

Figure 6.21 Use the main window's View menu to select which items you will view in your Tracks area.
© Apple Inc.

Because these items are simply selected or deselected and are described individually later in this chapter and in other chapters, this menu doesn't call for a definition of options here. The main thing to remember about the View menu is that when you need to toggle the view of any feature of the Tracks area, you use this local menu.

The Tracks Area Tool Menu

The Tracks area Tool menu contains a collection of tools for use in the Tracks area. Each of these tools has a different function when graphically manipulating and editing regions. In addition to the Tool menu in the local menu bar, you can press T to create a floating Tool menu at the current cursor position. Alternatively, you can right-click with your mouse if you have set right-click to open the Tool menu in the Editing tab of the General Preferences window, which you open by choosing Logic Pro > Preferences > General. When you open the Tool menu, you can access any of the tools either with the mouse or with the key command listed next to each tool. These key commands are listed here. Note that they work only when the Tool menu is open. Note that selecting a tool via key command or with the cursor closes the Tool menu. Figure 6.22 shows the Tool menu.

Figure 6.22 The Tool menu in the Tracks area. Each window and editor contains its own set of tools.
© Apple Inc.

Brief descriptions of each tool follow, from top to bottom:

▷ **Pointer:** This tool looks like an arrow pointing up and to the left. The Pointer tool should be familiar from most other computer applications and is the default tool in Logic. You can use it to select regions by clicking on one or more regions or dragging over a group of regions to create a "rubber band" or "lasso" that will select them all. The key command is T.

▷ **Pencil:** The icon for this tool resembles a pencil. This tool is used to add or alter the length of regions. The key command is T, then 2.

▷ **Eraser:** This tool looks like an eraser. It is used to remove (erase) any regions you have selected from the Tracks area. The key command is T, then 3.

▷ **Text:** This tool looks like a text-entry cursor. It is used to name regions. The key command is T, then 4.

▷ **Scissors:** The Scissors tool conveniently looks like a pair of scissors. It is used to split regions. You can hold the Option key down while splitting regions to divide the entire region into multiple equally spaced regions the same length as your initial split. The key command is T, then 5.

▷ **Glue:** This tool looks like a tube of glue. It is used to join selected regions into one single region, which is given the name and track position of the initial region. When the Glue tool is used to glue audio regions that were not originally next to each other, Logic will need to create a new audio file. The key command is T, then 6.

▷ **Solo:** The Solo tool is represented by the letter S. This tool solos any selected regions. The key command is T, then 7.

▷ **Mute:** The Mute tool is represented by the letter M. This tool mutes any selected regions. The key command is 8.

▷ **Zoom:** This tool resembles a magnifying glass. When you use this tool to select an area containing regions, Logic zooms in on that area. The key command is 9.

▷ **Fade:** This tool looks like a greater-than symbol (>). This tool, when dragged over two adjacent audio regions, creates a crossfade between them. It can also create fade-ins and fade-outs. See the next chapter for an explanation of crossfades. The key command is 0.

▷ **Automation Select:** The Automation Select tool resembles a bent arrow with a solid arrowhead, pointing up and to the left. The Automation Select tool can select automation data in the automation lane. Chapter 10, "Using Automation in Logic," discusses automation and the Automation Select tool in depth. The key command is Q.

▷ **Automation Curve:** The Automation Curve tool resembles a bent arrow with an open arrowhead, pointing up and to the left. The Automation Curve tool can create curves between two automation nodes. Chapter 10 discusses automation and the Automation Curve tool in depth. The key command is W.

▷ **Marquee:** This tool looks like a crosshair. The Marquee tool is a unique and powerful tool, as you'll see later in this chapter. Briefly, the Marquee tool is not limited to selecting entire regions, but can make selections within regions for subsequent editing. (The name *marquee* was adopted from graphics applications, in which some selection boxes featured moving, broken selection lines that often resembled an old theater marquee with rotating lights.) The key command is E.

▷ **Flex:** The Flex tool allows you to perform some Flex Time edits when Logic is not in Flex view. The Flex tool is covered in the section "Using the Flex Tool" later in this chapter. The key command is R.

TIP: Different windows and editors in Logic offer different selections of tools. That means the key commands you can use once a Tool menu is open change throughout Logic. Logic offers key commands to accomplish the function of many of these tools and offers key commands that enable you to select tools without having to use the Tool menu. For example, the Scissors tool is used in numerous editors. If you use the Scissors tool frequently, assigning a key command to directly access the Scissors tool can speed up your workflow. If you want to be as fast with Logic as possible, be sure to assign and use those direct key commands!

Global Menu Commands for the Main Window

In earlier versions of Logic, there were many more commands tucked in more local menus in the Arrange window. With Logic Pro X and the reorganization and renaming of so many different elements, including the Arrange window becoming the main window, more commands useful in the main window were moved up to new global menus. The global Track, Navigate, and View menus contain several commands for working with the main window and Tracks area. First, the Track menu.

The Track Menu

The Track menu contains commands for creating, sorting, and working with tracks. Figure 6.23 shows the Track menu.

Figure 6.23 The Track menu.
© Apple Inc.

Several of these commands have been covered previously in other chapters. The remaining Track menu commands are as follows:

▷ **Other:** The Other submenu has a couple commands not previously covered:

  ▷ **New Track for Overlapped Regions:** If you select a number of regions on a track lane that overlap, this command creates one new track for each region.

  ▷ **New Track for Selected Regions:** Similar to the New Track for Overlapped Regions command, this command creates a new track for each region you have selected. This command does not require regions to be overlapping.

▷ **Rename Track:** This command opens a text box in the selected track's track header, allowing you to rename the track. The key command is Shift+Return.

▷ **Delete Track:** This command deletes the selected track. The key command is Command+Delete. If nothing else is selected, you can also just press Delete.

▷ **Delete Unused Tracks:** This command deletes any tracks with no regions. The key command is Shift+ Command+ Delete.

▷ **Create Track Stack:** This command lets you create a Track Stack. A Track Stack is a combination of different tracks under the authority of a single main track that can be used for basic volume, mute, and solo control over a group of tracks, or as a collection of tracks all routed through the same Summing Track. Track Stacks are covered in detail later in this chapter in the section "Track Stacks." The key command for this is Shift+Command+D.

▷ **Flatten Track Stack:** Knowing about flattening take folders makes this command easier to understand without knowing much about Track Stacks. This is the command you use to "un-stack" a Track Stack, or free all the tracks in the selected Track Stack from their main track. This command also deletes the Track Stack's main track. The key command is Shift+Command+U.

▷ **Show Master Track:** This command shows the master track at the bottom of your track list. The master track contains no regions. It can be used to automate the main output channel strip in a mono or stereo project, or the master channel strip in a surround project. The key command for this is Shift+Command+M.

▷ **Replace or Double Drum Track:** This command lets you easily replace or double a drum track with sampled drum sounds. The Replace or Double Drum Track command is covered in the section "Replacing and Doubling Drum Tracks" section later in this chapter. The key command is Control+D.

▷ **Convert Regions to New Sampler Track:** This command lets you convert the selected region(s) to zones in an EXS24 instrument. The new EXS instrument will be loaded on a new software instrument track, which will contain a region with notes automatically placed to play back the converted regions at their original positions. This command is covered in more detail in the section "Converting Regions to Sampler Tracks" later in this chapter. The key command is Control+E.

▷ **Hide Track:** This command engages the Hide button (H) in the selected track header. The key command is Control+H. Hidden tracks are covered in the section "Hide Tracks" later in this chapter.

▷ **Unhide All Tracks:** This command disengages the Hide button for all tracks.

▷ **Show Hidden Tracks:** This command toggles tracks with their Hide buttons engaged show/hide status. The key command for this is H.

▷ **Sort Tracks By:** This is a submenu of track-sorting options. The Sort Tracks By options are as follows:

  ▷ **MIDI Channel:** If you choose this option, Logic sorts all the external MIDI and software instrument tracks in your Track list in order of their MIDI channel. Any aux channels in your Track list will also be sorted in order of the MIDI channel in their Track Inspector.

  ▷ **Audio Channel:** This option sorts audio tracks by their audio channel. MIDI channels, which don't have an audio channel, will be sorted to the top of your Track list.

  ▷ **Output Channel:** This option sorts audio tracks by their output channel. Tracks assigned to the same output will be sorted alphabetically. MIDI channels, which don't have an audio channel, will be sorted to the bottom of your Track list.

  ▷ **Instrument Name:** This option sorts tracks alphabetically by instrument name.

  ▷ **Track Name:** This option sorts tracks alphabetically by track name.

  ▷ **Used, Unused:** This option sorts tracks into groups that have regions and that do not have regions.

▷ **Assign Track Color:** This command opens the Color palette. Click a color to assign that color to the selected track.

▷ **Configure Track Header:** This command opens the Track Header Configuration window, which is covered in the section "Configuring the Track Header" later in this chapter.

The Navigate Menu

You already saw some of the powerful commands offered by the Navigate menu in Chapter 4, "Global Elements of Logic," and Chapter 5, "Transport Controls and Recording." In addition to these, there are a few more to explore at this time. Figure 6.24 shows the Navigate menu.

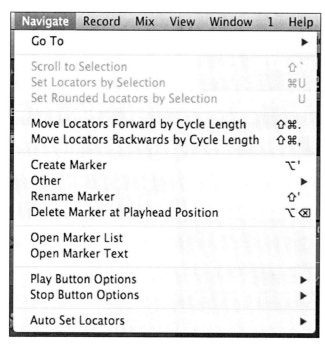

Figure 6.24 The Navigate menu.
© Apple Inc.

The remaining Navigate menu commands are as follows:

▷ **Go To:** The Go To submenu is covered after this bulleted list.

▷ **Scroll to Selection:** If you have selected a region that isn't currently displayed in your Tracks area because you are at a different location in your project, this command will take you back to the location of the selected region. The key command is Shift+`.

▷ **Set Locators by Selection:** This command will set the locators by the beginning and end of the selected region(s). The key command for this is Command+U.

▷ **Set Rounded Locators by Selection:** This command sets each locator to the nearest bar before and after the selected region(s). The key command is U.

▷ **Move Locators Forward by Cycle Length:** This command moves the locators forward across the Bar ruler by the current cycle length, with the new cycle region beginning at the end of the previous cycle region. The key command is Shift+Command+. (period).

▷ **Move Locators Backwards by Cycle Length:** This command moves the locators backward across the Bar ruler by the current cycle length, with the new cycle region ending at the beginning of the previous cycle region. The key command is Shift+Command+, (comma).

▷ **Auto Set Locators:** The Auto Set Locators submenu offers a few methods for automatically setting the locators. If you want to automatically set locators, select the Enable Auto Set Locators option. Then select which of the three methods will be used to set the locators: By Marquee, By Region, and By Note Selection. As you can see in Figure 6.25, you can have all three selected at once. The most recent selection takes precedence. In other words, if you select a MIDI region, the locators will be set at the beginning and end of that region. If the region is open in a MIDI editor, like the Piano Roll editor, and you select some notes in the Piano Roll editor in the selected region, the rounded extent of those notes will become the current locators setting. If you then make a Marquee selection in the Tracks area of another region, the Marquee selection will define the locators. Note that By Notes is the only option that rounds the locators to the nearest bar before and after the notes selection.

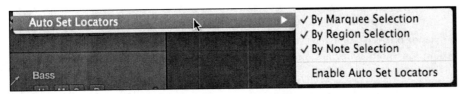

Figure 6.25 The Auto Set Locators submenu of the Navigate menu.
© Apple Inc.

The Go To submenu, partially covered in Chapter 4, gives you some commands for navigating your project to a direct location, via locators, selection boundaries, and, of course, markers. Figure 6.26 shows the Go To submenu.

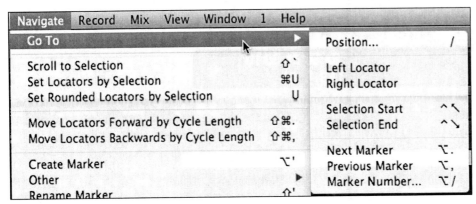

Figure 6.26 The Go To submenu of the Navigate menu.
© Apple Inc.

The commands are pretty straightforward. The Left Locator command moves your position in the Tracks area to the left locator; the Right Locator command to the right locator. Selection Start (Function+Control+left arrow) takes you to the beginning of the current selection, Selection End (Function+Control+right arrow) takes you to the end of the current selection. The marker commands were covered in Chapter 4. That leaves the Position command. Selecting the Position command or pressing the key command / (forward slash) opens the Go To Position dialog box, shown in Figure 6.27.

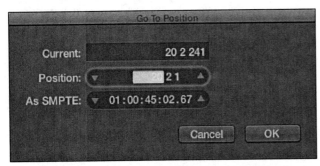

Figure 6.27 The Go To Position dialog box lets you navigate your project by manually entering a location.
© Apple Inc.

The Go To Position dialog box displays your current position and offers a Position field in which you can enter a new position in bars|beats|divisions|ticks by using the up and down arrows at either end of the Position field, by dragging the values in the Position field, or by double-clicking in the field and entering a value manually. When entering a value manually, place a space, a period, or a comma between the bar, beat, division, and ticks numbers. The SMPTE field lets you enter a new position using SMPTE timecode in the same manners as the Position field.

The View Menu

The global View menu, shown in Figure 6.28, gives you control over what elements are displayed in the main window.

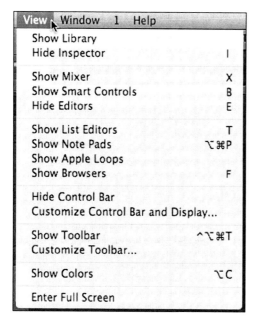

082411

Figure 6.28 The global View menu.
© Apple Inc.

The global View menu options are as follows:

▷ **Show/Hide Library:** This command toggles the display of the Library at the left side of the main window.

▷ **Show/Hide Inspector:** This command toggles the display of the Inspector pane at the left side of the main window. The key command is I.

▷ **Show/Hide Mixer:** This command toggles the display of the Mixer at the bottom of the main window.

▷ **Show/Hide Smart Controls:** This command toggles the display of Smart Controls at the bottom of the main window. Smart Controls are covered in the section "Smart Controls" later in this chapter. The key command is B.

▷ **Show/Hide Editors:** This command toggles the display of the editors at the bottom of the main window. If a MIDI region is selected, this command allows access to the Piano Roll, Score, and Step editors. If an audio region is selected, this command allows access to the Audio Track and Audio File editors. If a Drummer region is selected, this command allows access to the Drummer editor, covered later in this chapter. The key command is E.

▷ **Show/Hide List Editors:** This command toggles the display of the List Editors area at the right side of the main window. The key command is T.

▷ **Show/Hide Note Pads:** This command toggles the display of the Note Pads at the right side of the main window. The key command is Option+Command+P.

▷ **Show/Hide Apple Loops:** This command toggles the display of the Loops Browser at the right side of the main window.

▷ **Show/Hide Browsers:** This command toggles the display of the browsers at the right side of the main window. The key command is F.

▷ **Show/Hide Control Bar:** This command toggles the display of the control bar at the top of the main window.

▷ **Customize Control Bar and Display:** This command lets you customize the elements in the control bar and LCD display, as you learned in Chapter 5. Customizing the other elements in the control bar is covered later in this chapter.

▷ **Show/Hide Toolbar:** This command toggles the display of the Toolbar under the control bar at the top of the main window. The Toolbar is fundamentally an element of the control bar, meaning you have to show the control bar to show the Toolbar. The key command is Control+Option+Command+T.

▷ **Show/Hide Colors:** This command opens Logic's Color palette, useful for coloring tracks and regions. The key command is Option+C.

▷ **Enter Full Screen:** This command puts Logic in full-screen mode. You can also achieve this by clicking the arrows at the upper-right corner of the main window. In full-screen mode, you can access the global menus by moving your cursor to the top of your screen; they simply scroll down into view. To exit full-screen mode, press the Esc key.

Track Classes

By now you realize that all tracks are not created equal. Logic provides several different track classes. Each track contains different sorts of data and has a different purpose. Let's briefly go over them:

▷ **External MIDI tracks:** An external MIDI track is assigned to an external MIDI instrument or a MIDI channel of a multitimbral MIDI instrument and contains MIDI data. You can only record and play back MIDI information from an external MIDI track.

▷ **Audio tracks:** An audio track is a track assigned to an audio channel. It may contain, record, and play back audio information. An audio track doesn't have to contain audio data, however; you can create audio tracks to represent audio, bus, auxiliary, output, input, and other tracks that do not actually contain regions but are assigned to an audio channel. Reasons for creating these sorts of tracks are to access their channel strips in the main window Inspector pane, to include the multiple outputs of a software synthesizer with its software instrument track, to automate them using track automation, and so on.

▷ **Software instrument tracks:** These are also audio tracks, but of a special kind. A software instrument outputs audio produced by the instrument through Logic's audio engine. So a software instrument track uses an audio channel and has a channel strip similar to the channel strips of the other audio channel strips. However, because software instrument tracks contain instruments, the track itself contains only MIDI data in its regions that trigger the instrument. As such, the parameters and channel strip of a software instrument track look like an audio track, but the regions on a software instrument track look like that of a MIDI track.

▷ **Drummer tracks:** Drummer tracks are almost a hybrid of an audio track and a software instrument track. They are simultaneously less than and more than both track types. The Drummer track uses the Drum Kit Designer software instrument as a source for the audio it outputs, but it only uses its unique, self-generated Drummer regions. In other words, you cannot record to a Drummer track—it has no Record button. The regions the Drummer track creates in the Tracks area can only be edited in an extremely limited fashion, yet Drummer tracks have their own dedicated editor for working on their regions. A Drummer track's channel strip looks like a software instrument channel strip, as does its Track Inspector, but the Region Inspector is virtually devoid of options. Regardless, Drummer tracks are incredibly powerful tools that can help you quickly build an arrangement. They are covered in depth later in this chapter.

▷ **Folder tracks:** As explained, folder tracks use folders as containers for other classes of tracks. Tracks packed in folders can be arranged and edited as a single track. An advantage of this capability is that if you have a group of tracks that you want to keep together—for example, a full choir—you can put them all in a folder. Then, when you move, split, or otherwise change that folder track, all of your choir tracks will be moved and edited together; you need not operate on each individual track. Folders are also great organizational tracks in that packing tracks into folders can help keep your main window from becoming cluttered. There are commands in the Functions > Folder submenu to both pack folders (load a folder with tracks) and unpack folders (unload all the tracks in a folder onto the Tracks area). See the section "The Folder Submenu" earlier in this chapter for a description of those commands.

▷ **Master track:** The master track, when shown using the Track > Show Master Track command (Shift+Command+M), can be found at the bottom of the Track list. It contains no regions. Then what is it good for, you may ask? You can use the master track to automate the volume of your entire project. If your project is stereo, the master track affects the stereo outputs. If your project is in surround, it automates the master channel strip. You can also control the volume of your project using the Volume fader in the master track header. Additionally, the master track is a Track Stack, automatically adding any auxes assigned to the output of master fader to the master Track Stack. Track Stacks are covered in depth in the section "Track Stacks" later in this chapter.

Uses for Folder Tracks: Len Sasso, author of *Emagic Logic Tips and Tricks* (Course Technology PTR, 2003), offers a few expert uses for folder tracks:

Create a screenset with two main windows, one primary, and one secondary. Select your secondary main window's local View > Link > Content option. Any folder you select in the primary main window will now have its contents shown automatically in the secondary main window.

Sasso also explains how to unpack only part of a folder:

When you want to unpack only some of the regions in a folder, select the regions you don't want unpacked and pack them into a subfolder of their own. Then unpack the original folder and you will have the desired regions unpacked and the rest in their own folder. That's easier than trying to find and re-pack the desired regions in the full main window.

▷ **Metronome track:** This is the track reserved for the metronome in Logic, called click by default. You can use this track to adjust the parameters of your click to best assist your live performance. You will only want a single metronome track per project. Keep in mind that you don't actually need to have a metronome track in your Tracks area to use the metronome.

▷ **No Output track:** This special track, as its name implies, does not output any MIDI data to MIDI devices or audio data to audio outputs. Rather, this option is mostly used for storing synth SysEx data you don't want to send or as a temporary assignment for tracks you want to turn off momentarily.

You can change the class of a track and/or instrument of a track by right-clicking a track in the Track list. Place the cursor over the Reassign Track option and a menu will appear, containing all the previously discussed track classes and all your instrument and audio options divided into submenus based on the Environment layer in which they appear. Generally, you will use the Mixer submenu in the Reassign Track menu to change the class of a track. Figure 6.29 shows this menu of track classes. To change the track, simply select a new track class or instrument.

Figure 6.29 When you right-click on a track header, a menu will appear of all available track classes and instruments on the various Environment layers.
© Apple Inc.

Folders on Nonfolder Tracks: There is an exception to the preceding tip, as aforementioned author Sasso points out:

Normally folders are placed on special Folder Tracks, which are not assigned to particular channel strips, unlike other tracks. That's what Logic does automatically when you create a folder, but you can reassign the track to its own channel strip using the Reassign Track menu, and you can also move the folder to another track. When a folder is on a normal track, all of its output is routed to the channel strip assigned to that track. That holds for the No Output track as well.

The Control Bar

The control bar is a handy repository of buttons for opening different main window elements like the browsers and Smart Controls, for accessing the Quick Help field in the Inspector pane (which provides descriptions of elements in Logic when you place the cursor over them, a very useful feature when exploring Logic), and for accessing an extended Toolbar of commands. It also contains the Transport controls, as you learned in Chapter 5. In keeping with the overall customizable nature of Logic, you can configure the control bar to contain the buttons you find most useful, or you can hide the control bar entirely. Figure 6.30 shows the default control bar configuration. To hide the control bar, use the Hide Control Bar command in the global View menu.

Figure 6.30 The default control bar configuration, including the default Transport. The control bar can be configured to display buttons for different functions and commands or can be hidden from view.

© Apple Inc.

To configure the control bar, right-click any open space in the control bar and select Customize Control Bar and Display. This opens the Customize Control Bar and Display window shown in Figure 6.31.

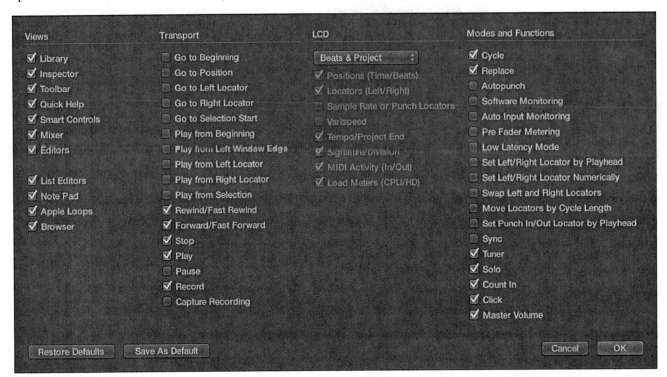

Figure 6.31 Right-clicking in the control bar and choosing Customize Control Bar and Display opens the Customize Control Bar and Display window.

© Apple Inc.

This is the same window used to customize the Transport. The Views column controls the control bar items. Simply select the items you wish to show in your Controls bar as you did with the Transport and click OK. You can also create your own default control bar and Transport by selecting all the items you want to access at the top of the main window and clicking Save As Default. If you have more items in your control bar than you have space on the screen at the top of your main window, some elements will be moved to a menu at the right end of the control bar. Click the area marked >> to access your other control bar items. The custom control bar options are self-explanatory, but there is one control bar feature that needs further attention: the Toolbar.

Accessing and Customizing the Toolbar

The Toolbar is a feature of the control bar that can be shown, hidden, and customized as needed. It contains buttons for executing commands in the main window, and a Nudge Value menu to give you quick access to nudge value settings. To access the Toolbar, shown in Figure 6.32, click the Toolbar button in the control bar or select View > Show Toolbar (Control+Option+Command+T).

Figure 6.32 The default Toolbar.

© Apple Inc.

The Toolbar opens directly beneath the control bar. As you can see in Figure 6.32, the default configuration offers a number handy commands, each one just a mouse click away. You can also customize the Toolbar to your liking. First, right-click in the Toolbar and select Customize Toolbar or select View > Customize Toolbar. This opens the Customize Toolbar dialog box, shown in Figure 6.33.

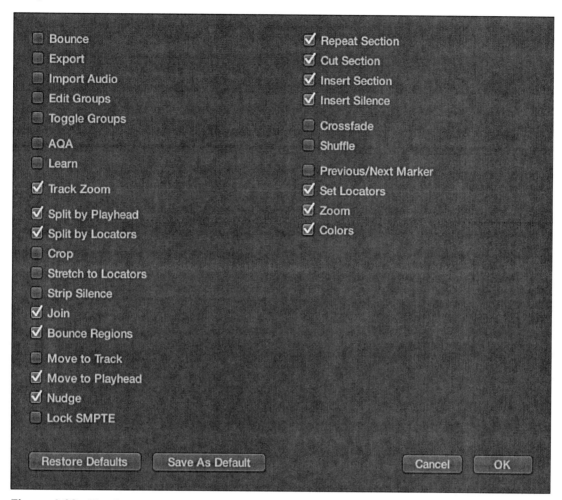

Figure 6.33 The Customize Toolbar dialog box. You can add buttons controlling a wide variety of commands to your Toolbar with this dialog box.
© Apple Inc.

As in the Customize Control Bar and Display window, you simply select the checkboxes of the commands you want in your Toolbar and click OK. You can use the Save As Default option to create your own default Toolbar. If you have more items in your Toolbar than you have space on the screen at the top of your main window, some commands will be moved to a menu at the right end of the Toolbar. Click the area marked >> to access your other Toolbar commands. Most of the commands available in the Toolbar are self-explanatory. The only one that really stands out as needing clarification is AQA. This is an abbreviation for Automation Quick Access, which is covered in Chapter 10.

Adding Tracks to the Main Window Track List

We already discussed how to add tracks to the main window Track list in Chapter 3, "The Logic Project." You can also use the Append Track to Track List command. If you want to append a new track to the very bottom of your Track list, you can do so by double-clicking in the empty space below the final track in your Track list. This creates a new track that is identical to whichever track you have selected in the Track list. You can also define a key command for this function in the Key Commands window.

The Main Window Inspector

We've already seen and discussed the different Track Inspector parameters in Chapter 3, but it bears repeating that every single track has two Inspectors. The main window Inspector also includes the Inspector channel strips, which display the signal flow channel strips for the selected track in the track list. Figure 6.34 shows both Inspectors and, because of the size of the Inspectors when open, the bottom of the Inspector channel strips.

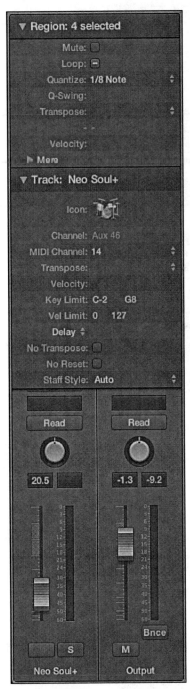

Figure 6.34 The Region Inspector, the Track Inspector, and the Inspector channel strips of a Drummer track. The Track Inspector should be familiar from Chapter 3. The Region Inspector contains playback parameters for MIDI regions. The Inspector channel strips show the signal flow of the selected track in the Track list.
© Apple Inc.

The upper area in the Inspector pane is the Region Inspector. It acts as the MIDI THRU Inspector if no region is selected. If any regions are selected, it acts on the region playback parameters for the selected regions. The second area is the familiar Track Inspector. Chapter 3 explained the track parameters, and the next section describes the region parameters.

Region Playback Parameters

Figure 6.34 shows the region playback parameters that you will find for a region on an external MIDI or software instrument track, and to auxes assigned to multi-timbral or multi-output instruments. They are called playback parameters because they do not affect recording. In addition, they are not written to the region itself, but only affect the way Logic plays back the track (unless you apply the Normalize Region Parameters command).

Descriptions of the parameters follow:

▷ **Mute:** Selecting this checkbox mutes the selected region(s) but not the parent track.

▷ **Loop:** Selecting this checkbox turns on "old-style" looping for that region. When activating old-style looping, the looped region will continually repeat for the length of the project or until another region on the same track interrupts the looping. When old-style looping is activated for a region, a number of regions with faded events representing the repeats of the looped region extend until the end of the project or until looping is interrupted by another region. You can also engage looping by pressing L. Looping is explained in more detail later in this chapter, in the "Looping Regions in the Tracks Area" section.

▷ **Quantize:** This is the quantize setting. To quantize MIDI data means to lock its playback to a beat count so that regardless of the timing of the data when it was created, it will be played back with the exact timing selected in the Quantize parameter. If you click to the right of the parameter, a menu will appear that offers you myriad beat and note options from which to choose. Quantizing is explored in more depth in Chapter 8.

▷ **Q-Swing:** This controls how tightly the quantization feature locks every second beat to its quantization grid to give the MIDI part a more pushed or laid-back feel. You can adjust this parameter from 1% to 99%, with values under 50% resulting in an early beat and values over 50% resulting in a delayed beat.

▷ **Transpose:** This parameter allows you to transpose the pitch of playback higher or lower by up to 96 semitones.

▷ **Velocity:** You can also offset the velocity of a MIDI track or region up or down. The range of velocity is the standard MIDI parameter range of 0–127. You can add or subtract up to 96 to or from that value, up to the maximum value of 127.

Advanced Region Parameters

If you click the disclosure triangle, labeled "More," at the bottom of the Region Inspector, the Region Inspector will expand to display the advanced region parameters, which offer more options than the standard region playback parameters. The advanced region parameters are shown in Figure 6.35. As you may have guessed from the name "advanced region parameters," these parameters offer control over some less typical functions.

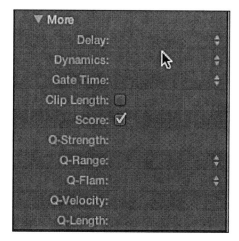

Figure 6.35 The advanced region parameters for the track in Figure 6.34.
© Apple Inc.

The advanced region parameters are as follows:

▷ **Delay:** This parameter offsets when a region plays back. The range of this parameter is −999 to 9,999 ticks. (A tick is the smallest time resolution in the sequencer, 1/3840 of a 1/4 note.) Double-click in the Delay field to access a text box for entering a Delay setting manually. Alternatively, click the arrows at the right end of the Delay field to open a menu that offers Delay settings in musically meaningful subdivisions, with the resulting delay in milliseconds listed as well. This parameter is useful if you are trying to align audio and MIDI data, and your MIDI seems to play back a tiny bit ahead of or behind the audio.

▷ **Dynamics:** Adjusting the Dynamics parameter affects the velocity, except that instead of offsetting the maximum value, Dynamics offsets the distance between the loudest and softest velocities in the region. This can compress or expand the difference in volume between the notes, affecting the perceived volume. Double-click in the Dynamics field to access a text box for entering a Dynamics setting manually. If you click the arrows at the right end of the Dynamics field, a menu will open that offers adjustment steps from 25% to 400%, with values below 100% decreasing the dynamics and values above 100% increasing the dynamics. The Fixed option plays back all the notes at the same velocity.

▷ **Gate Time:** This scales the note duration, forcing playback to be staccato (shorter) or legato (longer). This parameter offers a menu of adjustment steps from 25% to 400%, with values below 100% reducing note duration and values above 100% increasing note duration. The Fixed option will create an abrupt staccato effect, while Legato will remove all space between all notes in the selected region. Double-click in the Gate Time field to access a text box for entering a Gate Time setting manually.

▷ **Clip Length:** When the end of a MIDI region is reached, this parameter determines whether any notes that sustain past the end of the region will be played back to their completion or cut off. If the checkbox is selected, any sustaining notes are stopped. If the checkbox is deselected, the notes continue playing normally.

▷ **Score:** This parameter determines whether the MIDI region is available in the Score editor. Select this checkbox to make the region available in the Score editor. This parameter is of use when a MIDI region contains only nonmusical MIDI information, such as controller messages, and you don't need to display the region in the Score editor.

▷ **Q-Strength:** This parameter determines how close to move each note to the nearest quantization grid position. You can adjust the value from 0% to 100%, with 0% resulting in no movement of the note at all and 100% moving the note completely to the grid.

▷ **Q-Range:** If you set this parameter, notes that are farther away than the number of ticks you set are not quantized. The range can be from −3,840 to 3,840 ticks. There are some exceptions to this, however. A negative setting means that only those notes farther away are quantized; this is useful to quantize only those notes farther away from the grid than you would like. Also, a value of 0 basically turns off the Q-Range function, in which case all notes are quantized.

▷ **Q-Flam:** This parameter spreads out notes that fall on the same point; in other words, it rolls the chords. A positive value creates an upward roll; a negative value creates a downward roll. You can set the range from −3,840 to 3,840 ticks.

▷ **Q-Velocity:** This parameter sets how much the velocity values of a template MIDI region will affect the velocity of the notes. You can adjust this parameter from −99% to 127%, with negative numbers and numbers over 100% creating the greatest velocity deviation from the template MIDI region, 0% leaving the notes unaffected by the note velocities of the template MIDI region, and 100% meaning the notes adopt the note velocities of the template MIDI region completely.

▷ **Q-Length:** This parameter determines how the note lengths of a template MIDI region affect the note length of your MIDI region in the Tracks area. You can adjust this parameter from −99% to 127%, with negative numbers and numbers over 100% creating the greatest note length deviation from the template MIDI region, 0% leaving the notes unaffected by the note lengths of the template MIDI region, and 100% meaning the notes adopt the note lengths of the template MIDI region completely.

The Audio Region Inspector

If you select an audio region, a different Region Inspector will appear that contains parameters specific to audio regions. The Audio Region Inspector also includes advanced region parameters, which you access by clicking the disclosure triangle at the bottom of the Audio Region Inspector. Figure 6.36 shows the Audio Region Inspector with its advanced region parameters.

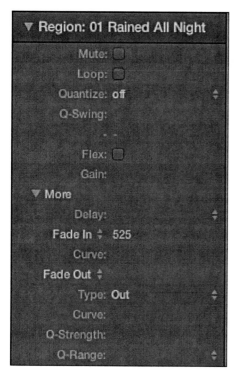

Figure 6.36 The Inspector of an audio region.
© Apple Inc.

Some parameters in this Inspector are the same as those you've already seen. The remaining parameters are as follows:

▷ **Mute:** Select this checkbox to mute the selected audio regions.

▷ **Quantize:** You can use the Quantize parameter to quantize audio regions based on Flex markers, similar to the Quantize setting described for the region playback parameters.

▷ **Flex:** This checkbox enables or disables Flex Time or Flex Pitch for the selected regions. It also can be used to "turn off" any Flex Time or Flex Pitch edits you have performed on the selected regions. Flex Time and Flex Pitch are covered later in this chapter.

▷ **Gain:** The Gain parameter lets you adjust the volume of the selected audio region, +/–30 dB.

▷ **Fade In:** You can adjust this parameter to determine the length in milliseconds of a fade-in at the beginning of an audio region.

▷ **Speed Up:** If you click on the Fade In parameter name, a menu will open in which you can select between the Fade In parameter and the Speed Up parameter. The Speed Up parameter creates an effect that sounds like tape speeding up to its proper playback speed, per the length in milliseconds you define, at the beginning of an audio region.

▷ **Curve:** This setting determines the strength and shape of the curve of the fade-in or speed up, if any.

▷ **Fade Out:** This parameter determines which kind of fade there will be at the end of your audio region.

▷ **Type:** The Type options are Out (for fade-out), X (for crossfade), EqP (for equal-power crossfade), or X S (for equal-strength crossfade).

▷ **Slow Down:** If you click on the Fade Out parameter name, a menu will open in which you can select between the Fade Out parameter and the Slow Down parameter. The Slow Down parameter creates an effect that sounds like tape slowing down from its proper playback speed, per the length in milliseconds you define, at the end of an audio region. The Slow Down setting only works with the fade type set to Out.

▷ **Curve:** This setting determines the strength and shape of the curve of the final fade or slow down, if any.

NOTE: Don't worry if you are completely unfamiliar with the concept of audio fades right now; you'll learn more about this in Chapter 7.

The Inspector Channel Strips

To make mixing and accessing mixing parameters more convenient, Logic displays the channel strip for the selected track below the parameters in the Inspector along with a second channel strip. The second channel strip is the signal flow channel strip. It can display any channel strip to which your primary channel strip is routed. In other words, you can have the second channel strip display the primary channel strip's output channel strip by simply clicking on the Output field of the primary channel strip, or to an aux channel strip by clicking on the Bus field on the primary channel strip for the desired aux. You need to have the Inspector turned on in the View menu (View > Inspector, or key command I) to see the Inspector channel strip. Figure 6.37 shows the Inspector channel strips of a software instrument track.

Figure 6.37 The Inspector channel strips of a software instrument track. This track is routed through a number of buses, but the aux channel strip for bus 1 is displayed to the right. You can select any output on the primary channel strip, and it will display in the second channel strip. As you can see, you'll need to close the Region or Track Inspector to fit the entire strip on the page on many monitors.
© Apple Inc.

The Inspector channel strips take up a lot of vertical space, so depending on how large your main window is and how many items you are viewing in the Inspector, the channel strips may not fit in the window and may appear cut off at the top of its frame. To fit both channel strips in the window, you might need to close other items in the Inspector by clicking on their disclosure triangles in the top-left of each box. A monitor with more vertical resolution would allow you to display all the items in the Inspector.

Configuring the Track Header

At the left side of each track lane is the track header, which contains a variety of track information and controls. As with so many other aspects of Logic, the track header is customizable. Perhaps you are using multiple control surfaces and need a quick visual reference for which tracks are tied to which control surface, or maybe you want to enable Volume and Pan controls on the track header. While some of the most fundamental tools are displayed in the track header by default, configuring the track header allows you to put tools you need at your fingertips. Figure 6.38 shows an audio track with the default track header.

Figure 6.38 An audio track with the default track header configuration.
© Apple Inc.

To configure your track headers, select Track > Configure Track Header or right-click on a track header and select Configure Track Header. Alternatively, press Option+T. This opens the Track Header Configuration dialog box, shown in Figure 6.39.

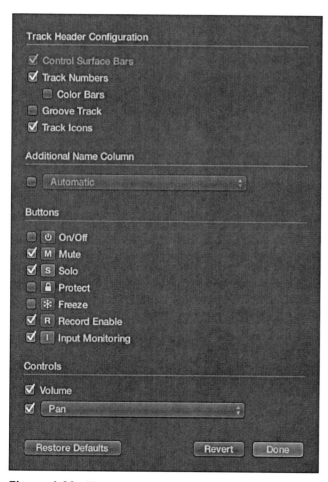

Figure 6.39 The Track Header Configuration dialog box. You can customize your track headers in this dialog box.
© Apple Inc.

Many of these options are explained in detail elsewhere in the book. For now, here is a quick description of the functions that each option represents:

▷ **Control Surface Bars:** Selecting this option displays the track control bars that show the tracks that are controlled by any connected control surfaces.

▷ **Track Numbers:** Selecting this option displays the track number for each track.

▷ **Color Bars:** If you have Track Numbers enabled, you can select this option to display the color bars for your tracks. You can assign colors to tracks using the Color palette, accessed via the global View > Show Colors command or by pressing Option+C.

▷ **Groove Track:** Enabling this option lets you click the track number area of a track to make that track the Groove Track, which is denoted by a yellow star in place of the track number. Once you select a track to be the Groove Track, checkboxes appear to the right of the other track numbers. These checkboxes let you select which tracks' timing follows that of the Groove Track. Tracks that follow the Groove Track cannot be quantized using the Region Inspector.

▷ **Track Icons:** If you select this option, track icons will be displayed in the track header. Track icons are covered in greater detail in the next section.

▷ **Additional Name Column:** This section provides another option for naming your tracks. The menu contains a list of options regarding the nature of the name(s) displayed for your tracks. The Additional Name Column section of the Track Header Configuration dialog box was covered in Chapter 3.

▷ **On/Off:** This button turns the track on and off, effectively muting it in the process. Turning a track off can be useful for managing system performance, freeing up CPU power for other purposes.

▷ **Mute:** This button mutes the track's parent channel strip. When you click this button, the track and any dependent tracks of the parent channel strip are muted, the regions' colors become grayer, and the button glows turquoise. Clicking it again unmutes the parent channel strip and any dependent tracks.

▷ **Solo:** This button will solo all the regions on the selected track. When you engage the Solo button, only other tracks with their Solo buttons engaged, or regions that have been soloed, will play back, and the Solo button will glow yellow. With Solo engaged, the LCD will become yellow, and a yellow outline will surround all the regions in the soloed track.

▷ **Protect:** This is the Track Protect switch. When clicked, this button locks the regions on the track in time and disallows recording on that track. (The R button vanishes.) When selected, the button glows green, and the icon changes to an image of a closed lock. When you click the button again, the track is no longer protected, and the icon returns to the image of an open lock.

▷ **Freeze:** The button with a snowflake icon is the Freeze switch (audio tracks, software instrument tracks, and Drummer tracks only). Clicking this button freezes the selected tracks. (See the "Freezing Tracks" section later in this chapter.) The button glows green when the Freeze switch is active for that track. If you click the button again, the track will unfreeze.

▷ **Record Enable:** This button allows the track to receive audio as soon as you begin recording. When you click the button, the track is record enabled, and the button glows red. Clicking it again disables record enable.

▷ **Input Monitoring:** Selecting the Input Monitoring button allows you to monitor audio signals through Logic when an audio track is not record enabled. When selected, the Input Monitoring button glows orange. The Input Monitoring button is displayed in the track header of audio tracks by default.

▷ **Volume:** Selecting Volume adds a volume slider to the track header, which also doubles as a level meter when in playback or recording.

▷ **Pan:** This option adds a Pan control to the track header, which can also be configured to act as a send control for any of the eight possible sends for the track using the Pan menu next to the Pan checkbox.

You can also enable and disable different options through the contextual menu available in the track header. Figure 6.40 shows the track header contextual menu.

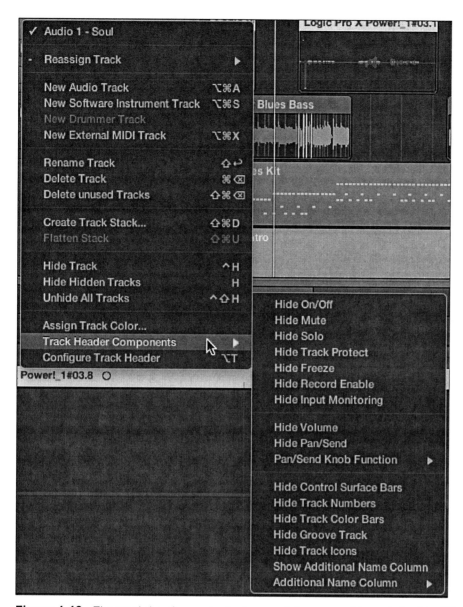

Figure 6.40 The track header contextual menu lets you enable and disable different track header options quickly and easily.
© Apple Inc.

As you can see in Figure 6.40, there are a number of additional commands available in the track header contextual menu, some that have already been covered, others that will be covered later in this chapter.

Unless you have a particularly large display, you will probably want to be fairly selective with the options you enable for your track headers. Figure 6.41 shows a track lane with every possible track header configuration option activated.

Figure 6.41 A track header with all options visible. As you can see, this takes up quite a lot of screen space.
© Apple Inc.

You can place the mouse pointer at the right edge of the Track list and use the Resize cursor that appears to expand or shrink the track header if you have all the track header components enabled. The Volume slider and Pan knob will disappear when you decrease the length of the track header, but all the buttons and the track icon will remain.

> **TIP:** If you want to toggle on or off multiple buttons of the same type, navigating to each track one by one to click its relevant track button will become quite time-consuming. Luckily, you can click and hold a button and then mouse up or down over the other similar track buttons to activate or deactivate multiple buttons at the same time. For example, suppose you want to mute 10 tracks. Rather than selecting each track individually and clicking each individual Mute button, you could click and hold the first Mute button, then slide your mouse over the other nine tracks to mute the rest of the tracks. Note that you can use this feature only on the same type of button. In other words, you can't click and hold on the Mute button of one track and then slide over the Solo button of another. Nonetheless, you'll find this feature to be a massive timesaver!

Track Icons

Every track can have an icon associated with it if you turn on Track Icons in the Track Configuration menu. This track icon represents the channel strip and/or Environment object to which that track is linked. Logic features excellent, high-resolution icons, as you can see in Figure 6.42.

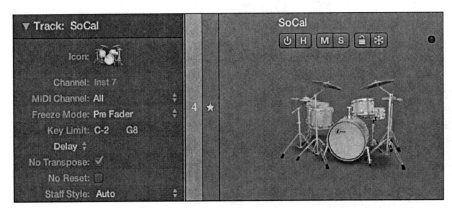

Figure 6.42 Here you can see the icon in the Drummer Track Inspector and a larger icon in a zoomed-out track lane.
© Apple Inc.

To assign an icon to a track, simply click and hold on the icon in the Track Inspector. A window with icons categorized by type will open, in which you can select the icon for your track.

Hide Tracks

Suppose you have tracks in the Track list that have project-related MIDI data, such as SysEx data, that you do not need to see in the Tracks area. Or perhaps you created a number of tracks for audio channel strips that you wanted to appear in the Mixer, but that you do not need to display in the Track list. Or maybe you just want to focus on a particular set of tracks and you wish to group the other tracks for quick hiding and unhiding. For situations where you have tracks in the Track list that you do not need or want to have visible, Logic offers the Hide Track feature.

There is a global Hide View button at the top of the Tracks area. It appears to the right of the New Tracks buttons and features an H, as you can see in Figure 6.43. When you click on the Hide View button, it glows green, and Hide buttons in the individual track headers become available. You can then activate the individual Hide buttons on the desired tracks, which will also glow green when activated. When you deactivate the global Hide View button, all those tracks with Hide activated will no longer be visible, and the Hide View button will glow orange to let you know that the Track list includes hidden tracks. The Hide button will also disappear from the remaining track headers. When you want to see the hidden tracks again or to have access to Hide buttons for your remaining tracks, simply reactivate the Hide View button.

Figure 6.43 The global Hide View button. It is currently green, indicating you can click on the Hide button on individual tracks to hide them.
© Apple Inc.

Several key commands relate to the Hide Track feature. Even when the global Hide View button is deactivated, you can still hide an individual track by using the Hide Current Arrange Track and Select Next Track key command, Control+H. You can toggle the state of the Hide View button using the key command H. Finally, there is a key command to unhide all tracks that resets the Hide buttons of each track, making them all visible, Shift+Control+H. You can also hide tracks assigned to groups that have Hide enabled in their Group Settings using the Toggle Hide Group key command, Control+Shift+Group Number (press the group number, 1 through 9). Groups are covered in Chapter 11, "Mixing in Logic." Keep in mind that hiding a track does not affect its playback in any way.

> **CAUTION:** Suppose you want to add or remove some measures from your entire project. An easy way to do this would be to select all your tracks in the Tracks area and then use the Snip/Insert Time commands from the local Region menu. Unfortunately, this way of adding or removing time skips over any hidden tracks. Be sure that if you have hidden tracks, you have clicked the Hide button so it is green when you use either of these commands.

Freezing Tracks

Freeze is one of the most powerful features in Logic. Most applications have some form of freeze function, but Logic was the first major sequencer to add Freeze. Freeze can extend the power of your computer if you find your CPU beginning to strain under the processing load of your project. You can also freeze your software instrument tracks on one computer, take your Logic project to a computer without those software instruments installed, and then play the project, including the missing instruments. If you use audio or software instruments, you may find yourself wanting to use Logic's Freeze function.

What Is Freeze?

When you start using audio effects and software instruments, particularly at high sample rates and bit depths, you'll quickly realize that real-time effects and synth processing can take up a large amount of CPU power. Each effect and synth takes up a different amount of CPU power, of course, but the more you use, the higher the load on your CPU. What happens when you reach the limit of your Mac's CPU capability? You get a System Overload error message, your project stops playing, and you need to turn off some of the synths or effects you have turned on.

This is where Freeze comes in. With a simple click of the Freeze button, Logic will make a temporary 32-bit floating-point audio file of your audio or software instrument track, including all effects and effects automation, and then link that track to the temporary audio file, bypassing all the effects (and the software instrument, if the track is a software instrument track). That means instead of your CPU having the heavy load of real-time synths and effects, it has only the lighter duty of playing back the referenced audio file. All the processing power required by the synth and the effects used by that track are now released.

You may want to use Freeze if you want to use effects and/or softsynths after you've run out of CPU power. Another very handy way to use Freeze is if you are trying to play back a Logic project created on a computer with greater power; you can use Freeze until the CPU load is reduced to the point that the project will play back. Keep in mind that if your project's real-time processing demands are not causing any processing problems, you do not need to freeze any tracks.

How to Freeze Tracks

Freezing tracks is incredibly easy. First, make sure that the Freeze button, which features a snowflake, is visible on your track. If it isn't, you can display it by selecting Track > Configure Track Header, pressing Option+T, or right-clicking on the track header and selecting Configure Track Header, and then checking the Freeze checkbox.

Once the button is visible, simply click on it. The button will glow green, as shown in Figure 6.44. Repeat this procedure for all the tracks in your project that you want to freeze. If you want to freeze many tracks at once, you can use the procedure described in the tip found in the "Configuring the Track Header" section earlier in this chapter to engage multiple Freeze buttons. The next time you issue the Play command (via the Transport, a key command, or a software controller), instead of beginning playback of your project, Logic will freeze all of the tracks that you have selected. If the region or regions on the tracks you are freezing don't extend to the length of your project, you can press Command+. (period) to stop the freeze process. Your tracks will be frozen, but you won't have to wait until Logic reaches the end of your project to get back to work. That's it!

Figure 6.44 An audio track with Freeze turned on. This button tells you that the plug-ins on this track will not be played back in real time, but instead the track is playing an audio file that is an exact duplicate of the track.
© Apple Inc.

There is a parameter to note in the Track Inspector: Freeze mode. There are two modes:

▷ **Source Only:** This freezes the software instrument or source audio file (including Flex Time and Flex Pitch adjustments), but not any of the plug-ins on the track. This is very useful if you have a very CPU-heavy software instrument and want to freeze the instrument, but you want to keep the plug-ins "live" so you can adjust them. Source Only also can be used if you have an audio track that is very heavily Flexed, as Flex takes up CPU resources when used in real time. In this mode, the Freeze button will turn blue.

▷ **Pre Fader:** This is the traditional Logic Freeze mode. The source audio or software instrument and all plug-ins (in other words, everything before the fader) will be frozen. This saves the most CPU and turns the Freeze button green.

When you freeze a track, you can no longer edit the track or adjust the automation of your effect or software instrument parameters. This is because the track is no longer playing back the regions in the track lane in real time, but is instead linking to the recorded file. If you selected Source Only mode for freezing, you can still adjust and add/remove plug-ins, but in Pre Fader mode you cannot. If you attempt to edit any of these parameters, Logic will display the error message, "Current track is frozen. Do you wish to unfreeze it?" As this message informs you, if you want to make further changes or edits to the regions, effects, or effects automation, just click the Unfreeze button in the message or click the Freeze button again to unfreeze the track. When you are finished editing your track, simply reactivate the Freeze button; the next time you activate Play, the track will refreeze with your changes. If you make an edit after unfreezing a track, the Undo command will undo the edit but will not refreeze your track, so be sure to freeze your track again even if your edits are undone.

Not every function of the track is frozen, however. You can still adjust the effect send level and destination, the pan and surround parameters, and the volume, and toggle the channel strip's mute and solo status (as well as automation for these features).

Keep in mind that because Freeze operates by printing files faster than real time, in order for Freeze to work, the audio engine and processors you are using must be capable of working faster than real time. Also, if you are using the I/O plug-in to access external hardware in real time, you cannot use Freeze.

Cycle Mode

Chapter 5 touched on Cycle mode, but now I'll go into it in detail. As you recall, Cycle mode allows you to loop a predefined section of your project continually. You might want to do this to listen critically to a specific section of your project, to practice performing a specific part of your project, to edit events only in a given section, and so on.

You can turn on Cycle mode in a number of ways:

 ▷ Click the Cycle button on the Transport.
 ▷ Press the Cycle key command C.
 ▷ Click the top of the Bar ruler.
 ▷ Define the cycle region.

When Logic is in Cycle mode, the playhead plays back the project only within the cycle region. When the playhead reaches the end of the cycle, it immediately returns to the beginning of the cycle, interrupting playback of whatever sounds are at the end of the cycle.

Combining Cycle Mode and Recording

One of the most powerful combinations of features in Logic is to use Cycle mode with recording. This can greatly facilitate creativity and frees you to improvise parts over a section of your project without worrying about creation and organization of tracks and so on. It can also be beneficial when recording takes, as you saw in Chapter 5. The Recording tab of the Project Settings window offers a number of preferences as to how cycle recording will operate within a given project. You can access these parameters by selecting File > Project Settings > Recording or by clicking and holding the Record button in the Transport and selecting Recording Settings from the menu that appears.

You already saw the Recording tab of the Project Settings window in Figure 5.38 of Chapter 5. Please refer to Chapter 5 if you would like more information on the Recording tab as a whole. Following are short explanations of each parameter that relates to Cycle mode MIDI recording (and MIDI recording only):

 ▷ **Create Take Folders:** This option tells Logic to automatically create a take folder when a second cycle has passed the first bar of the cycle region. Take folders and take recording were covered in detail in Chapter 5.
 ▷ **Join with Selected Regions:** This parameter merges the data from each recording pass into a single region on the track to which you are recording. If you do not select this option, Logic will create a new region for each recording pass.
 ▷ **Join When Cycling:** This setting allows you to record the first pass as a unique region. Then Logic merges all subsequent recording passes into another region. If you do not select this, Logic will create a new region for each recording pass.
 ▷ **Create Tracks When Cycling:** This option not only creates a new region for each recording pass, but creates a new track as well. The newly created tracks appear sequentially beneath the original track to which you began recording. Obviously, this function deactivates the merge options.
 ▷ **Create Tracks and Mute When Cycling:** If you select this option, each pass will be muted as soon as it is finished recording, so you will not have to listen to it when recording subsequent passes.

Defining the Cycle Region

There are a number of different ways to set the cycle region in Logic. The most straightforward method is to click in the top half of the Bar ruler and then drag your mouse to the point at which you want the cycle to end. As you drag the mouse, a gold bar will travel behind your mouse to the point at which you stop. This gold bar represents the cycle region. Figure 6.45 shows a defined cycle region.

Figure 6.45 The gold bar between measure 2 and measure 6 represents the defined cycle region.
© Apple Inc.

You can grab one of the edges of the cycle region to redefine it, even during playback! You can also click in the middle of the cycle region to move it. If you want to reset one of the cycle region boundaries to a specific point near that boundary, you can click on that point while holding down the Shift key. You can also drag a marker from the marker track or arrangement track into the upper portion of the Bar ruler to set the cycle region.

In addition to setting the cycle region graphically, you can set it by directly inputting the measure numbers into the position display of the Transport. You might also define several key commands to set the cycle region. If you do a key command search for *locator*, you will find a host of key commands that can set the cycle regions by objects, markers, and so on. Very few of these key commands are defined by default; it's up to you to decide which ones you want to use and then to define them. Also, don't forget about the commands regarding locators that are available in the Navigate menu, covered earlier in this chapter, including Auto Set Locators capabilities.

Using Skip Cycle

Skip Cycle is a variation of Cycle mode. Skip Cycle mode allows you to define a region that will be skipped over rather than used during playback. You can create a Skip Cycle region by using the Swap Left and Right Locators key command, =, or by right-clicking in the Bar ruler and selecting Swap Left and Right Locators in the contextual menu that opens. A Skip Cycle region is indicated by a gold striped black bar at the top of the Bar ruler, as shown in Figure 6.46.

Figure 6.46 Here a Skip Cycle region is defined between measures 2 and 6.
© Apple Inc.

When a Skip Cycle region is defined, Logic simply ignores that section of the project during playback or editing. The playhead jumps instantly from the beginning of the Skip Cycle region to the end and continues as if the section did not exist. When Skip Cycle mode is turned off, by turning on Cycle mode or by swapping the locators again, the region plays back as normal.

Looping Regions in the Tracks Area

We've already touched on the Loop parameter in the Region Inspector, and you've seen some of the commands related to looping in the Tracks area local menus. If you loop a region, Logic repeats that region again as soon as it ends. You will be able to see this visually on the track lane as well; boxes with grayed-out audio overviews or MIDI events the identical length of your original region will emanate from the end of your original region. This is illustrated in Figure 6.47.

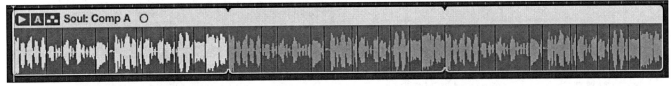

Figure 6.47 The boxes with grayed-out audio overviews attached to the take folder region offer visual feedback on the track lane that the region is looped.
© Apple Inc.

Looping Regions with the Loop Tool

The traditional method or old style of looping in Logic consists of selecting the Loop checkbox in the Region Inspector. You can also use the Toggle Loop command (default key command: L) to turn the Loop parameter on and off for a selected region. Once looping is engaged, boxes representing loops—repeats of your region—will extend from the selected region until they reach either the end of the project or another region in the same track lane. If you don't want the loop to extend to the end of the project, the old-style method of controlling how many measures a region will loop is to use the Pencil tool to create an empty region at some point in the track after a region that you want to loop, or create a new region with different events or audio at the desired location if that suits your arrangement. Then, when you turn on looping for the original region, it loops until it reaches that next region, and then the looping ends. As you move that new region around, you can extend or reduce the number of loops for that original region. You will also notice that as you extend or reduce the length of your project, those loops that extend to the end of your project will be extended or reduced along with the project length. You could also cut loops using the Marquee tool (covered in the section "Splitting and Resizing Regions Using the Marquee Tool" later in this chapter).

You can also loop regions directly in the Tracks area, which for distinction's sake I will call "new-style" looping. Users of GarageBand or other ACID-loop–style applications will be familiar with this method of looping. For users unfamiliar with this kind of looping, you are in for a treat because it couldn't be easier. Here's how it works:

1. Move the cursor to the upper-right edge of a region. The pointer becomes the Loop tool, as shown in Figure 6.48.

Figure 6.48 When you move the cursor to the upper-right edge of a region, it becomes the Loop tool.
© Apple Inc.

2. Drag the loop out as many measures as you wish (see Figure 6.49). The cursor info tag will indicate which region you are looping, where you are in your project, and how many times the region has been repeated. Note that the resolution to which you can drag a loop is determined by the Snap value, which is covered in the section "The Snap and Drag Menus" later in this chapter.

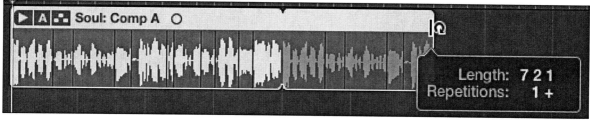

Figure 6.49 To loop your region, simply drag the region as far to the right as you would like your region to loop.
© Apple Inc.

That's it! Looping in Logic couldn't be simpler. If you want a loop to continue for an entire project or for so many measures that manually dragging the loop would be tedious, that's where the old style of looping comes in.

You can also use the Loop tool to edit any loop—old-style loops, new-style loops, and Apple Loops. If you simply move the mouse pointer to the upper third of a loop, it will turn into the Loop tool, as shown in Figure 6.50. You can then click on the loop to stop looping at that point. You can also drag the new end point exactly as you would a new-style loop. You can cut loops with the Loop tool regardless of whether they were looped using old- or new-style looping.

Figure 6.50 Moving the cursor to the upper third of any loop will turn the mouse pointer into the Loop tool. You can then split and drag the loop.
© Apple Inc.

If you want to operate on a loop that resides on a track in which the automation lane is showing, you must Option-drag the loop. This is because when the automation lane is in view, there is a very small area that must be shared by both looping and resizing functions. You will read more about resizing and track automation later in this chapter.

NOTE: One more time, just to be clear: There is no actual distinction made by the application between what I call "old-style" and "new-style" looping. I simply refer to these methods as such for the sake of upgraders who are familiar with traditional looping in Logic but unfamiliar with the updates to looping since Logic Pro 7.

Clicking on a loop selects the looped region and all its loops. Clicking and holding on a loop turns the cursor into a Hand tool, allowing you to grab and move the looped region. Clicking and holding on a loop's track turns the cursor to a rubber band, like normal. The Marquee tool is capable of making "rubber band" selections of portions of a loop.

The local Edit > Convert > Loops to Regions command, key command Control+L, changes all the loops from a selected region into new regions that are identical to the original region. The Edit > Convert > MIDI Loops to Aliases command changes all the loops from a selected region into new regions that contain no data but point to the original region.

TIP: Len Sasso, author of *Emagic Logic Tips and Tricks*, offered some tips on using folder tracks earlier in the chapter. He also has some tips specifically regarding using folder tracks for looping: "When you want to create a composite loop incorporating several regions," he explains, "pack the regions into a folder and loop the folder." In fact, if you use Propellerhead's ReCycle (REX) files, you will see that they use this same concept: REX files in Logic are folders packed with individual audio slices.

Creating Regions

At first, your tracks will not have regions on their track lanes. There are basically three ways for you to create regions in the Tracks area:

  ▷ You can record audio or MIDI onto your various tracks. (Refer to Chapter 5 for more information on recording.) Logic will create audio regions and MIDI regions consisting of what you record.
  ▷ You can use the Pencil tool to create regions. If you click with the Pencil tool in a MIDI track lane, an empty region one bar long will be created. If you click with the Pencil tool in an audio track, you will be presented with the Open File dialog box for you to choose an audio file to add to the Tracks area at the current cursor location. The created audio region will be the length of the audio file you select.
  ▷ You can create regions in the Tracks area by adding audio or MIDI files to your project by dragging them into the main window. You can drag MIDI files from the Finder directly into Logic or from the All Files Browser (discussed in Chapter 12, "Working with and Sharing Files"), and you can drag audio files from the Finder or the Project Audio Browser (discussed in Chapter 7). You can also use the Add to Tracks command in the Project Audio Browser.

Editing in the Tracks Area

After you create your Track list and you've got some regions in the Tracks area, you most likely will want to edit and rearrange them. As you would imagine, the Tracks area is ideal for rearranging regions. Every region displayed in the track lanes of the Tracks area is ready and waiting for you to manipulate using Logic Pro's powerful tools and features.

Making Selections

The first step in editing your project is to select one or more regions or portions of regions that you want to edit further. Selected regions will have lighter outlines and title bars. Figure 6.51 shows a number of selected regions in the Tracks area.

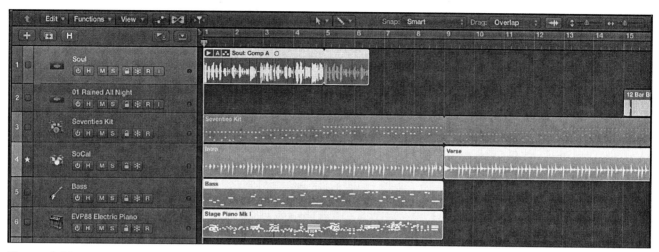

Figure 6.51 The Tracks area with several regions selected. The lighter color and title bar indicate which regions are selected.
© Apple Inc.

Logic offers a number of methods for selecting regions.

Selecting Regions Using Commands

You can use many different commands to select regions, such as the Select submenu commands. These commands were previously covered with the local Edit menu earlier in this chapter. If you do a search in the Key Commands window, you will also find many selection commands, some of which are unassigned.

The two most common key commands for selecting regions are the Select Next Region and Select Previous Region commands. The key commands move you to the following or previous region, using the right or left arrow, respectively. These commands select one region at a time. If you want to use the arrow keys to select more than one region, hold down the Shift key while navigating to the various regions with the arrow keys.

Selecting Regions Using the Pointer Tool

Clicking on any region in the Tracks area with the Pointer tool will select that region. Remember that if you have Track Automation view enabled, you will need to click on the top solid bar of any region you wish to select. Otherwise, you will inadvertently edit your automation. To select multiple regions, even on different tracks, Shift-click them. Clicking a track header selects all the regions on that track. Selecting multiple track headers by Shift-clicking them selects all the regions on the selected tracks. You can, however, disable this region selection behavior by deselecting the Select Regions on Track Selection checkbox in the Editing tab of the General Preferences window.

Another method of selecting regions is by using the Pointer tool to "rubber band" a group of regions. To do this, simply click the Pointer tool on an empty spot in the Tracks area near the objects you want to select and then drag a selection square over all the regions you want to select.

Making Selections with the Marquee Tool

The Marquee tool is unique in that instead of selecting a number of entire regions, it can select a *portion* of regions, as shown in Figure 6.52.

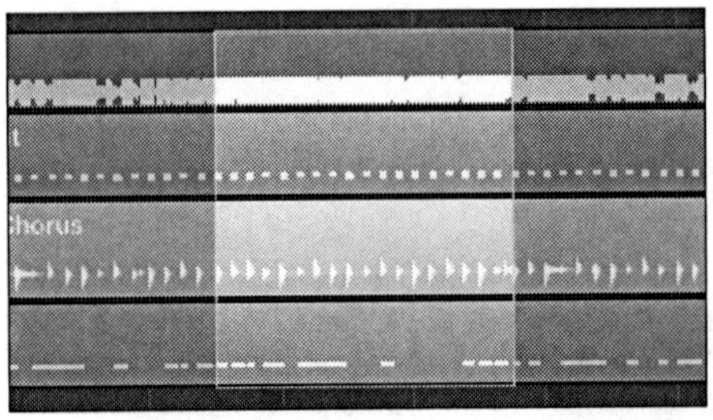

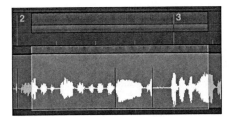

Figure 6.52 A marquee selection spanning a number of regions and tracks. The area in which the colors of the tracks are highlighted is the marquee selection.
© Apple Inc.

To use the Marquee tool, select the tool and then drag it over a portion of one or more regions. When you release the mouse button, the colors inside your selection area will be lightened; this is the selected area. You can press Control+Shift while selecting a marquee area to snap to either ticks or samples depending on your zoom level. Pressing Control while selecting a marquee area will snap to the current Division setting. By pressing Shift, you can adjust the borders of the current marquee selection from either the left or the right side (not up or down). Also, remember you can set the locators by your Marquee selection. When you have made a marquee selection and you click Play, playback of only the marquee selection occurs. If you click Record, the marquee area becomes an auto-punch region, and a red autopunch bar will be displayed under the Cycle area of the Bar ruler.

You also have the option to display the Marquee ruler, which sits below the Bar ruler and displays a gray-dotted bar over the area selected with the Marquee tool. To enable the Marquee ruler, select the local View > Marquee Ruler option.

Figure 6.53 shows the Marquee ruler and an area of a region selected with the Marquee tool.

Figure 6.53 The Marquee ruler displays a gray-dotted bar over the area selected with the Marquee tool. Note the auto-punch region beneath the Cycle area of the Bar ruler. Clicking Record when you have a marquee selection creates auto-punch locators.
© Apple Inc.

You can use the marquee stripe for a quick visual reference for the length of a selection you have made with the Marquee tool or for precise manipulation of the edges of the marquee selection. If you create a marquee selection by clicking and dragging on the Marquee ruler, all tracks are highlighted by the marquee selection. To adjust the borders of a marquee area with the Marquee ruler, drag the cursor to the edge you wish to alter. The cursor will become the Resize tool. The resolution you can achieve with the Resize tool depends on the Snap setting, which is covered in the section "The Snap and Drag Menus" later in this chapter. You can also move the marquee stripe across the Marquee ruler. Just place the cursor over the marquee stripe, and the cursor will change to a Hand tool. You can then drag the marquee stripe.

Almost every editing function that is available when you select entire regions is available when you select portions of regions with the Marquee tool. If you find yourself regularly working with the Marquee tool, consider selecting the Marquee Tool Click Zones checkbox in the Pointer Tool in Tracks Provides area of the Editing tab in the General Preferences window, shown in Figure 6.54. When you have Marquee Tool Click Zones enabled, the Pointer tool automatically becomes a Marquee tool in the bottom half of a region.

Pointer Tool in Tracks Provides: ☑ Fade Tool click zones
☑ Marquee Tool click zones

Figure 6.54 Selecting the Marquee Tool Click Zones checkbox in the Editing tab of the General Preferences window converts your Pointer tool to a Marquee tool automatically when you hover the cursor over the lower half of a region. © Apple Inc.

The More Tools, the Merrier: If you're comfortable with having a wide variety of contextual tools available when using the Pointer tool in the Tracks area, you should select both the Marquee Tool Click Zones checkbox and the Fade Tool Click Zones checkbox, which are found in the Pointer Tool in Tracks Provides section of the General Preferences Editing tab. This gives you the flexibility to have up to six tools at your immediate disposal in the Tracks area:

▶ **Pointer tool:** The Pointer tool, or whichever tool you have assigned using the left-most Tool menu in the Tracks area, is your default tool.

▶ **Command-click secondary tool:** The always available Command-click tool offers a secondary tool option.

▶ **Right mouse button:** When the Right Mouse Button menu in the Editing tab of the General Preferences window is set to Is Assignable to a Tool, you gain access to a third Tool menu. Assign your right-click tool using this third Tool menu.

▶ **Fade tool:** The Pointer tool becomes a Fade tool at the upper corner of audio region boundaries when the Fade Tool Click Zones checkbox is selected.

▶ **Marquee tool:** The Pointer tool becomes a Marquee tool in the bottom half of regions when the Marquee Tool Click Zones checkbox is selected.

▶ **Option-drag Zoom tool:** If you click-drag in an empty part of the Tracks area while pressing the Option key, the cursor becomes the Zoom tool. You can then lasso an area, and the Tracks area will zoom in to the lassoed area.

That doesn't even include the different Pointer modes like the Resize, Loop, and Hand tools! Even if you have your right-click preference set to open contextual menus, you can have five varied tools at your immediate disposal, plus the Tool menu a quick right-click away. As much as I encourage you to learn and use key commands, I also recommend using these different Pointer Tool in Tracks options along with a secondary tool setting and the Option-drag to Zoom facilities. The quicker you can work in Logic, the less time you spend not being creative!

Adjusting the Marquee Borders by Transient

One extremely powerful feature of the Marquee tool is that it can help you arrange and edit regions by transient. As mentioned during the discussion of the beat-mapping track in Chapter 4, transients are musically relevant peaks in audio material. You may want your marquee selection to fall not on the measure line but on the beat, or the upstroke of an acoustic guitar strum, or the accented stroke of a violin bow, and so on.

Previously, if you wanted to do this, you had no choice but to try to visually find the transients by looking at the zoomed-in audio region and then painstakingly set the marquee start and end on those transients. If you then realized that you set your marquee too long and you wanted your selection to be one transient shorter, or your marquee selection needed to be a couple transients longer, you had to grab the start or end of the marquee and try to visually reset it again. As you can imagine, this took a long time and wasn't always accurate. Fortunately, Logic Pro includes these four key commands:

▷ **Move Marquee End to Previous Transient:** This sets the end of the current marquee selection to the transient before the current marquee end. The key command is left arrow.

▷ **Move Marquee End to Next Transient:** This sets the end of the current marquee selection to the transient after the current marquee end. The key command is right arrow.

▷ **Move Marquee Start to Previous Transient:** This sets the start of the current marquee selection to the transient before the current marquee start. The key command is Shift+left arrow.

▷ **Move Marquee Start to Next Transient:** This sets the start of the current marquee selection to the transient after the current marquee start. The key command is Shift+right arrow.

These commands allow you to quickly shift the start and end points of the marquee selection to the transients you wish. Combined with the editing commands, these make the Marquee an even more precise editing tool.

The Tracks Area Grid

Most of what you'll be doing in the Tracks area will be editing and moving regions. For many users, the playhead and the Bar ruler offer enough of a guide. If you want more obvious guidelines, you're in luck. If you select View > Grid (or press Control+G), you will activate the Tracks area grid. This grid puts guidelines at every bar of your project. The resolution of the grid depends on your current zoom level and the numerator of the time signature of your project. Figure 6.55 shows a project with the grid turned on.

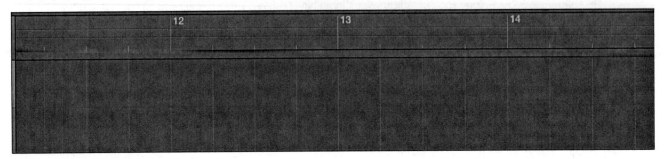

Figure 6.55 Here is a section of a Tracks area that has the grid activated. Due to the zoom level and the 4/4 time signature, you can see a grid line every 1/4 note.
© Apple Inc.

The grid is a purely visual tool. It does not affect region movement or editing at all, but it can assist you in moving regions and performing edits on specific grid positions. If the grid makes working in the Tracks area easier for you, turn it on whenever you need it.

Zooming in the Tracks Area

As you begin moving and editing regions, you'll find that you sometimes want an overview of a portion of the project, while other times you want to focus in on a very small area. To do this, you'll want to zoom in and out.Chapter 3 discussed using the zoom sliders in the upper-right of the Tracks area to adjust the size of the track lanes. Using the horizontal zoom increases or decreases the number of bars that are visible onscreen at a time. When your project is fully zoomed out, you can easily fit the entire length of the project on your monitor at once for arranging regions, and if you zoom in all the way, you'll be able to view each individual sample of your audio to enable very precise editing.

By now, it should be no surprise that Logic offers a full complement of key commands to facilitate zooming in addition to the zoom sliders. By default, pressing Command+arrow zooms in or out, horizontally or vertically, depending on the arrow key. There are also key commands to zoom in and out for individual tracks, to change instantly to user-definable zoom settings, to zoom to fit selection, and more. Be sure to do a search for *zoom* in the Key Commands window; you'll find a lot of fantastic timesaving key commands just waiting to be assigned.

Finally, you can select Auto Track Zoom either via the key command Control+Z or by choosing View > Auto Track Zoom. This automatically increases the vertical zoom of the selected track for as long as that track is selected. This command is useful if you want to keep your tracks vertically short to fit more tracks on the screen, but you want the specific track you are working on to be larger for more precise moves and edits.

Splitting and Resizing Regions

Two operations that go hand in hand with zooming are splitting and resizing regions. You can zoom out or in to get the optimal view of a section of project and then edit that section to suit your taste. This is one of the most important uses for sequencers, and Logic's main window offers users powerful and intuitive tools and commands for this purpose. This section describes some of the most popular commands, functions, and tips for splitting and resizing regions.

Splitting Regions

Logic offers a number of different functions and methods to split one region into two or more regions. Perhaps the most graphically intuitive way to split a region into two parts is to select the Scissors tool from the Tool menu and then click on a portion of a region. Logic then splits that region into two regions at the point at which you clicked. Figure 6.56 shows a region being split in two by the Scissors tool.

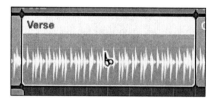 

Figure 6.56 Splitting a region with the Scissors tool. Left: the Scissors tool over a Drummer region in the Tracks area. Right: the resulting two Drummer regions.
© Apple Inc.

If you try to split a MIDI region that has a note that overlaps the split by more than 1/16 note, Logic will display a dialog box asking whether you want to keep, shorten, or split those notes. Select the option you prefer in the dialog box.

> ▷ Choosing Keep leaves the note lengths unaltered; you will simply have notes in the first region that play past the end of the region. (If you select the Clip Length option in the track's Region Inspector, however, the note will still be cut off.)
> ▷ If you select Shorten, the overlapping notes are truncated at the end of the first region.
> ▷ Selecting Split creates two notes to represent the original overlapping note: one note in the first region that is truncated at the end of the first region, and a new note at the beginning of the second region that consists of the remainder of the original note.

Logic also enables you to split a region into multiple regions using the Scissors tool. If you hold down the Option key while splitting your region, the Scissors tool will appear with a plus sign (+) above the teeth of the scissors, and it will split the region into multiple regions of equal size. Figure 6.57 illustrates this.

 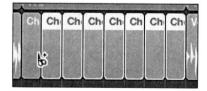

Figure 6.57 Using the Scissors tool to split a region into multiple regions. Left: the Scissors tool over a bar into a Drummer region. Right: the results of clicking with the Scissors tool while pressing the Option key.
© Apple Inc.

You can also use a number of commands to split regions. As explained, the Edit > Split submenu offers the commands Split Region by Locators and Split Region by Playhead, also available in the Toolbar. These commands split a selected region by using the locators in the Bar ruler or by using the playhead, respectively. You can also use the key commands for these commands, as well as the key command for Split Region by Rounded Playhead Position, which splits the region at the bar line nearest to the playhead.

NOTE: In the Editing tab of the General Preferences window is a SmartLoop Handling of Scissors and "Split by Playhead" checkbox. If you have this checkbox selected and you split a region that has been looped, the loop immediately following the split region will be turned into a copy of the original region and the original region will be split. This is a special feature in Logic called SmartLoop. Logic does not assume that just because you want to split a looped region you necessarily intend to split every single loop that comes after it. By creating a copy, Logic automatically keeps the loop identical to how it was before you split the looped region, giving you a "new" original for the following loops. This procedure of creating a copy, looping the copy, and then splitting the original used to require a number of steps and a fair amount of time. Now, Logic takes care of it automatically for you!

Resizing Regions

Splitting isn't the only way you can alter a region in the Tracks area; you can also resize it. Logic offers a few simple ways to resize regions. The most straightforward way is simply to move the pointer to the lower half of the edge of a region. The Pointer tool will become the Resize tool; you can then drag to the right or left to expand or shorten the region. The info tag beneath the cursor will display your action and position. Figure 6.58 shows a region being resized in this manner.

Figure 6.58 When you move the Pointer tool to the lower half of the right or left edge of a region, it turns into the Resize tool. You can drag right or left to lengthen or shorten selected regions. The info tag displays what you are doing.
© Apple Inc.

You can also resize multiple regions this way: Simply select a group of regions and then click and drag the lower-right corner of one of the selected regions to resize it. Logic will lengthen or shorten all the regions by the amount you adjusted the region that you clicked. If you want to adjust multiple regions to the same absolute length (meaning the same number of bars), even if they were originally of varying length, press the Option+Shift keys while resizing.

There are some limitations to your ability to resize regions, however. You cannot shorten a region out of existence—Logic will always retain at least a sliver of the region. Also, if you are expanding an audio region, you cannot lengthen it past the end of the audio file itself, because there is no audio after that point. However, you can expand a MIDI region past existing MIDI data.

If you shorten a boundary of a region that includes data, Logic will no longer consider that data part of that region. The data will not be deleted or modified in any way, however, and if you later lengthen the region, the original data will still be there, exactly as it was before you shortened the region.

Sometimes, however, when you adjust the length of a region, you may want to compress or expand the data inside to fit the new region boundary. If you have selected a region, you can do this by pressing the Option key while dragging the right region boundary.

You can also use two different commands to resize an audio region and compress or stretch its contents to fit: Time Stretch Region Length to Locators and Time Stretch Region Length to Nearest Bar, both available from the Edit local menu. These commands invoke the chosen time stretching algorithm to adjust the length of your audio region. Obviously, the Time Stretch Region Length to Locators command would require having Auto Set Locators by Region disabled. Compressing or stretching audio using any of these approaches is different from using Flex Time on an audio region. Flex Time editing is covered in detail in the section "Using Flex Time and Pitch" later in this chapter.

Other local menu functions, such as Remove Overlaps and Crop Outside Locators, are also useful for resizing regions. Review the subsections in the section "The Edit Menu" earlier in this chapter to learn about these commands. There are also unassigned key commands that will allow you to nudge the length of regions shorter or longer by varying degrees. If you find any of them useful, remember to assign key commands to them.

Splitting and Resizing Regions Using the Marquee Tool

The Marquee tool is a special tool—perhaps one of the most powerful editing tools available in Logic Pro—and thus gets its own section here. As described earlier in the section "Making Selections with the Marquee Tool," you can use the Marquee tool to select portions of regions, not just entire regions. Once you have made a selection with the Marquee tool, you can perform most region-based edit options, such as the following:

▷ **Erase:** Press Delete or click with the Eraser tool.

▷ **Move and Copy (with the Pointer tool):** To move a selection, drag it with the Pointer tool. To copy it, press the Option key while dragging the selection using the Pointer tool. (See the upcoming section "Moving and Copying Regions" for more information.)

▷ **Cut and Copy (with key commands):** Press Command+X for cut and Command+C to copy.

▷ **Paste:** To paste the region at the playhead, press Command+V.

▷ **Cut (at the selection border):** Click inside the selection with the Scissors tool.

▷ **Mute:** This can be done via a key command or the Mute tool. Both approaches result in a cut at the selection borders with the regions inside the selection borders muted.

▷ **Solo:** This can be done via a key command or the Solo tool. Both approaches result in a cut at the selection borders with the regions inside the selection being soloed.

Moving and Copying Regions

Now that you've split and resized some regions in the Tracks area, you probably want to arrange them! Moving regions around is certainly one of the central functions of the Tracks area, and it couldn't be simpler. Just select a region or regions, hold down the mouse button, drag your selection anywhere you want, and then drop the region or regions in the new location. Done!

Of course, Logic gives you many more options for moving regions. If you want to restrict the movement to either the horizontal or vertical axis (depending upon whether you initially move the region horizontally or vertically), there is a Limit Dragging to One Direction in Tracks checkbox in the Editing tab of the General Preferences window, which you access by choosing Logic Pro > Preferences > General. You can also toggle this feature on and off by pressing the Shift key while dragging. (In other words, if you've checked the preference, pressing Shift will allow normal movement, and if the preference is unchecked, you can press Shift to limit region movement to one axis.)

If you press Control while dragging a region, you can move the region in one-division increments. If you press Control+Shift while dragging a region, you can move the region in increments of one tick or one sample, depending on your zoom setting. Don't forget the various local Edit > Move commands covered earlier in this chapter. There are also unassigned key commands that you can use to nudge a region forward or backward by varying amounts. Search for *nudge* in the Key Commands window to find them. If you find any of them useful, be sure to assign keys to them.

Sometimes you may want to duplicate the data in a given region or regions in another location. Logic allows you to copy regions very easily. To move a copy of your selected region(s) instead of the original region(s), press the Option key while moving the region, leaving the original regions in their original positions. If you want the copied regions to be aliases (see upcoming tip) that point to the original regions instead of actual copies, press Option+Shift when moving the regions. You can also make multiple duplicates that will follow your selected region or regions by using the Repeat command either by pressing Command+R or by choosing the local Edit > Repeat option. This command presents you with a dialog box in which you may select the number of copies you want and specify whether you want them to be aliases or copies.

Moving and copying operations snap automatically to the Snap menu setting, discussed in "The Snap and Drag Menus" section later in this chapter. Also, remember that you can use the arrangement track to move and copy regions. Refer back to Chapter 4 for more information on using the arrangement track.

> **TIP:** Copying a region creates a completely new region with its own MIDI notes or audio data. It is a duplicate of the original region, but you can edit the original region without affecting the copy, and vice versa. An *alias*, however, looks like a copy of the original region, but it doesn't contain any data of its own. Instead, it is just a reference to the original region. That means any editing you do to the original will be reflected in the alias.

Aliases are perfect for when you want to ensure that each instance of your copied region exactly reflects the original region, because any edits and changes to the original affect all the aliases as well. If you want to edit an alias without affecting the original, you can always turn your alias into a real copy.

Editing Multiple Regions

There will probably be times when you will want to perform the same edits on multiple tracks. For example, you may want to remove a couple of bars from a multitrack drum performance and a guitar part and then drag the resulting regions one bar closer to each other. This kind of editing could take a bit of time, particularly if the tracks aren't all in order in the Track list. Fortunately, Logic allows you to group channel strips for just this kind of work.

To assign channel strips to a group, do the following:

1. Click the Group slot on a channel strip you wish to assign to a group. The Group slot is the empty dark-gray box between the Output and Automation Mode boxes on each channel strip.
2. Select an available group or create a new one in the menu that appears, which is shown in Figure 6.59. When you select a group for the first time, the Group Settings window shown in Figure 6.60 will open.

Figure 6.59 The Groups menu. You can assign channel strips to groups in this list.
© Apple Inc.

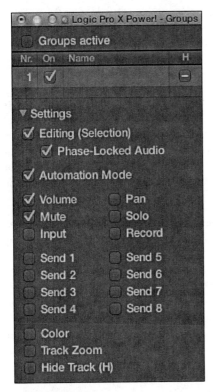

Figure 6.60 The Group Settings window.
© Apple Inc.

3. Select the Editing (Selection) option and close the Group Settings window. You can now assign other channel strips to that same group.

When you perform an edit on any single track assigned to a channel strip in the group, the same edit is performed on all tracks in the group. If you select an area of any region on a group track with the Marquee tool, the same area will be selected on all group tracks. If you select a whole region on a group track, all regions on group tracks that overlap the selected region anywhere along its length will be selected. You can then move or delete these regions collectively.

Groups can be used for many other functions, as you can see in Figure 6.60. Groups, the Group Settings window, and the Group box in the Inspector are covered in greater detail in Chapter 11.

Comping in Logic

Comping, or compiling pieces of different performances of the same material into one cohesive performance, used to involve a lot of work—keeping track of different performances on different tracks, selecting which parts to keep, editing sections into new regions, keeping the new edited bits organized, and so forth. Logic Pro gives you an incredibly powerful set of features that not only simplify the management of different takes, as explored in Chapter 5, but that also make creating audio comps from those takes a breeze thanks to Quick Swipe Comping.

Creating and Editing Comps

To begin, open an audio take folder by clicking its disclosure triangle at the upper-left corner. Next, enable Quick Swipe Comping by clicking the Quick Swipe Comping button at the upper-left corner of your audio region, by selecting Quick Swipe Comping in the Take Folder menu, or by using the key command Option+Q. Now you can use the Pointer tool to select sections from different takes. As you select a comp area from one take, that same area in every other take is deselected. Also, when you select different pieces of your takes to create your comp, the waveform in the top-most track in the audio take folder is updated to reflect those selections. Figure 6.61 shows an open audio take folder that has takes that have been comped. Note the cursor under the Take 4 heading—that's the cursor you use to create and edit comps.

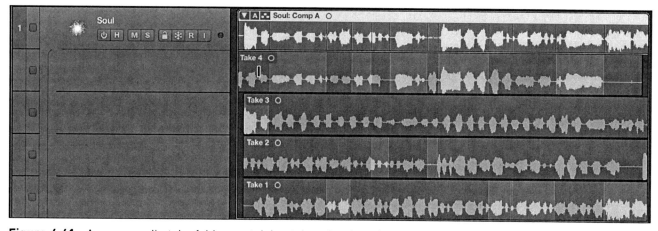

Figure 6.61 An open audio take folder containing takes that have been comped. Selecting an area of one take deselects that same area on all other takes, and the waveform in the top-most track updates to reflect the selection. © Apple Inc.

You can also create a take folder using the Functions > Folder > Pack Take Folder command (key command Control+Command+F). When you use this command on selected regions on different tracks, they are packed into a take folder using the channel strip of the top-most track. You can then create comps in your new take folder, but if you use this command on regions that are on the same track lane, then a comp is automatically created.

You can change the length of a comp section by dragging its border. If there are any comp sections that share that border with the section you are editing, they will automatically be resized. If you press Shift while shortening a comp section, adjacent comp sections will not be lengthened. You can also move a comp section. If you drag a comp section, you can move the entire section left or right. Any adjacent comp sections will be automatically resized.

When you create a comp, the various sections that make up the comp are automatically crossfaded per the settings in the Crossfades for Merge and Take Comping section of the General tab of the Audio Preferences window. You can access the Crossfades for Merge and Take Comping preferences by selecting Logic Pro X > Preferences > Audio. Figure 6.62 shows the Crossfades for Merge and Take Comping section of the General tab of the Audio Preferences window.

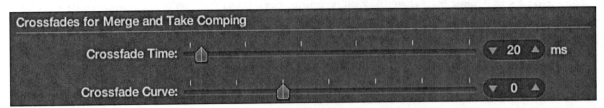

Figure 6.62 The Crossfades for Merge and Take Comping section of the General tab of the Audio Preferences window. You can determine how Logic crossfades the sections of any comps you create with the parameters in this section.
© Apple Inc.

The Crossfade Time parameter determines how long in milliseconds each crossfade will take. The Crossfade Curve parameter allows you to control the kind of curve Logic will use to crossfade your comps. A setting of 0 will give you linear crossfades, while positive or negative values will give you symmetrical, exponential fades.

After you have selected the various sections of your different takes that will make up your comp, you can quickly replace an individual section of your comp with the same section of a different take by clicking in the desired area of the desired take. If the take folder is closed, you can do this by right-clicking on the section in the take folder. A menu like the one shown in Figure 6.63 will appear, in which you can select the alternate take for use in that section.

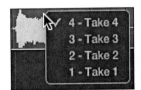

Figure 6.63 If you want to replace the take used for a particular section of your comp in a closed take folder with the audio from another take, simply right-click on that section in the take folder. You can select a different take from the menu that appears.
© Apple Inc.

To remove a comp section, simply Shift-click on that section on its parent take. If you Shift-click on a take's header, it will remove all comp sections from that take.

Treating Takes as Regions

Suppose you have found the exact comp you want from a set of takes, but there's one comp section that's just a little late. You can easily slice a take into sections via either of two commands found in a right-click contextual menu specific to audio takes folders—Slice at Comp Selection Borders and Trim to Active Comp Sections. Both of these commands fundamentally create new regions from the selected take that reside in the takes folder. The Slice at Comp Selection Borders command slices the take into separate regions defined by the borders of any comp selections for the particular take. Trim to Active Comp Sections slices the take into separate regions too, but it removes any regions that are not used as comps. You can see the effect of both of these commands in Figure 6.64.

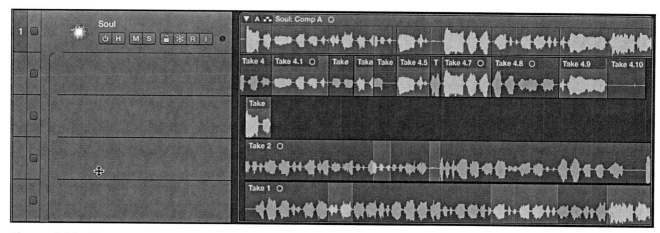

Figure 6.64 The top take in this takes folder, take 4, after using the Slice at Comp Selection Borders command has been divided into 11 regions. Five are derived from the comp sections from the take and six are from the remaining sections of the take. The next take has been reduced to one region derived from its comp section from the take using the Trim to Active Comp Sections command.
© Apple Inc.

You can now move these regions freely within the take folder using the mouse or any nudge commands. Note that you must turn off Quick Swipe Comping mode to move any of these take regions.

Saving Comps

You can store multiple comps created with the same take folder. Once you are satisfied with your comp, click on the triangle in the upper-right corner of the take folder to open the Take Folder menu and select New Comp. A new, freely editable comp will be created, and your previous comp will be saved. If you wish to rename a saved comp, open the Take Folder menu and select the desired comp. Then open the Take Folder menu again and select the Rename Comp command. This opens the Rename Comp dialog box, discussed with the Rename Take dialog box in Chapter 5.

Flattening and Merging Comps

After you have comped your takes and you have decided that you have a comp you want to use, you have the option to either flatten or flatten and merge your comp. Both of these commands are found in the Take Folder menu and are assignable to key commands. The Flatten command replaces your take folder with individual regions that encompass each take selection. Figure 6.65 shows regions that have been created by the Flatten command.

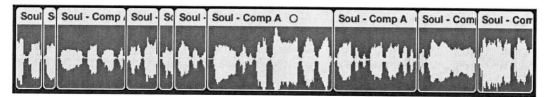

Figure 6.65 Regions created by the Flatten command in the Take Folder menu.
© Apple Inc.

The Flatten and Merge command takes the Flatten command one step further by merging the individual take selections into one region and creating a new audio file for that region. Figure 6.66 shows the effect of the Flatten and Merge command on the same comp used in Figure 6.65. What makes these commands so powerful is that the new regions created by these commands are fully editable and movable, just like any other region.

Figure 6.66 This region, created with the Flatten and Merge command, is from the same comp used in Figure 6.65.
© Apple Inc.

Exporting and Unpacking Takes and Comps

There are a few more commands for manipulating takes and comps that you may find useful: Export to New Track, Unpack, and Unpack to New Tracks. All three commands can be found in the Take Folder menu, and the two Unpack commands can also be found in the Functions > Folder submenu. Both Unpack commands place the contents of the take folder on individual tracks, getting rid of the parent take folder in the process. Takes are unpacked to individual tracks as whole regions, and comps are unpacked to individual tracks as regions representing each take selection. The Unpack command (Control+Command+U) places all takes and comps on their own track lanes, and they all use the parent take folder track's channel strip. The take or comp that was active when the folder was unpacked remains active, and all other takes and comps are muted. The Unpack to New Tracks command (Shift+Control+Command+U) functions like the Unpack command, except each new track is given its own channel strip with the configuration of the original take folder's channel strip. Figure 6.67 shows an unpacked take folder.

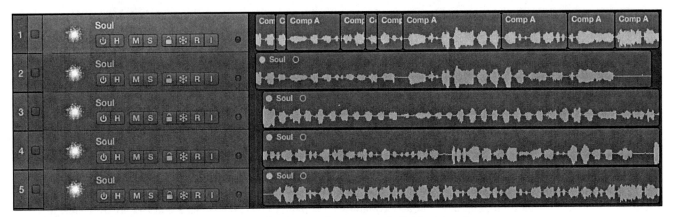

Figure 6.67 Unpacking a take folder sends all takes and comps to individual tracks.
© Apple Inc.

The Export to New Tracks command allows you to export an individual take or comp from the take folder to a new track with its own channel strip, but using the same settings as the channel strip of the parent track, while maintaining the existence of the parent take folder. You just need to select a take or comp and then select the Export to New Tracks command (or assign a key command), and the selected take or comp will be exported to a new track directly below the parent take folder in the Track list. If you export a comp, the take selections will be exported as individual regions.

The Snap and Drag Menus

To the left of the Tracks area Tool menu are two very important menus: Snap and Drag (see Figure 6.68). Both of these menus affect the way you can move regions around the Tracks area in Logic Pro. The following sections explain each menu in more detail.

Figure 6.68 The Snap and Drag menus of the main window.
© Apple Inc.

The Snap Menu

The Snap menu affects precisely where a region you move will "snap," or be affixed, in the Tracks area. You have a number of options for snap resolutions in this menu, designed to give you the ultimate say on where you want Logic to place your region. Your Snap menu options are as follows:

▷ **Smart:** Smart snap determines the snap resolution based on the zoom level of the Tracks area. For example, if you are zoomed out to see all 200 bars of your project, if you move a region, Smart snap will snap to even bars. However, if you are zoomed in so you can accurately see 1/32 notes, Smart snap will snap to 1/32 notes. The limit is the sample level.

▷ **Bar:** This option will always snap every region you move in one-bar increments relative to the region's start position, regardless of zoom level. If your region's position is 1 1 2 67, dragging your region one bar to the right will result in a position of 2 1 2 67.

▷ **Beat:** This option will snap to the denominator of your time signature (which determines the beat) relative to the region's start position, regardless of the zoom level. For example, if your project is in 4/4 time, Beat snap will snap your regions to 1/4-note increments; if your project is in 6/8 time, Beat snap will snap to 1/8-note increments. If you have time changes in your signature track, Beat snap will follow those signature changes and snap to the correct beat increment. As with the Bar snap setting, the Beat setting moves your regions by beats relative to the region's starting position.

▷ **Division:** This option snaps to the note value increments displayed in the Division display of the Transport window (1/16 notes, 1/8 notes, and so on) relative to the region's start position, regardless of the zoom level.

▷ **Ticks:** This option will always snap to ticks, regardless of the zoom level.

▷ **Frames:** Frames snap to SMPTE frames regardless of the zoom level. The exact snap will depend on which frame rate you have set in your synchronization options.

▷ **QF:** This option will always snap to quarter frames (one quarter the length of a full SMPTE frame) regardless of the zoom level.

▷ **Samples:** This option snaps at the sample level for extremely precise editing. You must be at extremely high zoom levels to use this snap resolution.

▷ **Snap Regions to Absolute Value:** Selecting this option snaps any move to the nearest absolute position described by the Snap value. In other words, if your region begins at 1 1 2 67, and your Snap value is set to Bar, any drag will move the region by an even bar. Moving the region to the immediate right would result in a position of 2 1 1 1.

▷ **Snap Regions to Relative Value:** Selecting this option snaps any move to the nearest relative position described by the Snap value. In other words, if your region begins at 1 1 2 67, and your Snap value is set to Bar, any drag will move the region by an even bar. Moving the region to the immediate right would result in a position of 2 1 2 67.

▷ **Snap Quick Swipe Comping to Absolute Value:** With this option enabled, all Quick Swipe Comping comps will be snapped to absolute values as defined by the Snap setting.

▷ **Snap Automation to Absolute Value:** With this option enabled, all automation, track-based or region-based, will snap to the absolute Snap value.

▷ **Automation Snap Offset:** Selecting this option enables Automation Snap Offset, which allows you to offset automation to compensate for any latency you may incur because of hardware, plug-in processing needs, or any other source of latency. Automation Snap Offset is covered in more detail in Chapter 10.

The Drag Menu

The majority of the Drag menu options determine how regions will react when two regions are moved into the same space, called *overlapping* (as the regions will then overlap each other). The exceptions are the Shuffle modes, which determine how regions respond when dragged or cut. The Drag menu options are as follows:

▷ **Overlap:** In this mode, two regions can overlap, with the region you are dragging covering the region being overlapped. Be careful not to lose one region behind another in this mode! You can always move regions to expose a region hidden due to overlapping.

▷ **No Overlap:** In this mode, two regions are not allowed to overlap. If you move a region into a position in which it would overlap another, the region that would be overlapped is simply resized. Remember, you can always resize regions back to their original state, so don't be afraid to use No Overlap mode.

▷ **X-Fade (Crossfade):** This mode acts like Overlap mode for MIDI regions. However, if you overlap two audio regions, Logic Pro will automatically generate a crossfade between the two regions, as shown in Figure 6.69. See Chapter 7 for more information on audio crossfades. You can see the crossfade graphically represented over the overlapping regions.

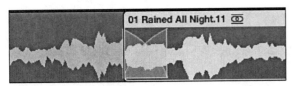

Figure 6.69 Logic will automatically create crossfades for overlapping audio regions with the Drag mode set to X-Fade.

© Apple Inc.

▷ **Shuffle R:** With Shuffle R mode enabled, if you move a region any distance to the right, it will automatically snap to the region to its immediate right, as shown in Figure 6.70. Obviously, if there is no other region to the right of the region you are moving, this will not happen.

Figure 6.70 As you can see from the two figures, in Shuffle R mode (left), if you move a region even a slight distance to the right, it will snap to the nearest region to its right. Shuffle L (right) mode is identical, but for regions you move left.

© Apple Inc.

▷ **Shuffle L:** Shuffle L mode operates identically to Shuffle R mode, except that if you move any region to the left, it will snap to the region to its immediate left. Shuffle L operates the same as the Pro Tools Shuffle mode. (Pro Tools does not have two shuffle modes—only one, which operates like Logic Pro's Shuffle L.)

Using Flex Time and Pitch

When you work with MIDI, moving around individual notes or groups of notes to improve their timing or pitch, tailoring them to exactly what you want, is easy. Indeed, there are many different tools you can use to accomplish this. Logic's many robust MIDI editors give you complete control over every detail of a MIDI performance, and time and pitch quantization let you easily align notes to a grid and a scale. Speeding up or slowing down a MIDI performance alters nothing about the pitch or timing of the performance.

Traditionally, audio has been much more difficult to deal with in these regards. Sampled sound is completely time reliant; making it "elastic" while maintaining an audio file's sound quality is challenging at best. Logic used to handle this solely through use of the Time and Pitch Machine, which is covered in Chapter 7. Basically, you needed to work very deliberately with your audio to get the desired effect without drastically altering the character of your recording. Then you had the issue of lining up parts of audio performances—in other words, quantizing the audio. Previously, to handle this kind of work, a lot of precision cutting and arranging of audio regions was necessary. For a single timing or pitch issue, this is no big deal, and this is still an easy and effective way to correct such a simple issue, but when you're dealing with entire sections that have "gotten off the grid," you're talking about a significant amount of tedious work.

Flex Time and Flex Pitch editing help make it much easier to manipulate the timing and pitch of your audio files and even give you the ability to actually quantize your audio to the same grid your MIDI performances use. Flex Time offers a number of different modes, which allow you to tailor its effect to each individual track you wish to flex, and it does this all nondestructively. Flex Pitch, on the other hand, is currently useful only on monophonic material.

Enabling Flex View

To work with Flex Time and Pitch, you need to enable Flex view. Flex view is a main window state that adds a Flex menu and Flex button to each audio track header, and therefore hides any automation lanes that may have been visible along with the automation controls in the track header. To enable Flex view, select Edit > Show Flex Pitch/Time, click the Flex button in the local Tracks area menus and buttons area, or use the key command Command+F. Figure 6.71 shows a track header with Flex view enabled.

Figure 6.71 Enabling Flex view gives you access to a Flex button and the Flex menu in each audio track header.
© Apple Inc.

The default Flex state for each audio track is off. You can enable Flex editing for a track by clicking its Flex button or by selecting a Flex mode. Clicking on the Flex menu reveals the different Flex modes available, which are assignable on a per-track basis (see Figure 6.72). When you select a Flex mode or enable the Flex button on a track for the first time, Logic will analyze the audio and create Flex markers—markers that generally denote meaningful points in your audio, such as higher amplitude transients, from which you can stretch or compress your audio. It will also analyze the pitch of your audio and create Flex Pitch bars for Flex Pitch editing. Transient markers are discussed in greater detail in Chapter 7; for now, the important thing to remember is that initially, Flex will use these Flex markers as the "pivot points" around which it will stretch or compress your audio. Flex Pitch bars are discussed later in this chapter.

Figure 6.72 The Flex button, highlighted in the upper-right corner of this image, lets you enable and disable Flex editing for the track. The Flex menu lets you choose the Flex mode you will use for the selected track.
© Apple Inc.

To perform Flex Pitch editing on your monophonic audio, select Flex Pitch in the Flex menu. The Flex Time modes are optimized for working on different types of material. Knowing which Flex Time mode to use with a particular kind of source will greatly improve the results you can achieve with Flex Time. I'll cover all the different Flex Time modes in more detail in the following sections; for now, here are brief descriptions of the different Flex Time modes:

▷ **Automatic:** This mode takes Logic's analysis of the material and automatically selects what it deems to be the appropriate Flex Time mode for the audio.
▷ **Monophonic:** Monophonic mode is great for flexing single vocal parts and other single-note passages.
▷ **Slicing:** Slicing mode allows you to flex your audio without applying any time compression or stretching. It works best with percussive sounds.
▷ **Rhythmic:** Rhythmic mode is great for flexing chordal rhythm parts.
▷ **Polyphonic:** Polyphonic mode is best used on chordal material, particularly less rhythmic material you want to flex.
▷ **Speed (FX):** Speed mode simply affects the playback speed of the source material. Your audio's pitch will be affected in Speed mode.
▷ **Tempophone (FX):** Tempophone mode provides an effect similar to a tape-based time-stretching device called the Tempophone.

You can also set the Flex mode in the Track Inspector of the selected track. There are added Flex parameters available in the Track Inspector for most Flex modes. In addition, remember that the only way to completely disable Flex mode for a track is to turn Flex mode off in the Track Inspector. You can disable Flex mode for individual regions by deselecting the Flex checkboxes in their Region Inspectors. Let's deal with the basics of Flex Time, such as creating and moving Flex markers, which are generally derived from transient markers. Then we'll look at each Flex Time mode's parameters in more detail. After that, we'll get into Flex Pitch editing.

Flex Time Editing Basics

The basics of Flex Time stretching or compressing are incredibly simple. You can stretch or compress an entire region if you wish, or you can just alter the timing of a small section of a region. Figure 6.73 shows a region with Flex view engaged. Note the white vertical lines—these are the transient markers.

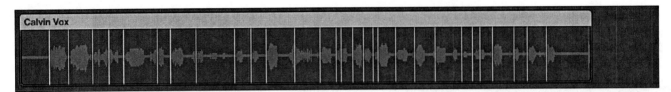

Figure 6.73 When Flex view is on, regions on tracks that have Flex Time enabled show vertical transient markers. Transient markers are points in your audio from which you can stretch or compress your audio.
© Apple Inc.

To stretch or compress an audio region on a Flex Time–enabled track, simply move your cursor to the beginning or end of the region and drag the region. Figure 6.74 shows the region in Figure 6.73 stretched to the next barline.

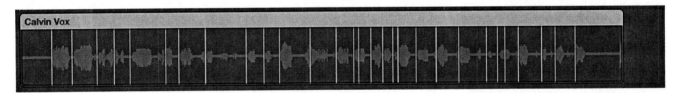

Figure 6.74 To stretch or compress an entire audio region, simply drag either end of the region.
© Apple Inc.

Stretching or compressing a section of your audio within a region is just as simple. First, drag the cursor into the top half of your Flex Time–enabled audio region. You'll notice the cursor changes to a vertical line. I'll discuss the function of that cursor mode in the next section. What you need to do now is drag the cursor near a transient marker. This changes the cursor from a simple vertical line to a line with a triangle at the top. When you see this cursor, shown on the left side of Figure 6.75, click your mouse, and a Flex marker will be created at the location of the selected transient marker, as shown on the right side of Figure 6.75.

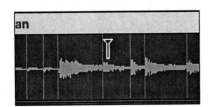 

Figure 6.75 Moving the cursor near a transient marker in a Flex Time–enabled audio region changes the cursor to a Flex marker tool. The Flex marker tool lets you change a transient marker to a Flex marker with a simple click of the mouse.
© Apple Inc.

Now you can drag the selected Flex marker left or right. Again, when you move the cursor over the Flex marker, the cursor mode changes to a tool that adds what look like miniature audio waveforms emanating from either side of the Flex marker tool, as shown in the right side of Figure 6.75. When the cursor changes to this mode, you can drag the selected Flex marker.

If you move your newly selected Flex marker, you'll notice something that could be problematic: The entire region is affected, not just the audio in the immediate area of the Flex marker. If this is all you could accomplish with Flex Time editing, it would make Flex Time editing less than "flexible." To affect the timing of a particular section of your audio region, you need to create Flex markers to either side of the Flex marker you wish to move. Obviously, that means if you are moving the beginning or end of a region, you only need to create one Flex marker to the right or the left, respectively.

In the middle of a region, you would need to create three Flex markers to flex a particular bit of audio—the Flex marker you wish to move and markers to create boundaries to either side. You can, of course, create these individually, and there may be times when that would be advantageous—for example, when flexing an area that encompasses multiple transient markers—but you can also use another cursor mode to accomplish this. Move the cursor to the bottom half of your Flex Time–enabled audio region. The Flex marker tool now has three vertical lines, as you can see in Figure 6.76.

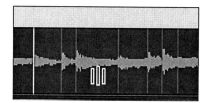

Figure 6.76 When you move the cursor to the lower half of a Flex Time–enabled region, the Flex marker tool has three vertical lines.
© Apple Inc.

As with the Flex marker tool in the upper half of an audio region, moving the tool next to a transient marker adds triangles to the top of each vertical line. Clicking your mouse will then create Flex markers for the selected transient marker and the transient markers immediately to the right and left of the selected transient marker, as shown in Figure 6.77.

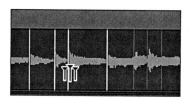

Figure 6.77 Clicking on the selected transient marker changes it and the transient markers to its immediate right and left into Flex markers.
© Apple Inc.

You can now move the middle Flex marker, which will affect only the audio between the outer Flex markers, which you can see in Figure 6.78.

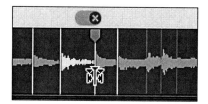

Figure 6.78 With three Flex markers now created, you can freely move the middle Flex marker and affect only the audio within the outer Flex markers.
© Apple Inc.

If you don't like your edits, you can always undo them. If you find that you want to reset all your edits to their original state, you can right-click on the region and select Reset All Flex Edits from the menu that appears.

Flex Markers Versus Transient Markers: If you think that Flex and transient markers are the same things, or you're confused about the difference, don't be alarmed—they *are* similar, and this can be quite confusing! Thankfully, once explained, it becomes obvious. You'll never forget again, and it will make all of Logic's Flex Time features make more sense.

As written, *transients* refer to the characteristics of the audio file—generally moments of peak amplitude that are rhythmically and musically important. Therefore, *transient markers* are part of the audio file, as they relate to the recorded material itself. These markers inform the time stretching algorithms how to work their magic.

Flex markers, however, relate to the Flex Time stretching and compression feature of Logic. So it is the Flex markers (and the Flex markers *alone*) that you use to stretch and compress your audio in the Tracks area. In other words, with few exceptions, if you are working with Flex Time in the Tracks area and Audio Track editor, you'll be working with Flex markers, and if you're working with audio transient markers, you'll be working in the Audio File editor. (More on transient markers in Chapter 7.)

You'll see in a moment that there are a few exceptions, such as creating Flex markers from another audio file's transient markers or using Flex with regions that don't have tempo information, but the preceding is true in all other cases. If you're "flexing" audio in the Tracks area, just worry about Flex markers.

Flexing your audio's time is just that simple, but there's a lot more depth in Flex Time editing than these simple elements. What if the transient markers don't line up with the points in your audio you want to flex? Let's find out.

Creating New Flex Markers

Creating your own Flex markers, independent of the transient markers Logic has created, is every bit as easy as it was to convert a transient marker into a Flex marker. Remember that when the Flex marker tool is in the upper half of a Flex Time-enabled audio region and is not near a transient marker, it is a single vertical line? To create a single Flex marker at a location you determine, simply move the Flex marker tool to the point in your audio where you would like to create a Flex marker and click your mouse. Figure 6.79 shows the same section of audio that we have been using since Figure 6.76, but notice the Flex marker created in a location where there was no transient marker.

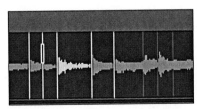

Figure 6.79 To create a new Flex marker, click your mouse in the upper half of your Flex Time–enabled region at the point you want to flex.
© Apple Inc.

Similarly, when you click the mouse in the lower half of your audio region away from a transient marker, a Flex marker will be created at that point and at the transient markers to the immediate right and left of that point, which you can see in Figure 6.80.

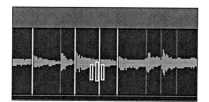

Figure 6.80 Clicking in the lower half of a Flex Time–enabled audio region away from a transient marker creates Flex markers at the point you click and at the transient markers to the immediate right and left.
© Apple Inc.

Creating Flex Markers with the Marquee Tool

You can also use the Marquee tool to create Flex markers. Here's how:

1. Select an area of your Flex Time–enabled audio region with the Marquee tool.
2. Switch to the Pointer tool.
3. Drag the cursor over the upper half of the audio region in the marquee area. The cursor becomes a Hand tool.
4. Click on the marquee area with the Hand tool. Flex markers will be created at the edges of the marquee area and at the transient markers to the immediate right and left, as shown in Figure 6.81.

Figure 6.81 When you click with the Hand tool on the upper half of a marquee selection in your Flex Time–enabled audio region, Flex markers are created at the edges of the marquee area and at the transient markers to the immediate right and left of the marquee region.
© Apple Inc.

When you click in the lower half of your marquee selection, Flex markers are created at the edges of the marquee area and at the point your clicked.

Creating Flex Markers from Another Audio Region's Transients

There may come a time when you're working on a project and you want to line up a Flex marker in one audio region with a transient marker in another audio region. Here's how:

1. Make sure the regions are on adjoining tracks.
2. Click on the region in which you would like to create the new Flex marker.
3. While pressing the mouse button, drag the cursor to the adjacent track, find the transient marker from which you'd like to create your new Flex marker, and release the mouse button.

When you drag the cursor over the second region, a Flex marker line will extend through both regions, allowing you to clearly see what you're doing, and the line will snap to the transient markers of the second region as you move the cursor. You can see this process in action in Figure 6.82. The left image in Figure 6.82 shows two Flex Time–enabled regions. The lower region has few transient markers in the selected area, and we'd like to create a new Flex marker from a transient in the upper region. Therefore, the left image shows the two regions before we do anything. The middle image shows the two regions as we drag the cursor from the lower region into the upper region. The right image shows the resulting Flex marker.

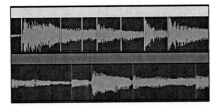 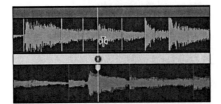 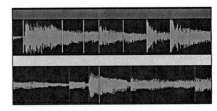

Figure 6.82 Left: The lower region has few transient markers, and we'd like to create a Flex marker at the exact location of a transient marker in the upper region. Middle: Clicking on the lower region and dragging the cursor to the upper region lets you snap the Flex marker tool to the transients in the upper region. Right: The Flex marker in the lower region is at the exact location of its parent transient marker in the region above.
© Apple Inc.

If you click on the lower half of the destination region and drag to the second region, three Flex markers will be created—two at the transient markers to the right and left of where you clicked and one in line with the parent transient marker in the second region. Note that regardless of where you click in the destination region, moving the cursor left or right as you select a parent transient will affect the audio in the destination region, so you want to begin by clicking in an area very close to the location of the parent transient to avoid any unnecessary impact on your audio.

Flexing Audio with an Unknown or Inconsistent Tempo: Flexing audio when Logic doesn't know the tempo of the audio material—either because the file has no tempo information, because it wasn't played to a click, or because it otherwise changes tempo—can lead to some pretty awful results. Luckily, with the Detect Tempo command and beat-mapping track, you can make Flex work wonders even in these difficult situations. Chapter 5 talked about the beat-mapping track, which lets you create a tempo map for an audio file that doesn't keep a consistent tempo. You can use this to generate tempo information and then embed that tempo information to the audio file.

First, refer to Chapter 5 on how to create a beat-mapping global track and use that to create a tempo map of your audio file. If your audio file is consistent in tempo, the Edit > Tempo > Detect Tempo of Selected Region command might be enough.

Once Logic has generated tempo information for the audio file, use the command Edit > Tempo > Export Tempo Information to Audio File. After you export the tempo information to the audio file, that tempo information will then be used to create transient markers when Logic subsequently detects transients in Flex mode. Now you should be able to flex your audio with good results!

Moving and Deleting Flex Markers

There will probably be times when you create a Flex marker, but you're not entirely happy with its exact location. You could always undo the action and create another Flex marker, or you could just move the one you have. To move a Flex marker, Option-drag the marker to the desired location, as in Figure 6.83. You can see the parent transient marker to the right of the moved Flex marker.

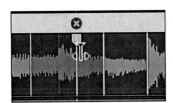

Figure 6.83 To move an existing Flex marker to a new location, Option-drag the marker.
© Apple Inc.

To delete a Flex marker, you can double-click it, click the circle with an × in it at the top of the Flex marker (refer to Figure 6.83), right-click on it and select Delete Flex Marker in the menu that appears, or click it with the Eraser tool. You can delete multiple Flex markers by dragging the Eraser tool across them. You can also delete Flex markers you have created in a region by right-clicking on the region and selecting Reset Manual Flex Edits from the contextual menu that opens.

Flex Pitch Editing Basics

Flex Pitch editing in the Tracks area is fairly basic compared to Flex Time editing. For one thing, you can really only work with monophonic material—at least that's the current limitation. There are other pitch-correction programs out there such as Melodyne editor that can work on polyphonic material, so if you need to work on polyphonic material, you're going to have to use other options for now. I'm pretty sure that when you see how easy it is to use Flex Pitch in the Tracks area, and then see how powerful the Flex Pitch editing tools are in the Audio Track editor (Chapter 7), that you'll be clamoring for Apple to introduce polyphonic Flex Pitch editing like I am.

To begin Flex Pitch editing, select Flex Pitch in the Flex menu in the track header for the track containing your monophonic audio. With the Flex button enabled, the Flex Pitch bars will be visible in the audio region, as shown in Figure 6.84.

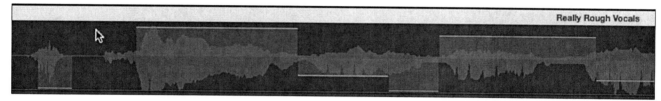

Figure 6.84 Flex Pitch bars appear in Flex Pitch editing–enabled audio regions, letting you drag notes to pitch.
© Apple Inc.

The Flex Pitch bars show how far away from pitch each analyzed note is, +/–50 cents, or up to a half a semitone sharp or flat. Flex Pitch editing in the Tracks area couldn't be simpler. Notes that are sharp extend above the center line, notes that are flat extend below. The center line denotes perfect pitch. To change the fine tuning of a note, simply drag its Flex bar with the cursor, which changes to a Resize cursor (see Figure 6.85). When you drag or click and hold a note, the audio at that location in your note plays, looping the current formant (formants are covered in the section "Flex Pitch Mode" later in this chapter). The pitch of the audio changes as you drag the Flex bar. The closer to the center line you drag the note, the more in tune it will be. A help tag will open telling you the pitch of the note and the fine-tuning adjustments you are making. Figure 6.85 shows the same audio from Figure 6.84 with Flex Pitch adjustments. Note the help tag with position, pitch, and fine-tuning info.

Figure 6.85 The same audio from Figure 6.84, but with some Flex Pitch edits, plus one in progress. Note the help tag offering position, pitch, and fine-tuning info.
© Apple Inc.

There are limitations to the pitch correction, though. Characteristics of a note like vibrato and pitch drift aren't forced in tune. Therefore, when you move a note toward absolute pitch, the note in its entirety is moved relative to itself, with the bits that are sharp or flat remaining just as sharp or flat as they were earlier relative to the new pitch setting. This may seem like cause for concern; you might have thought that Flex Pitch would completely correct your tuning issues. Rest assured, there's no need for alarm. Logic would rather preserve the intent of the performance first and give you the tools to edit further if need be. You'll find out just how extensively you can Flex Pitch edit audio in Chapter 7.

There are only a few other things to know about Flex Pitch editing in the Tracks area. First, if you keep dragging the fine tuning of a note up or down beyond the half semitone variance around the analyzed pitch, you can change the tuning of the note to the next pitch higher or lower, respectively. You can quickly tune a note by clicking it with the Resize cursor (the note will be highlighted like the note being edited in Figure 6.85), then right-clicking and selecting Set to Perfect Pitch from the menu that appears. This will adjust the note to the exact analyzed pitch, with the vibrato and pitch drift intact. You can select a region, right-click, and select Set All to Perfect Pitch to tune the entire region. You can undo Flex Pitch edits for a note by selecting the note and choosing Set to Original Pitch in the right-click menu, or select the region and choose Set All to Original Pitch in the right-click menu. You can select multiple notes to edit using any of the aforementioned methods using the same techniques you would for selecting multiple regions with the cursor: Shift-clicking, Command-clicking, and lassoing. Edits made to multiple selected notes are relative to the note you choose to drag. When you drag the selected note to perfect pitch, it is no longer editable, but if you continue to drag, the other notes will continue to be edited until they reach perfect pitch. Again, there are much more extensive editing facilities available in the Audio Track editor—some you may find very surprising.

Flex Mode Parameters

Each Flex mode, with the exception of Speed, has at least one parameter available in the Track Inspector. In addition, you can change the Flex mode of the selected track in the Track Inspector. Figure 6.86 shows the Track Inspector of a track in Slicing mode. Let's look at the parameters of the different Flex modes.

Figure 6.86   The Track Inspector for a track in Slicing mode.
© Apple Inc.

Slicing Mode

Slicing mode basically slices the audio and flexes it without stretching or compressing the audio. When a track is in Slicing mode, its Track Inspector offers the following parameters:

▷ **Fill Gaps:** Selecting Fill Gaps ensures that any gaps between slices are filled per the Decay parameter.
▷ **Decay:** The Decay parameter lets you set a decay time for the Fill Gaps parameter.
▷ **Slice Length:** This parameter lets you control the length of each slice as a percentage. When you set this parameter below 100%, you are effectively shortening each slice, so the Fill Gaps and Decay parameters are not available.

Rhythmic Mode

Rhythmic mode is good for rhythmic chordal parts. As such, flexing the audio can create some unwanted artifacts that the Rhythmic mode parameters help to mitigate. The Rhythmic mode parameters are as follows:

▷ **Loop Length:** This parameter lets you define the length as a percentage of the end of a time-stretched section of your audio that will be looped. This is similar to the looping that one might perform in the decay phase of a sampled instrument to help ensure a more natural decay phase.
▷ **Decay:** This parameter lets you define the decay time of any looping that will occur.
▷ **Loop Offset:** This parameter lets you move the start point of the looped section up to 100 ms earlier.

Monophonic Mode

Monophonic mode works best on monophonic sources. There is only one parameter for Monophonic mode: the Percussive checkbox. Select the Percussive checkbox if your source audio is more percussive, or staccato. Otherwise, leave this option deselected.

Polyphonic Mode

Polyphonic mode works best on more legato polyphonic material and is a very processor-hungry Flex mode. As with Monophonic mode, Polyphonic mode offers only a single parameter, Complex. Selecting Complex allows for more internal transients in your audio.

Tempophone Mode

Tempophone mode is not the mode you would want to use for natural-sounding flexing, as it produces a more grainy effect. Tempophone mode offers two parameters:

▷ **Grain Size:** This parameter defines the size of each grain of audio in milliseconds, from 0.10 ms to 500 ms.
▷ **Crossfade:** This parameter controls the amount of crossfade from one grain to the next. The lower the setting, the less crossfading you will hear.

Flex Pitch Mode

Flex Pitch mode offers two parameters:

▷ **Formant Track:** Formants are aspects of vocal sounds that, basically, allow us to distinguish vowels, the most resonant part of speech and singing. When shifting the pitch of audio, the formants are affected. The Formant Track setting lets you increase the frequency at which Logic looks for formants in your audio. The higher the Formant Track setting, the more frequently Logic looks for formants.
▷ **Formant Shift:** This parameter lets you tune the formants up or down, relative to the pitch of the audio. This can be useful for correcting artifacts created by Flex Pitch editing and making the audio sound more natural, particularly when changing the pitch drastically.

Using the Flex Tool

The Flex tool is useful for quick Flex edits of audio when you are not in Flex view—that is, when Flex view is disabled via the master Flex view commands, Command+F, or the Flex Edit button at the top of the Tracks area. It can use the transients detected in your audio as guides, much like you would see when creating three Flex markers with the Flex marker tool and moving the middle Flex marker. Figure 6.87 shows the Flex marker tool being used to flex a bit of audio.

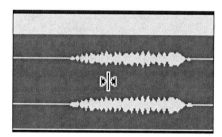

Figure 6.87 The Flex tool lets you flex your audio when you're not in Flex view.
© Apple Inc.

When the Flex tool nears a transient, its appearance changes, and you can then flex your audio at that transient. Figure 6.88 shows the Flex tool near a transient.

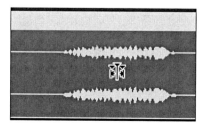

Figure 6.88 You can flex your audio at transients with the Flex tool, too.
© Apple Inc.

You can use the Marquee tool in conjunction with the Flex tool. Select an area of your audio region with the Marquee tool, switch to the Flex tool, and you can flex the selected area as you would when you click the upper half of a marquee selection in Flex view.

In addition, you can move Flex markers with the Flex tool in the same way you can when in Flex mode. Drag the Flex tool to a transient, as in Figure 6.88, and Option-drag the marker to the desired location.

Adding Files to the Tracks Area

As noted, recording audio and MIDI is not the only way to create regions. You can also add preexisting files into the main window in Logic. There are a number of ways to add files:

▷ As explained, if you click the Pencil tool in an audio track, Logic will present you with the Add File dialog box to select an audio file to add at the clicked position.

▷ By choosing File > Import > MIDI File or > Audio File (Shift+Command+I), you can import audio or MIDI files into Logic. The file will be placed at the nearest rounded playhead position.

▷ You can drag audio or MIDI files from your computer's desktop (or any file directory) onto your Tracks area. This method drops the dragged audio or MIDI file directly onto a track on the Tracks area. If it is an audio file, this method also adds the file to the Project Audio Browser.

▷ You can drag audio or MIDI files from the All Files Browser to the Tracks area. The All Files Browser is explained in detail in Chapter 12.

▷ If you are working with an audio file, you can add it to the Project Audio Browser using the Add Audio File command and then drag that file from the Project Audio Browser into the Tracks area or use the Add to Tracks command. These methods are explained in more detail in the next chapter.

Using Folders When Importing Standard MIDI Files: Sasso has another great tip for how folder tracks can assist when importing Standard MIDI Files into Logic:

If a Standard MIDI File (SMF) has multiple tracks, dragging it to the [Tracks area] will create a separate region for each track. To keep them together and well organized, first create an empty folder, then open it and drag the SMF into the main window displaying the folder's contents. If some of the resulting regions contain multiple channels, use Demix by MIDI Channel to further separate them.

Bouncing in Place

Bouncing tracks and regions in place, like freezing tracks and turning tracks off, is another great way to conserve system resources. A track or region that is bounced in place is given some of the same options that you see when you bounce your project, with added control over things such as volume and pan automation and whether new tracks are created for the bounced files. It allows you to bounce tracks directly into your project that you are "finished" with without the extra burden of deleting regions on your selected track or adding tracks to your project and dragging the bounced file into the new track and lining it up properly. It also allows you the flexibility to use external gear via the External Instrument or I/O plug-in.

Bouncing Tracks in Place

The Bounce Track in Place command lets you bounce an entire track and have the resulting bounce file automatically added back into the Tracks area. To use the Bounce Track in Place command, select the track you wish to bounce in place and then select File > Bounce > Track in Place or use the key command Command+Control+B. The Bounce Track in Place dialog box, shown in Figure 6.89, will open, giving you some options for how Logic will handle the bounce in place.

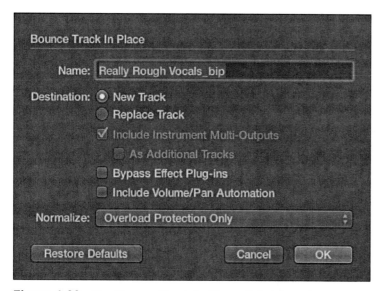

Figure 6.89 The Bounce Track in Place dialog box gives you a number of different options for controlling how Logic performs the bounce in place.
© Apple Inc.

The options in the Bounce Track in Place dialog box are as follows:

▷ **Name:** The Name field is automatically populated based on the track name, but you can rename the bounced file if you wish.

▷ **New Track:** If you select New Track as the destination for your bounced file, Logic will create a new track below the selected track, and the bounced file will be added to the new track.

▷ **Replace Track:** If you select Replace Track as the destination for your bounced file, Logic will bounce the selected track and place it on a new track that replaces the original track.

▷ **Include Instrument Multi-Outputs:** If you are bouncing a multi-output software instrument in place, selecting this command will also bounce the output of any dependent aux channels into your bounce file.

▷ **As Additional Tracks:** This option lets you create a separate bounce file for each multi-instrument aux output.

▷ **Bypass Effect Plug-Ins:** When you select this option, any effects plug-ins on the track will be bypassed for the bounce.

▷ **Include Volume/Pan Automation:** When you select this option, any volume or pan automation on the selected track will be performed during the bounce-in-place process.

▷ **Normalize:** The Normalize menu gives you options for normalizing the signal in the bounce, or finding the peak transient and increasing it to 0dBFs, and increasing the level of the rest of the file by the same amount. For more on the Normalize menu and its functions, see the section "Bouncing Your Mix" in Chapter 11.

Click OK, and the track will be bounced, with the resulting file(s) added back to the Tracks area per your instructions. Figure 6.90 shows a track before and after a bounce in place.

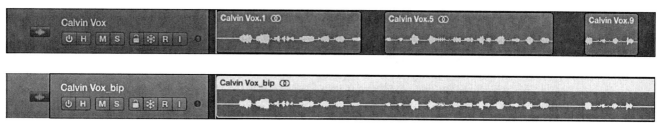

Figure 6.90 A track before and after using the Bounce Track in Place command.
© Apple Inc.

Bouncing Regions in Place

Bouncing regions in place is very similar to bouncing a track in place. This command allows you to selectively bounce the regions on a track either alone or in combination with other regions. To use the Bounce Regions in Place command, select the regions you wish to bounce in place and then select File > Bounce > Regions in Place or use the key command Control+B. The Bounce Regions in Place dialog box, shown in Figure 6.91, will open, giving you some options for how Logic will handle the bounce in place.

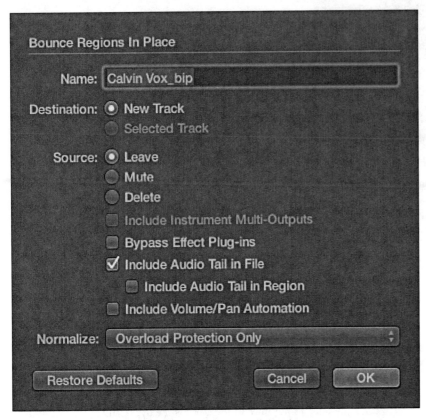

Figure 6.91   The Bounce Regions in Place dialog box.
© Apple Inc.

As you can see, some of the options in the Bounce Regions in Place dialog box are identical to those in the Bounce Track in Place dialog box shown in Figure 6.90. There are a few differences, though. The unique options in the Bounce Regions in Place dialog box are as follows:

▷ **Selected Track:** If you select Selected Track as the destination for your bounced file, Logic will bounce the selected regions and place them on the selected track.
▷ **Leave:** Selecting Leave keeps the parent regions intact and active after the bounce.
▷ **Mute:** Selecting Mute mutes the parent regions after the bounce.
▷ **Delete:** Selecting Delete deletes the parent regions from the main window after the bounce.
▷ **Include Audio Tail in File:** Selecting this option ensures that the bounce will continue until the very end of the region's audio tail, although the resulting region will match the length of the original region.
▷ **Include Audio Tail in Region:** This option ensures that the full extent of the audio tail will be included in the resulting bounce region.

Click OK, and the selected regions will be bounced and added back to the Tracks area per your instructions in the Bounce Regions in Place dialog box. Figure 6.92 shows two regions selected on one track and the bounce file that is produced when those regions are bounced in place.

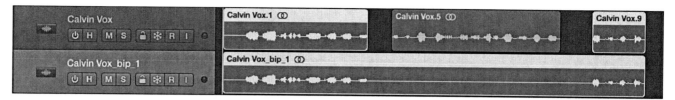

Figure 6.92 Two regions on the top track are selected and bounced in place, resulting in the new lower track and the new region on it.
© Apple Inc.

Bouncing All Tracks in Place

In addition to these track and region bounce-in-place functions, you can also bounce your entire project in place. Select File > Bounce > And Replace All Tracks. First you will be greeted with a warning dialog box inviting you to save your project. Since you're a smart Logic user, you'll select Yes because even though you save your projects regularly, it never hurts to save it one more time before performing a huge operation. After you select your save option, the Bounce Replace All Tracks dialog box, shown in Figure 6.93, will appear.

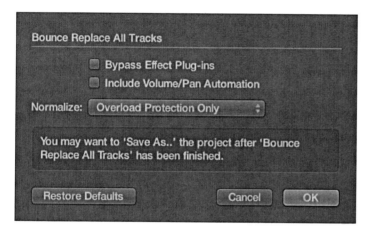

Figure 6.93 The Bounce Replace All Tracks dialog box.
© Apple Inc.

There are two options and one menu in the Bounce Replace All Tracks dialog box, which are identical in function to the same commands in the Bounce Track in Place dialog box. Click OK, and your entire project will be bounced in place!

Other Transient-Related Functions in the Main Window

The use of transient markers in Logic Pro is extensive, and the more you get used to working with them and their related processes, the more mileage you'll get out of Logic. There are a few more processes in the main window that use transient markers to perform their functions, and we'll explore those processes now.

Replacing and Doubling Drum Tracks

One very handy function in the main window that makes use of transient markers is the Drum Replacement/Doubling command found in the Track menu or accessed via the key command Control+D. When you run this command on a track, the regions on the track are analyzed for transients, a software instrument track with EXS24 loaded is created, and trigger notes in the correct places are created immediately below the selected track, as shown in Figure 6.94. In addition, the Drum Replacement/Doubling dialog box, shown in Figure 6.95, opens. The Library tab is also opened, allowing you to select a different replacement drum sound.

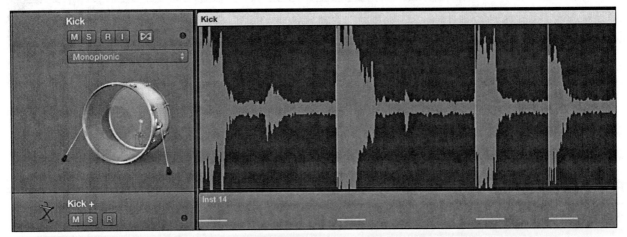

Figure 6.94 When you run the Drum Replacement/Doubling command, the regions on the selected track are analyzed for transients. A software instrument track is added directly below the selected track. A region with trigger notes in line with the transients derived from the audio track is created, and an EXS24 instance with the appropriate triggered drum sound is instantiated.

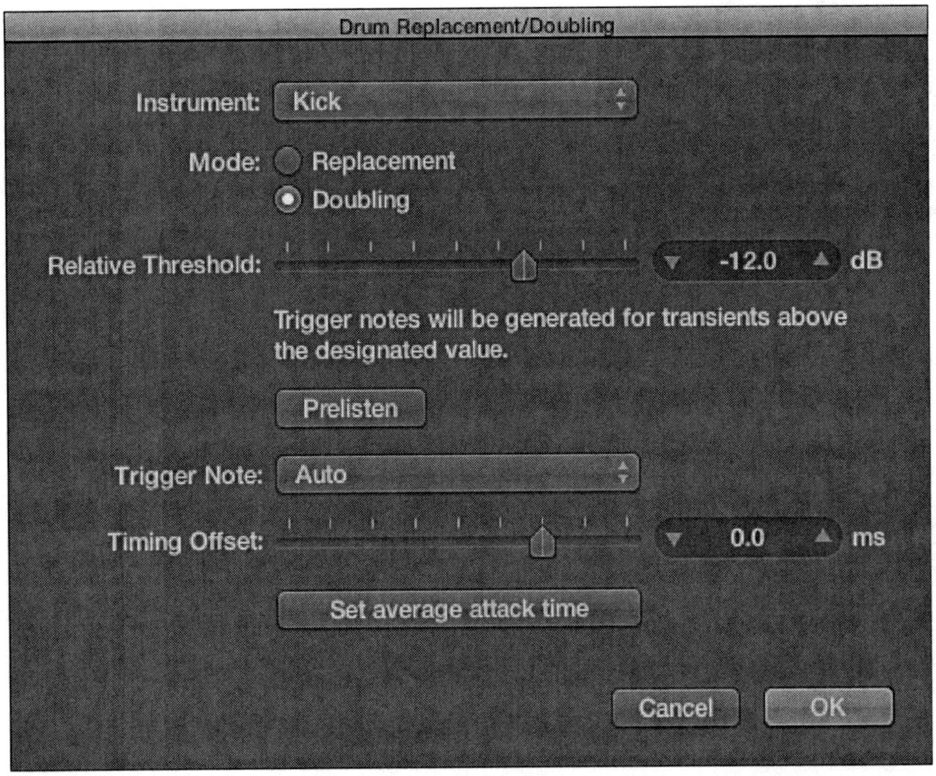

Figure 6.95 The Drum Replacement/Doubling dialog box.

The Drum Replacement/Doubling dialog box gives you a variety of options for defining how your drums are doubled or replaced:

▷ **Instrument:** The Instrument menu lets you define what kind of drum will be processed. The type of drum you define here will be loaded in the EXS24 instance on the related software instrument track. The Instrument menu options are Kick, Snare, Tom, and Other. You could therefore, for example, analyze a kick drum pattern but replace it with a snare drum if you wanted.

▷ **Replacement:** If you select Replacement, the original track will be muted, and the new software instrument track sound will replace the original sound.

▷ **Doubling:** If you select Doubling, the new software instrument sound will double the original audio track.

▷ **Relative Threshold:** The Relative Threshold control lets you define the threshold below which transients will be ignored. The lower the setting, the more transients will be doubled or replaced; the higher the setting, the fewer will be doubled or replaced.

▷ **Prelisten:** Clicking Prelisten lets you hear the results you will achieve with the current Drum Replacement/Doubling dialog box settings.

▷ **Trigger Note:** The Trigger Note menu lets you define what note will be triggered. This is particularly handy if you are going to use a custom drum kit for replacement or doubling or a drum at a non-standard note in Ultrabeat, for example. Auto sets the note based on the Instrument setting to the appropriate General MIDI note.

▷ **Timing Offset:** The Timing Offset setting lets you alter the placement of the replaced or doubled drums forward or backward in milliseconds.

▷ **Set Average Attack Time:** Clicking this button sets an offset for the slicing position for all regions on the parent audio track.

When you're finished tweaking the settings to achieve the desired result, click OK, and you're done!

Converting Regions to Sampler Tracks

You can also turn regions into EXS24 sampler instrument settings by executing the Convert Regions to New Sampler Track command in the Track menu, also accessible via the key command Control+E. When you select an audio region or regions and execute the Convert Regions to New Sampler Track command, the Convert Regions to New Sampler Track dialog box, shown in Figure 6.96, will open.

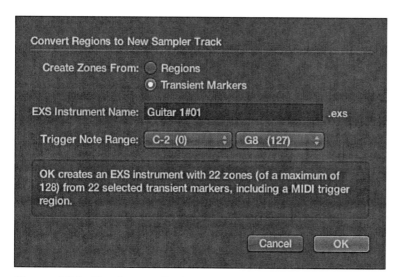

Figure 6.96 The Convert Regions to New Sampler Track dialog box.
© Apple Inc.

The options in the Convert Regions to New Sampler Track dialog box are as follows:

▷ **Regions:** When you select the Convert Zones from Regions option button, a new EXS24 zone will be created for each selected region.

▷ **Transient Markers:** When you select the Convert Zones from Transient Markers option button, the zones in the new EXS24 instrument will be created using the transient markers in the selected audio regions. The result is similar to what you would find in a ReCycle file, where the audio is sliced into "playable" bits.

▷ **EXS Instrument Name:** You can name your new EXS24 instrument here.

▷ **Trigger Note Range:** The Trigger Note Range menus let you define the upper and lower extent to which the newly created zones will be mapped in EXS24, from C-2 to G8.

When you click OK, the audio is processed per your instructions, a new software instrument track is created directly below the parent track with an instance of EXS24 loaded with your new sampler instrument, and a region is created on the new track with trigger notes created to play back your new instrument exactly like the parent audio region(s). You can see this in Figure 6.97.

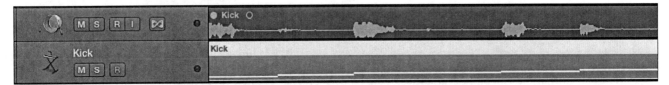

Figure 6.97 When you execute the Convert Regions to New Sampler Track command, a new software instrument track is created under the parent track, with your new sampler instrument loaded into EXS24. A region featuring the appropriate trigger notes for playing back your sampler instrument exactly like the parent audio region is also created.
© Apple Inc.

> **NOTE:** There isn't nearly enough room in this book to explore the EXS24 mkII and all the other professional, world-class software instruments that come with Logic Pro. However, if you are interested in more information on Logic Pro's instruments, *Using Logic Pro Synthesizers* by Kevin Anker (Cengage Learning, 2012) is the perfect companion to *Logic Pro X Power!*

Slicing Audio Regions at Transient Markers

There is one more command you can employ in the Tracks area that uses transient markers. To use it, right-click on a region and select the Slice at Transient Markers command. The selected region will be split into new regions at its transient markers, as shown in Figure 6.98. Note that the maximum initial length an audio region can be if you invoke this command is 32 bars.

Figure 6.98 An audio region before and after executing the Slice at Transient Markers command. You can see that the new regions all line up with the transient markers.
© Apple Inc.

There are many powerful things you can accomplish with transient markers. Now that you've seen some of them, you're probably thinking that all this is great, but what's the point if you can't customize your transient markers? No worries—Logic has this covered too in the Audio File editor, as you'll learn in the next chapter.

Track Stacks

Track Stacks are a new and very cool way of organizing tracks for automation and processing. There are two kinds of Track Stacks:

▷ **Folder Stacks:** A Folder Stack offers basic control of automation for volume, solo, and mute for its dependent tracks.

▷ **Summing Stacks:** A Summing Stack buses the output of all dependent tracks to an aux, which can be used for processing, automation, and layering multiple software instruments together.

You can combine audio, software instrument, external MIDI, and Drummer tracks in a Folder Stack. To use your external MIDI gear with a Summing Stack, you need to use the External Instrument plug-in on a software instrument track. You can create a Track Stack as a permanent fixture in your project, or you can create them and get rid of them as needed while working on your project. Once you create a Track Stack, their power and potential will become more apparent.

Creating Track Stacks

Creating a Track Stack is easy. First, select the tracks you want in a Track Stack in the Track list. Again, you can combine different types of tracks in a Track Stack. For instance, you could combine a kick drum on an audio track with a synth bass sound on a software instrument track because you want to process them and automate them identically, or a number of background vocal audio tracks with a software instrument string section and an external MIDI xylophone part that you will be soloing together and muting and soloing individually to analyze places you hear them conflicting. Part of the power of the Track Stack is that it takes all the tracks you select and organizes them in one location, so using them as a temporary way to group tracks together for editing is one of many effective ways to use Track Stacks. You can select as many or as few tracks as you'd like in your Track Stack.

After you select the tracks you want to stack, select Track > Create Track Stack or press Shift+Command+D. This opens the Track Stack dialog box, shown in Figure 6.99.

Figure 6.99 The Track Stack dialog box.
© Apple Inc.

As you can see, there are only two options in the Track Stack dialog box: Folder Stack and Summing Stack. Just in case you forget what the difference between the two types of Track Stacks is, you can click the Details disclosure triangle, and a description of the selected Track Stack type will be shown. If you want only basic automation control over the selected tracks, choose Folder Stack. If you want to route the outputs of all selected tracks to a single aux, select Summing Stack. Click Create, and the selected type of Track Stack will be created, as in Figure 6.100.

Figure 6.100 When you click Create in the Track Stack dialog box, a new Track Stack is created from the selected tracks. This figure shows a newly created Folder Stack.
© Apple Inc.

After you click Create, a new stack master track is created, which you can see in Figure 6.100. This is the container track—the one that you would use to solo or mute the entire stack and to automate the Track Stack. If you create a Folder Stack, the stack is named Sub. Summing Stacks are named Sum. You can rename a Track Stack by double-clicking on the name to open a text box and then typing the new name. To see the tracks contained in the Track Stack, click the disclosure triangle next to the icon in the Track Stack track header. Figure 6.101 shows the Track Stack from Figure 6.100 with its dependent tracks displayed.

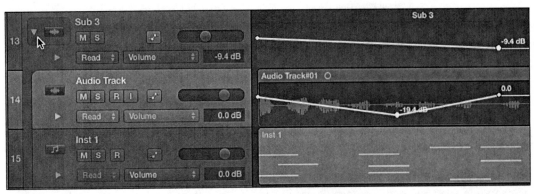

Figure 6.101 To see the dependent tracks of a Track Stack, click the disclosure triangle in the icon field of the Track Stack track header.
© Apple Inc.

There are a few things to note about Figure 6.101. First, this Track Stack contains an audio track and a software instrument track, and you can see their regions. There are no regions on the Folder Stack track. There is, however, volume automation on the Folder Stack track. There is also volume automation on the audio track. Although the Folder Stack track can be used to automate the volume, solo, and mute of its dependent tracks, you can still use automation on the Track Stack's other tracks as well. Because a Summing Stack routes the outputs of its dependent tracks to a single aux, you can automate any automatable parameter of any effects inserted on the aux, as well as volume, pan, solo, mute, and insert bypass for the aux on the stack master track. You can see that both of the track headers of the dependent tracks have a little gap on their left side that leads up to the stack master. This allows you to easily see what tracks are in a stack compared to the rest of the tracks in your Track list.

When you select a stack master track, as with any other track, its Inspector channel strips will be available in the Inspector. When you select a track in a stack, you will be able to access that track's channel strip and routing. The Folder Stack channel strip offers basic control, giving you access to automation settings, groups, volume, solo, and mute. No actual audio goes through the folder track fader; rather, it simply acts as a controller. The Summing Stack channel strip is a full-featured aux. The only options in the Track Inspector for a Track Stack are the Icon and MIDI Channel settings.

Flattening Track Stacks

Track Stacks are a great organizational tool. Sure, you can use them as a permanent fixture in your project, but as I mentioned, you can also use them as a temporary way of quickly organizing tracks for any number of purposes. Perhaps you want to briefly organize a bunch of disparate tracks in one place for editing purposes. Or maybe you want to audition some effects automation for a few tracks. Whatever the reason, once they've served their purpose, Track Stacks are easier to "delete" than they are to create.

When you're finished with a Track Stack, you can "flatten" it. Flattening a Track Stack is more similar to unpacking a folder than it is to flattening a comp. When you flatten a Track Stack, the stack master track is eliminated, and the tracks are flattened to their previous location in the Track list. To flatten a Track Stack, select Track > Flatten Stack or press Shift+Command+U. That's all there is to it! Figure 6.102 shows the Track Stack from Figure 6.101 after being flattened.

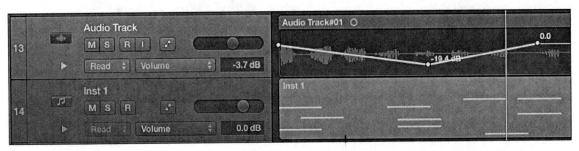

Figure 6.102 The tracks from the Track Stack in Figure 6.101 after the Track > Flatten Stack command is executed.
© Apple Inc.

Track Stacks allow for lots of flexibility and creativity in how you handle parts of your project. You may be envisioning different configurations of Track Stacks that you would love to be able to access across multiple projects. Fortunately, Logic Pro X allows for this via another great new feature: patches.

Working with Patches

So you've created some Track Stacks that are tailor made for your workflow across several types of projects on which you work regularly. For example, suppose you regularly record one particular drummer, and you have figured out the perfect Track Stack for mixing his kit and added it to your template. This Track Stack includes audio channels for all the mics you use, tailored audio FX for each channel, plus effects on the Sum aux of the stack and routings to your standard auxes to boot. Now all you want is to be able to quickly switch to your mix settings without having to load a whole bunch of settings on each channel strip. Alternatively, suppose you have a single software channel strip with an instance of Sculpture and Bass Amp Pro with some customized Smart Controls (covered later in this chapter), and you have sends set up to your usual auxes. The problem is, a channel strip setting doesn't save all of this information, just some of it. This (and more) is what patches can help you accomplish. With patches, you can have more complex collections of highly customized settings available to you, a click away in the Library!

Creating and Saving Patches

The process for creating and saving patches is simple, with the obvious caveat that setting up your Track Stacks and/or channel strips and customizing any effects, software instruments, routings, Track Stacks, and Smart Controls can be time consuming. Thankfully, because patches recall all that information, you only have to do this once per patch!

Once you have set up your track's channel strip or your Track Stack's channel strips, make sure the track or the stack master track you want to save as a patch is selected. Then open the Library by clicking the Library button in the control bar or by selecting the global View > Show Library option. Figure 6.103 shows the Library.

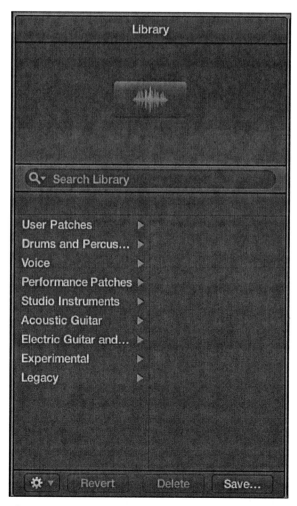

Figure 6.103 The Library is used for loading and saving patches.
© Apple Inc.

To save a patch, simply click the Save button in the bottom-right corner of the Library. A typical Save dialog box will open in which you can name your patch. The patch will be saved to the file path ~/Library/Application Support/Logic/Patches/*channel strip type*, or ~/Music/Audio Music Apps/Patches/*channel strip type* where *channel strip type* will be one of these directories: Audio, Aux, Instrument, or Output (depending on the kind of channel strip assigned to the track). Therefore, Track Stack patches are saved to the aux folder.

Loading Patches

Not only is the Library used for saving patches, it's also where you can search for, navigate to, and load patches. When you select a track in the Track list, all the channel strip settings and patches available for that track type are available in the submenus in the Library. Any patches and channel strip settings that you have made that are available for the selected track type will be available in the User Patches and User Channel Strip Settings submenus in the Library. Figure 6.104 shows the User Patches submenu for an audio track.

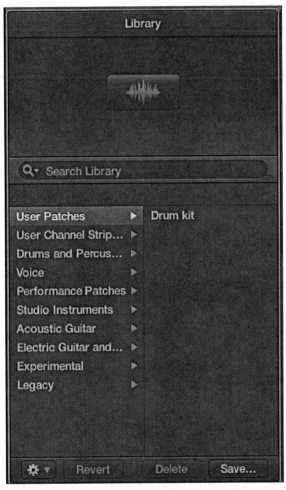

Figure 6.104 Browse and search for patches to load in the Library. The User Patches submenu is where you can find your custom patches.
© Apple Inc.

The user patch in Figure 6.104 reveals one other handy feature of patch loading. In the introduction to patches, I mentioned the notion of a Track Stack customized for mixing drums, and saving that Track Stack as a patch. Because that Track Stack contained nothing but audio tracks, when I select an audio track in the Track list, my drum kit mixing patch is available in the Library. If the drum kit patch is selected, the audio track is instantly converted into the drum kit Track Stack. That means you can quickly configure a new project with your custom Track Stack patches by loading audio Track Stacks directly to audio tracks, software instrument Track Stacks directly to software instrument tracks, aux Track Stacks directly to aux tracks you've added to the Tracks area, and output Track Stacks directly to output tracks you've added to the Tracks area. While this doesn't beat the convenience of a well-made template, it can let you quickly add new functionality to your template or help you reconfigure a project on the fly.

Merging Patches

So you came up with an incredibly happening audio effects signal path for guitar, complete with sends, that you saved as a patch, but you really want to hear how it would sound with your favorite Vintage Clav patch that you've tweaked with some MIDI effects (covered in Chapter 9, "Working with Software Instruments"). Sure, you could go through the trouble of loading all the settings for each audio and MIDI effect and for the Vintage Clav, or you could simply merge the patches. Patch merging offers loads of creative possibilities, letting you selectively apply aspects of one track to another track. Like every other aspect of patches, merging them is quickly and easily accomplished. First, select the track to which you want to transfer settings. Then click the Action menu in the lower-left corner of the Library and select Enable Patch Merging, as shown in Figure 6.105.

Figure 6.105 Select Enable Patch Merging in the Action menu in the Library to begin the patch-merging process.
© Apple Inc.

After you select Enable Patch Merging, the Patch Merging area, shown in Figure 6.106, opens at the bottom of the Library. There are four buttons available in the Patch Merging area: MIDI Effects, Audio Effects, Instruments, and Sends. Enable the aspects of a patch or a setting you'd like to transfer, and disable the things you don't want to be replaced. Finally, browse for and select the patch or setting in the Library from which you want to transfer settings, and the selected settings will be transferred to the selected track.

Figure 6.106 The Patch Merging area open in the Library.
© Apple Inc.

Figure 6.107 shows two channel strips before and after Patch merging. The channel strip to the left is selected, and audio effects settings from the channel strip right are merged to the selected channel strip. To disable patch merging, simply click the × in the upper-left corner of the Patch Merging area.

Figure 6.107 Note the channel strip on the left, before and after merging the audio effects of the channel strip to the right.
© Apple Inc.

Reverting and Deleting Patches

There are two other buttons at the bottom of the Library that can be useful: the Revert button and the Delete button. If you are editing any aspect of a patch or setting and you are unsatisfied with the results, you can revert to the original patch or setting by clicking the Revert button. To delete a patch or setting, browse or search in the Library for the patch or setting you want to delete, select it, and click the Delete button.

Smart Controls

Smart Controls are a new main window feature in Logic Pro X. They give you quick access to the some of the most important effects and software instrument parameters for the selected track. They are configured automatically for each channel strip, or you can create your own custom Smart Controls. To access Smart Controls, select the global View > Show Smart Controls option or press B. Figure 6.108 shows automatically generated Smart Controls for the software instrument and effects for the channel strip seen in a Mixer window to the left of the Smart Controls area in the main window.

Figure 6.108 Automatically generated smart controls for the software instrument and effects seen in the channel strip in the Mixer window to the left of the Smart Controls area in the main window.
© Apple Inc.

You can see in Figure 6.108 that the four controls to the left control the amplifier attack, decay, sustain, and release for the amp envelope of the EXS24 instrument; the autowah depth, attack, release, and compression ratio settings for the Fuzz-Wah effect; and the gain, EQ low, mid, and high parameters for the Guitar Amp Pro effect. To change the setting of a parameter, drag it. To change a setting with finer control, Shift-drag it. Although the selection of parameters may seem limited, they generally offer the most essential parameters you would expect to need to quickly access and edit. At the same time, you don't have to live with whatever Smart Controls Logic presents; you can edit which parameters a Smart Control affects.

Editing Smart Controls

Editing Smart Controls, like so many other things in Logic, is as easy as it is powerful. One reason to edit a track's Smart Controls is that you have a different idea of what controls would be the most essential to access. Another reason is that, because Smart Controls can be automated either through mouse input or via a hardware controller, you very well may want to totally remap the controls to parameters you want to automate. To edit Smart Controls, click the I button in the Smart Controls area to open the Smart Controls Inspector, shown in Figure 6.109.

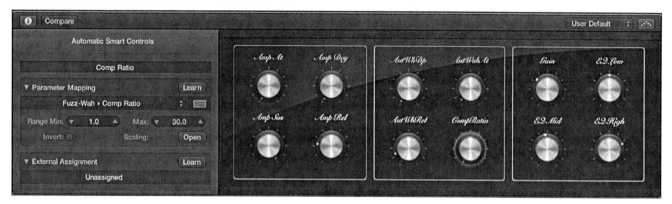

Figure 6.109 Use the Inspector in the Smart Controls area to edit Smart Controls.
© Apple Inc.

The options in the Smart Controls Inspector are as follows:

▷ **Layout:** If you click on the Layout menu—the area that reads "Automatic Smart Controls" in Figure 6.109—you'll see myriad Smart Controls layouts, suitable for particular instruments, effects types, and even amplifiers. If you compare Figure 6.108 and Figure 6.109, you'll see that they offer the exact same parameters. (It may be a little hard to tell because the font used for the Smart Controls in Figure 6.109 aren't the easiest to read at a smaller size.) To make the text for each Smart Control in Figure 6.108 more legible, I switched the layout setting to Modern Synth 12 using the Layout menu. You can change the layout as much as you'd like until you find the one that works best for your needs. The naming of the Layout menu options will give you a pretty good idea of what you can expect from each layout.

▷ **Name:** Click in the Name field (containing the text "Comp Ratio" in Figure 6.109) and type a new name to rename the Smart Control.

▷ **Parameter Mapping:** If you click in the field under the "Parameter Mapping" label, the Parameter Mapping menu, shown in Figure 6.110, opens. This menu offers options for mapping controls in custom layouts; options for adding, deleting, and copying mappings; and submenus for selecting which track, effect, or software instrument parameter will be mapped to the currently selected Smart Control. Parameters that cannot be automated can be found in the Non-Automatable submenu.

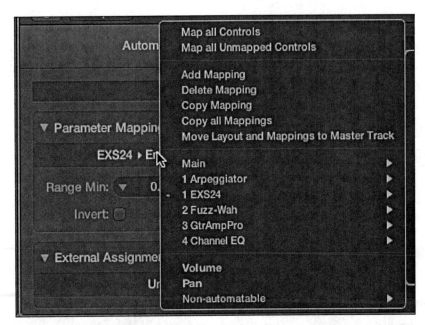

Figure 6.110 The Parameter Mapping menu.
© Apple Inc.

▷ **Range Min, Range Max, and Invert:** These parameters will change in purpose depending on your selection in the Parameter Mapping menu. For example, if you map a Smart Control to Pan, the range parameters allow you to control the minimum and maximum settings across the stereo field the control can access, with maximum and minimum values of +/−64 offered. Switch the control to a synth filter, and the values offered may be 0–100.

TIP: You can add more parameters to a Smart Control by selecting the Add Mapping control in the Parameter Mapping menu, allowing one Smart Control to affect multiple parameters.

▷ **Editor Window:** At the right end of the Parameter Mapping menu is the Editor Window button. If you click this button, the plug-in editor window for the currently selected parameter will open. This is useful in combination with the Learn button, discussed next.

TIP: You can also right-click on a Smart Controls interface element to open the plug-in with which it is associated.

▷ **Parameter Mapping Learn:** If you click the Editor Window button and then click the Parameter Mapping Learn button, the Parameter Mapping Learn button and the selected Smart Control glow orange. Click on any control in the plug-in editor window, and that parameter is automatically mapped to the selected Smart Control. You can select other Smart Controls and plug-in parameters and map as many or as few as you wish. Click the Parameter Mapping Learn button again to disengage Learn mode.

▷ **Scaling:** Click the Open button to open the Scaling window, shown in Figure 6.111. Here you can control how the selected Smart Control's values scale across its range. In the upper-left corner of the Scaling window are six preset scaling curves. Click a button to select that curve. The Range Min and Range Max parameters let you set the minimum and maximum values the selected Smart Control can access, like in the Inspector. The Invert button lets you invert the scaling. In other words, if the scaling of the curve in Figure 6.111 is inverted, the Smart Control produces its maximum value for the selected parameter with the Smart Control at its minimum setting, and the minimum value at its maximum setting. The Reset button lets you reset any edits you've made to the scaling curve. The Copy and Paste buttons let you copy and paste scaling curves, allowing you to copy the curve for one parameter to the curve of another parameter.

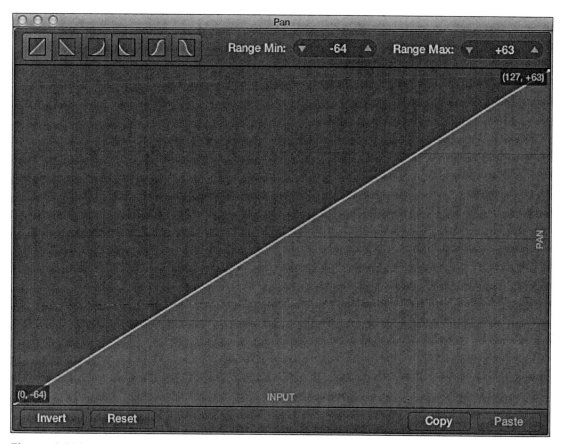

Figure 6.111 The Scaling window lets you dictate how a Smart Control's values scale across its range.
© Apple Inc.

TIP: You can use your mouse to edit the scaling curve. Drag at either end of the curve to change the Range settings of the curve. Click in the scaling curve area to move the scaling curve through that point. A help tag will follow the cursor throughout your movements in the scaling curve area, detailing the Smart Control Input value and the value that will be sent to the selected parameter at that Smart Control Input value, helping you to click in a meaningful location. A node on the curve, which can be moved by dragging, will be created at the location you clicked. The scaling curve will connect through that node using straight lines. Option-click on the line, either initially or after you have created nodes along the line, to be able to add curvature to the scaling curve. The selected part of the line will become dotted, and dragging it will add curvature to the line. You can see nodes and curves on the scaling curve in Figure 6.112.

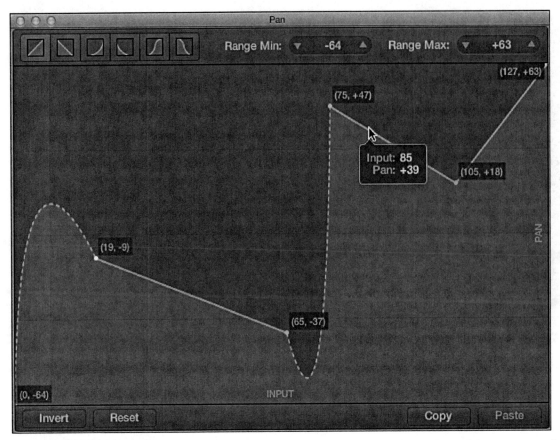

Figure 6.112 A pretty impractical scaling curve. It demonstrates the degree to which you can scale the control that a Smart Control has over a parameter. Note the help tag offering useful information next to the mouse pointer.

© Apple Inc.

▷ **External Assignment Learn:** If you want to map the currently selected Smart Control to a fader, knob, etc. on your hardware controller, click the External Assignment Learn button. The External Assignment Learn button and the selected Smart Control will glow orange. Move the desired element on your hardware controller to assign it to the selected parameter. Click the External Assignment Learn button again to get out of Learn mode. If you double-click in the External Assignment field, you will open the Controller Assignments window, covered in Chapter 3.

You can compare your edits with the original Smart Controls mapping by clicking the Compare button. To save Smart Controls you have edited, either save your channel strip as a channel strip setting in the Setting menu at the top of your channel strip or save your channel strip or patch as a patch.

You can also access the MIDI FX Arpeggiator in the Smart Controls area. To activate the Arpeggiator, click the Arpeggiator button at the upper-right corner of the Smart Controls area. You can select an Arpeggiator setting in the menu to the left of the Arpeggiator button. MIDI FX and the Arpeggiator are discussed in Chapter 9.

Drummer

The new Drummer track in Logic Pro X is one of those things that could have fit into a couple of chapters. When you create a Drummer track, a Drummer track, its parent channel strip, and two yellow eight-bar regions on the Drummer track are created, ready to be played. The Drummer channel strip includes the Drum Kit Designer software instrument, which provides reason to include this section in Chapter 9. What convinced me to include it in this chapter is the fact that not only are regions created on the Drummer track when you create a Drummer track, but the Drummer editor, which is the real key to its power, is integrated in the main window. You can see all this in Figure 6.113.

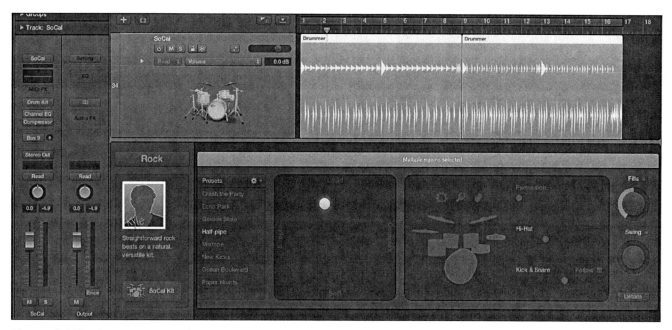

Figure 6.113 A newly created Drummer track, including the two regions that are automatically created, the Drummer editor at the bottom of the main window, and the Drummer channel strip in the main window Inspector.
© Apple Inc.

Drummer has a lot of unique characteristics. From its dedicated editor featuring a number of different "drummers" playing different styles, to its specialized software instrument, to its regions, Drummer tracks are just different enough that they need separate explanation.

Creating Drummer Regions

Drummer regions look unique—because they *are* unique. They don't really contain audio, although it appears as if they do. Rather, they contain MIDI data that triggers samples in the Drum Kit Designer plug-in in the Drummer channel strip.

You may notice in the Drummer track header that there is no Record button. Drummer tracks may be a hybrid audio and software instrument track, but you cannot record to a Drummer track via MIDI (although you can accomplish this by using Drum Kit Designer in a software instrument track). This begs the question, how the heck are you supposed to use the Drummer track if you can't record to it? The answer is that there are several methods for creating new Drummer regions.

The first method should be the most obvious: Click in the Drummer track with the Pencil tool. A new eight-bar Drummer region will be created at the spot you click. You can also copy and paste Drummer regions, with the new copied regions being pasted at the current playhead position just like other regions. You can also right-click at an empty spot in the Drummer track and select the Create Drummer Region command. A new eight-bar Drummer region will be created at the barline to the left closest to where you right-clicked. All three of these methods work just fine, but there are a few other methods for creating Drummer regions that are a little more powerful.

If creating eight-bar Drummer region after eight-bar Drummer region sounds a little tedious for a track that's 120 bars long, rest assured there are better methods. The simplest method is to right-click on an empty place in the Drummer track and select Populate with Drummer Regions in the menu that opens. The Drummer track will be filled with eight-bar Drummer regions from the end of the second initial Drummer region until the end of the project.

If creating nothing but eight-bar Drummer regions sounds a little limiting, there are a couple other methods of creating Drummer regions. The most flexible method involves the arrangement track. If you have a project whose arrangement has been decided, create arrangement track markers that follow your project's arrangement. If you create the arrangement markers before you create a Drummer track, the Drummer track will be created with regions that follow each arrangement marker in your project. If you already have a Drummer track created when you craft your arrangement markers, use the Populate with Drummer Regions command in the Drummer track right-click menu. Regions that match your arrangement will be created through the length of your arrangement, and they will be named per your arrangement markers. Figure 6.114 shows a Drummer track created by following the arrangement track.

Figure 6.114 Drummer track regions created based on existing arrangement track markers.
© Apple Inc.

One final method for creating a Drummer region: If you drag a MIDI region or alias onto a Drummer track (or better yet, Option-drag to move a copy of the region or alias), right-click on the region, and select Convert to Drummer Region from the menu that appears, a Drummer region the length of the MIDI region will be created. None of the MIDI data in the region will be used. Drummer regions generate their own data. This is of particular use if you haven't created an arrangement track but you have created MIDI regions that are more or less than eight-bars long that need Drummer accompaniment.

Resizing, Looping, Splitting, and Joining Drummer Regions

Although you can't directly edit the contents of a Drummer region like you can a MIDI region or an audio region, you can resize, loop, split, join, and otherwise edit the size of Drummer regions exactly as you would any other region. Refer to the sections dealing with editing regions earlier in this chapter for reminders of how to edit regions in this way.

The Drummer Editor

The content of a Drummer region cannot be directly edited, it can only be influenced. To influence the content of your Drummer regions, you need to use the Drummer editor. For a track with regions that you can't directly edit, the Drummer editor gives you fairly broad control over the content and vibe of your Drummer regions. To open the Drummer editor, double-click a Drummer region with the Pointer tool or select a region, regions, or the track header on a Drummer track and click the Editors button in the control bar (or press E). Figure 6.115 shows the Drummer editor.

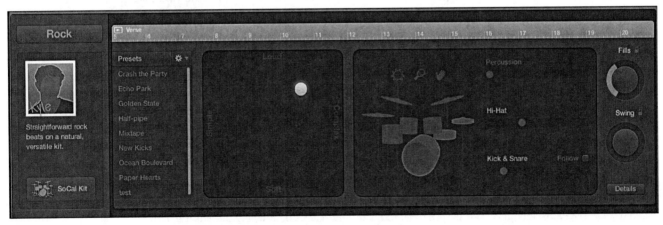

Figure 6.115 The Drummer editor.
© Apple Inc.

The Drummer editor works on the currently selected region or regions. If you have a single Drummer region selected, the Bar ruler at the top of the Drummer editor displays what region is selected and where it lies on the Bar ruler. You can click the Play button at the left end of the Bar ruler to play the selected Drummer region. If you create a Cycle region for the selected region (Auto Set Locators By Region Length comes in handy here), the Drummer region will Cycle when you click Play in the Drummer editor. This makes it easy to hear your Drummer edits, even though it takes a few seconds or even a few bars for your changes to audibly update.

Selecting a Drummer

As of this writing, Drummer includes 15 different virtual drummers over four different styles. First, select from one of the four available styles by clicking the Genre menu, which reads "Rock" in Figure 6.115. The currently available genres are Rock, Alternative, Songwriter, and R&B. When you select a genre, the available drummers for that genre are displayed, as in Figure 6.116.

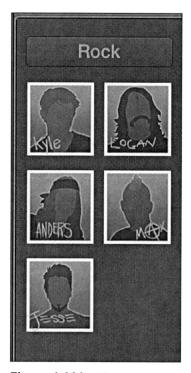

Figure 6.116 When you select a style, the available drummers for that style are displayed under the Genres menu. © Apple Inc.

Select a drummer by clicking on its picture. That loads the selected drummer for your Drummer track, and changes the content of your Drummer regions and the current Drum Kit Designer kit to match your selected drummer's style within their genre. When you select a drummer, information about him and his style is displayed under his picture (see Figure 6.115). It should be mentioned that the default installation of Logic Pro X includes a very limited selection of drum kits. If you select a drummer whose kit hasn't been downloaded, you will be prompted to download his kit. I highly recommend taking the time to download all the Drummer kits (along with their Producer Kits, mentioned later in this chapter).

Once you select a drummer, you can edit his kit by clicking the Editor Window button beneath the picture of your drummer. You can swap out drums, change entire kits, retune and dampen individual drums, and change individual drums' overall volume setting.

Drummer Presets

Each drummer has his own set of eight preset Editor configurations. These are available at the left end of the Drummer editor, as shown in Figure 6.117. Simply click on a preset to switch to that preset. Your Drummer regions will be updated to reflect this change. You can save custom presets using the Action menu at the top of the Presets list. After I cover how to edit your Drummer regions, I'll get into the Action menu.

Logic Pro® X Power!: The Comprehensive Guide

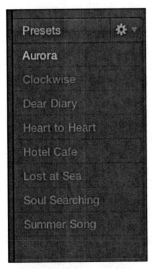

Figure 6.117 Select a preset for the current drummer in the Presets area of the Drummer editor.
© Apple Inc.

Editing Drummer Regions

Because you can edit individual regions or multiple regions, you may find it helpful to create a general vibe for your project by selecting the track header and using the Drummer editor parameters to edit the state of all the Drummer regions. Then, after listening, you can make further edits to specific regions. The Drummer editor may not let you specify *exactly* what you want in each drummer region (that's something you can do using Drum Kit Designer on a software instrument track), but what it can do is give you very musical, and very natural-sounding, drum performances that suit your project. The Drummer editor is pretty straightforward, and our discussion of it starts with the Drummer XY pad.

Using the Drummer XY Pad

The Drummer XY pad, found to the right of the Presets list and shown in Figure 6.118, gives you broad control over the content in the selected Drummer region(s). An XY pad gives you control over the relationship among four different parameters on a two-dimensional plane. You can see in Figure 6.118 that the left side of the XY pad is labeled "Simple," the right side is labeled "Complex," the top is labeled "Loud," and the bottom is labeled "Soft." As you move the yellow ball from left to right, the content of the selected Drummer region(s) becomes more complex. As you drag it from top to bottom, the drums are played softer. The upper-right corner provides the loudest and most complex drumming, and the lower-left corner provides the softest and simplest drumming for the selected region(s). The XY pad influences the vibe of your regions greatly, which is part of the reason I recommend clicking the track header to select all regions and establish an XY setting that fits the vibe of your song as a whole before getting into more specific tweaks, including XY pad setting, for individual regions.

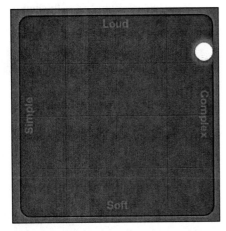

Figure 6.118 The XY pad in the Drummer editor.
© Apple Inc.

Using the Pattern Variation Controls

The Pattern Variation controls in the Drummer editor give you control over the various parts of the drum kit for the selected region(s), as well as the fills played and the swing feel of the drum performances. Figure 6.119 shows the Pattern Variation controls.

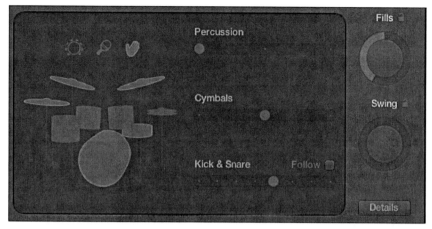

Figure 6.119 The Pattern Variation controls in the Drummer editor.
© Apple Inc.

The Pattern Variation controls are, on the whole, a reasonably simple set of controls. Any part of the drum kit that is highlighted is active for the selected region(s). To activate a part of the kit or a percussion instrument, click on it. Kick and snare are always available, and they can be activated and deactivated independently. You can have only one of these kit groups—Hi-Hat, Toms, and Cymbals— active at a time. You also have access to only one percussion instrument at a time. The sliders to the right of the kit offer pattern variations for the different drum kit elements. The Kick & Snare offers the most options, including six variations that produce beats typical for your time signature and tempo, plus a half-speed and a double-speed option, as you can see in Figure 6.120.

Figure 6.120 The Kick & Snare slider offers eight options.
© Apple Inc.

The slider above Kick & Snare will change based on your selection of Hi-Hat, Toms, or Cymbals as an element of the selected Drummer region(s). If you select Hi-Hats or Cymbals, there will be four pattern variations available. If you select Toms, there will be three pattern variations available. Each of the three percussion options offers three pattern variations.

You can also make your Kick & Snare follow the rhythm of another track in your project. If you click the Follow checkbox above the right end of the Kick & Snare slider, the slider disappears, and the Kick & Snare field becomes a menu. Click on the Kick & Snare field to select a track for the Kick & Snare in the selected Drummer region(s) to follow, as in Figure 6.121.

Figure 6.121 When you select the Follow option for the Kick & Snare in the current Drummer region, you can make the Kick & Snare follow the rhythm of another track in your project by selecting that track in this menu.
© Apple Inc.

If you look at the right end of the Pattern Variation controls in Figure 6.119, you can see two knobs, Fills and Swing. The Fills knob controls how prominent or frequent drum fills will be in the selected region. The lower the Fills setting, the fewer fills you'll get; the higher the setting, the more fills you'll get. The Swing knob controls the extent to which your region has a swing feel. At its lowest setting, the Drummer region plays very strict, straight time. As you increase the Swing setting, the swing feel increases. Once you find Fills and Swing settings you like for your Drummer region, you can click the lock icon next to the Fills and Swing knob names to prevent those parameters from being edited further. Click the lock icon again to unlock the knob for further editing.

You access the final Pattern Variation controls by clicking the Details button in the lower-right corner of the Drummer editor. Figure 6.122 shows the three Details parameters.

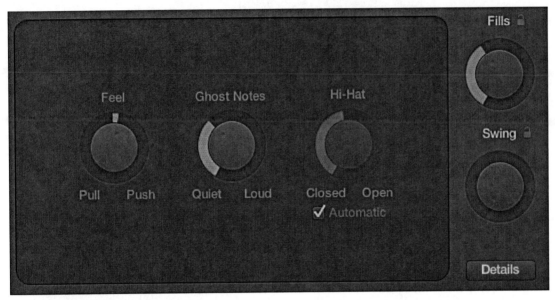

Figure 6.122 The Details parameters in the Pattern Variation controls area.
© Apple Inc.

> ▷ **Feel:** The Feel knob controls how behind the beat, on the beat, or ahead of the beat your Drummer region will feel. When the knob is centered, the feel is right on the beat. The closer the knob is set to Pull, the more the region will be behind the beat. The closer the knob is set to Push, the more the region will be ahead of the beat.
> ▷ **Ghost Notes:** The Ghost Notes knob controls the volume of any ghost notes in your Drummer region. The lower the setting, the quieter any ghost notes in the region will be.
> ▷ **Hi-Hat:** The Hi-Hat knob is editable only if you deselect the Automatic checkbox. If Automatic is selected, Drummer automatically decides how open or closed the Hi-Hat will be in your Drummer region (if the Hi-Hat is activated in the drum kit, of course). If you deselect Automatic, you can use the knob to make the Hi-Hat more opened or closed in your Drummer region.

As you edit many of the parameters in the Pattern Variation controls and the XY pad, the Drummer region(s) you are editing will visually change their content to reflect your changes to their actual musical content. Once you get a Drummer region to a state that you really like, you can save the Drummer editor settings as a preset.

Saving Drummer Presets and the Drummer Editor Action Menu

To save a Drummer preset, simply click the Action menu in the Drummer editor, shown in Figure 6.123, and select the Save Preset option.

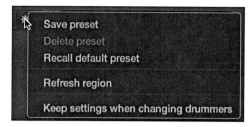

Figure 6.123 The Drummer editor Action menu.
© Apple Inc.

When you select Save Preset, a text field will open at the bottom of the Presets list. Enter a name for your preset, press Return, and your new preset will always be available for the currently selected Drummer. To delete a preset, select it in the Presets list and choose Delete Preset in the Action menu.

The Recall Default Preset command returns Drummer to the current drummer's default preset. The Refresh Region command lets you explore some alternate Drummer region performances based on your current Drummer editor settings.

Finally, enabling the Keep Setting When Changing Drummers option lets you audition your Drummer editor settings with other drummers. When this option is not enabled, switching drummers changes the Drummer editor settings to the new drummer's default preset.

TIP: If you really want to get the most out of Drummer, do yourself a favor and download all the Producer Kits available for Drummer. Although the amount of space they'll eat up on your storage drive is significant, the benefits are huge. When you load a Drummer Producer Kit, available in the Library after you download them, the Drummer track becomes a Drummer Track Stack. Instead of a single stereo Drummer track, opening the Drummer Track Stack reveals a host of tracks for each mic used in the original Drummer sampling session. This gives you full mixing, automation, and effects control over every element in the Drummer performance.

For added flexibility, load a Drum Kit Producer Kit on a software instrument track. The software instrument track will become a Drum Kit Track Stack, but without Drummer active. That means you can play and record MIDI performances to create your own drum track using Drum Kit Designer, but in a format that provides total control over the mixing possibilities of your performance—as you would get recording a real drummer!

Automation

Automation is one of Logic's more extensive features, and Chapter 10 examines it in depth. However, since most automation functions are in the main window, a brief explanation of automation follows.

Track-Based Automation

Track-based automation (TA) is the most powerful, accurate, and modern automation in Logic. With TA, your automation is not connected to the regions on a particular track lane, but to the actual track lane itself. This is how automation would function with an actual hardware mixer, in which you automate a mixer channel, not the material that is playing through the channel. It is possible, however, to tie TA to the regions on a track, which is explained in Chapter 10.

When you turn on track-based automation by choosing View > Track Automation or by pressing A, the track lane expands, and you will see the various automation options. Figure 6.124 shows a track with track-based automation visible.

Figure 6.124 This track has track-based automation turned on, and you can see volume automation data in the track lane.
© Apple Inc.

> **NOTE:** Because the automation lane takes up the majority of the track lane, when you want to edit, move, or resize regions, you'll need to be careful to click only in the top label portion of the region above the automation data. Otherwise, Logic assumes that you are trying to edit your automation data, not the region.

Region-Based Automation (MIDI Draw)

Before Logic introduced TA, the only method of automation was called Hyper Draw, now called MIDI Draw. MIDI Draw uses standard MIDI messages to automate MIDI data. These MIDI messages are directly tied to the region for which they were created; hence, MIDI Draw is also known as region-based automation (RA). Figure 6.125 shows a track with RA information visible.

Figure 6.125 This track has volume MIDI Draw (region-based automation) data displayed. Notice that the Track list does not show as much information for the RA data as for the TA data in Figure 6.124. Notice also that the RA information is included as an actual part of the region itself, unlike TA information, which is connected to the track.
© Apple Inc.

One of the main advantages to RA is that as you move regions around, RA automatically moves with them. In general, however, RA does not have the high resolution or show as much information on the Track list as TA does. You can turn RA data into TA data, as you will explore in Chapter 10.

Musical Typing

Finally, although this isn't technically a part of the main window, I'll mention Musical Typing (a truly dreadful name change from the former Caps Lock Keyboard) here because you may want to use it to record software instrument performances. Pressing Command+K or selecting Window > Show Musical Typing will bring up the onscreen keyboard shown in Figure 6.126.

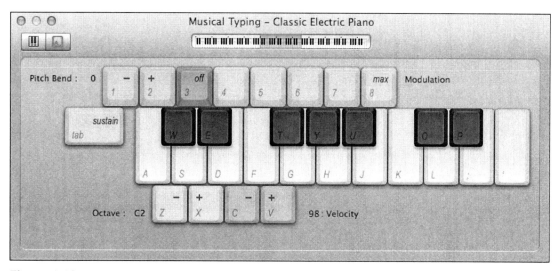

Figure 6.126 The Musical Typing keyboard.
© Apple Inc.

The Musical Typing keyboard is a real-time MIDI keyboard with a maximum of six notes of polyphony. You can use it to audition software instruments without having to reach for your MIDI controller. You can even use the Musical Typing keyboard to record a MIDI performance in real time! The numeric keys give you control over pitch bend and modulation, you can use the Tab key as a sustain pedal, and you can assign its octave and velocity with the four Z-row keys shown in Figure 6.126!

The Musical Typing keyboard clearly doesn't replace a full MIDI keyboard controller, but if you are on a plane, train, or automobile with no access to a real keyboard, Logic's Musical Typing keyboard is very convenient. If you want to record a MIDI performance using it, just select your software instrument track in the Tracks area, open the Musical Typing keyboard, start recording, and play!

The main window is perhaps the most complex window in Logic. There's a lot of information to digest here, but when you're comfortable with the main window, you'll be far along the path to being comfortable with Logic as a whole. The next chapter explores using audio and Apple Loops in Logic.

Working with Audio and Apple Loops

N OW THAT YOU'VE EXPLORED MANIPULATING AND EDITING REGIONS, it's time to address manipulating and editing the data within those regions. Logic's handling of audio has always been one of its most lauded features. In this chapter, you'll examine how Logic Pro X handles audio and Apple Loops, as well as some useful and creative tips and tutorials for using these features.

Let's start by going into greater detail about the various audio channel strips types available in Logic Pro X.

Types of Channel Strips

Logic offers many different types of audio channel strips. Software instrument and audio channel strips are automatically assigned their own Tracks area tracks, but you can assign any of the other audio channel strips to a Tracks area track. They will then appear as channel strips in the main window Inspector, in the Mixer, and in the Mixer layer of the Environment.

A brief description of the different types of channel strips follows:

▷ **Audio channel strips:** The audio channel strip is analogous to the standard audio track on a hardware mixer. You record, edit, and play back audio files on audio tracks. You will normally record or place audio onto an audio track in the Tracks area and then use the audio track as a playback track. Audio tracks can be mono, stereo, or surround. They can use a hardware input or a bus as an input. A Logic project can include up to 255 stereo, mono, or surround audio tracks.

▷ **Software instrument channel strips:** Like external MIDI tracks, software instrument tracks use MIDI regions instead of audio regions. Unlike external MIDI channel strips, software instrument channel strips actually pass the audio from software instruments through the effects and routing defined in each software instrument channel strip. Software instrument channel strips allow you to access the built-in or third-party plug-in software synthesizers that can be integrated into Logic. When you play back the MIDI regions of a software instrument, those MIDI regions trigger the DSP algorithms of the software instrument to generate sound. Software instruments can be mono, stereo, surround, or multi-output. Multi-output software instruments use aux objects for their additional outputs. (See Chapter 9, "Working with Software Instruments.") A Logic project can include up to 255 software instruments. Although the Drummer track uses its own channel strip, it is in essence a software instrument channel strip.

▷ **Aux channel strips:** Aux (auxiliary) channel strips in Logic do not record or play back audio regions. Instead, aux channel strips are routing destinations that can accept their input from a number of sources. They can accept the input of a bus, becoming a send destination for any send-capable channel strip. (See the upcoming "Channel Strip Components" section.) That also means you can assign the output of a channel strip to a bus and assign the input of an aux channel strip to that bus. If you assign the outputs of multiple channel strips to the same bus, you can then assign an aux channel strip's input to that bus and use the aux channel strip as a master fader for those channels. Aux channel strips can accept their input from a multi-output software instrument, so each aux channel strip becomes the destination of a different output from the software instrument, and can send and receive channel-specific MIDI information. If you are using Logic as a ReWire master, you use aux channel strips to bring the ReWire slave's audio into Logic. Finally, aux channel strips can take their inputs from your audio interface, allowing for complex routing of live audio. Aux channel strips can be bused to other aux channel strips via either their sends or their output assignment. Aux channel strips can be mono, stereo, or surround. Logic supports up to 255 aux channel strips.

▷ **Input channel strips:** Input channel strips are used as a live audio play-through track in Logic. Unlike audio tracks, on which you record audio and then play back audio regions, main window tracks with input channel strips are used for tracks that are always live—for example, a hardware synthesizer that you want to mix with the rest of your tracks in the Logic Mixer but you do not want to record onto an audio track. Input channel strips can be mono or stereo and can output in mono, stereo, or surround. The number of hardware inputs on your audio interface determines how many input channel strips are available in Logic.

▷ **Output channel strips:** Output channel strips are used to send audio to your external hardware. They are usually the output destination of your other channel strips. You can use output objects to "bounce" audio, which means to create an audio file that contains the summation of all the channel strips routing their output to that particular output channel strip. Output channel strips can be mono, stereo, or surround. The number of hardware outputs on your audio interfaces determines how many output channel strips are available in Logic.

▷ **Master channel strip:** Logic offers a master channel strip. This channel strip does exactly what it says: It serves as a master volume for your song. The master channel strip does not stream any audio or MIDI data itself; it simply is used to adjust volume. If you are doing a surround mix or are sending each track to a hardware mixer and using many output channel strips, having a master channel strip offers a convenient way to adjust the overall level.

▷ **External MIDI channel strip:** This isn't an audio channel strip at all, but it's included here for completeness, since it appears in the Mixer along with your other channels if you create external MIDI tracks. Like software instrument channel strips, these channel strips use MIDI data. If you are using a ReWire application with Logic and sending that application MIDI from Logic, you will use an external MIDI track assigned to your ReWire application. (Chapter 9 goes into using ReWire applications in more detail.) If you are using hardware synthesizers or other instruments and not using the External Instrument plug-in (again, see Chapter 9), the MIDI on this track will be directed to them.

The aforementioned channel strips are the only channel strips you'll ever need to use in Logic Pro X. However, there is one other channel strip type that existed in Logic 7 and is still included in Logic Pro X for compatibility purposes: the bus channel strip. I'm including its description here in case you are working on a project that began in Logic 7, but otherwise you will not need to use this channel strip. In fact, I'd strongly advise against using it, because it has been superseded by the much more flexible aux track, which you should use instead.

The bus channel strip does not play or record audio files at all. It is more of a patch bay track. Often, buses on mixers were push buttons that sent the audio on an audio channel to an auxiliary track or auxiliary output. Buses in Logic Pro X serve a similar purpose of being a patch bay between destinations for your audio, although in Logic you can also use an actual bus channel strip as a destination itself. Still, it's best to think of a bus as an internal routing between other channel strips in Logic because the more flexible aux channel strip has supplanted the bus channel strip. The bus channel strip offers no input choice, and offers no sends. Bus channel strips are, in effect, single destination objects with no routing options, while aux channel strips have incredibly flexible routing options.

Here are some of the things you can do with buses:

▷ You can have a bus route audio from other channel strips to hardware outputs.

▷ Aux and audio channel strips may use buses as their input source.

▷ Other channel strips can use their sends to route signal through or to a bus. As mentioned, buses do not have sends on their own channel strips because buses are the destination of sends from other channel strips, but you can put effects directly in the channel strip of a bus if you want. Bus channel strips can be mono, stereo, or surround. Logic offers up to 64 buses.

Channel Strip Components

You've seen the channel strip in previous chapters. Now that I've described the different channel strip types, I'll go over the components of the channel strip and the subtle differences in the strips for various channel strip types. The channel strip is mostly used during mixing, which is covered in Chapter 11, "Mixing in Logic." However, editing audio requires some knowledge of the channel strip. You can use the channel strip in Figure 7.1 as your reference.

Figure 7.1 An audio channel strip.
© Apple Inc.

Each of the components of this channel strip can be toggled on or off in the View menu in the Mixer or by right-clicking in the Mixer and selecting items from the menu that appears. The channel strips in the Mixer layer of the Environment are not as full featured as the channel strips in the main Mixer, and they look nothing like the channel strips in the Mixer. Both the Mixer and the Mixer layer of the Environment are covered in detail in Chapter 11. The following descriptions of the various components of the channel strip explain any differences that exist for a specific type of channel strip:

▷ **Channel strip Setting menu:** Each channel strip's Setting menu allows you to browse for and select, as well as manage, channel strip settings.

▷ **Gain Reduction meters:** Double-clicking inside this rectangle enables a real-time Gain Reduction meter (which is used by the Dynamics Audio FX Compressor, Limiter, and Adaptive Limiter, discussed in Chapter 11) inside the rectangle and instantiates the Compressor effect in the first Audio FX slot. (Audio FX slots are covered in this section.) If there is already a plug-in inserted in the first insert slot, you can Option-double-click inside the rectangle, and the Compressor will be instantiated in the first insert. If you have instantiated the Limiter or the Adapted Limiter instead, then any gain reduction those effects perform will be shown as your project plays. If the Gain Reduction meters are active in the channel strip, double-clicking on the Gain Reduction meter opens the respective Dynamics effect's editor. All audio and software instrument channel strips contain the Gain Reduction meter.

▷ **EQ graph:** If you double-click inside this rectangle, you will enable a thumbnail of the Channel EQ effect graph (using Logic's EQs is discussed in Chapter 11) inside the rectangle, and the Channel EQ effect is instantiated in the first Audio FX slot. If there is already a plug-in inserted in the first insert slot, you can hold the Option key down while double-clicking inside the rectangle, and the Channel EQ will be instantiated in the first insert. If you have instantiated the Linear Phase EQ, then the EQ graph from this effect will be shown in the EQ rectangle. If the thumbnail image of the Channel or Linear Phase EQ is already showing in the channel strip, double-clicking on the thumbnail opens the respective EQ's Editor window. All audio and software instrument channel strips contain the EQ section.

▷ **Input slot:** Below the EQ is the Input slot, which gives you combined control over the format and input of the channel strip. The Format button is on the left end of the Input slot. If the button is a single circle, the channel strip format is mono. If the button is a double circle, the channel strip format is stereo. Clicking the button toggles between mono and stereo. If you click and hold on an audio, aux, or bus channel strip's Format button, you can assign the channel strip to mono, stereo, left, right, or surround. If you select left or right, the Format button displays two separate circles, and the circle on the side you have chosen will be darkened. If you choose surround, the Format button will display five small circles. Software instrument channel strips do not have this button because the type of software synthesizer you selected will determine whether the software instrument channel strip is mono, stereo, or surround. The right side of the Input slot lets you assign an input for the audio or software instrument channel strip. Each channel strip type features a different method of handling its input slot:

> ▷ **Audio channel strips:** You may select any of your audio interface's physical inputs as the input for this slot. You may also select any bus. You can configure an audio channel strip as a surround channel strip if your audio interface has enough inputs. If you choose surround, the input configuration is dictated in the Input tab of the I/O Assignments pane of the Audio Preferences window, which was covered in Chapter 3, "The Logic Project."

> ▷ **Software instrument channel strips:** You may select any available software synthesizer as the input for this slot.

> ▷ **Aux channel strips:** You may select your hardware inputs, buses, ReWire channels, or multi-output instrument outputs as the input for this slot. You can also choose to use your hardware inputs in surround if your audio interface has enough inputs.

> ▷ **Input channel strips:** Input channel strips' input is determined by the selected hardware input in the input channel strip's Channel parameter in the Inspector of the Mixer layer in the Environment, so the Input slot does not appear in the input channel strip. Currently, you can only configure input channel strips in mono or stereo.

> ▷ **Output channel strips:** These channel strips do not have rectangles for input because they can be used only as destinations for other channel strips. They do have Format buttons, although outputs are limited to mono and stereo formats.

▷ **Audio FX slots:** These rectangles represent slots into which you can insert effects. Logic Pro comes with 67 built-in effects, and you can also use various third-party plug-in effects. (This is discussed further in Chapter 11.) To add effects to an Audio FX slot, click the Audio FX slot. A menu of effects opens. When you select an effect, it appears in that Audio FX slot and the insert glows blue, indicating the effect is functioning. You can have up to 15 effects per channel strip in Logic. If you see fewer than the maximum number of Audio FX slots on your channel strip, don't worry; when you fill the last slot on the screen, another slot will appear beneath it. This will continue until you reach the maximum number of effects. All audio and software instrument channel strips can have effects, although the nature of your project defines whether your output channel strips or the master channel strip has effects. Your master channel strip will not have effects unless you are working in surround, and then your outputs will not have the slots.

▷ **Sends:** Send knobs are used to route (send) a variable amount of the audio signal from channel strips through buses. When empty, sends appear as empty rectangles (slots) with empty circles next to them. When you click and hold on a send rectangle and add a send destination, not only does the destination appear in the slot, but a small dial appears in the circle to the right of the send for you to adjust the send level. If you see fewer than the maximum number of send rectangles on your channel strip, don't worry; when you fill the last send slot on the screen, another rectangle will appear beneath it. This will continue until you reach the maximum of eight sends. Because buses are the destinations of sends, bus channel strips do not have sends themselves—one major reason aux channel strips should be used rather than bus channel strips. When you assign an unused bus to a send, a new aux channel strip is automatically created as the destination for the bus. Bus channel strips are not automatically created—another reason to go with auxes.

▷ **Output setting:** The output for all channel strips, except actual output channel strips, can be any available bus or output channel strip. If you are using a channel strip in surround, the master channel strip will automatically function as its output. The hardware output is selected in an output channel strip's channel in the Inspector of the Mixer layer of the Environment, so output channel strips do not have an output rectangle. Changing a channel strip's output setting to an unused output automatically creates the selected output channel strip.

▷ **Group display:** This shows the group number of the selected channel strip. If the channel strip is not assigned to a group, this display is a darker gray than the rest of the channel strip. Groups are explained in Chapter 11. All types of channel strips, including external MIDI channel strips, may belong to groups.

▷ **Automation Mode display:** This display shows whether the channel strip is currently using Logic's track-based automation. If the channel strip is using automation, the display indicates whether the track is currently reading automation data or which mode it is using to write automation data. Automation is explained in Chapter 10, "Using Automation in Logic." All channel strips, including external MIDI channel strips, have automation slots.

▷ **Track icon:** The track icon, assigned in the Track Inspector in the main window and covered in Chapter 6, "The Logic Pro Main Window," appears beneath the Automation Mode display.

▷ **Pan knob:** The large rotary knob below the track icon is the Pan knob. This knob allows you to adjust the panorama—or stereo position—of the channel strip's audio in the stereo field. If you are in surround mode, you may adjust the channel strip's panorama on more than two axes. All channel strips except the master channel strip (but including external MIDI channel strips) have Pan knobs.

▷ **Volume slider:** This long slider below the Pan knob, directly to the left of the channel strip audio meter, allows you to adjust the volume of the channel strip. The box above the Volume slider displays the Volume slider setting. You can use it to manually enter a volume setting. To do so, double-click it and enter a value. All channel strips, including external MIDI channel strips, have Volume sliders.

▷ **Channel strip meter:** This meter displays a bar line that represents the volume of the audio passing through the channel strip. It changes with each variation in volume of the channel strip's audio. The small box above the channel strip meter displays the highest volume peak that the channel strip's audio has hit up to that point in the project in the Clip Detector, directly above the channel strip meter. The channel strip meter has a range from —60 dB to +0 dBfs. There are two display scale options for the channel strip meters: Sectional dB-linear and Exponential. The Exponential scale gives you a higher metering resolution the closer the signal gets to +0 dBfs. The Sectional dB-linear scale provides a very high level of resolution along the entire metering range. You can change the channel strip meters' display mode in the Mixer tab of the Display Preferences window. All audio and software instrument channel strips have audio meters.

▷ **Channel Mute button:** Clicking this button, marked with the letter M, mutes the channel strip, and all the tracks in the main window assigned to the muted channel strip are silenced. All channel strips have the Channel Mute button.

▷ **Channel Solo button:** Clicking this button, marked with an S, silences all other currently unsoloed channel strips; only those main window tracks assigned to the soloed track will be heard. All audio and software instrument channel strips have Solo buttons.

▷ **Input Monitoring button:** Enabling this button, marked with an I, allows you to monitor the signal through an audio channel strip without record-enabling the track.

▷ **Record-Enable button:** If you click this button, marked with an R, the audio channel strip is ready to record audio through your audio interface. Only audio channel strips have R buttons because they are the only channel strips that can record audio.

▷ **Bounce:** The Bounce (Bnc or Bnce) button is found only on output channel strips or, in the case of surround projects, the master channel strip. Clicking this button opens a dialog box that enables you to create a mono or stereo audio file from all the channel strips routed to that output channel strip or a surround bounce through the master channel strip. Bouncing is discussed further in Chapter 11.

▷ **Dim button:** This button, marked with a D, is found only on the master channel strip. Selecting the Dim button drops the level of your audio to the predetermined level set in the General tab of the Audio Preferences window.

The Project Audio Browser

The Project Audio Browser (formerly the Audio Bin) is, in a sense, a repository for recorded and imported audio files. You do not have to use every audio file listed in the Project Audio Browser in your project, but every audio file used in your project will be listed in the Project Audio Browser.

Logic Pro® X Power!: The Comprehensive Guide

The Project Audio Browser is far more than a simple list of files, however. The Project Audio Browser also keeps track of every audio region into which an audio file has been split. You can drag audio regions from the Project Audio Browser directly onto an audio track in the Tracks area. The Project Audio Browser also offers many ways to manage, group, and manipulate audio files and audio regions. The Project Audio Browser is available in the Browsers area of the main window and as its own window.

The Project Audio Browser window is unlike many other integrated browsers and their separate windows in that the Project Audio Browser window is slightly different in look and is a little more powerful in functionality than its integrated twin. If I mention that an operation can be performed in the Project Audio Browser, then that operation can performed in either the integrated Project Audio Browser or the Project Audio Browser window. But if I specifically mention that something can be done in the Project Audio Browser window, then that operation *cannot* be performed in the integrated Project Audio Browser. Figure 7.2 shows an integrated Project Audio Browser filled with audio files and audio regions. Figure 7.3 shows an Project Audio Browser window filled with the same audio files and regions.

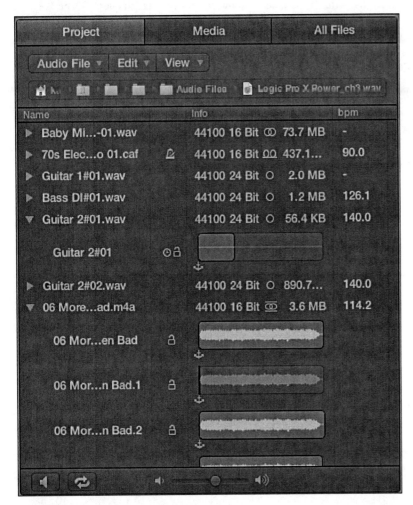

Figure 7.2 The Project Audio Browser.
© Apple Inc.

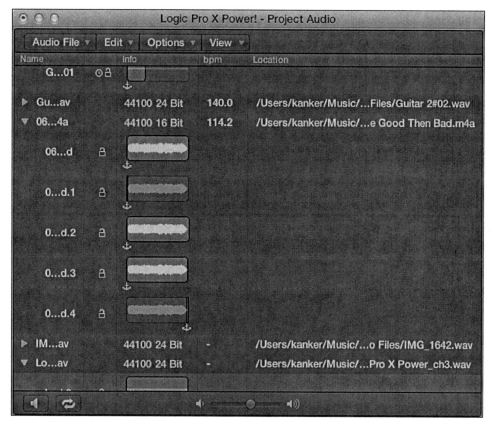

Figure 7.3 The Project Audio Browser window.
© Apple Inc.

The Project Audio Browser consists of local menus, buttons, and a Volume slider around its perimeter. The center contains an audio list containing the names of all your audio files and audio regions, along with text and graphic information about your audio regions represented in relation to the entire audio file to which they belong, sample rate, bit depth, size, BPM, and location information for all your audio files. To see the actual waveforms of your audio files and their anchor points, click the disclosure triangle for the file in the Name column; they will be displayed beneath the text in the Info column for the selected audio file. Let's start our exploration of the Project Audio Browser with the local menus.

The Project Audio Browser Local Menus

Like all windows and editors in Logic, the Project Audio Browser features its own local menus containing commands—in this case, commands that specifically affect audio and audio files. Keep in mind that for those commands that do not have key commands assigned by default, you can assign keys to them in the Key Commands window.

The Audio File Menu

The Audio File menu contains commands that operate on the audio files themselves. Figure 7.4 shows the Audio File menu of the Project Audio Browser.

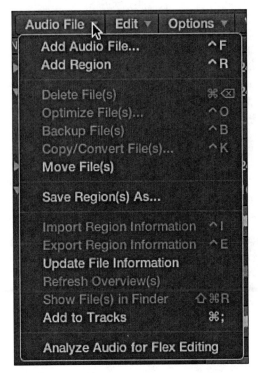

Figure 7.4 The Audio File menu of the Project Audio Browser.
© Apple Inc.

An explanation of the Audio File menu commands follows:

▷ **Add Audio File:** This command opens an Open File dialog box, which allows you to import audio files from your hard drive into the Project Audio Browser of your Logic project. You can then drag your file into the Tracks area or process it further in the Project Audio Browser. Logic can import files in WAV, Broadcast WAV, AIFF, CAF, SDII (Sound Designer II), MP3, and AAC format. The key command for this is Control+F.

▷ **Add Region:** If you select an audio file in the Project Audio Browser, this command creates a new audio region for that audio file. The new audio region will initially be the full length of the audio file, but you can adjust this length. The key command for this is Control+R.

▷ **Delete File(s):** This command deletes all selected files permanently from your storage drive. This is the only way to accomplish this within Logic. The key command for this is Command+Delete.

▷ **Optimize File(s):** This command deletes sections of audio files that are not used anywhere in your project. You can use this command to save hard drive space by eliminating unnecessary data, but make sure you don't accidentally erase a piece of audio that might prove useful. Because of this, you should use this command only when you are reasonably sure that you are completely finished with a song. The key command for this is Control+O.

▷ **Backup File(s):** This command creates a duplicate of all selected audio files. These files are given the extension .dup. Generally, because edits to regions are nondestructive (that is, they don't touch the file), this command is mostly useful if you are using time and pitch processing or editing samples, both of which affect the actual audio file itself. The key command for this is Control+B.

▷ **Copy/Convert File(s):** This command opens a dialog box in which you can duplicate or convert your selected audio file or files to AIFF, WAV, SDII, CAF, Apple Lossless, AAC, or MP3. For example, you could convert an AIFF file into a WAV file or an SDII file into an AIFF file. You can, of course, choose the original format and simply make duplicate files. This function is particularly useful when you want to export one or more files to a different format. You can also perform stereo conversion from a split format to an interleaved one or from an interleaved format to a split one; you can dither your audio file if you are changing bit rates; and you can choose to have the results of the process added to the Project Audio Browser. Figure 7.5 shows the Copy/Convert File As dialog box. These copy and conversion options are basically identical to the options you are given when you perform a bounce in Logic, which is covered in detail in Chapter 11. The key command for this is Control+K.

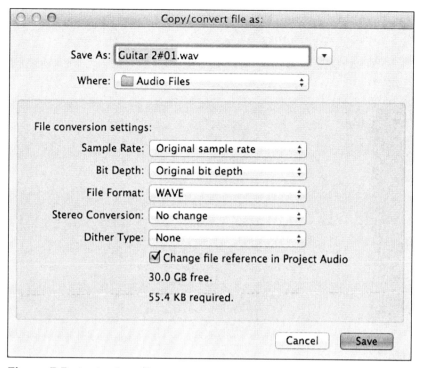

Figure 7.5 In the Copy/Convert File As dialog box, you can duplicate files and convert them from one format to another.
© Apple Inc.

▷ **Move File(s):** When you choose this command, a dialog box appears, prompting you for a new location on your hard drive to move one or more selected audio files in the Project Audio Browser. If you move audio files without using this command, Logic will not know the new location of your audio file and will prompt you to find it. If you use this command, Logic will be able to keep track of where you moved your audio files, even if you move the files to another storage drive.

▷ **Save Region(s) As:** This command allows you to save one or more specific audio regions as separate audio files. It opens a dialog box with identical commands to the Copy/Convert File As dialog box in Figure 7.5. This command is very useful if you want to export only those selected regions to another application.

▷ **Import Region Information:** This command allows you to import information from AIFF, CAF, WAV, and SDII audio regions you have added to your project. This allows you to add the information embedded in your audio file, such as position data, to the Project Audio Browser. The key command for this is Control+I.

▷ **Export Region Information:** This command allows you to export the information for the current audio file into the selected audio file. The key command for this is Control+E.

▷ **Update File Information:** If one or more of your audio regions is grayed out, that means Logic couldn't find the original audio file used by that audio region. If you select those grayed-out audio regions and choose this command, Logic presents a dialog box prompting you to navigate to the missing audio files. After using this command (and saving your song), Logic will remember the new file information.

▷ **Refresh Overview(s):** When you add a file to the Project Audio Browser, an overview, or graphical representation of the audio in the file, is created. If for some reason during the process of working with your audio, the overview does not represent your files, you can select this command to create a new overview for the file.

▷ **Show File(s) in Finder:** If you select one or more audio regions, this command will open Finder windows showing you the actual audio files on your hard drive to which these regions point. The key command for this is Shift+Command+R.

▷ **Add to Tracks:** You can select one or more audio regions and use this command to place them in the Tracks area. See the section "Adding Audio to the Tracks Area" later in this chapter for more details. The key command for this is Command+; (semicolon).

▷ **Analyze Audio for Flex Editing:** Although audio is analyzed for Flex Time and Flex Pitch editing in the Tracks area when you enable Flex editing for a track, this command lets you batch-process the flex analysis for some or all of your audio files at once.

The Edit Menu

This menu consists of some standard application editing functions and some functions specific to Logic. Figure 7.6 shows the Edit menu of the Project Audio Browser.

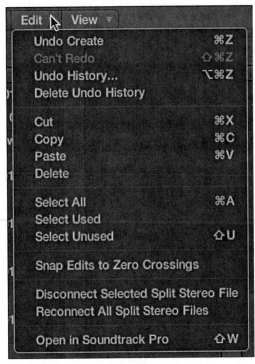

Figure 7.6 The Edit menu of the Project Audio Browser.
© Apple Inc.

The first eight commands in this menu—Undo, Redo, Undo History, Delete Undo History, Cut, Copy, Paste, and Delete—are the same commands you find in the global and local main window Edit menus. See the previous chapter for detailed information. Definitions of the rest of the commands follow:

▷ **Select All:** You can select every audio file and audio region in the Project Audio Browser with this command. The key command for this is Command+A.

▷ **Select Used:** This command selects all the audio regions that are currently used in your project.

▷ **Select Unused:** This selects all the audio regions that are not currently used in the Tracks area. The key command for this is Shift+U.

▷ **Snap Edits to Zero Crossings:** A zero crossing occurs when the amplitude of the audio wave is at the zero line. If you enable this option, all adjustments to audio regions fall at the nearest zero point. The advantage to this option is that you are far more likely to have seamless playback between two adjacent audio regions, since the amplitude of both audio regions will be at the zero crossing when they meet. The disadvantage is that this will sometimes interfere with where you want to make an edit if there doesn't happen to be a zero crossing at that point. Keep in mind that if you enable this option, it also holds true for audio region resizing and splitting in the main window.

▷ **Disconnect Selected Split Stereo File:** This command converts a split stereo file into two unlinked mono audio files. This is useful if you want to process or edit each side of the split stereo file separately.

▷ **Reconnect All Split Stereo File(s):** This command reconnects all unlinked mono files that used to be part of a split stereo file. This is especially useful when you import audio tracks that were originally split stereo files, but their link was broken in the process of exporting them from their original application.

▷ **Open in Soundtrack Pro:** If you have Apple's Soundtrack Pro on your system, you can use this command to open the selected audio in Soundtrack Pro. The key command for this is Shift+W.

The View Menu

The View menu offers options for viewing and sorting audio regions and audio files in the Project Audio Browser. Figure 7.7 shows the View menu of the Project Audio Browser.

Figure 7.7 The View menu of the Project Audio Browser.
© Apple Inc.

The various options in the View menu are as follows:

▷ **Files Sorted By:** This entry opens a submenu that enables you to select one of six options for sorting audio files in the audio list: None, Name, Size, Drive, Bit Depth, and File Type. When you re-sort your audio files, all the audio regions that originate from that file always move with the file. The default category is None, meaning your audio files are sorted by the order in which you added them. If you find it useful to have all your files in alphabetical order or in order of their file size, hard drive, or audio file bit depth, select the appropriate option.

▷ **Show File Info:** If this is checked, Logic displays the file information for all audio files in the audio list to the right of their names. The information displayed in the Project Audio Browser is, from left to right, the sample rate of the audio file, the bit rate, the file format, and the file size. The file format tells you whether the file is mono (single circle), stereo (overlapping circles), surround (five small circles), or an audio Apple Loop (an oval between two horizontal lines).

▷ **Show All Regions:** This command expands the disclosure triangle of all audio files so that all audio regions are displayed in the Project Audio Browser. The key command for this is Option+down arrow.

▷ **Hide All Regions:** This command contracts the disclosure triangle of each audio file so that none of the audio regions appears in the Project Audio Browser. The key command for this is Option+up arrow.

▷ **Sort Regions By:** This entry opens a submenu that enables you to check one of three options for sorting audio regions used by a given audio file: Start Point, Length, or Name. This sorts only the audio regions attached to each audio file; the files themselves do not change positions in the audio list.

▷ **Show Length As:** If you want to display the length of each audio region above the graphical representation of the region in the Project Audio Browser window, you can choose one of the options offered in the submenu that opens when you select this command. These are your options:

  ▷ **None:** This is the default. The audio region length is not displayed above the region.

  ▷ **Min:Sec:Ms:** This displays the length of the region in the following format: minutes:seconds:milliseconds.

  ▷ **Samples:** This command displays the number of samples in the region.

  ▷ **SMPTE Time:** This displays the length of the region in SMPTE timecode.

  ▷ **Bar/Beat:** This command displays how long the region is in bars and beats.

▷ **Create Group:** This command allows you to create a new grouping of audio files in the Project Audio Browser. Audio groups are discussed further in this chapter in the upcoming "Project Audio Browser Groups" section. The key command for this is Control+G.

▷ **Group Files By:** You can automatically create Project Audio Browser groups by grouping files by location, file attributes, or selection in tracks. Audio groups are discussed later in the chapter.

▷ **Delete Selected Groups:** This command deletes any selected Project Audio Browser group(s).

▷ **Show Region Use Count:** If this option is checked, there will be a number representing how many times that region appears in the Tracks area beside the overview of each audio region in the integrated Project Audio Browser.

The Options Menu

The Options local menu is available only in the standalone Project Audio Browser window. This menu contains one command: Strip Silence. The key command for this is Control+X. This command is also available in the Project Audio Browser if you right-click on a file. When you select an audio region, you can choose Strip Silence to scan the audio region for points in which the audio material is below a threshold you define, and then create a number of new audio regions out of those regions above the threshold. This command is extremely useful for removing any pauses in a recording. The section "Using Strip Silence" later in this chapter covers this command in more detail.

The Project Audio Browser Buttons

The bottom of the Project Audio Browser houses two buttons that affect how the Project Audio Browser operates, along with a Volume slider. Figure 7.8 shows the bottom of the Project Audio Browser.

Figure 7.8 The Project Audio Browser's buttons and Volume slider.
© Apple Inc.

The Project Audio Browser buttons do the following:

▷ **Playback button:** When the speaker icon in the Playback button is glowing green, the selected audio region plays back. If you have an audio file selected, the first audio region of that audio file plays back. If you have nothing selected, you cannot activate the button. If you click and hold the mouse button over any audio region, the cursor itself will become a speaker icon, your audio region will play back as long as you hold the button down, and the Playback button will remain lit during playback.

▷ **Cycle button:** With this button glowing yellow, the selected audio region cycles continuously. This is especially useful when you are adjusting loop points in the Project Audio Browser. (See the section "Using Cycling in the Project Audio Browser" later in this chapter.)

Cursor Modes in the Project Audio Browser Window

Although neither the integrated Project Audio Browser nor the Project Audio Browser window has a Tool menu, the cursor does serve a variety of functions in the Project Audio Browser window. Obviously, you can perform standard pointer functions in the Project Audio Browser window, such as selecting, dragging, and dropping files, but where you place the cursor over an audio region in the Project Audio Browser window changes the function of the cursor.

If you drag the cursor near either edge of an audio region, the cursor will change into a Resize cursor, which you can then use to change the start or end point of the region. If you keep the cursor inside the lower half of the region and move it in from a start point or an end point, the cursor will become a two-headed arrow. You can use this cursor mode to move the entire selected area that comprises the audio region over the parent audio file. If you move the cursor over the anchor-point indicator, which is the anchor icon under a region overview in the Project Audio Browser, the cursor will change into a finger, which allows you to drag the anchor to a new position in the selected audio region. Anchor points are covered in detail later in this chapter. If you have the cursor inside the top half of a region, it becomes a hand tool capable of dragging the region into the Tracks area (although you could just as easily drag the file by dragging its name).

Finally, if you drag the cursor over the top half of an audio region, the cursor will change into a speaker icon. If you click and hold on a region when the cursor is in speaker mode, the selected region will play from the point in the region that you clicked until either you release the mouse button or you reach the end of the region. If Cycle mode is engaged, then playback will begin at the point in the region where the cursor is, but the entire region will then loop until the mouse button is released.

Protecting Regions in the Project Audio Browser

Because there are so many different ways you could inadvertently edit your audio regions in the Project Audio Browser, Logic offers you the choice of protecting audio regions by locking them. A region that is locked in the Project Audio Browser cannot have its start or end point altered, and the anchor point is protected, too. To lock or unlock an audio region, simply click on the padlock icon next to the audio region's name in the Project Audio Browser. Figure 7.9 shows one locked audio region and one unlocked audio region in the Project Audio Browser.

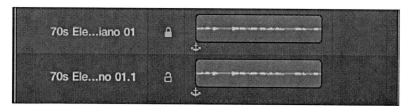

Figure 7.9 Locking audio regions protects them from inadvertent edits while you are working in the Project Audio Browser. Here you see one region that has been locked and another that is unlocked.
© Apple Inc.

You can still perform Strip Silence on a locked audio region, you can still edit a locked audio region in the Tracks area, and you can still delete a locked audio region from the Project Audio Browser. When an audio region is locked, the only cursor mode that is available for use with that region is the speaker cursor. (You can still drag it into the Tracks area by dragging its name field.)

The Prelisten Channel Strip

When you are working in the Project Audio Browser, any audio region you play back will by default play back through the prelisten channel strip, which is an audio channel strip that you can find in the Mixer next to the last audio channel strip when the Mixer is in the All view mode. (The Mixer and Mixer view modes are covered in detail in Chapter 11.) The prelisten channel strip is directly tied to the slider shown in Figure 7.8. The prelisten channel strip also services the Audio File editor, the Loops Browser, and the All Files Browser. Therefore, if you change the volume of the prelisten channel strip using the slider in the Project Audio Browser, for example, the slider in the Loops Browser will reflect that change. The Audio File editor and the Loops Browser are covered later in this chapter, and the All Files Browser is covered in Chapter 12, "Working with and Sharing Files."

At first, the need for a prelisten channel strip might seem counterintuitive. Why doesn't the Project Audio Browser simply play back each region using the audio channel to which that region is already assigned? Remember, the Project Audio Browser is a repository for all the audio files and regions that you have imported or recorded for your project, regardless of whether you use them. That means a good number of your audio regions may not be assigned to any audio channel. By offering an assignment of a single track for playback of everything in the Project Audio Browser, Logic ensures that each region, regardless of whether it is currently used in the project, will be able to play back. It also ensures that Logic is far more resource-efficient than if it had to constantly use resources to enable it to switch to any audio channel, turn on new effects processing, and so on for the various windows that use the prelisten channel. It also allows you to easily hear any changes you make to an audio file in the Project Audio Browser without any effects that may be instantiated on the audio file's parent channel strip.

Looking at it another way, the prelisten channel strip is not a limitation, but a feature. Many other DAWs don't include a prelisten channel strip at all. Instead, when you play audio from any editor or window except the main editor and Mixer, the audio is simply routed directly to the master outputs. You have no opportunity to adjust the volume, add effects, or otherwise process the "audition" channel. Logic gives you the ability to do that, thanks to the prelisten channel strip.

Still, if you want to monitor the audio files in the Project Audio Browser that have been assigned to a Tracks area track through their parent channel strips, you can right-click on the Playback button in the lower-left corner of the Project Audio Browser. This opens the contextual menu shown in Figure 7.10.

Figure 7.10 Right-clicking on the Playback button in the Project Audio Browser opens a contextual menu in which you can assign the playback routing of audio files in the Project Audio Browser.
© Apple Inc.

Selecting the Auto-Select Channel Strip option ensures that audio files that have been assigned to a main window track will play through their parent channel strip. Note that this playback setting applies to both the Project Audio Browser and the Audio File editor. If you change the playback setting in the Project Audio Browser, you also change the playback setting for the Audio File editor, and vice versa.

Adding Audio Files to the Project Audio Browser

Every time you record using Logic, the resulting audio file is automatically placed in the Project Audio Browser. Sometimes, however, you'll want to use audio in your song that you didn't record. If you want the audio to be in your song, you can, of course, add an audio file from the Tracks area, drag audio from the Finder to the Tracks area, or drag audio files from the All Files Browser. Sometimes, however, you'll want to have a number of prerecorded audio files available for your song but not placed in the Tracks area yet. In this case, you'll need to add them to the Project Audio Browser yourself. Luckily, this is very easy to do.

The easiest way to add audio to your song is simply to drag the audio files from your desktop or a Finder window into your Project Audio Browser. At that point, Logic creates an overview for the file, and it appears in your audio list like all the rest of your audio. You can select as many audio files as you want on your desktop or in the Finder; when you drag them into the Project Audio Browser, all of them will be added.

You can also use the Add Audio File command described previously. This command opens an Open File dialog box with one Logic-specific addition: a Play button. This button auditions the selected audio file on the prelisten channel. You can select one or more files to add; when you click the Add button at the bottom-right corner of the dialog box (or press Return), Logic will add any selected files to the audio list in the Project Audio Browser.

Exporting Audio from the Project Audio Browser

Sometimes, you may want to use an audio file you have recorded in Logic in another application. In that case, you'll want to export your audio. The usual way to export audio is to do a bounce, discussed in Chapter 11, or to export one or more tracks, discussed in Chapter 12. However, this section discusses a couple of options for exporting audio directly from the Project Audio Browser.

You can use the Copy/Convert File(s) or the Save Region(s) As commands to save your file in the same or a different format. When you select one of these commands, the resulting dialog box prompts you for a name and a destination for your file and then exports the audio file in the format you have selected.

Using Strip Silence

Earlier in this chapter, Strip Silence was mentioned. Now it's time to give this essential function a closer look. When you record an audio performance of an instrument that does not play constantly throughout the entire performance—for example, a vocal that weaves through the music or instruments that come and go for the duration of a song—your audio file will play back with moments of silence. At best, these moments take up unnecessary CPU cycles as Logic plays and processes segments of an audio file that are empty. At worst, the portions where your instruments or vocals aren't performing aren't truly silent at all, but are filled with background noise, guitar amplifier hiss, and the like. The Strip Silence command is designed to search your audio file for these segments of low or no audio and remove them from your song.

Strip Silence does not actually remove anything from the audio file on your hard drive. Because Logic plays audio regions in the Tracks area or Project Audio Browser, Strip Silence divides the selected audio region into several audio regions, leaving out those portions in which it did not detect any audio. The command allows you to set the threshold or minimum level for audio to be considered "not silence," so you have a certain amount of control over how many new audio regions the command will create. To access the Strip Silence window for a selected region, as shown in Figure 7.11, choose the Strip Silence command in the Project Audio Browser window or the Remove Silence from Audio Region command in the Tracks area Functions menu. Alternatively, use the key command Control+X.

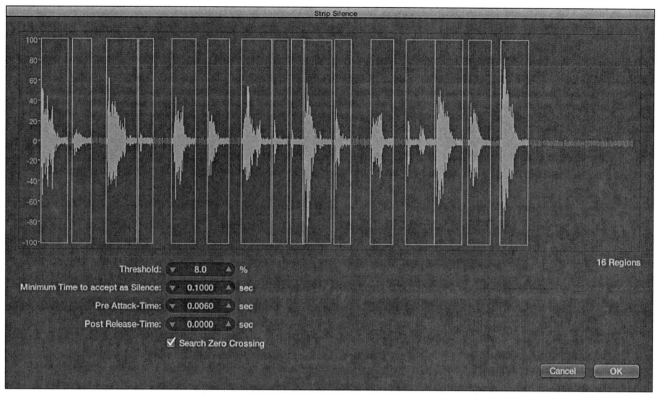

Figure 7.11 In the Strip Silence window, you can fine-tune the Strip Silence function.
© Apple Inc.

The Strip Silence window gives you a number of settings:

▷ **Threshold:** This is the amplitude above which Strip Silence detects the audio as audio and not as silence. Logic's default value is 4%, which is good for removing the silence in quiet tracks. If you have a noisier performance, such as a vocal that recorded a fair amount of background noise when there was no singing or a guitar amplifier with a loud hum or hiss when it wasn't playing, you will get better results if you set the threshold higher.

▷ **Minimum Time to Accept as Silence:** You don't want Strip Silence to detect any moment below a threshold as silence; otherwise, Logic will split up those nanoseconds between notes into their own audio regions! This parameter allows you to set how much time must pass before Logic detects silence. The default is 0.1 seconds, which is generally a very good setting. You might want to raise the setting if you find that Strip Silence is chopping off the decay of very quiet notes.

▷ **Pre Attack-Time:** This parameter ensures that Strip Silence will not cut off the attack of notes with slower amplitudes (or rise times). If you find that Strip Silence is cutting off your notes, increase this value.

▷ **Post Release-Time:** Similar to the preceding parameter, this setting is used to ensure that the decay of notes isn't removed. If you find that Strip Silence is cutting off your notes, increase this value.

▷ **Search Zero Crossing:** This command ensures that Logic always begins and ends audio regions at the point that the amplitude crosses the zero line. That way, no glitches or clicks will be audible at the beginning or end of newly created regions. You'll pretty much always want this option to be checked.

The actual operation of the command is quite simple:

1. Select an audio region.
2. Choose the Strip Silence command.
3. Use the graphic display of your waveform to adjust the settings. Your goal is for Logic to create exactly as many regions as you need, with no extra regions and without excess silence being included within the regions.
4. Click OK. The Strip Silence dialog box will close and your new regions will appear in the Tracks area and/or Project Audio Browser.

As you can see, Strip Silence is a powerful tool for quickly splitting the musically relevant portions of a performance or audio file into separate audio regions. If you want the silenced audio to also be removed from your hard drive after using Strip Silence, you can use the Edit > Select Unused command followed by the Audio Files > Optimize Files command in the Project Audio Browser. You can also use this function as a creative tool. For example, you can set the Pre Attack-Time and Post Release-Time parameters to cut off audio for a unique gated audio effect or to split different beats from a drum loop apart and then rearrange them to create an entirely new rhythm. Don't be afraid to experiment with Strip Silence. Creativity is the name of the game, and remember, you can always undo it later!

Using Strip Silence and Folder Tracks to Loop Audio: This information appears in the "Working with Audio and Apple Loops" chapter instead of the chapter on the main window so that it follows the section on the Strip Silence function, but this process really should be done completely in the Tracks area. Remember that the same command as the Strip Silence command in the Project Audio Browser appears in the local Tracks area Functions > Remove Silence from Audio Region menu path.

Sometimes you might want to use Strip Silence to remove the irrelevant segments of an audio region but retain the ability to manipulate the result as a single region. For example, suppose you want to loop a four-bar drum performance throughout the choruses of a song. You want to use Strip Silence to eliminate the noise between the beats, but trying to loop eight tiny audio regions representing a part of a whole would interfere with your looping. Folder tracks to the rescue! After using Strip Silence, you can place all resulting audio regions in a folder in the Tracks area by using the Functions > Folder > Pack Folder command in the Tracks area to pack that track into a folder. You can now manipulate the folder track as you would any other region in the Tracks area.

As you get more familiar with Logic, you can expand on this trick. For example, you could put each of the audio regions on a separate track, being careful not to alter their spacing from one another In fact, you'll find there's even an assignable key command, New Tracks for Selected Regions, that is really handy for this. You would select the right-most new region, use the key command to assign that region to a new track, then move to the previous region, select it, then use the key command to assign it to its own track, and so on. That way, you end up with each audio region on its own track. Now select the regions and pack them in a folder. Because each audio region in the folder gets its own channel strip, you could have different effects on every audio region, as well as submix the audio regions in the folder track. (More on mixing in Chapter 11.)

Using Cycling in the Project Audio Browser

As mentioned, you can loop playback of a region by clicking the Cycle button on the Project Audio Browser, selecting an audio region, then clicking on the Playback button (the one represented by the speaker icon). That audio region will then repeat until you disengage the Playback button. This may not seem particularly useful at first, but let's look at how you can use this functionality in the Project Audio Browser window in tandem with the Tracks area.

If you have an audio region in the Tracks area that just doesn't seem to begin and/or end where you'd like it to, and your attempts to resize it in the Tracks area are not giving you the desired results, the Project Audio Browser window is your answer. With the Loop button engaged, click the Playback button, and your region will repeat. Use the Project Audio Browser Resize cursor to adjust the start and end points of your audio region. The Tracks area track immediately reflects any changes you make, so you need not drag or move anything between windows.

Using this method to adjust regions can be a timesaver. If you have painstakingly set the locators, cycle, and/or autodrop points in the main window, this method gives you a way to loop the audio region you need to adjust without affecting any other aspect of your main window setup. Give it a try—you'll find using looping in the Project Audio Browser is a great way to resize individual audio regions.

Project Audio Browser Groups

Logic gives you the ability to organize audio files into groups inside the Project Audio Browser. You'll find this to be a great organizational help if you have lots of different types of audio material. For example, you could create one group called Guitars, one called Drums, one called Synths, and so on, and use these to keep your audio files organized within the Project Audio Browser.

Creating groups in the Project Audio Browser couldn't be easier. Simply select those audio files (not regions representing segments of a larger file, but regions representing a complete file) in the Project Audio Browser that you wish to group together and then select the View > Create Groups command. A text box will appear for you to name the new group, and the selected audio files will be placed inside the group. You can also use the Create Groups command without any audio files selected in the Project Audio Browser and then simply drag audio files into the group later. Finally, Logic can automatically group your audio files together by their location on your hard drive or their file attributes, or it can group those files selected in the Tracks area with the View > Group Files By commands. (If you already have groups created, you will be prompted about whether you want them to be deleted.)

The names of audio file groups will be in a bolder font than the names of your audio files, and the audio list will identify the group as an audio file group. (If you double-click this text, you can add your own comment.) Figure 7.12 shows the Project Audio Browser with two audio file groups created.

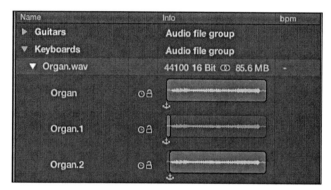

Figure 7.12 This Project Audio Browser has two audio file groups: Guitars and Keyboards. You can see the audio regions in the expanded Keyboards group with some of the region data hidden; the Guitars group has been collapsed, so its audio files are not displayed.
© Apple Inc.

You can open and close audio file groups by clicking on their disclosure triangles. You can also Option-click on a group triangle to open or close all the disclosure triangles within a group.

Keep in mind that audio file groups are strictly organizational groups. Grouping audio files does not affect their location on your hard drive, their use or placement in the Tracks area, and so on.

Adding Audio to the Tracks Area

The Project Audio Browser is a great organizational and processing tool for audio, but to actually use your audio in a project, you'll need to add it to the Tracks area. You can do this either by selecting one or more audio regions and dragging them from the Project Audio Browser (or the Finder) to the Tracks area or by using the Add to Tracks command. Regardless of which method you choose, the dialog box shown in Figure 7.13 will prompt you to instruct Logic how to handle the audio region(s).

Figure 7.13 The Add Selected Files to Arrange dialog box. Perhaps in a future update, this will be changed to the Add Selected Files to Tracks dialog box.
© Apple Inc.

Depending on your selections in this dialog box, Logic Pro will do the following:

▷ Create a new audio track in the Tracks area for each audio region you wish to add.
▷ Use the existing audio tracks in the Tracks area and add one audio region to each.
▷ Place all the audio regions you are adding to the Tracks area on the selected audio track.

As you can see, Logic makes adding audio from the Project Audio Browser to the Tracks area simple and intuitive, and gives you plenty of options to make sure it handles the audio the way you want it to.

The Logic Audio Editors

For years, the only heavy-lifting audio editing options in Logic have been in the Arrange window and in the Sample editor. In the Arrange window, you could edit regions, but you weren't actually changing the audio file itself, just how Logic referenced the file. The Sample editor allowed you to destructively edit the actual audio file itself. Logic Pro X has changed this paradigm. Along with the name changes to these two parts of Logic—the Arrange window to the main window and Sample editor to Audio File editor—comes a new audio editor, the Audio Track editor.

What's the difference between these two audio editors? Quite a bit, as you'll soon see. The main thing to understand is that the Audio Track editor simply works on the selected audio region in a similar manner to editing in the Tracks area. You simply edit Logic's handling of the file, the sections of the file it plays, and how it plays them. Work you perform on an audio file in the Audio Track editor does not transfer to other applications in which you may choose to use the file (unless, of course, you bounce the region or track) because it is not editing the file itself.

In contrast, the Audio File editor, like the Sample editor before it, does destructive editing to the actual audio file, permanently altering the audio file on your storage drive. This means that after you perform work on a file in the Audio File editor, opening the file in another application reflects the work you did without any need to bounce the result. While the Audio Track editor has access to global tracks, the Audio File editor does not. The Audio File editor does, however, have unique audio processing capabilities throughout Logic. Both editors have their uses, their advantages, and their disadvantages, and both will likely become essential to your workflow when handling audio. Let's dig into the Audio Track editor first, and then we'll get into the Audio File editor.

The Audio Track Editor

The Audio Track editor, shown in Figure 7.14, is in essence an extension of the Tracks area. Much of the editing power in the Audio Track editor is identical to that of the Tracks area. Indeed a task as simple as selecting an area in an audio region in the Audio Track editor selects that same area of the same region in the Tracks area. They are truly linked. This begs the question: Why bother with the Audio Track editor at all? First, it provides an instantly focused area in the main window where you can perform edits without having your vision field crowded by other regions on other tracks. Simply double-click an audio region in the Tracks area, and it will open in the Audio Track editor, ready for you to work on it. Second, and more importantly, the Audio Track editor is where you have access to Flex Pitch editing.

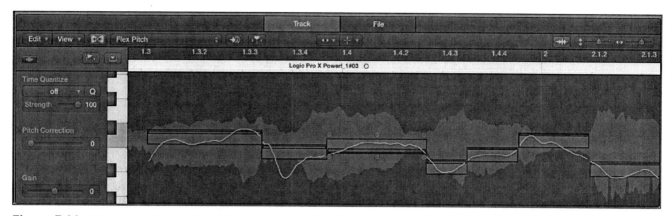

Figure 7.14 The Audio Track editor. There are many familiar components in the Audio Track editor. You can see the local menus, global tracks buttons, zoom controls, and so forth. We'll start by exploring the Audio Track editor local menus.
© Apple Inc.

Local Menus

As you can see in Figure 7.14, the Audio Track editor has two local menus, Edit and View. Many of the commands in these menus are identical to the same commands in the Tracks area Edit and View menus. When you use commands like Cut, Copy, and Paste in the Audio Track editor, they are immediately updated in the Tracks area; again, the Audio Track editor is fundamentally an extension of the Tracks area. For more information on these duplicate commands, review their descriptions in Chapter 6. For commands that may function a little differently, an explanation will be given here. First, the Edit menu.

THE AUDIO TRACK EDITOR EDIT MENU

The Audio Track editor Edit menu is shown in Figure 7.15.

Figure 7.15 The Audio Track editor Edit menu.
© Apple Inc.

This menu offers a few unique options:

▷ **Repeat Events:** This command is similar to the Repeat command in the Tracks area. You can repeat the selected region with this command. Additionally, when in Flex Pitch mode, you can select a Flex Pitch note, which is a more advanced version of the Flex Pitch bars in the Tracks area, and use this command to repeat the audio surrounding the selected note from its initial zero crossing to its final zero crossing. This command opens the Repeat Regions/Events dialog box, covered in Chapter 6. Repeating Flex Pitch notes is covered in the section "Flex Pitch Editing in the Audio Track Editor" later in this chapter.

▷ **Analyze Audio for Flex Editing:** This command analyzes the pitch and transients of the selected audio region.

▷ **Create MIDI Track from Flex Pitch Data:** Because Flex Pitch analyzes the pitch of monophonic audio files, translating that data to MIDI is a fairly straightforward operation. This command lets you convert that pitch data into MIDI data. When you use this command, a new software instrument track is created under the currently selected track header in the main window, along with a region containing MIDI notes derived from your audio. The Piano Roll editor, covered in Chapter 8, "Working with MIDI," opens in the main window, giving you the ability to immediately edit the new region. This command is great for doubling or replacing a monophonic audio region with a software instrument sound. Because the new software instrument track is placed under the currently highlighted track header, you can select the place in the Track list where you would like your new software instrument track to be, and then select the audio region you wish to use. I highly recommend you take the time to perform all the Flex Pitch editing you plan on doing before you use this command. The results you achieve with this command can be very surprising, depending on the accuracy of the pitch editing!

▷ **Open In:** If you have configured Logic to work with an external sample editor in the Audio File Editor tab of the Audio Preferences window, you can use this command to open the selected audio in your external sample editor. Setting up an external sample editor is covered in the section "Configuring Logic to Use an External Sample Editor" later in this chapter. The key command for this is Shift+W.

▷ **Snap Edits to Zero Crossings:** You learned about zero crossings earlier in this chapter. If you select this command, Logic always looks for the point at which the amplitude crosses the zero mark while you are editing. This is to ensure glitch- and click-free playback, but it might restrict you from making edits at the exact location you want.

THE AUDIO TRACK EDITOR VIEW MENU

The Audio Track editor View menu, shown in Figure 7.16, has only one command that is not in the Tracks area View menu: Show Local Inspector. This command is available only when the Audio Track editor is in Flex Pitch Editing mode. The Audio Track editor Inspector is covered later in this chapter in the discussion of Flex Pitch Editing, but if you're curious about what it looks like, it can be seen at the left end of the Audio Track editor in Figure 7.14.

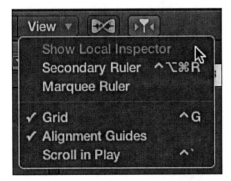

Figure 7.16 The Audio Track editor View menu.
© Apple Inc.

The Audio Track Editor Buttons

The Audio Track editor includes four buttons, shown in Figure 7.17.

Figure 7.17 The Audio Track editor buttons.
© Apple Inc.

The Audio Track editor buttons, from left to right, are as follows:

▷ **Show/Hide Flex:** Use this button to enable and disable Flex editing in the Audio Track editor. When Flex editing is engaged, a Flex Mode menu identical to the one found in audio track headers in the Tracks area is displayed to the right of the Show/Hide Flex button. You can see this in Figure 7.17.

▷ **MIDI IN:** As of this writing, with Logic Pro X 10.0.4, there is no use for the MIDI IN button in the Audio Track editor. This button is displayed only when Flex editing is enabled in the Audio Track editor.

▷ **Catch Playhead:** The Catch Playhead button enables Catch Playhead mode. If this button is lit, the Audio Track editor is linked to the current song position in the Tracks area, and vice versa. If there is no audio, the playhead simply stops at the end of the audio region. It is particularly helpful to leave this engaged in the Audio Track editor because edits and actions performed on the selected regions in either the Audio Track editor or the Tracks area are immediately reflected in both areas. It's especially helpful for keeping track of where you are in a region when your Tracks area and Audio File editor are using very disparate horizontal zoom settings.

▷ **Waveform Zoom:** This button lets you increase or decrease the vertical zoom of the waveform displayed in the Audio Track editor. If you click and hold on this button, a vertical slider appears, allowing you more control over the vertical waveform zoom. Clicking the button again returns the waveform to its previous zoom setting.

The Audio Track Editor Tool Menu

The Audio Track editor Tool menu, shown in Figure 7.18, contains all the tools found in the Tracks area Tool menu (with one exception that will be noted in the Audio Track editor Tool menu details to follow), plus two other unique tools.

Figure 7.18 The Audio Track editor Tool menu.
© Apple Inc.

The Audio Track editor Tool menu tools are as follows:

▷ **Pointer:** The Pointer tool is very versatile in the Audio Track editor. It can be used to drag the selected region along the timeline as in the Tracks area, but its real power comes when in Flex Edit mode, as you'll discover later in this chapter.

▷ **Pencil:** This tool is used to add or alter the length of pitch notes in Flex Pitch edit mode.

▷ **Eraser:** This tool can be used to erase the current Audio Track editor region, to erase Flex Pitch notes, and to erase Flex Time transients.

▷ **Text:** This tool looks like a text-entry bar. It is used to name regions in the Audio Track editor. Click under the region header with this tool to open a text box, which lets you rename the region.

▷ **Scissors:** This tool is used to split regions. You hold the Option key down while splitting regions to divide the entire region into multiple equally spaced regions the same length as your initial split. You can also use the Scissors tool to split Flex Pitch notes.

▷ **Glue:** This tool is used to join selected regions into one single region, which is given the name and track position of the initial region. The Glue tool can also be used to join Flex Pitch notes.

▷ **Solo:** This tool can be used to solo any selected regions when you aren't in Flex Edit mode.

▷ **Mute:** This tool mutes any selected regions when you aren't in Flex Edit mode.

▷ **Zoom:** This tool is used to zoom in on the region you're editing in the Audio Track editor.

▷ **Fade:** This tool, when dragged over two adjacent audio regions, creates a crossfade between them. It can also be used to create fade-ins and fade-outs. It works in the Audio Track editor only if Flex edit mode is turned off both in the Audio Track editor and the parent track in the Tracks area. Crossfades are covered later in this chapter.

▷ **Automation Select:** The Automation Select tool can select automation data in the automation lane. Although it doesn't appear in the Audio Track editor Tool menu, it does appear in the Audio Track editor shortcut menu when a Show Tools option is selected in the Right Mouse Button menu in the Editing tab of the General Preferences window. It also serves no purpose in the Audio Track editor.

▷ **Automation Curve:** The Automation Curve tool can create curves between two automation nodes. It also serves no purpose in the Audio Track editor.

▷ **Marquee:** This tool functions exactly as it does in the Tracks area when Flex Pitch edit mode is disabled. Marquee selections and edits in the Audio Track editor are immediately reflected in the Tracks area. You can also use the Marquee tool to make selections for Flex Time editing as you would in the Tracks area.

▷ **Flex:** The Flex tool allows you to perform some Flex Time edits when the Audio Track editor is not in Flex view.

▷ **Vibrato:** The Vibrato tool lets you adjust the extent of the vibrato drift from the analyzed pitch when Flex Pitch editing. The Vibrato tool is covered in more detail in the section "Flex Pitch Editing in the Audio Track Editor" later in this chapter.

▷ **Volume:** The Volume tool lets you adjust the gain of Flex Pitch notes when in Flex Pitch edit mode. The Volume tool is covered in more detail in the section "Flex Pitch Editing in the Audio Track Editor" later in this chapter.

The Audio Track Editor Zoom Controls

The Audio Track editor features a horizontal zoom control, unless you are in Flex Pitch edit mode, which add a vertical zoom control. Increasing Vertical zoom in Flex Pitch edit mode can make it easier to make adjustments to different Flex Pitch parameters, which are covered in the section "Flex Pitch Editing in the Audio Track Editor" later in this chapter.

Editing Audio Regions in the Audio Track Editor

Editing audio regions in the Audio Track editor is identical to editing audio in the Tracks area. In fact, using the Audio Track editor is the ideal way to focus on a single audio region or a selection of audio regions on a track without having to change the zoom setting in the Tracks area. You can resize regions at their edges, use the Scissors tool to split regions, use the Glue tool to join regions, use the Marquee tool and manipulate Marquee selections, and use the various Tracks area key commands to edit regions, among other things. When not in Flex edit mode you should, quite literally, treat the Audio Track editor as an extension of the Tracks area, letting you focus on a region or multiple regions of an audio track, using its independent zoom level from the Tracks area to let you work on the specifics of your audio edits while seeing the grander scheme of your arrangement. The more you get used to using the Audio Track editor in conjunction with editing in the Tracks area, the more efficient your workflow will become!

Flex Time Editing in the Audio Track Editor

Flex Time editing in the Audio Track editor also functions identically to Flex Time editing in the Tracks area. You can create and delete Flex Time markers, time stretch and compress by moving Flex Time markers, use the Marquee tool to flex audio, and use any of the Flex Time modes in the Audio Track editor. Mastery of the Flex Time editing procedures detailed in Chapter 6 is highly recommended. Just like editing audio regions, using the Audio Track editor can speed your workflow by giving you that additional focused area for performing Flex Time edits.

Flex Pitch Editing in the Audio Track Editor

This is where things get interesting in the Audio Track editor: with Flex Pitch editing. Although Flex Pitch editing in the Tracks area can be good for quick and dirty tweaks, and is sometimes all the editing that's needed, the Flex Pitch editing tools in the Audio Track editor are vast by comparison. Of course, you can analyze an audio region or regions on a track in the Flex Pitch editor and alter the pitch of those monophonic audio regions, but you can also use Flex Pitch notes to edit the extent of the analyzed vibrato, affect the formants in Flex Pitch notes to help make your tweaks sound more natural, alter the gain of Flex Pitch notes nondestructively, quantize your audio, and more. Flex Pitch notes look quite different from the Flex Pitch bars found in the Tracks area, as you can see in Figure 7.19.

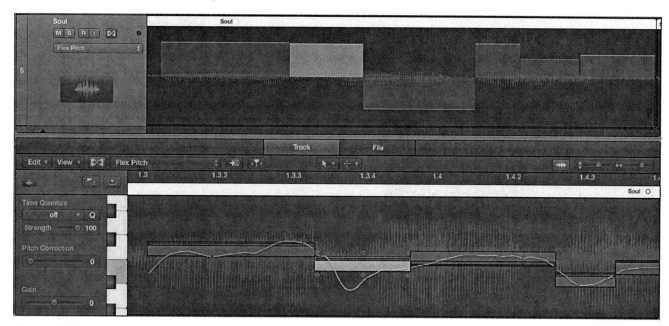

Figure 7.19 An audio region shown in the Tracks area and the Audio Track editor in Flex Pitch Editing mode. With both tracks at a similar horizontal zoom level, you can see how different Flex Pitch notes are compared to the Flex Pitch bars in the Tracks area.
© Apple Inc.

Note the vibrato line running through the Audio Track editor—each section of the line a part of its parent note—and the six circles surrounding the highlighted Flex Pitch note in the middle of the Audio Track editor. Along with the functions in the Audio Track editor Inspector and the Audio Track editor tools, these characteristics of Flex Pitch notes offer you extremely broad control for Flex Pitch editing.

CHARACTERISTICS OF FLEX PITCH NOTES

There are some fundamental characteristics of Flex Pitch notes—namely the vibrato line and the six Flex Pitch editing circles, or hotspots, surrounding a Flex Pitch note—that are central to deeper Flex Pitch editing. These characteristics and their functions are as follows:

- ▷ **Vibrato line:** The vibrato line shows the amount of analyzed vibrato or pitch drift for the note. You can edit the vibrato line using the pitch drift hotspots (covered next in this list) with the vibrato hotspot and the Vibrato tool, which are detailed later in this chapter in the section "Using the Vibrato Tool."
- ▷ **Pitch drift hotspots:** The hotspots at the upper-left and upper-right of a Flex Pitch note are the pitch drift hotspots. You can drag these to increase or decrease the amount of pitch drift at the beginning or end of a Flex Pitch note, respectively. These changes will be reflected in the amplitude of the vibrato line. Note that changing the pitch drift setting at either end of a Flex Pitch note will alter the pitch drift of any adjacent Flex Pitch notes.
- ▷ **Fine pitch hotspot:** The fine pitch hotspot is the hotspot in the center at the top of a Flex Pitch note. This hotspot functions like the Flex Pitch bar in the Tracks area. Drag it vertically to fine-tune the pitch of the Flex Pitch note. The more you alter the flex pitch hotspot's setting, the more or less blue you'll see in the note. Notes that are sharp will fill with blue from the bottom of the note.

▷ **Gain hotspot:** The Gain hotspot, found at the lower-left corner of a Flex Pitch note, lets you alter the gain of its Flex Pitch note by dragging it vertically. Use this hotspot to boost the volume of any bit of audio that's too quiet or to decrease the volume of something that's sticking out too much.

▷ **Vibrato hotspot:** The vibrato hotspot, at the center-bottom of the Flex Pitch note, allows you to alter the extent of the vibrato or pitch drift across the entire note by dragging it vertically. As with the pitch drift hotspots, any changes to the vibrato hotspot alter the pitch drift of adjacent notes.

▷ **Formant shift hotspot:** The formant shift hotspot, at the lower-right of the Flex Pitch note, lets you alter the extent of formant shift for a Flex Pitch note. Similar to the Formant Shift setting in the parent track, covered in Chapter 6, this hotspot lets you fine-tune the formant shift for its Flex Pitch note.

It is not essential to select a note to access its hotspots. Simply drag the cursor to the note, and its hotspots appear. When you put the cursor over a hotspot, the cursor becomes a Finger tool, and a help tag appears to show you the value of any changes you make. As you drag the hotspot the cursor becomes a −, as in Figure 7.20.

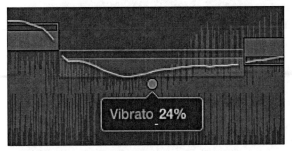

Figure 7.20 Using help tags, you can fine-tune the setting of a hotspot. Here, the Vibrato amount has been decreased to 24% of its original value. Note the extreme change in the vibrato line compared to Figure 7.19. You can also see how this affects the slope of the pitch drift of the adjacent Flex Pitch notes at their borders.
© Apple Inc.

Remember that you can increase or decrease the vertical zoom in the Audio Track editor. With so much visual feedback available for Flex Pitch notes, increasing the vertical zoom can really be helpful for fine-tuning a note. Figure 7.21 shows the same note in Figure 7.20 at the maximum vertical zoom setting.

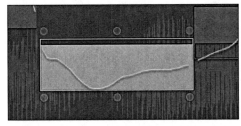

Figure 7.21 Use the vertical zoom control to enhance editing of Flex Pitch notes.
© Apple Inc.

TIP: You can use the same zoom key commands, Command+arrows, as in the Tracks area to adjust vertical and horizontal zoom when the Audio Track editor is in focus.

TIP: If you have made any edits to the vibrato line of a note using the Pitch Drift and/or vibrato hotspots or by using the Vibrato tool covered later in this chapter, you can easily undo all those edits and return the vibrato line of the selected note back to its original state by right-clicking on the note and selecting the Reset Pitch Curve command.

SELECTING AND EDITING MULTIPLE HOTSPOTS

One other very handy trick for using hotspots is to select multiple Flex Pitch notes and use the hotspots for one of the selected notes to edit the group. This can be done with the same methods you use to select multiple regions in the Tracks area:

▷ You can select multiple notes by dragging the mouse pointer and "lassoing" a collection of notes.
▷ You can Command-click non-contiguous notes.
▷ You can select the first note and Shift-click the last note you'd like to edit for a contiguous group of notes.
▷ You can use the keyboard at the left end of the Audio Track editor to select all notes of that pitch.
▷ You can Shift-click on the keyboard to select all notes of multiple pitches. (Note that this method does not select all pitches between two selected pitches. For example, you can use this method to select all C2 notes and all Bb1 notes, as shown in Figure 7.22.)

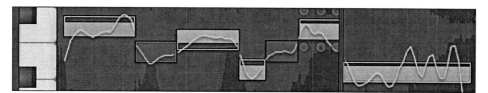

Figure 7.22 Shift-click to select all notes of various pitches using the Audio Track editor keyboard.
© Apple Inc.

Editing multiple selected notes can be useful for a variety of reasons. Perhaps the formant shift of all the notes of a pitch isn't to your liking. Maybe there were a couple of specific pitches a particular instrument produced that were consistently louder than all the rest, so instead of compressing the track, you quickly reduce the gain of all those notes. These methods for selecting multiple notes will be useful for many other Flex Pitch editing processes, as you'll soon see.

AUDITIONING FLEX PITCH NOTES

There can be several Flex Pitch notes found in a small area across the Bar ruler, even in one word of a vocal performance. It would be frustrating to have to set an extremely small Cycle region or chop your audio into a bunch of regions to use the Set Locators by Regions command and use Varispeed to slow playback enough to get meaningful feedback for edits you make—although it is a useful method. Fortunately, there is a quicker and easier way to audition your Flex Pitch notes. If you place the cursor over a Flex Pitch note, the cursor becomes a Hand tool. Click and hold with the Hand tool at any spot within the boundaries of a Flex Pitch note, and the audio at that exact location will play until you release the mouse button. Take care not to move the Hand tool horizontally when you do this or your note could be stretched or compressed. Move to a different place in the note, and you can hear the audio at that exact location. This allows you to truly fine-tune your edits across a Flex Pitch note in a way that is more effective than only hearing playback of the note. Keep both of these methods in mind as you learn more about editing Flex Pitch notes. You'll find that both methods have their uses, but that the Hand tool approach will generally be the most useful.

USING THE VIBRATO TOOL

The Vibrato tool gives you another means to adjust the vibrato line for a selected event(s). Its function is identical to the vibrato hotspots, but instead of having to drag a small hotspot, you can drag vertically anywhere in a selected note to alter the vibrato line for any selected notes. If you have multiple notes selected and you drag the Vibrato tool on a non-selected note, it will affect the Vibrato setting of the selected notes as well.

CHANGING THE GAIN OF NOTES

There are a few different methods available for changing the gain of notes in the Audio Track editor. The gain hotspot offers one method. You can also use the Volume tool. As with the Vibrato tool, you can use the Volume tool to edit the gain of any selected notes by dragging vertically anywhere in a selected note. If you have multiple notes selected and you drag the Volume tool on a non-selected note, it will affect the Gain setting of the selected notes as well. Using the gain hotspot or Volume tool gives you instant feedback because the size of the audio waveform scales immediately as you change the Gain setting. Don't forget to use the Waveform Zoom control to provide even more feedback for your Gain setting edits by increasing the zoom of the waveforms in the Audio Track editor.

There is one other method for changing the gain of notes: the Gain slider in the Audio Track editor Inspector, shown in Figure 7.23. As with the gain hotspot and the Volume tool, the Gain slider lets you change the volume of all selected notes. Drag the slider left to decrease the Gain setting, right to increase the Gain setting. Unlike the gain hotspot and the Volume tool, there is no instant feedback in the edited waveforms. You have to release the mouse button before the waveform is redrawn. Figure 7.24 shows two notes, one with its normal Gain setting, the other with its Gain setting reduced drastically. You can see that the two notes are connected—in this case, parts of the same vocal performance of a word. For this example in the real world, it would have been more desirable to select both notes and alter their gain collectively.

Figure 7.23 Use the Gain slider to change the volume of selected notes.
© Apple Inc.

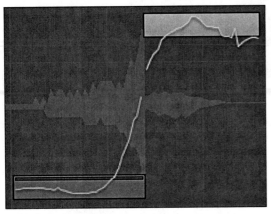

Figure 7.24 Two note events in the same word of a vocal performance. The first note has its normal Gain setting. The second note's Gain has been reduced drastically.
© Apple Inc.

CHANGING THE PITCH OF NOTES

The Audio Track editor offers multiple ways to alter the pitch of a note. Obviously, the fine pitch, pitch drift, and vibrato hotspot and the Vibrato tool can accomplish this, but there are a number of other ways to do this, too.

Changing the Fine-Tuning of Notes   The fine pitch hotspot can be used to increase or decrease the fine-tuning of a note. Not only can you drag the fine pitch hotspot to tune the note to the analyzed pitch, but you can keep dragging the hotspot up or down to move the note to other pitches. This is one way to correct the coarse-tuning of a note performed so poorly that the analysis returned a different pitch entirely.

In addition to the fine pitch hotspot, there is another method you can use to change the fine-tuning of notes. While there is no Pitch tool, there's something just as useful in the Inspector: the Pitch Correction slider in the Audio Track editor Inspector, shown in Figure 7.25.

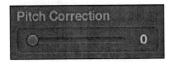

Figure 7.25   The Pitch Correction slider in the Audio Track editor Inspector.
© Apple Inc.

The Pitch Correction slider is limited to correcting the pitch in relation to the analyzed pitch. In other words, if your note is 15 cents sharp of the analyzed note, the Pitch Correction slider will only let you move the selected note down toward the analyzed note. You can't change the coarse-tuning of a note using the Pitch Correction slider.

Changing the Coarse-Tuning of Notes   To change the coarse-tuning of notes—in other words, move a note or notes to an entirely different pitch—simply drag a selected note to the desired pitch. This is an example of the usefulness of selecting multiple notes using the Audio Track editor keyboard. For example, suppose all the F3s performed in a region should have been E3s. If you click F3 in the keyboard to select all F3 notes and drag one of the selected notes to E3, all the selected notes will be moved to E3. This is one way to quantize the pitch of notes, but there are two other methods available.

Quantizing the Pitch of Notes   If you want to move notes in your audio region to pitch in an automated fashion, the Audio Track editor offers two options. The first option is very quick and easy: Right-click in the Audio Track editor to access its shortcut menu, shown in Figure 7.26. There are two options in the shortcut menu: Set All to Perfect Pitch and Set All to Original Pitch. If you select Set All to Perfect Pitch, all the notes in the Audio Track editor will be quantized to their analyzed pitch, although their vibrato/pitch drift will remain.

Figure 7.26   The Audio Track editor shortcut menu.
© Apple Inc.

Figure 7.27 shows some of the notes you've seen in other figures after being quantized to pitch. You can see that the notes are completely filled in, showing that they are pitched to their analyzed pitches. You can also see that although some notes are selected, the unselected notes have also been pitch quantized. To return notes back to their original pitch, select the Set All to Original Pitch option. Additionally, note that the vibrato line still varies the pitch of the note around the perfect pitches. If you want notes to be set to perfect pitch, it's sensible to quantize the pitch first, and then start editing vibrato, pitch drift, and formant shift, the idea being to handle the coarse changes before handling the finer edits.

Figure 7.27   Flex Pitch notes that have been quantized using the Set All to Perfect Pitch command in the Audio Track editor shortcut menu.
© Apple Inc.

The second option is to quantize pitches to scales using the Scale Quantize controls in the Audio Track editor Inspector, shown in Figure 7.28. There are two menus and one button for Scale Quantize operations. The first menu, labeled Off in Figure 7.28, offers all 12 keys and the Off setting. The second menu, labeled Major in Figure 7.28, offers 19 different scales that you can use to quantize the pitch of your audio.

Figure 7.28   The Scale Quantize controls in the Audio Track editor Inspector.
© Apple Inc.

To use these tools to quantize your pitches, follow these steps:

1. Select a key in the first menu.
2. Select a scale in the second menu.
3. Select any notes you wish to pitch quantize.
4. Click the Q button to apply the Scale Quantize settings to your selected notes. Figure 7.29 shows the notes from Figure 7.27 pitch-quantized to the key of G major.

Figure 7.29 The same notes shown in Figure 7.27 after using Scale Quantize to quantize their pitches to G major.
© Apple Inc.

You can compare the notes in Figures 7.27 and 7.29 with their pitch positions relative to the Audio Track editor keyboard. Note that all the notes in Figure 7.29 were selected to quantize them to G major after they had been set to perfect pitch. If you haven't quantized the selected notes to perfect pitch, your notes will be quantized to the selected scale relative to their original pitches.

You can also use the Q button with Scale Quantize set to Off to perform a Set All to Perfect Pitch operation only on selected notes. If you find any of your Scale Quantize results to be less desirable than the original analyzed Flex Pitch notes, you can use the Set All to Original Pitch command in the Audio Track editor shortcut menu or use the Undo command (Command+Z). Remember, the Audio Track editor edits your audio completely nondestructively, so experiment freely!

I recommend using the Set All to Perfect Pitch command or a Scale Quantize operation along with your other edits before using the Create MIDI Track from Flex Pitch Data command for optimal results. This won't necessarily prevent the need for further tweaks to the generated MIDI data, but as you'll deduce from the following sections about splitting, joining, moving, resizing, and quantizing the timing of notes, once your audio has been perfectly edited, the resulting MIDI region will require much less editing.

Splitting and Joining Notes

There may be times when the length of the Flex Pitch notes returned after analysis don't meet your expectations or make editing difficult. Perhaps the note is too long for you to fix a small section of a note to your satisfaction, or two events were returned where you would like to have one. If you find that to be the case, the Scissors and Glue tools are exactly what you need.

Use the Scissors tool to create two notes from one note by clicking with the Scissors tool at the desired location. If you click and hold with the Scissors tool, a vertical line appears, allowing you to line up your edit along the Bar ruler or along an exact part of your waveform. You can create as many notes from a single note as you wish using the Scissors tool. Be aware that if you haven't done any pitch editing, the new notes will be pitch shifted closer to their own new vibrato lines. The new notes will have their own hotspots for editing.

You can repair cuts you've made to notes or join analyzed notes together by selecting the notes you'd like to join and then clicking one of the selected notes with the Glue tool.

Moving and Resizing Notes

Moving and resizing notes not only gives you control over the size of the note itself, but it also performs some Flex Time–like expansion and compression at the same time. When you look at how Flex Pitch notes compare to Flex Time markers for the same bit of audio, you'll notice that transients aren't necessarily considered. The analyzed pitch is what's important, not what transients exist within the notes. What this means is that you have access to time stretching and compression based on an entirely different process.

Think about Flex Pitch editing a vocal track. Flex Pitch analysis returns notes. Often, one word may be sung across multiple notes, and words with multiple syllables may not produce transients clearly enough for Flex Time to return meaningful results. Because Flex Pitch analysis produces results for all the sung notes, and notes within a word can be split if need be, these unique results compared to Flex Time markers give you a different way to achieve time compression or stretching. You can lengthen and shorten them, either on their own or in relation to adjacent notes, to achieve a greater level of control of the performance in time, not just in pitch.

In essence, moving and resizing notes achieve similar results. You can use the Hand tool to stretch or compress a note by dragging a note horizontally. Dragging to the left stretches the note, dragging to the right compresses it. There is one limitation: You can only move the note in relation to the right end of the note. The right end of the note is fundamentally locked in place. If there is a note to the right within the waveform of the note being moved, it will be stretched or compressed compared to the moved note. Figure 7.30 shows the same notes from Figure 7.29 with the second note moved so that it is stretched, leaving the first note compressed.

Figure 7.30 The second note has been moved using the Hand tool, stretching it and compressing the first note.
© Apple Inc.

Resizing a note is more flexible. You can resize either end of a note using the Resize cursor, which appears when you move the cursor to an end of a note. As with moving a note, resizing a note affects the adjacent note to the side you resize.

QUANTIZING THE TIMING OF NOTES

One of the coolest features of Flex Pitch editing in the Audio Track editor has nothing to do with pitch. After a monophonic audio file has been analyzed and Flex Pitch notes have been created for the audio, the resulting notes contain pitch and length data, but they also have position data. That the notes are displayed not only as elements of their parent waveform but also against the length of the Bar ruler reveals this. The location data, by extension, makes it easy for Logic to quantize your audio. The Audio Track editor facilitates this in an incredibly simple and elegant manner using the Time Quantize controls in the Inspector, shown in Figure 7.31.

Figure 7.31 The Time Quantize controls in the Audio Track editor Inspector.
© Apple Inc.

If the Time Quantize parameters look familiar, it's because they function identically to the Quantize menu and Quantize Strength parameters in the region, covered in Chapter 6. The Quantize menu, labeled 1/16 note in Figure 7.31, has the same division options as the Time Quantize menu in the region. Likewise, the Strength slider has an identical purpose as the Strength setting does in the region, defining the extent to which notes are quantized exactly to the selected division setting in the Time Quantize menu. To quantize selected notes, simply set the quantize resolution in the Time Quantize parameters, adjust the Strength setting to taste, and click Q. Figure 7.32 shows notes shown quantized to 1/16 note resolution with a Strength setting of 100. You can see that they line up with the Bar ruler divisions at the top of the figure.

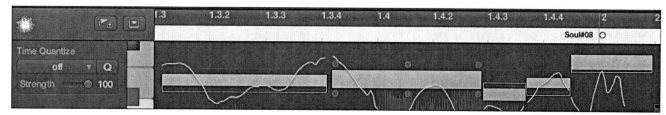

Figure 7.32 Use the Time Quantize controls in the Audio Track editor Inspector to quantize the timing of Flex Pitch notes.
© Apple Inc.

Hopefully now you can see the full scope of the power of Flex Pitch editing—and audio region editing in general—in the Audio Track editor. Not only can you fine-tune notes; edit their vibrato, gain, and formant shift; coarse-tune notes; quantize the pitch and time of notes; and time stretch and compress notes in the Audio Track editor, but you can also use it as a place to work with Flex Time and edit audio regions in exactly the same way as you would in the Tracks area, but in a much more focused environment. Now that you have a greater understanding of Logic's nondestructive audio-editing capabilities, let's take a look at the destructive audio editing section in Logic, the Audio File editor.

The Audio File Editor

Sometimes, resizing or editing audio regions won't be enough; you'll want to alter the audio data itself permanently. This is where the Audio File editor comes in. The Audio File editor operates on the actual data in the audio file. That means the Audio File editor's edits are destructive. They forever alter the contents of the actual audio file, unlike edits to audio regions, which are nondestructive, meaning that the audio data itself is never touched. Figure 7.33 shows the Audio File editor window.

Figure 7.33 The Audio File editor window.
© Apple Inc.

Double-clicking an audio region in the Tracks area opens that region in the main window's integrated audio editors. The Audio Track and Audio File editors open in the same pane in the main window; if the Audio Track editor is displayed, simply click the File tab to access the Audio File editor. When the Audio File editor is displayed, selecting an audio region in the Project Audio Browser opens that region in the Audio File editor. In either case, the region will be displayed inside the waveform overview and detailed waveform display. You can also launch the Audio File editor by choosing Window > Open Audio File editor, by using the key command Command+6, or by opening the integrated Audio File editor in the main window by pressing W. You can also drag the File tab in the integrated Audio File editor to open a separate Audio File editor window. As with the other windows, we'll start with a discussion of the Audio File editor's local menus.

Local Menus

The local menus provide file, editing, and processing commands specific to the Audio File editor. A description of the local menus follows.

THE AUDIO FILE MENU

This menu contains the file operations that are possible from the Audio File editor. Figure 7.34 shows the Audio File local menu of the Audio File editor.

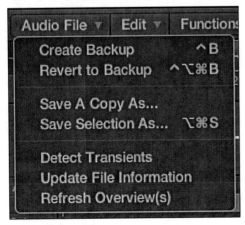

Figure 7.34 The Audio File menu of the Audio File editor.
© Apple Inc.

An explanation of the commands follows:

▷ **Create Backup:** Because the actions that you make in the Audio File editor are destructive, you may want to make a backup of your file so that if you do something you don't like, you still have your original audio. The key command for this is Control+B.

▷ **Revert to Backup:** If you've previously made a backup of your audio file, this command replaces your current processed and edited audio file with the backup. You can use this command if you've made a backup and are not happy with the changes you've made to your audio file. The key command for this is Control+Option+Command+B.

▷ **Save a Copy As:** You can create a copy of an audio file using this command.

▷ **Save Selection As:** Using this command, you can save only the portion of your file that you have selected with your mouse. The key command for this is Option+Command+S.

▷ **Detect Transients:** This command detects transients in your audio file and marks them with transient markers, which can aid you in general editing but also gives you a very powerful tool for customizing the transients for flexing, deriving a groove template from your audio, and for use with the Convert Regions to New Sampler Instrument command. You'll look into this in a little more detail in the section "Editing Transient Markers" later in this chapter.

▷ **Update File Information:** This updates the information that Logic has stored for the file you are editing. Saving your project performs this updating, but you can use this command to update the file information without saving the project.

▷ **Refresh Overview(s):** This command refreshes the waveform overview of the audio region you are editing in the Audio File editor.

THE EDIT MENU

The Edit menu contains functions that involve the selection and manipulation of audio and audio regions. Figure 7.35 shows the local Edit menu of the Audio File editor.

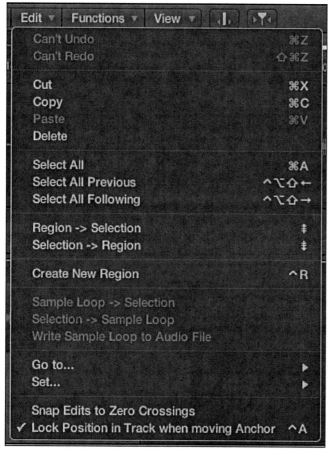

Figure 7.35 The Edit menu of the Audio File editor.
© Apple Inc.

Although the Audio File editor Edit menu has a number of familiar Edit menu commands, many of these commands function differently in the Audio File editor. Following are details about the commands in this menu:

▷ **Undo:** This command undoes the last action made to your audio in the Audio File editor. You can have as many levels of undo as you set in the Preferences > Audio > Audio File Editor tab. The key command for this is Command+Z.

▷ **Redo:** This command will redo the last undone action in the Audio File editor. Note that the Audio File editor Undo and Redo functions are unique to the Audio File editor (meaning you can't undo a main window action in the Audio File editor, whereas in a MIDI editor, for example, Undo will include windows outside the MIDI editor). The key command for this is Shift+Command+Z.

▷ **Cut:** This command removes a selected area of audio and places it on the Clipboard. The cut selection can be pasted only in the Audio File editor. The key command for this is Command+X.

▷ **Copy:** This command copies a selected area of audio and places it on the Clipboard. The copied section can be pasted only in the Audio File editor. The key command for this is Command+C.

▷ **Paste:** This command pastes audio from the Clipboard at the current locator position. Only audio that has been cut or copied from the Audio File editor may be pasted in the Audio File editor with the Paste command. The key command for this is Command+V.

▷ **Delete:** This command removes the selected audio from your audio file.

▷ **Select All:** This command selects your entire audio file. The key command for this is Command+A.

▷ **Select All Previous:** This command adds the area from the beginning of the audio file to the currently selected area. The key command for this is Control+Option+Shift+left arrow.

▷ **Select All Following:** This command adds the area from the end of the audio file to the currently selected area. The key command for this is Control+Option+Shift+right arrow.

▷ **Region -> Selection:** This command selects the entire audio region that you are currently editing. The key command for this is Page Up.

▷ **Selection -> Region:** This command redefines the existing region boundaries to match the selection. The key command for this is Page Down.

▷ **Create New Region:** This creates a new audio region from your current selection. The original audio region you are editing remains unchanged. The key command for this is Control+R.

▷ **Sample Loop -> Selection:** This function turns a loop you have loaded into the Audio File editor from the EXS24 Sampler into a normal audio selection that you can edit.

▷ **Selection -> Sample Loop:** This turns a selection of audio into a loop for use with Logic's EXS24 Sampler.

▷ **Write Sample Loop to Audio File.** This command saves an audio file from the contents of an EXS24 loop.

▷ **Go To:** The Go To submenu is covered in the following section, "The Go To Submenu."

▷ **Set:** The Set submenu will be covered in its own section, "The Set Submenu."

▷ **Snap Edits to Zero Crossings:** You learned about zero crossings earlier in this chapter. If you select this command, Logic always looks for the point at which the amplitude crosses the zero mark while you are editing. This is to ensure glitch- and click-free playback, but it might restrict you from making edits at the exact location you want.

▷ **Lock Position in Track When Moving Anchor:** With this command engaged, the left boundary of an audio region will stay fixed in its parent track regardless of any changes you make to an audio region anchor in the Audio File editor. If this is not engaged, anchor points will remain fixed in the audio regions in the Tracks area. The key command for this is Control+A.

The Go To Submenu   The Go To submenu gives you a variety of commands for quickly navigating to specific points in your audio file. Figure 7.36 shows the Go To submenu.

Figure 7.36   The Go To submenu.
© Apple Inc.

The functions in the Go To submenu are as follows:

▷ **Selection Start:** This command moves the waveform display and the highlighted area in the waveform overview to the beginning of the selected area of the audio region. The key command for this is Fn+Control+left arrow.

▷ **Selection End:** This command moves the waveform display and the highlighted area in the waveform overview to the end of the selected area of the audio region. The key command for this is Fn+Control+right arrow.

▷ **Region Start:** This command moves the waveform display and the highlighted area in the waveform overview to the beginning of the audio region. The key command for this is Control+Option+left arrow.

▷ **Region End:** This command moves the waveform display and the highlighted area in the waveform overview to the end of the audio region. The key command for this is Control+Option+right arrow.

▷ **Region Anchor:** This command moves the waveform display and the highlighted area in the waveform overview to the anchor point of the audio region. The key command for this is Control+Option+down arrow.

▷ **Previous Transient:** This command moves the waveform display and the highlighted area in the waveform overview to the closest transient before the current selection. The key command for this is Option+left arrow.

▷ **Next Transient:** This command moves the waveform display and the highlighted area in the waveform overview to the closest transient after the current selection. The key command for this is Option+right arrow.

The Set Submenu   The Set submenu gives you a variety of commands for assigning start, end, and anchor points for your audio file. Figure 7.37 shows the Set submenu.

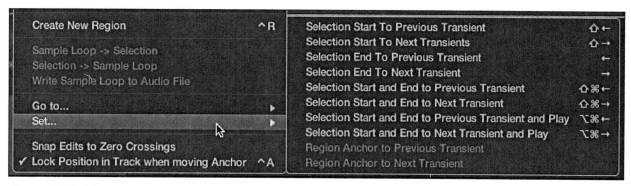

Figure 7.37   The Set submenu.
© Apple Inc.

The functions in the Set submenu are as follows:

▷ **Selection Start to Previous Transient:** This command moves the start of the selected area to the first transient immediately before the selected area. The key command for this is Shift+left arrow.

▷ **Selection Start to Next Transients:** This command moves the start of the selected area to the first transient immediately after the current start point of the selected area. The key command for this is Shift+right arrow.

▷ **Selection End to Previous Transient:** This command moves the end of the selected area to the first transient immediately before the current end of the selected area. The key command for this is left arrow.

▷ **Selection End to Next Transient:** This command moves the end of the selected area to the first transient immediately after the selected area. The key command for this is right arrow.

▷ **Selection Start and End to Previous Transient:** This command moves the start and end points of the selected area to the first transients immediately before the current start and end points, respectively. The key command for this is Shift+Command+left arrow.

▷ **Selection Start and End to Next Transient:** This command moves the start and end points of the selected area to the first transients immediately after the current start and end points, respectively. The key command for this is Shift+Command+right arrow.

▷ **Selection Start and End to Previous Transient and Play:** This command moves the start and end points of the selected area to the first transients immediately before the current start and end points, respectively, and then the selection is played. The key command for this is Option+Command+left arrow.

▷ **Selection Start and End to Next Transient and Play:** This command moves the start and end points of the selected area to the first transients immediately after the current start and end points, respectively, and then the selection is played. The key command for this is Option+Command+right arrow.

▷ **Region Anchor to Previous Transient:** This command moves the region anchor to the transient immediately before its current position.

▷ **Region Anchor to Next Transient:** This command moves the region anchor to the transient immediately after its current position.

THE FUNCTIONS MENU

The Functions menu consists of Audio File editor functions that process your audio in one way or another. These functions operate only on the area of your audio region that is selected. (If you want to process your entire file, choose Edit > Select All or use the key command Command+A first.) You can generally cancel any process in progress by pressing Command+. (period). Figure 7.38 shows the Functions menu of the Audio File editor.

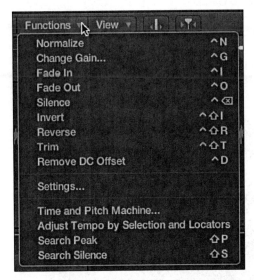

Figure 7.38 The Functions menu of the Audio File editor.
© Apple Inc.

These functions are as follows:

▷ **Normalize:** To normalize audio means to increase its level as much as possible without changing the dynamics or distorting the audio file. Logic does this by finding the loudest point in the currently selected audio, determining its distance from the maximum attainable level for the audio passage, and then increasing the audio for the entire selection by that amount. This way, the dynamics are preserved, the audio is not maximized to the point that it distorts, and the entire selection is louder by a specified amount. You can set the desired maximum level in the Settings dialog box. The key command for this is Control+N.

> **NOTE:** The Audio File editor Normalize feature is not the same as the Normalize feature in the Bounce dialog box. The Audio File editor Normalize feature operates directly on your audio file. That means it is destructive—it permanently changes the audio file—and it is limited to the bit depth (16- or 24-bit) of your audio file. The Normalize function in the Bounce dialog box is really a nondestructive, 64-bit, floating-point precision bitmapping function. It normalizes the audio in your bounced file but does not affect the audio in your project. Don't mix up the two! See Chapter 11 for more information on the Normalize feature of the Bounce dialog box.

▷ **Change Gain:** This command raises or lowers the level of the selected audio by a specified amount. You can determine this amount in the dialog box that appears when you select this command. You can choose to change the gain by either inputting a percentage of the current level or entering absolute decibels. If you click Search Maximum, Logic finds the highest peak in the selection and calculates how much it can safely raise the gain (much as it does with the Normalize function). You can also view the results in absolute, which shows you an absolute value rather than a percentage. Keep in mind that if you raise the gain more than 100%, you will clip your file, producing a very nonmusical digital clipping. The key command for this is Control+G.

▷ **Fade In:** This allows you to create a destructive fade-in at the front of your selection. This is in contrast to creating a fade-in in the Tracks area or Audio Track editor, which affects only how the audio region is played back and is nondestructive. You can adjust the curves of the fade-out in the Settings dialog box. The key command for this is Control+I.

▷ **Fade Out:** With this command, you can create a destructive fade-out at the end of your selection. This contrasts with creating a fade-out in the Tracks area or Audio Track editor, which affects only how the audio region is played back and is nondestructive. You can adjust the curve of the fade-out in the Settings dialog box. The key command for this is Control+O.

▷ **Silence:** Silence zeroes the amplitude of all audio data inside your selection. The key command for this is Control+Delete.

▷ **Invert:** This inverts the phase of the audio selection. In other words, what originally was the peak of the amplitude of the waveform becomes the bottom, and so on. This command doesn't affect the sound, but it can help fix phase cancellation problems with your audio file that become apparent during mixing. The key command for this is Control+Shift+I.

▷ **Reverse:** This command reverses the audio in your selection. (In other words, the audio plays backward.) The key command for this is Control+Shift+R.

▷ **Trim:** Trim erases any part of the current region outside of the area you have selected. Make sure you don't delete any areas that you'll need for your song! If you try to trim away portions of a region you are using in the Tracks area, a warning screen will appear, asking you to confirm that you want to do so. The key command for this is Control+Shift+T.

▷ **Remove DC Offset:** When you are using lower-quality audio hardware, it is common for stray direct current (DC) to be layered over your audio signal. This causes the waveform to look like it's not centered around the zero line, but is shifted vertically up or down. This can cause crackling and artifacts at the beginning and end of audio regions. This command removes the effect of DC and centers the audio around the zero bar. The key command for this is Control+D.

▷ **Settings:** Settings isn't a function itself, but rather a command that opens a dialog box of parameters for other functions. Figure 7.39 shows the Function Settings dialog box. Here, you can set the maximum value to which you want the Normalize function to increase the selection's level, either as a percentage of the maximum amplitude or in decibels. The dialog box also presents options to adjust the curves for the fade-in and fade-out. If you select their checkboxes and adjust the curve value from −100 to 100, the graphic display will change to illustrate the current shape of the curve.

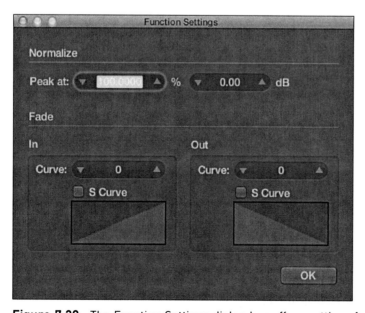

Figure 7.39 The Function Settings dialog box offers settings for the normalize, fade-in, and fade-out functions.
© Apple Inc.

▷ **Time and Pitch Machine:** The Time and Pitch Machine command enables you to independently adjust the tempo and pitch of your selected audio.

▷ **Adjust Tempo by Selection and Locators:** This command adjusts the tempo of your audio by stretching or compressing it to fit the length of the current locator positions while maintaining the integrity of its pitch. This is very similar to the global Edit > Tempo > Adjust Tempo Using Region Length and Locators command.

▷ **Search Peak:** If you select this option, Logic will search the currently selected audio for the sample with the greatest amplitude value and will center the cursor in the waveform display around this point. The key command for this is Shift+P.

▷ **Search Silence:** With this option, Logic searches the currently selected audio for silence and places the cursor at the start of the first section of silence detected. The key command for this is Shift+S.

THE VIEW MENU

The View menu offers you a number of options for changing the units of measurement on the waveform display and the way the audio wave itself is displayed. Figure 7.40 shows you the View menu of the Audio File editor.

Figure 7.40 The View menu of the Audio File editor.
© Apple Inc.

The View menu options are as follows:

▷ **Samples:** This displays the actual number of the sample or the samples you are currently viewing on the Bar ruler.

▷ **Min:Sec:Ms:** This shows the elapsed time on the Bar ruler.

▷ **SMPTE Time:** This displays the SMPTE position on the Bar ruler.

▷ **Bars/Beats:** This shows the musical location of the audio on the Bar ruler.

▷ **Transient Editing Mode:** This enables Transient Editing mode, allowing you to modify your audio file's transients. The key command for this is Control+T.

▷ **Amplitude Percentage:** This specifies that the vertical axis of the waveform display measures the amplitude of the audio wave as a percentage of the maximum amplitude.

▷ **Amplitude Sample Value:** This specifies that the vertical axis of the waveform display measures the amplitude of the audio wave in sample units.

▷ **Show as Sample & Hold:** This displays the actual data structure of the waveform (that is, the wave appears blocky, not rounded). This is very useful if you are using the Pencil tool to remove pops and clicks.

▷ **Scroll in Play:** This moves the audio file past a stationary playhead instead of moving the playhead across your audio file when you play the audio file. The key command for this is Control+`.

▷ **Show in Finder:** This opens a Finder window displaying the location on your hard drive of the audio file being edited. The key command for this is Shift+Command+R.

THE AUDIO FILE EDITOR TOOL MENU

The Audio File editor Tool menu contains the six tools available to you in the Audio File editor. Figure 7.41 shows the Audio File editor Tool menu.

Figure 7.41 The Audio File editor Tool menu.
© Apple Inc.

A description of how each tool functions in the Audio File editor follows:

▷ **Pointer:** Drag the Pointer tool across the audio in the waveform display to select audio.

▷ **Eraser:** The Eraser tool is used for removing transients from your audio file.

▷ **Hand:** The Hand tool allows you to reposition a selection box (made previously with the pointer) to the right or left.

▷ **Zoom:** Drag the selection "rubber band" over a portion of audio to increase the magnification of the selected audio down to the single-sample level. Double-click anywhere to return the selection to its original zoom resolution. If you have already used the zoom rectangles or key commands to zoom in on your audio, this tool has no further effect.

▷ **Solo:** This tool will scrub (play back slowly) a selection of audio as you drag across the file.

▷ **Pencil:** This tool will allow you to redraw the audio waveform at high zoom levels. If you are not at a high zoom level, the Pencil tool can be used as a Zoom tool to increase the zoom setting by rubber-banding an area of the waveform. The main use for this tool is to smooth out sudden sharp peaks in your audio, as these usually represent pops or clicks. This tool works well in tandem with Show as Sample & Hold, which enables you to see exactly which samples are peaking. Be very careful when redrawing waveforms, however—if you don't know what you are doing, you are likely to redraw a waveform incorrectly and compromise the sound of your audio.

The Audio File Editor Mode Buttons

On either side of the Tool menus are the Audio File editor's four mode buttons. In addition, two more buttons appear when you engage Transient Editing mode. Figure 7.42 shows the Audio File editor buttons.

Figure 7.42 The Audio File editor buttons.
© Apple Inc.

The functions of the Audio File editor buttons, going from left to right across the top of the Audio File editor, are as follows:

▷ **Transient Editing Mode:** The Transient Editing Mode button enables Transient Editing mode. This gives you the ability to increase and decrease the number of transients Logic uses when flexing audio and stretching Apple Loops. To do this, you use the minus (–) and plus (+) buttons that appear to the right of the Transient Editing Mode button when it's engaged. It also gives you the ability to move transient markers.

▷ **Catch Playhead Mode:** The playhead button enables Catch Playhead mode. If this button is lit, the Audio File editor is linked to the current song position. If there is no audio, the playhead simply stops at the end of the audio region.

▷ **Prelisten Mode:** The speaker icon represents Prelisten mode. If the Cycle button is also enabled, Logic will continuously play back your selection from start to finish. If the Cycle button is not also enabled, it will play through your selected audio one time. If the Prelisten button is not enabled, your selection will not play back. You can right-click on the

Prelisten button to open a shortcut menu that lets you select an auto-select channel strip or a prelisten channel strip as your ouptut options, like in the Project Audio Browser.

▷ **Cycle Mode:** If you enable Cycle mode, playback of the selected portion of audio repeats continuously if the Prelisten button is also enabled.

Volume Slider

The Volume slider, to the right of the Cycle button, controls the output volume of the prelisten channel strip.

The Audio File Editor Region Locators Display

To the left of the Volume slider is a position display that shows you the start point and length of the audio region in the Audio File editor using the unit display you selected in the local View menu. You obviously cannot place audio regions graphically using the Audio File editor, only numerically. When you open the Audio File editor from the Tracks area, the Bar ruler reflects the region's location in the main window; when you open the Audio File editor from the Project Audio Browser, the Bar ruler instead measures from the start of the audio region.

The Waveform Display

The main feature of the Audio File editor is the waveform display (see Figure 7.43). This is the main window you use to edit your audio and transients in the Audio File editor. You can use the zoom controls in the upper-right of the Audio File editor, as well as key commands and the Zoom and Pencil tools, to zoom in and out of your audio and display and edit your audio region down to single-sample accuracy.

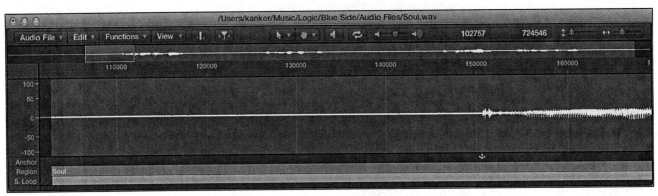

Figure 7.43 The waveform display of the Audio File editor. Notice the anchor point, the region area bar, and the sample loop bar of the audio region under the waveform.
© Apple Inc.

Beneath your audio on the waveform display is the anchor point, represented by a graphic version of a ship's anchor. The anchor point represents the first musically relevant point on which you want the audio region to pivot. It is the anchor point that gets placed at a specific time position when you drag regions around the Tracks area. For example, if your audio region begins with a fade-in, you might want to place the anchor point at the end of the fade-in so that the audio past the fade-in falls exactly on the bar as you move the region in the Tracks area. Notice in Figure 7.43 that the anchor point has been moved to the beginning of any meaningful audio in the region to allow it to lock to the grid in the Tracks area at exactly that point.

Beneath the anchor point is the region area, which displays a bar that runs the entire length of the selected region. You can change the start and end points of the region by dragging the ends of the region area bar with the Resize cursor, which automatically appears when you move the cursor over either end of the bar.

Under the region area is the Sample Loop (S. Loop) display. If you choose the Edit > Selection -> Sample Loop command, a sample loop bar similar to the region area bar will appear. You can change the length of the sample loop by dragging the ends of the sample loop bar in the same manner as the region area bar. When you select Edit > Write Sample Loop to Audio File, the sample loop information is added to the looped audio file's file header. This information can be used by other applications capable of reading loop data in the file header and, more importantly to Logic, by the EXS24 sampler instrument.

As you use the Audio File editor to process or edit your audio, the waveform display reflects your changes. Use the Bar ruler to ensure that the audio region is still positioned where you want it to be as you process and edit your audio.

Editing Transient Markers

Among the many editing functions that can be performed in the Audio File editor, transient marker editing gives you some of the most varied possibilities. Any action that involves using transient markers can be affected by judicious use of transient marker editing. From altering Apple Loops, to defining a groove template, to improving the reliability of your transient markers for flexing, to creating musically, technically, or creatively meaningful selections in the Audio File editor, Transient Editing mode can open multiple paths for the manipulation of a single audio file.

Before you begin working with a file's transient markers, choose the Detect Transients command from the Audio File menu. This will analyze your audio file for transients (which can take a while with longer audio files) and enable Transient Editing mode automatically. Figure 7.44 shows an audio file in the Audio File editor after running the Detect Transients command. Notice that the Transient Editing mode button has been selected, and that the minus and plus buttons are shown next to it.

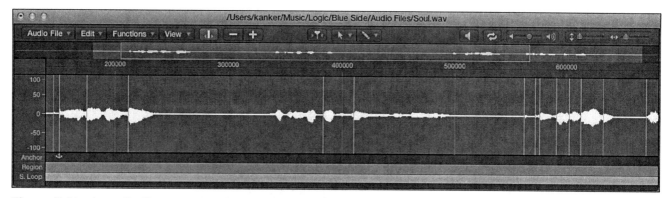

Figure 7.44 An audio file in the Audio File editor with transients displayed after running the Detect Transients command.
© Apple Inc.

Just looking at an audio file, or looking at it while it's playing back, can give you a good indication of whether you need to increase or decrease the number of transient makers in your audio file. You can quickly increase or decrease the number of transients for your audio file by clicking the plus or minus button, respectively. Figure 7.45 shows the same audio file with fewer transients detected.

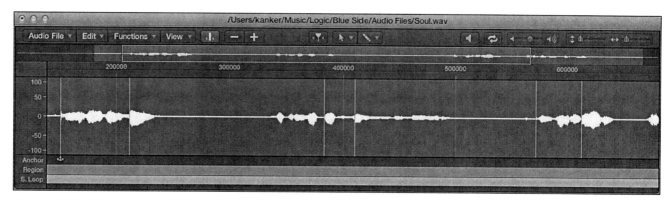

Figure 7.45 The same audio file as seen in Figure 7.44, but with fewer transients displayed.
© Apple Inc.

You create new transient markers with the Pencil tool while in Transient Editing mode. You can delete transient markers by double-clicking them, by clicking them with the Eraser tool, or by selecting the area containing the transient markers you wish to remove and pressing Delete.

When you move the mouse pointer near a transient marker, the pointer changes to a Transient Editing tool, which allows you to grab and drag a transient to a new position. Figure 7.46 shows the Transient Editing tool moving the transient marker to its left. You can toggle Transient Editing mode by clicking the Transient Editing Mode button or by using the key command Control+T.

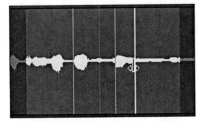

Figure 7.46 Use the Transient Editing tool to move transient markers.
© Apple Inc.

Time and Pitch Machine

The Time and Pitch Machine can change the tempo of audio by stretching or compressing that audio. In fact, when you stretch and compress audio in the Tracks area without using any Flex tools, you are technically invoking the tempo-adjusting function of the Time and Pitch Machine. When you access the Time and Pitch Machine in the Audio File editor—by selecting the local Functions > Time and Pitch Machine command—you can also transpose audio up or down in pitch. You can link these functions together, or they can be independent. Figure 7.47 shows the Time and Pitch Machine dialog box.

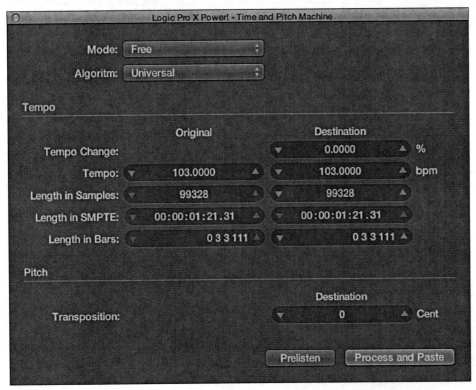

Figure 7.47 You can access the Time and Pitch Machine via the Audio File editor.
© Apple Inc.

Most parameters include a text field for the Original (current) value of the audio and a text field to input the desired new Destination value. If you know the specific numeric values you want to use for your parameters, you can enter those numbers in the text fields to the right. The parameters are as follows:

▷ **Mode:** The Mode menu in the Time and Pitch Machine contains two options: Free and Classic. Free mode indicates that tempo and pitch adjustments are independent. Classic mode means that pitch and tempo are adjusted together, like on an old tape machine, which gets higher in pitch when the tape speeds up and lower in pitch as the tape slows down.

▷ **Algorithm:** This selects which algorithm the Time and Pitch Machine uses to adjust the tempo of the audio. These options are already detailed in the section "The Time Machine Algorithm Submenu" in Chapter 6. Remember that any additional Time and Pitch Machine–compatible plug-ins you have installed will need to be 64-bit in order to integrate into Logic.

▷ **Tempo Change:** This parameter tells you how drastic your tempo change will be by giving you the percentage of change from the original tempo. For example, if the tempo of your original audio track was 120 BPM and you change the tempo to 240 BPM, the parameter will indicate a 100% tempo change. You cannot increase the Tempo Change parameter to more than 300% or reduce it by more than −75%.

▷ **Tempo:** The Original field lists the current tempo of your audio. You can input a new tempo in the Destination field. You can increase the tempo as much as 300% or decrease it as much as 75% depending on the algorithm used.

▷ **Length in Samples:** This is the exact length of the audio in samples. If you know exactly how many samples you want your processed audio to be, you can enter that value in the Destination field. You cannot adjust the number of samples so drastically that the result would be beyond the boundaries of the tempo restrictions mentioned for the Tempo setting.

▷ **Length in SMPTE:** The length of your audio in SMPTE frames is listed here. If you know exactly how many SMPTE frames you want your processed audio to be, you can enter that value in the Destination field. You cannot adjust the SMPTE frames beyond the boundaries of the Tempo setting's restrictions.

▷ **Length in Bars:** This is perhaps the most musically useful setting and the closest to the way the Time Machine is used in the Tracks area. Here you see how long your audio is in bars. You can enter the number of bars you want your audio to be in the Destination field. Again, you cannot adjust the bar length beyond the Tempo setting's restrictions.

▷ **Transposition:** Now you are getting into the transposition settings that affect pitch, not tempo. The Destination field allows you to enter the number of cents, or hundredths of a semitone, by which you want to adjust your audio. Positive numbers raise the pitch, whereas negative numbers reduce the pitch.

Because using the Time and Pitch Machine is destructive, Logic offers a Prelisten button to the left of the Process and Paste button. Prelisten gives you a sample of what your new audio will sound like before you commit to processing your audio and pasting the newly processed audio into your song.

NOTE: If you're transitioning from an earlier version of Logic, you're probably wondering what happened to the other Digital Factory options. Many of those options have been supplanted by newer and better methods of achieving the same results. For example, Audio to Score functions are handled by the Create MIDI Track from Flex Pitch Data command in the Audio Track editor, with universally better results. The same holds true for the Quantize Engine, which has been bested by the Time Quantize function in the Audio Track editor. To be honest, there is no need for the former Digital Factory options because the continued development of Logic has made them obsolete!

Setting Up Audio File Editor Undo Preferences

As you now see, the Audio File editor is a very powerful destructive audio editor. Because of this, you might be wondering what happens if you perform a process whose results are less than satisfactory, but you forgot to make a backup of your original audio file. Never fear! Not only does the Audio File editor have its own set of preferences that specifically deal with the facility and extent of the Undo command in the Audio File editor, but it also has its own Undo History that is separate from Logic's global Undo History! Unfortunately, given the destructive nature of the Audio File editor's processing, there is no way to open the Audio File editor's Undo History. You can access the Audio File editor's Undo Preferences by opening the Audio File editor tab of the Audio Preferences window, shown in Figure 7.48.

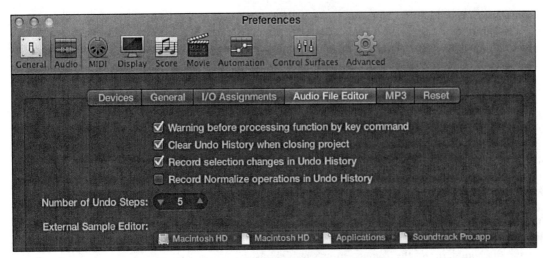

Figure 7.48 The Audio File Editor tab of the Audio Preferences window.
© Apple Inc.

The functions of the Audio File editor's Undo Preferences are as follows:

▷ **Warning Before Processing Function by Key Command:** Selecting this option ensures that when you use a key command to process audio in the Audio File editor, a warning dialog box will open, asking you whether you are sure you want to process the selected audio.

▷ **Clear Undo History When Closing Project:** With this option selected, the Audio File editor's Undo History is automatically cleared when you quit Logic or close the current project.

▷ **Record Selection Changes in Undo History:** This option enables or disables the Audio File editor's Undo capability for selection changes. It is best to leave this option selected.

▷ **Record Normalize Operations in Undo History:** This option allows you to record normalize operations in the Undo History. Since normalization is typically the last process performed on an audio file, when you leave this selection unchecked, the Undo History is automatically deleted when you normalize an audio file. Just to be on the safe side, if this option is not selected, Logic will open a dialog box that asks whether you want to add the normalize process to the Undo History when you invoke the Normalize command.

▷ **Number of Undo Steps:** You can set the number of Undo steps that are stored for the Audio File editor in this field by clicking on the up and down arrows, by clicking on the number and scrolling with your mouse, or by double-clicking in the field and entering a number manually.

▷ **External Sample Editor:** The final option is for setting up an external sample editor to use for processing and editing your audio files, and it's covered in the next section.

Configuring Logic to Use an External Sample Editor

Although Logic's Audio File editor is a great place to edit and process your audio files, you might be more comfortable performing those processes in another application. Logic makes this a piece of cake. To tell Logic which 64-bit application to use as an external sample editor, simply open the Audio File editor tab of the Audio Preferences window and click in the External Sample Editor field, shown in Figure 7.48. A file dialog box will open, allowing you to browse for your sample editor of choice.

Once you have selected an external sample editor, you can open audio regions from Logic in your external sample editor by pressing Shift+W. Your external sample editor will automatically launch and open with the selected audio region.

Audio Fades and Crossfades

There are three types of audio fades:

▷ Fade-ins, in which audio ramps up in volume from its beginning
▷ Fade-outs, in which audio ramps down in volume toward its end

▷ Crossfades, in which two audio regions fade into each other. Often, fading is used as a creative effect, such as fading out a song over a 20-second coda, building in an effect, or crossfading between two songs. Sometimes, however, you will want to use fades as tools to cover up clicks at the beginning or end of audio regions or caused by overlapping audio regions. These fades, rather than being seconds long, are usually measured in milliseconds. For these micro-fades, Logic allows each audio region to have one fade-in and one fade-out or crossfade associated with it. When a fade is associated with an audio region, the length of the fade will appear in the Region Inspector and the fade will appear as a light shading on the region itself, as shown in Figure 7.49.

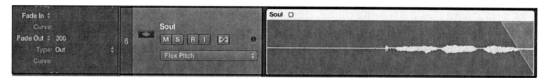

Figure 7.49 The audio region here has a fade-out that is 300ms long, as you can see on the region and in the Region Inspector.
© Apple Inc.

Creating Audio Fades

There are three ways to create fades in the Tracks area:

▷ By typing fade settings into the Region Inspector
▷ By using the Fade tool in the Tracks area Tool menu

TIP: Remember, as covered in Chapter 6, you can enable the Fade Tool Click Zones option in the Editing tab of the General Preferences window to have the Fade tool as a constantly available mode of the Pointer tool in the Tracks area.

▷ By setting the Tracks area Drag mode to X-Fade and overlapping two audio regions

You can also create fades—in, out, and cross—in the Audio Track editor using the Fade tool.

Fade Files

Whenever you set up a fade, Logic creates a fade file. This is a very short temporary audio file that contains just the faded segment. This file is stored in a Fade Files folder in your Project folder. These files cannot be edited. Whenever you adjust a fade in the main window, the fade file will be re-created.

Adjusting Audio Fades

If you want your fade to have a curve (in other words, instead of a linear increase or decrease in volume, a logarithmic increase or decrease) you can adjust the Curve parameter from –99 to 99 to create various symmetrical curves in the Region Inspector. This number determines the strength and direction of the curve. You can also select whether the right region fade will be a fade-out, a linear crossfade (X), an equal power crossfade (EqP) for crossfading between two regions that are not phase coherent (for example, two completely different instruments), or an S-shaped crossfade (X S) for material that is hard to crossfade with a standard-shaped crossfade. Sticking with a straight crossfade (X) will work in most situations, and you should try the other curves only if you find yourself getting audio dropouts with a linear crossfade. The Time and Curve parameters for the X-Fade drag mode's crossfades can be set in the General tab of the Audio Preferences dialog box.

You can also use the Fade tool to adjust the curve of a fade or crossfade. To do this, simply click and drag the fade using the Fade tool and to change its curve. You can also adjust the length of a fade by dragging the fade node at the end of a fade-in or the beginning of a fade-out. To delete a fade, just change the value of the Fade In or Fade Out parameter to 0 (zero) or Option-click on the fade with the Fade tool.

Apple Loops

If you are a new Logic user but are familiar with the Apple audio application GarageBand, you will already be familiar with Apple Loops. Users familiar with ACIDized WAV files will already have an idea of what Apple Loops can do, although Apple Loops go much further than ACIDized WAVs.

To put it simply, Apple Loops are special audio or MIDI regions that contain embedded pitch, tempo, channel strip, and even sample information.

Audio Apple Loops

Audio Apple Loops are AIFF or CAF audio files with specially embedded tempo and pitch information. Audio Apple Loops do the following:

▷ They automatically play at the current song tempo, regardless of the tempo at which the audio was originally recorded.
▷ They automatically adjust to the key of the current song, regardless of the key of the original performance.

Audio Apple Loops behave just like normal audio regions. You can loop them, resize them, cut them, and so on. They even appear in the Project Audio Browser like other audio regions. However, you *cannot* edit an Apple Loop in the Audio File editor because this would compromise the embedded information in the Apple Loop. If you want to edit an Apple Loop, make a copy of it that is a normal audio file and edit that. You can then convert the edited audio file into Apple Loop format. Creating Apple Loops is covered in the section "Creating Your Own Apple Loops" later in this chapter.

To add an audio Apple Loop to your Logic song, simply drag it into an audio track in the Tracks area as you would any other audio file. That's it! You don't need to set up anything—Logic automatically will handle it as an Apple Loop. You can even drag the audio Apple Loop to a blank area of the Tracks area, and a new track will be created.

Software Instrument Apple Loops

Software instrument Apple Loops are MIDI files with specially embedded information. In addition to their MIDI notes, software instrument Apple Loops include the following:

▷ **Channel strip settings:** This means the software instruments and effects that the loop uses will be instantly recalled as soon as you add the loop to a software instrument track. You can also drag a software instrument Apple Loop to a blank area of the Tracks area, and a new track will be created with the correct channel strip setting!
▷ **Sample information:** If the software instrument Apple Loop uses a sample-based instrument, all the samples it uses will automatically load and be ready for use.
▷ **Audio information:** If you drag a software instrument Apple Loop to an audio track, it will behave exactly as an audio Apple Loop!

To use a software instrument Apple Loop, just drag it into a MIDI, software instrument, or audio track. Remember that unlike audio Apple Loops, which work only on audio tracks, software instrument Apple Loops also contain an embedded audio version of the Apple Loop and can be used on either MIDI or audio tracks. If you drag a software instrument Apple Loop to a blank area of the Tracks area, it will create a software instrument track with the Apple Loop.

Software Instrument Apple Loops: Audio Versus Instrument Track? As mentioned, software instrument Apple Loops also include audio information and can be used on either audio or MIDI tracks. So when would you want to use a software instrument Apple Loop in an audio or MIDI track? There are advantages and disadvantages to both uses.

Software instrument Apple Loops allow you far more ability to adjust the software instrument, effects, and MIDI data in the loop itself. However, loading software instruments and effects can take up significant CPU power, depending on the individual plug-ins that are part of the loop.

Audio Apple Loops don't let you fine-tune the notes inside the loops themselves or the recorded tone of the loop, since it's a prerecorded audio performance that is looped. However, audio Apple Loops take up very little CPU, but they do take up RAM; the longer the loop, the more RAM they require.

If you don't need to adjust the loop itself, and you want to conserve CPU, you might want to place your software instrument Apple Loop on an audio track. However, if you want to adjust the instrument used in the loop itself or to conserve RAM, you want to load your software instrument Apple Loop onto a software instrument track.

The Loop Browser

Because Apple Loops are a special kind of file, there is a special kind of window to organize them. Those of you who are used to Soundtrack or GarageBand are already familiar with the concept of the Loop Browser. Basically, the Loop Browser allows you to search and audition your loops by various criteria. The Loop Browser can index more than just Apple Loops; if you have many ACID loops, for example, you can use the Loop Browser to index them as well. The Loop Browser is available in the Media area of the main window and can also be accessed by using the key command O. Figure 7.50 shows the Loop Browser.

Figure 7.50 The Loop Browser allows you to search for your Apple Loops via category, text search, and more.
© Apple Inc.

Browsing Loops

Searching for loops couldn't be simpler. You can either type in search words in the search field or click the category buttons to limit your search to various instrument and sound effects categories and genres (or both). If you prefer lists of categories instead of buttons, the buttons at the top left of the Loop Browser will switch you between button view and column view, shown in Figure 7.51. You can also select a scale and time signature of Apple Loop to look for and limit your search to specific Jam Packs in the Loops menu.

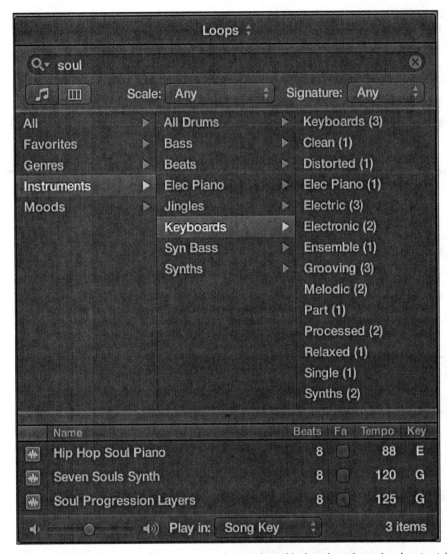

Figure 7.51 The Loop Browser in column view. Notice that there is also text in the text search field, further restricting the results.
© Apple Inc.

The left column in the results window displays either a blue audio wave or a green MIDI note to indicate whether the loop is an audio Apple Loop or a software instrument Apple Loop. To the right of the loop name is the Beats column, telling you how many beats are in the Apple Loop. If you want to store a loop in your Favorites category in the Loop Browser, just select the checkbox in the Fa column. The Tempo column displays the original tempo of the loop. Finally, the Key column tells you the original key of the loop, if any.

Auditioning Loops

To audition a loop, simply click the name of the loop (or anywhere on the same line). The loop will play back using the prelisten channel strip (as discussed), with the volume determined by the Volume slider at the bottom of the Loop Browser and the key determined by the Play In menu. The Play In menu gives you the option to play the loop in the song key, the loop's original key, or any other key you define. To stop the loop from playing, click the loop again.

Adding Loops to the Loop Browser

You add new loops to the Loop Browser by dragging them from the Finder to the results window of the Loop Browser. If you are adding a single Apple Loop, your Apple Loop will then be added to ~/Library/Audio/Apple Loops/User Loops/SingleFiles. If you add a folder with multiple Apple Loops, an alias of the folder will be added to ~/Library/Audio/Apple Loops/User Loops. If the Apple Loop is on a different drive, you will be asked whether you want to copy the loop to the Loop Browser's default loop location or if you'd rather that the Loop Browser just index your loop in its current location. After you make your selection, your loop will be entered into the Loop Browser's database and will be ready for use in Logic. If you are adding ACID loops, be sure to drag the entire folder (or CD) containing the ACID loops onto the Loop Browser because with Apple Loops, the folder name is used as the category name.

Adding Loops from the Loop Browser to Your Logic Song

If you find a loop you want to use in your song, simply drag it to an appropriate track in the Tracks area—an audio track for an audio Apple Loop (or another kind of loop, such as an ACID loop) or a software instrument Apple Loop, or a MIDI or audio instrument track for a software instrument Apple Loop. The loop will now be part of your song, and if it's an audio loop, it will be added to the Project Audio Browser as well.

If, for example, you want a number of audio loops in your song, but not necessarily placed in the Tracks area yet, you can also add audio loops directly to your Project Audio Browser. Just drag the audio loops to the Project Audio Browser like you would any other audio file.

Creating Your Own Apple Loops

At this point, you may be very excited by the potential of Apple Loops. It won't be long before you'll want to make your own Apple Loops. In Logic Pro X, you can create audio and software instrument Apple Loops quickly and easily.

Creating Apple Loops in Logic

In the main window, select the audio or software instrument region that you want to convert into an Apple Loop. Next, select Functions > Open in Apple Loops Utility. You can also drag an audio or software instrument region to the Loop Browser and drop it. Either action opens the dialog box shown in Figure 7.52.

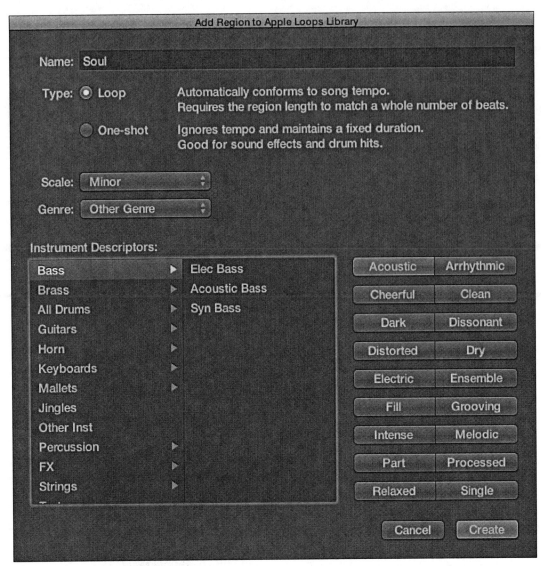

Figure 7.52 The Add Region to Apple Loops Library dialog box. You can use the options in this dialog box to name, tag, and otherwise define properties of your Apple Loop.
© Apple Inc.

The Add Region to Apple Loops Library dialog box allows you to tag your Apple Loop with the following information:

▷ **Name:** You can name your Apple Loop in this field.
▷ **Type:** The Type options define whether the Apple Loop will follow the tempo or key of any project it is used in (Loop) or play for its normal duration and pitch regardless of tempo or transposition (One-Shot). If you are trying to convert an audio region that is not an exact number of bars in length, then One-Shot will automatically be selected. If you want to use the audio region as a loop-type Apple Loop, then you need to process it in the Apple Loops Utility.
▷ **Scale:** This menu allows you to define the tonality of your Apple Loop.
▷ **Genre:** This menu allows you to define a genre for your Apple Loop.
▷ **Instrument Descriptors:** This consists of a list area, which allows you to define an instrument type for your Apple Loop, and a button area, which allows you to add other descriptive tags to your Apple Loop. In the list area, the list on the left allows you to define a general instrument family for your Apple Loop. Most of the general instrument families have a secondary list that appears in the list on the right when you select a general instrument family. This secondary list allows you to define a more specific instrument type. For example, in Figure 7.52, Bass is selected in the general instrument list on the left, and the list on the right contains three more specific options from which you can select: Elec Bass, Acoustic

Bass, and Syn Bass. In the button area, you can add up to nine of the descriptors to your Apple Loop. You can select only one descriptor from each horizontal pair of buttons, so if you chose Single from the first row, clicking on Ensemble would automatically deselect Single.

When you are finished tagging your Apple Loop, click the Create button. Your new Apple Loop will automatically be added to the Loop Browser.

> **NOTE:** When you make your own custom Apple Loop using the Open in Apple Loops Utility command, it uses the currently detected and edited transients from the Audio File editor to determine where to stretch your loop. So if you want to adjust the "stretch points" of your Apple Loop, you can use Transient Editing mode as described earlier to set and adjust the transients. If you create an Apple Loop without adjusting the transients, Logic simply creates its own grid based on the project's beat divisions.

Adding ACID Loops to the Loop Browser

ACID loops are audio loops that are designed to work in Sony Creative Software's ACID programs. ACID Loops are similar to Apple Loops in that they are designed to automatically adjust to the tempo and key of a project in an ACID program. They are in WAV format, unlike Apple Loops.

Suppose you have a bunch of ACID loops, but you want to find some way to integrate them into Logic. You can add the ACID loops to the Loop Browser; this allows you to manage all your loop libraries in one location. Because ACID loops aren't embedded with tags like Apple Loops are, you can't import ACID loops without the context of their folder structure. So, if you want to add ACID loops to the Loop Browser, simply drag the highest-level folder in your ACID loops' folder structure into the Loop Browser. You can now access your ACID loops in the Loop Browser.

Using ReCycle Files in Logic

ReCycle is a file format originally designed to work in Propellerhead Software's Reason program. A file that is in ReCycle format contains an audio file that has been sliced into smaller pieces to allow the file to be played back at different tempos with little degradation in sound quality.

Importing ReCycle Files into Logic

If you have some ReCycle files you'd like to incorporate into your Logic project, Logic offers you a variety of options regarding how the ReCycle file is handled. First, you need to import a ReCycle file by selecting File > Import Audio File, by pressing Shift+Command+I, or by right-clicking on an audio track in the main window and choosing Add Audio File from the menu that appears. Logic Pro can import ReCycle files with an .ryc, .rex, or .rx2 suffix. When you import a ReCycle file, the ReCycle File Import dialog box shown in Figure 7.53 opens.

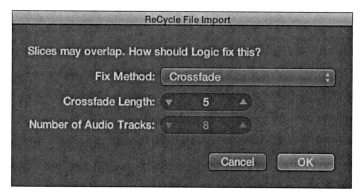

Figure 7.53 The ReCycle File Import dialog box.
© Apple Inc.

Because the ReCycle file probably will not match your project tempo, there is a possibility that the slices could overlap each other. Logic allows you to define how it handles your ReCycle file in the ReCycle File Import dialog box. The options in the Fix Method menu determine how Logic handles the imported ReCycle file. The different Fix Method menu options and their functions are as follows:

▷ **Don't Fix:** This option imports the files as they are, without performing any extra processing. If you import your ReCycle file using this option, the slices may overlap.

▷ **Crossfade:** If you select this option, Logic adds all the slices to the same audio track and automatically crossfades the slices per the Crossfade Length setting. The Crossfade Length setting is in milliseconds.

▷ **Add Tracks:** If you select the Add Tracks option, Logic will distribute the slices onto the original audio track, plus any additional tracks as defined in the Number of Audio Tracks field.

▷ **Render into Single File:** This option renders the ReCycle file into a single audio file per the current project tempo.

▷ **Render into Apple Loop:** Selecting this option imports the ReCycle file as an Apple Loop.

If you import the ReCycle file using the Don't Fix, Crossfade, or Add Tracks option, then Logic will create a ReCycle folder in the Tracks area on the selected track. You can then open the folder and manipulate the individual slices as audio regions.

Converting ReCycle Files into Apple Loops

As you know, you can import ReCycle files into Logic and have them converted into Apple Loops in the process. You can also use the All Files Browser to convert ReCycle files into Apple Loops. To convert ReCycle files into Apple Loops in the Browser, you need to navigate to the folder containing your ReCycle files in the All Files Browser. Next, select Convert ReCycle Files to Apple Loops from the Action menu at the bottom of the All Files Browser, as shown in Figure 7.54. After you select this command, a file browser dialog box appears, asking you to choose which folder to put your new Apple Loop(s) in.

Figure 7.54 The Action menu in the All Files Browser. Selecting Convert ReCycle Files to Apple Loops allows you to convert ReCycle files to Apple Loops in the All Files Browser.
© Apple Inc.

Now that you've explored how to work with Apple Loops and audio data inside audio regions, the next chapter will look at working with the MIDI data inside MIDI regions.

Working with MIDI

U NLIKE AN AUDIO FILE, MIDI files are simply numerical messages rather than actual sound. You can move, alter, program, and view those MIDI messages in many different ways. Thanks to these properties and Logic's origins as a MIDI-only application, there are far more editors and windows relating to MIDI information than to audio. Each MIDI editor offers its own unique view of MIDI data and allows you to work with your MIDI information in whichever way seems most comfortable. Logic offers perhaps the most comprehensive and powerful MIDI editing and re-imagining functions of any sequencer, and these obviously take some time to master.

This chapter is not going to explore every possible detail and use of every possible option in all the editors, but it will go over the functionality, operation, and potential of each one specifically enough for you to explore more deeply on your own.

MIDI Editors and MIDI Regions

You've already explored MIDI regions. Just as double-clicking an audio region brings you to the Audio Track editor in which you edit your audio, double-clicking a MIDI region opens the MIDI editor of your choice in the main window. To choose which MIDI editor opens automatically when you double-click a MIDI region, choose Logic Pro > Preferences > General, select the Editing tab, and open the Double-Clicking a MIDI Region Opens menu. Logic presents you with a menu of the four MIDI editors in Logic, as shown in Figure 8.1.

Figure 8.1 You can choose any of the four MIDI editors as the default editor in the Global Preferences.
© Apple Inc.

Logic defaults to opening up the Event editor when you double-click a MIDI region. You may prefer to use the Piano Roll editor or another editor, however. When you get used to the various editors and how you like to use Logic, you can change the default to reflect your personal working method.

Double-clicking a MIDI region in the main window is not the only way to view it in a MIDI editor. In addition, each editor can be viewed not only in the main window, but also in its own dedicated window. Most MIDI editors have Link functions, which allow you to keep one or more of the MIDI editors in your screenset, and those editors automatically contain the data from any MIDI region selected in the main window. The Event list, Piano Roll, and Score editors even allow you to view multiple regions at one time. There are also key commands you can use when selecting regions to open specific editors.

In addition, you can always open the various MIDI editors by using menu and key commands, regardless of what is selected on the main window.

The Piano Roll Editor

The Piano Roll editor offers a graphical piano roll–like view of MIDI data. It displays MIDI notes as colored bars in different positions, with different lengths, colors, and velocities. You can even use the Piano Roll editor to visually edit MIDI controller data (called MIDI Draw data), as you'll see later in this section. Figure 8.2 shows the Piano Roll editor.

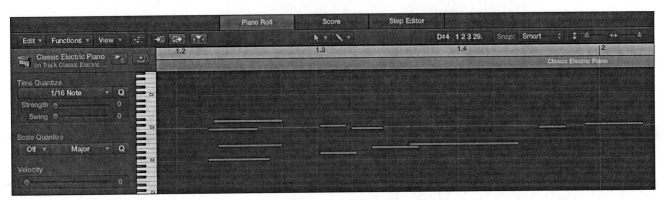

Figure 8.2 The Piano Roll editor allows you to edit your MIDI notes graphically.
© Apple Inc.

The Piano Roll editor contains now-familiar elements of local menus, buttons, a position display, and a Tool menu, but its most striking feature is the large window that displays the MIDI notes. The playhead moves across all the notes of the MIDI region as you play the song, much like a piano roll spins as a song plays. You can use the Piano Roll editor not only to edit notes but also to create MIDI parts. The Piano Roll editor also has zoom controls and a Bar ruler display, complete with global tracks to help you navigate and edit. Logic Pro X also brings a few new features to the Piano Roll: Time Quantize, Scale Quantize, and Velocity controls.

This section explores the various elements of the Piano Roll editor and how you can use them.

Local Menus

The Piano Roll editor contains three local menus: the Edit, Functions, and View menus. Figure 8.3 shows the local menus of the Piano Roll editor.

Figure 8.3 The local menus of the Piano Roll editor.
© Apple Inc.

The following subsections contain descriptions of each local menu.

The Edit Menu

The Edit menu contains options for moving and selecting data. Figure 8.4 shows the Edit menu of the Piano Roll editor.

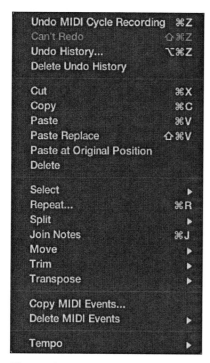

Figure 8.4 The Edit menu of the Piano Roll editor.
© Apple Inc.

The commands in this menu are as follows:

▷ **Undo:** This undoes your last action in the Piano Roll editor. The key command for this is Command+Z.

▷ **Redo:** This command redoes your last undone action in the Piano Roll editor. The key command for this is Command+Shift+Z.

▷ **Undo History:** This command opens the Undo History window. See the Tracks area local Edit menu for details. The key command for this is Option+Command+Z.

▷ **Delete Undo History:** Choose this command to delete the Undo History. See the main window local Edit menu for details.

▷ **Cut:** This removes all selected notes from the grid and places them in the Clipboard. The key command for this is Command+X.

▷ **Copy:** This command copies any selected MIDI notes into the Clipboard. The key command for this is Command+C.

▷ **Paste:** This command places any MIDI notes in the Clipboard on the grid at the current playhead position. The key command for this is Command+V.

▷ **Paste Replace:** This command replaces notes you select in the Piano Roll editor with those from the Clipboard. It pastes notes at the current playhead and replaces all notes within the time range of the pasted notes. The key command for this is Shift+Command+V.

▷ **Paste at Original Position:** This command places MIDI notes from the Clipboard back into the notes' original location. This is useful if you cut notes and decide you still want them where they were, or if you copy notes, subsequently delete them from their original positions, and decide you want them back. You can also use this command to paste notes in a region on a different MIDI or software instrument track as a means of doubling those notes with another instrument.

▷ **Delete:** Delete removes the selected MIDI information from the Piano Roll editor. You can also use the Delete key to delete the selected information.

▷ **Select:** The Select submenu is covered at the end of this bulleted list.

▷ **Repeat:** This command repeats the selected notes. It presents a small dialog box for you to select the number of repetitions, whether you want real or alias copies, and whether you want to quantize the copies (in other words, force the repeats to end on an exact bar line, even if the original does not). The key command is Command+R.

▷ **Split:** The Split submenu offers three options, two of which are similar to those found in the main window Edit > Split submenu. The Split submenu commands are as follows:

  ▷ **Notes at Playhead:** This command splits any selected notes at the current playhead position. The key command is Command+T.

  ▷ **Notes at Rounded Playhead:** This command splits any selected note at the bar nearest the playhead.

  ▷ **Notes at Locators:** This command creates a split in any selected notes at the current locator positions. The key command is Control+Command+T.

▷ **Join Notes:** This command lets you join selected notes of the same pitch together to make one note. The key command for this is Command+J.

▷ **Move:** The Move submenu contains commands for moving selected notes, similar to the Edit > Move submenu in the main window, covered in Chapter 6, "The Logic Pro Main Window." The Piano Roll Editor Edit > Move options are much fewer in number:

  ▷ **To Playhead:** This command moves the beginning of the selected note to the current playhead position. If multiple notes are selected, they will be moved as well, while maintaining their position compared to the left-most note. The key command for this is ; (semicolon).

  ▷ **Nudge Left:** This command lets you nudge selected notes to the left per the Edit > Move > Set Nudge Value To setting. The key command for this is Option+left arrow.

  ▷ **Nudge Right:** This command lets you nudge selected notes to the right per the Edit > Move > Set Nudge Value To setting. The key command for this is Option+right arrow.

  ▷ **Set Nudge Value To:** This submenu, identical to the Edit > Move > Set Nudge Value To menu path in the main window (covered in Chapter 6), lets you set the nudge value for the Piano Roll editor.

▷ **Trim:** The Trim submenu, shown in Figure 8.5, gives you the following options for trimming the length of notes in the Piano Roll editor:

  ▷ **Note to Remove Overlap with Selected:** This shortens any selected overlapping notes so they do not overlap. You must select both of the overlapping notes to correct a given pair of overlapping notes.

  ▷ **Note to Remove Overlap with Adjacent:** This shortens any selected overlapping notes so they do not overlap. It does not matter whether one or both of the overlapping notes is selected. The key command for this is \ (backslash).

  ▷ **Note to Remove Overlap for Repeated:** This shortens any selected repeated overlapping notes of the same pitch so they do not overlap. The first note in the overlap must be selected for this command to work.

  ▷ **Note Start to Playhead:** This command trims the start of any selected notes to the current playhead position. The key command for this is Command+[(left bracket).

  ▷ **Note End to Playhead:** This command trims the end of any selected notes to the current playhead position. The key command for this is Command+] (right bracket).

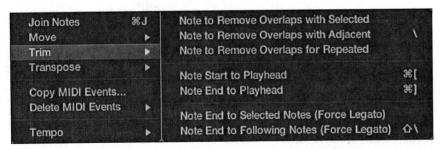

Figure 8.5 The Trim submenu of the Edit menu.
© Apple Inc.

▷ **Note End to Selected Notes (Force Legato):** This lengthens any note to extend to the beginning of any following notes. You must select both the initial notes to extend and the notes to which they will extend.

▷ **Note End to Following Notes (Force Legato):** This lengthens any note to extend to the beginning of any following notes. (This sort of smooth transition from one note to another without space in between is called *legato*.) The initial notes to be extended must be selected. The key command for this is Shift+\ (backslash).

▷ **Transpose:** The Transpose submenu offers the following commands for transposing selected notes.

    ▷ **+1 Semitone:** This command lets you transpose selected notes up one semitone. The key command for this is Option +up arrow.

    ▷ **−1 Semitone:** This command lets you transpose selected notes down one semitone. The key command for this is Option+down arrow.

    ▷ **+12 Semitones:** This command lets you transpose selected notes up 12 semitones, or one full octave. The key command for this is Shift+Option+up arrow.

    ▷ **−12 Semitones:** This command lets you transpose selected notes down 12 semitones, or one full octave. The key command for this is Shift+Option+down arrow.

▷ **Copy MIDI Events:** You can copy all MIDI events with this command. You will be presented with a dialog box asking you the range of notes to copy and how you want them to be copied.

▷ **Delete MIDI Events:** The Delete MIDI Events submenu offers the commands shown in Figure 8.6.

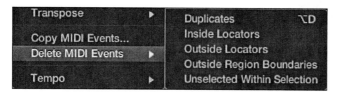

Figure 8.6 The Delete MIDI Events submenu of the Edit menu.
© Apple Inc.

These commands offer different options for erasing groups of MIDI events in the Piano Roll editor. Here is a brief description of each:

    ▷ **Duplicates:** This erases the second instance of all MIDI events that are duplicated by other MIDI events (in other words, same pitch, time, controller number, and so on). The key command for this is Option+D.

    ▷ **Inside Locators:** This command erases all MIDI events between the locators.

    ▷ **Outside Locators:** This erases all MIDI events not between the locators.

    ▷ **Outside Region Borders:** If you are editing more than one MIDI region in the Piano Roll editor, this command erases MIDI events inside the selected region that are outside the currently visible region boundaries. This is useful when a region has been resized. The other regions will not be affected.

    ▷ **Unselected Within Selection:** If one or more notes or events are unselected between the first and last selected notes, this command erases them.

▷ **Tempo:** The Tempo submenu offers a number of options for operating on the tempo of your project. The Tempo submenu is covered in detail in Chapter 13, "Advanced Tempo Operations."

The Select submenu, shown in Figure 8.7, contains a host of commands for selecting MIDI data in the Piano Roll editor.

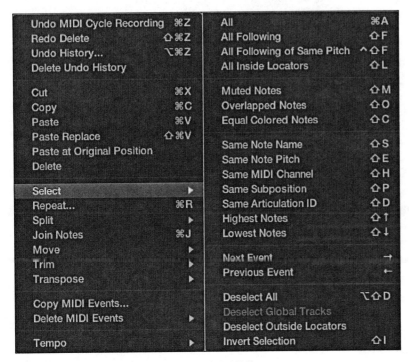

Figure 8.7 The Select submenu of the Edit menu.
© Apple Inc.

The Select submenu commands are as follows:

▷ **All:** This selects all the notes in the Piano Roll editor. The key command for this is Command+A.

▷ **All Following:** Use this command to select all the notes after the currently selected note. The key command for this is Shift+F.

▷ **All Following of Same Pitch:** Use this command to select all the notes of the same pitch after the currently selected note. The key command for this is Control+Shift+F.

▷ **All Inside Locators:** This command selects all the notes inside the two locators. The key command for this is Shift+L.

▷ **Muted Notes:** This command selects all notes that you have muted. The key command for this is Shift+M.

▷ **Overlapped Notes:** You can use this command to select all notes that overlap each other in time, such as chords. The key command for this is Shift+O.

▷ **Equal Colored Notes:** This command selects all notes with the same color, based on the Colors mode enabled in the local View menu. The key command for this is Shift+C.

▷ **Same Note Name:** This command selects all notes of the same name. For example, if you currently have a C selected, this command will select all C notes. The key command for this is Shift+S.

▷ **Same Note Pitch:** This selects all notes of the same pitch—for example, all D#4 notes. The key command for this is Shift+E. You can also select notes of the same pitch by clicking on that pitch in the keyboard at the left side of the Piano Roll editor.

▷ **Same MIDI Channel:** This selects all notes on the same MIDI channel. This is useful when viewing more than one MIDI track in the same Piano Roll editor. (See the section "Editing Multiple Regions in the Piano Roll Editor" later in this chapter for details on viewing options in the Piano Roll editor.) The key command for this is Shift+H.

▷ **Same Subposition:** A powerful selection option, this command selects all MIDI notes that have the same relative position in the Bar ruler. That means if you select a note directly on the bar line, you select all notes that fall on a bar line as well. If you select a note between the third and fourth bar, for example, you also select all notes that fall on that relative position between the third and fourth bar, and so on. The key command for this is Shift+P.

▷ **Same Articulation ID:** Articulations are a means of getting different timbres out of an instrument. For example, a violin can have many different bowing techniques. In this example, articulations allow you to access different bowing techniques from one software instrument. This is much more elegant than having one software instrument for long bowing and another one for tremolo. Different articulations have different IDs—MIDI commands that tell the software instrument to use a particular articulation. The Select Same Articulation ID command lets you select all notes using a particular articulation ID. Instead of having to select each note individually when trying out a different articulation, you can use this command to select them all at one time. The key command for this is Shift+D.

▷ **Highest Notes:** This command selects all the top-most notes across the length of your MIDI region. If your region contains a monophonic performance, such as a melody line, all the notes will be selected. The key command for this is Shift+up arrow.

▷ **Lowest Notes:** This command selects all the bottom-most notes across the length of your MIDI region. If your region contains a monophonic performance, such as a melody line, all the notes will be selected. The key command for this is Shift+down arrow.

▷ **Next Event:** This command lets you change your selection from the selected event to the next event to the right of it. The key command for this is right arrow.

▷ **Previous Event:** This command lets you change your selection from the selected event to the next event to the left of it. The key command for this is left arrow.

▷ **Deselect All:** This command deselects any selected events. The key command for this is Shift+Control+D.

▷ **Deselect Global Tracks:** This command deselects any selected global tracks.

▷ **Deselect Outside Locators:** This command deselects any selected events outside the right and left locators.

▷ **Invert Selection:** This command inverts the selection status of all the notes in the Piano Roll editor. In other words, if you have a single note selected, this command toggles between that single note and every note except that selected note. If you had previously used the Select Inside Locators command, Invert Selection alternates between all notes inside the selected locators and those outside those locators. The key command for this is Shift+I.

The Functions Menu

The Functions local menu contains commands that operate on other aspects of MIDI data in the Piano Roll editor. Figure 8.8 shows the Functions local menu.

Figure 8.8 The Functions menu of the Piano Roll editor.
© Apple Inc.

The functions included in this menu are as follows:

▷ **Mute Notes On/Off:** This command lets you mute and unmute the selected notes. The key command for this is Control+M.

▷ **Quantize Notes:** This command applies the current Time Quantize setting to the selected notes. The Time Quantize functions are covered in the section "The Piano Roll Editor Inspector" later in this chapter. The key command for this is Q.

▷ **Undo Quantization:** This removes any quantization that has been applied and returns the selected notes to their original location. The key command for this is Control+Command+Q.

▷ **Include Non-Note MIDI Events:** If you select this option, editing and moving notes also edits and moves any controller data acting on those notes.

▷ **Convert Sustain Pedal to Note Length:** If you use this command, Logic uses any sustain pedal MIDI controller data to adjust the lengths of the MIDI notes that the messages were sustaining.

▷ **Set MIDI Channel to Voice Number:** For selected notes, this places each voice (note of different pitch) on a separate MIDI channel.

▷ **Insert Instrument MIDI Settings as Events:** When you select regions on an external MIDI track, choosing the Insert Instrument MIDI Settings as Events command creates MIDI events for program, volume, and pan if they are checked in the Track Inspector and places those events in the selected region.

▷ **MIDI Transform:** One of Logic's most powerful MIDI tools is its MIDI Transform feature, which lets you transform data in nearly unlimited ways. The MIDI Transform submenu offers a selection of Transform presets, as shown in Figure 8.9. If you select one of these presets, you launch the MIDI Transform window, which is configured to run the task you have chosen. The MIDI Transform window is one of the more complex aspects of Logic and is examined further in the section "The MIDI Transform Window" later in this chapter.

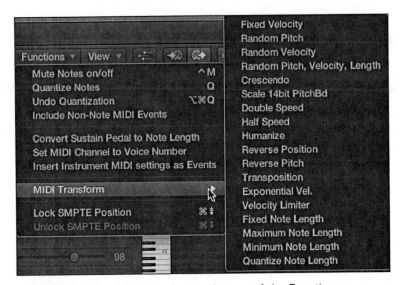

Figure 8.9 The MIDI Transform submenu of the Functions menu.
© Apple Inc.

▷ **Lock SMPTE Position:** This command locks the MIDI events to their current SMPTE positions. The key command for this is Command+Page Down.

▷ **Unlock SMPTE Position:** This releases the MIDI events from being tied to their current SMPTE positions. The key command for this is Command+Page Up.

The View Menu

The View menu allows you to alter the appearance of the Piano Roll editor and gives you access to the MIDI Draw functions. Figure 8.10 shows the View menu of the Piano Roll editor.

Figure 8.10 The View menu of the Piano Roll editor.
© Apple Inc.

The View menu options are as follows:

▷ **MIDI Draw:** As mentioned briefly in Chapter 6, MIDI Draw enables you to enter and edit MIDI controller data to automate a MIDI region. (MIDI Draw is also referred to as region-based automation, or RA.) Because the MIDI controller data is part of the region itself, when you are editing a region in the Piano Roll editor, you can edit the controller data as well.

This command displays a menu that offers a selection of possible MIDI controllers you may want to view alongside your note data, as shown in Figure 8.11. If you select one of these options, a controller data lane opens in the bottom half of the Piano Roll editor. This area is filled with any existing controller messages that you already have in the region, as shown in Figure 8.12.

Figure 8.11 The MIDI Draw submenu of the View menu.
© Apple Inc.

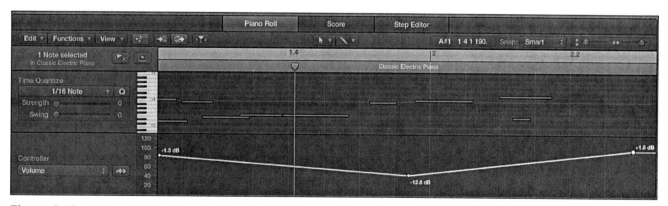

Figure 8.12 A Piano Roll editor showing the MIDI Draw window. Currently, the volume MIDI controller data is showing.
© Apple Inc.

TIP: You can adjust the height of the MIDI Draw area by dragging the bar between the MIDI Draw and Piano Roll areas up or down. You'll learn more about MIDI Draw in Chapter 10, "Using Automation in Logic."

▷ **Show/Hide Local Inspector:** This command shows or hides the Piano Roll editor Inspector, which contains the Time Quantize, Scale Quantize, and Velocity controls. The Piano Roll editor Inspector is covered later in this chapter.

▷ **Set Note Color:** This submenu offers commands for setting the note colors based on the following parameters:

   ▷ **Region Color:** This command displays the notes of each MIDI region with the same color from the Tracks area. This is most useful when more than one region is in the Piano Roll editor at the same time. (See the section "Editing Multiple Regions in the Piano Roll Editor" later in this chapter.)

   ▷ **Velocity:** When Velocity is selected, the velocity of each note in the Piano Roll editor is displayed in color, ranging from bluish-green at the lowest velocities to reddish-purple at the loudest velocities. Editing velocity in the Piano Roll editor is easy using the Velocity tool, which is covered in the next section. Velocity is the default view in the Piano Roll editor.

   ▷ **MIDI Channel:** This command allows you to display notes of the same MIDI channel with the same color. For example, if you decide to use the Set MIDI Channel to Voice Number command on a region, and you want to see what notes are on which MIDI channels, selecting MIDI Channel Colors makes the changes readily apparent.

▷ **Secondary Ruler:** As in the main window, the Secondary Ruler command in this menu adds a second Bar ruler to the Piano Roll editor, showing bars if the primary ruler is showing time and time if the primary ruler is showing bars. The key command for this is Control+Option+Command+R.

▷ **Global Track Protect Buttons:** This command adds track protect buttons in the global track headers. Enabling a track protect button on a global track header prevents you from accidentally editing global events on that global track when working in the Piano Roll editor. If you're displaying global tracks in the Piano Roll editor (using the Track > Global Tracks > Show Global Tracks command, the Global Tracks buttons, or the key command G), it's a good idea to protect the tracks unless you need to edit one.

▷ **Scroll in Play:** If you select Scroll in Play, instead of the playhead scrolling across the Piano Roll editor window, the playhead remains stationary in the center of the window and the MIDI data scrolls horizontally past it, from right to left. The key command for this is Control+`.

▷ **Auto Zoom:** If you select Auto Zoom, when you open a region in the Piano Roll editor, the horizontal zoom level is automatically set to a point at which the entire length of the region can be displayed.

The Piano Roll Editor Tool Menu

Because the Piano Roll editor is designed for graphic editing, it makes sense that the Piano Roll editor would have a rather extensive Tool menu of graphic editing tools. As in the main window, you can also assign secondary right-click tool in the Piano Roll editor and even a tertiary tool, per your Right Mouse Button preference setting. Figure 8.13 shows the Piano Roll editor Tool menu. You can also access the Piano Roll editor Tool menu by pressing T.

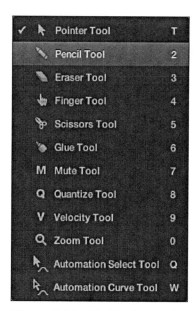

Figure 8.13 The Tool menu in the Piano Roll editor.
© Apple Inc.

Here is a description of the tools, in order from top to bottom.

▷ **Pointer:** This tool is the standard pointer for selecting and making "rubber band" selections of multiple notes. You can access this tool by pressing T.

▷ **Pencil:** The Pencil tool allows you to draw new notes into the Piano Roll editor. You'll learn how to use the Pencil tool later in this chapter, in the section "Inserting and Deleting Notes in the Piano Roll Editor." You can access this tool by pressing T, then 2.

▷ **Eraser:** This tool removes notes from the Piano Roll editor. You can access this tool by pressing T, then 3.

▷ **Finger:** This tool allows you to resize notes. You can access this tool by pressing T, then 4.

▷ **Scissors:** The Scissors tool splits notes into multiple notes. You can access this tool by pressing T, then 5.

▷ **Glue:** This tool merges adjacent notes, forming one note from multiple notes. You can access this tool by pressing T, then 6.

▷ **Mute:** The Mute tool mutes or unmutes notes in the Piano Roll editor. You can access this tool by pressing T, then 7.

▷ **Quantize:** The Quantize tool allows you to quantize only selected notes, leaving the rest of the region unquantized. This is very useful if you have a great performance, but with only a portion in which the timing is slightly off. You can use this tool to quantize just those few notes and not alter the rest of the performance. You can access this tool by pressing T, then 8.

▷ **Velocity:** The bar inside each note indicates the velocity of that note relative to the length of the note itself. In Velocity Colors mode, the bar for each note also displays its velocity using colors from purple through the rainbow to red. With the Velocity tool, you can raise or lower the velocity of one or more notes by selecting the note and then scrolling up or down with the mouse to shorten or lengthen the velocity bar inside the note or notes. When you adjust the velocity of all selected notes at once by clicking on any selected note and moving the mouse, every note retains its relative value compared to the other notes. (So if you raise the velocity of a loud note and a soft note, both will get louder, but the numeric difference between their velocities will remain the same.) You can also access this tool by pressing T, then 9.

▷ **Zoom:** For zooming in on a particular group of notes, use the Zoom tool to "rubber band" them and zoom in to the maximum level. Click anywhere that has no notes to return to the original zoom level. You can access this tool by pressing T, then 0.

▷ **Automation Select:** The Automation Select tool—represented by a bent arrow with a solid arrowhead, pointing upward and left—can select automation data in the Piano Roll editor MIDI Draw automation lane. Chapter 10, "Using Automation in Logic," discusses automation and the Automation Select tool in depth. You can access this tool by pressing T, then Q.

▷ **Automation Curve:** The Automation Curve tool—represented by a bent arrow with an open arrowhead, pointing upward and left—can create curves between two automation nodes in the Piano Roll editor MIDI Draw automation lane. Chapter 10 discusses automation and the Automation Curve tool in depth. You can access this tool by pressing T, then W.

Piano Roll Editor Buttons

At the upper-left corner of the Piano Roll editor are four Piano Roll editor buttons. Figure 8.14 shows those buttons.

Figure 8.14 The Piano Roll editor buttons.
© Apple Inc.

The functions of each of these buttons, going from left to right across the Piano Roll editor, are as follows:

▷ **MIDI Draw:** Clicking this button opens the MIDI Draw area of the Piano Roll editor.

▷ **MIDI IN:** When this button is engaged, you can use your MIDI controller to directly input MIDI into the Piano Roll editor. This is very useful for step input, which is explained later in this chapter, in the section entitled "MIDI Step Input."

▷ **MIDI OUT:** With this button engaged, you hear each note as you select and edit it. This is useful if you want to monitor what you are doing as you work in the editor.

▷ **Catch Playhead:** The button containing the now-familiar playhead icon is the Catch Playhead button. With this button engaged, the visible window in the Piano Roll editor always follows the playhead. You will almost always want this button engaged.

The Piano Roll Editor Inspector

The Piano Roll editor has been upgraded in Logic Pro X to include a few handy controls in the new Piano Roll editor Inspector, shown in Figure 8.15. These controls are Time Quantize, Scale Quantize, and Velocity.

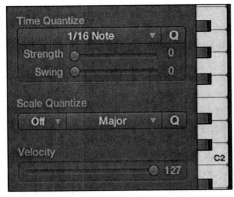

Figure 8.15 The Piano Roll editor Inspector gives you Time Quantize, Scale Quantize, and Velocity controls.
© Apple Inc.

Time Quantize

The Time Quantize functions are identical to the quantize parameters in the MIDI Region Inspector in the main window. To use Time Quantize in the Piano Roll editor, follow these steps:

1. Select the notes you wish to quantize.
2. Select the desired note value in the Time Quantize menu (directly under the words "Time Quantize," as shown in Figure 8.15). It offers the same values found in the Quantize menu in the MIDI Region Inspector.
3. Next, adjust the Strength and Swing settings. Although this Inspector features sliders instead of the hybrid click-drag and text entry fields found in the MIDI Region Inspector, these sliders function identically to the Q-Strength and Q-Swing parameters in the MIDI Region Inspector.
4. Click the Time Quantize Q button, and the selected notes are quantized per your settings!

Scale Quantize

Scale Quantize is a great tool for fixing little mistakes—for example, when you have played a few wrong MIDI notes in an otherwise great performance—or perhaps for auditioning what a region would sound like in a minor key rather than a major one. It lets you select notes in the Piano Roll editor, set a root key and a scale or mode to use built off that key, and quantize the pitches of the selected notes to that scale.

To set up Scale Quantize, follow these steps:

1. Select notes you'd like to quantize to a scale.
2. Select a root key in the Key menu (under the words "Scale Quantize" in Figure 8.15). It has options for all 12 keys, plus an Off setting to turn Scale Quantize off.
3. Select one of the scales offered in the Scale menu, as shown in Figure 8.16.

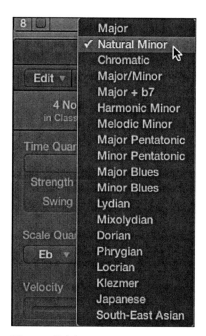

Figure 8.16 The Scale menu offers a wide array of scales for the Piano Roll editor's Scale Quantize function.
© Apple Inc.

For those of you familiar with music theory, most if not all of these scales should be familiar. As of this writing, when you select a scale, the selected notes are automatically quantized to the selected scale in the selected key. The Scale Quantize Q button is (currently) unnecessary. If you change the Key or Scale settings, the scale quantization will happen immediately. If you set the Key setting to Off, the selected notes will return to their original pitches.

Velocity

The Velocity slider lets you quickly alter the velocity setting of any selected notes. It does not create an absolute velocity value for the selected notes; rather it scales them up or down as you increase or decrease the Velocity setting.

You will probably find it useful to remember some of the different note selection techniques detailed earlier in this chapter when using these different functions. For example, it's pretty easy to see how selecting all notes of one pitch using the Edit > Select > Same Note Pitch command (Shift+E) would make it a breeze to change the velocity of all snare hits in a given MIDI performance, or how choosing Edit > Select > Same Note Name (Shift+S) would let you correct any stray Eb notes in a performance in C major. You could even time-quantize the performance of different parts of a drum kit using different Swing or Strength settings. The possibilities offered by the functions of the Piano Roll editor Inspector are endless!

Inserting and Deleting Notes in the Piano Roll Editor

You may already have a region filled with MIDI information from recording a MIDI performance. If, however, you want to enter MIDI data without recording and performing a MIDI part in its entirety, and if working with your music graphically appeals to you, the Piano Roll editor is *the* place to create MIDI performances in Logic. There are a couple ways to insert notes in the Piano Roll editor:

▷ You can use a MIDI controller, the computer keyboard, or onscreen keyboard to "step input" MIDI.
▷ You can use the Pencil tool to draw your MIDI performance onscreen.

To use one of these methods of inserting notes, first you must have an open MIDI region in the Piano Roll editor. This can be an empty region that you created in the Tracks area just so you could fill the region in the Piano Roll editor, or it could be a region that already contains MIDI data. In the following sections, you'll learn how to use each method of inserting notes.

MIDI Step Input

The Piano Roll editor (and the Score and Event list editors) allow you to use your hardware MIDI controller to input MIDI in step input or step recording mode. In this mode, you enter your MIDI performance one step at a time. This is useful if you want to create a MIDI performance that is beyond your technical ability to play in real time or if you know precisely which notes you want to input and you want to insert them quickly, but not in real time. Step input in Logic is fast and intuitive once you understand the basics, and it is a powerful tool when you know how to use it.

To use step input:

1. Make sure you have the MIDI IN button engaged so that the Piano Roll editor can receive external MIDI.
2. Make sure your LCD is set to Custom.
3. Set the Division value in the Transport for the length of notes you'll be playing. Click and hold on the Division display to access the Division menu, in which you select the Division value. The Division display in the Custom LCD is shown in Figure 8.17.

Figure 8.17 The Division display in the LCD in the Transport, Custom view. Click and hold on the Division display to access the Division menu, where you can select the Division value.
© Apple Inc.

4. Start playing your controller. Logic considers any notes you hold down at the same time to have been input at the same point, so you can play either single notes or chords. As soon as you release the key(s), the playhead advances by one division, and you will see the notes you performed (complete with the velocity with which you pressed the keys) onscreen. It's as simple as that!

As you'd expect, Logic offers more control over step input than the basic procedure I just described. You can adjust the Division setting using the Division display or key commands throughout the step-input process. So you could, for example, step input a few 1/8 notes, then a passage of 1/16 notes, then two 1/4 notes, then back to 1/8 notes. You can lengthen notes you have just input by using the sustain pedal or the Sustain Inserted Notes key command. You can also insert a rest by depressing the sustain pedal without inputting notes or by using the Rest key command. You can also step forward and backward via key commands, or you can press the Delete key to erase what you have just input and thus move the playhead backward. When the Piano Roll editor is in focus, the spacebar works as a step forward key command. I've made references to some of the key command options for step input; in fact, you can use step input entirely by means of key commands. In the Key Commands window, look for the Step Input Keyboard section. You will find key commands for everything, from all the notes and divisions to different velocity settings. Also, be aware that if you have the Piano Roll editor MIDI IN engaged and the Piano Roll editor is in focus, your computer keyboard will react as if you have engaged the Musical Typing keyboard. To use the key commands that overlap input keys used by the Musical Typing keyboard, you must either disable the MIDI IN button or use the Tab key or your mouse to shift focus to another area of the main window.

If you would rather use step input completely with the mouse, you can use Logic's Musical Typing keyboard (described in Chapter 6) or the Step Input keyboard. You can launch the Step Input keyboard either by selecting Window > Step Input Keyboard or via the key command Option+Command+K. The Step Input keyboard is shown in Figure 8.18.

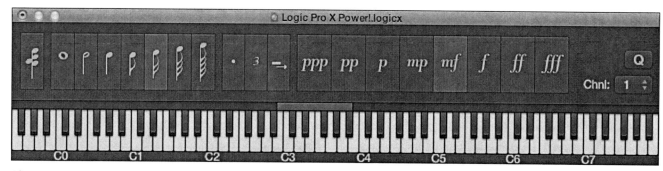

Figure 8.18 Use the Step Input keyboard to step input MIDI notes onscreen with the mouse.
© Apple Inc.

The Step Input keyboard includes buttons representing the various quantization settings, velocity ranges, a button for chord creation, and so on. As with MIDI hardware or keyboard input, you can adjust these features at any point while inputting, so you can create complex MIDI performances using the Step Input keyboard.

> **NOTE:** As mentioned, you can use the Musical Typing or Step Input keyboard to step input MIDI notes. Because the Step Input keyboard has so many more options relating to MIDI step input, I highly recommend you use it for step recording instead of the Musical Typing keyboard. The Musical Typing keyboard is designed more for real-time input of performances in the main window.

All these step-input methods and key commands offer rich and creative tools to create and develop MIDI performances. Feel free to experiment with them, and be sure to check out the available key commands. Don't think that step input is only for those who are not piano virtuosos. Even the best performers may just need to add a few notes to a MIDI region, and there's nothing faster than using step-input key commands!

Entering MIDI Notes with the Pencil Tool

You can also "draw" your MIDI performance using the Pencil tool. If you know exactly what you want, this is a great way to create MIDI parts quickly. When you click the Pencil tool in the Piano Roll editor, it creates a note at that pitch and the nearest division. The created note will be the same length and velocity as the previously created note, so if you created an 1/8 note, then used the Finger tool to lengthen it to a whole note, the next note you created would be a whole note. If you select a note with the Pointer tool and then use the Pencil tool to create notes, all subsequent notes will have the length and velocity of the previously chosen note. If you click and drag with the Pencil tool, you can shorten or lengthen the note you are creating.

Entering Notes Using the Piano Roll Shortcut Menu

The Piano Roll editor shortcut menu, which you can open by right-clicking in the Piano Roll editor, offers a Create Note command. This places a note at the current pitch and position of the mouse pointer.

Deleting Notes in the Piano Roll Editor

You can delete notes in the Piano Roll editor by pressing the Delete key to delete any selected notes or by using the Eraser tool. If you want to restore notes you have deleted, you can undo the action.

Resizing and Moving Notes in the Piano Roll Editor

After creating notes, resizing and moving notes are two of the things you will use the Piano Roll editor for most often. Because the Piano Roll editor is designed for graphic editing, it's no surprise that it includes tools to make these tasks as easy as possible. This section explores some of the methods for moving and resizing notes in the Piano Roll editor.

Resizing Notes

You can resize notes using a number of tools. To resize notes from the front, leaving the end point the same, you can grab a note from the lower-left corner (the cursor should change into a Resize cursor), hold down the mouse button, and drag right or left to move the beginning of the note forward or backward in the region. If you select multiple notes, when you click on the lower left of one note, you adjust the beginning point of all the selected notes.

The Finger tool is designed to allow you to adjust the length of one or more notes quickly. You can click on a single note to resize it, or you can select a group of notes and resize them all. As you hold down the mouse and drag right or left, the note becomes longer or shorter. You can resize a note to be as long as the entire MIDI region in the Piano Roll editor or as tiny as the smallest possible note division. Keep in mind that the smallest division to which you can graphically reduce a note depends on the zoom resolution of the Piano Roll editor. You can change the zoom level using the Zoom tool or the zoom sliders in the upper right of the Piano Roll editor, or via key commands.

If you hold down the Shift key while using the Finger tool to select multiple notes, every selected note will become the length of the last note selected. If you resize the notes while holding down the Shift key, the selected notes will all be the same length. If you hold down the Shift+Option key combination, all selected notes will end at the same point.

Moving Notes

You can move notes around the Piano Roll editor by selecting them with the Pointer tool and dragging them to a new location. When you hold the mouse button down with one or more notes selected, the mouse pointer turns into a hand to give you a visual cue that you can now move your notes around the Piano Roll editor. You can move at the highest resolution possible for the current zoom level by holding down the Control key as you move your notes (wait until the pointer turns into a hand before you press Control). To move at the single-tick level (the finest resolution possible in Logic) regardless of zoom level, hold down the Control+Shift keys.

> **TIP:** To make and move a copy of one or more notes, hold down the Option key while dragging your notes.

Editing Multiple Regions in the Piano Roll Editor

The most common use of the Piano Roll editor is to open a single MIDI region for editing. However, sometimes you might want to view and/or edit more than one region in the Piano Roll editor simultaneously. You can accomplish this very easily.

To view multiple regions in the Piano Roll editor, simply select the regions you want to view in the Tracks area; the contents of all your selected MIDI regions will appear in the Piano Roll editor. Lines delineating the start and end points of MIDI regions in the Tracks area will appear as thick vertical lines in the editing window, reflecting the colors of their parent region. If you have Region Colors engaged, the notes of the various regions will have the same colors in the Piano Roll editor as their regions do in the main window.

When showing multiple regions, you can make selections, resize, and move notes from more than one region as if they were all in the same region.

The Event List

The Event list is the oldest method of recording, storing, and entering MIDI data, both in general and in Supertrack, Logic's earliest predecessor. Given this long heritage, the Event list is extremely robust and feature-laden while admittedly looking a bit anachronistic. Put simply, the Event list features a scrolling text window containing MIDI information. You view, edit, and modify this information by changing the text in the list. Figure 8.19 shows the Event list window. You can also access the Event list in the List Editors area in the main window.

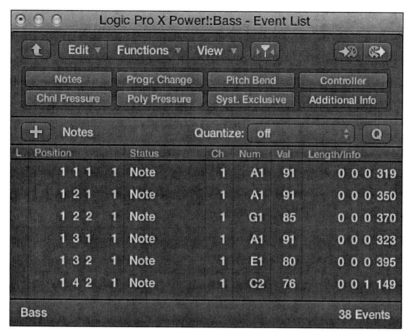

Figure 8.19 In the Event list, you can view and edit your MIDI data as text.
© Apple Inc.

The Event list displays the position of events, the specific type of event it is (which the list labels as "Status"), the MIDI channel of the event (Ch), any numerical values associated with that event, and the length or other relevant information about that MIDI event.

At first glance, it might seem as if editing music as text would be more tedious than creative. When you get used to the Event list, however, you'll find this is far from the reality. Often, you'll want to have a linked Event list even when using another editor or the main window, simply to view the detailed information available in the Event list. In some cases, some MIDI information, such as note release velocity, can be viewed and edited only in the Event list. And you might just find that when you know what you are doing, being able to quickly find and replace MIDI data as text is the most efficient method of editing available.

Let's start looking at this vital and powerful tool by going through its local menus.

Event List Local Menus

Like the Piano Roll editor, the Event list has three local menus: Edit, Functions, and View. You can see those menus in the upper-left area of the Event list in Figure 8.19.

The similarities between the Piano Roll editor's and the Event list's local menus don't end there. Because all MIDI editors are essentially working with the same data, many of the commands are also shared, as you will see in the following sections.

The Edit Menu

Figure 8.20 shows the Edit menu of the Event list. As you can see, this menu is exactly the same as the Edit menu in the Piano Roll editor. The submenus in the Edit menu also are identical in content. Refer to the descriptions of the commands in those sections of the chapter.

Figure 8.20 The Event list's Edit menu is identical to the Piano Roll editor's local Edit menu. (The Undo option displayed may be different, but that changes with each action.)
© Apple Inc.

The Functions Menu

Compare the Functions menu of the Event list in Figure 8.21 to the Functions menu in the Piano Roll editor. There are a couple of slight differences between them. First, the Event list editor Functions menu does not have the Include Non-Note MIDI Events command. That's because by its very nature, the Event list is purpose-built for working on all manner of MIDI data. Second, the Event list Functions menu includes a submenu: Note Events. This submenu contains the Convert Sustain Pedal to Note Length command and the Set MIDI Channel to Voice Number command. The Note Events submenu also contains one more command: Assign MIDI Channels Based on Score Split. This command splits selected notes to different MIDI channels based on the Auto Split Notes in Polyphonic Staff Styles setting in the Score Preferences. When you choose this command, notes above get one channel and notes below get another. The key command for this is Control+Shift+C. For information about the other commands in the Functions menu, refer to the description of the commands in the section "The Functions Menu," found in the section "The Piano Roll Editor" earlier in this chapter.

Figure 8.21 The Event list's Functions local menu shares most of the same options as the Piano Roll editor's Functions menu.
© Apple Inc.

The View Menu

Unlike the other two local menus in the Event list, the View menu offers selections unique to it. Figure 8.22 shows the View menu of the Event list.

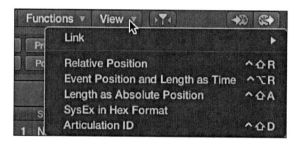

Figure 8.22 The View menu in the Event list.
© Apple Inc.

This menu offers a selection of commands that allow you to customize the display of events in the Event list:

▷ **Link:** The Link submenu contains Off, Same Level, and Content commands for linking the Event list to other areas and windows in Logic. The Link submenu functions were covered in Chapter 6.

▷ **Relative Position:** With this engaged, the position of notes does not reflect their position in the song, but their relative position inside the MIDI region you are editing. The key command for this is Control+Shift+R.

▷ **Event Position and Length as Time:** With this engaged, the Position and Length columns in the Event list display SMPTE units instead of bar units. The key command for this is Control+Option+R.

▷ **Length as Absolute Position:** If this is engaged, the Length display shows the absolute song position of the note-off message as opposed to the note length (which is the usual way of displaying length). The key command for this is Control+Shift+A.

▷ **SysEx in Hex Format:** If your Event list is displaying any system exclusive (SysEx) information for a hardware MIDI device, engaging this option displays the data in hexadecimal format. Consult your MIDI hardware unit's instruction manual for details of its SysEx implementation.

▷ **Articulation ID:** This command lets you add a column in the Event list for viewing and editing Articulation IDs. The key command for this is Control+Shift+D.

Event List Buttons

The Event list holds many more buttons than any window you have explored so far. Figure 8.23 shows the Event list buttons.

Figure 8.23 The Event list buttons allow you to select which data to show and which to filter out.
© Apple Inc.

Some of these buttons are familiar from other windows. Others are unique to the Event list and allow you to display only those specific types of MIDI messages with which you want to work. The familiar buttons located to the left of local menus include the following, from left to right:

▷ **Hierarchy:** Clicking this button when it is active will move you up a level in the Event list from a list of the events in a region to a list of the regions in the project.

▷ **Catch Playhead:** With this button engaged, the visible window in the Event list always follows the playhead position. You will almost always want this button engaged.

▷ **MIDI IN:** When this button is engaged, you can use your MIDI controller to input MIDI directly into the Event list. This was described earlier in this chapter in the section "MIDI Step Input."

▷ **MIDI OUT:** With this engaged, you hear the currently selected MIDI note that you are editing.

In addition to these buttons, there is another major set of buttons available in the Event list. These buttons allow you to filter what MIDI data you see in the Event list.

▷ **Notes:** With this button engaged, you will see the MIDI notes in the MIDI region that you are editing.

▷ **Program Change:** With this button engaged, you will see any program change messages in the MIDI region you are editing.

▷ **Pitch Bend:** With this button engaged, you will see any pitch bend messages in the MIDI region you are editing. Keep in mind that if your region has pitch bend information, you may find literally *hundreds* of pitch bend messages representing every instant the pitch bend wheel was touched, so disengaging this button can be very handy!

▷ **Controller:** With this button engaged, you will see any control change messages in the MIDI region you are editing. Like pitch bend data, continuous control change messages (modulation, for example) can overwhelm your Event list, making this another very useful filter.

▷ **Channel Pressure:** With this button engaged, you will see aftertouch messages in the MIDI region you are editing. Channel pressure is a continuous controller.

▷ **Poly Pressure:** With this button engaged, you will see any polyphonic key pressure messages in the MIDI region you are editing. Polyphonic aftertouch is also a continuous controller.

▷ **System Exclusive:** With this button engaged, you will see any system exclusive messages in the MIDI region you are editing. SysEx is comparatively expert-level MIDI data. Most users can disengage this button, but for those who work with SysEx a lot, SysEx viewing and editing in the Event list is invaluable.

▷ **Additional Info:** If this button is engaged, you will see extra information (the "full message") about the displayed MIDI messages. Again, this is relatively expert-level stuff.

Inserting and Deleting MIDI Messages in the Event List

As with the other MIDI editors, you can insert and delete MIDI information in the Event list. Because the Event list is a text editor, you do not have the visual cues that you do in the Piano Roll editor or the musical notation cues you have in the Score editor. Still, some people may find it convenient to add notes directly while using the Event list, and you can employ a number of methods.

First, you can use the same process described earlier in the section "MIDI Step Input" to input MIDI information into a MIDI performance one note at a time. The major difference is that you will not see a graphic representation of the note you have performed, but a line of text information instead.

You can also insert an event using the Create New Event button, marked with a plus symbol, in the bottom-left corner of the Event list (refer to Figure 8.23). You can create any kind of MIDI data listed previously for the Event list filter buttons. Simply select the type of data you'd like to create in the menu next to the Create New Event button, labeled "Notes" in Figure 8.23, and click the Create New Event button. The new event will be created at the current playhead position.

If you select an event and copy it (Command+C), the event is copied to the Clipboard. When you paste the event, a text entry box also appears, in which you can enter position values; this will be pasted in the new location.

You can delete MIDI events by selecting them and then pressing the Delete key. If you are not happy with any insertions or deletions you have made, you can always use the Undo command, or open the Undo History window if you have made a number of edits you dislike.

Moving and Adjusting the Values of MIDI Messages in the Event List

Even though you do not have the graphic bar to move, lengthen, or shorten for each note as you do in the Piano Roll editor, you can easily accomplish these things in the Event list, and with even more precision. The important thing to remember is that you are accomplishing everything through text entry, so you need to know the precise values of how much you want to resize a MIDI note or the exact position to which you want to move a MIDI event.

To move a single event, simply double-click its position data with the Pointer tool. A text entry box appears in which you type the new value. When you press Return, the event moves to the new location. If you select multiple MIDI messages, they all move relative to the event whose position you changed. So if you selected three MIDI notes that occurred on bar 1, bar 2, and bar 3, and you double-clicked on the note at bar 2 and changed its position to bar 3, the note at bar 1 would move to bar 2, and the note at bar 3 would move to bar 4.

The procedure for adjusting any other value, such as a MIDI event's length or velocity, is basically the same: You simply double-click the desired data with the Pointer tool, enter a new value in the text box using spaces, commas, or periods to differentiate bars/beats/divisions/ticks, and press Return. If you select more than one MIDI event, they all maintain their values relative to each other, just as previously described; all selected events maintain their relative length.

You can also adjust values and move events without entering text, but by selecting one or more events and then using the mouse as a vertical slider to adjust values up or down.

When adjusting values for a group of MIDI events with the mouse, if any selected event reaches its maximum or minimum value (remember, MIDI values are between 0 and 127), no further adjustments in that direction will be possible for any event in that group, so that each event may maintain its relative value. If you want to continue to change the events from the selected group that have not reached their maximum or minimum, you can do so by holding the Option key down while dragging one of those events. If you want to set the same value for all selected events, hold down Shift+Option while dragging one of the events.

The Quantize function works as you would expect: Select the events you want to quantize, select the desired Quantize setting, and click the Q button.

> **TIP:** You can easily use the Piano Roll editor and the Event list in tandem in the main window. When working in the Piano Roll editor, you can open the Event list in the main window by double-clicking a note in the Piano Roll editor. The Event list will open to the note you selected in the Piano Roll editor, ready for any editing you'd like to perform in the Event list!

The Step Editor

The Step editor, formerly called the Hyper editor, is another MIDI editor with a heritage that goes back to the early versions of Notator. It offers a unique way to build drum parts and to edit MIDI controller data graphically. It looks a bit like a cross between the Tracks area and the Piano Roll editor, with lanes for different notes or controller messages like tracks in the Tracks area, and vertical bars representing MIDI events. You can also view global tracks in the Step editor. Figure 8.24 shows a Step editor window.

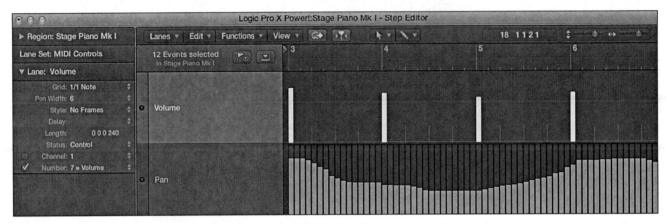

Figure 8.24   You can use the Step editor as a MIDI drum or controller editor; here it is being used as a controller editor.
© Apple Inc.

The Step editor not only offers a step-entry graphic editor for drums and controller messages, it also allows you to save combinations of event definitions and drum note names as lane sets, which you'll explore in the "Lane Sets" section later in this chapter. Due to the uniqueness of the Step editor, it is often overlooked. After reading this section, I hope you will feel comfortable enough to integrate it into your working method.

NOTE: What's the difference between the Step editor and MIDI Draw? Although both can operate on MIDI control messages, they serve different purposes. MIDI Draw is an automation-like protocol in which you can enter MIDI control data in the main window or the Piano Roll editor for specific MIDI regions. The Step editor is a grid-based editor that does allow for the input and editing of MIDI control data, but its grid-based editing does not allow for the smoothness of changes that are possible with MIDI Draw. MIDI Draw is not suited for one-off and non-continuous MIDI control—MIDI Draw wants to connect control messages together. On the other hand, you'll find the Step editor is far too tedious if you are trying to create automation-like effects—you'd be far better served using MIDI Draw or track-based automation. Additionally, the Step editor's grid-based editing facility is uniquely suited for drum programming.

Step Editor Local Menus

Like the Event list, the Step editor shares the Edit, Functions, and View menu commands with the other MIDI editors. There is one wholly unique menu, however: the Lanes menu. Let's look at the Step editor local menus.

The Lanes Menu

The local Lanes menu includes commands unique to the Step editor. Figure 8.25 shows the Lanes menu.

Figure 8.25 The Lanes menu of the Step editor.
© Apple Inc.

This local menu contains commands related to using and creating lane sets. The "Lane Sets" section later in this chapter explains in detail how to use lane sets. Following are descriptions of these commands:

▷ **New Lane Set:** This creates a new lane set.

▷ **New Lane Set for GM Drums:** This creates a new General MIDI drum lane set.

▷ **New Lane Set for Current Events:** This creates a lane set using the events currently selected in one of the MIDI editors. This is very useful if you have used MIDI Draw in other windows to add controller messages to MIDI regions, and you want to create a lane set with just those previously defined messages (events) represented.

▷ **Clear Lane Set:** This empties the current lane set.

▷ **Delete Lane Set:** This deletes the current lane set.

▷ **Create Lane:** This creates a new lane based on the event definition of the selected lane in the Step editor. Event definitions determine which MIDI event a given lane of the Step editor will edit. You can change the event definition of a lane in the Lane Inspector, which is covered in the section "The Lane Inspector" later in this chapter. The key command for this is Option+Command+N.

▷ **Delete Lane:** This deletes the selected lane(s) in the Step editor. The key command for this is Command+Delete.

▷ **Create Multiple Lanes:** You can automatically create lanes for all MIDI events or all selected events. When you choose this command, a dialog box appears, asking whether you want to create new lanes with definitions only for those events you have selected or for all events. Select the option you desire and press Return, and all those event definitions will appear in the Step editor.

▷ **Convert Lane:** This redefines the selected event definition, as well as all the events in its lane. The events retain their values after conversion. A pane appears in the main window showing the current Lane Inspector settings to the left of an identical Lane Inspector, which you can edit.

▷ **Copy Lane:** This command copies an event definition into the Clipboard. The key command for this is Control+C.

▷ **Paste Lane:** This pastes an event definition from the Clipboard. The key command for this is Control+V.

▷ **Select All Lanes:** This command selects all the lanes in the current lane set.

The Edit Menu

Figure 8.26 shows the Edit menu of the Step editor. As you can see, the Step editor shares its Edit menu with the Piano Roll editor and Event list. Refer to the previous section covering the Piano Roll editor's Edit menu for descriptions of these commands.

Figure 8.26 The Edit menu of the Step editor is the same as the Edit menus of the Piano Roll editor and Event list.
© Apple Inc.

The Functions Menu

Figure 8.27 shows the Functions menu of the Step editor. This menu has commands found in the Functions menu in the Piano Roll editor and the Event list. Refer to the previous sections covering the Functions menu for descriptions of these commands.

Figure 8.27 The Functions menu of the Step editor has commands found in the Piano Roll editor and the Event list.
© Apple Inc.

The View Menu

The View menu for the Step editor, shown in Figure 8.28, has options found in the Piano Roll editor and Event list editor View menus. Refer to the previous View menu sections for descriptions of these commands.

Figure 8.28 The View menu of the Step editor.
© Apple Inc.

The Step Editor Tool Menu

Figure 8.29 shows the Step editor Tool menu.

Figure 8.29 The Tool menu of the Step editor.
© Apple Inc.

The Line tool is unique to the Step editor, but the other four tools are standard. Descriptions of the five tools follow:

▷ **Pointer:** This is the standard Pointer tool for selecting and making "rubber band" selections of multiple notes.

▷ **Pencil:** The Pencil tool allows you to draw in new drum notes if you are using the Step editor as a drum editor or new controller information if you are using the editor to edit controller data. You'll learn how to use the Pencil tool later in this chapter.

▷ **Eraser:** This tool removes notes and controller data from the Step editor.

▷ **Line:** This tool is valuable if you want to make linear changes in your data. To use this tool, click and hold on the note or controller message that you want to begin your line, drag the line until you reach your end point, then release the mouse button. The velocity or controller data in any event between the line's end points will snap to the value at which the line bisected the event. In other words, if you want to fade up the velocity of drum hits slowly, you could click the crosshair on the first drum hit at the very bottom of the hit; then, at the end of the measure, click again, drawing a diagonal line up through your drum hits. The velocities of your drum hits now have the upward ramp formed by the Line tool, giving you an even, linear fade-in.

▷ **Zoom:** To zoom in on a particular area, use the Zoom tool to "rubber band" it. Then zoom in to the maximum zoom level. Click in any empty space in the editor to return to the original zoom level.

The Step Editor Buttons

Because the Step editor is unique in its functions, it relies less on the standard Logic window components. The Step editor has two basic function buttons common to the other MIDI editors: Catch Playhead and MIDI OUT. When working in the Step editor, you'll normally want these buttons on. For information on how these buttons work, refer to the section "The Piano Roll Editor Buttons" earlier in this chapter.

The Lane Inspector

Unlike the Piano Roll editor or the Event list, the Step editor has an Inspector. The Step editor's Lane Inspector contains parameters to define the currently selected lane in the Step editor. Every event definition has its own Inspector. Figure 8.30 shows an Inspector for the Volume lane.

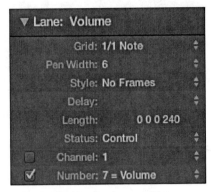

Figure 8.30 The Inspector for the volume events in the Step editor.
© Apple Inc.

The functions of these parameters are as follows:

▷ **Grid:** This determines the grid, or how many events will fit in one bar in the Step editor window. The size of the grid determines the resolution of the events.

▷ **Pen Width:** With this parameter, you can adjust the width of the bars that appear in the Step editor window. You can adjust this parameter between 1 and 16. In general, you'll want to find the value that almost completely fills the grid space but that still leaves a few pixels so you can differentiate the different bars. You need to determine the correct value based on your chosen grid resolution.

▷ **Style:** This parameter gives you two options for how data is displayed in the Step editor. No Frames displays the event as a vertical line. Framed Values displays the event as a vertical line with a hollow frame that fills the remainder of the lane, allowing you to see the event as a proportion of its full range. You can see the framed values displayed in the pan lane in Figure 8.24.

▷ **Delay:** With this parameter, you can offset all the events in a lane by a number of ticks. Simply double-click the left side of the Delay text box and enter a value. Positive values delay events; negative numbers advance events. If you click the right side of the Delay area by the up and down arrows, a menu appears in which you can select your note divisions.

▷ **Length:** The Length parameter determines how long added notes will be. The first number is the current division and the second is ticks. You will not normally need to set this unless you have some particularly long or short drum samples.

▷ **Status:** Here you can change the event definition from one type of message (note, volume, pitch bend, and so on) to another.

▷ **Channel:** Normally, the Step editor displays all matching MIDI events in the region being edited. If you set the Channel parameter and select the accompanying checkbox, the Step editor shows only those events on the selected channel. If the checkbox is unchecked, the parameter is ignored.

▷ **Number or Pitch (First Byte):** With this checkbox selected, this parameter determines what the initial byte (note pitch for notes, controller type for MIDI control messages) must be for the lane to display data. In other words, if this parameter is set for C#2, the editor displays only those notes that fall on C#2. Generally, for drum editing and specific MIDI control message events, you'll want this checkbox selected. For more generic columns (such as the All Velocities option), you'll want to leave this checkbox unchecked.

NOTE: Suppose you've become very comfortable working with Logic's editors in the main window. You've looked at the picture of the Step editor in Figure 8.24 and you've looked at the integrated Step editor in the main window, and you don't see the Step editor window's Inspector in the integrated Step editor. Instead of wasting what space you *do* have in the main window's Step editor, Logic uses the main window's own Inspector for controlling the currently selected lane!

Lane Sets

Lane sets are unique to the Step editor. They are basically stored lists of MIDI note or MIDI control message definitions, complete with parameters for each lane. Lane sets allow you to configure the editor for your specific needs. You can then save that configuration with all of your parameter settings, note names, and so on, and recall that configuration at will. If you like to use a few specific MIDI control events, you can create a lane set of only those event definitions. You can also have a lane set for your specific MIDI drum kit. Then, whenever you want to program drums, the exact setup that you need will be ready for you right in the Step editor.

Lane sets not only are powerful tools, but they are also very easy to use. You can access your available lane sets from the Lane Set menu in the Inspector. Simply click in the Lane Set field to open the menu and select the lane set you want to use. This menu also includes the commands for creating and clearing lane sets found in the Lanes menu. Figure 8.31 shows the Lane Set selection field.

Figure 8.31 All the lane sets you create are available in the Lane Set menu.
© Apple Inc.

Logic offers lane sets for MIDI controls and GM (General MIDI) drums, which you can use as they are or as templates for your own lane sets. Simply adjust each lane using the Lanes local menu and key commands, set the Lane Inspector for the event definitions in the Inspector to taste, use the Select All command, then choose New Lane Set for Current Events to create a lane set of your current configuration. (The section "Setting Up the Step Editor as a Drum Editor" later in this chapter describes this in more detail.) If you'd prefer to work from a blank slate, you can always start the process by using the New Lane Set command. You can name your lane set by selecting Rename Lane Set in the Lane Set menu, which presents you with a text box in which to enter a new name for the lane set. You need not worry about saving anything—Logic automatically saves each new lane set, so it's available in all of your projects.

Editing MIDI Control Messages Using the Step Editor

The Step editor is ideal for editing situations in which you want to see your controller data in a grid or in vertical bars. You can also view many different MIDI messages in one lane set and get an overall view of how your various MIDI messages, such as volume and pan messages, are interacting with each other.

You can use the Pencil tool to place MIDI events directly on the grid where you want them. If you want to create many messages at once, simply hold the mouse button down and move across the grid. As you move the mouse up or down, you draw in higher or lower values for your data. The bar for each note is solidly colored to represent how high the value of the event is. A totally solid event means the event has a value of 127, the highest MIDI value. If the solid portion of the bar is only a third of the way up the bar, the value may be only 42. After creating your data with the Pencil tool, you can use the Line tool to make smooth, linear value adjustments across an entire lane.

If you are used to viewing messages as continuous data, viewing them in the shape of static bars instead might seem tricky at first, but what you might think is continuous is actually nothing but a series of individual messages, each assigning a given controller a value at a particular position. After using the Step editor to edit those individual messages and values, you might just fall in love with having that level of control over your data!

Editing MIDI Notes (Drums) Using the Step Editor

A MIDI note is actually just a type of MIDI message that tells a sound module or software instrument to play a sound at a given pitch. That means the Step editor can be configured to edit MIDI note messages just as easily as MIDI control messages. Because the Step editor allows you to place notes directly on a grid, using the Step editor as a drum editor is a natural fit. If you enjoy programming drums in the computer rather than via a performance on a MIDI keyboard, drum controller, or MIDI percussion set, the Step editor offers you the ability to draw notes on a grid quickly, exactly where you want them. Thanks to lane sets, you can even name each lane with the name of the drum instrument the lane triggers. See the next section, "Setting Up the Step Editor as a Drum Editor," for specific details on using the Step editor with drums.

The procedure for using the Step editor to program drums is exactly the same as described previously for MIDI control messages: You draw in the event you want, in the lane you want, at the velocity you want. You'll see a bar line representing your drum hit and the velocity you selected. You can hold the Pencil tool down and roll over many positions to create multiple notes, and you can use the Line tool to create fade-ins, fade-outs, steady velocity at a particular value, and so on. If you like programming drum parts directly into Logic, you'll find the Step editor especially suited to your needs.

> **TIP:** Clearly, the Step editor assumes that if you want to program notes in its grid, they will be for drum parts—as its inclusion of a GM drum lane set and commands to create them illustrates. That doesn't mean you *must* use the Step editor for drum tracks. However, if you are programming heavily quantized MIDI parts and looking for that old-school "analog" step sequencer style of grid in which to place your arpeggiated synth pulses and techno hits, you just might find that the Step editor suits your needs as well.
>
> Simply create a GM drum lane set, which will give you a lane set with all notes; then erase the drum name in the Lane Inspector and give each event its standard note name. You'll end up with a lane set of notes without drum names. Rename the lane set, and you now have a MIDI step sequencer lane set, ready for you to program synths right to the grid!

Setting Up the Step Editor as a Drum Editor

If you happen to be using an external General MIDI drum module (or a synthesizer with GM drum assignments), then the Step editor is already set up for you. Just select the GM drums lane set, and you're done! Everything is already configured for you. However, it's possible that you are using a software instrument or a more advanced drum module that may not follow the GM convention for drums. In this case, you should start with the GM drum kit set, but you'll want to customize it to your specific instrument.

If your software instrument or drum module matches some or all of the GM drum notes, customizing your lane set will be a breeze. Simply select those event definitions that you don't need and choose Lanes > Delete Lane or use the default key command, Command+Delete (refer to Figure 8.25). You can delete more than one definition at a time by Shift-clicking multiple lanes.

Very often, your drum instrument may match its main drums with the names in the GM drum kit, but not all of them. For example, the kick, snares, and most cymbals may match up between your instrument and the GM drum kit lane set, but your instrument's crash sound may be in the GM drum kit lane for RIDE 2. Thankfully, the Step editor lets you easily change the names of event definitions. To do this, in the Lane Inspector, simply click on the lane name and type in the new name. Figure 8.32 shows the name of the KICK 2 event definition being changed.

Figure 8.32   Click the lane name in the Lane Inspector to quickly change its name.
© Apple Inc.

If you find that your instrument doesn't match any of the GM drum kit names, you can create a brand-new lane set specifically using the notes of your instrument. To do this, select a MIDI region of notes, open that region in the Step editor, and select New Lane Set for Current Events from the Lanes menu. As Figure 8.33 shows, this will leave you with a new lane set containing one lane for each MIDI note in your MIDI region. The event definitions will be named for their MIDI note by default. The lane set will have the same name as your MIDI region. You can rename both the lane set and event definition names in the Lane Inspector.

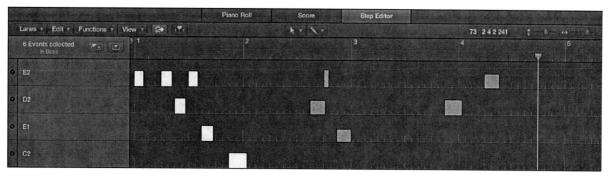

Figure 8.33 When you use the New Lane Set for Current Events command, a new lane set named after your MIDI region is created with one lane for each MIDI note.
© Apple Inc.

TIP: Suppose you're creating your own lane set from the New Lane Set for Current Events command, and you want to ensure that you have a lane for every single drum hit. In this case, create a MIDI region that contains one note for each drum hit. You can even play each drum hit in the order from first to last that you want the lanes to appear in your new lane set. Then select that MIDI region, open it in the Step editor, and select New Lane Set for Current Events. This creates a lane for every single hit, with the first note appearing in the top lane and the last note appearing in the bottom lane.

TIP: Even if you are using a software instrument such as Ultrabeat that already has a built-in step sequencer, you might want to use the Step editor. Most software instruments with step sequencers only allow a single-step division setting to be used at once; in other words, you can't have a 1/4-note grid for your kick drum, a 1/16-note grid for your snare, a 1/32-note grid for your hi-hats, and so on. The Step editor gives you that level of flexibility. Give it a try!

The Score Editor

As cutting edge as Logic is, musicians who like working with notation are not left out in the cold. One of the most powerful editors in Logic is the Score editor, which offers traditional music notation recording, editing, and score printing. Even if you don't feel at home using computers to manipulate MIDI performances, you will find the Score editor to be the "digital music notation paper" you always wanted, where you can perform, move, erase, redraw, and print out sheet music with the ease that only a computer can bring. Figure 8.34 shows the Score editor.

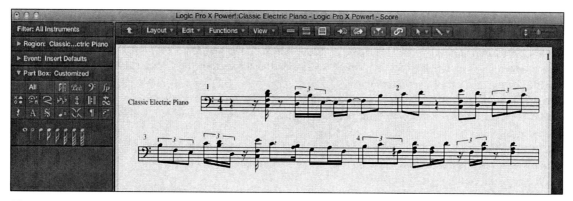

Figure 8.34 The Score editor.
© Apple Inc.

If you do not read and write music notation, you might find this editor superfluous to your working method. However, if you do use—and sometimes even think in—music notation, you'll find the Score editor to be one of Logic's most important features, with advantages over other sequencers that do not offer the power and flexibility of Logic's notation facilities.

> **NOTE:** This section is not intended to teach music theory or the reading and writing of music notation. Instead, the purpose is to introduce those already familiar with these concepts to the way that Logic allows users to write and edit music in notation form—and I do mean *introduce*. The Score editor is perhaps the deepest editor in Logic, because music notation itself is truly an advanced symbolic language, with all the inherent complexity and flexibility that implies. If this chapter inspires you to explore music notation on your own, great! Music theory will always help your music productions, regardless of genre.

Score Editor Local Menus

Because of the comprehensive nature of music notation, the Score editor has a lot of commands relating to how to format, lay out, and enter musical information. To accommodate this, the Score editor has a unique Layout menu. The other local menus are shared with the other MIDI editors, but there are some Score editor–specific commands in these menus. The sections that follow describe the various options available in the local menus.

Layout Menu

The Layout menu contains options for how to format your score. Figure 8.35 shows the Layout menu.

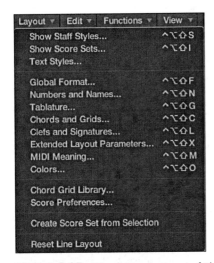

Figure 8.35 The Layout menu of the Score editor.
© Apple Inc.

The various options are as follows:

▷ **Show Staff Styles:** This command opens the Staff Styles window, which allows you to access Logic's predesigned staff styles as well as create your own. The Staff Styles window is described in the section "Staff Styles" later in this chapter. The key command for this is Control+Option+Shift+S.

▷ **Show Score Sets:** This command brings up the Score Sets window, which allows you to create score sets for grouping MIDI instruments from the Tracks area as you want them to appear in your score. The key command for this is Control+Option+Shift+I.

▷ **Text Styles:** This command opens the Text Styles window, which allows you full control of any text on your score. The Text Styles window is covered in the section "Text Styles" later in this chapter.

▷ **Global Format:** This command opens the Score Project Settings window to the Global tab, which allows you to configure the page setup for printing, the spacing of your score, the chord symbols, and so on. (See Figure 8.36.) You can also access the Score Project Settings window by choosing File > Project Settings > Score. The key command for this is Control+Option+Shift+F.

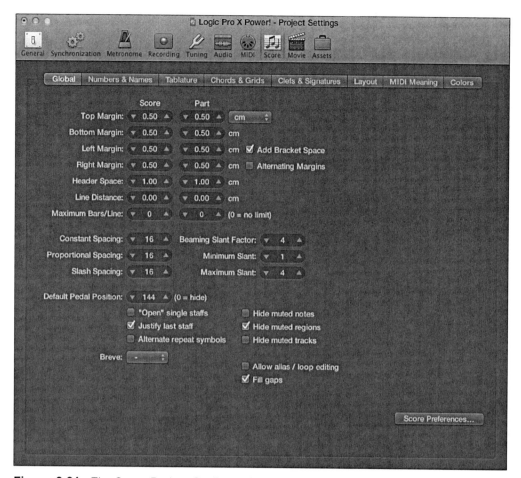

Figure 8.36 The Score Project Settings window open to the Global tab.
© Apple Inc.

▷ **Numbers and Names:** This command opens the Score Project Settings window to the Numbers & Names tab, in which you can configure page numbers, bar numbers, and instrument names for printing and so on. (See Figure 8.37.) The key command for this is Control+Option+Shift+N.

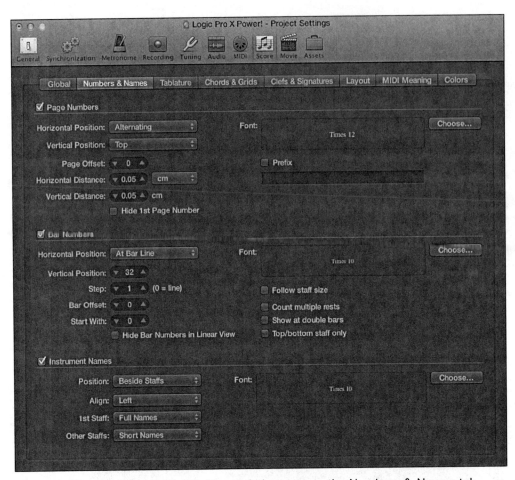

Figure 8.37 The Score Project Settings window open to the Numbers & Names tab.
© Apple Inc.

▷ **Tablature:** This command opens the Score Project Settings window to the Tablature tab, which allows you to configure how Logic will format guitar tablature and similar features. (See Figure 8.38.) The key command for this is Control+Option+Shift+G.

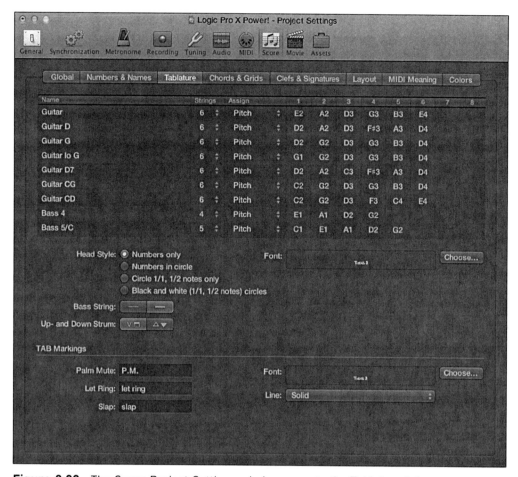

Figure 8.38 The Score Project Settings window open to the Tablature tab.
© Apple Inc.

▷ **Chords and Grids:** This command opens the Score Project Settings window to the Chords & Grids tab, which allows you to configure the way Logic displays chord symbols and to define settings for the way tablature is displayed. (See Figure 8.39.) The key command for this is Control+Option+Shift+C.

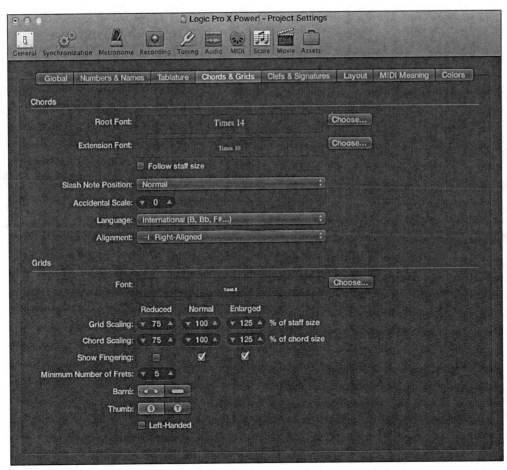

Figure 8.39 The Score Project Settings window open to the Chords & Grids tab.
© Apple Inc.

▷ **Clefs and Signatures:** This command opens the Score Project Settings window to the Clefs & Signatures tab. This window offers parameters for how Logic displays clefs, key signatures, time signatures, and octave symbols. (See Figure 8.40.) The key command for this is Control+Option+Shift+L.

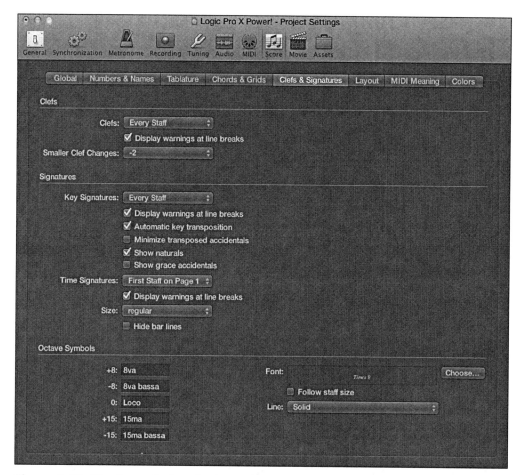

Figure 8.40 The Score Project Settings window open to the Clefs & Signatures tab.
© Apple Inc.

▷ **Extended Layout Parameters:** This command opens the Score Project Settings window to the Layout tab. This window offers extra parameters for more esoteric and aesthetic display options. (See Figure 8.41.) The key command for this is Control+Option+Shift+X.

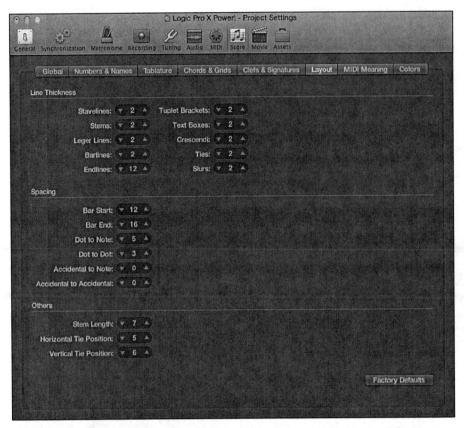

Figure 8.41 The Score Project Settings window open to the Layout tab.
© Apple Inc.

▷ **MIDI Meaning:** This command opens the Score Project Settings window to the MIDI Meaning tab. This window lets you assign MIDI values to score symbols. (See Figure 8.42.) The key command for this is Control+Option+Shift+M.

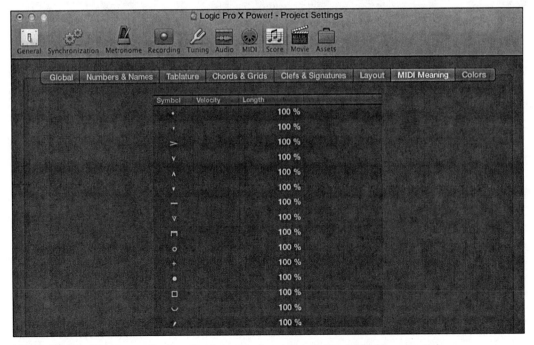

Figure 8.42 The Score Project Settings window open to the MIDI Meaning tab.
© Apple Inc.

▷ **Colors:** This command opens the Score Project Settings window to the Colors tab. This window lets you assign colors to pitch and velocity, as well as construct your own user palettes. (See Figure 8.43.) The key command for this is Control+Option+Shift+O.

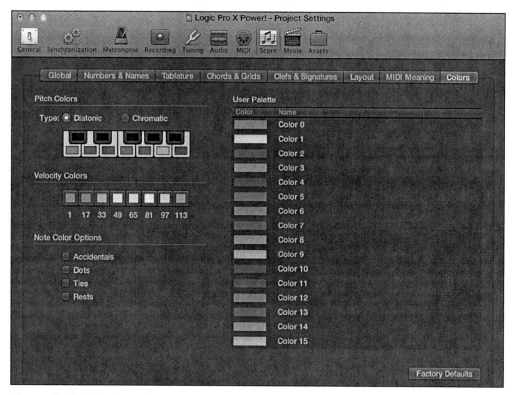

Figure 8.43 The Score Project Settings window open to the Colors tab.
© Apple Inc.

▷ **Chord Grid Library:** Selecting Chord Grid Library opens the Chord Grid Library, a repository of thousands of guitar tablatures. The Chord Grid Library will be covered in detail in "The Chord Grid Library" section later in this chapter.

▷ **Score Preferences:** This command launches the global Score Preferences dialog box. You can also open this dialog box by choosing Logic Pro > Preferences > Score or by clicking on the Preferences menu in the Toolbar and selecting Score. The Score Preferences dialog box includes preferences for how you want the Score editor to operate. The specific settings that you want will depend completely on how you use the Score editor—for example, do you use it more for editing or just for printing? Many score preferences options are self-evident if you are familiar with music notation. Figure 8.44 shows the Score Preferences dialog box.

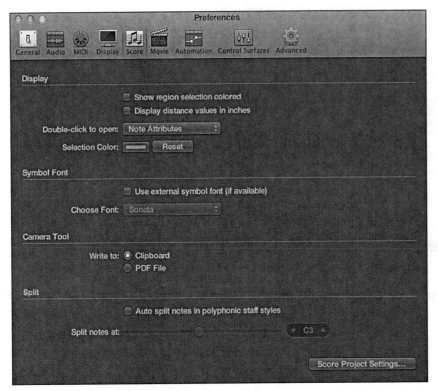

Figure 8.44 The Score Preferences dialog box allows you to define how the Score editor will behave in all of your projects.

© Apple Inc.

▷ **Create Score Set from Selection:** This creates a new score set from all the instruments assigned to the MIDI regions you have selected.

▷ **Reset Line Layout:** You can reset the layout of the notation lines with this command.

Printing a Score That Includes Both a Transposed and a Non-Transposed Instrument: Noted film and television composer Jay Asher, author of *Going Pro with Logic Pro 9* (Course Technology PTR, 2010), is a long-time Logic user who, as he puts it, "lives in the Score editor." Asher shares with us a very helpful tip he learned for printing scores that begin on a non-transposing instrument and switch to a transposing instrument:

Let us say you need to print out a part that begins on a non-transposing (C) instrument—for example, the oboe—and then switches to a transposing instrument—for example, the English horn, which transposes up a 5th (+7). You could highlight all the notes in one of the editors and manually transpose them, but the result would be that the notes would sound different when played back. Here's how you can do it without changing the sound:

1. Make sure that your Score editor is showing the default instrument set All Instruments.
2. If your oboe and English horn parts are already different MIDI regions on the same main window track, you can skip to step 4.
3. Cut the MIDI region into two MIDI regions and put them on the same main window track.
4. Make sure that both have the proper transposition—in our example, none for the oboe sequence, and +7 for the English horn.
5. Open the Score editor. Make sure that you are in Full Score mode in Page Edit view and select both MIDI regions by holding the Shift key while selecting.

6. In the Layout local menu, choose Create Score Set from Selection. This will create a new score set (which you can rename if you would like).
7. Then double-click anywhere in the white area around the MIDI regions.
8. Switch to Print view.

The result is [a single] score part with both MIDI regions properly transposed for a [professional musician] to read, and your MIDI parts will sound [as they did originally]. Remember, of course, to insert text to [inform] the player...when he is playing one instrument (oboe, in our example) and when he switches (to English horn, in our example).

The Edit Menu

As Figure 8.45 illustrates, the Edit menu in the Score editor is fundamentally the same as in the other MIDI editors. Although you can refer to the subsection covering the Piano Roll editor's Edit menu to learn about the various functions of the Edit menu, there is one in particular that is unique to the Score editor that needs attention. At the bottom of the Score editor Edit menu is the Diatonic Insert command. When you are using the Pencil tool, engaging Diatonic Insert limits you to inserting only notes that are diatonically correct for the current key. You can alter the notes chromatically once they have been inserted, however. Note that this function does not work for MIDI input notes, only drawn notes.

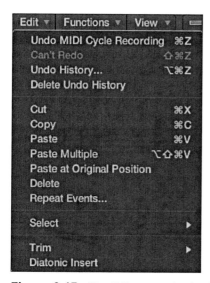

Figure 8.45 The Edit menu in the Score editor is similar to the Edit menu in all the other MIDI editors in Logic.
© Apple Inc.

The Functions Menu

The options of the Functions menu, shown in Figure 8.46, are also similar to the other MIDI editors with a few notable exceptions:

Figure 8.46 The Functions menu in the Score editor.
© Apple Inc.

▷ **Quantization:** Figure 8.47 shows the Quantization submenu. The Quantization submenu gives you options to control the quantization of events in the Score editor:

Figure 8.47 The Quantization submenu of the Functions menu in the Score editor.
© Apple Inc.

▷ **Quantize Events:** This command applies the current quantization setting to the selected events. The key command for this is Q.

▷ **Undo Quantization:** This removes any quantization that may have been applied and returns the selected notes to their original location. The key command for this is Option+Command+Q.

▷ **Fix Displayed Note Positions:** This command fixes the display quantization of the notes in your project, allowing you to export it to another notation program, maintaining the display quantization settings.

▷ **Fix Displayed Note Positions and Durations:** This command fixes the display quantization of the notes and their duration.

▷ **Delete MIDI Events:** The Delete MIDI Events submenu, covered in the main window Edit menu section in Chapter 6, provides commands for deleting notes based on the following selection methods: Duplicates, Inside Locators, Outside Locators, Outside Region Boundaries, and Unselected Within Selection.

▷ **Note Events:** The Note Events submenu is identical to the Note Events submenu in the Event list editor. For details on these commands, refer to the Event list editor's "Functions Menu" section earlier in this chapter.

▷ **Copy MIDI Events:** You can copy all MIDI events with this command. You will be presented with a dialog box asking you the range of notes to copy and how you want them to be copied.

▷ **Note Attributes:** The Note Attributes submenu is filled with note and score symbol display parameters that you can set individually per note, regardless of your settings in other menus. It contains nine menus with more than 40 options for altering the attributes of the selected note or notes. To apply any of these options, select one or more notes and/or symbols in the editor display, then choose the desired option from this menu. For example, you can change the direction of the stem of a note, shift a sharp note to its enharmonic flat note, or change the display color of a note with commands from this menu. Figure 8.48 shows the Note Attributes submenu.

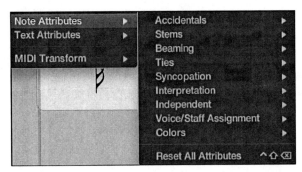

Figure 8.48 The Note Attributes submenu. This Functions menu submenu contains different options to change the attributes of a selected note or symbol.
© Apple Inc.

> NOTE: It's beyond the scope of this book to cover all the possible note and symbol attribute alterations in this menu. If you write music notation and need to alter note attributes, you should find it easy to locate the desired attributes in this menu.

▷ **Text Attributes:** The Text Attributes submenu should look familiar to anyone used to word-processing and desktop-publishing applications. The Text Attributes submenu offers a standard selection of text-formatting options from which to choose any of your installed fonts, size, style, left/right alignment, and so on, for use with lyrics, notes on your score, and more. Figure 8.49 shows the Text Attributes submenu.

Figure 8.49 The Text Attributes submenu offers you the use of your currently installed fonts and basic style options for score text.
© Apple Inc.

▷ **MIDI Transform:** This submenu gives you access to presets in the MIDI Transform window, which is covered later in this chapter.

The View Menu

The View menu contains options for configuring your view of the Score editor. Figure 8.50 shows the View menu.

Figure 8.50 The View menu of the Score editor.
© Apple Inc.

The various options available in the View menu are as follows:

▷ **Link:** The Link submenu is identical to the ones found in the Event list and Step editor View menus. The Score editor also includes a Link button.

▷ **Colors:** This submenu offers options to colorize notes by pitch, velocity, or voice assignment. You can also force a note to be black and white instead of colorized.

▷ **View Mode:** This submenu offers three view modes for the Score editor. Linear view shows your score part on a single line. Wrapped view appears more like a normal score layout. Page view is your actual printer-ready score layout. The key command for Page view is Control+P.

▷ **Page Display Options:** This submenu offers additional page layout display options when Page view is selected, like the ability to adjust your margins.

▷ **Show Local Inspector:** Engaging this option displays the Score window's Inspector to the left of the edit area in the Score editor window. As of this writing, this command does not open or close the Inspectors shown in Figure 8.34, which can be shown or hidden using the key command I. Instead, it opens an Inspector containing the same Time Quantize, Scale Quantize, and Velocity controls found in the Piano Roll editor. Refer to the section "The Piano Roll Editor Inspector" for more information on these controls. This command is only available when the Score editor is in Linear view mode.

▷ **Show Region Headers:** Selecting this option wraps each region in the Score editor with its own region header, complete with the name and correct coloring from the parent Tracks area regions. This can be very handy when working with multiple regions across multiple tracks, for example.

▷ **Go to Page:** When you are in Page view, selecting this option opens the Go to Page dialog box. There, you can enter a page number and click OK or press Return, and the selected page will be displayed. The key command for this is Control+/ (forward slash).

▷ **Duration Bars:** Duration bars are similar to the bars for notes in the Piano Roll editor. They provide a visual, editable representation of the length of each note. You can choose to disable the display of duration bars, display them only for notes you have selected, or display them for all notes.

▷ **Guides:** This submenu gives you a variety of options for displaying vertical dotted-line guides, which can help you align objects in the score as you work on its layout. You can turn guides off or display them for dragged objects, selected objects, or all objects. If you want to clean up your score to look as professional as possible, guides are an invaluable aid.

▷ **Explode Folders:** This separates folder tracks into their component tracks. The key command for this is Control+F.

▷ **Explode Polyphony:** This separates into separate staves the various separate voices playing together. The key command for this is Control+X.

▷ **Scroll in Play:** If this is engaged, instead of the playhead scrolling through the Score editor, the score scrolls past the stationary playhead.

▷ **Secondary Ruler:** Like in the main window, the Secondary Ruler command adds a second bar ruler to the Score, with bars if the primary ruler is showing time and time if the primary ruler is showing bars. The key command for this is Control+Option+Command+R.

▷ **Show Global Tracks:** You can toggle the global tracks on or off with this command when Page view is off. The key command for this is G.

▷ **Configure Global Tracks:** This command opens a menu that lets you toggle on or off individual global tracks you wish to view. The key command for this is Option+G.

▷ **Global Track Protect Buttons:** If this is selected, Track Protect buttons will appear on the global tracks.

▷ **Show Instrument Names:** This determines whether the name of the instrument to which your MIDI region is assigned is displayed. The key command for this is Control+Shift+N.

▷ **MIDI Draw:** Just like the Piano Roll editor View menu option, this command creates a track lane beneath the Score editor where you can view, edit, and create MIDI Draw or MIDI control message information. Figure 8.51 shows a Score editor displaying the MIDI Draw lane.

Figure 8.51 The MIDI Draw View option selected in the Score editor, displaying volume automation. Region headers are also enabled in this image.

© Apple Inc.

The Score Editor Tool Menu

Because the Score editor is geared toward both graphic editing and printing, its Tool menu is the largest of all the MIDI editors, housing 17 tools. Figure 8.52 shows the Score editor Tool menu.

Figure 8.52 The Score editor Tool menu.
© Apple Inc.

Many of these tools are familiar, but a few are unique to the Score editor. Following are descriptions of these tools from top to bottom:

▷ **Pointer:** The standard Pointer tool is for selecting and making "rubber band" selections of multiple notes.

▷ **Pencil:** The Pencil tool allows you to insert new notes into the Score editor and to create nodes in the MIDI Draw area.

▷ **Eraser:** This tool removes notes from the Score editor.

▷ **Text:** With this tool, you can enter text into your score.

▷ **Layout:** Use this tool to move objects around in your score without actually affecting the timing of the parent MIDI event.

▷ **Zoom:** If you want to zoom in on a particular group of notes, use the Zoom tool to "rubber band" them. You then zoom in to the maximum zoom level. Click anywhere there are no notes to return to the original zoom level.

▷ **Voice Separation:** This tool allows you to separate polyphonic voices into different staves by drawing a dividing line. For this tool to be effective, you must be using a polyphonic staff style.

▷ **Solo:** This tool solos or unsolos notes in the Score editor.

▷ **Mute:** The Mute tool mutes or unmutes notes in the Score editor.

▷ **Resize:** This tool can adjust the size of objects in the Score editor.

▷ **Quantize:** The Quantize tool allows you to quantize only selected notes, leaving the rest of the region unquantized. This is very useful if you have a great performance with only one portion in which the timing is slightly off. You can use this tool to quantize just those few notes to improve the readability of the score and leave the rest of the performance alone.

▷ **Velocity:** With the Velocity tool, you can raise or lower the velocity of one or more notes graphically, by selecting the note and then scrolling up or down with the mouse to increase or decrease the velocity of the selected note. When you adjust the velocity of all selected notes at once by clicking on a single note and moving the mouse, every note retains its value relative to the other notes. (So, if you raise the velocity of a loud note and a soft note, both become louder, but the soft note becomes the same amount softer.) You can hold down Option+Shift to adjust all selected notes to the same velocity.

▷ **Camera:** Use the Camera tool to select sections of your score and export them into graphics files.

▷ **Scissors:** The Scissors tool can be used to cut a score piece into multiple regions, and in the signature track for cutting bars into smaller divisions, creating time-signature changes in the process.

▷ **Glue:** This tool works in the signature track to merge measures, affecting the time signature of those measures in the process. You can also glue notes of the same pitch together to create notes of longer duration.

▷ **Automation Select:** The Automation Select tool—represented by a bent arrow with a solid arrowhead, pointing upward and left—can select automation data in the Score editor MIDI Draw automation lane. Chapter 10 discusses automation and the Automation Select tool in depth.

▷ **Automation Curve:** The Automation Curve tool—represented by a bent arrow with an open arrowhead, pointing upward and left—can create curves between two automation nodes in the Score editor MIDI Draw automation lane. Chapter 10 discusses automation and the Automation Curve tool in depth.

The Score Editor Buttons

The Score editor offers nine buttons, five of which are common to the other editors in Logic. Figure 8.53 shows the Score editor buttons.

Figure 8.53 The Score editor buttons.
© Apple Inc.

Following are descriptions of the buttons, moving from left to right:

▷ **Hierarchy:** This button takes you from a view of the selected region(s) to a master Score view of all the project's regions.

▷ **Linear View:** This button lets you see your score in Linear view, where you will do the bulk of your editing.

▷ **Wrapped View:** This button lets you see your score in Wrapped view.

▷ **Page View:** This button lets you see your score in Page view, a full-page overview of how your score will print out. Page view was not really designed for real-time input or editing operations, but for final finishing touches before printing.

▷ **MIDI Draw:** This button opens the MIDI Draw area in the Score editor. The MIDI Draw button is available only in Linear view.

▷ **MIDI IN:** The MIDI IN button engages step input mode, described earlier in this chapter in the section "The Piano Roll Editor."

▷ **MIDI OUT:** With this engaged, you hear the currently selected MIDI note or event change (if you are working with pitch bend data, for example) while you are working.

▷ **Playhead Catch:** With this button engaged, the edit area in the Score editor will always follow the playhead position. You will almost always want this on.

▷ **Link:** Engaging this button ensures that the editor always displays the same content as the top-most window. Double-clicking or Option-clicking the Link button while the Playhead Catch button is also engaged activates Contents Catch mode, in which the Score editor always shows the contents of the currently playing MIDI region as the song plays.

The Score Editor Inspector

As you can see in Figure 8.54, the Score editor's Inspector is loaded with options. Two of them are Inspectors for the region being edited in the Score editor. You can also see the Time Quantize, Scale Quantize, and Velocity controls found in the Piano Roll editor. Refer to the section "The Piano Roll Editor Inspector" earlier in this chapter for more information on those controls. The following sections describe the Score Inspector parameters.

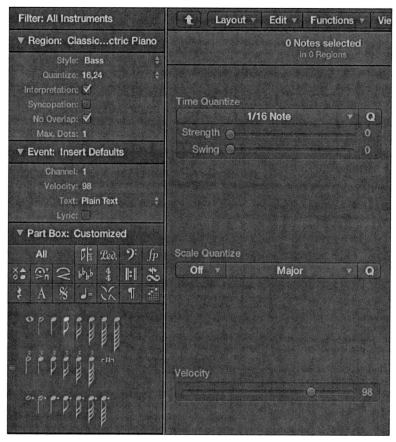

Figure 8.54 The Score editor Inspector.
© Apple Inc.

The Filter Menu

The Filter menu lets you select what score set or instrument is displayed in the Edit area. You can also access the Show/Hide Score Sets Window command in this menu. To access this menu, click in the Filter field.

The Region Inspector

The Region Inspector, located directly underneath the Filter menu, contains parameters that configure the rhythmic display of the selected MIDI region. Figure 8.55 shows the Region Inspector.

Figure 8.55 The Region Inspector.
© Apple Inc.

Descriptions of the parameters follow:

▷ **Style:** This parameter indicates the staff style used for the score display of the selected MIDI region. Clicking to the right of the parameter name opens a menu of all available staff styles from which you can choose.

▷ **Quantize:** The Quantize parameter determines the shortest note value that the currently selected region can display. The value can be either a single number, called a binary quantization, or two numbers (a binary and a ternary value), called a hybrid quantization. As with the Style parameter, you choose your desired value from the menu that appears when you click to the right of the parameter name. This quantize parameter affects only the display of notes in the Score editor, not their quantize setting within their parent region.

▷ **Interpretation:** With Interpretation enabled, the Score editor displays notes with length values that fall on the beat to make the score easier to read. The display is far less precise than when Interpretation is disabled and the Score editor shows notes at their true length. At the same time, when Interpretation is disabled, your Score can be *too* accurate, showing every possible miniscule division of the beat that was played. You can also turn this feature on or off on a per-note basis by choosing the appropriate option in the Functions > Note Attributes menu or via a key command. Generally, you probably want to leave Interpretation on.

▷ **Syncopation:** If Syncopation is enabled, instead of displaying syncopated notes as several tied notes, the Score editor displays them as a single note. As with the Interpretation option, you can turn this feature on or off per note by choosing the appropriate option in the Functions > Note Attributes submenu or via the key command.

▷ **No Overlap:** This prevents the overlapping of notes in the display. Unless you want to display visually repeated and overlapping notes, you will want to keep this option on.

▷ **Max. Dots:** The Max. Dots option determines how many dots Logic allows a single note to display. You can change unwanted dotted notes by inserting user rests.

The Event Inspector

Each event in the Score editor gets its own parameter set. The Event Inspector displays those parameters for each individual event (note, rest, time signature, and so on) in your score. Figure 8.56 shows the Event Inspector.

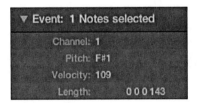

Figure 8.56 The Event Inspector.
© Apple Inc.

Depending on whether you have selected a note or a non-note event, the Event Inspector displays different options. Following are all the possible parameters that can appear in this box:

▷ **Channel:** The selected event is on the MIDI channel set in this parameter. In general, your entire MIDI region should send all of its notes on the same channel, but you might want to send a few notes to other devices. An exception is if you are working on a drum score and you are sending different drum instruments on different MIDI channels.

▷ **Pitch:** This sets the pitch of the selected note. This parameter appears only when notes are selected.

▷ **Velocity:** This parameter is for setting the MIDI velocity (the volume of the event). If the event is a rest, even though the parameter contains a value, it is still sending silence.

▷ **Length:** This parameter sets the length of the note. It appears only when notes are selected.

▷ **Text:** Use this parameter to select a text style from the menu that appears when you click on it. You'll learn about text styles in the "Text Styles" section later in this chapter. This parameter does not appear for note events.

▷ **Lyric:** You should select this checkbox if you are writing lyrics above this event. If not, uncheck it. This parameter does not appear for note events.

The Part Box

The Score editor Inspector contains a unique notation toolset underneath the Event Inspector called the part box—so named because it contains various parts you might like to use in a score. Figure 8.57 shows the part box.

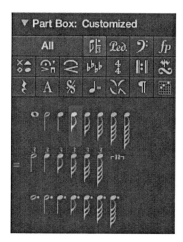

Figure 8.57 The Score editor part box.
© Apple Inc.

The part box is so expansive that the entire box fits into the Score editor only at the highest resolutions of very large displays. Figure 8.57 shows only a portion of the part box. This isn't a problem, however, because the top portion of the part box consists of 19 Group buttons. As you click different buttons, different sections of the part box move to the top of the box under the Group buttons, so the specific section of the part box you need is never more than one click away. You can also click in the Part Box field to access and create part box sets—combinations of groups that suit your workflow.

Inserting parts from the part box couldn't be easier: Simply select the group(s) you need, click on a part you want to add to your score, and then drag it to the location in your score where you want to place the part. Alternatively, use the Pencil tool to insert a part. You can drag the left half of the Part Box field to open a floating part box, which can be freely resized. Additionally, you can use key commands to switch among the parts in the part box.

Staff Styles

You can think of staff styles as similar to style sheets in word-processor or desktop-publishing applications: They contain a set of formatting and layout preferences for you to apply when needed. You can access staff styles from the Layout local menu or via the key command Control+Option+Shift+S. Figure 8.58 shows the Staff Style window.

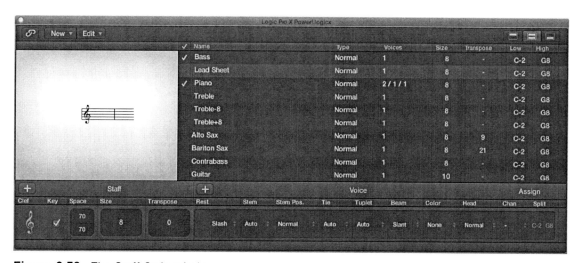

Figure 8.58 The Staff Style window.
© Apple Inc.

The Staff Style window allows you to select one of the default staff styles or to create your own. These staff styles are then accessible through the Region Inspector in the Score editor or the instrument Inspector in the main window for every MIDI instrument.

You can create your own staff styles by selecting Duplicate or by choosing one of the varieties of new staff styles from the New local menu. After designing your style by typing new values and/or using the Pointer click-drag values, you can double-click the name of the style you have been creating to type your own name. That staff style then appears in every menu of staff styles.

Text Styles

Just as there is a Staff Style window to create format and layout templates for your score, there is also a Text Styles window for creating text-formatting templates. Figure 8.59 shows the Text Styles window, accessible from the Lanes menu.

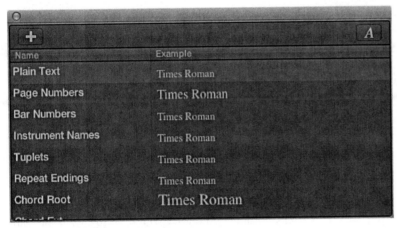

Figure 8.59 The Text Styles window.
© Apple Inc.

Clicking on a text style in the Example column or clicking the A button opens a typical Fonts window, which lets you select a font, size, and formatting style. You can also access the Fonts window from the Functions > Text Attributes local menu command in the Score editor window. You can edit the selected text style in the Fonts window or create your own by clicking the plus (+) button in the Text Styles window and defining the new style's attributes in the Fonts window. Your new text style will appear at the bottom of the Text Styles window and at the bottom of the Text Styles menu.

A Brief Primer on Working in the Score Editor

After reading all the information on the various menus and tools in the Score editor, it would be unfair to leave you without even the slightest knowledge of how to use any of those tools to create your own scores. Although it is well outside of the scope of this book to go into much more depth on this very powerful editor, I can at least give you a couple of basic building blocks, starting with the Chord Grid Library.

The Chord Grid Library

The Chord Grid Library contains thousands of preconfigured chords in tablature. It's an easily searchable database, but it also offers you a great deal of latitude to create and edit chord grids of your own using tunings of your own creation. The Chord Grid Library window has three different tabs: Instrument Editor, Chord Grid Selector, and Chord Grid Editor. You can open the Chord Grid Library by selecting Chord Grid Library in the Layout menu. We'll start by looking at the Instrument Editor tab.

The Instrument Editor Tab

The Instrument Editor tab of the Chord Grid Library window lets you create, delete, import, and export different instruments for which you can create chord grids. Although it only has a standard six-string guitar instrument configuration in standard tuning to begin with, you can create an instrument with up to 16 strings tuned almost any way you can imagine. Figure 8.60 shows the Instrument Editor tab.

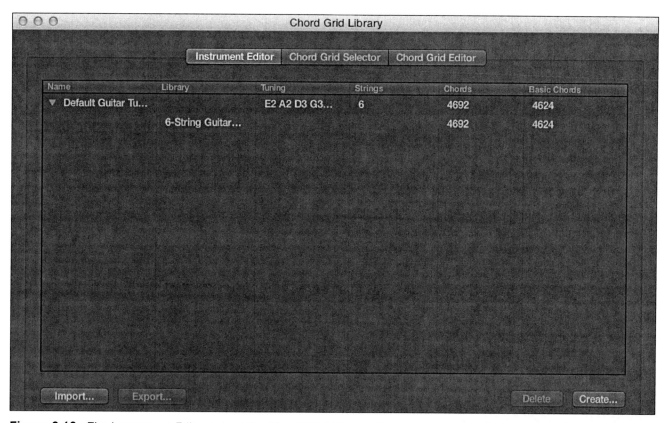

Figure 8.60 The Instrument Editor tab of the Chord Grid Library. You can create new instruments with up to 16 strings in any number of tunings in the Instrument Editor tab.
© Apple Inc.

To create a new instrument, click the Create button in the lower-right corner of the window. This opens the Create Library dialog box, shown in Figure 8.61.

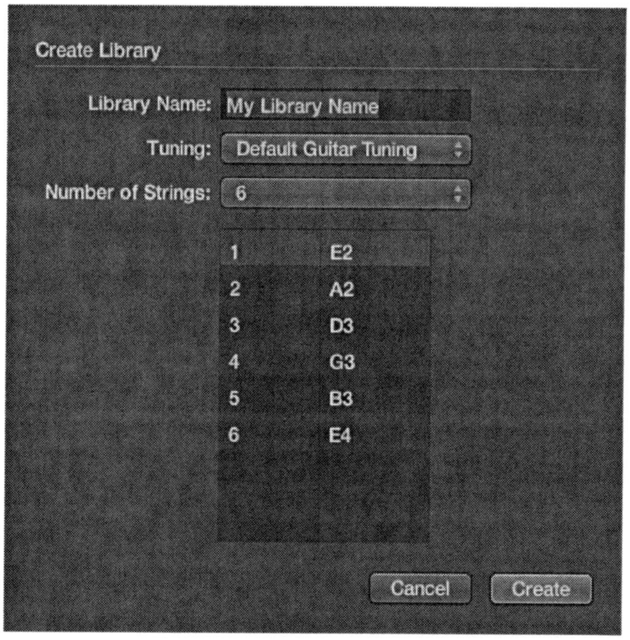

Figure 8.61 The Create Library dialog box.
© Apple Inc.

The Create Library dialog box offers the following options:

▷ **Library Name:** To name your library, select the text in the text box and type your new library name.
▷ **Tuning:** The Tuning menu allows you to select a tuning to use as a starting point. At first, there is only the Default Guitar Tuning option, but as you add your own libraries, they will appear in this list. This menu may become unavailable depending on the settings in the Number of Strings menu.
▷ **Number of Strings:** Use this menu to define the number of strings for your new instrument, from 1 to 16.
▷ **Tuning area:** The Tuning area lets you define the tuning for each string of your new instrument. Simply double-click the pitch name for the string you wish to alter and enter the new pitch name manually. Be sure to enter the right octave number for the string, too! After you have finished defining the properties of your new instrument, click the Create button, and your new instrument will be added to the Instrument Editor tab. You can rename an instrument or library in the Instrument Editor tab by double-clicking the name you want to edit, entering the new name, and pressing Return.

You can delete an instrument in the Instrument Editor tab by selecting it and clicking the Delete button in the lower-right corner. Clicking Import or Export opens a typical file browser dialog box in which you can search for an instrument file to import or choose a directory into which you will export, respectively.

THE CHORD GRID SELECTOR TAB

The Chord Grid Selector tab lets you browse for, view, and even hear any chord in the Chord Grid Library. Figure 8.62 shows the Chord Grid Selector tab.

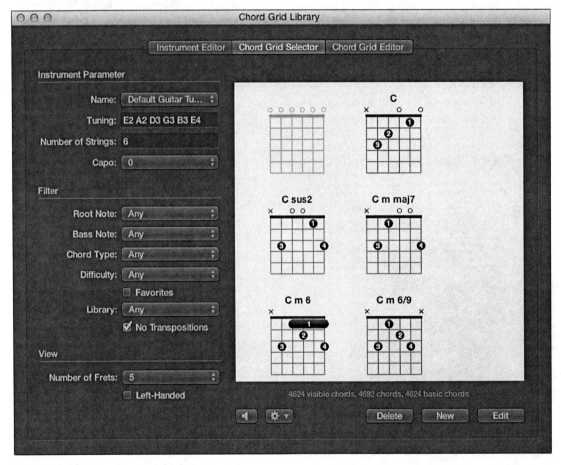

Figure 8.62 The Chord Grid Selector tab.
© Apple Inc.

The Chord Grid Selector tab has a bunch of different menus, enabling you to browse for a very general set of chord grids or extremely specific ones quickly and easily. The Chord Grid Selector tab's options are as follows:

▷ **Name:** Select the instrument whose chord grids you wish to view in this menu.

▷ **Tuning:** This field displays the tuning for the selected instrument.

▷ **Number of Strings:** This field displays the number of strings for the selected instrument.

▷ **Capo:** You can assign a capo setting for the selected instrument in this menu, anywhere from the first fret to the 12th.

▷ **Root Note:** This menu allows you to assign a root note for the chord grids you are looking for, filtering out all chord grids with different root notes. You can also select Any, which displays all chord grids, or Undefined, which displays any undefined chord grids.

▷ **Bass Note:** This menu allows you to assign a bass note for the chord grids you are looking for, filtering out all chord grids with different bass notes. You can also select Any, which displays all chord grids, or Undefined, which displays any undefined chord grids.

▷ **Chord Type:** This menu allows you to assign a chord quality—such as major, minor, or any other of a wide variety of chord types—for the chord grids you are looking for, filtering out all chord grids of different chord types. You can also select Any, which displays all chord grids, or Undefined, which displays any undefined chord grids.

▷ **Difficulty:** This menu allows you to filter the chord grids based on their difficulty: Easy, Medium, or Advanced. You can also select Any, which displays all chord grids, or Undefined, which displays any undefined chord grids.

▷ **Favorites:** Selecting this checkbox allows you to display only those chord grids tagged as favorites.

▷ **Library:** This menu allows you to select whether to display the chord grids from any library for your selected instrument or from a specific library.

▷ **No Transpositions:** This checkbox allows you to exclude chord grids that have been transposed.

▷ **Number of Frets:** This menu lets you define the number of frets shown for each chord grid—four, five, or six.

▷ **Left-Handed:** Selecting the Left-Handed checkbox reverses the chord grids so they appear as they would on a left-handed guitar.

You can select any chord grid simply by clicking on it. If you want to hear what that particular chord grid looks like, click the Playback button at the bottom of the Chord Grid Selector tab. You can even decide how chord grids will be played when you click the Playback button by using the self-explanatory options in the Playback Action menu immediately to the right of the Playback button. The Playback Action menu is shown in Figure 8.63.

Figure 8.63 The Playback Action menu lets you define how chord grids will be played when you click the Playback button.
© Apple Inc.

To delete a chord grid, select the chord grid and click the Delete button. You can edit a chord grid by selecting it and clicking the Edit button, and you can create a new chord grid by clicking the New button. Either one of these actions opens the Chord Grid Editor tab.

THE CHORD GRID EDITOR TAB

The Chord Grid Editor tab allows you to create new chord grids, edit existing ones, and save them to the desired library. Figure 8.64 shows the Chord Grid Editor tab. As you can see, the parameters to the left of the window are almost identical to those in the Chord Grid Selector tab, but instead of using them to filter chord grids, you use them to classify the chord grid you are editing.

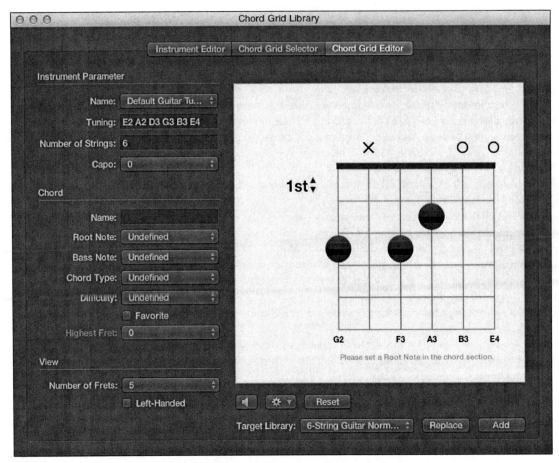

Figure 8.64 The Chord Grid Editor tab.
© Apple Inc.

To add a note to a chord grid, simply click on the desired string and fret. A dot will appear. You can move the dot by clicking and dragging it. You can assign the new note a fingering by right-clicking on the dot and selecting a finger number from the menu that opens. To create a barre, click and hold on one of the desired outer strings and drag the mouse across the chord grid to the desired end of the barre. If you click and drag vertically, a selection box will be drawn, allowing you to select multiple notes to edit. Above the chord grid in Figure 8.64, you'll notice an X (meaning don't play that string) and a couple Os (meaning let the open string ring). You can change from an X to an O by clicking on the X, and vice versa. Finally, you can assign the lowest fret for the chord grid by clicking on the number to the left of the chord grid—1st in Figure 8.64. This opens a menu from which you can select any fret number from 1 to 15.

The Clear button at the bottom of the window lets you clear the entire chord grid. If you have performed any edits, it becomes a Reset button, letting you return the chord grid to its original state. The Target Library menu lets you determine which library the chord grid will be added to when you've finished creating or editing it. The Replace button replaces the original chord grid with your edited chord grid. The Add button adds it to the selected chord grid library.

Inserting and Deleting Events in the Score Editor

Although the Score editor deals with MIDI information as traditional notation instead of as text or piano roll–like graphics, you can still use some of the same familiar event-entry methods that are available in the other MIDI editors.

As with the Piano Roll editor and the Event list, you can use the process described in the "MIDI Step Input" section to input MIDI information into the Score editor. Before you do, make sure you have disabled the Interpretation setting in the Display Inspector and that you have set the Quantize setting to the smallest note value you'll be using. You can set the playhead by dragging it to the position you want.

To enter notes in the Score editor with a mouse, make sure you have the Notes button selected in the part box, as in Figure 8.57. You can then drag a note of the desired value directly onto the staff and place it at the appropriate location. As you drag the note across the staff, a help tag appears, showing you the MIDI channel, pitch, velocity, and position of the note. You can also use the Pencil tool to add events to the Score editor by selecting the note value you wish to use in the part box and clicking in the staff at the position and pitch you want the event to be. Be aware that the Quantize setting determines the smallest note value you can enter with the mouse, too.

What if you need to add a tempo marking or a slur to your score? You can add any of these other notation symbols to your score directly from the part box. Just drag the symbol to the location where you want it, and it's added to the score just like a note.

If you insert a chord grid from the part box, a two-tab version of the Chord Grid Library will open, offering the Chord Grid Selector and Chord Grid Editor tabs. You can drag the desired chord grid from the Chord Grid Selector tab directly to the inserted chord.

Deleting events from the Score editor is just as easy as it is in the other editors. Simply select the notes you want to delete and either press Delete or click on the note with the Eraser tool.

Moving and Adjusting Events in the Score Editor

You've finished your score and you notice a few things you want to adjust. Perhaps there is a wrong note, or a note isn't lining up where you'd like it. Maybe a note you entered via step input isn't long enough. Making these adjustments in the Score editor is quick and easy.

CHANGING THE LENGTH OF EVENTS IN THE SCORE EDITOR

Entering events into the Score editor via step input creates notes that are the same length as the Quantize setting you selected earlier. To alter the length of a note you have entered, you simply select the note and change it to the desired length using the Length setting in the Event Inspector or via key commands. You can also enable duration bars in the View menu and edit the length of notes using the Resize cursor as you would in the Piano Roll editor. Figure 8.65 shows some notes in the Score editor with duration bars enabled. Notice the Resize cursor next to one of the very light gray duration bars.

Figure 8.65 You can edit the length of notes in the score using duration bars.
© Apple Inc.

CHANGING THE PITCH OF EVENTS IN THE SCORE EDITOR

Adjusting the pitch of a note in the Score editor couldn't be easier. Simply select the note(s) you want to change and drag it vertically to the correct pitch. As you hold down the mouse button, a help tag will appear, telling you what pitch the note is currently on and how far you have transposed it. You can also use the Pitch parameter in the Event Inspector to alter a note's pitch or do so via key commands.

ADJUSTING THE LAYOUT OF EVENTS IN THE SCORE EDITOR

Once you have all of your events at the correct time and pitch in the Score editor, the score itself might have a few places that aren't as easily readable in Page view as you would like. Perhaps a couple of notes are a little too close together, or a bar is smaller than you would like it to be. This is where the Layout tool, seen in the Tool menu in Figure 8.52, comes in handy.

The Layout tool allows you to adjust the position of events in the Score editor graphically while maintaining their timing. Select the Layout tool from the Tool menu, grab the event(s) you want to adjust, and then drag them horizontally to their correct location. A help tag will appear, telling you how far you have moved the event. The entire bar that the event is in will adjust some as a result of the move. A little bit of experimentation with the Layout tool will make anticipating the effects of these adjustments much more intuitive. Also, don't forget to enable guides to help you align elements of your score. Figure 8.66 shows an element of a score with guides enabled.

Figure 8.66 Notice the dotted vertical line below the *sforzando* marking. Enabling guides makes it easy to line up elements of your score with the note to which you intend them to relate.
© Apple Inc.

For Further Score Editor Information...

The Score editor is the deepest MIDI editor in Logic, and there is far more to delve into than space in this book allows. As you see, just the preceding explanation of the surface functionality of the Score editor has already taken more figures and pages of this book than any other MIDI editor has! Going into minute detail could easily fill half this book. Instead, let me point you to two resources for further information on the Score editor. The first, of course, is the Logic Pro X manual itself, which includes more than 100 pages on the Score editor. For a really excellent guide on how to use the Score editor, I recommend Johannes Prischl's *Logic Notation Guide*, which has more than 200 pages of explanation, tutorials, valuable Logic Environments, and more to help you get the most out of the Score editor. The book is only available through the author's website: http://prischl.net/LNG/. Prischl wrote this guide for an earlier version of Logic, so you'll notice that the look of the Score editor is different. However, the fundamental workflow and functionality of the Score editor hasn't changed much over the years. Although his examples will look different, the methodology and procedures are fundamentally the same, and his Environments still work (although they may need conversion through Logic 7 to a usable format). I cannot recommend his book highly enough for those who want a more complete Score editor reference.

The MIDI Transform Window

The MIDI Transform window is not exactly a MIDI *editor*, but it offers you the ability to alter (or transform) large amounts of MIDI data at once. You can consider it a MIDI event batch processor window if you want. If that sounds a bit complicated, that's because its functionality can be incredibly far-reaching. You can use it for processes as straightforward as changing every instance of one note in a selected MIDI region into another note, or you could set up a very complex map, which would filter out only specific notes of a specific velocity and map them to selected new notes. Logic comes with a number of transform sets that are preconfigured for many popular transformations, and you can create your own transform sets. The MIDI Transform window is one of those features in Logic that you may use very rarely, but when you can use it, knowing how to will allow you to automate the transformation of your MIDI data in ways that would take forever manually.

Users often overlook the MIDI Transform window. For one thing, it's not an editor, so it's not absolutely necessary to the basic recording and editing of music. Another reason users frequently overlook the Transform window is that it initially appears to be very mathematical in nature and not very intuitive. Figure 8.67 shows a MIDI Transform window.

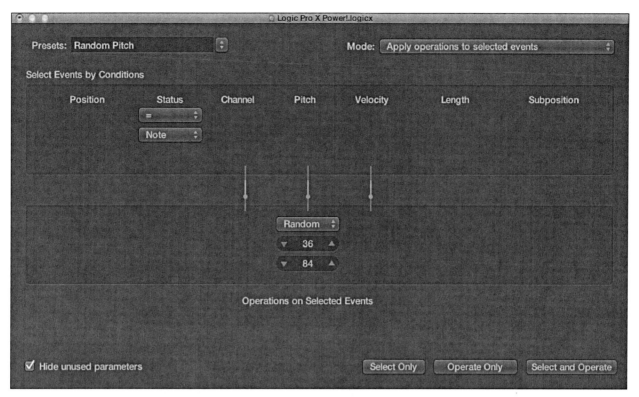

Figure 8.67 You can use the MIDI Transform window to make batch transformations of MIDI data.
© Apple Inc.

Unless you already have a mathematical understanding of MIDI data and values, the MIDI Transform window doesn't seem very inviting, does it? Despite its initial complexity, however, it is a very powerful weapon to have in your arsenal. The goal of this section is to demystify the MIDI Transform window for you!

How the MIDI Transform Window Works

The MIDI Transform window becomes easier to grasp when you have a general idea of how it works. Remember that at its root, MIDI represents musical ideas mathematically, and the MIDI Transform window uses the form and flow of a mathematical formula to operate on your data.

You'll start by setting the operation mode from the Mode menu in the upper-right area of the window. The mode you choose determines how the transformation will affect the selected events. The different modes are described in the next section, "Setting the MIDI Transform Mode."

Next, you set up the conditions for the transformation, defining which events to transform. You set up these conditions in the area labeled "Select Events by Conditions." You'll learn how to do this in the section titled "Setting Up Transform Conditions" later in this chapter. After you have set up your conditions, you define the operation that you want to execute. You can select the various parameters of your operation in the area labeled "Operations on Selected Events." You'll learn how to set these parameters later in this chapter, in the section "Setting Up Transform Operations."

Finally, you perform your transformation by clicking on one of the buttons at the bottom of the window. The different buttons are described in the "Action Buttons of the MIDI Transform Window" section later in this chapter.

Setting the Transform Mode

In the upper-right area of the MIDI Transform window is the Mode menu. Apply Operations to Selected Events is the mode showing in Figure 8.67. The modes available in this menu are as follows:

▷ **Apply Operations to Selected Events:** In this mode, the operation that you set up in the Mode menu is applied to the events you select via the conditions you set. This is the default mode.

▷ **Apply Operations and Delete Unselected Events:** When the only events you want to remain after the transformation are those events that are operated on, choose this option. It operates on the selected events and deletes any other events in the region.

▷ **Delete Selected Events:** In this mode, you can use the MIDI Transform window as a programmable delete function. You set up which events to select in the Select Events by Conditions area. When you apply the transformation, those events are deleted.

▷ **Copy Selected Events, Then Apply Operations:** If you don't want to modify your original events but you do want to add transformed events to your region, you can do so in this mode. This mode copies your selected events and then operates on those events, so you retain the original events and add the transformed copies of those events.

Setting Up Transform Conditions

The Select Events by Conditions area of the MIDI Transform window gives you seven parameters with which to define those events you want to select. Figure 8.68 shows you the Select Events by Conditions area.

Figure 8.68 The Select Events by Conditions area in the MIDI Transform window allows you to focus precisely on the exact events you want to transform.
© Apple Inc.

Notice that all the parameters offer menus filled with options for that parameter. Sometimes, an option includes an additional menu in which you can enter a further value. This allows you to precisely configure the condition you want for selecting events. The various parameters and your options for setting them are as follows:

▷ **Position:** This option is for setting the time position in the song of your selection relative to the conditions you set. In other words, should Logic select only those notes that happen at an earlier or equal time to your conditions, or should it also select those that are unequal to the time position you are setting? Or should it select those events that are equal or those events inside a specific time range (map) of values? Figure 8.69 shows the menu of all your options.

Figure 8.69 The Position options. Use this menu to determine which notes to select relative to the value determined by your conditions.
© Apple Inc.

> NOTE: Remember that your MIDI data is mathematical at its base, so it's easy to create mathematical relationships between the conditions you set up and to specify how you want those conditions to determine which notes to select.

▷ **Status:** First, the menu allows you to choose whether you want your selection conditions to be equal to a specific kind of MIDI event or to apply to all MIDI events. If you choose to limit your conditions to one type of MIDI event, another menu appears from which you can choose your event type. Figure 8.70 shows the list of event types.

Figure 8.70 In this menu, you can choose the event type to which you want to limit your selection conditions.
© Apple Inc.

> NOTE: Note events are the most commonly chosen, but you can also choose fader (automation) events, meta events, MIDI program changes, and other common MIDI performance events.

▷ **Channel:** Here you can specify whether you want the conditions to apply to events on all MIDI channels, only channels equal to or less than the recorded MIDI channel of the event, and more. This menu has the exact same options as the Position menu.

▷ **Pitch:** The menu under the title is the same menu as displayed for the Position and Channel parameters. This menu allows you to specify the range of pitches, controller number, and so on of the selected notes or controller numbers relative to the conditions you are setting. When you make a Pitch menu selection, one or two text entry boxes will open underneath this menu. You can define a single value or a range of values for selection using these text entry boxes. If the event you selected in the Status menu is a note, then you type the note you want in this box. If you selected a control message type in the Status menu, you input the controller number here.

▷ **Velocity:** The menu under the title is the same menu as displayed for the Position, Channel, and Pitch parameters. This menu allows you to specify the range of the velocity or controller value relative to the conditions you are setting. When you make a Velocity menu selection, one or two text entry boxes will open underneath this menu. You can define a single value or a range of values for selection using these text entry boxes. If the event you selected in the Status menu is a note, then in this box you type in the velocity you want for the note. If you selected a control message type in the Status menu, you input the controller value here.

▷ **Length:** Here you can determine what the relative length of the events selected by your conditions should be, whether the events all need to be equal or unequal in length, and more. This option presents the same menu as displayed for the Position, Channel, Pitch, and Velocity parameters. This field is irrelevant except for with regard to note events.

▷ **Subposition:** This parameter determines whether events must have the same subposition inside a bar as other selected notes. Once again, this parameter features the same menu as the Position, Channel, Pitch, Velocity, and Length parameters.

Setting Up Transform Operations

In the Operations on Selected Events area, shown in Figure 8.71, you can specify any changes that you want executed on those MIDI events that match all the conditions you set in the Select Events by Conditions area.

Figure 8.71 The Operations on Selected Events area is where you specify which transformations you want to perform on the events selected by the conditions you set.
© Apple Inc.

Notice the menus in the Operations on Selected Events area directly beneath each parameter In the Select Events by Conditions area. Each menu in the Operations on Selected Events area directly affects the parameter above it. (You can refer to Figure 8.67 for a view of the whole Transform window.) In other words, if you want your transformation to operate on the pitch of a note, you would use the menu under the Pitch condition. The default for each of the menus is Thru, which specifies that no operation is performed. Figure 8.72 shows the Operations menu and all of the possibilities for transformations it offers. This Operations menu is the same menu for every column in the Operations on Selected Events area except Status.

Figure 8.72 The Operations menu. Every column but Status uses this same menu.
© Apple Inc.

Figure 8.72 shows all the ways in which you can operate on your data. As soon as you select an option, a text box appears below for you to type in the value that you want for the operation. A brief explanation of the options follows:

▷ **Thru:** This parameter passes the selected events through without altering them.
▷ **Fix:** The parameter is fixed (changed) to the value you choose.
▷ **Add:** This option adds the value you choose to the event.

▷ **Sub:** This subtracts the value you choose from the event.

▷ **Min:** If any events that met your conditions have values in this column less than the number you set for this parameter, Logic changes the event values to the number you set here.

▷ **Max:** If any events that met your conditions have values in this column that exceed the value you set, this value replaces those event values.

▷ **Flip:** You can flip, or reverse, data around a set point. If the value of the event in this column is above the flip value, Logic reduces the value below the flip point by the same amount it was originally over it. If the value in the selected event is below the flip point, Logic raises it above the flip point by as much as it originally had under it.

▷ **Mul:** The event is multiplied by the value you choose.

▷ **Div:** The event is divided by the value you choose.

▷ **Scale:** In this complex action, two text entry boxes appear below the Operations on Selected Events area, one above the other. Logic first multiplies the value of events that match your conditions by the top number and then adds the bottom number to the result.

▷ **Range:** This limits the range of values to the lower and upper values entered in the text boxes.

▷ **Random:** This generates random values for the events that match the conditions, within limits that you set.

▷ **+− Rand.:** This adds to the event a random number between zero and a value you set. You can use either a positive or a negative number as a value.

▷ **Reverse:** This option reverses the value of the event within its parameter range (so a velocity of 13 becomes 115, for example).

▷ **Quantize:** This quantizes the event to a multiple of the value you choose.

▷ **QuaMin:** This is a combination of the Quantize and Min operations. The operation quantizes the event, but if the quantized value falls below the value you choose, Logic replaces the value with the minimum value you choose.

▷ **Expon.:** This scales the parameter value according to an exponential function. The value you choose shapes the curve of the exponential function. A positive value scales exponentially; a negative value scales logarithmically.

▷ **Cresc:** If you have selected "inside" as your value for your condition above, this operation creates a smooth alteration between the set boundaries.

▷ **Rel. Cres.:** This has a similar effect as Cresc. does, except it takes the original values of your selected event into account to create a more natural crescendo and preserve the original feel of the MIDI event.

▷ **Use Map:** When you select this option, the map at the bottom of the MIDI Transform window becomes interactive, and you can select, deselect, and map different values as you see fit. Figure 8.73 shows the Universal Map under a Velocity operation. You use this map by typing a value in each text box in the lower-left (such as 81 in the first box and 67 in the second box), by scrolling the numbers in the text boxes, or by clicking in the map itself. The vertical columns represent every permissible value, and the blue lines represent the location to which that value is currently mapped.

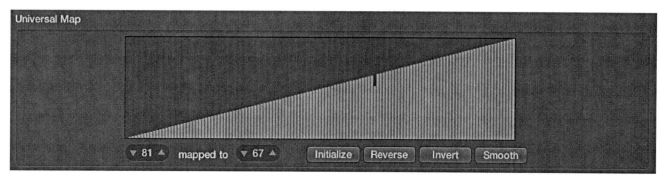

Figure 8.73 The MIDI Transform Universal Map can be used to map one parameter value to another, only operate on specific values within the map, and more.
© Apple Inc.

Action Buttons of the MIDI Transform Window

The bottom of the MIDI Transform window contains a couple of general controls, the parameter to hide any menus you aren't using in the Select Events by Conditions and Operations on Selected Events areas, and the action buttons. These three action buttons give you a number of different ways to use the Transform window. Figure 8.74 shows the three action buttons of the MIDI Transform window.

Figure 8.74 The action buttons of the MIDI Transform window.
© Apple Inc.

Once you have your conditions and operations defined, you must click one of these buttons to begin the transformation. These buttons are as follows:

▷ **Select Only:** This selects all the events that fulfill your conditions, but it will not operate on them. This is useful if you want to use the Transform as a programmable selection tool or if you want to verify that your conditions select the right events.

▷ **Operate Only:** This button processes any selected events according to the Operations on Selected Events area settings, regardless of the Select Events by Conditions area settings. This is useful if you have already manually selected all the events you want to be operated on.

▷ **Select and Operate:** This button selects events according to your Select Events by Conditions area settings and processes those events according to the Transform mode and your Operations on Selected Events area settings.

MIDI Transform Sets

As mentioned, in the top-left corner of the MIDI Transform window is the MIDI Transform Sets menu. These transform sets are already configured for many popular transformations to save you the trouble of having to set up each transformation from scratch. You can simply select the transform set and modify any specific parameters to suit your needs, and you're ready to process your data. Figure 8.75 shows you the menu of available transform sets.

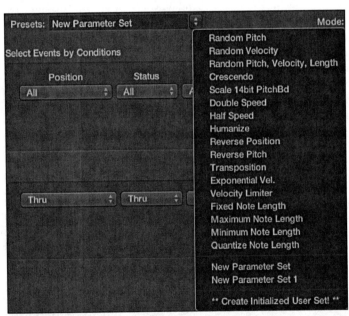

Figure 8.75 The menu of available transform sets. At the bottom of the menu is the option to create your own transform set.
© Apple Inc.

You may also find that there are specific transformations that you like to do regularly. Logic allows you to save your own transformations as transform sets. Notice the last item on the Transform Sets menu is named **Create Initialized User Set!** If you select this option, a dialog box opens, asking whether you would like to create a new transform parameter set or rename the current set. If you choose to create a new set, you can configure your transformation any way you want, and Logic will automatically save your settings in this new transform set. You can rename it by clicking the name and changing it to anything you want.

Working with Software Instruments

W ITHOUT A DOUBT, one of the most exciting developments in the world of computer music is the software synthesizer. Knowing a bit about the development of software synthesis will help you understand the philosophy, uses, and limitations of software instruments, so the next few paragraphs will explain how software instruments came to be and what they are.

From the late 1960s through the 1980s, synthesizers were electronic devices that used physical oscillators and filters to make sound. These devices sounded spectacular (at least to synthesizer enthusiasts!) but were incredibly bulky and expensive. Starting at the end of the 1970s and into the 1980s, the first steps in digital synthesizers were being made—in effect, a dedicated computer chip that had specially written software to control sound production, including the development of "virtual" oscillators and filters. Digital synthesizers took over in the 1980s and 1990s, and even though these synthesizers were housed in rackmount boxes or in keyboards, it was in fact the software that was doing the synthesis.

With the rise of home computers in the 1980s and 1990s, programmers began to experiment with writing programs that used the built-in sound potential of the computer for making music. Although fun and innovative, these initial forays into desktop software synthesis were limited by the primitive sound-delivery components, CPU power, and memory. As the 1990s progressed, however, computers became more powerful and more sophisticated. With digital signal processing (DSP), programmers began to bring their understanding of programming hardware digital synthesizers to bear in the desktop computer world. Some of the standalone software synthesizers developed in these days, while rudimentary, were orders of magnitude better than anything previously available. In the late 1990s, Steinberg blew the computer-music world off its collective feet when the second version of its audio plug-in format, Virtual Studio Technology (VST), allowed for not only audio processing plug-ins, but also synthesizer plug-ins. These were small pieces of code that "plugged in" to the host audio sequencer, accepted MIDI data, and translated that MIDI data into sound. All this happened just like with any hardware synthesizer, but completely inside the computer, with no cabling required, with sample-accurate timing, and with total integration into your software mixing environment. The computer-music world has never been the same.

As time passes, software synthesizers keep getting better and better, reaching the quality of hardware synthesizers and in many cases surpassing it in terms of ease of use, integration into computer recording environments, and their ability to draw on the vast amount of processing power in modern computers. There is a downside to all of this, however: The more processing we ask our computers to do, the sooner they run out of power for other things. For example, suppose that simply playing back, editing, and mixing your 32-track audio and MIDI project required 30 percent of your available CPU power. Now suppose that you wanted to add your favorite software synthesizer plug-in, which requires 25 percent of your available CPU by itself. As you can see, your computer could comfortably handle only two such processor-intensive software synthesizers with your project.

Logic is very efficient with CPU resources and offers the Freeze and Bounce in Place functions described in Chapter 6, "The Logic Pro Main Window," to help manage CPU resources even further. This enables you to get more power out of your computer than ever before. But, as you can see, although software synthesizers are a spectacular new development in the computer-music world, they require some compromises and, occasionally, careful resource management.

Logic and Software Instruments

Emagic embraced the idea of software synthesizers (softsynths) very early. In fact, Emagic's release of its ES1 synthesizer and EXS24 24-bit software sampler represented two of the very first integrated synthesizers available for any sequencer. Unlike VST plug-ins, Logic's own softsynths are not additional programs that can be integrated into Logic. Rather, Logic's software instruments are actual extensions of the main Logic application and are already 100-percent integrated into the application. In addition to offering Logic's own software instruments, Logic can also accept third-party 64-bit softsynths compatible with Apple's Audio Units format. These plug-ins are called *components* on your hard drive because Audio Units are technically a "component" of the audio architecture of the Macintosh OS X operating system.

Although incorporating softsynths is typical in the modern DAW, the software instrument channel strip object (the Environment's extension of the software instrument) sets Logic apart. Not only does it allow you to insert a software instrument and enter MIDI data onto its associated Tracks area track, producing audio from the software instrument, but it also allows you to apply any of the large array of MIDI tools in the Environment to your softsynths and to insert MIDI and audio effects in the channel strip to enhance or affect the softsynth's output.

> **NOTE:** For a complete guide and "master class" tutorial on how to use Logic Pro's many excellent built-in synthesizers, pick up *Using Logic Pro's Synthesizers* by Kevin Anker (Course Technology PTR, 2012).

Accessing Logic Software Instruments

Logic's own software instruments don't need any special installation; they are part of the Logic code itself. This means there's no procedure necessary to install them; your installation of Logic includes all of them. Be aware, though, that—like Apple Loops, Space Designer, and Drummer—EXS24 has a lot of additional content available for download that you very well may want to install by opening the Logic Pro X menu and choosing the Download Additional Content command.

Remember, when you create a new software instrument track, if you have Open Library checked in the New Tracks dialog box, a default software instrument channel strip will be created that includes the Vintage Electric Piano instrument. If you want to start a software instrument track from scratch, deselect the Open Library option and you'll get a new, empty software instrument channel strip.

To instantiate any of Logic's softsynths into an empty software instrument channel, simply click the Instrument slot of the channel strip. A menu appears, allowing you to select the Logic instrument you want from its submenu. Each submenu lists the available channel format options for the instrument, such as Mono, Stereo, Multi-Output, and 5.1 (surround). Simply select the Logic instrument in the format you want to use, and it will be loaded into the software instrument channel strip. The channel strip will automatically be configured to the correct format. Figure 9.1 shows Logic's Vintage Clav being instantiated into a software instrument channel strip in the main window.

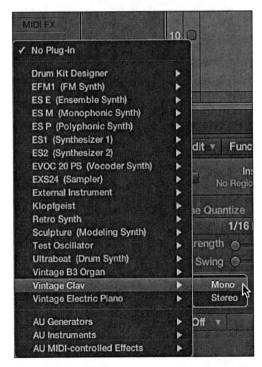

Figure 9.1 This main window channel strip for a software instrument track shows Logic's Vintage Clav softsynth being selected from the Instrument menu.
© Apple Inc.

The selected software instrument automatically opens its graphic editor when you instantiate it, giving you full access to all the parameters and functions of the instrument. Figure 9.2 shows the graphic editor of Logic's ES1 software instrument and its parent channel strip.

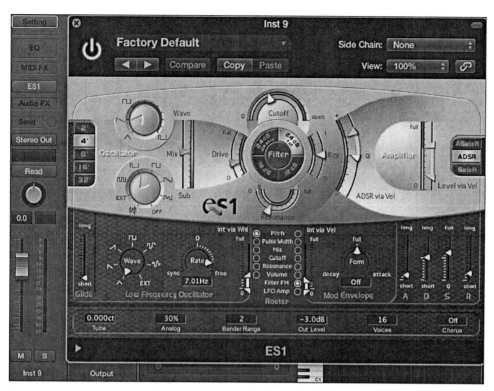

Figure 9.2 A software instrument channel strip with Logic's built-in ES1 softsynth instantiated. If you double-click on the Instrument slot displaying the name of the instrument, you launch the graphic editor for that instrument.
© Apple Inc.

Using the Instrument Slot Buttons

After you have a software instrument instantiated on your channel strip, the Instrument button gains three functions:

▷ You can turn the instrument on and off using a power button on the left end of the Instrument slot.
▷ If you close the editor and want to access it again, you can click on the middle of the Instrument slot of the software instrument, which shows two sliders when you hover the cursor over it. The softsynth's graphic editor will reopen.
▷ If you want to change the instrument, you can access the Instruments menu on the right end of the Instrument slot by clicking on the arrows. Figure 9.3 shows these buttons in the Instrument slot.

Figure 9.3 After an instrument is loaded on a software instrument channel strip, the Instrument slot offers three buttons allowing you to turn the instrument on and off, open or close the graphic editor, or browse the instrument menu for another instrument.
© Apple Inc.

Loading Instruments and Settings Using the Library

You can use the Library in the main window to select and load a setting for the currently selected software instrument track by browsing through the available Library options or by using the Search Library function. In the process of selecting a setting, you can even switch the instrument and effects used by the selected software instrument track—for example, selecting a setting in the Clav directory when the current software instrument is the Vintage B3 Organ.

Installing and Accessing Non-Logic Software Instruments

You need to install any third-party 64-bit software instruments into either the local (system-wide) or user (yours specifically) Components folder of your Macintosh. The exact method of installation depends on whether the developer included an installer application that automatically places files where they need to go or whether you need to manually move the plug-in file, with the extension .component, to where it belongs.

If you have to install a plug-in manually, the local Components folder resides at /Library/Audio/Plug-ins/Components, and the user Components folder is at ~/Library/Audio/Plug-ins/Components. It shouldn't make a difference which location you choose or whether your components are split among both Components folders. Logic sees all Audio Unit plug-ins in both folders.

You instantiate third-party softsynths into software instrument channel strips using the same procedure as with Logic's softsynths, except that you navigate the AU Instruments portion of the Instrument menu. The AU Instruments menu contains additional submenus that divide software instruments into groups based on the manufacturer of the instrument. Figure 9.4 shows the Zebra2 software synthesizer by u-he being selected.

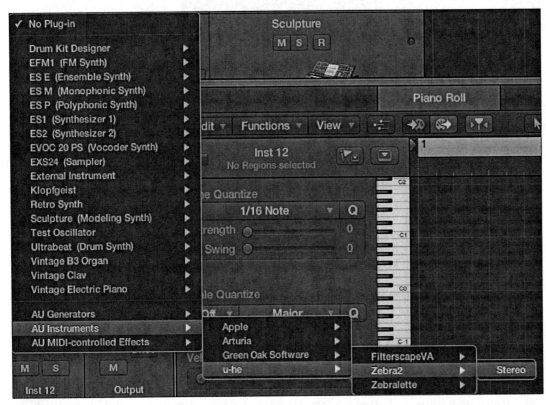

Figure 9.4 A third-party synthesizer—in this case, Zebra2 by u-he—is being instantiated on this software instrument channel strip.
© Apple Inc.

Just as with the Logic softsynths, the Instrument slot gives you access to the three buttons—power, graphic editor launcher, and Instrument menu—once a plug-in is instantiated.

Method Tip: Using the External Instrument to Connect MIDI Synthesizers: Considering how many software instruments and effects Logic comes with, it is impossible for this book to go into them all. However, one of Logic's software instruments is so special that it warrants going over. And it's not even a true software instrument, in that it makes no sound itself.

Many times, you might want to send MIDI performances to an external MIDI device, such as a MIDI sound module or a MIDI synthesizer, and then send the stereo audio from your MIDI hardware back into the Logic Mixer to be processed and summed with all your other tracks. This used to take a fair amount of preparation. You needed to create an instrument or multi-instrument object for your MIDI hardware device in the Environment. This object would then need to have a track created for it in the Arrange window in order for Logic to record MIDI from and send MIDI to the device. Then you needed to configure audio channels for the audio outputs of your MIDI device.

The External Instrument plug-in is designed expressly for this situation. You still need to have created an instrument, multi-instrument, or mapped-instrument track for your MIDI device. Select either a mono or a stereo external instrument in a software instrument channel strip's Instrument slot. The plug-in editor gives you only a few options. First, set its MIDI channel to your instrument, multi-instrument, or mapped-instrument's MIDI channel. Then set its input to the input(s) on your audio interface into which you plugged your MIDI hardware device and adjust the input volume.

That's it! You now have a single track that both sends and receives information from your hardware MIDI device. Keep in mind that you can use only one (mono) or two (stereo) outputs of your MIDI hardware with this instrument. There is not a multichannel option.

Plug-in Window Controls

Software instruments and audio effects (which are discussed in Chapter 11, "Mixing in Logic") use the same basic form of plug-in window. Each plug-in window features Link, Bypass, Compare, Copy, and Paste buttons, two arrow buttons, and either two or three pull-down menus, as shown in Figure 9.5.

Figure 9.5 The two varieties of controls you'll find on software instrument plug-in windows. They are identical except for the number of pull-down menus. Software instrument windows (left) typically have two menus; some software instruments (right) have side chains, which gives them three menus, with the Side Chain menu offset from the others.
© Apple Inc.

The elements of the plug-in window in which your software instrument will open are described in the following sections.

Plug-in Window Buttons

There are seven buttons at the top of the plug-in window. From left to right they are as follows:

▷ **Power:** The power button turns the plug-in on and off. This has the same effect as using the power button or Option-clicking in the plug-in's Instrument slot in the channel strip in which the plug-in is instantiated.

▷ **Next Setting and Previous Setting:** These are the two arrow buttons, which allow you to select the next or previous preset.

▷ **Compare:** The Compare button allows you compare any changes you have made to a plug-in's settings to the last saved setting.

▷ **Copy:** Use this button to copy a plug-in's setting.

▷ **Paste:** Use this button to paste a copied plug-in setting.

▷ **Link:** This button, at the upper-right of the plug-in window, looks like two chain links. By default, the Link button is disengaged, so multiple plug-in windows can be on the screen simultaneously. If the Link button is engaged, only a single plug-in window at a time is allowed onscreen. This is useful if you have a limited amount of screen space. You can also open a number of windows with the Link button disengaged and then engage the Link button on one of the open plug-in windows so that all subsequent plug-ins will appear in this window.

Plug-in Window Menus

The plug-in window contains either two or three menus in its top bar, depending on the capabilities of the plug-in.

▷ **View menu:** This menu always contains these two options: Editor, which offers the standard graphic editor view of plug-ins, and Control, which simply lists the parameters of the synth and offers a slider with number field or a menu for each parameter. Most plug-ins have too many parameters to offer useful graphic feedback in Control view, so you'll almost always want to use the Editor view. Control view is particularly suited to fine-tuning particular parameters. When in Editor view, you also have extra parameters that let you resize the graphic editor from 50% to 200% in increments of 25%. You can also resize the graphic editor by click-dragging the lower-right corner of the window.

▷ **Side Chain menu:** Some softsynths can process the audio from an audio channel. To do this, you will need to use the Side Chain menu to select which audio channel to process. Side chains are discussed in detail in Chapter 11.

▷ **Settings field:** The Settings field is the pull-down menu to the right of the Next Setting and Previous Setting buttons. This menu has commands for loading and saving Logic plug-in setting files. These files store the current parameter conditions of your plug-in, which you can then reload later and even reuse in other songs. This is useful for creating your own unique collection of commonly used settings for your various plug-ins. As you save your settings, they appear in this pull-down menu for easy access. The presets for Logic's own instruments and effects are listed at the bottom of this menu as well. Plug-in settings are stored in the Plug-In Settings folder inside the ~/Music/Audio Music Apps directory, as well as in the Logic Application Support folder. You can also manually add settings collected from other users by copying them to this folder. This field also displays the name of the currently selected preset. Note that many third-party plug-ins have their own methods for loading and saving presets and do not rely on the host application for preset handling. You can still use the commands in this menu if you want to create and manage settings for a plug-in within Logic's preset hierarchy rather than the plug-in's.

Extended Parameters

Not all of Logic's plug-ins have every parameter available in their Editor view. In such cases, a disclosure triangle at the bottom-left corner of the plug-in window allows you to open an extended parameters area, giving you access to any remaining controls the plug-in offers. Figure 9.6 shows the bottom of EFM1 with the extended parameters area opened.

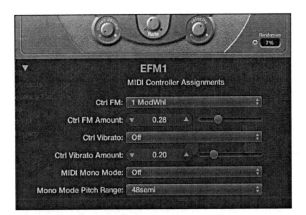

Figure 9.6 The extended parameters area of the EFM1 plug-in. Some Logic plug-ins have parameters that are not found in the plug-in's Editor view but are available by clicking on the window's disclosure triangle in the lower-left corner.

© Apple Inc.

Software Instruments and the Environment

As discussed, a software instrument channel strip is both a channel strip object and a MIDI object. As such, you can route software instrument objects to other MIDI objects to create unique MIDI effects and routings, just like you can any other MIDI device. If this sounds interesting to you, I'd encourage you to spend time exploring the Environment.

Using Multi-Output Software Instruments

The vast majority of the software instruments you use will be either mono or stereo instruments. Moreover, you'll probably only need stereo outputs from softsynths that allow for more than two outputs. However, sometimes you might want to have an independent output for each sample from a sampler, each voice of a synthesizer, or each drum from a drum instrument to allow for more precise mixing, processing, or automation control. For these situations, you can instantiate a multi-output instrument in a software instrument channel strip.

Logic is far more efficient than other DAWs in the management of resources when using software instruments. The price for this efficiency, unfortunately, is that accessing the additional outputs of softsynths takes a few more steps than in other applications. Most other applications automatically create every allowable output channel for multiple-output instruments as soon as you instantiate the plug-in. This is very convenient because there are no steps required to access the additional outputs. There are two drawbacks to this, however. The first is that if your instrument is set up to allow 32 outputs, your Mixer will be cluttered with 32 additional output channels, making it huge and unwieldy—especially if you only wanted to use, say, four outputs! The other drawback is that all of those unused outputs may drain your computer's CPU power and RAM. Logic allows you to activate only those outputs that you will actually use, conserving both screen real estate and computer resources, but giving you this flexibility means that activating the additional outputs requires some configuration.

The first step is to make sure that you have instantiated a multi-output softsynth like EXS24 in a software instrument channel strip by selecting the Multi Output option. Then, you may need to change the output assignments in the softsynth's graphical interface. For details, consult the documentation for your specific software instrument.

Next, open the Mixer and use the plus (+) button on the multi-output instrument's channel strip to add as many aux channels as you need for routing your multi-output instrument. Figure 9.7 shows the plus button on a multi-output channel strip in the Mixer. After you have used the plus button to add aux channel strips to the Mixer, the minus (–) button next to it is enabled, allowing you to delete that multi-output instrument's dependent aux channels one by one.

Figure 9.7 Use the plus button to add more aux channel strips to the Mixer for the outputs of a multi-output instrument. Use the minus button to delete any unused auxes you created for the multi-output instrument.
© Apple Inc.

Now you need to assign your aux channels to the outputs of the multi-output instrument. In addition to submenus for hardware inputs and available buses in each aux channel strip's Input pull-down menu, you will find a menu of all the outputs available for your multi-output instrument. If the aux channel's Format button shows a single circle, mono outputs are displayed; if the Format button shows two overlapping circles, stereo outputs are displayed. Choose the output (or outputs, if you are using stereo) that you want this aux channel to use as its input(s). Figure 9.8 shows an aux channel's input being assigned to a multi-output instrument's output.

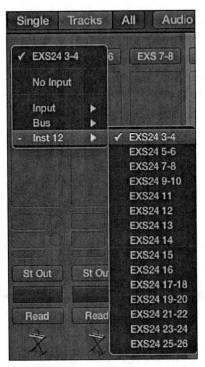

Single | Tracks | **All** | Audio

✓ EXS24 3-4   6   EXS 7-8

No Input

Input ▶
Bus ▶
- Inst 12 ▶   ✓ EXS24 3-4
    EXS24 5-6
    EXS24 7-8
    EXS24 9-10
    EXS24 11
    EXS24 12
    EXS24 13
    EXS24 14
    EXS24 15
St Out   St Ou   EXS24 16
    EXS24 17-18
    EXS24 19-20
Read   Read   EXS24 21-22
    EXS24 23-24
    EXS24 25-26

Figure 9.8 To access the additional outputs of multi-output instruments, create an aux channel and select the desired output from its input menu. Here, the EXS24 output 3–4 is chosen as the input for this aux channel.
© Apple Inc.

If your Mixer's display mode is set to Tracks, the new aux channel strips will be shown directly to the right of their parent multi-output channel strip. Different Mixer display modes will be covered in detail in Chapter 11; for the moment, you can find the display mode buttons at the top center of the Mixer window's local menu bar. (Some of these are shown in Figure 9.8.) Figure 9.9 shows the Ultrabeat multi-output instrument channel strip in the Mixer. Note that in addition to the main software instrument channel strip that serves as the main stereo output pair, this multi-output instrument has been configured with two additional mono aux channel strips and then a stereo aux channel strip. This is the power of Logic: Only six of Ultrabeat's 24 outputs were needed, and the configuration matches exactly the user's desired combination of mono and stereo outputs.

082411

Figure 9.9 The multichannel Ultrabeat has been configured to include the main outputs, two additional mono outputs, and an additional stereo output. If you need more outputs, you can easily continue creating aux objects and choose more Ultrabeat outputs, to the limit of the instrument's capacity.
© Apple Inc.

The Tracks area track for this multi-output instrument is where you will record, program, and edit the MIDI data that will operate the software instrument. The multi-output instrument's own outputs will be the "master outputs." That means, depending on how the specific softsynth you are using operates, it may serve as your master stereo output or it may be a summation output of all the other outputs for the entire instrument. You'll need to consult your instrument's documentation for specifics on how it utilizes its master outputs.

For multi-output instruments, you won't need to have any of the additional outputs in the Tracks area if you don't want them there. However, you might want to put some or all of them in the main window to automate those outputs. Automation is discussed in Chapter 10, "Using Automation in Logic." You can add your aux channels to the main window in a couple of different ways. In the Mixer, you can right-click on an aux channel strip and choose Create Track from the resulting menu, as shown in Figure 9.10. Alternatively, select the aux for which you want to create a track and press Control+T. (Note that this key command works only in the Mixer.)

Figure 9.10 To create a Tracks area track for an aux in the Mixer, simply Control-click on an aux channel strip and choose Create Track from the menu or press Control+T.
© Apple Inc.

In the main window, you can also change a newly created track or a currently unused one to an aux channel by right-clicking on the track header. Under the Mixer submenu of the Reassign Track Object menu, go to the Aux submenu and select the aux channel you want, as shown in Figure 9.11.

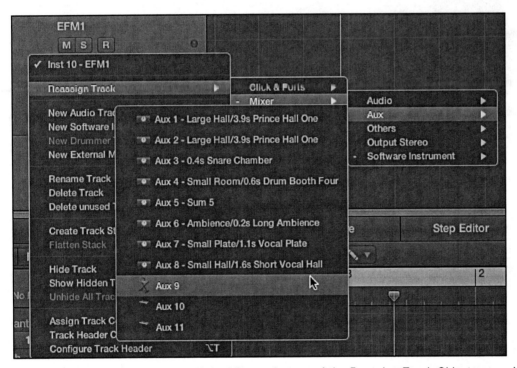

Figure 9.11 The Aux submenu of the Mixer submenu of the Reassign Track Object menu. You can assign a Tracks area track to the aux channel output of a multi-output instrument using this menu.
© Apple Inc.

Another way to add your multi-output instrument's dependent aux channels to the main window is to do the following:

1. Create a new channel of any type in the Tracks area for each aux you want to add.
2. Open the Environment Mixer.
3. Select the aux channels you want to add to the main window and then drag them to the Tracks area over the new tracks. You will see boxes highlighting the track headers of the channels that the aux channels will be affecting.
4. Once you have selected the desired tracks, release the mouse button. The selected tracks will automatically be changed to aux channels.

Be careful, though—if you release the aux over any channel, even one with regions on it, it will be converted into an aux channel. If this happens, you can simply undo the action (press Command+Z). You can also assign any aux to an automation mode, and it will automatically be added in the Tracks area.

This is a perfect example of the "Logic way." It might take a little extra initial configuration, but when you understand how it works and how to do it, not only is it simple, but you can really take advantage of the power and flexibility it offers over other applications!

Using Multitimbral Software Instruments

Some software instruments allow for multitimbral operation, meaning they'll allow you to load completely different plug-in settings, presets, and so on for each different MIDI channel the instrument can receive. Not all instruments allow for this—in fact, Apple doesn't currently make any software instruments that are multitimbral—but if you *do* have some Audio Units instruments that allow this function, here's how you would access them from within Logic. One method is to simply have the MIDI regions on your software instrument track send different MIDI events to different MIDI channels. For example, you could create a single MIDI region with a bass line sending to MIDI channel 1 and a high lead part sending to MIDI channel 2. Your software instrument will take care of routing the different notes to the proper MIDI channels.

This technique comes in handy for scoring, when you might want several voices in a single MIDI region going to different channels. However, if you want separate tracks for each MIDI part being routed to different channels, you can easily create them in the main window. Here's how:

1. Open the New Tracks dialog box to create a new software instrument. To do so, either click the plus button in the upper-left corner of the Tracks area or press the Option+Command+N key command.
2. Specify the number of new tracks you wish to create.
3. Select the Multi-timbral checkbox in the Details area of the New Tracks dialog box, as shown in Figure 9.12. The initial channel strip and region parameters will be identical for all of the new tracks because the exact same software instrument channel strip is being used on all the newly created software instrument tracks.

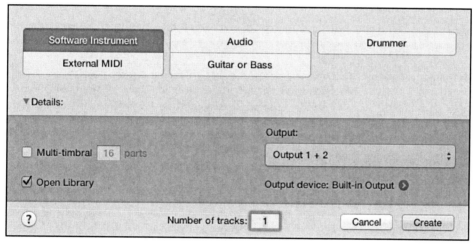

Figure 9.12 The New Tracks dialog box. Selecting the Multi-timbral checkbox creates the defined number of multitimbral instruments and their dependent tracks in the Tracks area.
© Apple Inc.

Now you can create new MIDI regions on these tracks and send those MIDI regions to different MIDI channels of your multichannel software instrument. This way, you have the MIDI parts for each channel separated on different tracks.

Using MIDI FX

Among the many new features in Logic Pro X, one of the coolest is MIDI FX. In previous versions of Logic, if you wanted an arpeggiator—for example, to arpeggiate a synth that didn't have its own built-in arpeggiator—you had to build one in the Environment. The more complicated the arpeggiations, the more complicated an Environment layer you would have to construct. Although there are still many things that can be accomplished only in the Environment, the inclusion of these nine new MIDI FX reduces the need for most users to ever have to worry about the Environment significantly. These MIDI FX are very versatile and programmable, and you can have up to eight MIDI FX instantiated per software instrument channel strip. To access Logic's MIDI

FX, click the MIDI FX slot, below the EQ thumbnail, on a software instrument channel strip. Figure 9.13 shows the MIDI FX menu.

Figure 9.13 The MIDI FX menu, found only in software instrument channel strips.
© Apple Inc.

Although it's outside the scope of this book to cover these MIDI FX in depth, the following are brief descriptions of each MIDI FX:

▷ **Arpeggiator:** This is the MIDI FX available when you access Smart Controls for a software instrument. It can produce very simple or extremely complex arpeggiations.

▷ **Chord Trigger:** This lets you trigger chords with a single MIDI note.

▷ **Modifier:** This lets you reassign an incoming MIDI control change message, such as velocity, to another controller.

▷ **Modulator:** This lets you create custom LFO modulation and envelopes to affect the selected MIDI control change parameters.

▷ **Note Repeater:** This has similar effect on MIDI notes as a delay effect has on audio.

▷ **Randomizer:** This lets you define a MIDI control change parameter whose incoming signal will be randomized.

▷ **Scripter:** This includes an editor that lets you use JavaScript to create custom MIDI FX processes, which the Scripter plug-in will then run. If you are familiar with software samplers that use scripting to enhance and expand the performance of those samplers, then you have at least some notion of what Scripter can do, the important difference being that Scripter woks with *any* software instrument.

▷ **Transposer:** This can be used for simple transposition, but can also be used similarly to the Scale Quantize parameter in the Piano Roll editor, forcing incoming MIDI notes to the defined key and scale selection.

▷ **Velocity Processor:** This lets you create alternate velocity curves for incoming MIDI messages.

When you select a MIDI FX plug-in, its graphic editor window will open, letting you edit the parameters of the plug-in, save those settings, and load factory and user settings. MIDI FX plug-ins have the same buttons and menus found at the top of software instruments' graphic editor windows. This can be seen in Figure 9.14, which shows the Arpeggiator MIDI FX. Most of the MIDI FX plug-ins also have an Extended Parameters area. I encourage you to explore the Logic Pro Instruments manual, available as an option in the Logic Pro X Help menu, to learn more about using these incredible MIDI FX plug-ins. If you work with MIDI a lot, you will likely find at least one or two of these effects quite useful!

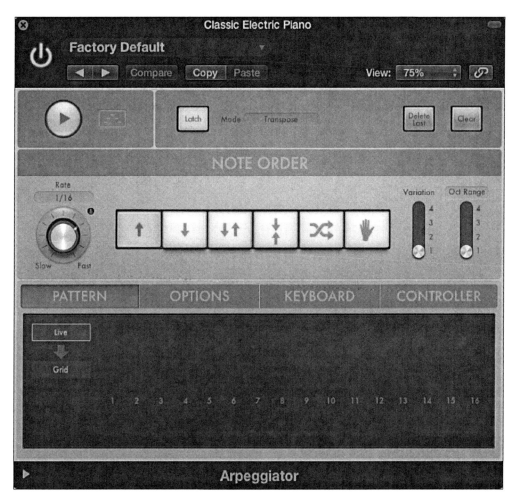

Figure 9.14 The Arpeggiator MIDI FX plug-in graphic editor window.
© Apple Inc.

Using ReWire 2 Instruments

Chapter 3, "The Logic Project," briefly described how to create ReWire instruments, but now we'll go into more detail. As mentioned, ReWire 2 is a protocol developed by Propellerhead Software through which one program can access and control another music software program, with both applications running on the same computer. ReWire 2 slaves function as software instruments because all their processing is done inside the host computer, but they are different from software instruments in the sense that they are not part of the Logic application like Logic's own softsynths, nor are they literally "plugged in" to the Logic application like third-party plug-ins. So although all the connections that Logic needs to make are "virtual connections" that do not require hardware interfaces and cables, Logic must still create these connections *out* of Logic *into* another application. The Environment's ReWire object, therefore, is a virtual MIDI cable between Logic and the ReWire 2 application, and is also a virtual audio cable between Logic and the ReWire 2 application. This section explains how to configure these objects to use a ReWire 2 application with Logic.

Working with ReWire 2 Applications

ReWire 2 has two modes: master and slave. Generally, the application launched first is the default ReWire master, and the ReWire 2 application launched subsequently is the ReWire slave. The master application controls the synchronization between the two applications, and the sound from the ReWire slave application plays through the ReWire master application. Logic is only capable of being a ReWire master, so be sure that the ReWire 2–capable application you want to use can be operated in ReWire 2 slave mode. Also, because Logic Pro X is a 64-bit application, any ReWire slave you use with Logic must also be 64-bit.

No special configuration is required to initialize ReWire operation. Be sure to launch Logic first, then launch your ReWire 2 slave application. The application should automatically load in ReWire slave mode.

Creating ReWire Instruments for MIDI Transmission

Before you can use Logic with your ReWire slave, you need to create and configure the necessary tracks in the Tracks area. First, create as many new external instrument tracks as you will need for your ReWire slave, as discussed in Chapter 3. Next, open the Library, as shown in Figure 9.15.

Figure 9.15 The Library in the main window. You can see your ReWire-capable applications in the Library when you select an external instrument track.
© Apple Inc.

After a ReWire slave has launched, you will see a list of the available ReWire sources in the Library, as shown in Figure 9.16. You can assign a ReWire slave instrument to an external instrument track by simply clicking on the name of the desired instrument.

Figure 9.16 You can select the desired ReWire instrument directly in the Library in the main window.
© Apple Inc.

If at any time you want to change a ReWire track's settings, you can do so in the Inspector. Following are descriptions of each parameter:

▷ **Type:** The Type menu lets you select the type of external instrument, including ReWire and QuickTime.
▷ **Device:** This refers to the specific ReWire 2 application to which the ReWire instrument is connecting. For example, if you were using three different ReWire 2 applications, all three applications would appear in this pull-down menu, and you could select which of the three applications to connect this ReWire instrument to.
▷ **Bus:** This parameter allows you to choose which ReWire bus to use from your available ReWire buses.

▷ **Channel:** This parameter specifies the MIDI channel on which you want your ReWire instrument to send and receive MIDI data. Clicking the Channel menu would show a mixture of available MIDI channels and Reason instruments assigned to different channels, so picking the right channel for the desired instrument is effortless.

In the Devices tab of the Audio Preferences dialog box, which you access by clicking the Logic Pro menu, choosing Preferences, and selecting Audio, you will find a menu for ReWire mode with two options: Playback and Live. For normal use, leave this setting in Playback mode. If you are going to use your ReWire slave for live performance of its instruments over the ReWire connection, set the ReWire mode to Live. This diverts extra CPU resources to ensure the best possible synchronization between Logic and your ReWire application during live performance. If you use ReWire applications extensively, even if not strictly for live use, you will want to keep the Live option selected. Note that by default, Logic Pro X has ReWire turned off, so you will need to set the ReWire mode parameter to use ReWire.

Setting Up ReWire Objects for Audio Transmission

Now that you have set up your ReWire instrument's MIDI connection between Logic and your ReWire 2 application, you need to create and configure aux channels to receive audio from the ReWire slave. To create a new aux, simply open the Mixer either in the main window or in its own window, open the Mixer's local Options menu, select Options, and choose Create New Auxiliary Channel Strips. Alternatively, press Control+N. You can then define the ReWire bus of your aux channel strip using the Input menu, shown in Figure 9.17.

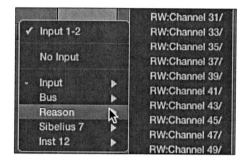

Figure 9.17 Use the Input menu in an aux channel strip to define the ReWire bus of your aux channel strip.
© Apple Inc.

You can now use Logic's internal effects on your ReWired audio. You can also add the aux channel to the Tracks area to use automation on your ReWired audio.

Using Automation in Logic

I N THE EARLY DAYS OF RECORDING, if you wanted to capture the sound of moving one of the controls—for example, to create a wild stereo panning effect with an instrument, to have sound fade out gradually, or simply to level out the volume of a track that fluctuated wildly in level—you would need to move the control carefully by hand while the mixdown was happening. Any error in movement meant starting the whole thing over from scratch, and there was no way to exactly repeat anything. If you wanted to repeat the move for a new mixdown, the only option was to do it again manually and hope that the result was close to that of the original mixdown.

In the 1970s, large mixing consoles began to offer *automation*—a way to write, rewrite, and save these moves in memory so that as you mixed your material, it would automatically make your move for you. This was not only more convenient, but it meant that you could audition, change, and repeat any move an infinite number of times, and it would be the same each time. This opened the door not only for more accurate mixing, but also for much more creative mixing by experimental artists who wanted to use the studio itself as an instrument.

With the advent of computer sequencers, automation has become an even more powerful tool, available to all. You can use automation to turn static effects into living, dynamic parts of a track's sound; you can tailor the volume of a track exactly to the source material; you can perfect mixes to previously unimaginable accuracy; and you can use your DAW not only as a tool, but as an instrument in its own right. Logic's automation system is fairly intuitive, but it still takes a while to get used to its "logic!"

Types of Automation

As discussed in Chapter 6, "The Logic Pro Main Window," there are two ways to automate your song data in Logic. Both methods are useful and are very similar in many ways, but each has distinct advantages and disadvantages.

The first method is called *track automation* (*TA*), so named because the automation data is stored with the Tracks area track lane. This paradigm of storing the automation data with the track harkens back to the days of hardware mixing consoles, where you automated a specific channel of the mixer. TA allows for incredibly high (sample-accurate) resolution, which gives you precise control over automation points and lines. Because TA is the more recent and powerful automation system, you will probably use TA for most of your automation in Logic.

Unlike using a hardware mixing console, where the console doesn't know what type of data you are sending through a channel, a computer *does* know what sort of data you have in your song. That means that unlike a hardware console, a computer sequencer doesn't need to automate a channel, but can instead include automation information as part of the audio or MIDI region itself. This type of automation in Logic is called *MIDI Draw* (formerly called Hyper Draw), which is a *region-based automation* (*RA*). Emagic developed Hyper Draw long before TA, back when all automation of MIDI hardware and audio tracks was based on MIDI (hence the term MIDI Draw, as it is basically a lane set of the MIDI control messages). That means RA is limited to controlling parameters that have MIDI control message values, as you learned in Chapter 8, "Working with MIDI," and that RA's values are limited to the standard MIDI range of 0–127 (as opposed to TA's 32-bit resolution). While RA is definitely limited compared to TA, it still has its uses.

Both forms of automation can be used together, so you can have a region in which you've automated some plug-in parameters using MIDI Draw as well as done some track-based automation. When you have Track Automation view enabled, there will be a disclosure triangle on the left side of the track; if you click on the triangle, you can get as many additional lanes for viewing MIDI Draw and for viewing, creating, and editing track automation as you need. Figure 10.1 shows a track that has track-based automation and another where the MIDI region itself has some RA on it. You can even turn RA into TA and vice versa, as you'll explore later in this chapter. But be careful not to use TA and RA for the same parameter—the results will be random and unusable.

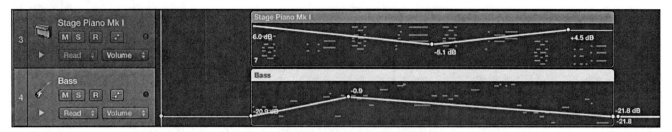

Figure 10.1   This shows both MIDI Draw (region-based automation) and track-based automation. You can see the Stage Piano Mk I region with volume RA above the Bass region with TA automating its volume. You can use both of them interchangeably, depending on your needs. Because TA is the newer and more robust automation system, you will most likely use TA more often.

© Apple Inc.

Using Track-Based Automation

Using TA couldn't be simpler. If you've already turned on track-based automation using the Show/Hide Automation button in the main window or by using the Mix > Show Automation command, the automation display is visible for all your tracks. If you haven't done that, click the Show/Hide Automation button, select Mix > Show Automation, or press the A key. Once you show automation, each track header gets its own Enable Automation button, letting you activate automation on a per-track basis. You can also use the Control+Command+O key command to toggle automation for the selected track. To turn off automation for all tracks while leaving automation mode on, use the Control+Shift+Command+O key command. Figure 10.2 shows a few tracks in the Track List. Two tracks have Automation view enabled, one does not have automation enabled, and only one of the tracks actually has any automation. You can also see the Show/Hide Automation button next to the View menu.

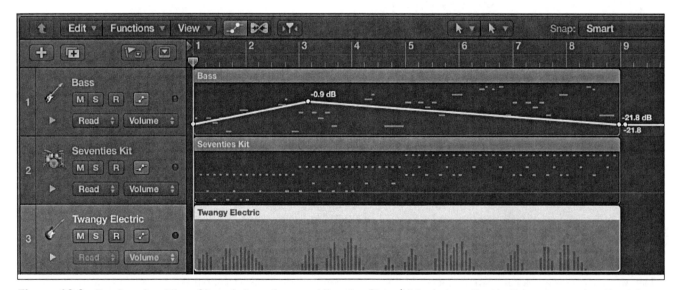

Figure 10.2   By choosing Mix > Show Automation, enabling the Show/Hide Automation button, or pressing the A key, you ensure that each track in the Track List contains track-based automation controls. Note that only the first of the three visible tracks actually has automation data visible in the track lane, the second track is ready to be automated, and the third track has automation disabled.

© Apple Inc.

The menu on the right of each track header is the Automation Parameter menu. Here you can select from all the available parameters for all the automatable elements of the track itself (volume, pan, solo, mute, send, insert bypass, and so on), from Smart Controls, as well as each automatable plug-in and software instrument parameter. Choose from this menu the parameter you want to automate. Figure 10.3 shows the submenus in the Automation Parameter menu.

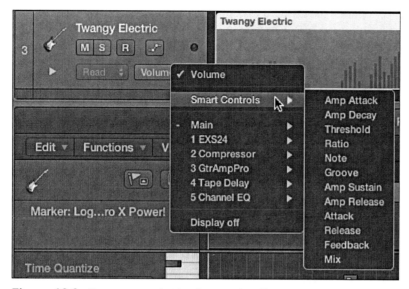

Figure 10.3 You can see in the Automation Parameter menu of this track that in addition to the shortcuts to Display Off and Volume, there are hierarchical menus to choose to display parameters from the main track, Smart Controls, software instruments, or effects.
© Apple Inc.

As you automate more parameters, they appear in the automation lane behind the currently live parameter. Volume appears as a yellow line, pan as a green line, and other parameters appear in a range of other colors.

There are two ways to create automation: in real time or in the track lane (non-real time). Both methods yield excellent results, and you'll find that both are useful, even when working with one automation parameter on a track. If you want to create automation in real time, you need to choose the automation mode in the Automation Mode menu to the left of the Automation Parameter menu. There are four automation modes:

▷ **Read:** This mode tells Logic to "read" the automation data on the track. When you play your song, Logic automates your track. You cannot write automation data in real time in this mode, but you can create and edit automation data in the track lane itself (as explained later in the section "Manipulating Automation Data"). You can set all tracks to Read using the Shift+Control+Command+R key command.

▷ **Touch:** In Touch mode, if you "touch" an element of the channel strip with your mouse or a hardware control surface, such as the Avid Artist Control or Mackie controller, Logic starts writing automation data for that element. This is real-time, live automating, so any move you make is recorded live into Logic's track automation, although you can of course edit the data later. As soon as you release the mouse or the control surface or stop "touching" the onscreen element, Logic stops writing automation data and returns the chosen parameter to its original value at the playhead position where you quit "touching" the parameter. For example, if you are in Touch mode and, during playback, you use the mouse to click on the Pan knob and move it from its current value—say, −25—you will write pan automation data in real time. When you release the mouse button, you will stop writing pan automation data, and the pan value will return to −25 at the current playhead position, at a rate defined by the Ramp Time parameter in the Automation Preferences window. Keep in mind that if you already have pan data written in the specific place in which you wrote new data, the new data recorded in Touch mode will overwrite the previous data. Touch mode is the standard mode for real-time onscreen or software controller automation. You can set all tracks to Touch using the Shift+Control+Command+T key command.

▷ **Latch:** Latch mode is like Touch mode except that once you click your mouse or move your control surface to start writing automation, Logic continues to write new data for that parameter even after you release the control. Only when playback stops will Logic stop writing automation for that parameter. Latch mode is desirable when you know that after a certain point in your song, you want to overwrite all the remaining data for a particular parameter. You can set all tracks to Latch using the Shift+Control+Command+L key command.

▷ **Write:** Write mode deletes all existing track automation as the playhead passes it. If you write new data, the new data is recorded. If you do not write new data, Write mode acts as a "real-time eraser" of previous automation data, which it replaces with nothing. Write mode is useful only if you want to start your mix over without using any of the Delete commands described later in this chapter. You will probably find this mode to be less useful than the other automation modes.

After setting the parameter you want to display and the automation mode you wish to use, all that's left to do is to actually write the automation data!

You can automate in real time by clicking on the various elements of the channel strip (Volume fader, Pan knob, Solo button, Mute button, insert and send slots) or the graphic interface of a plug-in or software instrument, then adjusting those elements by dragging them (or just clicking on them, if the parameter is controlled by a button) as your project plays. As you change the values of various elements, you will create automation points, which are points in which the value of an automatable parameter has changed. When you do real-time automation, as you might imagine, you may create hundreds of these points at a time in a mix with lots of complex motion.

You can also use a control surface, such as the Avid Artist controllers, Mackie Control, or any other MIDI hardware controller that you have set up, using the Learn Controller Assignment function described in Chapter 3, "The Logic Project." In this case, you would use the hardware controls on your controller to manipulate the onscreen channel strip and plug-in elements. If you are used to hardware mixers, automating by using a controller will seem more natural to you. Also, unlike with a mouse, using hardware controllers gives you the ability to manipulate more than one parameter at the same time. Finally, some hardware controllers offer 10-bit or greater resolution in their faders and knobs, which means that you'll be able to make finer-resolution moves with the controller than you could with a mouse.

If you don't want to automate in real time, you can also directly add automation points (points) and drag them up and down with your mouse in the track lane itself. This offers more precise placement of automation data than real-time mixing but also less feedback, because you can't hear what you're doing as you make the move.

You can also quickly create points on the borders of a selected region or regions by using two commands found in the Mix > Create Automation menu: Create 1 Automation Point at Region Borders (Shift+Control+Command+1) and Create 2 Points at Region Borders (Shift+Control+Command+1). There are also key command–only commands for creating one or two points at every region border of the selected track: Control+Command+1 and Control+Command+2, respectively. The benefit of these commands is that they create new points at the precise region borders, allowing you to easily control any automatable parameters on a per-region basis. With one point at each region border, you can create single-region fades, panorama movement, or filter sweeps without having to worry about creating precisely placed points on a region border. With two points at each region border, you can add quick volume, compressor threshold, or individual EQ band gain changes that affect only the region(s) you choose to automate. In essence, these commands bring region-based automation–like benefits to the more flexible track-based automation.

Automation Parameter Versus Parameter Write: Although you need to select a parameter for the automation lane to display automation data, in fact you can write automation data for any parameter that is automatable, even if it is not currently being displayed. For example, say you select Volume as the parameter displayed in the automation lane. Then, while in Touch mode, you write some volume automation data, but you also make some panning moves. Logic will write both the volume and the pan moves, even though the automation lane will reflect only the volume moves while you are recording automation data.

Keep in mind that you are not limited to any one method of writing automation data. You can use the mouse to automate volume in a track in real time, then add a few more points and adjust them in the track lane, and use one of the Create Points commands on a few of the track's regions. This is discussed further in the upcoming "Expert Automation Editing" section.

Method Tip: Viewing Multiple Automation Lanes: A track's automation lane lets you choose only one live parameter to display. However, you can automate more than one parameter at a time with a software controller. What if you want to view more than one parameter that you are automating? As mentioned, you can view multiple parameters on separate displays by clicking the small disclosure triangle at the bottom-left of a track displaying automation to open a new track lane to display another automation parameter. The new automation display lane will contain a plus sign (+) button, which opens another track automation lane when clicked. You can use this technique to open as many new automation display lanes as you need for each track you are automating. Click the disclosure triangle to collapse the automation lanes. Figure 10.4 shows a track that is displaying more than one automation lane this way.

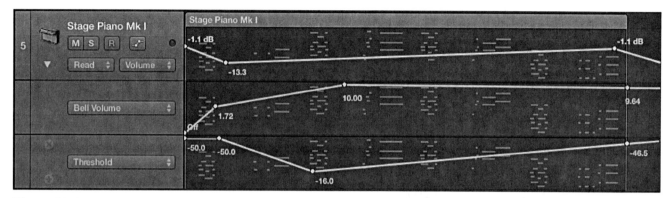

Figure 10.4 This track displays volume automation on its track lane. By clicking the triangle in the lower-left corner, the user created two additional automation display lanes automating elements of plug-ins on the track's parent channel strip.
© Apple Inc.

A Tale of Two View Modes: Both Automation and Flex Time views offer view modes that add information to every track in the main window. That means Automation view and Flex view are mutually exclusive. In other words, you can't have the Automation view displaying on one track and the Flex view displaying on another track simultaneously. If you have both Flex and Automation enabled, you can toggle between both views with main window buttons and key commands.

Manipulating Automation Data

Because you can write automation either by using the mouse or a hardware controller in real time or by simply adding it to a Tracks area track while not in playback, you can use the methods in this section to alter existing data or to create new data. All you need to do is turn on track-based automation and select a parameter in the Automation Parameter menu.

Using the Pointer Tool

To move a point, simply grab it with the Pointer tool and then move the point in any direction you want. Notice that the position line representing the continuous parameter value simply shifts positions and values depending on where you move the point. If you click somewhere on the automation line in the automation lane in which there isn't currently a point, Logic creates a point in that location, which you can manipulate as described. You can also create points using the Pencil tool.

The Pointer tool can manipulate automation data in additional ways:

▷ Double-clicking on a point deletes it.
▷ Clicking and holding on a line between two points enables you to move the line by dragging it.
▷ If you click and hold a point and then press the Shift key, you restrict the movement of the point to one plane, horizontal or vertical, whichever direction you move first.
▷ If you click and hold a point and press the Control key, you gain fine control of the point in the vertical plane, moving 0.1 units at a time.
▷ Option-clicking selects the area from the point to the right of the pointer to the last point on the track lane.
▷ Option-double-clicking selects all automation data in the current track lane.
▷ You can move a selected area by clicking and dragging anywhere in that selected area.
▷ If you Option-drag the selection, it will copy selected automation data to the new location.
▷ Shift+Control-clicking in an automation lane changes the pointer into the Automation Curve tool, discussed in the next section.

To change the value of a group of points, simply alter the value of one of the selected points inside the selected area. All the selected points then change by the same amount. If you click on a line away from a point but inside a selected area, or you alter the value of either of the two points at the edges of the selected area, you alter the values proportionally to where you clicked, but the values do not change by the same absolute amount.

Using the Automation Tools

You can also use the Automation tools described in the section "The Tracks Area Tool Menu" in Chapter 6. There are two Automation tools: Curve and Select. Figure 10.5 shows the Automation tools in the Tool menu.

Figure 10.5 The Automation Select tool is the solid arrow with the jagged stem. The Automation Curve tool is the open arrow with the jagged stem.
© Apple Inc.

In Curve mode, you can use the Automation tool to grab the line between any two points and bend it into a curve. Logic offers a number of preset curve types: convex, concave, and S-curves. Which variety of curve you create depends on where on the line you start your bend and in which direction you bend the line.

In Select mode, the Automation tool can make "rubber band" selections in the automation lane. If you click outside the automation lane in a region title bar, you select all the automation that falls within that region, up to the right-most point if that point falls outside the region. You can make noncontiguous selections of automation with this tool by holding down the Shift key while selecting additional automation data on the track. You can also extend a selection by Shift-clicking on a point in front of or behind an existing selection; everything from the selected area to the point you clicked is then selected.

Expert Automation Editing

As you would expect, Logic offers myriad key commands to control various automation functions. Figure 10.6 shows a sampling of the automation key commands. I would encourage you to search for "automation" in the Key Commands window to see the full extent of the assigned automation key commands, much less the unassigned commands!

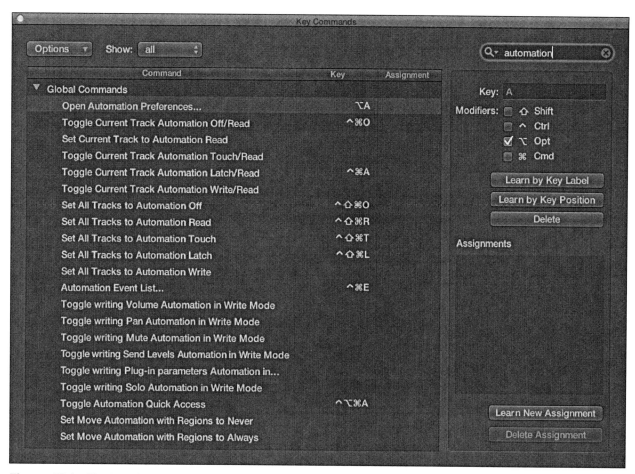

Figure 10.6 The Key Commands window showing some automation-related commands.
© Apple Inc.

Feel free to assign keys to any of the options you want. You'll find using Logic's automation even faster and more natural when you master the key commands. The Automation Event List key command, Control+Command+E, opens the Event List window to show all automation data for the selected track. These views of automation data are normally invisible. The Automation Event List is an "expert option" because unless you know what you are doing, you will probably find it too confusing to be of much use. If you want to explore it, however, the following subsection describes it briefly.

Logic Pro® X Power!: The Comprehensive Guide

Automation Event List

You can view automation data in the Automation Event List, just like other command data, such as MIDI control messages. Because automation data is technically a special proprietary type of data known as *fader messages*, you'll notice that the Automation Event List consists exclusively of fader and control data, depending on what the entry is automating. Figure 10.7 shows an Automation Event List.

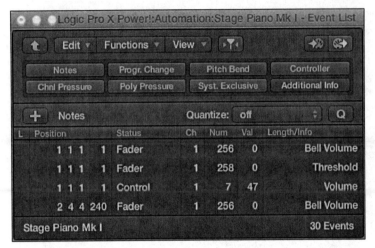

Figure 10.7 An Automation Event List. Because this is displayed in the Event List Editor, you have all the options previously described in Chapter 8 to edit your automation data.
© Apple Inc.

As you can see, the Automation Event List is a specialized view in the Event List Editor. Therefore, you can use all the options and techniques described in Chapter 8 regarding the Event List Editor to edit your MIDI automation. You may find the Automation Event List useful if you know exactly what you want to edit or if you are more comfortable editing data numerically rather than graphically.

Moving Automation Data from One Parameter to Another

If you have automation data written for one parameter but you'd like to move it to another parameter—say you automated a filter cutoff for a software instrument, and now you want that data to control the envelope level—you can do this easily. With the parameter you want to move displayed in the automation lane, press the Command key while opening the Automation Parameter menu. (Be sure to continue pressing the Command key after you release the mouse button.) Now when you choose a destination parameter, a dialog box appears, asking whether you want to convert (move) the current automation to the new parameter or copy and convert it, which leaves the data you have recorded in the current parameter but also adds it to the new parameter. Select the option you prefer, and that's it!

Moving Automation with Regions

As with so many other things, Logic gives you options for controlling its behavior when you move regions on tracks that contain automation. To define how Logic handles automation data when you move a region, choose Logic Pro > Preferences > Automation, or press Option+A. Figure 10.8 shows the Automation Preferences window.

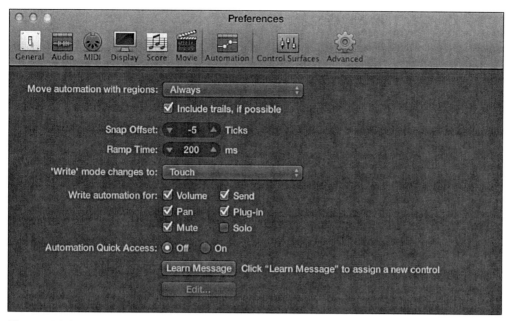

Figure 10.8 The Automation Preferences window.
© Apple Inc.

The Move Automation with Regions menu gives you three options: Never, Always, and Ask. If you select Never, Logic will not move any associated automation data when you move a region. If you select Always, Logic will always move all associated automation data when you move a region. If you select Ask, then Logic will open a dialog box asking whether you would like to move the automation data with the region. It is generally best to select Ask because this gives you the power to choose what happens to automation data on a per-case basis.

Snapping Automation

If you want to snap automation points to a grid, you can select Snap Automation to Absolute Values from the Snap menu in the main window, shown in Figure 10.9.

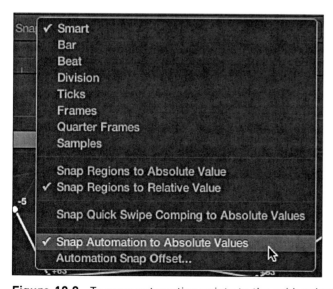

Figure 10.9 To snap automation points to the grid, select Snap Automation to Absolute Values from the Snap menu in the main window.
© Apple Inc.

You can offset the placement of points created with Snap Automation to Absolute Values enabled by changing the Snap Offset value in the Automation Preferences window (refer to Figure 10.8). Changing the Snap Offset value will automatically offset the snap position of newly created points by the defined number of ticks.

Deleting and Converting Automation Data

Eventually, you may find yourself wanting to completely rid a track of all the automation for a given parameter you have recorded and start over. Perhaps you want to attach your track-based automation to a track's regions, or maybe you want to convert MIDI control information into TA. Luckily, Logic allows you to delete automation and convert between RA and TA easily.

THE MIX > DELETE AUTOMATION SUBMENU

The Mix > Delete Automation submenu, shown in Figure 10.10 gives you options for deleting automation data.

Figure 10.10 The Mix > Delete Automation submenu.
© Apple Inc.

Here is a brief description of these commands:

▷ **Delete Visible Automation on Selected Track:** This command erases all the automation data on the selected track for the parameter in the Parameter Display. The key command is Control+Command+Delete.

▷ **Delete All Automation on Selected Track:** This command erases all automation data on the selected track. The key command is Control+Shift+Command+Delete.

▷ **Delete Orphaned Automation on Selected Track:** This command erases all orphaned automation data from the selected track. The key command for this is Control+Shift+Delete.

▷ **Delete Redundant Automation Points:** Selecting this command removes any redundant points. For example, suppose you are automating the volume of a track and you have created a few points in a row that share the same value. Using the Delete Redundant Automation Points command will remove all but the first and last of these points. The key command for this is Control+Delete.

▷ **Delete All Automation:** This command erases all automation data on all tracks.

THE MIX > CONVERT AUTOMATION SUBMENU

You can find the basic commands to convert automation data by choosing the Mix > Convert Automation submenu, shown in Figure 10.11.

Figure 10.11 The Mix > Convert Automation submenu.
© Apple Inc.

Here is a brief description of these commands:

▷ **Convert Visible MIDI Draw to Track Automation:** This command converts the MIDI Draw information currently displayed into TA data. When you use this command, TA data in the automation lane replaces the MIDI Draw display inside your region. The key command is Control+Command+Up Arrow.

▷ **Convert Visible Track Automation to MIDI Draw:** You can convert your currently displayed TA data to MIDI Draw with this command. When you use this command, your TA data turns into MIDI Draw information that is part of the region. The key command is Control+Command+Down Arrow.

▷ **Convert All MIDI Draw to Track Automation:** This command converts all of a region's MIDI Draw information into TA data. When using this command, TA data in the automation lane replaces the MIDI Draw display inside your region. The key command is Control+Shift+Command+Up Arrow.

▷ **Convert All Track Automation to MIDI Draw:** You can convert all your current TA data to MIDI Draw with this command. When you use this command, your TA data turns into MIDI Draw information that is part of the region. Because MIDI Draw is MIDI data, keep in mind you'll need a MIDI region under the TA for this to work. (For audio tracks, you can always create a MIDI region on an external MIDI or software instrument track, then move it under the TA with your mouse.) The key command is Control+Shift+Command+Down Arrow.

Automation Quick Access

Sometimes, you may want to record a single parameter live to track automation as part of a MIDI performance. For example, say you want to perform a synthesizer track, but you want to record your pitch shifting as TA instead of as MIDI Draw information. You can, of course, record the information as normal MIDI and then convert it to TA using one of the commands discussed previously, but Logic offers you an even more elegant shortcut: Automation Quick Access. This feature allows you to use any single hardware controller able to send MIDI data to write track-based automation data. Automation Quick Access is very easy to set up, thanks to Logic's very intuitive Learn function.

To configure and engage Automation Quick Access, open the Automation Preferences dialog box that contains the Automation Quick Access controls shown in Figure 10.12. To do so, choose Mix > Automation Preferences or press Control+Option+Command+A. You can, of course, also access this window via the Automation Preferences window.

Figure 10.12 The Automation Preferences window contains the options to configure Automation Quick Access.
© Apple Inc.

You'll immediately notice that the bottom of the Automation Preferences window consists of settings for Automation Quick Access. All you need to do is click the large Learn Message button at the bottom of the window. As soon as you engage this button, Logic is ready to "learn" the specifications of the controller you want to use as your Automation Quick Access control. The text to the right of the button reads, "Slowly move/turn the control up and down you want to assign." In other words, simply take hold of the control you want to assign, slowly adjust the control to its maximum value, and then adjust the control to its minimum value.

That's it! Click Done, and you're ready to use your control to input TA data. You can now engage or disengage Automation Quick Access by selecting Mix > Enable Automation Quick Access or by pressing Control+Option+Command+A.

Mixing in Logic

11

WHENEVER YOU HAVE MORE THAN ONE TRACK IN YOUR DAW, you will have to mix together the different tracks so you can hear all the various tracks out of the same set of speakers or headphones. The simplest form of mixing is when you sum (in other words, add the different audio streams of) all your audio to the same outputs so all your different tracks play from the same speakers. For example, you could take a song with material on 16 different audio channels and combine them into a single stereo output so you can listen to all 16 channels through your stereo monitors. After you do this, your audio will have been mixed together. However, mixing music is far more of an art than simply that. You can adjust the volume and position of your audio in a stereo or surround panorama for each track. You can process your tracks through effects individually or in groups. You can process the song as a whole through effects. And, of course, you can *bounce*—or print—the mix to a single audio file.

Logic offers some of the most comprehensive and intuitive options and features for mixing that are available in the digital realm. Logic can build a mixer for you from the tracks you have in your main window, or you can build your own mixer in the Environment. You can route your audio directly to your outputs or use myriad creative methods to group tracks for mixing and processing. You can insert effects directly into a given audio track, send your audio to other channels for processing, or change the output of your tracks to group them with others for processing. You can bounce your audio down to a file in real time so you can hear exactly what is going into the file, or you can bounce the audio offline when you know exactly what you have and you don't need to hear it again. Logic does all this using channel strips that offer you a complete view of each track's settings at a glance.

This chapter will not teach you how to create a professional radio-ready mix of your music. It will, however, explain how you can use Logic to achieve the best mix you can and offer some techniques for using Logic to mix in creative and exciting ways.

Mixer or Mixer Layer?

As discussed, channel strip objects in Logic show a complete channel strip reminiscent of a hardware mixer channel strip. Logic gives you two options for how you can arrange these channel strips. The first is to allow Logic to put together your mixer for you. As mentioned in Chapter 3, "The Logic Project," Logic creates a mixer, called—wait for it—the *Mixer*, based on the tracks you have in the main window. The other way you can create a mixer is to do so manually, by adding your own channel strip objects to the Mixer layer of the Environment window and organizing them yourself. Each method has its advantages and disadvantages, and they are not mutually exclusive; because any channel strips in the Mixer represent channel strip objects in the Environment, both mixers coexist in the same project. You may prefer to access either or both, depending on your workflow and the specific project on which you are working. The specific features of each mixer are described in this section.

The Mixer

The Mixer is a very powerful tool in Logic. Not only does it reflect all of the MIDI and audio tracks you have in the main window, but it automatically reflects all channel strip objects in your project that you have created in the Environment. You can access the Mixer from the Window global menu by selecting Window > Open Mixer or by pressing the key command Command+2. You can also open it inside the main window by pressing X. Figure 11.1 shows the Mixer window.

Figure 11.1 The Mixer reflects all the tracks you have in your project.
© Apple Inc.

One of the best features of the Mixer is that Logic automatically configures it for you. There is no setup at all to do. As you add tracks to the main window, the Mixer automatically reconfigures, too. Also, the Mixer is the only mixer screen that shows MIDI channel strips, so if you use a fair number of MIDI tracks, the Mixer allows you to see channel strips for your MIDI tracks alongside your audio channel strips.

You can use the channel strip Filter buttons at the top of the Mixer to filter the types of channel strips in the Mixer (omit the audio tracks, instruments, outputs, MIDI tracks, and so on). You can also use the Single, Arrange, and All View buttons to change your view in the Mixer.

The Mixer's biggest weakness is that it is limited to only a single horizontal row of channel strips. You could, however, open multiple Mixers, each set to a different channel strip type, and arrange them as you see fit. Also, if you want to rearrange the order of tracks in the Mixer, you'll need to reorganize the tracks in the Tracks area.

The Mixer Layer of the Environment

You can create channel strip objects in the Environment. By simply adding multiple channel strip objects in the Environment window, you can create your own custom-configured Environment Mixer layer. The Layer menu includes a command to open the Mixer layer; this command opens an Environment window to the Mixer layer of the Environment. Normally, this is where Logic keeps all your channel strip objects, but if you create your own Mixer on a new layer, the Mixer Layer command will not open your custom mixer. The Mixer layer in the Environment can have any shape you want and can include as many or as few channel strip objects in any given layer as you want (with the caveat, of course, that all the tracks in your song will have objects created for them on some Environment layer). Figure 11.2 shows the Mixer layer of the Environment for the same project as in Figure 11.1.

Figure 11.2 The Mixer layer of the Environment offers great flexibility but doesn't automatically adapt to the tracks in your main window like the Mixer does.
© Apple Inc.

The main advantage of building Mixers in the Environment is that you can create and organize them however you like, allowing your Mixer to reflect exactly how you want to work. The Mixer layer does not reflect your main window, however. This can create extra navigation headaches. For example, if your Mixer layer contains 64 audio track channel strips and then three software instrument channel strips, but your song uses only 16 audio tracks and two software instruments, you'll have to scroll from audio track 16 through 48 empty audio tracks to your three software instruments—or continually create Mixer layers reflecting what your song looks like. By contrast, the Mixer can be filtered to contain only your 16 audio tracks, so you'll have no extra tracks to navigate. On the other hand, in the Mixer layer, you can instantly rearrange any of the objects, so you can simply move your Mixer around or open new layers for different channel strip objects. Of course, because the Mixer layer contains only channel strip objects, it does not show you any of the external MIDI tracks in your Tracks area. The Environment channel strips also lack certain features available in Mixer channel strips, like access to MIDI FX on software instrument channel strips and the Compressor/Limiter Gain Reduction meter, which you'll learn about later in this chapter.

Adding Input Channel Strips

Although most audio tracks can be added to your Logic project in the main window, input channel strips still need to be added in the Environment. In the Mixer layer of the Environment, open the New local menu and choose Channel Strip > Input. A new input channel strip object will be created in the Mixer layer.

You can add as many mono input channel strips as your audio interface has inputs. If you change an input channel strip's format to stereo, it will use two of your audio interface's hardware inputs. Therefore, if your audio interface has eight inputs, you could have eight mono input channel strips in Logic, four stereo input channel strips, or any other combination of stereo and mono input channel strips that does not exceed your audio interface's eight total hardware inputs.

What's in a Name?: Although Logic Pro is full of many great features that have simplified previously tedious and confusing tasks, possible new sources of confusion are the names *Mixer* and *Mixer layer*.

In earlier versions of Logic, the Mixer was known as the *Track Mixer*, and it reflected only what was in the Arrange window (now called the main window). The Mixer layer of the Environment was known as the *Audio Mixer*, and it was where you needed to create and configure your audio objects (now known as channel strip objects), which you could then transform into the kind of customized workspace for which Logic is famous. The problem back then was that you needed to add all your audio objects to the Arrange window to have access to them in the Track Mixer, and you didn't have access to MIDI tracks in the Audio Mixer.

Now, in addition to the ability to quickly and easily create any type of track in the main window and have that reflected in the Mixer, the Mixer also automatically reflects anything you add to the Mixer layer of the Environment. The Mixer layer, on the other hand, is still crippled by its inability to incorporate external MIDI tracks, among other things. That means the Mixer will be your preferred mixer in Logic, with the Environment's Mixer layer being reserved for special customization and incorporation of Environment widgets.

The problem is keeping track of which Mixer is which. Unless I state that something is to be done in "the Mixer layer of the Environment" or in some way refer specifically to "the Mixer layer," then "the Mixer" refers to the Mixer that opens in its own window or inside the main window, with its own local menus.

The Mixer Local Menus

Like all windows in Logic, the Mixer includes its own local menus with commands specific to itself. The following sections describe the Mixer local menus and their options.

The Edit Menu

The Mixer Edit menu contains the typical Edit menu commands, but it does add a few Mixer-specific commands, which you can see in Figure 11.3.

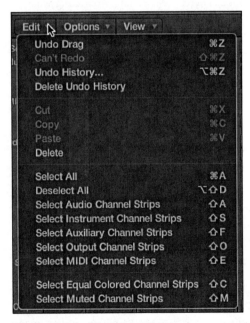

Figure 11.3 The Mixer Edit menu.
© Apple Inc.

The unique Mixer Edit commands are pretty self-explanatory, offering commands for the selection of specific channel strip types, such as Select Audio Channel Strips, and two other commands for selecting particular groups of channel strips:

▷ **Select Equal Colored Channel Strips:** This selects all channel strips of the same color as the currently selected channel strip. The key command for this is Shift+C. You can assign colors to your channel strips by opening the Colors window (the global View > Show Colors path, or Option+C), selecting a channel strip, and clicking on a color. This also updates the associated track color in the Tracks area.

▷ **Select Muted Channel Strips:** This selects all muted channel strips. The key command for this is Shift+M.

The Options Menu

The Options menu consists of a few miscellaneous functions you may want to use. Figure 11.4 shows the Options menu of the Mixer.

Figure 11.4 The Options menu of the Mixer.
© Apple Inc.

Here are brief descriptions of these functions:

▷ **Create New Auxiliary Channel Strip:** This command creates a new auxiliary channel strip. The key command for this is Control+N.

▷ **Create Tracks for Selected Channel Strips:** This command adds any selected Mixer channel strips to the Tracks area. For example, you can use this command to add aux tracks to the Tracks area from aux channel strips in the Mixer. The key command for this is Control+T.

▷ **Send All MIDI Mixer Data:** This command sends all the Mixer-related information that is on MIDI tracks to your MIDI devices.

▷ **Enable/Disable Groups:** This command allows you to temporarily disable groups and reenable them. Groups are covered in detail in the section "Mixer Groups" later in this chapter. The key command for this is Shift+G.

▷ **Change Track in Record Mode:** If you select this option, changing a setting on any channel strip while recording automatically selects that track. If you keep this option deselected, you can change the settings on any channel strip during recording without changing the track that is selected.

▷ **Change Track in Play Mode:** If you select this option, changing a setting on any channel strip during playback automatically selects that track. If you keep this option deselected, you can change the settings on any channel strip during playback without changing the track that is selected.

▷ **I/O Labels.** This command opens the I/O Labels window, shown in Figure 11.5. In this window, you can assign names to your inputs, outputs, and buses, which can be provided by Logic (channel), your driver, or you. Double-clicking in the Long and Short columns allows you to assign long and short user I/O labels. The Reset menu gives you options to reset all the labels or to reset them by specific channel type: input, output, or bus. Note that these labels are a global setting and will apply across all projects. You can also access this window by selecting Mix > I/O Labels.

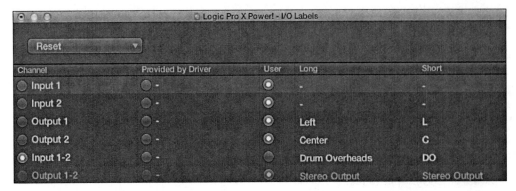

Figure 11.5 The I/O Labels window.
© Apple Inc.

> **NOTE:** The Mix menu was discussed in Chapter 10, "Using Automation in Logic." Mix menu commands that were not covered in Chapter 10 will be covered later in this chapter.

The View Menu

The View menu offers a number of options that relate to MIDI tracks and the overall look of the Mixer. Figure 11.6 shows you the View menu.

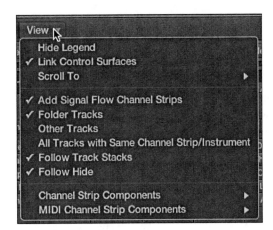

Figure 11.6 The View menu of the Mixer.
© Apple Inc.

The various options in the View menu are as follows:

> **Show/Hide Legend:** This command lets you toggle the Mixer's legend, which can be seen at the far left of the Mixer in Figure 11.1.

> **Link Control Surfaces:** If you have a hardware control surface connected to Logic, selecting this option ensures that the track selected in the Mixer always reflects the channel you have selected on your control surface.

> **Scroll To:** This submenu includes options that allow you to jump to various track types in your Mixer. It includes the same group of track types as the channel strip filter buttons. These navigation options can be very useful if you have a large Mixer and you keep your track types organized together. If your Mixer is small or you mix up your track varieties, you most likely will not use these options. You can also assign key commands for these options, with which you can navigate among the track varieties even more quickly.

> **Add Signal Flow Channel Strips:** Selecting this option allows you to see the entire signal flow of channel strips, of a selected channel strip in Single view, or of all Tracks area channel strips in Tracks view.

▷ **Folder Tracks:** Select this option if you want folder tracks to get channel strips in the Mixer. Deselect this option if you do not.

▷ **Other Tracks:** Select this option if you want other types of tracks that do not have any mixing options, such as a No Output track, to get channel strips in the Mixer.

▷ **All Tracks with Same Channel Strip/Instrument:** If selected, this option gives you a separate channel strip in your Mixer for each track that accesses the same object. With this option deselected, if more than one track is assigned to the same object, you will see only a single channel strip for that instrument in the Mixer.

▷ **Follow Track Stacks:** When in Tracks view, the Follow Track Stacks command toggles the display of the channel strips of the dependent tracks in Track Stacks based on whether the dependent tracks are shown or collapsed per the disclosure triangle in the track master header.

▷ **Follow Hide:** When in Tracks view, selecting Follow Hide toggles the display of tracks that are hidden or unhidden in the Tracks area.

▷ **Channel Strip Components:** This submenu, shown in Figure 11.7 gives you control over exactly what components of your channel strip are shown in the Mixer. In the descriptions of the options in this submenu, any option that deals with an audio channel strip also applies to aux, bus, input, and output channel strips. The Channel Strip Components submenu options are as follows:

  ▷ **Type and Number Label:** If this option is selected, the Mixer displays the channel strip type and number at the top of your channel strips.

  ▷ **Setting Menu:** If this option is selected, the Mixer displays the Setting menu near the top of each audio/software instrument channel strip in the Mixer.

  ▷ **Gain Reduction Meter:** If this option is selected, the Mixer displays Gain Reduction meters in each audio/software instrument channel strip.

  ▷ **EQ Thumbnails:** If this option is selected, the Mixer displays the channel EQ thumbnail of each audio/software instrument channel strip.

  ▷ **MIDI Effects:** If this option is selected, the Mixer displays the MIDI FX of each software instrument channel strip.

  ▷ **Input/Instrument:** If this option is selected, the Mixer displays the input/instrument of each audio/software instrument channel strip, respectively. Be aware that the left side of the Input field for any audio, aux, or output channel strip contains the Format button for that channel strip, which lets you change the format of the channel strip—mono, stereo, or surround. Hiding the Input/Instrument slots also hides the Format buttons.

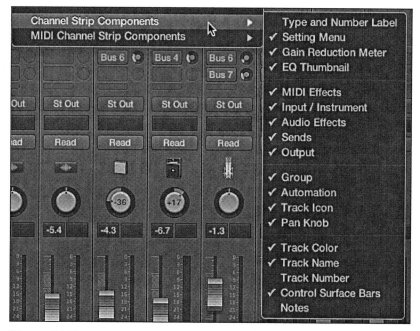

Figure 11.7 The Channel Strip Components submenu.
© Apple Inc.

▷ **Audio FX:** If this option is selected, the Mixer displays the Audio FX of each audio/software instrument channel strip.

▷ **Sends:** If this option is selected, the Mixer displays the sends of each audio channel strip.

▷ **Output:** If this option is selected, the Mixer displays the output of each audio/software instrument channel strip.

▷ **Group:** If this option is selected, the Mixer displays the group of each channel strip.

▷ **Automation:** If this option is selected, the Mixer displays the automation mode of each channel strip.

▷ **Track Icon:** If this option is selected, the Mixer displays the track icon of each channel strip.

▷ **Pan Knob:** If this option is selected, the Mixer displays the Pan knob of each channel strip.

▷ **Track Color:** If this option is selected, the Mixer displays the track colors for each channel strip.

▷ **Track Name:** If this option is selected, the Mixer displays the track name of each channel strip.

▷ **Track Number:** If this option is selected, the Mixer displays the track number of each channel strip.

▷ **Control Surface Bars:** If this option is selected, the Mixer displays which channel strips are being controlled by your control surface.

▷ **Notes:** If this option is selected, the Mixer displays a Track Notes field under each channel strip. You can double-click on a Track Notes field to create or edit a note; those changes will be reflected in the parent track's notes.

▷ **MIDI Channel Strip Components:** This submenu allows you to select or deselect individual components in the MIDI track. You can toggle the Instrument Name, Program, Bank, and Assign 1–5 controls for MIDI track strips by selecting or deselecting the relevant components.

Mixer Buttons

The Mixer has a number of buttons alongside the local menus. Figure 11.8 shows the Mixer buttons.

Figure 11.8 The Mixer buttons.
© Apple Inc.

The Mixer buttons, from left to right, are as follows:

▷ **Hierarchy:** Clicking the Hierarchy button, found at the left end of Figure 11.8, moves you up a level in your project's hierarchy when working with folder tracks.

▷ **Mixer View buttons:** The Mixer View buttons allow you three different Mixer display options. You can also use the Cycle through Mixer Views key command, Shift+X. The buttons are as follows:

  ▷ **Single:** This button displays the selected Tracks area track's channel strip, as well as the signal flow of the selected track.

  ▷ **Tracks:** This button displays the channel strips of all Tracks area tracks. If you have selected the Add Signal Flow Channel Strips option, then all the other channel strips that the Tracks area tracks used will also be displayed.

  ▷ **All:** This button displays all the channel strips in your project.

▷ **Mixer Filter buttons:** The Mixer Filter buttons allow you to toggle the display of specific channel strip types. You can toggle audio, software instrument (Inst.), aux, bus, input, output, master, and MIDI channel strips independently using these buttons. If you think you'll use these filters often, remember to assign them their own key commands.

▷ **Channel Strip Size buttons:** The Channel Strip Size buttons, shown at the right end of Figure 11.8, offer two channel strip sizes: Narrow (left button) and Wide (right button). Narrow channel strips offer the ability to fit more channel strips onscreen. Wide channel strips make it much easier to read things like audio FX names, track names, and track notes.

Recording Audio from the Mixer

NOTE: Throughout the rest of this chapter, everything discussed applies to either the Mixer or the Mixer layer.

You may choose to set up your audio recordings directly from the Mixer. This process consists of two steps.

The first step is to select the physical input(s) on your audio interface that you want to use from the Input box of your channel strip. When you click and hold the box, a menu of all available inputs will appear (see Figure 11.9). From this menu, select the input you want to use.

Figure 11.9 From the Input menu, choose the hardware input you want to use for this track.
© Apple Inc.

Next, click the R button at the bottom of the channel strip. The R button flashes red, as you can somewhat discern from Figure 11.10. This indicates that when you click Record on the Transport, the track will record audio.

Figure 11.10 When you click the R button at the bottom of an audio track channel strip, it flashes red to indicate that the channel is now armed for recording.
© Apple Inc.

Repeat the preceding two steps for each track on which you want to record audio, remembering that only one track per input can be armed at any given time. After that, just click the Record button on the Transport (via mouse, hardware controller, or key command) and record away!

Basic Mixing: Summing Volume and Panorama

The most basic mixing that you'll want to do is simply to adjust the volume of one track in comparison to another and to place tracks at different points across the stereo field, or panorama. If this is all you'll ever want to use the Logic's Mixer for, then this section will tell you all you'll ever need to do to mix in Logic.

Volume Summing

Because each individual track is usually recorded with an ear toward getting the best recording of that specific source material, you almost never will initially record your tracks at the perfect level in relation to each other. This is why, since the beginning of recorded music, engineers have brought the level of one track up in a mix, while perhaps bringing another track down. The result is creating the perfect balance among all the various sounds in the mix.

You adjust the volume of a channel by moving the onscreen Volume fader on its channel strip. If you are using a mouse, you'll generally be able to adjust only one fader at a time, but if you have a hardware control surface, you may be able to adjust many faders at once. The numbers inside the fader represent either how many decibels you have added or subtracted from the initial volume of the track or the current MIDI volume, from 0 to 127. Figure 11.11 shows a Mixer in which the Volume faders have been adjusted to different levels to create a pleasing overall volume balance.

Figure 11.11 Mixing the volume of your tracks is as easy as sliding the Volume faders with your mouse or controller. You can also adjust the volume numerically.
© Apple Inc.

Option-clicking a Volume fader sets it to its null value, or the center point at which no adjustment is made. This is 0 dB for decibel faders and 100 dB for MIDI data faders. Clicking the number field in a fader allows you to enter a volume value numerically. Note that you will generally want to enter a negative value if you are entering a Volume setting manually.

Remember, if you have customized your Transport to include the Pre-Fader button, and you have pre-fader metering engaged, you'll only see the input values of your track in the meter and not the impact of the Volume fader on the track's level.

Panning

The other basic mixing technique you'll find yourself wanting to do is placing tracks at different spots in the stereo panorama. This is known as panning. Panning can make tracks more distinct by placing them in a stereo location in which there is no other sound competing for the space. The technique can make mixes come alive by making the material sound as if it is coming from all over the stereo spectrum instead of having all sounds originating from the exact middle of the listening field. The Pan knob is above the Volume number fields, and you can adjust the pan value for any track by moving the knob to the right or left with either your mouse or a hardware control surface. Pan values range from −64 (full left) to +64 (full right), with 0 being the exact middle. Figure 11.12 shows a pair of tracks that have been panned differently to enhance the mix.

Figure 11.12 To adjust the pan of a track, rotate its Pan knob to the desired setting. You can also enter a pan value numerically.
© Apple Inc.

You can double-click the Pan knob to enter a pan value numerically, and Option-clicking on the Pan knob returns the pan value to the center. Keep in mind that you can automate these volume and pan settings as explained in the previous chapter so that your mix can be dynamic, with automatic changes happening exactly on cue.

The Direction Mixer Plug-In

If you adjust the Pan knob on a stereo track, you aren't really panning the signal between left and right, because the stereo signal already exists in both channels. Instead, you are adjusting the balance between the two channels. Sometimes this can work like panning, but sometimes it won't. If you want more control over the track's stereo panorama, check out Logic Pro's built-in Direction Mixer effect, found in the Imaging submenu of an Audio FX slot. You can see the Direction Mixer interface in Figure 11.13.

Figure 11.13 The Direction Mixer effect.
© Apple Inc.

The Direction Mixer will allow you to not only adjust the balance of the signal, but also adjust the width of the stereo image and its location between the two channels. To apply this effect to a stereo signal, select LR as the input. You can then change the perceived width of the stereo signal with the Spread control and the perceived location of the signal with the Direction knob. You can also double-click in either parameter's numerical display to enter a value directly.

This effect is also designed to decode mid-side audio recordings. To decode mid-side recordings with the Direction Mixer, select MS as your input. If you're wondering what mid-side recording is, you probably shouldn't select MS as your input, but the short answer is that mid-side configuration refers to a method for setting up two microphones, one with a figure-eight pattern and another with a cardioid pattern, to accurately record space and depth—but the resulting tracks need to be decoded in order to be used effectively. You can find a discussion of this and other multiple microphone techniques in *Getting Great Sounds: The Microphone Book* by Tom Lubin (Course Technology PTR, 2008).

The Binaural Panner

The Binaural Panner is a very powerful, very flexible stereo imaging tool. It adds spatial directional clues to your audio, giving your source a depth or presence in a mix that a typical pan control can't achieve. To add a Binaural Panner to a mono or stereo channel strip, click on the channel strip's Output box and select Binaural. The Pan knob will be replaced with the Binaural Pan control shown in Figure 11.14. Double-clicking on the Binaural Pan control opens the Binaural Panner window, shown in Figure 11.15.

Figure 11.14 Selecting the Binaural option in a channel strip's Output box replaces the typical Pan knob with the Binaural Pan control.
© Apple Inc.

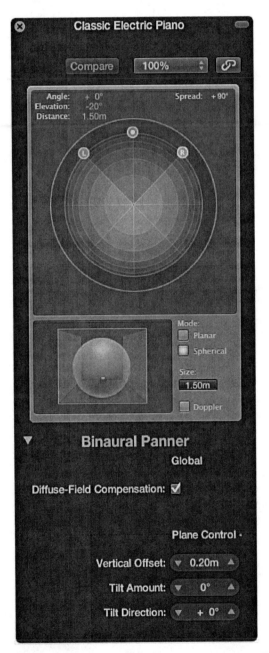

Figure 11.15 The Binaural Panner window. Double-clicking the Binaural Pan control opens this plug-in–style window.
© Apple Inc.

You can drag the L or R dots to change the width of the stereo image. The middle circle determines the perceived direction and distance from which the sound will come. If you hold the Command key while dragging the blue dot, you can change the position of your audio while maintaining the same distance. Holding Option+Command while dragging the L or R dot locks the angle so you can tweak the distance.

The Binaural Panner has two modes: Planar and Spherical. Selecting Planar limits the motion of the controls to a plane. The Extended Parameters area of the Binaural Panner interface gives you three Planar mode controls: Vertical Offset, Tilt Amount, and Tilt Direction. These parameters give you control over orientation of the circular plane relative to the listener. Spherical mode, which you can see in Figure 11.15, allows you to simulate the positioning of sound in space.

The Size parameter defines the maximum size of the plane or sphere that the Binaural Panner will allow. The Doppler parameter simulates the pitch shifting that a listener experiences as his distance from a source changes, known as the Doppler effect. The Diffuse Field Compensation parameter in the Extended Parameters region delivers a more neutral sound to the listener.

The Binaural Panner's effect is most obvious when listening through headphones. That said, the power of the effect is such that you might be tempted to try it on a number of tracks through your studio monitors. To get the most out of the Binaural Panner, send all the channels strips you have set to Binaural through the same aux or output channel strip. In an Audio FX slot of the destination channel strip, instantiate the Binaural Post-Processing plug-in, found in the Imaging submenu and shown in Figure 11.16.

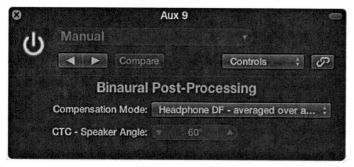

Figure 11.16 The Binaural Post-Processing plug-in.
© Apple Inc.

Set the Compensation mode to Speaker CTC–Cross Talk Cancellation. Then, set the CTC–Speaker Angle parameter to match the angle at which you have your studio monitors.

When using the Binaural Post-Processing plug-in, turn off the Diffuse Field parameter in all of your Binaural Panners. The Binaural Post-Processing plug-in will handle this operation for all of your Binaural Panner channels, freeing up CPU power.

Busing Tracks in Logic

When you play back your audio material in Logic, the most direct signal path your audio can follow for you to hear it is for the source audio channel strip to output its audio directly to the output channel strip connected to your hardware. Logic offers you more signal path options than this, however. As discussed in Chapter 7, "Working with Audio and Apple Loops," these are basically parallel mixers that allow you to send a portion of your signal to another channel strip or to output a track into another Mixer channel strip for further grouping and processing instead of having to output that track directly to your hardware.

Using Aux Channel Strips

Aux channel strips are perhaps the most powerful and flexible channel strips in the Mixer. Clicking the Input box of an aux channel strip opens the Input menu for the aux channel strip, as shown in Figure 11.17. Notice that the aux channel strip can accept a hardware input, a bus, a ReWire output, or a multichannel output from a software instrument. Using an aux channel strip for multi-output software instruments and ReWire outputs was discussed in Chapter 9, "Working with Software Instruments." The next two sections address using aux channel strips with live inputs and bus inputs.

Figure 11.17 When you click on the Input box of an aux channel strip, you access its Input menu.
© Apple Inc.

Using Aux Channel Strips with Live Inputs

Sometimes you may want to record some audio without effects but hear your source audio with some effects on it while recording. One way to do this is to set up an aux channel strip with a live input as its input source. This allows you to use an aux channel strip as a true auxiliary mixer in which one set of audio goes to your hard disk and another goes to the speakers or headphones.

To use an aux channel strip this way, select one of your live inputs as the input for the aux channel strip. As soon as the source starts to play, you will hear the audio through the aux channel strip, as well as any audio track or input channel strip through which the audio is routed. Figure 11.18 shows an example of a setup with both an audio track and an aux channel strip using the same input for a source.

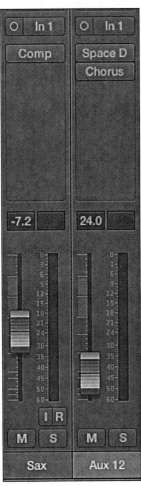

Figure 11.18 Here, an audio track will record using audio hardware interface input 1, while an aux channel is also getting its input from input 1. The aux channel is being used to add chorus and reverb effects.
© Apple Inc.

Such a setup is particularly useful when you have software monitoring turned off so that Logic is not monitoring the actual track doing the recording, and only the aux channel strip is playing back the source material during recording. This is also very useful if your vocalist likes to hear some effects while recording—for example, a bit of reverb or chorus—that are separate from whatever effects you're actually tweaking on the vocal track's audio channel strip. By setting up an aux track with effects, the vocalist will hear the performance through the aux with effects, but Logic will record the performance on the audio track without effects.

Using Aux Channel Strips with Buses

Often, you might want to assign a group of channels to a bus so you can use an aux channel strip to process all the tracks together and serve as a master fader for the group without using a Track Stack. In other words, say your song has 24 tracks of drums (a full drum kit, miked using 12 microphones), plus audio recorded directly through your audio interface without miking, plus software instruments. In addition to having individual controls for each track, you may want a master fader for a group of them, or to apply effects to all the channels once (such as putting them all through the same reverb to put the entire band in the same "room"). Logic allows you to set up an aux channel strip to serve this purpose by using its buses as a virtual patch bay between your source channels and the aux channel strip.

To do this, first you need to set the output setting of your source channels to a bus. Then set the input of your aux channel strip to the same bus to which you have set the output of the source channels. Figure 11.19 shows a simple setup in which two tracks are using an aux track as their bus destination.

Figure 11.19 The two channel strips on the left are software instrument tracks with their outputs set to bus 10. The channel strip on the right is an aux channel strip with its input set to bus 10. The aux channel strip can now be used as a master fader for the two source tracks, and effects can be added to both tracks via the aux.
© Apple Inc.

If you end up using aux channel strips as master group faders, as in Figure 11.19, I highly recommend you use aux channel strips as described here. Having the option to use sends on your master group fader is definitely worth it!

It's also important to note that multiple aux channel strips can use the same bus as an input and that any aux can be bused to another aux. That means you can create some complex and creative routings, all automated in the main window, if you desire!

Using a Send to Feed an Aux Channel Strip

If you want to use a send to feed audio to an aux channel strip, simply click and hold a Send box, and a menu of all your available buses will appear. Select the bus you want and turn the Send knob to send to the bus the amount of audio you want. You then assign the destination aux channel strip's input to the desired bus. Figure 11.20 shows the menu of a Send box with all the buses available for you to choose.

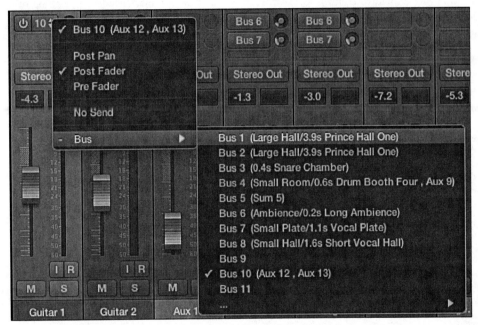

Figure 11.20 To send audio to an aux channel strip using a send, simply select the bus you want from the Send menu and then adjust the Send knob to send the desired amount of signal to the bus. Assign the input of an aux channel strip to the send's bus.
© Apple Inc.

The Send menu includes Post Fader, Pre Fader, and Post Pan options. If you select Post Fader, Logic feeds your audio through the send *after* the Volume fader has adjusted its level. If you select Pre Fader, Logic feeds the audio through the send *before* the fader adjusts the volume of the channel. If you select Post Pan, Logic feeds your audio through the send *after* both the Volume fader and the Panorama knob have been adjusted. To turn off a send, you can click on its power button. Your Send box will stop glowing blue, indicating that it is turned off. It still retains the bus you chose for it, so clicking the power button again will reengage it.

Busing audio to sends is especially useful when you want to use time- and modulation-based effects, such as delay, chorus, and reverb, to process your audio. Because you rarely want to process all your audio using these effects, you can insert the effect into the audio FX box of an aux channel strip and send a variable amount of your audio to that aux channel strip, adjusting the Send knob until you get just the right balance for your music. Figure 11.21 shows a Drummer track using a send to add a reverb that is inserted in an aux channel strip. Inserting effects in an Audio FX slot is discussed in more detail later in this chapter.

Figure 11.21 The channel strip on the left is for a Drummer track. The Drummer channel strip is using a send to feed the second channel strip, which is an aux channel strip in which Logic's built-in Space Designer impulse response reverb is instantiated. By adjusting the Send knob on the Drummer channel strip, you can control how much reverb is added to the Drummer audio.
© Apple Inc.

Output Channel Strips

Output channel strips are the final destination for your audio. They connect directly to your hardware audio interface. You can have as many output channel strips as you have physical outputs on your audio hardware. Output channel strips have Audio FX slots for effects but no sends. This is because output channel strips portion out audio to hardware, not to additional processing channels within Logic. Output channel strips also don't have Input boxes, as they are destinations for any audio that they receive. These objects include the Bounce button (labeled "Bnc" or "Bnce" depending on your channel strip width setting), which allows you to sum all the audio going to that output channel strip into a file on your hard disk.

Usually, a song has only a single output channel strip, which represents the hardware output that leads to your speaker system. Figure 11.22 shows an output channel strip for the main outputs to the audio hardware.

Figure 11.22 This output channel strip is hardwired to the main stereo outputs for the hardware interface used with this project.
© Apple Inc.

Sometimes you might want to use more than the main output channel strip. If you are mixing surround audio, for example, you may need 6–12 outputs, each sending to a discrete input on a hardware surround encoder. Perhaps you are not doing all your mixing in Logic, but sending tracks from Logic into a large studio mixing console. Or maybe you are sending out various tracks to various hardware processors and bringing the audio back into Logic for mixing. Whatever your use, you will use output channel strips to interface Logic with your audio hardware.

Using Effects

Mixing is not simply a matter of bringing together multiple source signals. Sometimes, you'll want to process them as well. You can process audio in all sorts of ways. You can compress and distort audio; add EQ, delays, modulation, and reverb; link a track to external hardware for additional processing; and more. In traditional hardware studios, you need to cable an audio channel to a hardware effects processor to process a channel with effects. Just as software sequencers feature software mixers, they also feature software effects.

Effects in Logic generally have their own graphic editor that displays the parameters of the effect and often some visual representation of the current effect settings. This is called the Editor view. Figure 11.23 shows the Editor view of a Logic effect.

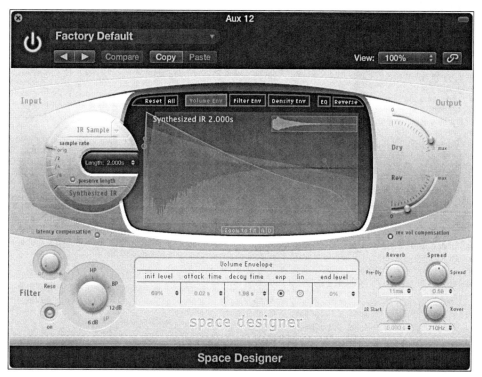

Figure 11.23 This is the graphic control window of Logic's built-in reverb effect, Space Designer. Not only are the parameters given graphic controls, but the impulse response audio file and volume envelope are represented graphically, too.
© Apple Inc.

Notice that the plug-in window for effects has the same controls already discussed in Chapter 9 regarding software instruments. The menus and functions are identical in their operation, and the windows are fully resizable. You will most often want to work with your effects in Editor view because this is where you get the most pleasing user experience, as well as graphical feedback. Sometimes, however, if you know exactly what you want and you just want to adjust a parameter numerically, or if you are working with older effects without graphics, you might want to use Controls view. As Figure 11.24 shows, when an effect is in Controls view, the controls are nothing but sliders and value fields, menus, and checkboxes for the different parameters. You still have full control over your effect. Indeed, when you are looking to enter values very specifically, you might accomplish this most quickly in Controls view, but you do not get the aesthetic experience or graphical feedback that the Editor view offers. Also, with an effect as extensive as Space Designer, you'll find yourself scrolling through a massive number of parameters looking for the one you want to tweak. This section explores using audio effects in Logic's Mixer and offers some tips and suggestions for using effects in a mix.

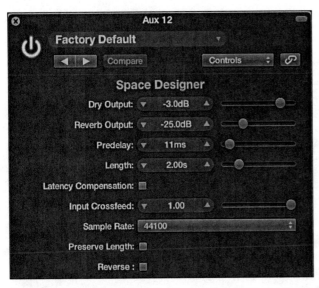

Figure 11.24 This is the section of the Controls view of the Space Designer from Figure 11.23. It displays only a slider for each parameter.
© Apple Inc.

Logic Effects

Apple ships Logic with a huge collection of professional-quality effects, which you can access from within Logic's Mixer. You will often hear Logic's effects referred to as plug-ins, since almost all other software effects are separate applications that are "plugged in" to a host digital audio sequencer, such as Logic. Logic's effects, while accessed the same way as third-party plug-ins, are in fact built into the code of the application itself, just like Logic's own softsynths. This is why you cannot access Logic's effects in other applications that allow effects plug-ins, other than in Apple's MainStage.

To access a Logic effect, click and hold on an Audio FX slot in a channel strip. A menu opens, listing the effects by type, such as Modulation, Dynamics, and Reverb. Once you select an effect type, a submenu opens, displaying the individual effects of the selected type. If the channel is mono, the menu that appears will offer you a mono effect, a mono -> stereo effect, or possibly both. If your channel is stereo, your default option is a stereo effect. You can force it to present mono effects by Option-clicking on the effect slot. Similarly, you can Option-click on a mono channel's effects slot to force it to present only stereo effects. To instantiate a Logic effect, simply choose a Logic effect from the menus offered, as shown in Figure 11.25. After you select the effect you want and release the mouse button, the effect appears in the Audio FX slot in the channel strip, and the plug-in window opens in Editor view, ready to be configured.

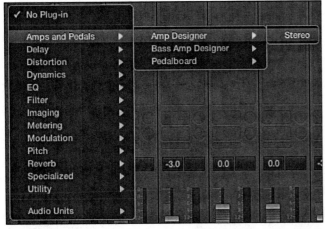

Figure 11.25 To select a Logic effect, follow the menus and select the Logic effect you desire—in this case, Amp Designer.
© Apple Inc.

Logic gives you a complete selection of all the effects you will need in modern music production, including all the standard dynamics-based effects (such as compression and limiting), time-based effects (such as delay and reverb), modulation effects (such as chorus and flange), and many unique offerings (such as Spectral Gate and Delay Designer). With 13 categories of built-in effects available, you'll find most, if not all, of what you need for effects in Logic.

As with the Input field for softsynths, Logic's Audio FX slots include power buttons to the left, a center area for accessing the plug-in window, and a menu access area to the right of the Audio FX field.

Logic Effects with Channel Strip Components

There is not enough space in this book to go over how to use each effect included with Logic Pro X. However, there are few plug-ins that interact with the channel strip differently than the others: the Channel EQ, the Linear Phase EQ, and the different Dynamics plug-ins that affect the Gain Reduction meter. These unique interactions are explained in the following sections.

Using the Channel and Linear EQ

As stated, Logic Pro X includes two professional-quality equalizer plug-ins: the Channel EQ and the Linear Phase EQ. Both are filters that can adjust the frequency response of your audio, and they look and operate identically. The main difference is that the Linear Phase EQ maintains the exact phase relationship of the frequencies of your audio material, which are altered at extremes using non-linear phase EQ algorithms. In other words, it does a better job of maintaining the integrity of your material the more intensely you apply equalization.

The price of this advanced linear phase algorithm is both increased CPU overhead and increased processing delay. Processing delay is discussed later in this chapter, in the section "Plug-In Delay and Logic's Plug-In Delay Compensation" section. The point is, you'll want to be judicious in your use of Linear Phase EQs.

If you have the EQ Thumbnails parameter turned on in the Mixer or in an audio channel strip's Inspector in the Mixer layer, the top of the channel strip has a rectangular box that displays a thumbnail representation of the current EQ curve, as in Figure 11.26. This EQ thumbnail box offers you easy access to the Channel EQ and Linear Phase EQ plug-ins and a visual reference of the current EQ curve. When the EQ thumbnail box is empty, it is just a plain gray slot like any other empty slot in a channel strip.

Figure 11.26 A channel strip's EQ thumbnail box above the Inserts parameter. This box is where you can access your Channel EQ and see the current EQ curve.
© Apple Inc.

To activate the Channel EQ, you can simply double-click inside the thumbnail box. Logic opens a plug-in window in Editor view for the Channel EQ plug-in, places a thumbnail of the grid display of the new Channel EQ in the EQ thumbnail box, and instantiates the Channel EQ plug-in into the top-most available Audio FX slot. You can force the Channel EQ to the top-most slot by Option-double-clicking on the EQ thumbnail field.

You cannot click in the box to instantiate the Linear Phase EQ, but if you add a Linear Phase EQ effect on your own, it also will show its grid in the EQ thumbnail box. As you adjust the parameters in the Channel or Linear Phase EQ, this thumbnail box reflects the EQ curve that is created in the plug-in window. This offers you a quick visual reference as to how you have EQed that channel. If you need to make an adjustment, you can double-click the EQ thumbnail box to open the Channel or Linear Phase EQ (depending which you have instantiated).

If you have multiple Linear Phase or Channel EQ effects in one track, only the top-most EQ will have its grid showing in the EQ thumbnail box.

The Gain Reduction Meters

If you have chosen to view Gain Reduction meters, all audio and software instrument channel strips will feature a small Gain Reduction meter above the EQ thumbnail box. This allows you to monitor the amount of gain reduction performed by the first

Compressor, Limiter, or Adaptive Limiter effect inserted in an Audio FX slot on a channel strip. Figure 11.27 shows a Gain Reduction meter at work.

Figure 11.27 The Gain Reduction meter lets you monitor the amount of gain reduction the first Compressor, Limiter, or Adaptive Limiter effect is performing on any track with one of these Dynamics plug-ins instantiated.
© Apple Inc.

Similar to the EQ Thumbnails area, if you double-click on an empty Gain Reduction meter, an instance of Compressor is opened by default, along with its plug-in window in Editor view. Option-double-clicking in the Gain Reduction meter slot forces the Compressor to the top effects slot. If you instantiate a Compressor, Limiter, or Adaptive Limiter effect on a channel without one of those Dynamics plug-ins already instantiated, the Gain Reduction meter for that channel strip will become active for the new Dynamics plug-in.

Effects Side Chains

Some effects, such as Logic's Compressor, Expander, and AutoFilter, as well as some third-party plug-ins, have what is called a side-chain input. A side chain is an input to an effect or plug-in that allows another audio track to trigger that effect or plug-in. You can use side chains to configure an effect to activate only when a signal from the side-chain input is present. One example of this would be to have a compressor on a bass track triggered by a kick drum on another track, so that the bass is compressed only when the kick drum appearing at the side-chain input sounds to create a tighter feel for the rhythm. Side chains are also very useful for ducking (making a signal softer when another signal is present), for vocoder effects and instruments (where an audio channel is sent into the side chain of a vocoder software instrument to "play" the vocoder), and so on. The side-chain input looks like an additional menu on the plug-in window control bar, as shown in Figure 11.28.

Figure 11.28 The side-chain input can be seen on the Compressor effect in Logic as a new menu on the far right of the control bar.
© Apple Inc.

To select a track to use as the side-chain input, simply select an available audio source from the menu, as shown in Figure 11.29. The track you choose triggers the operation of the effect.

Figure 11.29 To use one of these available tracks as the side-chain trigger, select it from the menu.
© Apple Inc.

The more audio tracks, inputs, and buses you have active, the more potential side-chain input sources you'll have. Not all plug-ins or effects have side-chain inputs, but for those that do, it opens a whole new creative way to use effects.

Using the Side-Chain Input to Rescue Lackluster Kick Drums: Producer, co-author of *Logic 7 Ignite!*, and Logic guru Don Gunn offers his expert method for how you can use the side-chain input feature to add "guts" to a kick drum performance that isn't punchy enough:

> *If you find yourself mixing a song and the kick drum just isn't providing the bottom end you'd like, there's an easy way to create low-frequency content. This tip utilizes Logic's software instruments as well as the side chain feature on the Noise Gate plug-in. With your kick drum track in the Mixer, assign an unused bus to one of the sends. Next, create a software instrument track and assign the track a software instrument of your choice for generating low tones. Any of the built-in Logic synthesizers work, but using a multi-oscillator synth, with one oscillator set to generate a sine wave, as well as a secondary sine sub-oscillator for additional fatness, works better. Now insert a Noise Gate plug-in on the Software Instrument track and assign the side-chain input to the bus that was assigned to the send on the kick drum track. If you play this track as it is currently set up, you will still only hear the original kick drum; for the instrument to produce sound, it needs a note that is affected by the incoming signal via the Noise Gate side chain. Create a note and make its length be the duration of the kick drum region that needs reinforcement. One benefit to this technique is that you can have the kick drum trigger a note that is in key with your song, helping to reinforce the notes being played by the bass part. At this point, when the song is played back, the kick drum will trigger the side chain on the Noise Gate to open, allowing the tone of the synthesizer to go to the output. Using the envelope controls in the Noise Gate (Attack, Hold, Release), you can make the tone of the synthesizer longer or shorter; give the note a short, clipped attack; or have the low-frequency material swell in behind the original kick drum. You can also adjust the sensitivity of the Noise Gate with the Threshold and Reduction parameters. Experimentation is the key, and while this Drum Replacement/Doubling function gives you one great tool for beefing up a kick drum, the side-chain method can produce results that other methods just can't achieve!*

Audio Units Effects

You may want to use an effect not included with Logic, or you may prefer to use a different version of an effect than the one Logic provides. To this end, all versions of Logic allow you to use third-party effects plug-ins as well as third-party software instruments. As discussed, these third-party applications literally "plug in" to Logic's Mixer and offer extended processing functionality from within Logic. There are a number of different plug-in formats with which different sequencers are compatible. Logic Pro X is compatible with Apple's native Audio Units (AU) format.

To access third-party effects, you follow the same basic procedure as you use with Logic effects. The difference is that instead of selecting Logic effects, you select Audio Units and then choose your effect from the list of manufacturers. Figure 11.30 shows a third-party Audio Units effect being selected.

Figure 11.30 To select a third-party Audio Units effect, you follow the same general procedure as when selecting a Logic effect, except that you follow the menu of Audio Units plug-ins.
© Apple Inc.

The Audio Units Manager

As you can imagine, there are hundreds of third-party Audio Units effects available, some of which come in bundles that are quite inexpensive. Remember when buying AU plug-ins to make sure they are 64-bit plug-ins. Although Logic has been a 64-bit app since 2009, many commercial plug-ins have not been ported to 64-bit. In spite of this, you may find that in no time flat your lists of available AUs will become huge! Thankfully, Logic Pro X includes an integrated way to manage your Audio Units plug-ins. This is called the Audio Units Manager (see Figure 11.31). To launch the Audio Units Manager, select Logic Pro X > Preferences > Audio Units Manager.

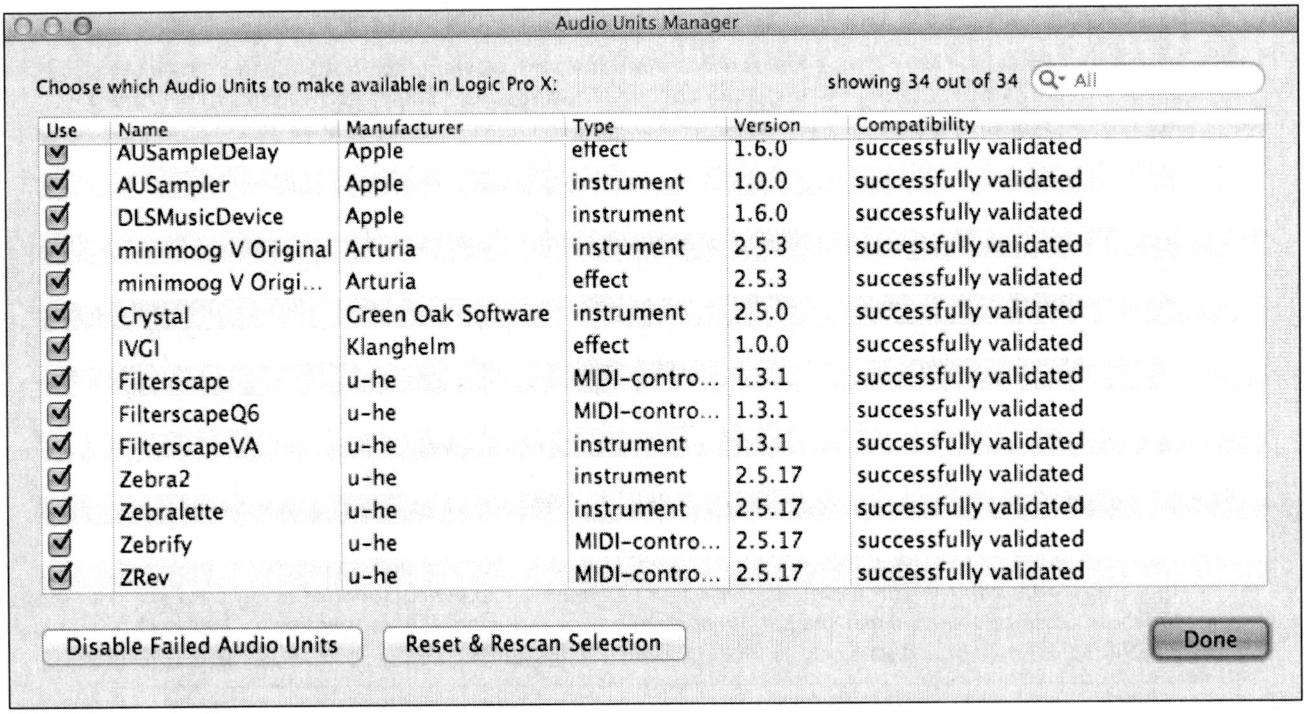

Choose which Audio Units to make available in Logic Pro X: showing 34 out of 34   Q▾ All

Use	Name	Manufacturer	Type	Version	Compatibility
☑	AUSampleDelay	Apple	effect	1.6.0	successfully validated
☑	AUSampler	Apple	instrument	1.0.0	successfully validated
☑	DLSMusicDevice	Apple	instrument	1.6.0	successfully validated
☑	minimoog V Original	Arturia	instrument	2.5.3	successfully validated
☑	minimoog V Origi…	Arturia	effect	2.5.3	successfully validated
☑	Crystal	Green Oak Software	instrument	2.5.0	successfully validated
☑	IVCI	Klanghelm	effect	1.0.0	successfully validated
☑	Filterscape	u-he	MIDI-contro…	1.3.1	successfully validated
☑	FilterscapeQ6	u-he	MIDI-contro…	1.3.1	successfully validated
☑	FilterscapeVA	u-he	instrument	1.3.1	successfully validated
☑	Zebra2	u-he	instrument	2.5.17	successfully validated
☑	Zebralette	u-he	instrument	2.5.17	successfully validated
☑	Zebrify	u-he	MIDI-contro…	2.5.17	successfully validated
☑	ZRev	u-he	MIDI-contro…	2.5.17	successfully validated

[Disable Failed Audio Units]   [Reset & Rescan Selection]   [Done]

Figure 11.31 The Audio Units Manager. You can select and deselect the checkboxes to specify which AUs will be available in the plug-in menus in Logic Pro X.
© Apple Inc.

The Audio Units Manager displays each of your Audio Units plug-ins in a row, one after the other. The Audio Units Manager contains six columns:

▷ **Use:** Select this checkbox if you want a plug-in to appear in the plug-in menus within Logic. Deselect this checkbox if you do not.

▷ **Name:** This is the name of the Audio Units plug-in.

▷ **Manufacturer:** This is the name of the developer of the Audio Units plug-in.
▷ **Type:** This column tells what kind of plug-in each Audio Units plug-in is, such as effect, instrument, or MIDI-controlled effect.
▷ **Version:** This column contains the version number of each Audio Units plug-in.
▷ **Compatibility:** This column tells you whether the plug-in passed, failed, or crashed Apple Computer's Audio Units Validation scan. Audio Units Validation is covered in the next section.

Using the Logic Audio Units Manager couldn't be easier. If you don't need an AU to appear in the plug-in menus within Logic, deselect the checkbox in the Use column. If you want to reactivate a plug-in that you deactivated, reselect its checkbox. When you're finished, simply click the Done button at the bottom-right of the Audio Units Manager to close it.

The Audio Units Manager includes one additional, vital function besides Audio Units management. It also scans your Audio Units for compatibility with the Audio Units format and deactivates them for you if they fail or crash validation. This is explained in more detail next.

Initial AU Scan

Apple wants Logic Pro X to be the most stable audio application possible. To ensure this, Apple takes pains to test the application rigorously before release. Unfortunately, third-party plug-ins are not within Apple's power to test and debug. In the past, this has meant that plug-ins that often didn't "play nice" with Logic could crash Logic, or in some cases, bring down your entire computer! To help mitigate this, Apple created a free diagnostic application for developers: the AU Validation Tool. This tool basically runs a number of diagnostic tests on an Audio Units plug-in in an attempt to ensure that it properly complies with the Audio Units format specifications and will not destabilize the host application.

When you first run Logic Pro X and every time you install a new Audio Units plug-in, Logic will scan the plug-in with the AU Validation Tool to test the plug-in for compatibility and stability. Normally, all you will see is a progress bar indicating that scanning is taking place, and that's it. When Logic Pro opens, your new plug-in will typically be available in the appropriate menus.

Sometimes, however, you may find that a plug-in you installed does *not* appear in the menu. This most likely means that the plug-in failed validation. At this point, if you open the Audio Units Manager, you will find that your plug-in is not checked along with the message that it failed or crashed validation.

If you believe that the scan results were somehow incorrect, you have the option to click the Reset & Rescan Selection button. The Audio Units Manager will then rescan just the selected AU plug-in and present you with the results. If the plug-in still fails validation, I highly recommend that you contact the developer with this information. If you want to be extra helpful, you can even copy and paste the rescan results into an email and send it directly to the developer, saving them from having to run it themselves. It is up to the developer to release an update that complies with the Audio Units specifications. When they do, Logic will scan the updated plug-in, it will pass the scan, and your plug-in will work properly!

Activating Incompatible AU Plug-Ins

What if you absolutely, desperately need to use an incompatible Audio Units plug-in in Logic—say, to finish a project on deadline? For these emergency situations, you can, if you want to, activate an incompatible plug-in in Logic. To do so, simply select its Use checkbox, just like a compatible plug-in. Plug-ins that you activate this way are filtered into their own special menu for incompatible plug-ins in the Audio FX and instrument slot menus.

I *highly* recommend against activating incompatible plug-ins unless you absolutely have no choice. The whole purpose of scanning Audio Units plug-ins is to try to ensure that Logic Pro will not be destabilized by an errant plug-in. If you activate a plug-in that crashes or fails validation, you defeat the whole purpose of the scan! This is truly a feature of last resort. Waiting for an update that successfully passes AU validation is always the best policy.

Using Audio FX

Audio effects are really simple to use, as you have seen. Simply select an effect for an Audio FX slot, and you're ready to use it! Bypassing an insert effect is just as easy. To bypass an effect, click the power button in its Audio FX slot. The effect will stop glowing, indicating the effect is bypassed.

Saving or Loading Channel Strip Settings

In addition to being able to save and load individual effects settings, Logic gives you the option to save and recall entire configurations of channel strip inserts—including software instruments. If you click and hold the Setting box on a channel strip, a menu like the one is Figure 11.32 will appear, offering you options to save, load, and navigate channel strip settings.

Figure 11.32 Clicking the Setting box on a channel strip opens the Setting menu, where you can manage and navigate channel strip settings.
© Apple Inc.

The functions of the commands in the Setting menu are as follows:

▷ **Next Channel Strip Setting:** This command changes the configuration of the channel strip to the next channel strip setting. The key command is Shift+] (right bracket).

▷ **Previous Channel Strip Setting:** This command changes the configuration of the channel strip to the previous channel strip setting. The key command is Shift+[(left bracket).

▷ **Copy Channel Strip Setting:** This command allows you to copy an entire channel strip configuration to the Clipboard so you can paste it into another channel strip. The key command is Option+Command+C.

▷ **Paste Channel Strip Setting:** This command allows you to paste an entire channel strip setting from the Clipboard into a channel strip. The key command is Option+Command+V.

▷ **Reset Channel Strip:** This command allows you to quickly remove all plug-ins and send routings from a channel strip.

▷ **Save Channel Strip Setting As:** This command allows you to save your own channel strip settings. When you save a channel strip setting, a Save dialog box like the one in Figure 11.33 opens.

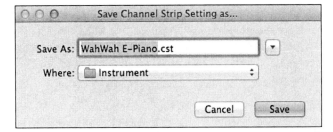

Figure 11.33 The Save Channel Strip Setting As dialog box.
© Apple Inc.

> **TIP:** It is helpful to create a new folder structure inside the default folder to organize your channel strip settings. Otherwise, all your channel strip settings will show up as a list in the Setting menu. Figure 11.34 shows a Setting menu with two instances of the same software instrument channel strip setting—one saved in the default Instrument folder and another saved in a folder created inside the Instrument folder.

Figure 11.34 This Setting menu shows one channel strip setting directly in the menu and another that has been nested in a submenu. Creating subfolders in the Save Channel Strip Setting As dialog box allows you to create submenus in the Setting menu, which will help you keep your channel strip settings organized.
© Apple Inc.

▷ **Save as Performance:** This command allows you to save your channel strip setting as a performance, which enables you to recall the channel strip setting via a MIDI program change message. Selecting this command opens the Save Channel Strip Setting as Performance dialog box shown in Figure 11.35. Simply name your performance, enter the program change number you wish to use in the Program Number field (0–127), and click OK. You can now use a program change message with the number you selected to recall your channel strip setting. Be aware that the program change message must be transmitted on MIDI channel 1.

Figure 11.35 The Save Channel Strip Setting as Performance dialog box. Saving your channel strip setting as a performance gives you the ability to recall your channel strip setting via a MIDI program change message.
© Apple Inc.

▷ **Delete Channel Strip Setting:** This command allows you to delete the current channel strip setting.

Beneath the Setting menu commands you'll find submenus full of channel strip settings. Channel strip setting files include all the insert effects instantiated on the channel strip (complete with their effects settings as they were saved). If you are on a software instrument channel strip, it will include the software instrument as well. The beauty of channel strip settings is that you can save configurations of channel strip inserts that you use regularly—for example, if you have a particular set of plug-ins you like to use to process vocals. You can save them as a channel strip setting and have quick access to your favorite configuration at all times. Logic Pro comes with a very wide variety of factory preset channel settings for you to explore as well. Give them a listen!

> **NOTE:** With all the different settings and patches available, it may be a bit confusing keeping them all straight. Think of them like measuring cups, where one nests inside another. When you load a plug-in, you can access a setting or save a setting for that plug-in in its own Settings menu. Your saved settings for that plug-in are available in any Logic project. You can have multiple plug-ins on the same channel strip, working in concert, that you can save as a channel strip setting for use in any project. Finally, you have patches—multiple channel strips and Track Stacks, with different channel strips featuring unique combinations of plug-in settings, channel strip settings, and bus routings to auxes full of their own settings. Your patches are also available in any project. Logic gives you the ability to work from the simplest individual plug-in to massive routings, all portable across your projects. The more you get used to using these varying and expanding approaches to saving and recalling individual plug-in presets, preset groups of plug-ins on a channel strip, and entire preset collections of channel strips, their plug-ins, and their routings, the more you will get out of Logic!

Using Send Effects

Using a send to add effects to a track is a bit more complicated than using audio effects on your source channel strip. This is because sends don't directly connect to effects; instead, they connect through buses to aux channel strips. To use a send to add effects, you assign a send to a bus, then add the effect you desire in an Audio FX slot of the aux channel whose input is assigned to that bus. You control how much of your audio signal is bused to the aux via the Send knob.

Plug-In Delay and Logic's Plug-In Delay Compensation

Most effects do their processing nearly instantly. Some, however, do not. They may involve highly complex mathematical processes, like convolution reverbs, such as with Logic's Space Designer. Or they might have a "look ahead" feature, by which the effect increases its accuracy by scanning the recorded audio—literally "looking ahead" before it processes it, which requires that the effect hang on to the audio signal for a while instead of instantly processing it. Some Audio Units plug-ins run on FireWire or on PCI Express or ExpressCard DSP devices, such as the UAD-2 cards; it takes time to get the audio out to these devices.

The point is, some devices and plug-ins introduce a delay into your signal path. This can be a real problem. For example, if you have two tracks that are both in sync with each other and set to play at bar 1.0.0.0, but one track has plug-ins that introduce 2,000 samples of delay, that track will play late and out of sync. If you are not careful, plug-in delay can really ruin your song.

Luckily, Logic tries to make things a bit easier for people. There is a Compensation menu in the General tab of the Audio Preferences window for plug-in delay compensation, as shown in Figure 11.36.

Figure 11.36 The Compensation menu in the General tab of the Audio Preferences window. You can determine how plug-in delay compensation will work in your project from this menu.
© Apple Inc.

There are three options in the Compensation menu:

▷ **Off:** This means there will be no plug-in delay compensation. If you're not using any plug-ins that need compensation, then this is the preferred setting.

▷ **Audio and Software Instrument Tracks:** Selecting this will automatically adjust any of your audio and software instrument tracks to be in sync with any other audio and software instrument tracks that have delay-causing effects on them.

▷ **All:** Selecting this allows you to compensate for delay-inducing plug-ins across your entire project, including outputs and auxes. All is the default plug-in delay compensation mode of Logic Pro X.

Keep in mind that plug-in delay compensation works only during playback, not during recording. If you have no choice but to record with plug-ins that cause some processing delay, be sure to use Low Latency mode, as explained in Chapter 5, "Transport Controls and Recording."

Final Notes on Using Effects

Using effects is arguably one of the most dramatic ways to alter an audio mix. Sometimes, the effects become instruments themselves, and their processing is an integral part of the music. But as with all things, it's very easy to get carried away both musically and computationally.

Keep in mind that your computer has only a finite amount of CPU power. If you try to process every track to death in a large project, you'll most likely overtax your computer to the point that your project no longer plays back. And if you *really* overdo it, you might so overextend your resources that your project won't play unless you engage Freeze for every track! Also, don't forget to use Bounce in Place whenever possible. Once a track is finished, there's no point in having it steal more CPU cycles than are absolutely necessary.

If you are using a fair number of software instruments and effects in a given song, keep a close watch on your system performance to make sure your computer is up to your demands. You can get a gauge of Logic's audio CPU and hard disk usage from the load meters in the Transport, which you can open in their own windows by double-clicking on them. This is another advantage to using some effects on aux channel strips and having tracks access them via sends. You can have more than one track access the same aux, thereby saving you from having to instantiate that same effect on more than one track.

Beware of the pitfall of EQing and effecting one track until it is perfect when played by itself, but muddies everything up when placed in the context of the mix. That infinite delay line that you love so much might just start getting jumbled when you bring in 24 more tracks and it's been repeating for 90 seconds! Even as you work on perfecting individual tracks, always try to keep a holistic view of what you want the completed project to sound like. Logic Pro's signal analysis effects—Correlation Meter, MultiMeter, and Level Meter—can help you get a better picture of your material, where there is too much signal energy, and where you might want to adjust your mix to sound more open or less overloaded. The saying "less is more" definitely applies to mixing!

Lastly, remember that there are no hard and fast rules as to how to add effects to a mix. Listen to effects on a lot of your favorite CDs, read magazines and books that discuss effects placement and usage in detail (Cengage Learning sells a fair number of books on mixing; go to cengage.com to check them out), and, of course, don't forget to experiment on your own!

Muting Channels

From Chapter 6, "The Logic Pro Main Window," you're already familiar with the Mute button on each track in the main window. That button mutes or unmutes either a single track or all tracks routed to a single channel strip. To mute the dependent tracks of a channel strip, you must turn those tracks off using the power buttons in their track headers. Each channel strip also has a Mute button at its bottom, as shown in Figure 11.37. Clicking this button mutes or unmutes the channel in question. Muting a channel strip also mutes the Mixer output of all dependent tracks of the muted channel strip.

Figure 11.37 The button with the M is the Mute button for this channel strip. If mute is engaged, the button on the channel strip glows light blue.
© Apple Inc.

Soloing Channels

Each channel strip except for output channel strips has a Solo button like the one in Figure 11.38. When the Solo button is engaged, all other channel strips, other than dependent aux channel strips and output channel strips, are silenced unless they have their Solo buttons engaged. When one or more tracks are soloed, the M in the Mute buttons of the non-soloed tracks flash.

Figure 11.38 When the Solo button of a channel strip is activated, all non-soloed channel strips are silenced except for output and aux channel strips. The Solo button will glow yellow when activated.
© Apple Inc.

Solo does not silence output channel strips because output channel strips are necessary for the soloed tracks to be heard. Also, soloing channels is strictly an audio function; MIDI tracks are not muted unless their audio is routed into Logic. Additionally, soloing a channel strip that is bused to an aux channel strip does not mute the dependent aux, as you can see in Figure 11.39.

Figure 11.39 Soloing a channel strip that is bused to an aux channel strip does not mute the dependent aux. Here you can see a signal in the level meters of the soloed channel strip, its dependent aux channel strip, and the output channel strip.
© Apple Inc.

If you are using an aux as the destination of a send and do not wish to hear the processing you are applying on the aux while soloing a parent channel strip, you can mute the aux.

Soloing an aux channel strip passes all audio routed to that aux through to its output. If the parent channel strips are assigned to an output channel strip, then their output signal is muted. This can be very handy for dialing in the settings on insert effects with precision. In Figure 11.40, aux 12 is using bus 18 as an input. The three channel strips to the left of aux 12 are sending signal to aux 12 through bus 18. Notice that while there is no signal registering in any of the software instrument's level meters, aux 12 is sending signal to the output channel strip.

Figure 11.40 When you solo an aux channel strip that is the destination of a send, the dry signal of its parent channel strips is muted. The aux still receives signal from its parent channel strips through its input bus and sends its soloed signal to the output channel strip.
© Apple Inc.

It's important to note that the Solo button in the Mixer interacts with the Solo buttons in the main window in a similar way to the Mute buttons. Also, Option-clicking a currently unsoloed channel strip will solo that particular channel strip and turn solo off on any currently soloed channel.

Because of the many different ways that soloed channels can interact, you may want to solo safe certain channels in your project. What does solo safe mean, you ask? Good question....

Solo Safe Mode

If you want to make sure that no matter which tracks are soloed, you never silence certain tracks, effects, buses, and so on, you can make them solo safe to exempt them from being silenced. Control-clicking the Solo button turns on Solo Safe mode for a given channel strip. You can tell whether a track is in Solo Safe mode because its Solo button will have a line through it, as in Figure 11.41. Control-clicking the Solo button a second time disengages Solo Safe mode.

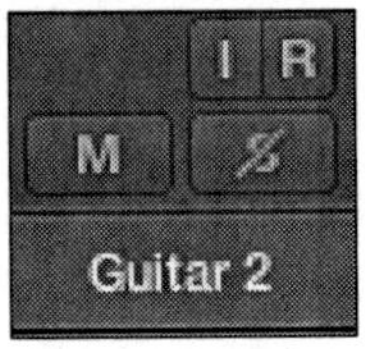

Figure 11.41 A red line through a deactivated Solo button on a channel strip indicates the channel strip is in Solo Safe mode.
© Apple Inc.

Mixer Groups

Sometimes you may want to link some properties of different channel strips. For example, you might want the volume, solo, and mute functions of all your drum tracks to change together as a group, or you might want to link the Pan control of a group of tracks that are all panned to the same location. The Group function allows you to do this and more. You can use the Group function not only to group Mixer operations, but also to link Tracks area functionality for group editing.

The Group slot is the dark-gray display window directly below the Output field in each channel strip, as shown in Figure 11.42. This is where you can select and create groups. You can create as many as 32 groups, and channels can belong to multiple groups.

Figure 11.42 Directly under the Output menu and above the Automation Mode menu is the Group slot. In this figure, the channel strip is assigned to group 1.
© Apple Inc.

Assigning Channels to Groups

To assign a channel to a group, click in the Group slot on the channel strip. A menu will appear with the numbers (and names, if assigned) of any current Mixer groups, as well as the option to create a new group, and to open the Group Settings window. If you are creating your first group in a project, select Group 1: (new). After you have created more groups by selecting Group *x*: (new), where *x* is any number from 2–32, you can assign a channel strip to any available group. The number of the group you have selected appears in the Group display of your channel strip. Figure 11.43 shows the Group menu with group 1 already created and group 2 ready to be created.

Figure 11.43 In the Group menu, you can choose the number of the group to which you want to assign your channel, create a new group, or open the Group Settings window.
© Apple Inc.

You can assign a channel to more than one group by holding down Shift while selecting groups in the menu. If you Option-click in the Group slot, the last group selection is applied to the current channel strip. This is especially handy for quickly assigning a large number of channel strips to the same group.

Group Settings

You can access the Group Settings window in a few ways. If you assign a group to a channel, the Inspector in the main window will add a Groups Inspector. You can drag the Groups Inspector header to open a separate but identical Group Settings window. You can also select the Open Group Settings option in the Group menu or use the key command Option+Shift+G. Figure 11.44 shows the Groups Inspector in the main window Inspector.

Figure 11.44 The groups Inspector is identical to the Group Settings window.
© Apple Inc.

The Group Settings window contains a list of options, each with a checkbox (except for the Name option). If you select the checkbox next to an option, that option will be set to the group. So, if you adjust the control or do any editing or automation in one channel in the group, that action affects all channels in the group. The following list describes the various options.

> ▷ **Groups Active:** This checkbox allows you to turn all groups on or off globally.
> ▷ **Groups list:** This list lets you control the following group options.
>> ▷ **Nr:** This column displays the available group numbers.
>> ▷ **On:** To turn on an available group, select its checkbox in this column.
>> ▷ **Name:** Double-click in the Name field to access a text box in which you can type a name for your group. The first seven or eight letters of the group's name will appear in the Group display in the channel strip, along with the group number.
>> ▷ **H:** Selecting a group's H checkbox hides that group. If one or more tracks in the group are already hidden, the checkbox will display a dash in it, but you still have the ability to hide all the group's tracks by clicking on the checkbox. This is different from using an individual track's Hide function, because you have to access the Group Settings window to toggle a group's Hide status.
> ▷ **Settings area:** The Settings area lets you configure what functions affect your group as a whole. The group settings are as follows:
>> ▷ **Editing (Selection):** With this option selected, if you select a region on one track in the group in the Tracks area, every track in the group will have any regions at the same relative time in the song selected.
>> ▷ **Phase-Locked Audio:** With this option selected, a group that has Editing (Selection) enabled will remain phase-locked if you quantize its audio. If you are Flex editing grouped tracks, this option must be enabled.
>> ▷ **Automation Mode:** Changing the Automation mode of one member of the group changes all of them.
>> ▷ **Volume:** Changing the Volume fader of one channel strip in the group changes all of them. Note that these are relative changes, so if two channels in the group are at different volumes, Logic raises or lowers both volumes by the amount of the change to the group, but they retain their relative difference in volume.
>> ▷ **Mute:** If one channel in the group is muted/unmuted, every channel in the group is muted/unmuted.
>> ▷ **Input:** With Input selected, all tracks in the group will use the same Input setting.
>> ▷ **Pan:** Logic adjusts the pan of every channel in the group if you adjust one channel's pan. As with the Volume option, all channels retain their relative differences from each other.
>> ▷ **Solo:** If one channel in the group is soloed/unsoloed, every channel in the group is soloed/unsoloed.
>> ▷ **Record:** Record-enabling/disabling one channel in the group record-enables/disables all the channels in the group.
>> ▷ **Send 1–8:** As with the Volume and Pan options, if you check any of these sends, Logic links them.
>> ▷ **Color:** If you assign a color to one member of the group, all of them are assigned that color.
>> ▷ **Track Zoom:** Adjusting the zoom of one track in the group adjusts the zoom of all the tracks in the group.
>> ▷ **Hide Track:** If you hide one track in the group using a track's H button, all members of the group are hidden.

When you link the automation of a group, any track can be the "master" that you use to control the mode. And if you draw or write automation for any linked parameter, Logic writes the automation for each individual track in the group. Therefore, if you later ungroup your tracks, they will still have the automation you wrote. There is also a "clutch" to disable group links temporarily, if you want to adjust one single track without affecting the rest of the group. You can access the Toggle Group Clutch command by pressing Shift+G. The numbers in the Group slot change color from yellow to gray as a visual cue that the group clutch is engaged.

Creating Temporary Groups by Selecting Multiple Channel Strips

There is a very down-and-dirty way to make a change to more than one fader without going through the process of creating a group. If you just want to adjust the Volume faders of four channel strips, for example, you can select them all, either by Shift-clicking on them or via a "rubber band" selection with the Pointer tool (if they are contiguous) in the Mixer. Logic Pro indicates which channels are selected by their color; they will all be light gray instead of dark gray. Once selected, you can adjust an attribute on one of them, and all of the selected tracks will also adjust. You can click anywhere outside the selected channel strips to deselect the channel strips.

Bouncing Your Mix

At any point in the mixing process, you might want to "bounce" your mix down to a stereo (or surround) master mix. This is different from Logic's Bounce in Place function, where you bounce individual tracks and automatically add them back to the project. The goal of bouncing here is to provide a usable, listenable audio file outside of Logic. The term *bounce* originated from the days in which this process required you to play your audio from a multitrack tape machine and then re-record your mixed audio onto a stereo tape deck—hence "bouncing" the audio from one tape deck onto another. With computer recording, however, bouncing to a file requires far less setup and effort, so you no longer need to wait until your mix is complete to bounce tracks. You can bounce mixes regularly during the mixing process to listen to them on different systems, to share your mixes with others, and so on.

Because bouncing consists of outputting your mix, Logic puts the Bounce button on the bottom-right of output channel strips, as well as the master channel strip when you are working in surround. It is the button labeled "Bnc" or "Bnce," depending on your Mixer's width setting. Figure 11.45 shows the Bnc button width, because the Mixer is in narrow channel strips.

Figure 11.45 Click the Bounce (labeled "Bnc" or "Bnce") button of an output channel strip to display the Bounce dialog box and create an audio file of your mix.
© Apple Inc.

There are two other ways to bounce your mix. You can select the global Bounce command from File > Bounce > Bounce Project or Section, or use the key command Command+B. This will bounce outputs 1–2. If you have one or more output channel strips, you can click the Bounce button on an output channel strip to bounce its dependent audio tracks.

The Bounce Dialog Box

When you select the command to bounce audio by any of the aforementioned means, the Bounce dialog box appears, as shown in Figure 11.46. This dialog box contains all the options to bounce your mix down to a file.

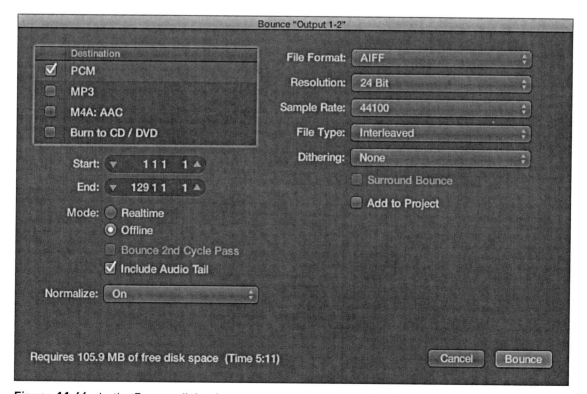

Figure 11.46 In the Bounce dialog box, you can set the parameters for how to bounce your mix.
© Apple Inc.

First, you need to select the file type for your bounce:

▷ **PCM:** This option bounces a standard, uncompressed audio file into AIFF, Broadcast WAV, or Sound Designer II format.

▷ **MP3:** This bounces to the MP3 compression format.

▷ **M4A: AAC:** This bounces to either the AAC or the Apple Lossless compression format. The selected subformat will be listed after M4A, such as M4A: AAC.

▷ **Burn to CD/DVD:** This burns your Logic project onto a recordable CD or DVD.

Below the Destination section, Logic lets you enter the start and end positions of your bounce by dragging in the Start or End field, by clicking on the arrows for the desired field, or by clicking in the desired field and entering a value manually. If you have Cycle mode engaged, the start and end positions will reflect the cycle region. If you have Cycle mode disengaged and have a region selected in the main window, the start and end positions will reflect the boundaries of the selected region. Otherwise, the start and end positions will reflect the length of the entire project, as set in the Custom Transport view.

Bounce Mode Options

Once you have your start and end positions set, you can choose between Realtime or Offline mode. In Realtime mode, Logic plays the selection you want to bounce and prints the file as it is playing. The advantage of this mode is that you get to hear exactly how the bounced file will sound, and you can include the signals from input channel strips. However, it can be slow if the file is long. In Offline mode, Logic bounces your mix internally, so any external sound sources or DSP cannot be included in your bounce, with the exception of ReWire. (ReWire sources are internal to your computer, after all.) If your Logic song is not taxing your CPU, offline bouncing can be much faster than real-time bouncing. If your song squeezes every last bit of your CPU to do complex processing, offline may actually be the only way to perform a bounce. If you find this is the case, yet you want to perform a real-time bounce to ensure the bounce sounds exactly as you wish as it's occurring, bounce your most taxing tracks in place to ease the CPU hit, and perform a real-time bounce.

Below the Realtime/Offline option buttons are two checkboxes that let you dictate a couple of very specific aspects of your bounce. The first option, Bounce 2nd Cycle Pass, works when you are bouncing a cycle region. Logic will play through one cycle of the region and then bounce the second cycle. The tails from effects such as reverbs and delays from the first pass will end up bounced at the front of the second cycle. The other option, Include Audio Tail, automatically lengthens the bounce to include all effect tails. For final mixes in particular, this option should be checked to avoid clipping your track's end prematurely.

Normalize Options

Below the Bounce mode options is the Normalize menu, shown in Figure 11.47.

Figure 11.47 The Normalize menu.
© Apple Inc.

The Normalize menu gives you three options for normalizing your bounce: Off, Overload Protection Only, and On. Normalizing means a file is scanned to find its highest peak, and the level of that peak is increased to the highest possible level (technically, 0 dBFS) without clipping, and the level of the rest of the audio is raised by the same amount. If you select Off, your bounce will not be normalized. If you select On, your bounce will be normalized in the manner described. If you select Overload Protection Only, Logic will perform a specialized normalization in which the file is scanned for overloads, and those peaks will be decreased to 0 dBFS, leaving the rest of your bounce unaltered. The Normalize feature in the Bounce dialog box is really a special feature. Be sure to read the following sidebar on it for all the details.

When to Use Logic's Floating-Point Bounce: The Normalize functions in the Bounce dialog box are actually quite special: They use floating-point math instead of fixed-point math. That means they normalize the floating-point audio information and then map each bit to its optimal level in the final fixed-point audio file. The result is that the full dynamic range of Logic's 64-bit floating-point audio engine is preserved much more accurately than with the traditional fixed-point Normalization feature, such as the one found in Logic's own Audio File editor. Traditional fixed-point normalization methods may result in distortion or audio degradation, but the floating-point Normalize features of the Bounce dialog box will never compress, limit, or distort your audio.

So does this mean that you should always normalize your bounces? It depends. Here are some guidelines:

▶ If your peak levels are already at 0 dBFS, the floating-normalize feature will do absolutely nothing, so there is no point.
▶ If you're delivering your final bounce to a mastering engineer, he generally won't want your peak levels to be at 0 dBFS, so in this case, don't normalize your bounce.
▶ If the levels of your audio are above 0 dBFS (in other words, if it sounds like your track is digitally clipping), be sure to normalize using the Overload Protection Only option. It will remap your audio to 0 dBFS, your audio will not be clipped anymore, and your overall bounce will maintain its accuracy.
▶ If you are bouncing a single track to be reused in your Logic project and you want to make sure you bounce at the optimal level, use the On setting.
▶ If you're bouncing particularly dynamic material to a compressed file format, such as MP3 or AAC, using the Normalize feature will help you get optimal dynamic range into the compressed file.

As you can see, while normalization is not a cure-all or something you always want to use when you bounce, Logic's exceptional floating-point Normalize features are extremely useful in the right circumstances.

Near the bottom of the Bounce dialog box, Logic informs you how much disk space you'll need for your bounce and how long your file will be. You also have options to create a new folder for your bounces, to cancel the operation, and to commence the bounce.

You can bounce to multiple file formats by selecting the Destination checkboxes of more than one file type. The Bounce parameters to the right of the Destination section will change depending on which destination is highlighted (click outside the checkbox area to highlight a Destination option). The parameters for each bounce destination are explained in the following subsections.

Bounce to PCM

This bounce destination includes bouncing to uncompressed AIFF, Broadcast Wave, or Core Audio Format files. Figure 11.48 shows the PCM destination parameters.

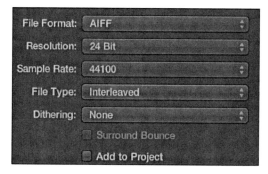

Figure 11.48 The PCM bounce destination parameters.
© Apple Inc.

The parameters for this bounce are as follows:

▷ **File Format:** This is where you select AIFF, Broadcast Wave (WAV), or Core Audio Format (CAF) for your PCM bounce. There is no sonic difference among the different formats. What format you bounce to is ultimately guided by compatibility. If you're bouncing audio that will be imported into another DAW or across platforms, you'll want to bounce in the most compatible format for the destination application. For example, WAV is the native audio format on PCs. If you are sending audio files to someone who is working on a PC, it will probably make the most sense to bounce your audio to WAV format. In general, if you are only working with the audio on your Macintosh, AIFF and CAF are the native formats, although AIFF is ubiquitous.

▷ **Resolution:** Here you can choose the file bit depth for your bounce. Your choices are 8, 16, and 24 bit. You will almost never want to print an 8-bit bounce. If you are going straight to CD, you might want to print a 16-bit file with dither if you recorded to 24 bit (see the description of the Dithering option later in this list). Normally, you'll want to archive your mix at 24 bits, which is the highest bit rate that Logic currently allows.

▷ **Sample Rate:** You can select the sample rate for your bounced file here. Logic will default to the same sample rate as your Logic song, but you can change it to any of 12 different sample rate options between 11 kHz and 192 kHz. If you select a different sample rate from the sample rate of your song, Logic will sample rate convert your bounced file using its very high quality sample rate conversion algorithms. Similar to the Resolution setting, you will generally print a file no lower than 44.1 kHz.

▷ **File Type:** This option is available only if you are bouncing a stereo file. If your destination file is for an application that cannot import interleaved files and requires split stereo files (meaning you bounce one file for the left track and another for the right), select Split. Unless you know you need split stereo files, leave this set to Interleaved. If you are bouncing a mono file, this will be grayed out.

▷ **Dithering:** If you are bouncing 24-bit audio to a 16-bit file for CD or compressed format uses (for example, MP3 or Internet), you'll want to turn on dithering. Normally, when you save 24-bit audio into a 16-bit file, the 8 bits that don't make it to the 16-bit file are simply those that happen to be filling the lowest bits of the audio stream. Unfortunately, sometimes you have desired audio in those bits, and this truncation can end up sounding harsh. Dithering adds imperceptible amounts and frequencies of noise to your file so that the noise "pushes" all the desired audio into the 16 bits that are saved, and only the noise is eliminated. As you can imagine, not all dither is created equal. Logic includes the industry-standard POW-r dithering algorithms. There are three algorithms—the first is plain, and the second and third have various amounts of noise shaping to attempt to tailor the dither even more to your audio material. Logic also includes the Apogee UV22HR dithering algorithm. Use the algorithm that sounds best with your material. If you are bouncing 24-bit files, leave dithering off.

▷ **Surround Bounce:** If you are bouncing for a surround mix, Logic will bounce to any of the six surround formats it supports. If you turn on Surround Bounce, this grays out the Add to iTunes Library option. Logic doesn't do any actual surround encoding or decoding, so if you plan to do a surround bounce, you need additional hardware or software (such as Compressor, which is included in the Logic Studio bundle) to play and encode the bounced files in the proper format. Unless you need to bounce surround files, you should leave this set to Off.

▷ **Add to Project:** This checkbox allows you to add the bounced file to the Project Audio Browser for reuse in your Logic song. This is very useful if you are bouncing only a small portion of audio to capture some effects processing or you are doing a real-time bounce to record audio from inputs and you want the result to be available for later use.

Bounce to MP3

MP3 (or MPEG-1 audio layer 3) currently reigns as the ubiquitous compression format for sharing music across platforms. Figure 11.49 shows you the MP3 destination parameters.

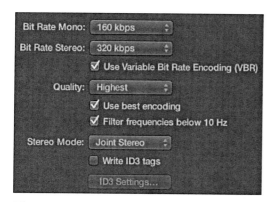

Figure 11.49 The MP3 destination parameters.
© Apple Inc.

The parameters for this bounce are as follows:

▷ **Bit Rate (Mono/Stereo):** You can select bit rates between 32 Kbps and 320 Kbps. Typically, bit rates of 160 Kbps or 192 Kbps offer the best balance between quality and file size for MP3 compression. The quality improvement for bit rates above 192 Kbps is minimal—you'd be better off bouncing to PCM. For mono voice sources delivered to MP3, the bit rates can generally be set lower.

▷ **Use Variable Bit Rate Encoding (VBR):** Select this checkbox if you want to use variable bit rate encoding instead of constant bit rate encoding. Variable bit rate encoding compresses simpler passages more heavily than more harmonically rich passages, which in theory encodes better-quality MP3s at a smaller file size.

▷ **Quality:** If you use VBR encoding, this menu allows you to select the quality of your variable bit rate. Generally, you should keep this set to Highest. Reducing the quality speeds up the conversion process, but at the expense of audio quality. Additionally, modern computers render MP3s extremely quickly. There's no benefit to choosing a lower setting.

▷ **Use Best Encoding:** If you deselect this checkbox, you gain encoding speed at the price of audio quality. Again, you should always keep this setting selected.

▷ **Filter Frequencies Below 10 Hz:** Frequencies below 10 Hz are usually not reproduced by speakers and are not audible to human ears anyway. Such frequencies can, however, create a muddier MP3. If you select this checkbox, Logic removes those frequencies, leaving slightly more data bandwidth for the frequencies that people can hear and resulting in an improvement in perceived quality.

▷ **Stereo Mode:** You can choose between Joint Stereo and Normal Stereo modes. The differences are very subtle, if any, so go ahead and experiment to see which sounds better on your source material. Don't be surprised if both sound the same. This option is not available for mono bounces.

▷ **Write ID3 Tags:** MP3 files can have ID information, such as song title, artist, and so on, encoded with the audio. If you want to enter this information for your bounce, select this checkbox.

▷ **ID3 Settings:** If you select the Write ID3 Tags checkbox, this button will become available. Click it to open a window in which you can enter the song title, artist, album, genre, and other information. ID3 tags are useful if you plan to share your MP3 or you want the information to display in iTunes. Otherwise, there's no need to bother.

Bounce to M4A: AAC

Advanced Audio Coding (AAC) and Apple Lossless are the "next generation" of audio encoding, based on the MP4 (MPEG-4) format, the successor to MP3. Figure 11.50 shows you the M4A: AAC destination parameters.

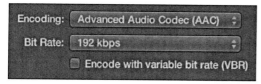

Figure 11.50 The M4A: AAC destination parameters.
© Apple Inc.

AAC produces better audio quality at the same bit rate as MP3. Apple Lossless is a format that compresses the audio to a smaller file size than an uncompressed format with absolutely no loss of data or quality. AAC and Apple Lossless files can be decoded by iTunes (and, therefore, iPods, iPads, and iPhones), and by QuickTime on Mac OS X and Windows PCs. AAC is also compatible with some other media players and is used by the iTunes Music Store for its commercially available songs.

When you select M4A in the Destination area, there are only three visible options.

▷ **Encoding:** You can choose to encode your audio in AAC or Apple Lossless format.
▷ **Bit Rate:** You can choose the bit rate of your AAC file from between 16 Kbps and 320 Kbps. Typically, a bit rate of 160 Kbps or 192 Kbps offers the best balance between quality and file size for AAC compression. The quality improvement for bit rates above 192 Kbps is minimal. If you are bouncing in Apple Lossless format, this option is grayed out.
▷ **Encode with Variable Bit Rate (VBR):** Select this checkbox if you want to use variable bit rate encoding instead of constant bit rate encoding. Variable bit rate encoding compresses simpler passages more heavily than more harmonically rich passages, which in theory encodes better-quality AACs at a smaller file size. If you are bouncing in Apple Lossless format, this option is grayed out.

Bounce to CD/DVD

This option lets you bounce your Logic project directly to a CD or DVD—in other words, to burn it. This option does not allow you the complete facilities for properly mastering a commercial CD. If you want to quickly bounce your Logic project to a CD-R/CD-RW or DVD to audition it in various stereo or surround systems, to share with friends, and so on, this option will do the trick. Figure 11.51 shows the Burn destination parameters.

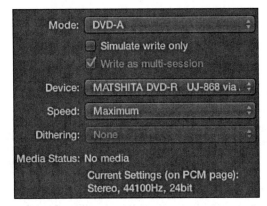

Figure 11.51 The Burn destination parameters.
© Apple Inc.

The parameters for this bounce are as follows:

▷ **Mode:** This menu allows you to choose between CDDA (Compact Disc Digital Audio) and DVD-A (Digital Versatile Disc Audio).
▷ **Simulate Write Only:** If you want to try a test run to make sure everything is set up and working properly to do a CDDA or a DVD-A burn, select this checkbox.
▷ **Write as Multi-Session:** If you select this checkbox, you will be able to write other files to a CD-R after you burn your Logic project. If this checkbox is deselected, Logic will "close" the CD-R when it is finished. If you want to use your CD-R for more material, select this checkbox. Otherwise, leave it deselected. If you are bouncing to DVD-A, this option is grayed out.
▷ **Device:** This menu allows you to select any connected CD or DVD burner.
▷ **Speed:** This menu allows you to select the maximum speed your CD or DVD burner can write to disc or any lower speed your drive is capable of. How many options appear here will depend on your model of drive.
▷ **Dithering:** Refer to the "Dithering" bullet in the "Bounce to PCM" section earlier in this chapter.
▷ **Media Status:** This tells you what kind of disc is in the selected drive.

The Current Settings (on PCM Page) section at the bottom informs you of your current PCM settings for a bounce. The current PCM bounce settings are what will be bounced to CD or DVD, regardless of whether PCM is checked or not. If you want a different sample rate and bit depth for your CD or DVD bounce, change those settings for the PCM bounce settings.

Including MIDI Tracks in Your Bounce: Clearly, bouncing your audio tracks from an output channel strip includes only audio. What if you want to include the output of your MIDI hardware modules in your bounce file?

There are two ways to go about this. The first method requires that before you do your final bounce, you record the output of your external MIDI hardware into audio tracks in Logic. This takes extra time but allows you to move and edit your newly recorded external MIDI audio as you would any other audio performance, which you may enjoy. Once your external MIDI has been committed to audio tracks, Logic bounces them with all your other audio tracks. This is especially easy if you use the External Instrument effect as described in Chapter 9.

If you want to keep your MIDI hardware in the MIDI realm as long as possible and never record it as audio, one way to do this is simply to delay the aforementioned step until right before you print your final bounce. However, if you know that you'll never want to record your MIDI in advance, you can instead create input channel strips for all your MIDI hardware modules. Because input channel strips are audio channel strips, you can mix, process, and bounce them to a file just like the audio on any other audio channel strip. Using input channel strips requires that you have as many physical hardware inputs as you have MIDI module outputs you want to use. Creating input channel strips is a bit more complicated because you can't create them in the main window; you can only create them in the Mixer layer of the Environment. But using the Mixer layer of the Environment, you can create an entire "input mixer" if you want, for just this sort of thing.

Also, to compensate for your audio hardware latency, you may need to adjust the Delay transmission by setting, which you can access by choosing File > Project Settings > Synchronization and clicking the MIDI tab. If you don't know exactly how much latency your audio hardware has, and its documentation lists no approximations in milliseconds, you can use trial and error to determine the point at which your audio sounds in sync with your MIDI.

Surround Mixing

In addition to allowing for the usual stereo mixing, Logic Pro X includes complete, comprehensive, and arguably best-in-class support for surround mixing, including surround effects, panning, and bouncing functions. Logic supports the most common surround formats (such as quad, Pro Logic, 5.1, and 7.1) and even some additional, more esoteric surround formats. To access Logic's surround functions, you must have audio hardware with more than two physical outputs. Logic also offers surround upmixing and downmixing in software.

Changing an audio channel strip from a mono or a stereo channel to a surround channel is very simple. Click and hold the Format button; then, in the menu that opens, select Surround, as shown in Figure 11.52.

Figure 11.52 If you want an audio channel strip to be a surround object, select Surround from the Format menu.
© Apple Inc.

When an audio channel strip is placed in Surround mode, its Panorama dial is replaced by a special Surround control, as shown in Figure 11.53. The surround speakers are represented by white dots and the pan position by a green dot. You can grab the green dot and rotate it anywhere around the Surround control. Note that you can mix stereo and surround objects in the same Logic song with no restrictions.

Figure 11.53 After placing an audio channel strip in Surround mode, its Pan dial changes into a special Surround panorama control.
© Apple Inc.

The Surround Panner Window

If you double-click the Surround control on a surround channel, you will open a Surround Panner window, shown in Figure 11.54. This gives you a more detailed view of the surround panorama, as well as access to the surround format, LFE Level setting, and Center Level setting.

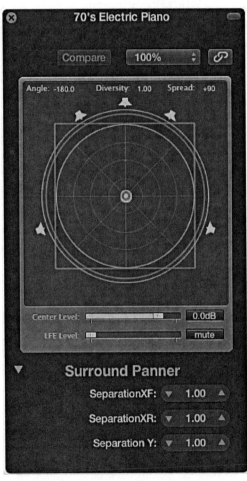

Figure 11.54 In the Surround Panner window, you can access the surround format, LFE Level setting, and Center Level setting, and also see a more detailed image of the surround panorama.
© Apple Inc.

The Surround Panner window offers you more options than just grabbing and moving your signal in the surround panorama. To lock the diversity, you can press the Command button while dragging the blue dot. You can also press Command+Option while dragging lock the angle, and you can press Option to reset the angle and radius to the exact center.

The slider at the bottom of the window is the LFE (Low Frequency Enhancement) Level control. Generally, the LFE channel is a subwoofer, but it doesn't have to be. This slider controls how much of the signal from this channel is directed toward the LFE channel. The Center Level slider determines signal level at the dead center of the surround panorama.

The extended parameters area offers three controls:

▷ **Separation XF:** Separation XF changes the separation of the front left and right channels.
▷ **Separation XR:** Separation XR changes the separation of the rear left and right channels.
▷ **Separation Y:** Separation Y changes the separation of the front and rear speakers.

Assigning Surround Channels to Audio Outputs

You determine which physical output will correspond to which surround channel in the Output screen of the I/O Assignments tab of the Audio Preferences window. You can access the Audio Preferences window from the global menus by choosing Logic Pro > Preferences > Audio. Clicking the I/O Assignments tab opens the Output screen by default (see Figure 11.55).

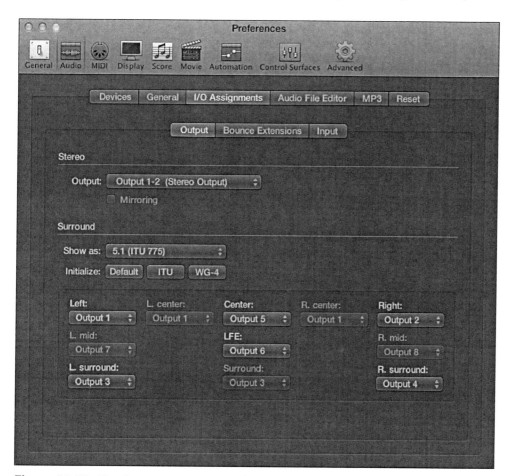

Figure 11.55 The Output screen of the I/O Assignments tab of the Audio Preferences window.
© Apple Inc.

In the Show As menu, you can select which surround format Logic will output. At this point, the appropriate menus are accessible for assigning your hardware outputs to the surround channels dictated by your chosen surround format. You might want to place a low-pass filter effect into the Audio FX slot of the output object that is your LFE, since that is the standard LFE cutoff for surround subwoofer channels. The three buttons under the Show As menu allow you to automatically select the Default, ITU, or WG-4 configuration of hardware outputs rather than having to set each menu manually.

Applying Surround Effects

Logic supports the use of surround effects, and some of Logic's own effects have native 5.1 support. You can insert stereo 5.1 effects on stereo channel strips and 5.1 effects on surround channel strips, such as surround software instrument channel strips and master channel strips.

Applying Surround Effects to a Surround Channel Strip

Inserting a surround effect on a surround channel strip is just as easy as inserting a stereo effect in a stereo channel strip. Simply select an Insert slot, navigate to the effect you would like to insert, and then select whichever format the plug-in offers for your project's surround format, such as 5.1 or Multi Mono, as shown in Figure 11.56.

Figure 11.56 A Multi Mono effect being instantiated on a surround channel strip.
© Apple Inc.

When you instantiate a Multi Mono effect, you'll notice that the plug-in window's Editor view offers new tabs that are unavailable on stereo or mono effects (see Figure 11.57).

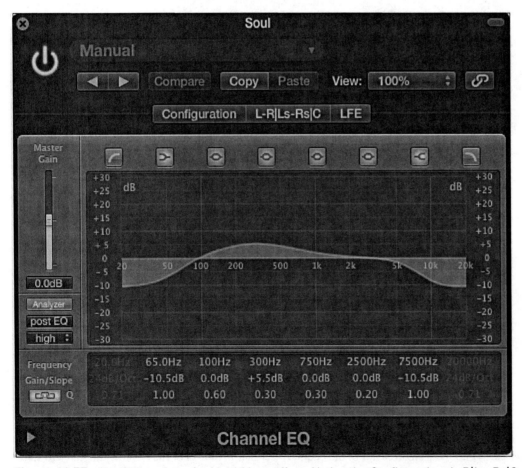

Figure 11.57 The Editor view of a Multi Mono effect. Notice the Configuration, L-R|Ls-Rs|C, and LFE tabs.
© Apple Inc.

The Configuration tab allows you to alter the content and number of the remaining tabs. Clicking the Configuration tab reveals a new set of controls in the plug-in window, as shown in Figure 11.58.

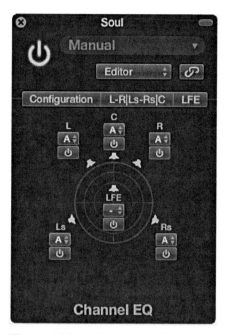

Figure 11.58 Clicking the Configuration tab reveals a new set of controls in the plug-in window.
© Apple Inc.

The Link menus under each surround channel in the Configuration tab allow you to assign each channel to a linked group: A, B, C, or –. Each Link group has its own tab, which appears as channels are added to that group. Each tab basically allows the effect to act as a dedicated effects unit for the channels assigned to that tab. The – option assigns the selected channel to its own individual tab. You can see in Figure 11.59 that the L, C, and R channels have all linked in the same tab; that the Ls and Rs channels are each assigned to discrete tabs; and that the LFE channel is bypassed. That means the L, C, and R channels are being processed with the same plug-in setting, while the Ls and Rs channels can each be processed separately within the same plug-in instance and the LFE channel undergoes no processing. You can save these configuration and effects settings as presets for recall at a later time.

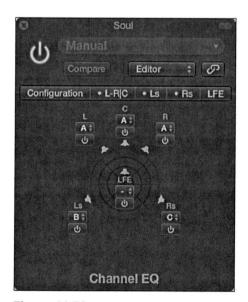

Figure 11.59 The L, C, and R channels coming through this effect have been linked to group A, allowing them to be processed together. The Ls and Rs tabs are being processed individually, while the LFE channel is not being processed.
© Apple Inc.

Note that when you use the side chain on a side chain–capable plug-in, the source audio is routed to all surround channels and the side-chain detection is linked, so that the plug-in can maintain the integrity of the surround image.

Applying Surround Effects to a Mono or Stereo Channel Strip

If your audio interface supports six or more outputs, inserting a Mono > Surround or Stereo > Surround plug-in on a mono or stereo channel whose output has automatically been assigned to Surround changes the level meters of the channel to surround metering, as shown in Figure 11.60. The Mono > Surround or Stereo > Surround option should reflect your project's surround format, meaning that if your project is in 5.1, then a surround plug-in inserted on a stereo channel will be instantiated as a Stereo > 5.1 format plug-in.

Figure 11.60 A mono audio channel strip whose output has been set to Surround. When you instantiate a Mono > Surround or Stereo > Surround effect in an Audio FX slot, like Delay Designer in this instance, the level meters switch to surround metering. Note that the Format button of the channel strip still displays the mono symbol.
© Apple Inc.

Effects that are inserted before the Mono > Surround or Stereo > Surround effect maintain the channel strip's original format. Effects inserted after the Mono > Surround or Stereo > Surround effect can be either Multi Mono or Surround, depending on what format(s) the plug-in supports.

Using the Down Mixer Plug-In

The Down Mixer plug-in, found in the Utility submenu of the master channel strip's Audio FX slots, allows you to change the format of the master channel strip from Surround to Stereo, Quad, or LCRS (Pro Logic). This gives you the ability to quickly check how your surround mix sounds in another format. Figure 11.61 shows a Down Mixer 5.1 To Stereo instance. The level controls allow you to change the levels of different channel groupings, along with the overall signal level.

Figure 11.61 The Down Mixer plug-in. This master channel strip plug-in allows you to quickly check the compatibility of your surround mix in different formats.
© Apple Inc.

The Surround Compressor

There is one other Logic effect worth mentioning: the Surround Compressor. Although it is outside the scope of this book to go into detail about the Surround Compressor, it bears mentioning because this effect is available only on surround channel strips. It functions like any typical compressor, but it is specifically designed for surround application, with the Link menus of a Multi Mono plug-in available directly in its Editor view.

Bouncing in Surround

As mentioned, you can choose to bounce in surround by selecting Surround Bounce in the Bounce dialog box. Logic gives the files the extensions shown in the Bounce Extensions screen in the I/O Assignments tab of the Audio Preferences window, as shown in Figure 11.62.

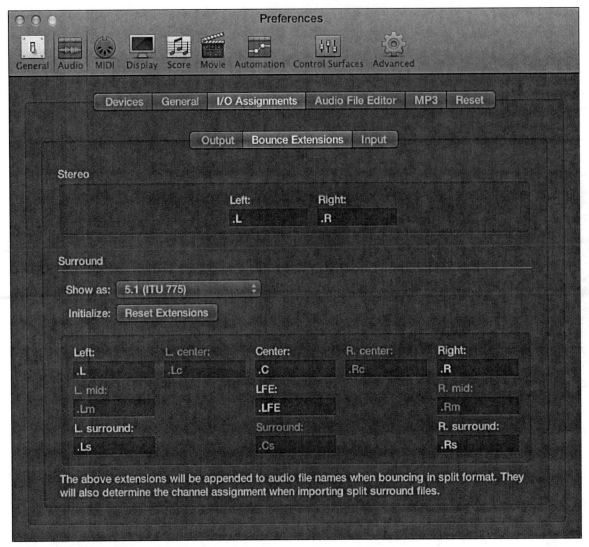

Figure 11.62 The Bounce Extensions screen of the I/O Assignments tab of the Audio Preferences window.
© Apple Inc.

Mixing Using Control Surfaces

Setting up a control surface with Logic was discussed in Chapter 3. But considering that most control surfaces are geared toward mixing, I wanted to briefly bring them up again here.

Depending on how you like to work, these devices can be a godsend. They let you manipulate more than one fader, Pan knob, and so on at a time. Control surfaces usually let you adjust plug-in parameters as well, and as with faders, you can control multiple parameters simultaneously. You can use a control surface to record automation for one or more tracks at a higher resolution than you can using a mouse. They usually include Transport controls to start and stop the song. The more advanced controllers also include shortcut buttons for advanced automation, editing, and other useful functions. As you can see, control surfaces can help you mix both more quickly and more accurately.

Control surfaces range from small plastic devices with a few knobs and sliders that cost less than most Audio Units plug-ins, to completely professional full-size mixers that cost hundreds of thousands of dollars. This book can't possibly cover all the different types of control surfaces and ways in which control surfaces can be connected and used with Logic Pro. However, I did want to mention a few controllers.

The Avid Artist series of controllers for audio applications consists of the Artist Control, the Artist Mix, and the Artist Transport. These controllers look like Mac products for good reason: Apple was involved in their development before Avid bought the original manufacturer, Euphonix, and they were created with Logic in mind. Avid has a long and well-earned reputation for making high-end, professional audio products, and if you can afford these controllers, you won't be disappointed.

The Artist Control was designed to be a complete editing and mixing "brain" that gives you one-button touchscreen access to as many editing, arranging, and mixing features as you like. You can add Artist Mix units for a system offering as many high-quality, touch-sensitive motorized faders as you need. Euphonix also invented its own high-end, two-way communication protocol between control surface and software program, called EuCon. Avid has continued that protocol, which is supported by most media applications, including Logic. You can learn more about the Avid Artist series at www.avid.com.

Many years ago, the controller that initially blew open the controller market was the Logic Control, designed by Mackie. Today's Mackie MCU Pro series of controllers is the direct descendant of that original Logic-only control surface. And this controller truly is universal: Most software and controller devices support Mackie Control emulation (including the Avid Artist series). The Mackie Controllers (or the Mackie Control protocol) are not as robust as the Avid Artist series, but they are extremely capable. You can read more about them at www.mackie.com/products/mcupro.

Working with and Sharing Files

12

A T THIS POINT, YOU SHOULD HAVE A PRETTY SOLID FOUNDATION IN HOW TO SET UP, COMPOSE, AND MIX A PROJECT IN LOGIC. You're now ready to start learning about file management within Logic. Some general aspects of file management, such as creating new documents and opening and saving files, should already be familiar to you, although Logic Pro X offers a new way to save your project—as a wholly self-contained package. Other more specialized operations, such as exporting your project to a variety of standard formats, require a little more explanation. This chapter should hit on everything you need to know to manage your project's files properly in Logic.

Creating New Projects

As explained in Chapter 3, "The Logic Project," Logic can be configured to launch to your default template. You can also have Logic launch with an empty project or to the Templates dialog box, among other options. Normally, new songs are based on one of these starting points. Your template is your "virtual studio," representing an ideal configuration for the way you like to work, but what if you have a number of ideal configurations based on the specific project? Luckily, Logic lets you create and save multiple templates for access at any time.

Templates

Chapter 3 discussed templates in some detail. A template is a powerful way to have a preferred Logic configuration ready to go whenever you need it, and having multiple templates allows you to have a number of different Logic configurations at your disposal. For example, you might want one virtual studio setup for compositions with lots of software instruments, one for recording lots of audio tracks simultaneously, one for different video setups if you do sound-to-picture, and so on. Or, you might have more than one Mac and want different templates based on the different monitor sizes and CPU power of each machine, or perhaps you use a laptop and require one template for when you're on the go and another for when you have a second monitor connected.

Logic Pro X comes with a number of templates, which are installed in the /Library/Application Support/Logic/Project Templates directory. You will notice that there are different base configurations optimized for composing, recording, working in surround, and so on. You can also save any project you create as a template by opening the File menu and choosing Save As Template. After you name the project in the dialog box that appears, your project will be saved in the ~/Music/Audio Music Apps/Project Templates directory. You can create a subfolder structure in the Project Templates folder to organize multiple templates if you wish. Every time you create a new project template, the template you created will appear in the list of available templates in the New dialog box either on startup or when you use the New command.

Using the New Command to Create New Songs

Obviously, the easiest way to create a new project is to simply start working in your default template and then save it as a new project later. However, if you set the Startup Action Preference (discussed in the "Configuring Logic's Startup Action" section later in this chapter) in the Project Handling tab of General screen of the Preferences window (which you access by opening the Logic Pro menu, choosing Preferences, and clicking General) to Automatically Open Most Recent Project, for example, you will not get your default template or an empty project on startup. Also, you may want to start a new song from one of your other templates or one of the templates included with Logic. In these situations, you'll want to use the New command from the global File menu.

When you select the New command, the Project Chooser opens, as shown in Figure 12.1.

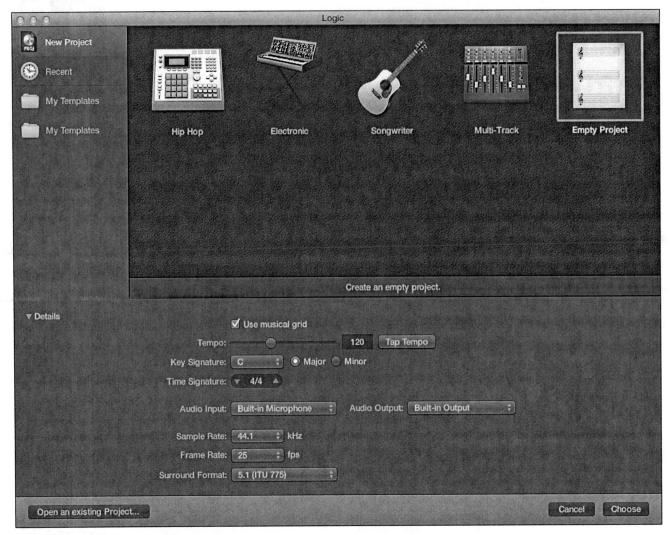

Figure 12.1 The Project Chooser.
© Apple Inc.

From here, you can select the project template you want to use from the various menus of project templates. You can also open the Details area at the bottom of the dialog box and begin setting up different parameters such as Tempo, Key Signature, Time Signature, Audio Input, Audio Output, Sample Rate, Frame Rate (for video work), and Surround Format (if you're working in surround; if you aren't, don't worry about this setting). There is also a button in the bottom-left corner, the Open an Existing Project button, that lets you browse for an existing project.

Saving Logic Projects

In versions of Logic before Logic 8, songs were saved independently of their various dependent files, or assets. To save a song with its assets, you had to specifically tell Logic to save the song as a project. Logic would then create a folder hierarchy containing all the assets you wanted saved in the project. Since Logic Pro 8, the project is the default format. Logic Pro X adds the option to save your project as a self-contained package. Let's look at the different Save options.

The Save Dialog Box

To save your project in Logic, open the File menu and choose Save or press Command+S. The first time you save your Logic project, the Save dialog box, shown in Figure 12.2, will open.

Figure 12.2 The Save dialog box. In addition to determining the file path and name of your Logic project, you can choose which of its assets to save in the Project folder.
© Apple Inc.

The Save dialog box looks very similar to a typical Save dialog box you might see in any application—until you look at the area below the file browser. There are a number of different options for how you can organize and save the files in your project. These options are divided into two sections: Organize My Project As and Copy the Following Files into Your Project.

The Organize My Project As options are as follows:

▷ **Package:** When you select this option, Logic saves your project and any of the project assets you select as a package. A package differs from a folder in that it is entirely self contained, with the file structure hidden from view in the Finder, much like an application, a GarageBand project, or your iPhoto Library. These are packages that contain and hide their dependent files. Because the file structure is hidden when you save a project as a package, the file structure is also hidden from Spotlight. That means you can't search for any of the included assets in the Finder using Spotlight. You can always right-click on a package and select Show Package Contents from the menu that opens to access the file structure of a package and search for files contained in the package manually.

▷ **Folder:** Selecting this option saves your Logic project and any project assets you select in a folder, giving you full, quick, and easy access to any and all files saved with the project.

The Copy the Following Files into Your Project options are as follows:

▷ **Audio Files:** When you select this option, Logic saves all the audio files used in your project in the project package or in the Audio Files subfolder of the Project folder.

▷ **EXS Instruments and Samples:** This option allows you to save any EXS instrument files (.exs) and their dependent samples used in your project in the project package or in the Sampler Instruments and Samples subfolder of the Project folder. Unless the Include Apple Sound Library Content option is selected, this will only save EXS samples not included in the Apple Sound Library.

▷ **Ultrabeat Samples:** You can save any Ultrabeat samples used in your project in the project package or the Project folder by selecting this option. Ultrabeat samples are then added to the Samples subfolder of the Project folder. Unless the Include Apple Sound Library Content option is selected, this will only save Ultrabeat samples not included in the Apple Sound Library.

▷ **Space Designer Impulse Responses:** This option saves any Space Designer impulse responses you use in the project in the project package or in the Impulse Responses folder in the Project folder.

▷ **Movie File:** This option saves any QuickTime movies used in the project in the project package or in the Movie Files folder in the Project folder. If you select this option, Logic will open a dialog box asking whether you really want to store a copy of your movie in the Project folder.

▷ **Include Apple Sound Library Content:** This option lets you save all your user samples, plus any Apple sound library content in the project package or the Project folder. Selecting this option automatically selects the EXS, Ultrabeat, and Space Designer options.

You may not want—or even need—to use all these options all the time. What these options do is allow you to create an easily portable version of your project encompassing all the files associated with it. This is perfect for backing up important projects, transferring projects between computers, and even transferring projects to other Logic users. You can therefore ensure that all necessary assets are not only included with your project but also are located in the directory structure in which Logic expects to find them.

Changing Your Project's Included Assets

Suppose you've saved your project. Since then, you've decided you need to use an instance of Ultrabeat in your project. You'd like to save the Ultrabeat samples in the Project folder, but you didn't allow for that the first time you saved your project. If you have already saved your project and you decide you need to reconfigure the assets that Logic is saving, simply open the File menu, choose Project Settings, and select Assets. Alternatively, select Assets from the Settings menu in the Toolbar. This opens the Assets tab of the Project Settings window, shown in Figure 12.3.

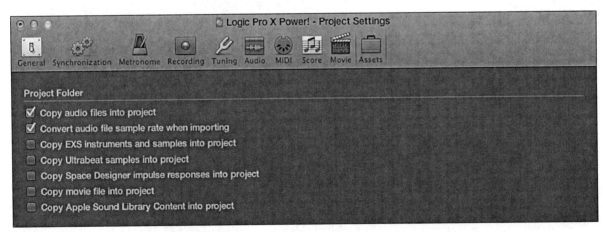

Figure 12.3 The Assets tab of the Project Settings window.
© Apple Inc.

The asset options in the Assets tab of the Project Settings window are identical to those in the Save dialog box, with one exception: Convert Audio File Sample Rate When Importing. This option is a good one to leave enabled. If you import audio into your project that is of a different sample rate than your project, it will not play correctly. Suppose your project sample rate is 44.1 kHz and you import a one-second audio file whose sample rate is 48 kHz. If you do not have Convert Audio File Sample Rate When Importing selected, Logic will read 41,000 samples of the 48,000 samples contained in the imported audio in one second, reading the remaining 7,000 samples in the first 7/48 of the next second. Your audio will play back too slow—and flat to boot. Unless you're looking for that sort of effect (to each their own), having Logic handle the sample-rate conversion automatically will save you a lot of headaches.

Saving Backups of Your Project

Logic automatically creates a backup of your project file each time you save your project. Each backup of your project is numbered and automatically saved inside the project file itself. These backups are available in the File > Revert To menu path.

To save your Logic project with a new name or in a new directory, or even to switch it to a package or a folder, open the File menu and choose Save As or press Shift+Command+S. You can also save a copy of your project by opening the File menu and choosing Save a Copy As. In either case, a dialog box identical to the original Save dialog box will appear, in which you can type a new name for your file and select a directory in which to save your project. If you use the Save a Copy As option, the Organize My Project As options are not accessible.

These methods of backing up a project are similar to those used in other software applications. Although Logic does automatically create backups of your projects, it is still wise to manually back up projects (and even templates) as a normal part of your work routine.

Saving Alternatives of Your Project

It's pretty common when working on music, either for yourself or for a client, to experiment with different mixes or arrangements. Sometimes—for example, in the case of commercials—it's pretty much a requirement for the job. Project alternatives are an amazingly handy way to create alternative mixes and arrangements of your project without having to bother with extra file-management headaches.

Saving an alternative is as easy as opening the File menu, choosing Alternatives, and selecting New Alternative. When you do, a simple Save as New Alternative dialog box opens. The only option in the dialog box is to name your alternative. By default, it uses your project name and adds a number to the title, ascending from 1 as you add more alternatives. Although the numbers make it easy to quickly save an alternative, it's a good idea to change the alternative name to something more meaningful, like "[Your Project] Mix No Voice" or "[Your Project] Extended Arrangement." Alternatives share assets with the original project because they are in fact a part of the project.

When you add an alternative, it is added to the Alternatives submenu of the File menu, allowing you to quickly switch from one alternative to another. If you need to rename or delete an alternative, open the File menu, choose Alternatives, and select Edit Alternatives. This opens a dialog box that lets you accomplish those things easily.

Configuring Logic's Startup Action

Logic offers you a number of options as to what occurs when you launch the program. Opening the Project Handling tab of the General Preferences window allows you to access the Startup Action menu, shown in Figure 12.4.

Figure 12.4 The Startup Action menu in the Project Handling tab of the General Preferences window.
© Apple Inc.

The options in the Startup Action menu are as follows:

▷ **Do Nothing:** Selecting this option allows you to choose what you do each time you launch Logic. You can decide to create a new project, open a recent project, open a template from the Templates dialog box, and so on.

▷ **Open Most Recent Project:** If you select this option, each time you launch Logic, it will open the project on which you last worked.

▷ **Open Existing Project:** If you select this option, Logic will display the Open dialog box to the most recent save location when launched.

▷ **Create New Project from Template:** If you select this option, Logic will display the Project Chooser when launched.

▷ **Create New Empty Project:** If you select this option, Logic will launch an empty project.

▷ **Create New Project Using Default Template:** If you select this option and have assigned a default template, Logic will open your default template upon startup.

▷ **Ask:** If you select Ask, every time you open Logic, a dialog box containing the preceding options will appear. Select the option you prefer and click OK. If you select Cancel, Logic will remain open, and you can select a project using any method you prefer—the Open command, the New command, the Open Recent menu, and so on.

Obviously, the best startup action for your workflow is a matter of personal preference, but often, a well-thought-out default template is the perfect starting point.

The Project Management Menu

You have a number of project-related options beyond simply saving Logic projects and their assets to Project folders or project packages and then opening the projects within them. Figure 12.5 shows the Project Management submenu of the File menu. The options in this submenu give you the ability to do a little housecleaning to your project if the need arises.

Figure 12.5 The Project Management submenu of the File menu.
© Apple Inc.

Clean Up

You can clean up Project folders by deleting unused files with the Clean Up command. If you select Clean Up from the Project Management submenu of the File menu, the Clean Up Project: Options dialog box opens, as shown in Figure 12.6.

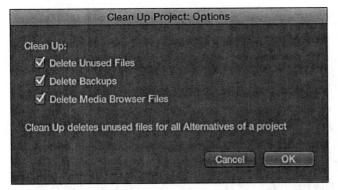

Figure 12.6 The Clean Up Project: Options dialog box gives you options for what types of files will be deleted from your project when you use the Clean Up command.
© Apple Inc.

The Clean Up Project: Options choices are as follows:

▷ **Delete Unused Files:** Selecting this option will let you delete all unused files in all project alternatives. Delete Backups is automatically selected when you use this option.

▷ **Delete Backups:** This option lets you delete all backups for all project alternatives.

▷ **Delete Media Browser Files:** This option lets you delete all files shared to the Media Browser.

Clicking OK opens the Clean Up Project window, which lists any files in the Project folder or project package that are currently unused in your song, as shown in Figure 12.7.

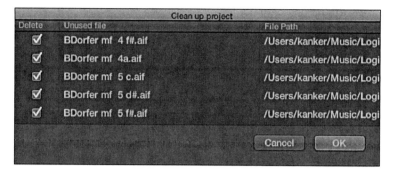

Figure 12.7 The Clean Up Project window allows you to delete unused files from your Project folder or project package.
© Apple Inc.

Select which files to delete and which unused files you wish to keep; then click OK. Logic will clean up your project for you.

Consolidate

If you have been working with a project that has managed to link to files all over your hard drive or otherwise become disorganized, you can choose Consolidate from the Project Management submenu of the File menu to bring your Logic song and associated files together. After selecting this command, you will be presented with the Consolidate Project: Options dialog box, which offers the same asset-handling options as the Save As Project dialog box (see Figure 12.8).

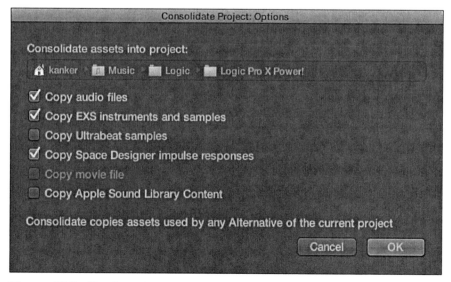

Figure 12.8 The Consolidate Project: Options dialog box.
© Apple Inc.

After your project is consolidated, you can use all the other project-related functions (such as cleaning up and opening its settings) to further operate on the consolidated folder.

Rename

If you want to rename a project, choose the Rename command from the Project submenu of the File menu. This command is very useful if you save a project before you name your song and you want to rename it all in one go. Figure 12.9 shows the Rename Project dialog box.

Figure 12.9 The Rename Project dialog box.
© Apple Inc.

Show in Finder

The Show in Finder command in the Project Management submenu of the File menu is useful when you need to access your project's folder or package in the Finder. For example, suppose you just finished work on your project and you want to back up the file to an external storage drive. If you execute the Show in Finder command, a Finder window will open to your project's location!

The Project Settings Menu

The Project Settings menu can be found in the File menu. Most of the Project Settings are covered in depth in other chapters. These settings affect the current project only. You can configure these settings as you desire and save them to your template project to ensure that each time you start a new project, you are using your preferred settings. The Import Project settings command found in the Project Settings menu is discussed later in this chapter.

Opening or Importing Projects and Files

In Logic Pro, the Open dialog box not only opens Logic and GarageBand Projects, but also lets you import all the formats that Logic can import. When you open the File menu and choose Open or press Command+O, Logic displays a typical Open dialog box. Logic Pro X can open the following file types:

▷ **Logic projects:** This includes projects created in Logic 5 or later.
▷ **GarageBand projects:** Any GarageBand projects can be opened in Logic.
▷ **MIDI files:** Logic can open Standard MIDI File (SMF) files.
▷ **AAF files:** Advanced Authoring Format (AAF) files are currently supported by high-end professional audio applications, such as Pro Tools HD.
▷ **XML (Final Cut Pro) files:** Extensible Markup Language (XML) files allow you to integrate Logic Pro with Apple's video-editing application, Final Cut Pro.

If you are opening a song from an earlier version of Logic, a dialog box tells you that Logic is converting the file to the newer song format. Note that Logic Pro X can open Logic songs created only in Logic 5, Logic 6, Logic 7, Logic 8, Logic 9, or Logic X. If you need to open a song created in Logic 4 or earlier, the song must first be opened and saved in a version of Logic 5, Logic 6, or Logic 7. (Be aware that pre–Logic 5 projects do not open in Logic 8 or 9, either.) Once you save an older Logic project in Logic Pro X, you can only open the new project file in Logic Pro X.

If you open the File menu and choose Open Recent, Logic will display the submenu shown in Figure 12.10. This Open Recent submenu lists all Logic songs that you have opened; you can simply select your song from this submenu.

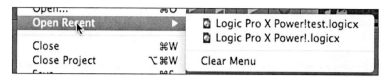

Figure 12.10 The Open Recent submenu in the global File menu.
© Apple Inc.

If your Open Recent submenu gets too long and unwieldy, you can choose the Clear Menu option at the bottom of the Open Recent submenu to reset the list.

Importing Files into Logic

Although the Open dialog box can both open and import files, Logic also contains an Import command, which you can access by opening the File menu and choosing Import. The Import menu lets you import any of the file types Logic can open. You can also import audio files using the Import menu. The main difference between opening and importing is that when you use the Open command, Logic Pro opens a new project, whereas with the Import command, Logic attempts to import the file into the currently open project. If it cannot add the imported material to the current song, it will open a new project, just like the Open command.

You can also import SMF files by dragging them onto the main window in Logic. When you open an SMF file this way, Logic will place it in your Tracks area. One track for each MIDI channel is created, and any data on that track appears in the track lane as a single MIDI region.

Logic also includes a specialized window called the All Files Browser, discussed next.

Using the All Files Browser

The All Files Browser is available in the Browsers area of the main window. The key command to open the Browsers area is F, and the All Files Browser is available in the All Files tab of the Browsers area. The All Files Browser is akin to having a Finder window incorporated into Logic—and in fact, the Browser is kept automatically in sync with your drives via Spotlight, the Finder's built-in search technology. Figure 12.11 shows the All Files Browser. You can use the All Files Browser to search for and add any file type supported by Logic.

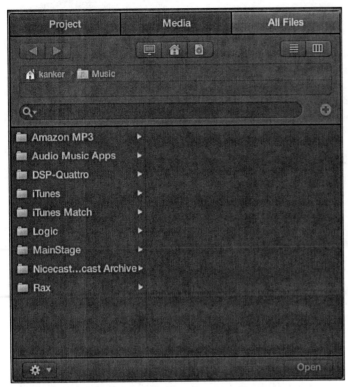

Figure 12.11 The All Files Browser in the Browsers area of the main window in Column view. The All Files Browser functions similarly to a Finder window.
© Apple Inc.

The All Files Browser has a very simple interface. Its main function allows you to quickly search for and add files to your Logic project. The All Files Browser has two view modes: List view and Column view. These two views are similar to List view and Column view in the Finder. You switch between these two views using the two buttons in the upper-right corner of the All Files Browser. Figure 12.11 shows the All Files Browser in Column view.

To the left of the View buttons are the Bookmark buttons. These buttons are, from left to right, the Computer button, the Home button, and the Project button. Selecting one of these buttons moves the All Files Browser to that particular level of your computer's file hierarchy.

Beneath the View buttons in the All Files Browser is the Path field. The Path field displays the current file hierarchy. You can navigate up the levels of the file path of your project using the Path field. When you select a different level in the file hierarchy, the All Files Browser shows the files and folders contained in that level, similar to a Path menu in a Save dialog box.

In the upper-left corner are two buttons with arrows in them, the Back and Forward buttons. These buttons allow you to move backward and forward through your navigation history in the All Files Browser, independent of file path.

The All Files Browser also includes a Search field. Clicking the magnifying glass in the left end of the Search field opens a list of your recent All Files Browser searches. To the right of the Search field is a plus symbol (+) in a circle. Clicking the plus symbol opens a set of advanced search parameters, as shown in Figure 12.12.

Figure 12.12 Clicking the plus symbol next to the Search field opens a set of advanced search parameters.
© Apple Inc.

You can use these parameters to narrow and fine-tune your search to specify things such as the file type, sample rate, bit depth, format, and so on. You can add more search parameters by clicking the plus symbol next to the advanced search parameters, or you can remove search parameters by clicking the minus (–) symbol.

When you find the file(s) you are looking for, select the files and click the Add button to add the selected file(s) to the Tracks area. Audio files are also added to the Project Audio Browser. Selecting a movie opens the Open Movie dialog box, covered in Chapter 14, "Working with Video."

When you select an audio file, the bottom of the All Files Browser adds a couple familiar features: the Speaker button, which allows you to preview audio files in the All Files Browser, and a volume slider. There is also an Actions menu at the bottom of the All Files Browser, which was mentioned briefly in Chapter 7, "Working with Audio and Apple Loops." Figure 12.13 shows the Actions menu of the All Files Browser.

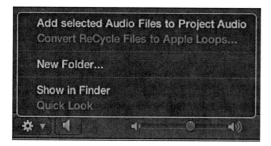

Figure 12.13 The Actions menu of the All Files Browser.
© Apple Inc.

The Actions menu contains the following options:

▷ **Add Selected Audio Files to Project Audio:** Using this command will add the files selected to the Project Audio Browser.

▷ **Convert ReCycle Files to Apple Loops:** This command, which was covered in detail in Chapter 7, allows you to convert the selected ReCycle audio files into Apple Loops.

▷ **New Folder:** Selecting New Folder opens a dialog box in which you can name your new folder. After you name the new folder, it is added to the currently displayed folder in the All Files Browser.

▷ **Show in Finder:** This command opens a Finder window with the selected file displayed.

▷ **Quick Look:** If you have selected a Logic project document, this option allows you to see a Quick Look of the project in its most recent saved state, just as you would see with Quick Look in the Finder.

Importing Track Settings from Other Projects

One of the really handy features in Logic is the ability to import different settings directly from other Logic projects. After selecting a Logic project in the All Files Browser or opening the File menu, choosing Import, and selecting Logic Projects, clicking the Import button opens a window that gives you access to any available project alternatives. Once you select a project alternative you wish to explore, the All Files Browser switches to Track Import view, shown in Figure 12.14.

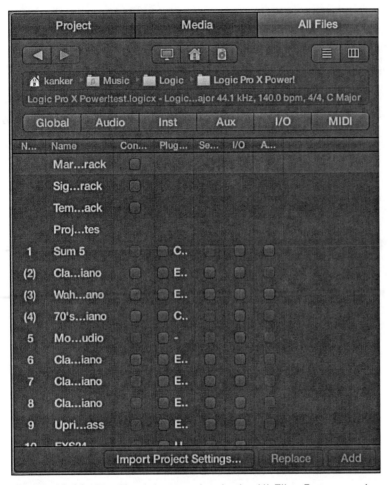

Figure 12.14 The Track Import view in the All Files Browser, where you can import settings from individual tracks in other Logic projects directly into your current Logic project.
© Apple Inc.

The Track Import view shows all the tracks in the selected project, including the marker, signature, and tempo global tracks. You can select what type of settings will be imported from each individual track by selecting the appropriate checkboxes. You can also filter the types of tracks that are displayed using the Global, Audio, Inst, Aux, I/O, and MIDI filter buttons that appear at the top of the list of tracks, similar to the way you can filter tracks in the Mixer. The columns and options of the Track Import view are as follows:

- ▷ **Num:** The Num column displays track numbers in the selected project, where applicable.
- ▷ **Name:** This column displays the name of each track in the selected project.
- ▷ **Content:** If you select Content and click the Add button, the region data or global track data for the selected track(s) will be imported, and a new track will be created for each imported track. The channel strip settings for any track imported via the Content option will not be imported.
- ▷ **Plug-ins:** If you select Plug-ins and click Add, the region data (if applicable) and channel strip settings will be imported for each selected track to new tracks.
- ▷ **Sends:** If you select Sends and click Add, you will be prompted to either add a new aux that matches the aux selected in the All Files Browser or select an aux in your current project to convert to the aux selected in the All Files Browser.
- ▷ **I/O:** If you select I/O and click Add, tracks that share an I/O configuration will be imported, creating new tracks in the Tracks area with empty channel strips.
- ▷ **Auto:** If you select Auto and click Add, the automation data for the selected track(s) will be imported into new tracks in the Tracks area with empty channel strips.
- ▷ **Notes:** The Notes option lets you import notes for the selected track.

You can select multiple options per track, and all the selected options for a track will be imported to a single track. You can click on one option for a track and press the right arrow key on your keyboard to select all options for the selected track. Pressing the left arrow key deselects all options on the selected track. Selecting any option for a track in a Track Stack automatically selects all options for all tracks in the Track Stack.

The Replace button at the bottom of the Track Import view transfers that data to the currently selected tracks in the main window, replacing all data of the selected types on the selected track. Otherwise, click the Add button to import everything you have selected into the current project.

The Import Project Settings Window

There may be times when you want to import different settings from other projects, such as screensets, staff styles, or lane sets. To browse for a Logic project in a typical file browser, open the File menu, choose Project Settings, and select Import Project Settings. To import a project, select it in this file browser and click Import. After you click Import, or after you click the Import Project Settings button at the bottom of the Track Import view, the Import Project Settings dialog box opens, as shown in Figure 12.15.

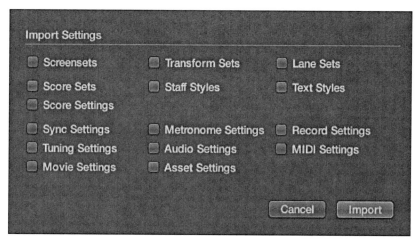

Figure 12.15 The Import Project Settings dialog box.
© Apple Inc.

The settings from which you can choose are as follows:

▷ Screensets
▷ Transform Sets
▷ Lane Sets
▷ Score Sets
▷ Staff Styles
▷ Text Styles
▷ Score Settings
▷ Sync Settings
▷ Metronome Settings
▷ Record Settings
▷ Tuning Settings
▷ Audio Settings
▷ MIDI Settings
▷ Movie Settings
▷ Asset Settings

Simply select the settings you wish to import and click Import. The chosen settings will be imported into the current project.

Exporting Files from Logic

If you want to export your Logic project in a different format for use in a different application (or an earlier version of Logic), Logic offers an Export submenu in the global File menu. Figure 12.16 shows this submenu.

Figure 12.16 The Export submenu in the global File menu features options for exporting files from Logic into different formats.
© Apple Inc.

The export options are as follows:

▷ **Region to Loop Library.** Selecting a region and using the Region to Loop Library command opens the Add Region to Apple Loops Library window. This command and the Add Region to Apple Loops Library window were covered in Chapter 7.

▷ **Region as Audio File:** This command allows you to export the selected audio or software instrument region as an audio file. When selected, this command opens the Region as Audio File dialog box, shown in Figure 12.17. In addition to the normal Save As dialog box features, this dialog box gives you a number of different options regarding how Logic will bounce your regions. These options are as follows:

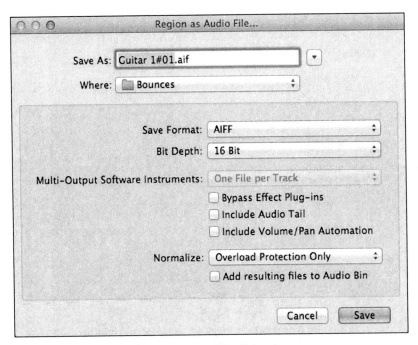

Figure 12.17 The Region as Audio File dialog box.
© Apple Inc.

▷ **Save Format:** Use this menu to select the save format for your exported audio file: AIFF, CAF, or Broadcast Wave.

▷ **Bit Depth:** Select the bit depth (8-, 16-, or 24-bit, or 32-bit float) of your exported audio file in this menu.

▷ **Multi-Output Software Instruments:** This menu offers two options: One File per Track and One File per Channel Strip. The One File per Track option creates one bounce file for the selected multi-output software instrument track in the Tracks area. The One File per Channel Strip option creates one file for every channel strip a multi-output software instrument utilizes, including aux channel strips. Exporting a Multi-Output Software Instrument region to audio automatically selects the Include Volume/Pan Automation option.

▷ **Bypass Effect Plug-Ins:** Selecting this option lets you bypass the effect plug-ins for the exported audio file.

▷ **Include Audio Tail:** When you select this option, the exported audio file is automatically lengthened to include any effects tails, similar to the Include Audio Tail option in the Bounce dialog box.

▷ **Include Volume/Pan Automation:** With this option selected, all volume and pan automation that occurs over the selected region will be performed during the export.

▷ **Normalize:** The Normalize menu offers the same options for export as the Normalize menu in the Bounce dialog box: On, Off, and Overload Protection Only. With On selected, the exported file will be normalized. With Off selected, the exported file will not be normalized. With Overload Protection Only selected, the file will be scanned for peaks over 0 dBFS. Those peaks will be reduced to 0 dBFS, and the rest of the file will not be altered.

▷ **Add Resulting Files to Audio Bin:** Select Add Resulting Files to Audio Bin to have the exported audio added to the Project Audio Browser. ("Audio Bin" is what the Project Audio Browser was named in Logic 9; as of this writing, this detail has not been updated to current Logic Pro X terminology.)

When you click Save, Logic will perform an offline bounce of the selected region.

▷ **Selection as MIDI File:** To export MIDI data from Logic, first select one or more MIDI regions (across as many tracks as you'd like); then choose this option or press Option+Command+E. A dialog box will prompt you to choose a name and a directory for your exported file, and your MIDI selection will be exported with a .mid extension to denote that it is a Standard MIDI File (SMF) file. By default, Logic exports SMFs in Format 1, where the file can contain one or more MIDI tracks. In the Project Handling tab of the Global Preferences window, shown in Figure 12.4, there is an option to export single MIDI as Format 0. Format 0 SMFs consist of one multichannel track. To export a Format 0 SMF, you would first need to merge all your MIDI regions into one region on one track. First, select all your MIDI regions; then open the Edit menu, choose Join, and select Regions, or press Command+J. You can now export your MIDI file as a Format 0 SMF.

▷ **Track as Audio File:** This command allows you to export the selected audio or software instrument track as an audio file. Selecting this command brings up a dialog box identical to the one shown in Figure 12.17. Logic Pro will do an offline bounce of the selected track that begins at the project's beginning and ends at the project's end. The key command for this is Command+E.

▷ **All Tracks as Audio Files:** This command allows you to export all of your audio and software instrument tracks as separate audio files. Selecting this command or pressing Shift+Command+E brings up a dialog box identical to the one shown in Figure 12.17. The export options you specify will be applied to every track you export. For example, you can't choose different formats and/or bit depths for different tracks; they will all have the same format and bit depth. Logic Pro will do an offline bounce of each track that begins at the project's beginning and ends at the project's end.

▷ **Project as AAF File:** When you choose to export your song as a new, professional Advanced Authoring Format (AAF) file, you are presented with a specialized Save AAF File As dialog box, shown in Figure 12.18. In addition to the normal Save As dialog box options, this dialog box offers four Audio File Export Settings:

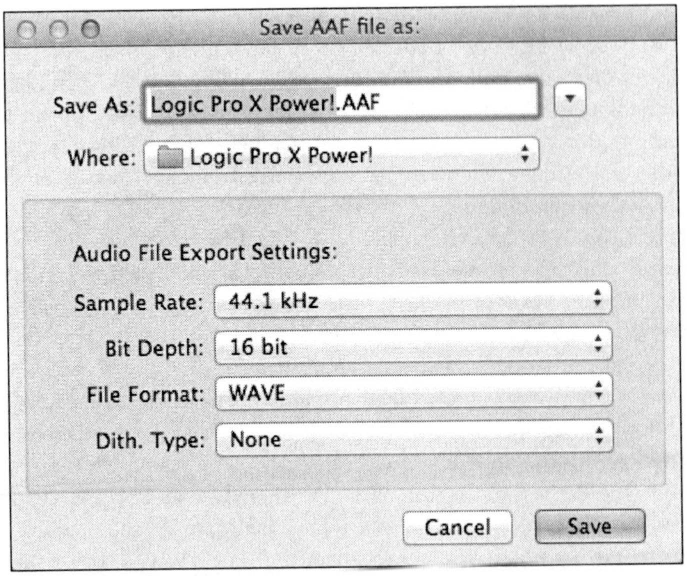

Figure 12.18 The Save AAF File As dialog box.
© Apple Inc.

In addition to the normal Save As window options, this dialog box offers four Audio File Export Settings:

▷ **Sample Rate:** You can select a sample rate from 44.1 kHz to 96 kHz.
▷ **Bit Depth:** You can select a bit depth of either 16 or 24 bit.
▷ **File Format:** You can select either the WAVE or AIFF format for your audio files.
▷ **Dither Type:** If you have selected 16-bit audio files from 24-bit originals, you should select one of the available dither algorithms to dither your files.

When you are finished setting up the AAF audio file export settings, click Save, and Logic will export your Logic song as an AAF.

▷ **Project to Final Cut Pro/XML:** This option will save your Logic song in Extensible Markup Language (XML) for use in Final Cut Pro. When you select this option, it will present you with a Save As dialog box that has two options: Include Video in Export and Export as Final Cut Compound Clip. Simply name your file, choose if you will include the video and export the project as a Final Cut compound clip, choose where to save your XML file, and press Return. Logic will save your song as an XML file that you can then import into Final Cut Pro.
▷ **Score as MusicXML:** The Export Score as MusicXML command lets you export your project's score in an industry-standard format that is compatible with many DAWs and scoring applications. When you select this option, a simple Save As dialog box opens.

Sharing Audio to iTunes, the Media Browser, and SoundCloud

As you are working on a project, and particularly when you are finished with it, you very likely will want to share your audio on the Internet or to other applications, like iTunes or Final Cut Pro. The Share submenu of the File menu, shown in Figure 12.19, helps you accomplish these things without having to bounce the file. Let's check out the different sharing options.

Figure 12.19 The Share submenu of the File menu.
© Apple Inc.

Sharing to iTunes

Perhaps the most common destination for bounced audio is iTunes. Listening to audio, putting it on an iOS device, and burning it to disc is what we do with iTunes. Logic Pro X lets you share audio directly to iTunes. When you open the File menu, choose Share, and select To iTunes, the Share to iTunes dialog box, shown in Figure 12.20, opens.

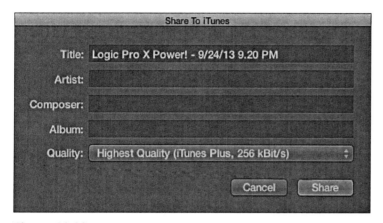

Figure 12.20 The Share to iTunes dialog box lets you add metadata to the audio being shared to iTunes and to select the audio quality.
© Apple Inc.

The Share to iTunes dialog box lets you add metadata to the audio you are sharing to iTunes, including the title, artist, composer, and album, making it easy to find and sort in iTunes. If you need to add additional metadata, you can accomplish that in iTunes using the Get Info command (right-click on the file in iTunes).

You can also select the quality of the audio that will be shared to iTunes. There are five Quality options in the Quality menu:

▷ Low Quality (64 kBit/s)
▷ Medium Quality (128 kBit/s)
▷ High Quality (192 kBit/s)
▷ Highest Quality (256 kBit/s)
▷ Uncompressed (AIFF)

The first four options share your audio in the compressed AAC format. What quality setting you choose is determined by your source audio and how critical the delivery format is. For example, a spoken-word audio file could be shared at 64 kBit/s with little if any audible degradation of the source audio, particularly for private consumption. If you're looking to listen to a mix of a song with everything from bass to high guitar or keyboard parts, anything less than 192 kBit/s would degrade the audio too much, while 256 kBit/s and especially AIFF would be the preferred audio quality.

After you have filled in the metadata fields and chosen a quality setting, click Share. Logic will bounce your audio and share it to iTunes, and iTunes will open and play your shared file. Note that when you share a file with Cycle engaged, the Cycle region will be shared.

Sharing to the Media Browser

Sharing to the Media Browser makes it easy to make your bounced audio available to other Apple applications like iMovie. To share to the Media Browser, open the File menu, choose Share, and select the To Media Browser. This opens the Share to Media Browser dialog box, shown in Figure 12.21.

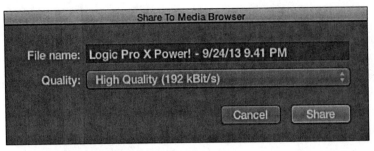

Figure 12.21 The Share To Media Browser window.
© Apple Inc.

The Share to Media Browser dialog box lets you name the file and select the file's quality, with the same quality settings as in the Share to iTunes dialog box. When you're finished choosing your settings, click Share; the project is bounced and shared to the Media Browser.

Sharing to SoundCloud

SoundCloud (www.soundcloud.com) is one of the most popular sites on the Internet for individuals and bands to share their music with the world. Logic Pro X lets you share your projects directly to SoundCloud. Don't worry if you don't have a SoundCloud account; the first time you open the File menu, choose Share, and select the To SoundCloud command, a dialog box opens that lets you either log in to your SoundCloud account or create a new one. After you log in or create a new account, the Share to SoundCloud dialog box, shown in Figure 12.22, will open.

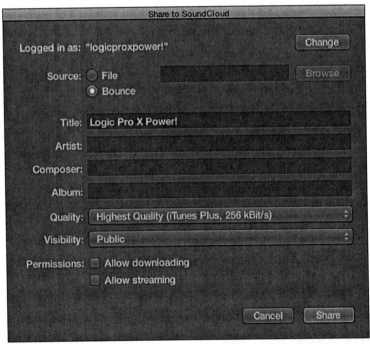

Figure 12.22 The Share to SoundCloud dialog box lets you share your project audio directly to the Internet.
© Apple Inc.

The Title, Artist, Composer, Album, and Quality options are identical to those offered in the Share to iTunes window. There are some options unique to the Share to SoundCloud dialog box, however. Those options are as follows:

▷ **Logged In As:** The Logged In As area shows you the username of the SoundCloud account to which you currently have access.

▷ **Change:** Click the Change button if you need to log in to a different SoundCloud account to share the project audio.

▷ **Source:** Source gives you two options: File and Bounce. If you select File, you can click the Browse button to open a file browser in which you can select an audio file to share to SoundCloud. If you select Bounce, you will share the audio from your project to SoundCloud when you click the Share button.

▷ **Visibility:** The Visibility menu lets you select whether your shared audio will be public or private.

▷ **Permissions:** The permissions options let you determine whether your shared audio can be downloaded and/or streamed.

Once you have configured all the Share to SoundCloud options, click Share. Assuming you are connected to the Internet, your project audio will be bounced and uploaded to SoundCloud!

Advanced Tempo Operations

13

T EMPO, MEANING SPEED AND TIMING, is one of the most important elements in music. Tempo management can be as simple as agreeing on the tempo of a song and asking all the musicians to play in time, or it can be as complicated as keeping track of multiple tempo changes throughout a musical movement—or even continuous tempo changes. With digital audio sequencers being the nerve center for both electronic and acoustic, programmed and performed tracks, it becomes vital that the sequencer keeps everything synchronized and gives the user the tools to fully implement whatever tempo requirements he has.

Luckily, Logic is up to the task. Logic offers many different tempo functions and, in typical Logic fashion, many ways to use them, depending on your own personal style. It can sync with external hardware through a number of common protocols, and it keeps perfect internal sync.

We have already discussed the most innovative and intuitive controls Logic gives you over tempo: the tempo and beat-mapping tracks, discussed in detail in Chapter 4, "Global Elements of Logic." By contrast, in this chapter, you'll explore Logic Pro's other tools to work with tempo and synchronization.

Tempo Operations Versus Flex Time: If you're not familiar with the musical concept of tempo, I forgive you for thinking that "tempo operations" are part of Logic Pro's Flex Time functions. After all, Flex Time is supposed to adjust audio to the tempo, right? But in fact, it is the reverse: Flex Time relies on Logic's facility with tempo. Here's a quick explanation.

As explained, Logic includes lots of functions to manage the tempo—that is, the speed and timing—of your *project*. Flex Time is a subset of features that lets you manage the tempo of your *audio regions*. So for example, say you use Flex Time's quantize features to adjust your audio to the song tempo. Flex is relying on Logic's tempo operations to define and manage the project tempo, which then determines how Flex will quantize the "flexed" audio region. As you can see, because Flex relies on Logic's tempo management to work its magic, Logic's tempo operations are far more than simply an aspect of Flex Time.

The Tempo Display

The first step in tempo management is to know what the tempo is. As discussed in Chapter 5, "Transport Controls and Recording," the tempo is shown in the Tempo display in the LCD area of the transport in the control bar. Figure 13.1 shows this.

Figure 13.1 As you recall from Chapter 5, the Tempo display in the LCD area in the transport shows the current song tempo. Chapter 5 also explained how to change the display preferences for the Tempo display if you want.
© Apple Inc.

The Tempo display will show the current song tempo even if an external device to which Logic is synced is determining the tempo. If your Logic project has only a single tempo, and Logic is the master of any external devices (or if you have no external devices and Logic is the only tempo master), the easiest way to set the tempo is simply to double-click the tempo in the Tempo display and manually enter the correct number. For more involved tempo manipulation, Logic offers a number of methods to edit tempo.

Recording and Editing Tempo

Whether you want to add only a few subtle tempo changes or a complex set of evolving tempos for different movements, Logic gives you a number of methods to record and edit tempo changes. This section discusses the variety of ways you can perform or program tempo changes.

Programming Tempo Changes on the Tempo Track

The tempo track discussed in Chapter 4 not only displays any tempo changes in your song, but also gives you an intuitive track on which to enter your tempo changes. Please refer to the section titled "The Tempo Track" in Chapter 4 for the complete details.

Recording Tempo Changes

To record tempo changes while you are performing (for example, by adjusting a Tempo slider on external hardware), make sure the Allow Tempo Change Recording checkbox is selected in the Recording screen of the Project Settings window. To access this screen, open the File menu, choose Project Settings, and click the Recording option. Figure 13.2 shows this preference turned on.

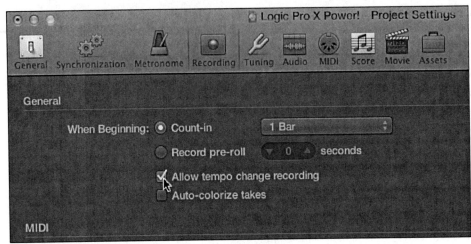

Figure 13.2 Select the Allow Tempo Change Recording checkbox in the Recording screen of the Project Settings window if you want to record tempo changes in real time.
© Apple Inc.

After you select this checkbox, any tempo changes you make while recording will be saved into the tempo track, which is the internal list of tempo changes that Logic maintains to manage a song's tempo. The next subsections discuss the two ways to access, add to, and edit that tempo track.

Tap Tempo and the Tempo Interpreter

If you want to record your tempo live, perhaps the best way to do so is to tap your tempo into Logic as you are performing. To accomplish this, Logic includes a Tap Tempo key command (which you would need to assign) and a Tempo Interpreter window.

To access the Tempo Interpreter window, in the Tracks area or Tempo List editor, open the Edit menu, choose Tempo, and select Tempo Interpreter. Alternatively, click and hold the Sync button on the transport (see Chapter 5) to reveal its pull-down menu and select Open Tempo Interpreter. Figure 13.3 shows the Tempo Interpreter window.

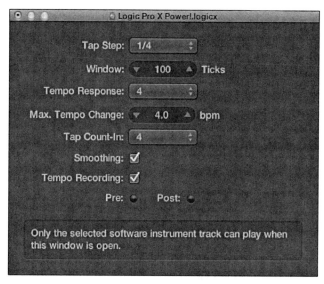

Figure 13.3 The Tempo Interpreter window.
© Apple Inc.

This window enables you to configure how Logic will interpret those tempos that you tap in with the Tap Tempo key command. A description of the parameters follows.

▷ **Tap Step:** This sets the note value that Logic will assign to each of your taps. Generally, the best possible selection is 1/4 notes. Smaller figures will give you too much variation, and larger divisions will not accurately capture the tempo.

▷ **Window (Ticks):** This adjusts how much of a window in time there is in which taps will be interpreted as tempo taps. In other words, if you set a huge window, only taps that are a very large number of ticks apart will be counted as taps for determining tempo. If you set a tiny window, nearly every tick will be counted. In general, you'll want this value to be large enough that double-clicks or ghost-clicks won't be counted but anything else will.

▷ **Tempo Response:** This sets Logic's internal sensitivity for tempo changes. The higher the value, the more responsive Logic will be—meaning, the more often Logic will change the tempo of the song. If you are hoping for a constant tempo, a value of 2 should work. If you are expecting some tempo changes, a value of 4 is recommended.

▷ **Max. Tempo Change:** You probably don't want wild changes in your song. You should set as small a value as possible here so that any inconsistencies in your tapping don't result in outlandishly large tempo variations.

▷ **Tap Count-In:** This enables you to tap a count into your song. Type in the number of taps you want as a count (if any).

▷ **Smoothing:** If you select this checkbox, any jumps in tempo will be smoothed out. If you want your taps to be followed exactly, do not select this checkbox.

▷ **Tempo Recording:** This will create a real-time Tempo List editor if you are creating tap tempo events in Record mode. Normally, you will not need this, so you'll want to leave it off.

▷ **Pre and Post:** These have to do with how your taps are displayed onscreen. If you select the Pre option, every tap that is input will be displayed. If you select the Post option, only those taps that are in the accepted timeframe defined in the Window parameter above will be displayed. Accepted taps flash yellow; unaccepted taps flash red. If you do not select either option, of course, no taps will flash at all.

In the General screen of the Synchronization window, you will need to set the Sync Mode menu to Manual and ensure that the Auto-Enable External Sync and Tap Tempo checkbox is selected, as shown in Figure 13.4. To access this screen, open the File menu, choose Project Settings, and click Synchronization. Alternatively, click and hold the Sync button in the transport and select Synchronization Settings. You can also change the sync mode by clicking and holding the Sync button and selecting the desired sync setting.

Figure 13.4 The Synchronization screen of the Project Settings window. Under the General tab, set the Sync Mode setting to Manual and select the Auto-Enable External Sync for Logic checkbox to recognize tap tempo.
© Apple Inc.

Remember, you will need to assign a key command or MIDI command to record tempo this way.

Real-Time Tempo Fader

One of the special Environment fader objects is a Tempo fader. To create this object, in the Environment, open the local New menu, choose Fader, select Specials, and choose Tempo Control. You can use this fader to create real-time tempo changes in Logic by using the mouse to adjust the fader value. The range of this fader is 50–177 BPM.

If you only want to adjust the tempo during playback, you do not need to cable the fader to anything. You can simply click and drag the fader, and the playback tempo will change. However, if you want to record your tempo changes or control the fader from something like a hardware MIDI device's pitch bend wheel (you can set this to another controller if you like, but using the pitch bend wheel generally works best during a MIDI performance), you'll need to connect the fader between the physical input and sequencer input objects. Fortunately, when you create the Tempo fader, a window opens, reminding you how to cable the tempo fader!

If you'd like to configure a MIDI controller for your Tempo fader, select Control in the Tempo fader's Object Inspector, set the channel to the correct MIDI channel, and set the 1 parameter to the desired MIDI controller number.

Tempo List Editor

The Tempo List editor is available in the Lists area of the main window and as a floating window. You can create and edit tempo events in a text-based format using the Tempo List editor. If you click and hold the transport's Sync button, you can select Open Tempo List from the pull-down menu, which will open the Tempo List editor. You also can access the Tempo List editor via the Tracks area and the Lists area Tempo List editor by opening the Edit menu, choosing Tempo, and selecting Show Tempo List, via the Option+Shift+T key command, or by clicking and dragging the Tempo heading in the Lists area. Figure 13.5 shows the Tempo List editor.

Event	Marker	Tempo	Signature
Edit ▾	Options ▾	▸Y◂	Additional Info
+		Tempo Set: Untitled	
Position	**Tempo**	**SMPTE Position**	
1 1 1 1	98.0000	01:00:00:00.00	
17 1 1 1	95.0000	01:00:39:04.47	
33 1 1 1	98.0000	01:01:19:15.09	
49 1 1 1	93.0000	01:01:58:19.56	

Figure 13.5 The Tempo List editor.
© Apple Inc.

You will notice that this basically looks like a standard Event list. You can manipulate the events in the Tempo List editor similarly to how you would in a normal Event list, as described in Chapter 8, "Working with MIDI." You can add tempo events at the current playhead position by clicking the Create New Tempo Event button (the plus sign [+] below the Tempo List Edit menu). A new tempo event will appear, which you can edit by double-clicking on any parameter (Position, Tempo, or SMPTE Position). Press Return to enter the data. Also, you can click on any of the parameters and drag up or down with your mouse to change the value. If you have created any tempo curves in the tempo track, engaging the Additional Info button will display more events along the tempo curves. Finally, you can delete tempo events by pressing the Delete key or using the Eraser tool.

> **TIP:** Sometimes, you may want more than a single Tempo List editor in order to experiment with different tempos, changes in different places, and so on. To facilitate this, Logic allows you to store several alternative Tempo List editors, called tempo sets. The Tempo Set menu, accessible in the Tempo List editor or by clicking on Tempo in the tempo track header, lets you create, delete, and rename tempo sets, and also select what tempo set is in use. Remember that because the Tempo List editor and the global tempo track are showing the same information in different ways, any changes you make to tempo events in one editor will show up in the other editor.

Tempo Operations

You can access the Tempo Operations window in a number of ways. You can open the Edit menu in the Tracks area and Tempo List editor, select Tempo, and choose Tempo Operations. You can also open the Tempo Operations window from the pull-down menu accessible from the Sync button, as with the Tempo editors. Figure 13.6 shows the Tempo Operations window.

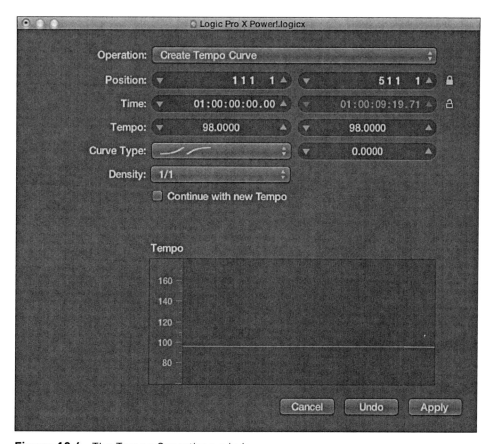

Figure 13.6 The Tempo Operations window.
© Apple Inc.

As with the tempo track and Tempo List editor already discussed, the Tempo Operations window provides another option for creating and editing tempo changes. To use the Tempo Operations window, you'll need to make a selection in another Tempo List editor; your tempo will be shown in the window. You might have to re-open the Tempo Operations window to reflect any recent tempo changes.

The Operation pull-down menu, shown in Figure 13.7, contains the six functions possible in the Tempo Operations window.

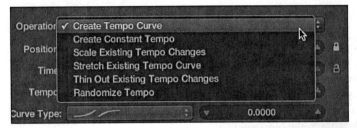

Figure 13.7 The Operation pull-down menu lists the six functions possible in the Tempo Operations window.
© Apple Inc.

The following sections describe each of the Tempo Operations window functions. You will find that most of these processes can be accomplished more quickly and intuitively in the tempo track.

Create Tempo Curve

This function enables you to create a tempo curve. To generate a curve, first choose one of the three curves available from the Curve Type pull-down menu, shown in Figure 13.8.

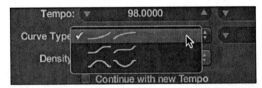

Figure 13.8 The Curve Type pull-down menu in the middle left of the Tempo Operations window contains the three curve shapes that you can choose for your tempo curve.
© Apple Inc.

After you've chosen a curve, adjust the Position or Time settings to set the start position and end position of your tempo change curve. Below those parameters, enter the starting and ending tempos you want in the tempo track. Finally, set the Curvature parameter in the field to the right of the Curve Type menu, which determines the curve on which your tempo will speed up or slow down, depending on whether you enter a positive or a negative number. Values between 1.0000 and −1.0000 are allowed. After that, clicking the Apply button will create your tempo curve.

If you need more tempo events for a smoother curve, you can enter a smaller note denomination in the Density parameter. Figure 13.9 shows a descending tempo curve created using 1/8 notes.

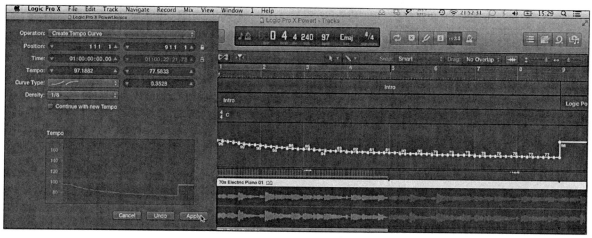

Figure 13.9 This curve was created by the Create Tempo Curve operation generating one tempo event every 1/8 note over the area specified by the chosen parameters.
© Apple Inc.

You can select the Continue with New Tempo checkbox if you want your song to maintain the tempo at which your curve ends. If you want to revert to the original song tempo after your curve, leave this checkbox unchecked.

As you can see, creating tempo curves on the tempo track is *far* simpler than using the Tempo Operations window!

Create Constant Tempo

If you want to eliminate all tempo events for a given area and simply set one tempo for a given length of time, this operation will do it. As you can see in Figure 13.10, the only options with this function are the Position and Time settings for the start and end positions your constant tempo should be set and the Tempo field to enter what the tempo should be.

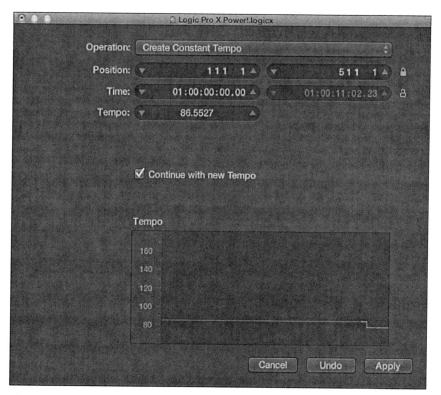

Figure 13.10 The Create Constant Tempo screen of the Tempo Operations window.
© Apple Inc.

You can use the Continue with New Tempo checkbox to either maintain this tempo for the rest of the song or revert to the original tempo after your section of constant tempo. Again, this process has been superseded by the tempo track.

Scale Existing Tempo Changes

This lets you adjust currently existing tempo functions proportionally. You can set the Position and Time settings to determine the start and end positions across which you want your scaling to occur. You then enter the percentage of scaling you want to apply to the current tempo events and the average tempo. Figure 13.11 shows the Scale Existing Tempo Changes settings.

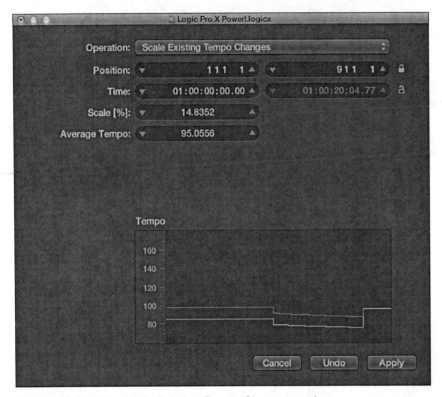

Figure 13.11   The Scale Existing Tempo Changes settings.
© Apple Inc.

Stretch Existing Tempo Curve

This enables you to shrink or elongate an existing tempo curve. You can adjust New End Position and New End Time settings as well as the percentage of stretching you want as you adjust the length of the existing tempo curve. Figure 13.12 shows the Stretch Existing Tempo Curve screen.

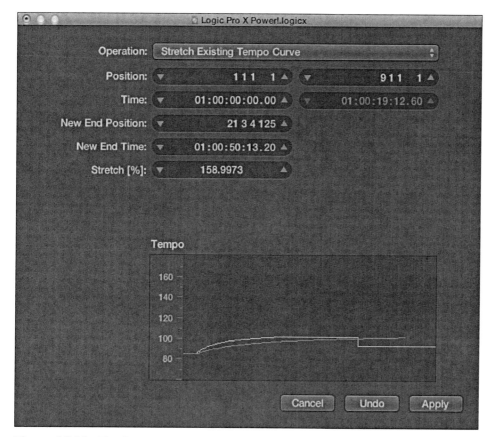

Figure 13.12 The Stretch Existing Tempo Curve settings.
© Apple Inc.

Thin Out Existing Tempo Changes

This lets you remove tempo events from a given length of time. You can set the position or time at which you want the thinning to occur and the density of events you want to remain after processing. Figure 13.13 shows the Thin Out Existing Tempo Changes screen.

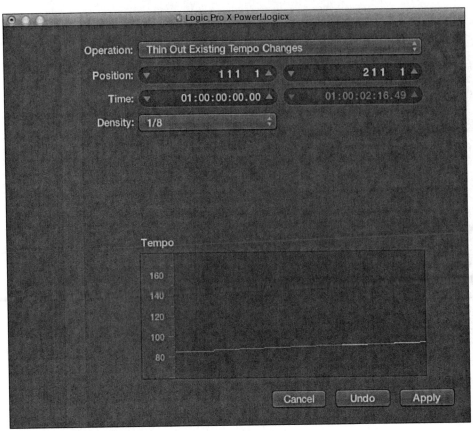

Figure 13.13 The Thin Out Existing Tempo Changes settings.
© Apple Inc.

This is something that the Tempo Operations window might come in handy for. The tempo track doesn't offer a simpler way to thin out specific tempo changes, and manually deleting tempo events from the Tempo List editor could be time consuming.

Randomize Tempo

Finally, you can randomize your tempo—create a random deviation in beats per minute (BPM) from your current tempo. The Position and Time parameters determine the start and end positions of the section of random tempo deviation, and the Density setting defines how many program changes will appear per bar. The Randomize parameter defines the extent the random tempos will deviate from the current tempo(s) of the defined region, with larger positive and negative values creating larger deviations. Figure 13.14 shows the Randomize Tempo screen.

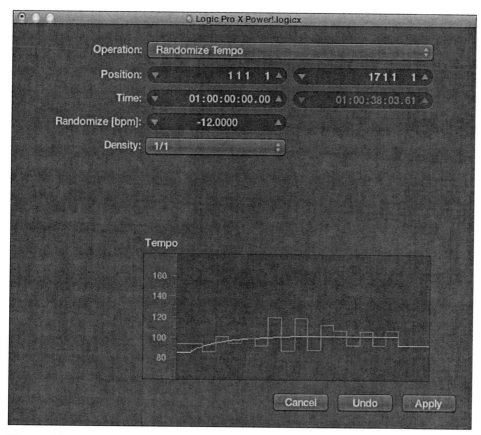

Figure 13.14 The Randomize Tempo settings.
© Apple Inc.

This is another thing that you might want to use the Tempo Operations window for, because the tempo track doesn't lend itself to randomizing tempo changes.

Matching the Project Tempo to an Audio Region

There might be times when you want to build a song, or even just a section of a song, around an audio clip. For example, suppose you have a two-bar bass pattern, but you don't know its tempo. Now you have a problem: how to set the project's tempo to a value that matches the tempo of your audio. Logic allows you to set your project's tempo to match your audio region with ease.

First, you need to select the audio region you will use to define the tempo. Next, set the locators either in the Bar ruler or in the transport to start at the beginning of your audio region and end at a musically meaningful location, typically the end of a bar. Using the two-bar bass pattern as an example, you would set the cycle length to two bars, as shown in Figure 13.15.

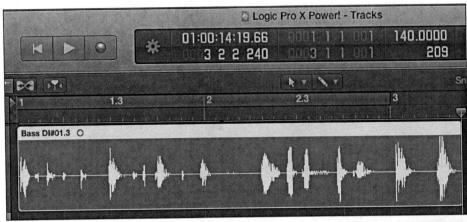

Figure 13.15 To match the project tempo to an audio region, first set the locators to match the length you want your audio region to define.
© Apple Inc.

Next, open the local Tracks area Edit menu, select Tempo, and choose Adjust Tempo Using Region Length and Locators. This opens the dialog box shown in Figure 13.16, which asks whether you want to change the project's global tempo or simply change the tempo inside the locators.

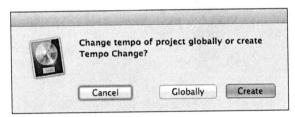

Figure 13.16 The Change Tempo of Project Globally or Create Tempo Change dialog box.
© Apple Inc.

Selecting the Globally option changes the entire project tempo to match that of your audio region. Selecting the Create option allows you to change the tempo of the area inside the locators only. Figure 13.17 shows the end result of this process: The selected audio region now fits the locators, and the project's tempo has changed to reflect the length of the audio region.

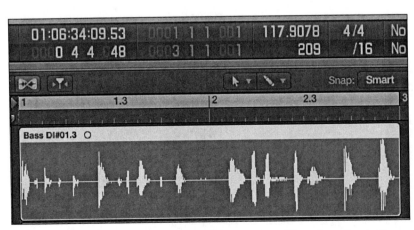

Figure 13.17 After matching the tempo to an audio region, the audio region fits the locators, and the project's tempo has changed.
© Apple Inc.

Using Beat Detection to Adjust the Project Tempo

Using beat detection as a guide, you can have Logic analyze a region and offer a number of suggestions for possible tempos derived from the selected region. First you need to select one or more regions. Use the Transients buttons in the Beat Mapping global track header to adjust the beat detection sensitivity. The more sensitive the beat detection, the more tempo options Logic will present to you when you invoke the Adjust Tempo Using Beat Detection command. You can access this command by opening the Tracks area local Edit menu, choosing Tempo, and selecting Adjust Tempo Using Beat Detection or by pressing the Option+Command+T key command. The Adjust Tempo Using Beat Detection command opens the Adjust Tempo Using Beat Detection dialog box, shown in Figure 13.18. (To open the Advanced Options area, click its disclosure triangle.)

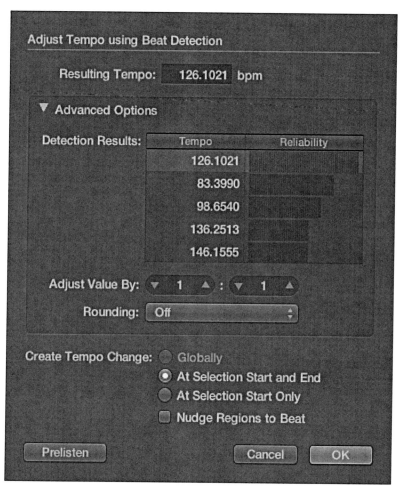

Figure 13.18 The Adjust Tempo Using Beat Detection dialog box.
© Apple Inc.

The parameters in the Adjust Tempo Using Beat Detection dialog box are as follows:

▷ **Resulting Tempo:** The Resulting Tempo field displays the tempo that will result from using the settings assigned throughout the rest of the Adjust Tempo Using Beat Detection dialog box.

▷ **Detection Results:** The Detection Results area lists the potential results from which you can choose. The more transients you have detected, the more results you will see. The Tempo column lists the tempo of each result and the Reliability column shows bars to demonstrate graphically the extent to which Logic believes a particular tempo to be correct. Logic automatically selects the first result. To select a different result, simply click on the desired result. The Resulting Tempo field will update to reflect the tempo of the selected result.

▷ **Adjust Value By:** The Adjust Value By fields enable you to set a ratio that will affect the value in the Resulting Tempo field. A ratio of 3:1 will triple the tempo. A ratio of 1:3 will cut the tempo to one third of its original setting. You can set each Adjust Value By field from 1 to 16 by clicking and dragging in the desired field, by clicking the up or down arrows in the desired field, or by double-clicking in the desired field and entering a value manually.

▷ **Rounding:** The Rounding menu lets you define the type of rounding Logic will apply to the tempo value the Adjust Tempo Using Beat Detection command creates. Figure 13.19 shows the Rounding menu.

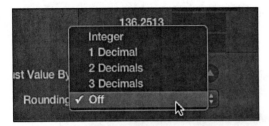

Figure 13.19 The Rounding menu lets you define what type of rounding, if any, will be applied to the tempo value resulting from the Adjust Tempo Using Beat Detection command.
© Apple Inc.

If you select Off, the tempo will not be rounded. Selecting 1 Decimal, 2 Decimals, or 3 Decimals will round the tempo to tenths, hundredths, or thousandths place, respectively. Selecting Integer rounds the tempo to a whole number.

▷ **Create Tempo Change:** Create Tempo Change gives you three options to define the extent to which the Adjust Tempo Using Beat Detection command affects the project tempo. If you select the Globally option, the tempo of the entire project will be altered to reflect the result of the Adjust Tempo Using Beat Detection command. If you select At Selection Start and End, the tempo of the area defined by the selected region(s) will be altered to reflect the result of the Adjust Tempo Using Beat Detection command, and the previous tempo will begin again at the end of the selected region(s). If you select At Selection Start Only, the tempo of the project will be altered at the beginning of the first selected region to reflect the result of the Adjust Tempo Using Beat Detection command. That tempo will remain in effect through the end of the project unless there is another tempo change event later in the project.

▷ **Nudge Regions to Beat:** With this checkbox selected, all selected regions will be nudged by the same amount as it takes to move the first transient in the first selected region to the closest beat.

▷ **Prelisten:** Click the Prelisten button to hear the tempo change the Adjust Tempo Using Beat Detection command will create before finalizing the command.

Once you have set the parameters in the Adjust Tempo Using Beat Detection dialog box to your liking, click the OK button, and the project tempo will change!

Detecting the Tempo of an Audio Region

You can use Logic's beat detection to detect the tempo of an audio region by opening the local Edit menu, choosing Tempo, and selecting Detect Tempo of Selected Region. This opens the Detect Tempo of Audio Regions dialog box, shown in Figure 13.20.

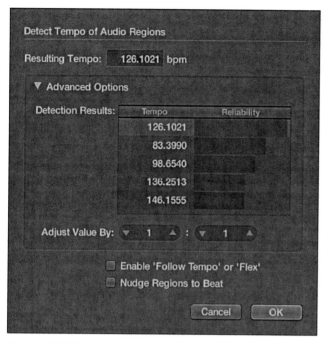

Figure 13.20 Use the Detect Tempo of Selected Region command to use beat detection find out the possible tempos of an audio region.
© Apple Inc.

You can see that the Detect Tempo of Audio Regions dialog box looks similar to the Adjust Tempo Using Beat Detection dialog box (refer to Figure 13.18). It includes many of the same advanced options, which you access by clicking the disclosure triangle. The Resulting Tempo, Detection Results, Adjust Value By, and Nudge Regions to Beat functions are identical to those in the Adjust Tempo Using Beat Detection dialog box. There is one other command unique to the Detect Tempo of Audio Regions dialog box, however: Enable 'Follow Tempo' or 'Flex.' Selecting this option automatically enables the Follow Tempo checkbox in the selected region's Region Inspector when you click the OK button. The selected region will then automatically be adjusted to match the project's tempo.

Working with Tempo Data in Audio Files

Logic automatically saves tempo data into audio files bounced or exported from Logic. The Tempo submenu in the local Edit menu gives you three options for handling this data, as shown in Figure 13.21.

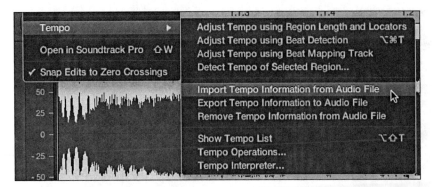

Figure 13.21   The Tempo submenu offers three options for dealing with tempo information in audio files.
© Apple Inc.

▷ **Import Tempo Information from Audio File:** Simply select an audio region, select this command, and the tempo data from the region will automatically be added to the global tempo track.

▷ **Export Tempo Information to Audio File:** You can export data from the tempo track into an audio region by selecting this command.

▷ **Remove Tempo Information from Audio File:** This command removes all tempo data from the selected region.

Working with Video

14

F OR THOSE INVOLVED IN SCORING COMMERCIALS, industrial videos, motion pictures, games, or any other visual medium that integrates music and/or sound, Logic provides features to enable you to synchronize your music production with the video. Logic does not enable you to edit your video; for that you need a video production application, such as Apple's world-class Final Cut Pro—and, as you saw in Chapter 12, "Working with and Sharing Files," you can export your Logic Pro project to Final Cut Pro/XML via the Export command. Logic Pro will, however, enable you to open your video, view your video alongside your Logic project, and lock your music to particular frames of video.

Logic supports Apple's QuickTime format for digital video. QuickTime is not only the Macintosh standard, but the format of choice among professionals. If you want to use video with Logic, make sure it is in the QuickTime format.

Opening Movies

There are number of ways to open a QuickTime video in Logic:

▷ Open the File menu, choose Movie, and select Open Movie.
▷ Press Option+Command+O.
▷ Click on the Movie track name and select Open Movie in the Movie menu.
▷ Click anywhere in the movie track with the Pencil tool and select Insert Movie.
▷ Right-click in the video track and choose the Open Movie option from the menu that appears.

If you use any of these methods, you will be presented with the Open File dialog box, with the Movies folder displayed by default, to choose your video. When you open your video, the Open Movie dialog box will appear, giving you two options: Open the Movie and Extract the Audio Track. Figure 14.1 shows the Open Movie dialog box.

Figure 14.1 The Open Movie dialog box.
© Apple Inc.

Although these functions are pretty self-explanatory, realize that you can use the commands independently to open only the video content of the movie by deselecting the Extract the Audio Track checkbox, or import only the audio by deselecting the Open Movie checkbox.

When you click OK to open the movie (regardless of the Extract the Audio Track setting), it will appear in its own window along with your Logic song. Figure 14.2 shows a video opened as part of a Logic song.

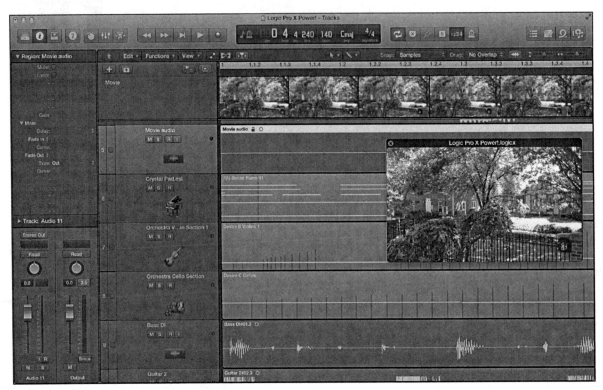

Figure 14.2 After you click OK in the Open Movie dialog box, you will be able to view a QuickTime movie along with your Logic project.
© Apple Inc.

If you wish to preview a movie before opening it, you can do so in the Movies tab of the Media Browser. To remove a movie from your project, use the Remove Movie command, which will be located in all the same menus as the Open Movie command. You can adjust the image size via the Movie Options menu, which is discussed in the following section.

Movie Options

If you right-click anywhere on your QuickTime Movie window, you will be presented with the Movie Options menu, shown in Figure 14.3.

Figure 14.3 You can access the Movie Options menu by right-clicking anywhere on your QuickTime Movie window.
© Apple Inc.

This menu gives you a number of resizing and synchronization options:

▷ **0.25 Size:** Display your movie at one quarter its original size.

▷ **0.5 Size:** Display your movie at half its original size.

▷ **Original Size:** Display your movie at its original size.

▷ **2× Size:** Display your movie at double its original size.

▷ **3× Size:** Display your movie at triple its original size.

▷ **Fullscreen:** Display your movie in a full-screen window.

▷ **Keep Aspect Ratio:** If you resize your Movie window, the aspect ratio of the video will be maintained.

▷ **Center:** This will place your Movie window in the middle of your screen. (If you have multiple monitors, your video will be placed in the middle of the monitor it is currently on.)

▷ **Movie Project Settings:** This opens the Movie Project Settings window. This window is described in the "Movie Project Settings" section, later in this chapter.

Movie Scene Markers

Movie scene markers are special markers locked to a specific SMPTE time. They were discussed in Chapter 4, "Global Elements of Logic," in the section on the video track. You can also create them via the Create Movie Scene Markers submenu. (Open the Navigate menu, choose Other, and choose Create Movie Scene Markers, as shown in Figure 14.4.)

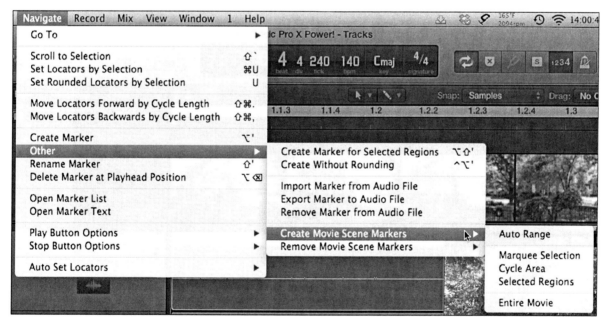

Figure 14.4 The Create Movie Scene Markers submenu gives you a variety of options for creating markers for your QuickTime movie.

© Apple Inc.

The Create Movie Scene Markers submenu commands function more or less the same as the Detect Cuts button on the movie track, discussed in Chapter 4. They search for scene cuts in your QuickTime movie and create movie markers in the marker track. Unlike the movie track Detect Cuts button, the Create Movie Scene Markers submenu commands can restrict Logic to looking for cuts within a cycle range, a Marquee tool selection, or a region selection.

You can delete movie markers via a dialog box that opens if you remove the movie from your project. You can also remove them by opening the Navigate menu, choosing Other, selecting Remove Movie Scene Markers, and choosing one of the commands in the submenu that appears. The Remove Movie Scene Markers submenu offers the same options for marker removal as the Create Movie Scene Markers submenu does.

> **NOTE:** Remember that Chapter 4 discussed the movie track, which is the global track that lets you view video thumbnails of your QuickTime movies along with your song. Also, your movie markers will show up on the marker track, another important global track. Remember to use these features in tandem with the Movie window.

> **TIP:** As experienced film and TV composers know, a hit point that is exactly on a cut to the frame will actually seem to sound a little early, which is why they frequently delay it by one to six frames. Although a movie scene marker's SMPTE position cannot be edited, it can be converted to a standard marker using the Convert to Standard Marker command in the Marker list's Options menu, and then adjusted as desired. Editing movie markers in the Marker list makes the process quick and easy.

Movie Project Settings

Among the various Project Settings is the Movie Project Settings window. To access this window, open the File menu, choose Project Settings, and select Movie or press Option+P and select the Movie screen. You can also right-click in the Movie window and select Movie Project Settings. Figure 14.5 shows the Movie Project Settings dialog box.

Figure 14.5 The Movie Project Settings dialog box.
© Apple Inc.

The options of this dialog box are as follows:

▷ **Movie Start:** The Movie Start setting allows you to offset the start of your video file in SMPTE units to match a particular bar position.

▷ **Movie Volume:** You can use this slider to adjust the level of your video's audio.

▷ **Follow Tempo:** Selecting the Follow Tempo checkbox allows your QuickTime movie to follow tempo change events using the Basis Tempo parameter as its baseline.

▷ **Basis Tempo:** The Basis Tempo parameter defines the base tempo for any tempo changes the video may undergo when the Follow Tempo option is active.

Movie Preferences

As you can see in Figure 14.5, there is a button on the bottom right of the Movie Settings window to open the Movie Preferences window. You can also access the Movie Preferences window by opening the Logic Pro X menu, choosing Preferences, and selecting Movie. Figure 14.6 shows the Movie Preferences window.

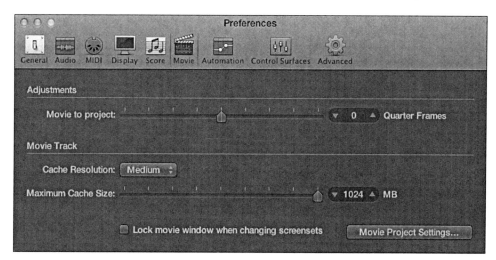

Figure 14.6 The Movie Preferences window.
© Apple Inc.

The Movie Preferences window includes the following options:

▷ **Movie to Project:** This is a global setting to fine-tune exactly which quarter frame your movie will start on. You can either adjust the slider or type in a number. The range is −48 to 48 quarter frames.

▷ **Cache Resolution:** This determines the resolution of video thumbnails stored in the temporary internal memory cache. Your options are Low, Medium, High, and Best. Obviously, the higher the quality, the more detail in your video thumbnails, but the more memory they take up.

▷ **Maximum Cache Size:** This determines how large your cache for video thumbnails can be. The memory is only filled when movie data is displayed.

▷ **Lock Movie Window When Changing Screensets:** If you work with video a lot and want movies you work with to be locked in position on the screen when changing screensets, engage this option.

Importing Audio from a QuickTime Movie

If you want to use the soundtrack from a QuickTime movie in your Logic project, you can use the Import Audio from Movie command to bring the QuickTime audio into your song. To use the command, open the File menu, choose Movie, and select Import Audio from Movie. When you do, Logic will automatically bounce the audio from the movie, perform any necessary sample-rate and format conversions, and add the new audio file to your Project Audio Browser using the name of the movie as the name of the new audio file. A new audio track will be created at the top of the Tracks area, and the audio from the movie will be placed on this track.

Exporting Audio to a QuickTime Movie

If you wish to add the bounced audio from your project into a QuickTime movie soundtrack using the Export Audio to Movie command, you will be presented with the Location and Name of New Movie dialog box, where you can also choose your export options, as shown in Figure 14.7.

Figure 14.7 The Location and Name of New Movie dialog box is where you set the location of your movie, name it, and set your export preferences.
© Apple Inc.

The available audio formats are Linear PCM, AAC, and Apple Lossless. Sample rates range from 44.1 to 96 kHz. Available bit depths are 16 and 24.

After you have chosen a location and a name to save your new QuickTime movie, you are prompted to specify which, if any, soundtracks from the original QuickTime movie should be included in the new QuickTime movie file. Figure 14.8 shows this window.

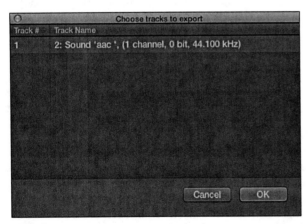

Figure 14.8 You can select which original tracks from the original QuickTime movie to include in the new QuickTime movie.
© Apple Inc.

Finally, Logic will bounce your Logic song (just as if you'd pressed the Bnc button on an output channel strip; opened the File menu, selected Bounce, and chosen Project or Section; or pressed Command+B) and then save that bounced audio to your new QuickTime movie.

Index

Index

Index

Index

Index

Index

Index

Index

Index

Index